Moral Choices:
Ethical Theories and Problems

(9,10)

8,11

Moral Choices:
Ethical Theories and Problems

Joseph Grčić
Philosophy Department
University of Florida

West Publishing Company
St. Paul   New York   Los Angeles   San Francisco

Joseph Grčić (pronounced ′gər-sich) teaches philosophy at the University of Florida. He attended
City College of New York and received his Ph.D.
from the University of Notre Dame. He has published articles on ethics and political philosophy
in various journals including *Kant-Studien, Journal of Value Inquiry,* and *The Southern Journal of
Philosophy.*

Designer: Paula Shuhert
Copyeditor: Charlene Brown
Compositor: Parkwood Composition Service, Inc.
Cover designer: Lois Stanfield
Chapter opening illustrations from: *JAPANESE DESIGN MOTIFS,*
  Matsuya Piece-Goods Store, Dover Publications, Inc., N.Y., 1972.

Indexers: David and Linda Buskas, Northwind Editorial Services

COPYRIGHT © 1989   By   WEST PUBLISHING COMPANY
                        610 Opperman Drive
                        P.O. Box 64526
                        St. Paul, MN 55164–0526

Printed in the United States of America
96   8 7 6 5 4 3

Library of Congress Cataloging-in-Publication Data

Moral choices: ethical theories and problems/[edited by] Joseph Grčić.

    p.   cm.
    Includes bibliographies and index.
    ISBN 0-314-47163-4
    1. Ethics.   I. Grčić, Joseph.
BJ1012.M629   1989   88-28129
170—dc19   CIP

TEXT IS PRINTED ON 10% POST
CONSUMER RECYCLED PAPER

Printed with Printwise
Environmentally Advanced Water Washable Ink

For my parents: Ljubo and Matija Grčić

Contents

Preface

Human consciousness and rationality give rise to the awareness of alternatives and the possibility of choice. The possibility and inevitability of choice call for rules and guidelines by which to choose. What these rules and guidelines should be is the subject matter of ethics and of the anthology before you.

This collection of readings is the result of several years of teaching courses on contemporary moral problems and applied ethics. Articles were selected on the basis of the moral significance of their content, the cogency of argumentation, the clarity of expression, and the general interest students have shown in the topics chosen. Every chapter presents a balanced selection of readings representing the focal positions on the spectrum of opinion. As such, the discussion of the moral problem represented includes opinions that may be roughly characterized as conservative, moderate, and liberal, depending on how far they diverge from the prevailing status-quo thinking on the matter.

The structure and content of this collection has several features that instructors and students may find useful. First, it not only contains a wide sampling of readings on significant moral questions but it also incorporates selections from the classic ethical theories, thus bringing together in one volume all that is necessary, in terms of reading materials, for most courses on ethics and moral problems. Second, it comprises readings on such increasingly popular areas of discussion as virtues, love and personal relations, the contribution of psychology to our understanding of ethics, comparison of Eastern and Western religious ethics, and the relation of ethics to the overall question of the meaning of life. Third, relevant Supreme Court cases are represented to remind students that philosophical issues exist outside of the classroom and that they permeate every aspect of intellectual life. Fourth, each reading is accompanied by questions to help students understand and evaluate the arguments presented. Fifth, examples of hypothetical moral dilemmas present complex theoretical problems in concrete situations in order to stimulate discussion. Finally, the introductory essays, while presenting the basic issues of each problem, also provide some of the historical background and cultural context within which philosophical problems arise and evolve.

A project such as this could not have been completed without the support and suggestions of many. I am grateful to R. M. Hare, Robert Baum, Ellen Haring, and Robert D'Amico, of the University of Florida and especially to Michael Bayles of Florida State University for their support and assistance. I'd like to thank the following people for reviewing the text: Jann Benson, Colorado State University; Jeffrey Berger, Community College of Philadelphia; John Ford, University of Louisville; David Mayo, University of Minnesota at Duluth; Lynn Pasquerella, University of Rhode Island; and Robert Trotter, William Jewell College. I must also acknowledge my deep appreciation for the loyalty and guidance that Jim Sterba has shown to me from the very beginning. Finally, I must thank Jane Bacon, Peter Marshall and Mélina Brown-Hall of West Publishing Company for their patience, editorial and production advice throughout this project.

Moral Choices
Ethical Theories and Problems

Introduction

W hat is reality, and how should human beings live in that reality? Humankind differs from other creatures in having the desire and the ability to ask and answer these questions. Rather than being passive figures in the natural landscape, we are transformers of that landscape. We recreate the world through the power of our minds and our imaginations as we attempt to understand the meaning of life.

Philosophy

The human desire to know the causes and laws underlying reality gave rise to philosophy in approximately 500 B.C. The philosophers of the ancient Greek city of Athens were the first to fully articulate the meaning of *philosophy* as 'love of wisdom.' *Wisdom,* according to the ancient Greeks, means knowledge of the world, of the self, and of how best to live in the world. The philosophical way of looking at the world revolutionized human thinking because it radically rejected the mythical and traditional approaches that went before it. While others continued to rely on the darkness of superstition and the slavery of custom, the Greek philosophers looked to reason to explain the world. To be rational means to believe and to act on the basis of the largest set of available evidence and experience. This experience must be stated and organized according to the rules of logic, which are the rules of correct reasoning. The rules of logic demand (1) the avoidance of ambiguity and vagueness in our definitions of terms, (2) consistency in our beliefs (something cannot be true and false at the same time), and (3) choice of the more complete and comprehensive explanation over the narrow and limited one. Being rational means to accept our fallibility (i.e., the realization that we could be mistaken), to have an open mind, to listen to new ideas and evidence, and to be willing to give up false beliefs and to accept new and more rational beliefs.

This way of understanding reality sharply contrasts with the primitive mythical approach. Myths and primitive religions explain reality in terms of personal or personlike forces behind nature such as gods or supernatural beings. Different primitive cultures, however, developed quite different and inconsistent views about the nature of these gods, how the world came about, and why things happen in the way they do. Primitive mythical thinking differs from philosophy in that mythical thinking (1) is not fully rational in that it is based on beliefs unwarranted by available evidence, (2) violates basic rules of logic, (3) stresses unquestioning loyalty to its central beliefs and authority figures, and (4) is a closed system of ideas that resists revision or dialogue with opposing systems of belief. Major religions today (Judaism, Christianity, Islam) share some of the traits of mythical thinking but differ in being less anthropomorphic (supreme being is less human-like) usually monotheistic and more concerned in presenting their belief systems as coherent and rational. Philosophy, on the other hand, is rational and logical, recognizes no authority except reason, and is open to constant questioning and rational criticism of beliefs and institutions with the intent of acquiring greater knowledge. The critical and questioning aspect of philosophy serves as an important check against false beliefs. The mind must be cleansed of prejudice and falsehood for true learning to begin.

In addition to critically questioning erroneous beliefs and interpretations, the goal of philosophy is to understand how all things fit together. In this respect, philosophy is an attempt to make sense of the collective, or total, experience of humankind. This means bringing together the findings of science, religion, ethics, and politics into a comprehensive and consistent picture of reality. One's philosophy informs one's sense of the overall meaning of existence. To pursue philosophy is to pursue knowledge of self, of reality, and of how to live in that reality in a rational and systematic manner. If life is a journey through reality, and wisdom means having an accurate map of reality, then the better our map, the more likely it is that we will make more of our lives.

Ethical Rules

Every society or human community is organized according to various kinds of rules and standards for behavior. These rules only apply to certain kinds of entities or beings. They do not apply to inanimate objects such as stones or even to animate objects such as trees. They do not apply to these types of beings because rules are reasons by which behavior is guided, and reasons presuppose a rational mind. Moral rules apply primarily to conscious rational beings, for only they have a choice about how to act. Inanimate objects and lower animals behave according to their natural or genetic structure, not by awareness of possibilities and the ability to decide on one of these possibilities by the use of reasons. This is why morality presupposes free choice or free will: If reasons cannot make a difference in the behavior of something, morality is irrelevant.

Morality exists, then, because people have the ability to reason and to choose, but this is not the complete story. No need for moral rules would exist if human beings were fully altruistic (unselfishly concerned for the welfare of others). Because persons are morally limited and often ignore the welfare of others, conflict results. This conflict is significant because all persons are, more or less, vulnerable to being harmed by others, (i.e., we are not deities beyond the reach of the actions of others). This vulnerability suggests the next crucial component of morality, the fact that human beings are roughly equal in their physical, intellectual, and moral abilities, weaknesses, and needs. We are all born helpless and need the care of others to survive, in the early years at least. If we had not needed others to meet our survival and other needs, our species may not have evolved as a social animal, and morality may not have been conceived. Our social nature, combined with human limitations, our similarity of needs, and the scarcity of desired objects, goods, or conditions (e.g., food, wealth, jobs, status, or love), creates situations of conflict that moral rules, in concert with other rules, help to limit, resolve, or minimize.

Some of these rules concern customs about how to dress, what to eat, how to address others politely, and how to treat others in terms of rights and duties. Clearly, not all of these rules are equally important. The rule that requires men to shake hands at first meeting other men and the rule of Western fashion that prohibits men from wearing dresses are clearly not as important as the rule against murder. Moral rules are rules that have the greatest importance or *override* all other rules. The rules against murder and rape override rules of self-interest, beauty, or etiquette. Moral rules have priority because they are essential for the existence and welfare of the community, as seen by that community. Some philosophers would argue that moral rules override all other rules because they concern the most basic human needs and desires (murder is wrong, for it conflicts with the basic desire to live) and the necessary conditions for people to live together in an organized way (lying is wrong, for random and general disregard for the truth makes communication impossible, which undermines the ability of the society to deal with enemies and to survive in the long term).

Most of us remember in our childhood, when we did something wrong, our parents saying disapprovingly, "What if everyone did that?" This question suggests that moral rules can be applied to all persons, or are *universalizable*. Some rules apply only to persons who perform a certain job (e.g., a police officer has the right to direct traffic, to ask you to stop, and so forth, whereas ordinary citizens normally do not have this right). Some rules apply to persons who play a position in a game (hence, a goalie in soccer has the right to use his or her hands in a way in which other players do not). Moral rules, unlike rules of games or employment, are said to apply to all rational persons. Universalizability does not mean that all moral rules are universally believed and followed. Rather, the concept of universalizability is meant to convey that moral rules are logically distinct from statements about

matters of taste, for example (I prefer vanilla ice cream, and you prefer chocolate). Disagreements about matters of taste do not fundamentally affect the relations between persons in the way that moral disagreements do. Furthermore, the fact that a rule is commonly believed and practiced does not mean that it is morally correct; racist and sexist attitudes were at one time virtually universally assumed to be true, yet most people today believe them to be immoral. Universalizability is a logically necessary condition for something to be a candidate for a moral rule, but it alone is not sufficient. It expresses the form that moral statements must have; their specific content will depend on the moral theory one accepts (e.g., the theory of Aristotle, Aquinas, Kant, Mill, or another).

The meaning of universalizability can be better understood by considering unethical behavior. Immoral action occurs at least in part when one makes oneself the exception to a rule. A student who cheats on an exam, for example, assumes that others have studied but attempts to achieve an equal or better evaluation than his or her classmates without studying. As the cheating example suggests, immoral actions are often parasitic in nature (i.e., they involve taking advantage of others or denying them equal status as persons). Moral rules, then, are such that if something is right for one to do under some given circumstances, then it must be right for all to do the same kind of action under the same kind of circumstances. Or, in other words, universalizability is based on the equality and rationality of persons. It means that one would be willing to be on the receiving end of a moral action. This is the idea expressed by the Golden Rule (Do unto others as you would have them do unto you), which is part of many religious and nonreligious codes of ethics.

In addition to their overriding and universalizable nature, moral rules, according to many philosophers, also concern the welfare of others. If some action has no impact on the well-being of others, but only on the agent, then the action is said to be a matter of prudence, not morality. Most moral and immoral acts concern and have an impact on the welfare of others. Ethics is the branch of philosophy that defines morality and determines the meaning and rational justification of the right way to live, the correct values, and the correct way in which to treat others.

Ethical Egoism

Ethical egoism is the view that morality requires everyone to pursue his or her self-interest. This is a theory of morality because it states that everyone (universal) should pursue his or her self-interest (which is overriding). Those who support ethical egoism claim that this view is most compatible with human nature; they claim that all persons are by nature inclined to promote their self-interest. This statement about human nature is called psychological egoism, which is to say that all persons exclusively seek their own welfare, pleasure, or benefit.

Ethical egoism is subject to various criticisms. Some claim that one cannot argue for ethical egoism on the basis of psychological egoism because even if our nature *is* to pursue our interest, one cannot derive an 'ought' (morality) from an 'is' (a statement of fact). The is/ought dichotomy argument contends that to argue what one ought to do from human nature is simply logically incorrect, for one could also argue, for example, that we should overcome our nature. Also, to say that all persons always pursue their own interest does not even seem to be factually correct. Humans do actually sometimes feel and act out of compassion and sympathy for others. The egoists could say at this point that even when we act altruistically to benefit others, we do so because the act may give us pleasure. That helping others brings us pleasure may well be true, but it is not obvious that we act compassionately only *because* it gives us pleasure.

What happens when the interests of different persons conflict? How is the conflict resolved by ethical egoists? Moral theory is supposed to help us resolve conflicts in terms of, for example, the greatest happiness or by using consistent rules or by divining God's will, but ethical egoism doesn't seem to have a way to resolve conflict since the self-interest of all individuals is equal. How can it be in my self-interest for others to pursue their interest? Wouldn't my interest be promoted more fully if they pursued not their self-interest but mine? Such doubts continue to plague ethical egoism.

Normative and Non-Normative Ethics

The study of ethics can be divided into normative and non-normative areas. Normative ethics is concerned with developing rational rules, guidelines, or standards according to which we should live our lives. This branch of ethics would involve the rational evaluation of statements such as, 'Do not kill,' 'Do not lie,' and 'Do not steal.' Non-normative ethics has two aspects: metaethics and descriptive ethics. Metaethics concerns the meaning of ethical terms such as 'right,' 'good,' and 'obligation.' Does 'good' mean that which is commanded by God, or does it mean that which maximizes happiness? Descriptive ethics deals with how people actually behave, not with whether such behavior is right or wrong. Sociological studies such as Kinsey's famous survey in the 1940s and 1950s about sexual behavior in America is a good example of descriptive, non-normative ethics.

Normative ethical theories can be helpfully categorized as teleological or deontological. Teleological theories (from the Greek *telos,* meaning purpose or goal) hold that the ultimate criterion of moral goodness is either the sum total of good over evil *consequences* that the action brings about (e.g., Mill) or whether it promotes individual functioning and development (e.g., Aristotle). A teleologist holds that an action is moral if it is a means to the appropriate moral goal.

A deontological approach (from *deon,* Greek for duty) holds that the morality of an action is not primarily determined by its consequences but by certain *intrinsic* features of the intention or mental aspect of the contemplated action. A deontologist emphasizes doing one's duty and the nature of our motives and intentions, not the consequences that may result from our actions. On this view, moral correctness means to follow certain universal rules or to be true to a moral insight, such as honesty, regardless of the consequences.

Whether one takes a teleological or a deontological approach, all moral theories make moral distinctions among various acts. All moral systems specify what is *obligatory* (i.e., what persons must do) and what is *prohibited* (or what persons must not do). It is also generally agreed that 'ought implies can,' or that no one can be obligated to do the impossible; one cannot be obligated to swim the Atlantic Ocean or to memorize the contents of the Library of Congress.

In addition, a duty or obligation can be *prima facie* or *actual*. A prima facie (at first sight) duty is a duty only if certain conditions apply. For example, we have a duty to return borrowed items, but one may not return an insane person's gun, for the consequences could be injury to the person or to others. Hence, the duty in this case is prima facie only and is overriden by our actual duty to prevent harm.

Some actions may be morally correct but not necessarily obligatory. Most of our routine daily acts, such as either bringing one's lunch or going to a restaurant, fall into this category. Another set of acts that are permitted but not obligatory includes risking one's life to save someone else or dedicating one's life to helping the poor. This type of behavior that goes above and beyond what most people are expected to do is called *supererogatory* behavior. What specific acts are obligatory, prohibited, permitted, or supererogatory depends on the particular theory one adopts.

Criteria for Theories of Ethics

A theory is a set of systematically related statements that explain or justify some area of human experience or reality. To explain something means to show the logical and causal connections between elements of our experience or events in nature. Ethical theories, like most theories, must meet certain criteria to be rationally acceptable:

1. The most basic criterion of an acceptable ethical theory is the requirement for clear, well-defined concepts. Concepts are the building blocks of theories, and ambiguity at this level will infect the whole theory with vagueness and imprecision. In a good ethical theory, we need a clear definition of concepts such as 'good' and 'right.' A theory uses these concepts to form statements. An example of an ethical statement is 'Lying is wrong.'

2. A good theory will have consistent statements. Consistency is a basic requirement of logic because two contradictory statements could not both be true and because contradictory statements would give conflicting suggestions about how we should act. In ethics, statements vary according to degrees of generality. The more general statements are called principles (such as 'Persons deserve respect'). From principles, one can derive more specific statements called rules. Rules based on the principle of respect for persons might include 'Do not lie' or 'Do not murder.'

3. A theory may have clear concepts and consistent statements but be very limited in its ability to tell us how to act in a given situation. A good theory must be complete. That is, it should help us to decide how to act in all significant problem areas of life.

4. A good theory should have simplicity. That is, it should not have more statements than necessary to be complete. Simplicity also means that the rules and principles can be learned and understood by most people, for that is the function of an ethical theory, to provide guidelines for all rational persons.

5. In addition to clarity of concepts, consistency, completeness, and simplicity, a theory must be based on the fullest set of available, relevant evidence and facts for it to be rationally acceptable. A theory based on falsehoods, irrelevant claims, or limited evidence is, to that degree, weak and not rationally acceptable.

These purely logical considerations for the rational evaluation of theories must be combined with certain rational mental attitudes. That human beings are prone to make hasty generalizations, (i.e., to generalize from a few cases or limited experience) is common knowledge. This tendency of jumping to conclusions must be avoided. Second, emotion can cloud and diminish our reasoning ability; therefore, we should not decide important issues while under the influence of strong feelings. Third, rationality requires that we resist the temptation to assume that our society's values are necessarily correct; we must accept the possibility of our own error. Accepting the possibility of fallibility means that we evaluate theories with an open mind and are willing to listen to the ideas of others. Finally, attitudes about what one should believe should be ultimately based not on a personal authority but on reason. Authority cannot be the final basis of truth, for we must always ask how the authority in question justifies his or her belief.

Truth and Ethics: Relativism

In the above discussion of a good ethical theory, the essential element of 'truth' seems to have been left out. Shouldn't the most important criterion for evaluation of an ethical theory be its truth? How can we determine whether a statement like 'Do not lie' is true? Some philosophers have claimed that only statements that claim to describe the physical world, or the way reality is (e.g., 'The world is round'), can be true or false. Ethical statements do not state the way reality *is* but the way it *ought* to be, and no way to test the truth of such a statement appears to exist. 'Do not lie' does not describe the world (we all know that people do lie) but prescribes how we should act. How then can we show whether this is a correct moral rule?

Moral relativism is the view that ethics and moral rules cannot be universally or objectively true for all people at all times. For example, today science and mathematics are universal; there is no Christian math or Jewish chemistry or Moslem biology. Yet, a Christian morality exists that is distinct from Jewish and Moslem morality. Why? Relativists believe that moral right or wrong is always relative to a particular culture and a particular time and that no absolute system of ethics can be known to be true for all time (as 'two plus two equals four' is true, presumably, forever). Sumner defends moral relativism in our readings. Mill, Kant, and Aristotle argue for different versions of *ethical absolutism,* the view that there is an objective and true morality that all societies should adopt.

Critics of moral relativism see it as a flawed theory. First, they point out that although there is no universally accepted objective theory today, one may be known in the future. At one time, agreement did not exist concerning the science of astronomy, but some astronomical theories are now widely accepted. Second, human nature, which is generally considered universal at least in its basic biological characteristics, is a limit to what can be considered moral or immoral. As indicated above, 'ought implies can.' Hence, that which is beyond the capability of human nature (for example, no person could count the grains of sand on all the beaches or drink the Pacific Ocean) can never be a moral duty. Human nature is such that it gives rise to certain needs and desires, such as survival and security, which all moral systems do recognize to some extent. The needs for survival require a prohibition against murder. The needs for social coexistence and order require a general principle against lying (specific rules may vary) to ensure effective communication. These universal needs explain the common core that most moral systems have. Another way of expressing this point is to say that there is widespread agreement about many moral principles such as 'Murder is wrong' or 'Stealing is wrong,' but the specific rules that follow from these principles can vary according to the social circumstances of individuals and the 'facts' as they believe them to be.

Moral beliefs are beliefs based on other beliefs. Quite often, religious teaching is the foundation upon which other beliefs are constructed. For example, Muhammad allowed a man to have four wives at a time, but Jesus did not. As long as religious differences exist, moral differences probably will also. Moral beliefs can also be based on nonreligious beliefs (e.g., if a white male believes that blacks and women are by nature inferior in their reasoning capacity, he may also believe that they do not deserve equal moral status with white men). As evidence and experience prove such beliefs to be false, our moral beliefs must change to reflect this. Advances in scientific knowledge and in our understanding of nature may cause our moral beliefs to become more alike.

Differences in social and historical circumstances can also give rise to different moral rules. Morality can be understood as a way of adapting to one's environment so as to best meet one's needs. If the circumstances change, the morality of some actions could also change. For example, if the population were to grow to such an extent that starvation was a real possibility, the morality of actions such as abortion, contraception, or homosexuality could change as a result. Changing circumstances usually occasion a change in the noncore morality; the core morality based on relatively unchanging needs (i.e., survival, security, and communication) does not change significantly.

Finally, if moral relativism is true, we cannot objectively say that Gandhi, for example, was a better man than Hitler. If a moral theory does not allow us to make such comparisons and determinations, how useful is it? If all ways of living are equally satisfactory in the view of reality they assume and the quality of life they bring forth, then relativism is true; otherwise, it is not. The final verdict on moral relativism will depend on whether the absolutists such as Kant, Mill, or Aristotle adequately defend their theories.

Philosophers who, like the relativists, believe that moral statements cannot be objectively and universally true or false hold what is called the *noncognitivist* position in ethics. Noncognitivism is essentially the result of a philosophical movement known as *logical positivism* that emerged during the early part of this century. This movement maintains that for a statement to be true or false, it must be either empirical (scientifically proven to be true) or a matter of definition (e.g., 'Bachelors are unmarried adult males'). Otherwise, it is meaningless. Given this understanding of what constitutes meaningful discourse, the *emotivists,* a major group of noncognitivists, claimed that moral statements are merely expressions of emotion or attitude, nothing more. To say that killing innocent persons is wrong is, for the emotivists, to say that one dislikes killing the innocent and not at all to say something that can be shown to be objectively true in the scientific sense.

Emotivism has been widely criticized. Critics have pointed out that individuals can and do hold moral beliefs contrary to their emotional attitudes, which are partly a function of upbringing and personal tastes. Emotivism also seems to deny the role of reason in changing people's moral beliefs. Even though morality is often associated with strong feelings, it does not follow that the meaning of morality is reducible to emotion.

Others, such as Aristotle, Kant, and Mill, are *cognitivists.* They believe that moral statements can be as objectively true as scientific statements (e.g., 'The world is round'). Aristotle, for example, would argue that moral statements such as 'Be just' or 'Be courageous' are true because they recommend a way of life that is required in order to achieve what we all seek, which, according to Aristotle, is happiness. For him, ethics is a necessary means to the good life of happiness, or well-being. Teleologists, like Aristotle, claim that ethical statements are 'true' if they help us to live the kind of life we desire or to reach our goal. Philosophers who believe moral values are a description of some natural property or state like pleasure or happiness are termed *naturalists* or *descriptivists.*

Another approach in determining the truth of moral claims is called *intuitionism.* Intuitionists hold that ethics is a branch of knowledge independent from science or any other discipline. Moral statements are known to be true or false by an inner mental light or insight called intuition. These intuitive statements are self-evident (i.e., they are known to be true in and of themselves).

Intuitionism is no longer as popular as it once was. To claim to know something by intuition is nothing more than to believe something without giving reasons for one's belief. Intuitionism takes morality out of the realm of rationality. Some philosophers have pointed out that intuitionism assumes that words like 'good' refer to properties of objects, whereas in reality they do not describe a property at all but prescribe a course of action. Intuition may be nothing more than the way our conscience has been shaped by our culture, which would explain why individuals in different cultures disagree about morality. Intuitionism seems to make morality mysterious and suggests no way to resolve moral disputes.

Rights

One of the central concerns of moral philosophy is the question of the nature and extent of human rights. In ancient cultures and continuing through the Middle Ages, the idea of human rights was virtually nonexistent; the focus was on duties and obligations. Starting at about the seventeenth century, philosophers and politicians became increasingly involved with the idea of rights. The problem of human rights can be divided into the question of definition (What is a right?) and justification (Are there any rights, and how are they supported?).

Various definitions of rights have been proposed. Some define a right as a liberty or a choice about behaving in a certain way with which others must not interfere. The right to free speech, for example, means that others must not shut us up. A right, then, confers a corresponding duty on the part of others that they refrain from obstructing us in exercising that right. This liberty or choice is construed by others as a valid claim based on some moral or legal principle. More generally, we can say a moral right specifies the correct moral relation between persons that requires individuals to act or refrain from acting in specified ways.

Moral rights must be distinguished from legal rights. A *moral right* is a right justified by a moral principle, whereas a *legal right* is justified by a legal principle. The right to free speech, for example, can be considered a moral right in that, according to J. S. Mill, it follows from the principle of utility (see chapter 3). But it is also a legal right in the United States, for it is protected by the Constitution. Something can be a moral right and not a legal right if it is not recognized by the state as a right. For example, when the United States practiced slavery, the moral right of the black slave to freedom was not legally recognized as a right. Similarly, something can be a legal right but not a moral right if the law is unjust, as in the case of the legal right of the slaveholder to buy and sell slaves.

Some moral rights are sometimes referred to as *human,* or *natural, rights.* This formulation suggests that certain rights (e.g., life and liberty) are universal and apply to all people, regardless of whether or not they are recognized by the particular government one happens to live under. Kant and Mill would argue that persons have certain rights because all persons are equal in their capacity to choose, to reason, and to experience happiness or pain. If moral rights are rights that one has simply because one is a person, they are said to be inalienable, (i.e., they cannot be sold or justifiably taken away without reducing the essential humanity of the person).

There is growing consensus that persons have certain basic moral rights that require others to abstain from interfering with the right holder. The rights to free speech, worship, and the like are often categorized as *negative rights* in that they are liberties that require others not to restrict our behavior. The concept of rights has in more recent human history been expanded to include what some refer to as *positive rights,* rights to goods or services such as education, health, an adequate standard of living, and so forth. These kinds of rights require not that others abstain from acting in a given way but that they act to provide goods and services to meet basic human needs. These rights are more controversial, although some philosophers have attempted to justify them by appealing to the principle of utility or to some original contract or agreement.

Why Be Moral?

Correct moral theories tell us what is right, but why should we do what is right? To many, being moral seems to mean not having fun and not getting the best out of life. If this is true, why should we be moral? In his great classic *The Republic,* Plato tells the story of a shepherd Gyges who finds a ring that can make him invisible. While invisible, he commits all kinds of immoral and selfish acts and is never punished. Wouldn't all of us be immoral if we could get away with it as Gyges did?

What kind of world would we live in if everyone were immoral, if nobody cared for others or restrained their behavior and self-interest? First of all, none of us would be here. Since we are all born helpless, without the care and protection of adults we would die. Our own existence then is due to the moral or caring acts of others. Parents and children, however, can be caring toward each other but immoral to the rest of humanity. Of course, much of morality is translated into law and enforced by the police and the courts, which is why many people do not act immorally. This being the case, it is in one's self-interest to be moral. However, if we imagine a world without any government or police, then clearly a world in which everyone were immoral would be a world of total fear, violence, evil, suffering, chaos, and death. Clearly, no one would want to live in such a world. However, another possibility exists. What if everyone were moral except you? Wouldn't this be the ideal situation, as Gyges presumably found out?

To be sure, one would have to be immoral in such a way that others did not find out, for if they did, they would surely punish you. To this point, many religions have an answer. The religious answer to the question "Why be moral?" is based on the idea that God knows all of our acts and will reward and punish us in the afterlife. Today, some persons either reject all religion as false or see that the correct moral life has intrinsic, or its own, rewards.

The nonreligious defenders of morality agree with Plato and Aristotle that a truly moral life is one in which the long-term rewards are in fact usually in our interest. Plato argued that the immoral person lacks inner harmony and is constantly dissatisfied, irrational, and therefore unhappy. Aristotle argued that a moral person will have long-term goals in mind and will exercise self-control when necessary to avoid short-term gain that goes contrary to long-term benefit. This is why Aristotle claimed that a moral life is necessary for happiness because happiness is a life-long goal and requires that we live in a certain way in order to have a happy life, not just a happy youth or a happy year. He believed that much of immorality is actually short-sightedness that defeats our overall interests and welfare. Happiness involves having self-control in the pursuit of pleasure, enjoying the company of friends, and being trusted and respected by others, which is impossible unless we are moral toward them.

Many philosophers accept many of Plato's and Aristotle's ideas but add to them other considerations. First, the obvious point must be made that in fact no ring of Gyges exists. The ring allowed Gyges to escape the consequences of his actions, but to be a successful immoralist in the real world would require an intelligence and deception beyond the abilities of most people. This is the basis of that old saying, "What a tangled web we weave when first we practice to deceive." The idea is that to be a successful liar requires a memory and an intelligence that most of us do not have. Liars contradict them-

selves eventually and are thus discovered. To forever escape the consequences of our actions, good or bad, is impossible. This is what Hindus and Buddhists call the *law of karma*. The best way to seem moral is to be moral.

Some might object to this viewpoint and argue that many immoral persons seem to have had happy lives. Here, several points must be made. First, we cannot know with certainty how happy others really are; their outward happy appearance may mask an inner dissatisfaction and regret. Second, one can grant the point to a degree and say that those happy immoralists could possibly have been even happier had they been moral. Again, remember that we are here assuming the correct moral theory, not any given moral status quo; in an immoral society, rejecting what society prescribes to be 'good' may be morally correct. Aristotle's point concerning happiness is also relevant here: He noted that moral goodness is necessary for happiness but not sufficient to insure it. Unhappiness can arise from sources unrelated to morality, such as bad luck, illness, poverty, and other circumstances.

Some psychologists, such as Maslow (see chapter 4), believe that a life of caring for others will make our life more meaningful and will increase our sense of our own value. Our self-esteem, or sense of our own value, is strengthened through moral action because in that action we participate in a larger sphere of existence beyond that of our own selfishness. This larger sphere is the sphere of life-enhancing values such as justice, goodness, and knowledge. Without this sense of value, our life may become a cycle of boredom and emptiness (see readings chapter 14). Individuals who pursue their own pleasure exclusively without concern for the welfare of others often encounter the 'paradox of hedonism' (i.e., the egotistical pursuit of one's own happiness often results in one's unhappiness). This paradox results, according to Aristotle, Mill, and others, because the self-centered and other-ignoring life denies our social nature, our need for the recognition and approval of others. The correct moral theory, as suggested earlier, is one in which our needs can be met in a way that also satisfies the needs of others. This is why moral communities experience less violence, suffering, and human conflict than immoral ones. As Plato suggested, the correct moral theory promotes an inner personal harmony and peace as well as social harmony. Human happiness seems to be tied up with our social nature; we need others not only to survive but also to feel good about surviving.

Suggested Readings

Brody, Baruch. *Beginning Philosophy.* Englewood Cliffs, N.J.: Prentice-Hall, 1977.

Cornman, James W., and Keith Lehrer. *Philosophical Problems and Arguments.* New York: Macmillan, 1974.

Frankena, William. *Thinking About Morality.* Ann Arbor: University of Michigan Press, 1980.

Hare, R. M. *Moral Thinking.* Oxford, England: Oxford University Press, 1981.

Singer, Peter. *Practical Ethics.* London: Cambridge University Press, 1979.

Stevenson, Leslie. *Seven Theories of Human Nature.* Oxford, England: Clarendon Press, 1974.

Taylor, Paul. *Principles of Ethics.* Belmont, Calif.: Dickenson, 1975.

Thiroux, Jacques P. *Ethics: Theory and Practice.* Encino, Calif.: Glencoe Publishing Co., 1977.

Woodhouse, Mark B. *A Preface to Philosophy.* Belmont, Calif.: Wadsworth, 1980.

Morality and Religion

M ost of us first encounter morality in the context of religion. In addition to providing a general theory of the origin and nature of reality, religions also offer moral guidelines by which to live. These guidelines often take the form of God's (or gods') commandments, which we must follow if we are to please God, be saved, or be happy in this life or the next. The religious view usually holds that God or a Supreme Being created the universe. As the creator, God has the authority to make demands on how we should live. Human life is part of God's overall plan, and our happiness is assured if we live to fulfill that plan. The view that moral right and wrong are defined solely by God is usually called the *divine command theory*, or *theological voluntarism*.

Background

Religion is a complex phenomenon difficult to define precisely. Nevertheless, certain common characteristics of religion may be observed:

1. Most religions include belief in supernatural beings who are usually credited with having caused and with ruling the natural world. As such, religion is a general theory about the origin and purpose of reality and life.
2. Rituals and ceremonies such as sacrifices, communion, readings from sacred texts, and prayers (communication with the gods) are integral components of the religious experience. These rites are usually associated with a high degree of emotion and mystery.

3. The supernatural beings also require human beings to adhere to a certain standard in their behavior or be subject to punishment. Moral duties and commandments are also a part of religion.

4. Most religions stress the need to believe in its doctrines in order to be saved and happy. They do not approve of doubt and scepticism concerning the major holy texts, personalities, or decrees.

Human history has witnessed an immense array of contrasting systems of religious belief. Most anthropologists agree that probably the earliest form of religion was that of animism. *Animism* is a primitive religious form in which most or all things in the world are believed to be animated with spirits or souls that exist in them. These spirits can move outside of their normal places of residence and are usually invisible to humans but can influence human life for better or worse. Consequently, primitive people seek to please these spirits through rituals and prayers.

Human religious evolution generally, though not universally, moves from animism to *polytheism.* Polytheism is a form of religion consisting in the belief in many gods or deities. These gods are usually differentiated by their special powers and functions. The ancient Greeks, Egyptians, and Hindus, among others, had different gods to control the heavens, natural occurrences, events, and places. In polytheism, gods become personified or are more person-like, though more removed from nature, than the spirits of animism. As in animism, polytheistic gods provide an identity to a people and help to perpetuate the existence of the community by declaring divine punishment for those who violate its traditions and customs. The Code of Hammurabi, for example, one of the most ancient legal and moral codes, was, according to tradition, given to King Hammurabi over four thousand years ago by the sun god Shamash.

The gradual change in polytheistic religions usually involves the emergence of a superior god among the other gods. Eventually, polytheism evolves into *monotheism*, the belief in one supreme deity. The causes of this shift are difficult to determine, but the unity and interrelatedness of nature may point to a single force as the explanation for its order. Monotheism was also spread through holy wars and missionaries. As in polytheism, monotheism helps to give even greater social unity to communities.

Religion in all of its manifestations is one way to explain reality. Some philosophers think that the evolution of religion from animism to polytheism to monotheism will next move to *atheism,* the belief in no gods at all. They argue that religion is a crude science that has been replaced by modern science. Others, including Freud, believe that religion is based on fear, guilt, and ignorance. Freud argued that religion is an illusion based on our unmet needs for an all-loving, cosmic "father" to help us deal with death, disease, and injustice in this world. Still others see religion as a way of maintaining social unity and order in the face of individual self-interest that, if unchecked, would tear apart the social fabric.

Buddha

The founder of Buddhism, Siddhartha Gautama (563–483 B.C.), was born in northeast India. He lived an aristocratic life and eventually married and had children. At about the age of thirty, he became dissatisfied with his life, left his home, and wandered about seeking truth about life, suffering, and death. Tradition tells us that at one point in his quest for wisdom he sat for forty-nine days under a tree until he acquired enlightenment, thus receiving the title Buddha, the Enlightened One.

The wisdom Buddha discovered eventually became known as the Four Noble Truths: (1) Life is suffering, (2) The cause of suffering is desire, (3) Desire can be overcome, and (4) The Eightfold Path is the way to destroy desire. This Eightfold Path is a summary of Buddhist ethics and includes the following precepts: (1) Right knowledge: understanding the Buddhist philosophy, especially the Four Noble Truths, (2) Right thought: avoiding ill will and desire, (3) Right speech: not lying or boasting, (4) Right conduct: not killing living things, not stealing and not being sexually impure, (5) Right vocation: not being a butcher or selling alcohol, (6) Right efforts: avoiding evil thoughts and keeping good ones, (7) Right mindfulness: reflecting on our thoughts to see their origin in desire, and (8) Right concentration: reaching the highest form of insight through meditation and enlightenment. Meditation plays a central role in Buddhism; the highest form of life is one totally dedicated to achieving enlightenment through meditation. Those who dedicate their lives in this manner live together in monasteries and practice celibacy, the total abstaining from sex. Those who cannot meet the challenge of this highest form of life are allowed to marry but have an obligation to support the monks through donations. In the Sermon on Abuse, Buddha teaches that we must return good for evil, thus anticipating the command of Jesus to turn the other cheek.

Buddha claimed his teachings were based on rational reflection and discipline, not on some special personal divine revelation. In this respect, he differs from Moses, Jesus, Muhammad, and other founders of religions. When one fully realizes these truths and follows the life of the Eightfold Path, one ends the cycle of rebirth, or *reincarnation,* and achieves enlightenment, or nirvana. *Nirvana,* or ultimate reality, is a concept Buddha did not fully explain. He did claim that the "self" is not a substance that exists beyond the death of the body but that the consequences of our actions do continue to exist as karma, an invisible force. This force is said to unify the death of one person and the rebirth of that person in the next life. When one reaches enlightenment, the karmic energy is destroyed and rebirth ends.

Buddhist thinking has been immensely influential throughout history. Some do not consider Buddhism a religion because it does not assert the reality of a personal deity, but others believe Buddha is that deity. If Buddhism is a philosophy, it fails to explain fully what karma is and how it exists. What is nirvana? If it is the absence of desire, is it also the absence of individual awareness? If so, how does it differ from natural death? Is Buddhism a life-denying religion that grew out of a society filled with poverty, disease, and despair? If so, is it at all relevant to our time?

Muhammad

Muhammad (A.D. 570–632) was born in Mecca (now in Saudi Arabia) and grew up as a poor orphan. Up to about age forty, Muhammad lived a traditional life with his wife and children in a polytheistic society. One day he began to see visions and hear voices that he eventually came to believe were from the angel Gabriel who was giving him messages from Allah, the one and only God. Though initially rejected, Muhammad and his teachings gained support, and he became a political as well as a religious leader. Muhammad's teachings are recorded in *the Koran,* the holy scripture of Islam.

Muhammad believed his writings were the final revelations of God, revelations that started with the Jews and Jesus. He considered Moses, Jesus, and the other main figures in the *Bible* to be genuine prophets who he, Muhammad, superseded by completing God's revelation. Moslems, Jews, and Christians share similar beliefs about the oneness of God (the creator of nature and man, whose commandments must be obeyed if one is to be happy in this life or the next). Muhammad's ethical code is reminiscent of the Ten Commandments of Moses. Both codes prohibit murder, lying, and adultery and require that we help the poor. Unlike Moses, Muhammad allowed polygamy with up to four wives per husband, and unlike Jesus, he did not look favorably on a life of celibacy but rather praised marriage as the fulfillment of human life. Muhammad required the faithful to abstain from alcohol and pork, hold firmly to the belief in the one God Allah, pray five times a day, and make a pilgrimage to Mecca, the birthplace of Muhammad, at least once in a lifetime.

Moses

Moses was born in Egypt in about 1300 B.C. According to the Old Testament, Moses, in response to God's command, led the Jews out of Egypt to the promised land. He is said to be the author of the first five books of the Old Testament, which states that Moses received the Ten Commandments from God, the creator of the universe and a fatherlike figure who demands obedience. The importance of obeying and worshiping God on the Sabbath and the prohibitions against murder, theft, adultery, lying, and envy are made clear and absolute. No reasons are given why we must keep these commandments other than that God will bless those who do and punish those who don't.

Jesus

Jesus (8/6 B.C.–A.D. 30), the founder of Christianity, was born in what is now Israel. He is usually referred to as Jesus Christ, the Messiah, or the Savior. Almost all the information we have about him comes from the New Testament. He claimed to be the Son of God whose mission was to save humankind through his death and teachings. The New Testament states that he was crucified, died, and rose from the dead and then ascended to heaven.

The picture of God that the New Testament presents is somewhat different from the strict, disciplinarian God of the Old Testament. The God of Jesus stresses that His basic relationship to humanity is that of love and concern. In his Sermon on the Mount, Jesus praises the poor and the humble and warns the rich and powerful that their way of life may not be pleasing to God. He commands us to love our enemies and to be compassionate to all. Again, as in the Ten Commandments, the reasons given are that this is God's will and the key to our ultimate happiness. On this view, moral principles are knowable to us not on the basis of our own thinking things through but on our faithful submission to the authority and wisdom of God.

Thomas Aquinas

St. Thomas Aquinas (A.D. 1225–1274) was a major Christian philosopher and theologian who sought to give morality and religion a more rational foundation. Many of his ideas came from the ancient Greek philosopher Aristotle (384–322 B.C.). Aquinas, as a Christian, believed that nature and humans were created by God and that God has a purpose for humanity, namely to achieve moral perfection and to be with God in heaven forever.

Aquinas saw the universe as a perfectly structured whole in which all things have a purpose. The highest structure is that of *eternal law,* the law of God's reason or mind, which rules the entire creation. *Divine law* is the law that is revealed to us in the Bible. This law helps us to achieve salvation by fully revealing to us what the natural law cannot. *Natural law* is the moral law revealed to us by reason. Finally, *human law* consists of laws made by people through political authorities to give specific guidelines for human life. Aquinas's hierarchical system must be in perfect harmony, hence human law cannot be inconsistent with natural or divine law.

Aquinas argued that since all things created by God are good, so is human nature. The fundamental principle of Aquinas's theory of natural law is 'Do good and avoid evil.' 'Good' is defined as those things persons naturally pursue. Human needs and natural inclinations are thus good, and we should follow them under the guidance of reason. For example, our sexual nature is the basis of marriage and the procreation of children and so is good. Our need for companionship is the basis of friendship and society in general. Our desire for self-preservation is the grounding for the rules against murder and suicide. Similarly, Aquinas would argue that premarital sex, adultery, and homosexuality are wrong because the first two are contrary to the proper procreation and nurture of children in the context of a stable family and the latter cannot bring forth offspring at all. Aquinas further argues that because human nature is everywhere the same and unchanging, therefore the basic moral principles are universal and unchanging (though not always recognized as such by all cultures).

Although Aquinas's views may have a great deal of merit and may be a step ahead of the purely command-oriented morality of the Bible, still certain questions can be raised. Given the findings of Charles Darwin's theory of evolution, which holds that all living things change through time, can we still say today that human nature is unchanging? Hasn't science shown that the evolving human is a very plastic creature whose nature can be shaped by environmental, social, and cultural conditions? If the environment does mold human nature and make it less universal and more particular, can the same moral rules apply to all persons? Is the procreation of children good if the planet becomes overpopulated? Is procreation the only or even primary purpose of sexuality? Is it always right to follow our nature? Shouldn't we sometimes try to overcome or to subdue our nature? Can one argue from the facts of human nature (the 'is') to a moral 'ought'? Isn't our love of power, money, and pleasure also natural? Why then shouldn't we pursue these to our fullest capacity? Questions such as these have led some to abandon Aquinas's theory or to reform it in several ways.

Reflections on Religious Morality

Amidst these religious traditions, agreement and disagreement on moral values is apparent. The disagreements range over the entire spectrum of morality. Attitudes toward sexuality, for example, range from a preference for virginity and celibacy to the approval of premarital sex and polygamy. However, although disagreements are widespread, they are not total and absolute. The moral principles found in the Ten Commandments of Moses, the Sermon on the Mount of Jesus, the Eightfold Path of the Buddha, and the Decalogue of Islam are in agreement that murder, lying, harming, and stealing (specific rules and exceptions may vary) are wrong. This similarity is also found in the Law of Manu (compiled between 200 B.C. and 100 A.D.) of Hinduism, which states, "Abstention from injuring creatures, truthfulness, and abstention from unlawful appropriating the goods of others, purity and control of the organs, Manu has declared to be the summary of the law of the four castes." (10:63) Most of these religions also accept a form of the Golden Rule, although some apply a double standard to men and women. The universality of these moral principles can hardly be construed as accidental. As suggested in chapter 1, reflection would show that rules against murder, lying, and other kinds of violence must be maintained if any community is to survive in a way that meets human needs. If this is so (i.e., if the basic moral principles can be justified on the basis of human needs and the necessary conditions for peaceful coexistence), why search for other and transcendental justifications? These kinds of considerations have led philosophers to seek the foundations of morality in other than religious dogma.

Plato

Plato (428/427–348/347 B.C.), one of the greatest Greek philosophers, criticizes the idea that morality is based on religion. In Plato's *Euthyphro,* Socrates (470–399 B.C.) discusses the meaning of piety, or moral goodness, with Euthyphro, who is suing his father for murder. Socrates's basic question is "Do Gods love what is good, or does their loving make it good?" Euthyphro answers that the gods love piety because it is good; their loving it does not make it good. Socrates is quick to point out that, in that case, the good is good independently of the gods' will. In other words, morality is independent of the commandments of gods. What then makes something good or moral? This dialogue does not give us an answer.

Bertrand Russell

Bertrand Russell (1872–1970) attacks religiously based morality in a radical manner. His first point is that to believe in the existence of God is irrational, and if there is no God, then obviously no morality can be based on His will. Second, he claims that Jesus and his moral teachings were flawed. He particularly finds the idea of hell, the eternal punishment for sinners, as too cruel and inhumane for a loving God to actually use.

Plato and Russell bring out some important issues concerning the relationship of morality to religion. Two possibilities seem to exist: Either God commands us to do something because it is good, or something is good because God commands it. If the former possibility is true, then God's will does not define morality. If the latter is true, then several questions follow. First, as Russell asked, is there a God? If so, whose god is it, that of the Jews, of the Christians, or of some other religious group? Second, if God's will is all that determines morality, then God could will that murder is right. Third, how could we say that God is good? To do so would be to say that God follows God's commands, but an evil God could make commands, too. Why did God pick these particular commands and not others? Why should we obey them? To obey out of mere fear of punishment seems tyrannical and arbitrary. Finally, we need a prior sense of what moral goodness is in order to decide whether some action of command does indeed come from God. For example, Charles Manson, a convicted murderer now in prison, claimed to be God, yet this claim can be dismissed on the grounds that his behavior was inconsistent with the values that most believers hold even God cannot violate.

What of those who say, "If there is no God, then all is permitted; there is no right or wrong." This issue is addressed in the next two chapters; philosophers and psychologists as diverse as Aristotle, Kant, Mill, Freud, Maslow, and others consider whether morality has a this-worldly justification.

Two Sermons

Buddha (563–483 B.C.) The founder of Buddhism was born in Nepal, near India, as Siddhartha Gautama, and received the title of "Buddha, The Enlightened One," after achieving the highest form of insight through meditation. As evidence that he had indeed achieved total enlightenment, several miracles are attributed to the Buddha. In one miracle, he is said to have risen into the air and the cut his body into pieces. The pieces fell to earth and were then joined together again.

Buddha

The Sermon at Benares

On seeing their old teacher approach, the five bhikkhus[1] agreed among themselves not to salute him, nor to address him as a master, but by his name only. "For," so they said, "he has broken his vow and has abandoned holiness. He is no bhikkhu but Gotama, and Gotama has become a man who lives in abundance and indulges in the pleasures of worldliness."

But when the Blessed One approached in a dignified manner, they involuntarily rose from their seats and greeted him in spite of their resolution. Still they called him by his name and addressed him as "friend Gotama."

When they had thus received the Blessed One,

he said: "Do not call the Tathāgata by his name nor address him as 'friend,' for he is the Buddha, the Holy One. The buddha looks with a kind heart equally on all living beings, and they therefore call him 'Father.' To disrespect a father is wrong; to despise him, is wicked.

"The Tathāgata," the Buddha continued, "does not seek salvation in austerities, but neither does he for that reason indulge in worldly pleasures, nor live in abundance. The Tathāgata has found the middle path.

"Neither abstinence from fish or flesh, nor going naked, nor shaving the head, nor wearing matted hair, nor dressing in a rough garment, nor covering oneself with dirt, nor sacrificing to Angi, will cleanse a man who is not free from delusions.

"Reading the Vedas, making offerings to priests, or sacrifices to the gods, self-mortification by heat

From *The Wisdom of China and India,* ed. Lin Yutang. © 1942 and renewed in 1970 by Random House, Inc. Reprinted by permission of the publisher.

1. A "bhikkhu" is a monk.

or cold, and many such penances performed for the sake of immortality, these do not cleanse the man who is not free from delusions.

"Anger, drunkenness, obstinacy, bigotry, deception, envy, self-praise, disparaging others, superciliousness and evil intentions constitute uncleanness; not verily the eating of flesh.

"A middle path, O bhikkhus, avoiding the two extremes, has been discovered by the Tathāgata—a path which opens the eyes, and bestows understanding, which leads to peace of mind, to the higher wisdom, to full enlightenment, to Nirvāna!

"What is that middle path, O bhikkhus, avoiding these two extremes, discovered by the Tathāgata—that path which opens the eyes, and bestows understanding, which leads to peace of mind, to the higher wisdom, to full enlightenment, to Nirvāna?

"Let me teach you, O bhikkhus, the middle path, which keeps aloof from both extremes. By suffering, the emaciated devotee produces confusion and sickly thoughts in his mind. Mortification is not conducive even to worldly knowledge; how much less to a triumph over the senses!

"He who fills his lamp with water will not dispel the darkness, and he who tries to light a fire with rotten wood will fail. And how can any one be free from self by leading a wretched life, if he does not succeed in quenching the fires of lust, if he still hankers after either worldly or heavenly pleasures. But he in whom self has become extinct is free from lust; he will desire neither worldly nor heavenly pleasures, and the satisfaction of his natural wants will not defile him. However, let him be moderate, let him eat and drink according to the needs of the body.

"Sensuality is enervating; the self-indulgent man is a slave to his passions, and pleasure-seeking is degrading and vulgar.

"But to satisfy the necessities of life is not evil. To keep the body in good health is a duty, for otherwise we shall not be able to trim the lamp of wisdom, and keep our mind strong and clear. Water surrounds the lotus-flower, but does not wet its petals.

"This is the middle path, O bhikkhus, that keeps aloof from both extremes."

And the Blessed One spoke kindly to his disciples, pitying them for their errors, and pointing out the uselessness of their endeavors, and the ice of ill-will that chilled their hearts melted away under the gentle warmth of the Master's persuasion.

Now the Blessed One set the wheel of the most excellent law rolling, and he began to preach to the five bhikkhus, opening to them the gate of immortality, and showing them the bliss of Nirvāna.

The Buddha said:

"The spokes of the wheel are the rules of pure conduct: justice is the uniformity of their length; wisdom is the tire; modesty and thoughtfulness are the hub in which the immovable axle of truth is fixed.

"He who recognizes the existence of suffering, its cause, its remedy, and its cessation has fathomed the four noble truths. He will walk in the right path.

"Right views will be the torch to light his way. Right aspirations will be his guide. Right speech will be his dwelling-place on the road. His gait will be straight, for it is right behavior. His refreshments will be the right way of earning his livelihood. Right efforts will be his steps: right thoughts his breath; and right contemplation will give him the peace that follows in his footprints.

"Now, this, O bhikkhus, is the noble truth concerning suffering:

"Birth is attended with pain, decay is painful, disease is painful, death is painful. Union with the unpleasant is painful, painful is separation from the pleasant; and any craving that is unsatisfied, that too is painful. In brief, bodily conditions which spring from attachment are painful.

"This, then O bhikkhus, is the noble truth concerning suffering.

"Now this, O bhikkhus, is the noble truth concerning the origin of suffering:

"Verily, it is that craving which causes the renewal of existence, accompanied by sensual delight, seeking satisfaction now here, now there, the craving for the gratification of the passions, the craving for a future life, and the craving for happiness in this life.

"This, then, O bhikkhus, is the noble truth concerning the origin of suffering.

"Now this, O bhikkhus, is the noble truth concerning the destruction of suffering:

"Verily, it is the destruction, in which no passion remains, of this very thirst; it is the laying aside of, the being free from, the dwelling no longer upon this thirst.

"This, then, O bhikkhus, is the noble truth concerning the destruction of suffering.

"Now this, O bhikkhus, is the noble truth concerning the way which leads to the destruction of sorrow. Verily! it is this noble eightfold path; that is to say:

"Right views; right aspirations; right speech; right behavior; right livelihood; right effort; right thoughts; and right contemplation.

"This, then, O bhikkhus, is the noble truth concerning the destruction of sorrow.

"By the practice of lovingkindness I have attained liberation of heart, and thus I am assured that I shall never return in renewed births. I have even now attained Nirvāna."

And when the Blessed One had thus set the royal chariot wheel of truth rolling onward, a rapture thrilled through all the universes.

The devas left their heavenly abodes to listen to the sweetness of the truth; the saints that had parted from life crowded around the great teacher to receive the glad tidings; even the animals of the earth felt the bliss that rested upon the words of the Tathāgata: and all the creatures of the host of sentient beings, gods, men, and beasts, hearing the message of deliverance, received and understood it in their own language.

And when the doctrine was propounded, the venerable Kondanna, the oldest one among the five bhikkhus, discerned the truth with his mental eye, and he said: "Truly, O Buddha, our Lord, thou hast found the truth!" Then the other bhikkhus too, joined him and exclaimed: "Truly, thou art the Buddha, thou hast found the truth."

And the devas and saints and all the good spirits of the departed generations that had listened to the sermon of the Tathāgata, joyfully received the doctrine and shouted: "Truly, the Blessed One has founded the kingdom of righteousness. The Blessed One has moved the earth; he has set the wheel of Truth rolling, which by no one in the universe, be he god or man, can ever be turned back. The kingdom of Truth will be preached upon earth; it will spread; and righteousness, good-will, and peace will reign among mankind."

The Sermon on Abuse

And the Blessed One observed the ways of society and noticed how much misery came from malignity and foolish offences done only to gratify vanity and self-seeking pride.

And the Buddha said: "If a man foolishly does me wrong, I will return to him the protection of my ungrudging love; the more evil comes from him, the more good shall go from me; the fragrance of goodness always comes to me, and the harmful air of evil goes to him."

A foolish man learning that the Buddha observed the principle of great love which commends the return of good for evil, came and abused him. The Buddha was silent, pitying his folly.

When the man had finished his abuse, the Buddha asked him, saying: "Son, if a man declined to accept a present made to him, to whom would it belong?" And he answered: "In that case it would belong to the man who offered it."

"My son," said the Buddha, "thou has railed at me, but I decline to accept thy abuse, and request thee to keep it thyself. Will it not be a source of misery to thee? As the echo belongs to the sound, and shadow to the substance, so misery will overtake the evil-doer without fail."

The abuser made no reply, and Buddha continued:

"A wicked man who reproaches a virtuous one is like one who looks up and spits at heaven; the spittle soils not the heaven, but comes back and defiles his own person.

"The slanderer is like one who flings dust at another when the wind is contrary; the dust does but return on him who threw it. The virtuous man cannot be hurt and the misery that the other would inflict comes back on himself."

The abuser went away ashamed, but he came again and took refuge in the Buddha, the Dharma, and the Sangha.[2]

---

2. *Dharma,* the Law of the Path of Buddhist teachings; *Sangha,* the Buddhist Church. These, with Buddha, constitute the "three refuges."

Study Questions

1. Is Buddhism a philosophy or a religion?

2. Is the ethic of Buddha most similar to Moses, Jesus, or Muhammad?

3. As a theory of how to live, is Buddhism life denying?

4. If no self survives the death of the body, what meaning could reincarnation or nirvana have?

The Koran

Muhammad (A.D. 570–632) Born in Mecca (now in Saudi Arabia), Muhammad, the Prophet, was the founder of Islam. The Moslem calendar starts in the year 622, the year of Muhammad's escape (the Hegira) from Mecca to the city of Medina. The Koran, the holy book of Islam, was, according to tradition, dictated to Muhammad by an angel of Allah, or God. Though Muhammad never claimed to be anything more than a man who was chosen to be Allah's messenger, miracles such as splitting the moon in half, healing the blind, and journeying to heaven on a horse are attributed to him by some followers.

Muhammad

The Chapter of the Night Journey.[1]

(XVII. Mecca.)

In the name of the merciful and compassionate God.

Celebrated be the praises of Him who took His servant a journey by night from the Sacred Mosque[2] to the Remote Mosque,[3] the precinct of which we have blessed, to show him of our signs! verily, He both hears and looks.

And we gave Moses the Book and made it a guidance to the children of Israel: 'Take ye to no guardian but me.'

Seed of those we bore with Noah (in the ark)! verily, he was a thankful servant!

And we decreed to the children of Israel in the Book, 'Ye shall verily do evil in the earth twice,[4] and ye shall rise to a great height (of pride).'

[5] And when the threat for the first (sin) of the two came, we sent over them servants of ours, endued with violence, and they searched inside your houses; and it was an accomplished threat.

---

1. Also called "The Children of Israel."
2. The Kaabah at Mecca.
3. The Temple at Jerusalem.
4. The two sins committed by the Jews, and for which punishments were threatened and executed, were, first, the murder of Isaiah and the imprisonment of Jeremiah, and second, the murder of John the Baptist.

Translated by E. H. Palmer. © 1900 by Oxford University Press.

Then we rallied you once more against them, and aided you with wealth and sons, and made you a numerous band.

'If ye do well, ye will do well to your own souls; and if ye do ill, it is against them!

'And when the threat for the last came[5]—to harm your faces and to enter the mosque as they entered it the first time, and to destroy what they had got the upper-hand over with utter destruction.'

It may be that thy Lord will have mercy on you;—but if ye return we will return, and we have made hell a prison for the misbelievers.

Verily, this Qur'ân [Koran] guides to the straightest path, and gives the glad tidings to the believers [10] who do aright that for them is a great hire; and that for those who believe not in the hereafter, we have prepared a mighty woe.

Man prays for evil as he prays for good; and man was ever hasty.

We made the night and the day two signs; and we blot out the sign of the night and make the sign of the day visible, that ye may seek after plenty from your Lord, and that ye may number the years and the reckoning; and we have detailed everything in detail.

And every man's augury[6] have we fastened on his neck; and we will bring forth for him on the resurrection day a book offered to him wide open. [15] 'Read thy book thou art accountant enough against thyself to-day!'

He who accepts guidance, accepts it only for his own soul: and he who errs, errs only against it; nor shall one burdened soul bear the burden of another.

Nor would we punish until we had sent an apostle. And when we desired to destroy a city we bade[7] the opulent ones thereof; and they wrought abomination therein; and its due sentence was pronounced; and we destroyed it with utter destruction.

How many generations have we destroyed after Noah! but thy Lord of the sins of his servant is well aware, and sees enough.

Whoso is desirous of this life that hastens away, we will hasten on for him therein what we please,—for whom we please. Then we will make hell for him to broil in—despised and outcast.

[20] But whoso desires the next life, and strives for it and is a believer—these, their striving shall be gratefully received.

To all—these and those—will we extend the gifts of thy Lord; for the gifts of thy Lord are not restricted.

See how we have preferred some of them over others, but in the next life are greater degrees and greater preference.

Put not with God other gods, or thou wilt sit despised and forsaken.

Thy Lord has decreed that ye shall not serve other than Him; and kindness to one's parents, whether one or both of them reach old age with thee; and say not to them, 'Fie!' and do not grumble at them, but speak to them a generous speech. [25] And lower to them the wing of humility out of compassion, and say, 'O Lord! have compassion on them as they brought me up when I was little!' Your Lord knows best what is in your souls if ye be righteous, and, verily, He is forgiving unto those who come back penitent.

And give thy kinsman his due and the poor and the son of the road; and waste not wastefully, for the wasteful were ever the devil's brothers; and the devil is ever ungrateful to his Lord.

[30] But if thou dost turn away from them to seek after mercy from thy Lord,[8] which thou hopest for, then speak to them an easy speech.

Make not thy hand fettered to thy neck, nor yet spread it out quite open, lest thou shouldst have to sit down blamed and straitened in means. Verily, thy Lord spreads out provision to whomsoever He will or He doles it out. Verily, He is ever well aware of and sees His servants.

---

5. Supply, "we sent foes."
6. That is, "fortune" or "fate," literally, "bird." The Arabs, like the ancient Romans, used to practice divination from the flight of birds.
7. Bade them obey the Apostle.

8. That is, if you are compelled to leave them in order to seek your livelihood; or if your present means are insufficient to enable you to relieve others.

And slay not your children for fear of poverty; we will provide for them; beware! for to slay them is ever a great sin!

And draw not near to fornication; verily, it is ever an abomination, and evil is the way thereof.

[35] And slay not the soul that God has forbidden you, except for just cause; for he who is slain unjustly we have given his next of kin authority; yet let him not exceed in slaying; verily, he is ever helped.

And draw not near to the wealth of the orphan, save to improve it, until he reaches the age of puberty, and fulfil your compacts; verily, a compact is ever enquired of.

And give full measure when ye measure out, and weigh with a right balance; that is better and a fairer determination.

And do not pursue that of which thou hast no knowledge; verily, the hearing, the sight, and the heart, all of these shall be enquired of.

And walk not on the earth proudly; verily, thou canst not cleave the earth, and thou shalt not reach the mountains in height.

Study Questions

1. What are some similarities and differences among the ethics of Moses, Muhammad, and Jesus?

2. Why do you suppose that Muhammad allowed polygamy and Jesus, Moses, and Buddha did not?

The Ten Commandments

Moses (1300 B.C.) Born in Egypt, Moses was the Jewish religious leader who led the Jews out of Egyptian slavery to the promised land, Israel. He has also been identified as the author of the first five books of the Old Testament.

Moses

Then God delivered all these commandments:

"I, the Lord, am your God, who brought you out of the land of Egypt, the place of slavery. You shall

not have other gods besides me. You shall not carve idols for yourselves in the shape of anything in the sky above or on the earth below or in the waters beneath the earth; you shall not bow down before them or worship them. For I, the Lord, your God, am a jealous God, inflicting punishment for their fathers' wickedness on the children of those who hate me, down to the third and fourth generation;

but bestowing mercy down to the thousandth generation, on the children of those who love me and keep my commandments.

"You shall not take the name of the Lord, your God, in vain. For the Lord will not leave unpunished him who takes his name in vain.

"Remember to keep holy the sabbath day. Six days you may labor and do all your work, but the seventh day is the sabbath of the Lord, your God. No work may be done then either by you, or your son or daughter, or your male or female slave, or your beast, or by the alien who lives with you. In six days the Lord made the heavens and the earth, the sea and all that is in them; but on the seventh day he rested. That is why the Lord has blessed the sabbath and made it holy.

"Honor your father and your mother, that you may have a long life in the land which the Lord, your God, is giving you.

"You shall not kill.

"You shall not commit adultery.

"You shall not steal.

"You shall not bear false witness against your neighbor.

"You shall not covet your neighbor's house. You shall not covet your neighbor's wife, nor his male or female slave, nor his ox or ass, nor anything else that belongs to him."

Study Questions

1. Are the Ten Commandments a complete moral system?

2. What would Buddha say about Moses' laws?

3. Which, if any, of the commandments can be defended rationally without any reference to God?

4. Can Moses' law help us to resolve the issues of abortion, capital punishment, euthanasia, or pornography?

The Sermon on the Mount

Jesus

Coming down the mountain with them, he stopped at a level stretch where there were many of his disciples; a large crowd of people was with

Jesus (8/6 B.C.–A.D. 30) Jesus (the Christ, Savior, or Messiah) was born in Bethlehem and was the founder of Christianity. The New Testament presents him as the Son of God who performed many miracles, including healing the sick, restoring the dead to life, as well as walking on water. He was condemned to die by crucifixion, and according to the Gospels (books of the New Testament that tell the life story of Jesus), he rose from the dead and ascended into heaven.

them from all Judea and Jerusalem and the coast of Tyre and Sidon, people who came to hear him and be healed of their diseases. Those who were troubled with unclean spirits were cured; indeed, the whole crowd was trying to touch him because power went out from him which cured all. Then, raising his eyes to his disciples, he said:

> "Blest are you poor; the reign of God is yours.
> Blest are you who hunger; you shall be filled.
> Blest are you who are weeping; you shall laugh.

"Blest shall you be when men hate you, when they ostracize you and insult you and proscribe your name as evil because of the Son of Man. On the day they do so, rejoice and exult, for your reward shall be great in heaven. Thus it was that their fathers treated the prophets.

> "But woe to you rich, for your consolation is now.
> Woe to you who are full; you shall go hungry.
> Woe to you who laugh now; you shall weep in your grief.

"Woe to you when all speak well of you. Their fathers treated the false prophets in just this way.

Love of One's Enemy

"To you who hear me, I say: Love your enemies, do good to those who hate you; bless those who curse you and pray for those who maltreat you. When someone slaps you on one cheek, turn and give him the other; when someone takes your coat, let him have your shirt as well. Give to all who beg from you. When a man takes what is yours, do not demand it back. Do to others what you would have them to do you. If you love those who love you, what credit is that to you? Even sinners love those who love them. If you do good to those who do good to you, how can you claim any credit? Sinners do as much. If you lend to those from whom you expect repayment, what merit is there in it for you? Even sinners lend to sinners, expecting to be repaid in full.

"Love your enemy and do good; lend without expecting repayment. Then will your recompense be great. You will rightly be called sons of the Most High, since he himself is good to the ungrateful and the wicked.

"Be compassionate, as your Father is compassionate. Do not judge, and you will not be judged. Do not condemn, and you will not be condemned. Pardon, and you shall be pardoned. Give, and it shall be given to you. Good measure pressed down, shaken together, running over, will they pour into the fold of your garment. For the measure you measure with will be measured back to you."

He also used images in speaking to them: "Can a blind man act as guide to a blind man? Will they not both fall into a ditch? A student is not above his teacher; but every student when he has finished his studies will be on a par with his teacher.

"Why look at the speck in your brother's eye when you miss the plank in your own? How can you say to your brother, 'Brother, let me remove the speck from your eye,' yet fail yourself to see the plank lodged in your own? Hypocrite, remove the plank from your own eye first; then you will see clearly enough to remove the speck from your brother's eye.

"A good tree does not produce decayed fruit any more than a decayed tree produces good fruit. Each tree is known by its yield. Figs are not taken from thornbushes, nor grapes picked from brambles. A good man produces goodness from the good in his heart; an evil man produces evil out of his store of evil. Each man speaks from his heart's abundance. Why do you call me 'Lord, Lord,' and not put into practice what I teach you? Any man who desires to come to me will hear my words and put them into practice. I will show you with whom he is to be compared. He may be likened to the man who, in building a house, dug deeply and laid the foundation on a rock. When the floods came the torrent rushed in on that house, but failed to shake it because of its solid foundation. On the other hand, anyone who has heard my words but not put them into practice is like the man who built his house on the ground without any foundation. When the torrent rushed upon it, it immediately fell in and was completely destroyed."

1. Is Jesus' idea of "turning the other cheek" a realistic moral rule?

2. If it were followed, would evil end up controlling the earth?

3. How does the moral theory of Jesus compare to those of Moses and Buddha?

Reason and Divine Law

Thomas Aquinas (A.D. 1225–1274) Born in Italy, Thomas Aquinas was a major Christian philosopher, theologian, and saint. He wrote many treatises, including Summa Theologica *and* Summa Contra Gentiles.

St. Thomas Aquinas

Question XC. On the Essence of Law

First Article. Whether Law is Something Pertaining to Reason?

We proceed thus to the First Article:—Objection 1. It would seem that law is not something pertaining to reason. For the Apostle says (*Rom.* vii. 23): *I see another law in my members,* etc. But nothing pertaining to reason is in the members, since the reason does not make use of a bodily organ. Therefore law is not something pertaining to reason. . . .

From *Introduction to St. Thomas Aquinas,* ed. Anton C. Pegis. By permission of the A. C. Pegis Estate.

On the contrary, It belongs to the law to command and to forbid. But it belongs to reason to command, as was stated above. Therefore law is something pertaining to reason.

I answer that, Law is a rule and measure of acts, whereby man is induced to act or is restrained from acting; for *lex* [law] is derived from *ligare* [to bind], because it binds one to act. Now the rule and measure of human acts is the reason, which is the first principle of human acts, as is evident from what has been stated above. For it belongs to the reason to direct to the end, which is the first principle in all matters of action, according to the Philosopher. Now that which is the principle in any genus is the rule and measure of that genus: for instance, unity in the genus of numbers, and the first movement in the genus of movements. Consequently, it follows that law is something pertaining to reason....

Second Article. Whether Law is Always Directed to the Common Good?

We proceed thus to the Second Article:—Objection 1. It would seem that law is not always directed to the common good as to its end. For it belongs to law to command and to forbid. But commands are directed to certain individual goods. Therefore the end of law is not always the common good.

Obj. 2. Further, law directs man in his actions. But human actions are concerned with particular matters. Therefore law is directed to some particular good.

Obj. 3. Further, Isidore says: *If law is based on reason, whatever is based on reason will be a law.* But reason is the foundation not only of what is ordained to the common good, but also of that which is directed to private good. Therefore law is not directed only to the good of all, but also to the private good of an individual.

On the contrary, Isidore says that *laws are enacted for no private profit, but for the common benefit of the citizens.*

I answer that, As we have stated above, law belongs to that which is a principle of human acts, because it is their rule and measure. Now as reason is a principle of human acts, so in reason itself there is something which is the principle in respect of all the rest. Hence to this principle chiefly and mainly law must needs be referred. Now the first principle in practical matters, which are the object of the practical reason, is the last end: and the last end of human life is happiness or beatitude, as we have stated above. Consequently, law must needs concern itself mainly with the order that is in beatitude. Moreover, since every part is ordained to the whole as the imperfect to the perfect, and since one man is a part of the perfect community, law must needs concern itself properly with the order directed to universal happiness. Therefore the Philosopher, in the above definition of legal matters, mentions both happiness and the body politic, since he says that we call those legal matters *just which are adapted to produce and preserve happiness and its parts for the body politic.* For the state is a perfect community, as he says in *Politics* i.

Now, in every genus, that which belongs to it chiefly is the principle of the others, and the others belong to that genus according to some order towards that thing. Thus fire, which is chief among hot things, is the cause of heat in mixed bodies, and these are said to be hot in so far as they have a share of fire. Consequently, since law is chiefly ordained to the common good, any other precept in regard to some individual work must needs be devoid of the nature of a law, save in so far as it regards the common good. Therefore every law is ordained to the common good.

Reply Obj. 1. A command denotes the application of a law to matters regulated by law. Now the order to the common good, at which law aims, is applicable to particular ends. And in this way commands are given even concerning particular matters.

Reply Obj. 2. Actions are indeed concerned with particular matters, but those particular matters are referable to the common good, not as to a common genus or species, but as to a common final cause, according as to the common good is said to be the common end.

Reply Obj. 3. Just as nothing stands firm with regard to the speculative reason except that which is traced back to the first indemonstrable principles, so nothing stands firm with regard to the practical reason, unless it be directed to the last end which is the common good. Now whatever stands to reason in this sense has the nature of a law.

Third Article. Whether the Reason of Any Man Is Competent to Make Laws?

We proceed thus to the Third Article:—Objection 1. It would seem that the reason of any man is competent to make laws. For the Apostle says (*Rom.* ii.14) that *when the Gentiles, who have not the law, do by nature those things that are of the law,... they are a law to themselves.* Now he says this of all in general. Therefore anyone can make a law for himself....

On the contrary, Isidore says, and the *Decretals* repeat: *A law is an ordinance of the people, whereby something is sanctioned by the Elders together with the Commonalty.* Therefore not everyone can make laws.

I answer that, A law, properly speaking, regards first and foremost the order to the common good. Now to order anything to the common good belongs either to the whole people, or to someone who is the viceregent of the whole people. Hence the making of a law belongs either to the whole people or to a public personage who has care of the whole people; for in all other matters the directing of anything to the end concerns him to whom the end belongs. . . .

Fourth Article. Whether Promulgation is Essential to Law?

We proceed thus to the Fourth Article:—Objection 1. It would seem that promulgation is not essential to law. For the natural law, above all, has the character of law. But the natural law needs no promulgation. Therefore it is not essential to law that it be promulgated. . . .

I answer that, As was stated above, a law is imposed on others as a rule and measure. Now a rule or measure is imposed by being applied to those who are to be ruled and measured by it. Therefore, in order that a law obtain the binding force which is proper to a law, it must needs be applied to the men who have to be ruled by it. But such application is made by its being made known to them by promulgation. Therefore promulgation is necessary for law to obtain its force.

Thus, from the four preceding articles, the definition of law may be gathered. Law is nothing else than an ordinance of reason for the common good, promulgated by him who has the care of the community.

Reply Obj. 1. The natural law is promulgated by the very fact that God instilled it into man's mind so as to be known by him naturally. . . .

Question XCI. On the Various Kinds of Law

First Article. Whether There Is an Eternal Law?

We proceed thus to the First Article:—Objection 1. It would seem that there is no eternal law. For every law is imposed on someone. But there was not someone from eternity on whom a law could be imposed, since God alone was from eternity. Therefore no law is eternal. . . .

I answer that, As we have stated above, law is nothing else but a dictate of practical reason emanating from the ruler who governs a perfect community. Now it is evident, granted that the world is ruled by divine providence, as was stated in the First Part, that the whole community of the universe is governed by the divine reason. Therefore the very notion of the government of things in God, the ruler of the universe, has the nature of a law. And since the divine reasons' conception of things is not subject to time, but is eternal, according to *Prov.* viii. 23, therefore it is that this kind of law must be called eternal. . . .

Second Article. Whether There Is in Us a Natural Law?

We proceed thus to the Second Article:—Objection 1. It would seem that there is no natural law in us. For man is governed sufficiently by the eternal law, since Augustine says that *the eternal law is that by which it is right that all things should be most orderly.* But nature does not abound in superfluities as neither does she fail in necessaries. Therefore man has no natural law.

Obj. 2. Further, by the law man is directed, in his acts, to the end, as was stated above. But the directing of human acts to their end is not a function of nature, as is the case in irrational creatures, which act for an end solely by their natural appetite; whereas man acts for an end by this reason and will. Therefore man has no natural law.

Obj. 3. Further, the more a man is free, the less is he under the law. But man is freer than all the animals because of his free choice, with which he is endowed in distinction from all other animals. Since, therefore, other animals are not subject to a natural law, neither is man subject to a natural law.

On the contrary, The *Gloss* on *Rom.* ii. 14 *(When the Gentiles, who have not the law, do by nature those things that are of the law)* comments as follows: *Although they have no written law, yet they have the natural law, whereby each one knows, and is conscious of, what is good and what is evil.*

I answer that, As we have stated above, law, being a rule and measure, can be in a person in two ways: in one way, as in him that rules and measures; in another way, as in that which is ruled and measured, since a thing is ruled and measured in so far as it partakes of the rule or measure. Therefore, since all things subject to divine providence are ruled and measured by the eternal law, as was stated above, it is evident that all things partake in some way in the eternal law, in so far as, namely, from its being imprinted on them, they derive their respective inclinations to their proper acts and ends. Now among all others, the rational creature is subject to divine providence in a more excellent way, in so far as it itself partakes of a share of providence, by being provident both for itself and for others. Therefore it has a share of the eternal reason, whereby it has a natural inclination to its proper act and end; and this participation of the eternal law in the rational creature is called the natural law. Hence the Psalmist, after saying (*Ps. iv. 6*): *Offer up the sacrifice of justice,* as though someone asked what the works of justice are, adds: *Many say, Who showeth us good things?* in answer to which question he says: *The light of Thy countenance, O Lord, is signed upon us.* He thus implies that the light of natural reason, whereby we discern what is good and what is evil, which is the function of the natural law, is nothing else than an imprint on us of the divine light. It is therefore evident that the natural law is nothing else than the rational creature's participation of the eternal law.

Reply Obj. 1. This argument would hold if the natural law were something different from the eternal law; whereas it is nothing but a participation thereof, as we have stated above.

Reply Obj. 2. Every act of reason and will in us is based on that which is according to nature, as was stated above. For every act of reasoning is based on principles that are known naturally, and every act of appetite in respect of the means is derived from the natural appetite in respect of the last end. Accordingly, the first direction of our acts to their end must needs be through the natural law.

Reply Obj. 3. Even irrational animals partake in their own way of the eternal reason, just as the rational creature does. But because the rational crea-ture partakes thereof in an intellectual and rational manner, therefore the participation of the eternal law in the rational creature is properly called a law, since a law is something pertaining to reason, as was stated above. Irrational creatures, however, do not partake thereof in a rational manner, and therefore there is no participation of the eternal law in them, except by way of likeness.

Third Article. Whether There Is a Human Law?

We proceed thus to the Third Article:—Objection 1. It would seem that there is not a human law. For the natural law is a participation of the eternal law, as was stated above. Now through the eternal law *all things are most orderly,* as Augustine states. Therefore the natural law suffices for the ordering of all human affairs. Consequently there is no need for a human law....

On the contrary, Augustine distinguishes two kinds of law, the one eternal, the other temporal, which he calls human.

I answer that, As we have stated above, a law is a dictate of the practical reason. Now it is to be observed that the same procedure takes place in the practical and in the speculative reason, for each proceeds from principles to conclusions, as was stated above. Accordingly, we conclude that, just as in the speculative reason, from naturally known indemonstrable principles we draw the conclusions of the various sciences, the knowledge of which is not imparted to us by nature, but acquired by the efforts of reason, so too it is that from the precepts of the natural law, as from common and indemonstrable principles, the human reason needs to proceed to the more particular determination of certain matters. These particular determinations, devised by human reason, are called human laws, provided that the other essential conditions of law be observed, as was stated above. Therefore Tully says in his *Rhetoric* that *justice has its source in nature; thence certain things came into custom by reason of their utility; afterwards these things which emanated from nature, and were approved by custom, were sanctioned by fear and reverence for the law.*

Reply Obj. 1. The human reason cannot have a full participation of the dictate of the divine reason, but according to its own mode, and imperfectly.

Consequently, just as on the part of the speculative reason, by a natural participation of divine wisdom, there is in us the knowledge of certain common principles, but not a proper knowledge of each single truth, such as that contained in the divine wisdom, so, too, on the part of the practical reason, man has a natural participation of the eternal law, according to certain common principles, but not as regards the particular determinations of individual cases, which are, however, contained in the eternal law. Hence the need for human reason to proceed further to sanction them by law. . . .

Fourth Article, Whether There Was Any Need for a Divine Law?

We proceed thus to the Fourth Article:—Objection 1. It would seem that there was no need for a divine law. For, as was stated above, the natural is a participation in us of the eternal law. But the eternal law is the divine law, as was stated above. Therefore there is no need for a divine law in addition to the natural law and to human laws derived therefrom. . . .

I answer that, Besides the natural and the human law it was necessary for the directing of human conduct to have a divine law. And this for four reasons. First, because it is by law that man is directed how to perform his proper acts in view of his last end. Now if man were ordained to no other end than that which is proportionate to his natural ability, there would be no need for man to have any further direction, on the part of his reason, in addition to the natural law and humanly devised law which is derived from it. But since man is ordained to an end of eternal happiness which exceeds man's natural ability, as we have stated above, therefore it was necessary that, in addition to the natural and the human law, man should be directed to his end by a law given by God.

Secondly, because, by reason of the uncertainty of human judgment, especially on contingent and particular matters, different people form different judgments on human acts; whence also different and contrary laws result. In order, therefore, that many may know without any doubt what he ought to do and what he ought to avoid, it was necessary for man to be directed in his proper acts by a law given by God, for it is certain that such a law cannot err.

Thirdly, because man can make laws in those matters of which he is competent to judge. But man is not competent to judge of interior movements, that are hidden, but only of exterior acts which are observable; and yet for the perfection of virtue it is necessary for man to conduct himself rightly in both kinds of acts. Consequently, human law could not sufficiently curb and direct interior acts, and it was necessary for this purpose that a divine law should supervene.

Fourthly, because, as Augustine says, human law cannot punish or forbid all evil deeds, since, while aiming at doing away with all evils, it would do away with many good things, and would hinder the advance of the common good, which is necessary for human living. In order, therefore, that no evil might remain unforbidden and unpunished, it was necessary for the divine law to supervene, whereby all sins are forbidden. . . .

Fifth Article. Whether There Is But One Divine Law?

We proceed thus to the Fifth Article:—Objection 1. It would seem that there is but one divine law. For, where there is one king in one kingdom, there is but one law. Now the whole of mankind is compared to God as to one king, according to *Ps.* xlvi. 8: *God is the King of all the earth.* Therefore there is but one divine law. . . .

I answer that, As we have stated in the First Part, distinction is the cause of number. Now things may be distinguished in two ways. First, as those things that are altogether specifically different, *e.g.,* a horse and an ox. Secondly, as perfect and imperfect in the same species, *e.g.,* a boy and a man; and in this way the divine law is distinguished in Old and New. Hence the Apostle (*Gal.* iii. 24, 25) compares the state of man under the Old Law to that of a child *under a pedagogue;* but the state under the New Law, to that of a full grown man, who is *no longer under a pedagogue.*

Now the perfection and imperfection of these two laws is to be taken in connection with the three conditions pertaining to law, as was stated above. For, in the first place, it belongs to law to be directed to the common good as to its end, as was stated above. This good may be twofold. It may be a sensible and earthly good, and to this man was directly ordained by the Old Law. Hence it is that, at the very outset of the Law, the people were invited to the earthly kingdom of the Chananæans (*Exod.* iii. 8, 17). Again it may be an intelligible and heavenly good, and to this, man is ordained by the New Law. Therefore, at the very beginning of His preaching, Christ invited men to the kingdom of heaven, saying (*Matt.* iv. 17): *Do penance, for the kingdom of heaven is at hand.* Hence Augustine says that *promises of temporal goods are contained in the Old Testament, for which reason it is called old; but the promise of eternal life belongs to the New Testament.*

Secondly, it belongs to law to direct human acts according to the order of justice; wherein also the New Law surpasses the Old Law, since it directs our internal acts, according to *Matt.* v. 20: *Unless your justice abound more than that of the Scribes and Pharisees, you shall not enter into the kingdom of heaven.* Hence the saying that *the Old Law restrains the hand, but the New Law controls the soul.*

Thirdly, it belongs to law to induce men to observe its commandments. This the Old Law did by fear of punishment, but the New Law, by love, which is poured into our hearts by the grace of Christ, bestowed in the New Law, but foreshadowed in the Old. Hence Augustine says that *there is little difference between the Law and the Gospel—fear* [timor] *and love* [amor]. . . .

Question XCIV. The Natural Law

Second Article. Whether the Natural Law Contains Several Precepts, or Only One?

We proceed thus to the Second Article:—Objection 1. It would seem that the natural law contains not several precepts, but only one. For law is a kind of precept, as was stated above. If therefore there were many precepts of the natural law, it would follow that there are also many natural laws.

Obj. 2. Further, the natural law is consequent upon human nature. But human nature, as a whole, is one, though, as to its parts, it is manifold. There-

fore, either there is but one precept of the law of nature because of the unity of nature as a whole, or there are many by reason of the number of parts of human nature. The result would be that even things relating to the inclination of the concupiscible power would belong to the natural law.

Obj. 3. Further, law is something pertaining to reason, as was stated above. Now reason is but one in man. Therefore there is only one precept of the natural law.

On the contrary, The precepts of the natural law in man stand in relation to operable matters as first principles do to matters of demonstration. But there are several first indemonstrable principles. Therefore there are also several precepts of the natural law.

I answer that, As was stated above, the precepts of the natural law are to the practical reason what the first principles of demonstrations are to the speculative reason, because both are self-evident principles. Now a thing is said to be self-evident in two ways: first, in itself; secondly, in relation to us. Any proposition is said to be self-evident in itself, if its predicate is contained in the notion of the subject; even though it may happen that to one who does not know the definition of the subject, such a proposition is not self-evident. For instance, this proposition, *Man is a rational being,* is, in its very nature, self-evident, since he who says *man,* says *a rational being;* and yet to one who does not know what a man is, this proposition is not self-evident. Hence it is that, as Boethius says, certain axioms or propositions are universally self-evident to all; and such are the propositions whose terms are known to all, as *Every whole is greater than its part,* and, *Things equal to one and the same are equal to one another.* But some propositions are self-evident only to the wise, who understand the meaning of the terms of such propositions. Thus to one who understands that an angel is not a body, it is self-evident that an angel is not circumscriptively in a place. But this is not evident to the unlearned, for they cannot grasp it.

Now a certain order is to be found in those things that are apprehended by men. For that which first falls under apprehension is *being,* the understanding of which is included in all things whatsoever a man apprehends. Therefore the first indemonstrable principle is that *the same thing cannot be affirmed and denied at the same time,* which is based on the notion of *being* and *not-being:* and on this principle all others are based, as is stated in *Metaph.* iv. Now as *being* is the first thing that falls under the apprehension of the practical reason, which is directed to action (since every agent acts for an end, which has the nature of good). Consequently, the first principle in the practical reason is one founded on the nature of good, viz., that *good is that which all things seek after.* Hence this is the first precept of law, that *good is to be done and promoted, and evil is to be avoided.* All other precepts of the natural law are based upon this; so that all the things which the practical reason naturally apprehends as man's good belong to the precepts of the natural law under the form of things to be done or avoided.

> "Law is a rule and measure of acts, whereby man is induced to act or is restrained from acting..."

Since, however, good has the nature of an end, and evil, the nature of the contrary, hence it is that all those things to which man has a natural inclination are naturally apprehended by reason as being good, and consequently as objects of pursuit, and their contraries as evil, and objects of avoidance. Therefore, the order of the precepts of the natural law is according to the order of natural inclinations. For there is in man, first of all, an inclination to good in accordance with the nature which he has in common with all substances, inasmuch, namely, as every substance seeks the preservation of its own being, according to its nature; and by reason of this inclination, whatever is a means of preserving human life, and of warding off its obstacles, belongs to the natural law. Secondly, there is in man an incli-

nation to things that pertain to him more specially, according to that nature which he has in common with other animals; and in virtue of this inclination, those things are said to belong to the natural law *which nature has taught to all animals,* such as sexual intercourse, the education of offspring and so forth. Thirdly, there is in man an inclination to good according to the nature of his reason, which nature is proper to him. Thus man has a natural inclination to know the truth about God, and to live in society; and in this respect, whatever pertains to this inclination belongs to the natural law: *e.g.,* to shun ignorance, to avoid offending those among whom one has to live, and other such things regarding the above inclination.

Reply Obj. 1. All these precepts of the law of nature have the character of one natural law, inasmuch as they flow from one first precept.

Reply Obj. 2. All the inclinations of any parts whatsoever of human nature, *e.g.,* of the concupiscible and irascible parts, in so far as they are ruled by reason, belong to the natural law, and are reduced to one first precept, as was stated above. And thus the precepts of the natural law are many in themselves, but they are based on one common foundation.

Reply Obj. 3. Although reason is one in itself, yet it directs all things regarding man; so that whatever can be ruled by reason is contained under the law of reason.

Third Article. Whether All the Acts of the Virtues are Prescribed by the Natural Law?

We proceed thus to the Third Article:—Objection 1. It would seem that not all the acts of the virtues are prescribed by the natural law. For, as was stated above, it is of the nature of law that it be ordained to the common good. But some acts of the virtues are ordained to the private good of the individual, as is evident especially in regard to acts of temperance. Therefore, not all the acts of the virtues are the subject of natural law....

I answer that, We may speak of virtuous acts in two ways: first, in so far as they are virtuous; secondly, as such and such acts considered in their proper species. If, then, we are speaking of the acts of the virtues in so far as they are virtuous, thus all virtuous acts belong to the natural law. For it has been stated that to the natural law belongs everything to which a man is inclined according to his nature. Now each thing is inclined naturally to an operation that is suitable to it according to its form: *e.g.,* fire is inclined to give heat. Therefore, since the rational soul is the proper form of man, there is in every man a natural inclination to act according to reason; and this is to act according to virtue. Consequently, considered thus, all the acts of the virtues are prescribed by the natural law, since each one's reason naturally dictates to him to act virtuously. But if we speak of virtuous acts, considered in themselves, *i.e.,* in their proper species, thus not all virtuous acts are prescribed by the natural law. For many things are done virtuously, to which nature does not primarily incline, but which, through the inquiry of reason, have been found by men to be conducive to well-living.

Reply Obj. 1. Temperance is about the natural concupiscences of food, drink and sexual matters, which are indeed ordained to the common good of nature, just as other matters of law are ordained to the moral common good …

Fourth Article. Whether the Natural Law Is the Same in All Men?

We proceed thus to the Fourth Article:—Objection 1. It would seem that the natural law is not the same in all. For it is stated in the *Decretals* that *the natural law is that which is contained in the Law and the Gospel.* But this is not common to all men, because, as it is written (*Rom.* x. 16), *all do not obey the gospel.* Therefore the natural law is not the same in all men. …

On the contrary, Isidore says: *The natural law is common to all nations.*

I answer that, As we have stated above, to the natural law belong those things to which a man is inclined naturally; and among these it is proper to man to be inclined to act according to reason. Now it belongs to the reason to proceed from what is common to what is proper, as is stated in *Physics* i.

The speculative reason, however, is differently situated, in this matter, from the practical reason. For, since the speculative reason is concerned chiefly with necessary things, which cannot be otherwise than they are, its proper conclusions, like the universal principles, contain the truth without fail. The practical reason, on the other hand, is concerned with contingent matters, which is the domain of human actions; and, consequently, although there is necessity in the common principles, the more we descend towards the particular, the more frequently we encounter defects. Accordingly, then, in speculative matters truth is the same in all men, both as to principles and as to conclusions; although the truth is not known to all as regards the conclusions, but only as regards the principles which are called *common notions.* But in matters of action, truth or practical rectitude is not the same for all as to what is particular, but only as to the common principles; and where there is the same rectitude in relation to particulars, it is not equally known to all.

It is therefore evident that, as regards the common principles whether of speculative or of practical reason, truth or rectitude is the same for all, and is equally known by all. But as to the proper conclusions of the speculative reason, the truth is the same for all, but it is not equally known to all. Thus, it is true for all that the three angles of a triangle are together equal to two right angles, although it is not known to all. But as to the proper conclusions of the practical reason, neither is the truth or rectitude the same for all, nor, where it is the same, is it equally known by all. Thus, it is right and true for all to act according to reason, and from this principle it follows, as a proper conclusion, that goods entrusted to another should be restored to their owner. Now this is true for the majority of cases. But it may happen in a particular case that it would be injurious, and therefore unreasonable, to restore goods held in trust; for instance, if they are claimed for the purpose of fighting against one's country. And this principle will be found to fail the more, according as we descend further towards the particular, *e.g.,* if one were to say that goods held in trust should be restored with such and such a guarantee, or in such and such a way; because the greater the number of conditions added, the greater the number of ways in which the principle may fail, so that it be not right to restore or not to restore.

Consequently, we must say that the natural law, as to the first common principles, is the same for all, both as to rectitude and as to knowledge. But as to certain more particular aspects, which are conclusions, as it were, of those common principles, it is the same for all in the majority of cases, both as to rectitude and as to knowledge; and yet in some few cases it may fail, both as to rectitude, by reason of certain obstacles (just as natures subject to generation and corruption fail in some few cases because of some obstacle), and as to knowledge, since in some of the reason is perverted by passion, or evil habit, or an evil disposition of nature. Thus at one time theft, although it is expressly contrary to the natural law, was not considered wrong among the Germans, as Julius Cæsar relates.

Reply Obj. 1. The meaning of the sentence quoted is not that whatever is contained in the Law and the Gospel belongs to the natural law, since they contain many things that are above nature; but that whatever belongs to the natural law is fully contained in them. Therefore Gratian, after saying that *the natural law is what is contained in the Law and the Gospel,* adds at once, by way of example, *by which everyone is commanded to do to others as he would be done by.*

Study Questions

1. How could Darwin's theory of evolution affect Aquinas's theory?

2. If human nature is more "plastic" than Aquinas seems to believe, so that different social and personal environments produce quite different individuals, what then happens to his ethic?

Euthyphro

Plato (428/427–348/347 B.C.) Born in Greece as Aristocles, this philosopher is known by his nickname, "Plato," which means "barrel-chested." He was a student of Socrates and a teacher to Aristotle. His writings are mostly in the form of dialogues of which there are about thirty, the most famous being The Republic.

Plato

Persons of the Dialogue

Socrates   Euthyphro
Scene:—The Porch of the King Archon.

From *The Dialogues of Plato* v. 2, B. Jowett, translator. © 1892 by Macmillan Publishing Co.

Euthyphro. Why have you left the Lyceum, Socrates? and what are you doing in the Porch of the King Archon? Surely you cannot be concerned in a suit before the King, like myself?
Socrates. Not in a suit, Euthyphro; impeachment is the word which the Athenians use.

Euthyphro. What! I suppose that some one has been prosecuting you, for I cannot believe that you are the prosecutor of another.

Socrates. Certainly not.

Euthyphro. Then some one else has been prosecuting you?

Socrates. Yes.

Euthyphro. And who is he?

Socrates. A young man who is little known, Euthyphro; and I hardly know him: his name is Meletus, and he is of the deme of Pitthis. Perhaps you may remember his appearance; he has a beak, and long straight hair, and a beard which is ill grown.

Euthyphro. No, I do not remember him, Socrates. But what is the charge which he brings against you?

Socrates. What is the charge? Well, a very serious charge, which shows a good deal of character in the young man, and for which he is certainly not to be despised. He says he knows how the youth are corrupted and who are their corruptors. I fancy that he must be a wise man, and seeing that I am the reverse of a wise man, he has found me out, and is going to accuse me of corrupting his young friends. And of this our mother the state is to be the judge. Of all our political men he is the only one who seems to me to begin in the right way, with the cultivation of virtue in youth; like a good husbandman, he makes the young shoots his first care, and clears away us who are the destroyers of them. This is only the first step; he will afterwards attend to the elder branches; and if he goes on as he has begun, he will be a very great public benefactor.

Euthyphro. I hope that he may; but I rather fear, Socrates, that the opposite will turn out to be the truth. My opinion is that in attacking you he is simply aiming a blow at the foundation of the state. But in what way does he say that you corrupt the young?

Socrates. He brings a wonderful accusation against me, which at first hearing excites surprise: he says that I am a poet or maker of gods, and that I invent new gods and deny the existence of old ones; this is the ground of his indictment.

Euthyphro. I understand, Socrates; he means to attack you about the familiar sign which occasion-ally, as you say, comes to you. He thinks that you are a neologian, and he is going to have you up before the court for this. He knows that such a charge is readily received by the world, as I myself know too well; for when I speak in the assembly about divine things, and foretell the future to them, they laugh at me and think me a madman. Yet every word that I say is true. But they are jealous of us all; and we must be brave and go at them.

Socrates. Their laughter, friend Euthyphro, is not a matter of much consequence. For a man may be thought wise; but the Athenians, I suspect, do not much trouble themselves about him until he begins to impart his wisdom to others; and then for some reason or other, perhaps, as you say, from jealousy, they are angry.

Euthyphro. I am never likely to try their temper in this way.

Socrates. I dare say not, for you are reserved in your behaviour, and seldom impart your wisdom. But I have a benevolent habit of pouring out myself to everybody, and would even pay for a listener, and I am afraid that the Athenians may think me too talkative. Now if, as I was saying, they would only laugh at me, as you say that they laugh at you, the time might pass gaily enough in the court; but perhaps they may be in earnest, and then what the end will be you soothsayers only can predict.

Euthyphro. I dare say that the affair will end in nothing, Socrates, and that you will win your cause; and I think that I shall win my own.

Socrates. And what is your suit, Euthyphro? are you the pursuer or the defendant?

Euthyphro. I am the pursuer.

Socrates. Of whom?

Euthyphro. You will think me mad when I tell you.

Socrates. Why, has the fugitive wings?

Euthyphro. Nay, he is not very volatile at his time of life.

Socrates. Who is he?

Euthyphro. My father.

Socrates. Your father! my good man?

Euthyphro. Yes.

Socrates. And of what is he accused?

Euthyphro. Of murder, Socrates.

Socrates. By the powers, Euthyphro! how little does

the common herd know of the nature of right and truth. A man must be an extraordinary man, and have made great strides in wisdom, before he could have seen his way to bring such an action.

Euthyphro. Indeed, Socrates, he must.

Socrates. I suppose that the man whom your father murdered was one of your relatives—clearly he was; for if he had been a stranger you would never have thought of prosecuting him.

Euthyphro. I am amused, Socrates, at your making a distinction between one who is a relation and one who is not a relation; for surely the pollution is the same in either case, if you knowingly associate with the murderer when you ought to clear yourself and him by proceeding against him. The real question is whether the murdered man has been justly slain. If justly, then your duty is to let the matter alone; but if unjustly, then even if the murderer lives under the same roof with you and eats at the same table, proceed against him. Now the man who is dead was a poor dependant of mine who worked for us as a field labourer on our farm in Naxos, and one day in a fit of drunken passion he got into a quarrel with one of our domestic servants and slew him. My father bound him hand and foot and threw him into a ditch, and then sent to Athens to ask of a diviner what he should do with him. Meanwhile he never attended to him and took no care about him, for he regarded him as a murderer; and thought that no great harm would be done even if he did die. Now this was just what happened. For such was the effect of cold and hunger and chains upon him, that before the messenger returned from the diviner, he was dead. And my father and family are angry with me for taking the part of the murderer and prosecuting my father. They say that he did not kill him, and that if he did, the dead man was but a murderer, and I ought not to take any notice, for that a son is impious who prosecutes a father. Which shows, Socrates, how little they know what the gods think about piety and impiety.

Socrates. Good heavens, Euthyphro! and is your knowledge of religion and of things pious and impious so very exact, that, supposing the circumstances to be as you state them, you are not afraid lest you too may be doing an impious thing in bringing an action against your father?

Euthyphro. The best of Euthyphro, and that which distinguishes him, Socrates, from other men, is his exact knowledge of all such matters. What should I be good for without it?

Socrates. Rare friend! I think that I cannot do better than be your disciple. Then before the trial with Meletus comes on I shall challenge him, and say that I have always had a great interest in religious questions, and now, as he charges me with rash imaginations and innovations in religion, I have become your disciple. You, Meletus, as I shall say to him, acknowledge Euthyphro to be a great theologian, and sound in his opinions; and if you approve of him you ought to approve of me, and not have me into court; but if you disapprove, you should begin by indicting him who is my teacher, and who will be the ruin, not of the young, but of the old; that is to say, of myself whom he instructs, and of his old father whom he admonishes and chastises. And if Meletus refuses to listen to me, but will go on, and will not shift the indictment from me to you, I cannot do better than repeat this challenge in the court.

Euthyphro. Yes, indeed, Socrates; and if he attempts to indict me I am mistaken if I do not find a flaw in him; the court shall have a great deal more to say to him than to me.

Socrates. And I, my dear friend, knowing this, am desirous of becoming your disciple. For I observe that no one appears to notice you—not even this Meletus; but his sharp eyes have found me out at once, and he has indicted me for impiety. And therefore, I adjure you to tell me the nature of piety and impiety, which you said that you knew so well, and of murder, and of other offences against the gods. What are they? Is not piety in every action always the same? and impiety, again—is it not always the opposite of piety, and also the same with itself, having, as impiety, one notion which includes whatever is impious?

Euthyphro. To be sure, Socrates.

Socrates. And what is piety, and what is impiety?

Euthyphro. Piety is doing as I am doing; that is to say, prosecuting any one who is guilty of murder, sacrilege, or of any similar crime—whether he be your father or mother, or whoever he may be—that makes no difference; and not to prosecute them is impiety. And please to consider, Socrates, what a notable proof I will give you of the truth of my words, a proof which I have already given to others:—of the principle, I mean, that the impious, whoever he may be, ought not to go unpunished. For do not men regard Zeus as the best and most righteous of the gods?— and yet they admit that he bound his father (Cronos) because he wickedly devoured his sons, and that he too had punished his own father (Uranus) for a similar reason, in a nameless manner. And yet when I proceed against my father, they are angry with me. So inconsistent are they in their way of talking when the gods are concerned, and when I am concerned.

Socrates. May not this be the reason, Euthyphro, why I am charged with impiety—that I cannot away with these stories about the gods? and therefore I suppose that people think me wrong. But, as you who are well informed about them approve of them, I cannot do better than assent to your superior wisdom. What else can I say, confessing as I do, that I know nothing about them? Tell me, for the love of Zeus, whether you really believe that they are true.

Euthyphro. Yes, Socrates; and things more wonderful still, of which the world is in ignorance.

Socrates. And do you really believe that the gods fought with one another, and had dire quarrels, battles, and the like, as the poets say, and as you may see represented in the works of great artists? The temples are full of them; and notably the robe of Athene, which is carried up to the Acropolis at the great Panathenaea, is embroidered with them. Are all these tales of the gods true, Euthyphro?

Euthyphro. Yes, Socrates; and, as I was saying, I can tell you, if you would like to hear them, many other things about the gods which would quite amaze you.

Socrates. I dare say; and you shall tell me them at some other time when I have leisure. But just at present I would rather hear from you a more precise answer, which you have not as yet given, my friend, to the question, What is 'piety'? When asked, you only replied, Doing as you do, charging your father with murder.

Euthyphro. And what I said was true, Socrates.

Socrates. No doubt, Euthyphro; but you would admit that there are many other pious acts?

Euthyphro. There are.

Socrates. Remember that I did not ask you to give me two or three examples of piety, but to explain the general idea which makes all pious things to be pious. Do you not recollect that there was one idea which made the impious impious, and the pious pious?

Euthyphro. I remember.

Socrates. Tell me what is the nature of this idea, and then I shall have a standard to which I may look, and by which I may measure actions, whether yours or those of any one else, and then I shall be able to say that such and such an action is pious, such another impious.

Euthyphro. I will tell you, if you like.

Socrates. I should very much like.

Euthyphro. Piety, then, is that which is dear to the gods, and impiety is that which is not dear to them.

Socrates. Very good, Euthyphro; you have now given me the sort of answer which I wanted. But whether what you say is true or not I cannot as yet tell, although I make no doubt that you will prove the truth of your words.

Euthyphro. Of course.

Socrates. Come, then, and let us examine what we are saying. That thing or person which is dear to the gods is pious, and that thing or person which is hateful to the gods is impious, these two being the extreme opposites of one another. Was not that said?

Euthyphro. It was.

Socrates. And well said?

Euthyphro. Yes, Socrates, I thought so; it was certainly said.

Socrates. And further, Euthyphro, the gods were admitted to have enmities and hatreds and differences?

Euthyphro. Yes, that was also said.

Socrates. And what sort of difference creates enmity and anger? Suppose, for example, that you and I, my good friend, differ about a number; do differences of this sort make us enemies and set us at variance with one another? Do we not go at once to arithmetic, and put an end to them by a sum?

Euthyphro. True.

Socrates. Or suppose that we differ about magnitudes, do we not quickly end the difference by measuring?

Euthyphro. Very true.

Socrates. And we end a controversy about heavy and light by resorting to a weighing machine?

Euthyphro. To be sure.

Socrates. But what differences are there which cannot be thus decided, and which therefore make us angry and set us at enmity with one another? I dare say the answer does not occur to you at the moment, and therefore I will suggest that these enmities arise when the matters of difference are the just and unjust, good and evil, honourable and dishonourable. Are not these the points about which men differ, and about which when we are unable satisfactorily to decide our differences, you and I and all of us quarrel, when we do quarrel?

Euthyphro. Yes, Socrates, the nature of the differences about which we quarrel is such as you describe.

Socrates. And the quarrels of the gods, noble Euthyphro, when they occur, are of a like nature?

Euthyphro. Certainly they are.

Socrates. They have differences of opinion, as you say, about good and evil, just and unjust, honourable and dishonourable: there would have been no quarrels among them, if there had been no such differences—would there now?

Euthyphro. You are quite right.

Socrates. Does not every man love that which he deems noble and just and good, and hate the opposite of them?

Euthyphro. Very true.

Socrates. But, as you say, people regard the same things, some as just and others as unjust,—about these they dispute; and so there arise wars and fightings among them.

Euthyphro. Very true.

Socrates. Then the same things are hated by the gods and loved by the gods, and are both hateful and dear to them?

Euthyphro. True.

Socrates. And upon this view the same things, Euthyphro, will be pious and also impious?

Euthyphro. So I should suppose.

Socrates. Then, my friend, I remark with surprise that you have not answered the question which I asked. For I certainly did not ask you to tell me what action is both pious and impious: but now it would seem that what is loved by the gods is also hated by them. And therefore, Euthyphro, in thus chastising your father you may very likely be doing what is agreeable to Zeus but disagreeable to Cronos or Uranus, and what is acceptable to Hephaestus but unacceptable to Herè, and there may be other gods who have similar differences of opinion.

Euthyphro. But I believe, Socrates, that all the gods would be agreed as to the propriety of punishing a murderer: there would be no difference of opinion about that.

Socrates. Well, but speaking of men, Euthyphro, did you ever hear any one arguing that a murderer or any sort of evil-doer ought to be let off?

Euthyphro. I should rather say that these are the questions which they are always arguing, especially in courts of law: they commit all sorts of crimes, and there is nothing which they will not do or say in their own defence.

Socrates. But do they admit their guilt, Euthyphro, and yet say that they ought not to be punished?

Euthyphro. No; they do not.

Socrates. Then there are some things which they do not venture to say and do: for they do not venture to argue that the guilty are to be unpunished, but they deny their guilt, do they not?

Euthyphro. Yes.

Socrates. Then they do not argue that the evil-doer should not be punished, but they argue about the fact of who the evil-doer is, and what he did and when?

Euthyphro. True.

Socrates. And the gods are in the same case, if as you assert they quarrel about just and unjust, and some of them say while others deny that injustice is done among them. For surely neither God nor man will ever venture to say that the doer of injustice is not to be punished?

Euthyphro. That is true, Socrates, in the main.

Socrates. But they join issue about the particulars—gods and men alike; and, if they dispute at all, they dispute about some act which is called in question, and which by some is affirmed to be just, by others to be unjust. Is not that true?

Euthyphro. Quite true.

Socrates. Well then, my dear friend Euthyphro, do tell me, for my better instruction and information, what proof have you that in the opinion of all the gods a servant who is guilty of murder, and is put in chains by the master of the dead man, and dies because he is put in chains before he who bound him can learn from the interpreters of the gods what he ought to do with him, dies unjustly; and that on behalf of such an one a son ought to proceed against his father and accuse him of murder. How would you show that all the gods absolutely agree in approving of his act? Prove to me that they do, and I will applaud your wisdom as long as I live.

Euthyphro. It will be a difficult task; but I could make the matter very clear indeed to you.

Socrates. I understand; you mean to say that I am not so quick of apprehension as the judges: for to them you will be sure to prove that the act is unjust, and hateful to the gods.

Euthyphro. Yes indeed, Socrates; at least if they will listen to me.

Socrates. But they will be sure to listen if they find that you are a good speaker. There was a notion that came into my mind while you were speaking; I said to myself: 'Well, and what if Euthyphro does prove to me that all the gods regarded the death of the serf as unjust, how do I know anything more of the nature of piety and impiety? for granting that this action may be hateful to the gods, still piety and impiety are not adequately defined by these distinctions, for that which is hateful to the gods has been shown to be also pleasing and dear to them.' And therefore, Euthyphro, I do not ask you to prove this; I will suppose, if you like, that all the gods condemn and abominate such an action. But I will amend the definition so far as to say that what all the gods hate is impious, and what they love pious or holy; and what some of them love and others hate is both or neither. Shall this be our definition of piety and impiety?

Euthyphro. Why not, Socrates?

Socrates. Why not! certainly, as far as I am concerned, Euthyphro, there is no reason why not. But whether this admission will greatly assist you in the task of instructing me as you promised, is a matter for you to consider.

> *"That thing or person which is dear to the gods is pious, and that thing or person which is hateful to the gods is impious ..."*

Euthyphro. Yes, I should say that what all the gods love is pious and holy, and the opposite which they all hate, impious.

Socrates. Ought we to enquire into the truth of this, Euthyphro, or simply to accept the mere statement on our own authority and that of others? What do you say?

Euthyphro. We should enquire; and I believe that the statement will stand the test of enquiry.

Socrates. We shall know better, my good friend, in a little while. The point which I should first wish to understand is whether the pious or holy is beloved by the gods because it is holy, or holy because it is beloved of the gods.

Euthyphro. I do not understand your meaning, Socrates.

Socrates. I will endeavour to explain: we speak of carrying and we speak of being carried, of leading and being led, seeing and being seen. You know that in all such cases there is a difference, and you know also in what the difference lies?

Euthyphro. I think that I understand.

Socrates. And is not that which is beloved distinct from that which loves?

Euthyphro. Certainly.

Socrates. Well; and now tell me, is that which is carried in this state of carrying because it is carried, or for some other reason?

Euthyphro. No; that is the reason.

Socrates. And the same is true of what is led and of what is seen?

Euthyphro. True.

Socrates. And a thing is not seen because it is visible, but conversely, visible because it is seen; nor is a thing led because it is in the state of being led, or carried because it is in the state of being carried, but the converse of this. And now I think, Euthyphro, that my meaning will be intelligible; and my meaning is, that any state of action or passion implies previous action or passion. It does not become because it is becoming, but it is in a state of becoming because it becomes; neither does it suffer because it is in a state of suffering, but it is in a state of suffering because it suffers. Do you not agree?

Euthyphro. Yes.

Socrates. Is not that which is loved in some state either of becoming or suffering?

Euthyphro. Yes.

Socrates. And the same holds as in the previous instances; the state of being loved follows the act of being loved, and not the act the state.

Euthyphro. Certainly.

Socrates. And what do you say of piety, Euthyphro: is not piety, according to your definition, loved by all the gods?

Euthyphro. Yes.

Socrates. Because it is pious or holy, or for some other reason?

Euthyphro. No, that is the reason.

Socrates. It is loved because it is holy, not holy because it is loved?

Euthyphro. Yes.

Socrates. And that which is dear to the gods is loved by them, and is in a state to be loved of them because it is loved of them?

Euthyphro. Certainly.

Socrates. Then that which is dear to the gods, Euthyphro, is not holy, nor is that which is holy loved of God, as you affirm; but they are two different things.

Euthyphro. How do you mean, Socrates?

Socrates. I mean to say that the holy has been acknowledged by us to be loved of God because it is holy, not to be holy because it is loved.

Euthyphro. Yes.

Socrates. But that which is dear to the gods is dear to them because it is loved by them, not loved by them because it is dear to them.

Euthyphro. True.

Socrates. But, friend Euthyphro, if that which is holy is the same with that which is dear to God, and is loved because it is holy, then that which is dear to God would have been loved as being dear to God; but if that which is dear to God is dear to him because loved by him, then that which is holy would have been holy because loved by him. But now you see that the reverse is the case, and that they are quite different from one another. For one (θεοφιλὲς) is of a kind to be loved because it is loved, and the other (ὅσιον) is loved because it is of a kind to be loved. Thus you appear to me, Euthyphro, when I ask you what is the essence of holiness, to offer an attribute only, and not the essence—the attribute of being loved by all the gods. But you still refuse to explain to me the nature of holiness. And therefore, if you please, I will ask you not to hide your treasure, but to tell me once more what holiness or piety really is, whether dear to the gods or not (for that is a matter about which we will not quarrel); and what is impiety?

Euthyphro. I really do not know, Socrates, how to express what I mean. For somehow or other our arguments, on whatever ground we rest them, seem to turn around and walk away from us.

Socrates. Your words, Euthyphro, are like the handiwork of my ancestor Daedalus; and if I were the sayer or propounder of them, you might say that my arguments walk away and will not remain fixed where they are placed because I am a descendant of his. But now, since these notions are your own, you must find some other gibe, for they certainly, as you yourself allow, show an inclination to be on the move.

Euthyphro. Nay, Socrates, I shall still say that you are the Daedalus who sets arguments in motion; not I, certainly, but you make them move or go round, for they would never have stirred, as far as I am concerned.

Socrates. Then I must be a greater than Daedalus: for whereas he only made his own inventions to move, I move those of other people as well. And the beauty of it is, that I would rather not. For I would give the wisdom of Daedalus, and the wealth of Tantalus, to be able to detain them and keep them fixed. But enough of this. As I perceive that you are lazy, I will myself endeavour to show you how you might instruct me in the nature of piety; and I hope that you will not grudge your labour. Tell me, then,—Is not that which is pious necessarily just?

Euthyphro. Yes.

Socrates. And is, then, all which is just pious? or, is that which is pious all just, but that which is just, only in part and not all, pious?

Euthyphro. I do not understand you, Socrates.

Socrates. And yet I know that you are as much wiser than I am, as you are younger. But, as I was saying, revered friend, the abundance of your wisdom makes you lazy. Please to exert yourself, for there is no real difficulty in understanding me. What I mean I may explain by an illustration of what I do not mean. The poet (Stasinus) sings—

'Of Zeus, the author and creator of all these things,
     You will not tell: for where there is fear there is also reverence.'

Now I disagree with this poet. Shall I tell you in what respect?

Euthyphro. By all means.

Socrates. I should not say that where there is fear there is also reverence; for I am sure that many persons fear poverty and disease, and the like evils, but I do not perceive that they reverence the objects of their fear.

Euthyphro. Very true.

Socrates. But where reverence is, there is fear; for he who has a feeling of reverence and shame about the commission of any action, fears and is afraid of an ill reputation.

Euthyphro. No doubt.

Socrates. Then we are wrong in saying that where there is fear there is also reverence; and we should say, where there is reverence there is also fear. But there is not always reverence where there is fear; for fear is a more extended notion, and reverence is a part of fear, just as the odd is a part of number, and number is a more extended notion than the odd. I suppose that you follow me now?

Euthyphro. Quite well.

Socrates. That was the sort of question which I meant to raise when I asked whether the just is always the pious, or the pious always the just; and whether there may not be justice where there is not piety; for justice is the more extended notion of which piety is only a part. Do you dissent?

Euthyphro. No, I think that you are quite right.

Socrates. Then, if piety is a part of justice, I suppose that we should enquire what part? If you had pursued the enquiry in the previous cases; for instance, if you had asked me what is an even number, and what part of number the even is, I should have had no difficulty in replying, a number which represents a figure having two equal sides. Do you not agree?

Euthyphro. Yes, I quite agree.

Socrates. In like manner, I want you to tell me what part of justice is piety or holiness, that I may be able to tell Meletus not to do me injustice, or indict me for impiety, as I am now adequately instructed by you in the nature of piety or holiness, and their opposites.

Euthyphro. Piety or holiness, Socrates, appears to me to be that part of justice which attends to the gods, as there is the other part of justice which attends to men.

Socrates. That is good, Euthyphro; yet still there is a little point about which I should like to have further information, What is the meaning of 'attention'? For attention can hardly be used in the same sense when applied to the gods as when applied to other things. For instance, horses are said to require attention, and not every person is able to attend to them, but only a person skilled in horsemanship. Is it not so?

Euthyphro. Certainly.

Socrates. I should suppose that the art of horsemanship is the art of attending to horses?

Euthyphro. Yes.

Socrates. Nor is every one qualified to attend to dogs, but only the huntsman?

Euthyphro. True.

Socrates. And I should also conceive that the art of the huntsman is the art of attending to dogs?

Euthyphro. Yes.

Socrates. As the art of the oxherd is the art of attending to oxen?

Euthyphro. Very true.

Socrates. In like manner holiness or piety is the art of attending to the gods?—that would be your meaning, Euthyphro?

Euthyphro. Yes.

Socrates. And is not attention always designed for the good or benefit of that to which the attention is given? As in the case of horses, you may observe that when attended to by the horseman's art they are benefited and improved, are they not?

Euthyphro. True.

Socrates. As the dogs are benefited by the huntsman's art, and the oxen by the art of the oxherd, and all other things are tended or attended for their good and not for their hurt?

Euthyphro. Certainly, not for their hurt.

Socrates. But for their good?

Euthyphro. Of course.

Socrates. And does piety or holiness, which has been defined to be the art of attending to the gods, benefit or improve them? Would you say that when you do a holy act you make any of the gods better?

Euthyphro. No, no; that was certainly not what I meant.

Socrates. And I, Euthyphro, never supposed that you did. I asked you the question about the nature of the attention, because I thought that you did not.

Euthyphro. You do me justice, Socrates; that is not the sort of attention which I mean.

Socrates. Good: but I must still ask what is this attention to the gods which is called piety?

Euthyphro. It is such, Socrates, as servants show to their masters.

Socrates. I understand—a sort of ministration to the gods.

Euthyphro. Exactly.

Socrates. Medicine is also a sort of ministration or service, having in view the attainment of some object—would you not say of health?

Euthyphro. I should.

Socrates. Again, there is an art which ministers to the shipbuilder with a view to the attainment of some result?

Euthyphro. Yes, Socrates, with a view to the building of a ship.

Socrates. As there is an art which ministers to the housebuilder with a view to the building of a house?

Euthyphro. Yes.

Socrates. And now tell me, my good friend, about the art which ministers to the gods: what work does that help to accomplish? For you must surely know if, as you say, you are of all men living the one who is best instructed in religion.

Euthyphro. And I speak the truth, Socrates.

Socrates. Tell me then, oh tell me—what is that fair work which the gods do by the help of our ministrations?

Euthyphro. Many and fair, Socrates, are the works which they do.

Socrates. Why, my friend, and so are those of a general. But the chief of them is easily told. Would you not say that victory in war is the chief of them?

Euthyphro. Certainly.

Socrates. Many and fair, too, are the works of the husbandman, if I am not mistaken; but his chief work is the production of food from the earth?

Euthyphro. Exactly.

Socrates. And of the many and fair things done by the gods, which is the chief or principal one?

Euthyphro. I have told you already, Socrates, that to learn all these things accurately will be very tiresome. Let me simply say that piety or holiness is learning how to please the gods in word and deed, by prayers and sacrifices. Such piety is the salvation of families and states, just as the impious, which is unpleasing to the gods, is their ruin and destruction.

Socrates. I think that you could have answered in

much fewer words the chief question which I asked, Euthyphro, if you had chosen. But I see plainly that you are not disposed to instruct me—clearly not: else why, when we reached the point, did you turn aside? Had you only answered me I should have truly learned of you by this time the nature of piety. Now, as the asker of a question is necessarily dependent on the answerer, whither he leads I must follow; and can only ask again, what is the pious, and what is piety? Do you mean that they are a sort of science of praying and sacrificing?

Euthyphro. Yes, I do.

Socrates. And sacrificing is giving to the gods, and prayer is asking of the gods?

Euthyphro. Yes, Socrates.

Socrates. Upon this view, then, piety is a science of asking and giving?

Euthyphro. You understand me capitally, Socrates.

Socrates. Yes, my friend; the reason is that I am a votary of your science, and give my mind to it, and therefore nothing which you say will be thrown away upon me. Please then to tell me, what is the nature of this service to the gods? Do you mean that we prefer requests and give gifts to them?

Euthyphro. Yes, I do.

Socrates. Is not the right way of asking to ask of them what we want?

Euthyphro. Certainly.

Socrates. And the right way of giving is to give to them in return what they want of us. There would be no meaning in an art which gives to any one that which he does not want.

Euthyphro. Very true, Socrates.

Socrates. Then piety, Euthyphro, is an art which gods and men have of doing business with one another?

Euthyphro. That is an expression which you may use, if you like.

Socrates. But I have no particular liking for anything but the truth. I wish, however, that you would tell me what benefit accrues to the gods from our gifts. There is no doubt about what they give to us; for there is no good thing which they do not give; but how we can give any good thing to them in return is far from being equally clear. If they give everything and we give nothing, that must be an affair of business in which we have very greatly the advantage of them.

Euthyphro. And do you imagine, Socrates, that any benefit accrues to the gods from our gifts?

Socrates. But if not, Euthyphro, what is the meaning of gifts which are conferred by us upon the gods?

Euthyphro. What else, but tributes of honour; and, as I was just now saying, what pleases them?

Socrates. Piety, then, is pleasing to the gods, but not beneficial or dear to them?

Euthyphro. I should say that nothing could be dearer.

Socrates. Then once more the assertion is repeated that piety is dear to the gods?

Euthyphro. Certainly.

Socrates. And when you say this, can you wonder at your words not standing firm, but walking away? Will you accuse me of being the Daedalus who makes them walk away, not perceiving that there is another and far greater artist than Daedalus who makes them go round in a circle, and he is yourself; for the argument, as you will perceive, comes round to the same point. Were we not saying that the holy or pious was not the same with that which is loved of the gods? Have you forgotten?

Euthyphro. I quite remember.

Socrates. And are you not saying that what is loved of the gods is holy; and is not this the same as what is dear to them—do you see?

Euthyphro. True.

Socrates. Then either we were wrong in our former assertion; or, if we were right then, we are wrong now.

Euthyphro. One of the two must be true.

Socrates. Then we must begin again and ask, What is piety? That is an enquiry which I shall never be weary of pursuing as far as in me lies; and I entreat you not to scorn me, but to apply your mind to the utmost, and tell me the truth. For, if any man knows, you are he; and therefore I must detain you, like Proteus, until you tell. If you had not certainly known the nature of piety and impiety, I am confident that you would never, on behalf of a serf, have charged your aged father with murder. You would not have run such a risk of doing wrong in the sight of the gods, and you would have had too much respect for the opinions of men. I am sure, therefore, that you know the nature of piety and impiety. Speak out then, my dear Euthyphro, and do not hide your knowledge.

Euthyphro. Another time, Socrates; for I am in a hurry, and must go now.

Socrates. Alas! my companion, and will you leave me in despair? I was hoping that you would instruct me in the nature of piety and impiety; and then I might have cleared myself of Meletus and his indictment. I would have told him that I had been enlightened by Euthyphro, and had given up rash innovations and speculations, in which I indulged only through ignorance, and that now I am about to lead a better life.

Study Questions

1. If God is irrelevant logically from ethics, why should we be moral?

2. If Socrates had lived in a society with a monotheistic, instead of a polytheistic, religion, would he have had a different understanding of the relationship of morality to the divine?

3. If Socrates is right in that morality is independent of the will of gods, why do so many cultures claim that their morality comes from a god or gods?

Why I Am Not a Christian

Bertrand Russell (1872–1970) Born in England, Bertrand Russell taught philosophy at Cambridge University. In 1938 he moved to the United States and taught philosophy in several American universities. Russell received the Nobel Prize in Literature in 1950 for his numerous books on all aspects of philosophy.

Bertrand Russell

I

The subject [of this paper] is "Why I Am Not a Christian." Perhaps it would be as well, first of all, to try to make out what one means by the word

Christian. It is used these days in a very loose sense by a great many people. Some people mean no more by it than a person who attempts to live a good life. In that sense I suppose there would be Christians in all sects and creeds; but I do not think that that is the proper sense of the word, if only because it would imply that all the people who are not Christians—all the Buddhists, Confucians, Mohammedans, and so on—are not trying to live a good life. I do not mean by a Christian any person who tries to live decently according to his lights. I think that you must have a certain amount of definite belief before you have a right to call yourself a Christian. The word does not have quite such a full-blooded meaning now as it had in the times of St. Augustine and St. Thomas Aquinas. In those days, if a man said that he was a Christian it was known what he meant. You accepted a whole collection of creeds which were set out with great precision, and every single syllable of those creeds you believed with the whole strength of your convictions.

What Is a Christian?

Nowadays it is not quite that. We have to be a little more vague in our meaning of Christianity. I think, however, that there are two different items which are quite essential to anybody calling himself a Christian. The first is one of a dogmatic nature—namely, that you must believe in God and immortality. If you do not believe in those two things, I do not think that you can properly call yourself a Christian. Then, further than that, as the name implies, you must have some kind of belief about Christ. The Mohammedans, for instance, also believe in God and in immortality, and yet they would not call themselves Christians. I think you must have at the very lowest the belief that Christ was, if not divine, at least the best and wisest of men. If you are not going to believe that much about Christ, I do not think you have any right to call yourself a Christian. Of course, there is another sense, which you find in *Whitaker's Almanack* and in geography books, where the population of the world is said to be divided into Christians, Mohammedans, Buddhists, fetish worshipers, and so on; and in that sense we are all Christians. The geography books count us all in, but that is a purely

geographical sense, which I suppose we can ignore. Therefore I take it that when I tell you why I am not a Christian I have to tell you two different things: first, why I do not believe in God and in immortality;[1] and, secondly, why I do not think that Christ was the best and wisest of men, although I grant him a very high degree of moral goodness.

But for the successful efforts of unbelievers in the past, I could not take so elastic a definition of Christianity as that. As I said before, in olden days it had a much more full-blooded sense. For instance, it included the belief in hell. Belief in eternal hell-fire was an essential item of Christian belief until pretty recent times. In this country, as you know, it ceased to be an essential item because of a decision of the Privy Council,[2] and from that decision the Archbishop of Canterbury and the Archbishop of York dissented; but in this country our religion is settled by Act of Parliament, and therefore the Privy Council was able to override their Graces and hell was no longer necessary to a Christian. Consequently I shall not insist that a Christian must believe in hell.

II

The Existence of God

To come to this question of the existence of God: It is a large and serious question, and if I were to attempt to deal with it in any adequate manner I should have to keep you here until Kingdom Come, so that you will have to excuse me if I deal with it in a somewhat summary fashion. You know, of course, that the Catholic Church has laid it down as a dogma that the existence of God can be proved by the unaided reason. That is a somewhat curious dogma, but it is one of their dogmas. They had to introduce it because at one time the freethinkers adopted the habit of saying that there were such and such arguments which mere reason might urge against the existence of God, but of course they knew as a matter of faith that God did exist. The ar-

---

1. [In this essay Russell does not take up the issue of immortality. He does so in a companion essay. Both of these essays were published in *Why I Am Not a Christian and Other Essays.*—Eds.]
2. [In England, a body of advisors whose function it is to advise the sovereign in matters of state.—Eds.]

guments and the reasons were set out at great length, and the Catholic Church felt that they must stop it. Therefore they laid it down that the existence of God can be proved by the unaided reason, and they have had to set up what they considered were arguments to prove it. There are, of course, a number of them, but I shall take only a few.

1. The First-Cause Argument
Perhaps the simplest and easiest to understand is the argument of the First Cause. It is maintained that everything we see in this world has a cause, and as you go back in the chain of causes further and further you must come to a First Cause, and to that First Cause you give the name of God. That argument, I suppose, does not carry very much weight nowadays, because, in the first place, cause is not quite what it used to be. The philosophers and the men of science have got going on cause, and it has not anything like the vitality it used to have; but, apart from that, you can see that the argument that there must be a First Cause is one that cannot have any validity. I may say that when I was a young man and was debating these questions very seriously in my mind, I for a long time accepted the argument of the First Cause, until one day, at the age of eighteen, I read John Stuart Mill's Autobiography, and I there found this sentence: "My father taught me that the question 'Who made me?' cannot be answered, since it immediately suggests the further question 'Who made God?'" That very simple sentence showed me, as I still think, the fallacy in the argument of the First Cause. If everything must have a cause, then God must have a cause. If there can be anything without a cause, it may just as well be the world as God, so that there cannot be any validity in that argument. It is exactly of the same nature as the Hindu's view that the world rested upon an elephant and the elephant rested upon a tortoise; and when they said, "How about the tortoise?" the Indian said, "Suppose we change the subject." The argument is really no better than that. There is no reason why the world could not have come into being without a cause; nor, on the other hand, is there any reason why it should not have always existed. There is no reason to suppose that the world had a beginning at all. The idea that things must have a beginning is really due to the poverty of our imagination. Therefore, perhaps, I need not waste any more time upon the argument about the First Cause.

2. The Natural-Law Argument
Then there is a very common argument from natural law. That was a favorite argument all through the eighteenth century, especially under the influence of Sir Isaac Newton and his cosmogony. People observed the planets going around the sun according to the law of gravitation, and they thought that God had given a behest to these planets to move in that particular fashion, and that was why they did so. That was, of course, a convenient and simple explanation that saved them the trouble of looking any further for explanations of the law of gravitation. Nowadays we explain the law of gravitation in a somewhat complicated fashion that Einstein has introduced. I do not propose to give you a lecture on the law of gravitation, as interpreted by Einstein, because that again would take some time; at any rate, you no longer have the sort of natural law that you had in the Newtonian system, where, for some reason that nobody could understand, nature behaved in a uniform fashion. We now find that a great many things we thought were natural laws are really human conventions. You know that even in the remotest depths of stellar space there are still three feet to a yard. That is, no doubt, a very remarkable fact, but you would hardly call it a law of nature. And a great many things that have been regarded as laws of nature are of that kind. On the other hand, where you can get down to any knowledge of what atoms actually do, you will find they are much less subject to law than people thought, and that the laws at which you arrive are statistical averages of just the sort that would emerge from chance. There is, as we all know, a law that if you throw dice you will get double sixes only about once in thirty-six times, and we do not regard that as evidence that the fall of the dice is regulated by design; on the contrary, if the double sixes came every time we should think that there was design. The laws of nature are of that sort as regards a great many of them. They are statistical averages such as would emerge from the laws of chance; and that makes this whole business of natural law much less impressive than it formerly was. Quite apart from

that, which represents the momentary state of science that may change tomorrow, the whole idea that natural laws imply a lawgiver is due to a confusion between natural and human laws. Human laws are behests commanding you to behave a certain way, in which way you may choose to behave, or you may choose not to behave; but natural laws are a description of how things do in fact behave, and being a mere description of what they in fact do, you cannot argue that there must be somebody who told them to do that, because even supposing that there were, you are then faced with the question, "Why did God issue just those natural laws and no others?" If you say that he did it simply from his own good pleasure, and without any reason, you then find that there is something which is not subject to law, and so your train of natural law is interrupted. If you say, as more orthodox theologians do, that in all the laws which God issues he had a reason for giving those laws rather than others—the reason, of course, being to create the best universe, although you would never think it to look at it—if there were a reason for the laws which God gave, then God himself was subject to law, and therefore you do not get any advantage by introducing God as an intermediary. You have really a law outside and anterior to the devine edicts, and God does not serve your purpose, because he is not the ultimate lawgiver. In short, this whole argument about natural law no longer has anything like the strength that it used to have. I am traveling on in time in my review of the arguments. The arguments that are used for the existence of God change their character as time goes on. They were at first hard intellectual arguments embodying certain quite definite fallacies. As we come to modern times they become less respectable intellectually and more and more affected by a kind of moralizing vagueness.

3. The Argument from Design

The next step in this process brings us to the argument from design. You all know the argument from design: Everything in the world is made just so that we can manage to live in the world, and if the world was ever so little different, we could not manage to live in it. That is the argument from design. It sometimes takes a rather curious form; for instance,

it is argued that rabbits have white tails in order to be easy to shoot. I do not know how rabbits would view that application. It is an easy argument to parody. You all know Voltaire's remark, that obviously the nose was designed to be such as to fit spectacles. That sort of parody has turned out to be not nearly so wide of the mark as it might have seemed in the eighteenth century, because since the time of Darwin we understand much better why living creatures are adapted to their environment. It is not that their environment was made to be suitable to them but that they grew to be suitable to it, and that is the basis of adaptation. There is no evidence of design about it.

> *"Religion is based, I think, primarily and mainly upon fear."*

When you come to look into this argument from design, it is a most astonishing thing that people can believe that this world, with all the things that are in it, with all its defects, should be the best that omnipotence and omniscience have been able to produce in millions of years. I really cannot believe it. Do you think that, if you were granted omnipotence and omniscience and millions of years in which to perfect your world, you could produce nothing better than the Ku Klux Klan or the Fascists? Moreover, if you accept the ordinary laws of science, you have to suppose that human life and life in general on this planet will die out in due course: It is a stage in the decay of the solar system; at a certain stage of decay you get the sort of conditions of temperature and so forth which are suitable to protoplasm, and there is life for a short time in the life of the whole solar system. You see in the moon the sort of thing to which the earth is tending—something dead, cold, and lifeless.

I am told that that sort of view is depressing, and people will sometimes tell you that if they believed that, they would not be able to go on living. Do not believe it; it is all nonsense. Nobody really worries much about what is going to happen millions of years hence. Even if they think they are worrying much about that, they are really deceiving themselves. They are worried about something much more mundane, or it may merely be a bad digestion; but nobody is really seriously rendered unhappy by the thought of something that is going to happen to this world millions and millions of years hence. Therefore, although it is of course a gloomy view to suppose that life will die out—at least I suppose we may say so, although sometimes when I contemplate the things that people do with their lives I think it is almost a consolation—it is not such as to render life miserable. It merely makes you turn your attention to other things.

4. *The Moral Arguments for Deity* Now we reach one stage further in what I shall call the intellectual descent that the theists have made in their argumentations, and we come to what are called the moral arguments for the existence of God. You all know, of course, that there used to be in the old days three intellectual arguments for the existence of God, all of which were disposed of by Immanuel Kant in the *Critique of Pure Reason;* but no sooner had he disposed of those arguments than he invented a new one, a moral argument, and that quite convinced him. He was like many people: In intellectual matters he was skeptical, but in moral matters he believed implicitly in the maxims that he had imbibed at his mother's knee. That illustrates what the psychoanalysts so much emphasize—the immensely stronger hold upon us that our very early associations have than those of later times.

Kant, as I say, invented a new moral argument for the existence of God, and that in varying forms was extremely popular during the nineteenth century. It has all sorts of forms. One form is to say that there would be no right or wrong unless God existed. I am not for the moment concerned with whether there is a difference between right and wrong, or whether there is not: That is another question. The point I am concerned with is that, if you are quite sure there is a difference between right and wrong, you are then in this situation: Is that difference due to God's fiat or is it not? If it is due to God's fiat, then for God himself there is no

difference between right and wrong, and it is no longer a significant statement to say that God is good. If you are going to say, as theologians do, that God is good, you must then say that right and wrong have some meaning which is independent of God's fiat, because God's fiats are good and not bad independently of the mere fact that it is not only through God that right and wrong came into being, but that they are in their essence logically anterior to God. You could, of course, if you liked, say that there was a superior deity who gave orders to the God who made this world, or could take up the line that some of the gnostics took up—a line which I often thought was a very plausible one— that as a matter of fact this world that we know was made by the devil at a moment when God was not looking. There is a good deal to be said for that, and I am not concerned to refute it.

5. *The Argument for the Remedying of Injustice* Then there is another very curious form of moral argument, which is this: They say that the existence of God is required in order to bring justice into the world. In the part of this universe that we know there is great injustice, and often the good suffer, and often the wicked prosper, and one hardly knows which of those is the more annoying; but if you are going to have justice in the universe as a whole you have to suppose a future life to redress the balance of life here on earth. So they say that there must be a God, and there must be heaven and hell in order that in the long run there may be justice. That is a very curious argument. If you looked at the matter from a scientific point of view, you would say, "After all, I know only this world. I do not know about the rest of the universe, but so far as one can argue at all on probabilities one would say that probably this world is a fair sample, and if there is injustice here the odds are that there is injustice elsewhere also." Supposing you got a crate of oranges that you opened, and you found all the top layer of oranges bad, you would not argue, "The underneath ones must be good, so as to redress the balance." You would say, "Probably the whole lot is a bad consignment"; and that is really what a scientific person would argue about the universe. He would say, "Here we find in this world a great deal of injustice, and so far as that goes that is a reason for supposing that justice does not rule in the world; and therefore so far as it goes it affords a moral argument against deity and not in favor of one." Of course I know that the sort of intellectual arguments that I have been talking to you about are not what really moves people. What really moves people to believe in God is not any intellectual argument at all. Most people believe in God because they have been taught from early infancy to do it, and that is the main reason.

Then I think that the next most powerful reason is the wish for safety, a sort of feeling that there is a big brother who will look after you. That plays a very profound part in influencing people's desire for a belief in God.

III

The Character of Christ

I now want to say a few words upon a topic which I often think is not quite sufficiently dealt with by rationalists, and that is the question whether Christ was the best and the wisest of men. It is generally taken for granted that we should all agree that that was so. I do not myself. I think that there are a good many points upon which I agree with Christ a great deal more than the professing Christians do. I do not know that I could go with Him all the way, but I could go with Him much further than most professing Christians can. You will remember that He said, "Resist not evil: but whosoever shall smite thee on thy right cheek, turn to him the other also." That is not a new precept or a new principle. It was used by Lao-tse and Buddha some 500 or 600 years before Christ, but it is not a principle which as a matter of fact Christians accept. I have no doubt that the present Prime Minister,[3] for instance, is a most sincere Christian, but I should not advise any of you to go and smite him on one cheek. I think you might find that he thought this text was intended in a figurative sense.

Then there is another point which I consider excellent. You will remember that Christ said, "Judge not lest ye be judged." That principle I do not think you would find was popular in the law courts of

3. Stanley Baldwin.

Christian countries. I have known in my time quite a number of judges who were very earnest Christians, and none of them felt that they were acting contrary to Christian principles in what they did. Then Christ says, "Give to him that asketh of thee, and from him that would borrow of thee turn not thou away." That is a very good principle.... I cannot help observing that the last general election was fought on the question of how desirable it was to turn away from him that would borrow of thee, so that one must assume that the Liberals and Conservatives of this country are composed of people who do not agree with the teaching of Christ, because they certainly did very emphatically turn away on that occasion.

Then there is one other maxim of Christ which I think has a great deal in it, but I do not find that it is very popular among some of our Christian friends. He says, "If thou wilt be perfect, go and sell that which thou hast, and give to the poor." That is a very excellent maxim, but, as I say, it is not much practiced. All these, I think, are good maxims, although they are a little difficult to live up to. I do not profess to live up to them myself; but then, after all, it is not quite the same thing as for a Christian.

1. Defects in Christ's Teaching Having granted the excellence of these maxims, I come to certain points in which I do not believe that one can grant either the superlative wisdom or the superlative goodness of Christ as depicted in the Gospels; and here I may say that one is not concerned with the historical question. Historically it is quite doubtful whether Christ ever existed at all, and if He did we do not know anything about Him, so that I am not concerned with the historical question, which is a very difficult one. I am concerned with Christ as He appears in the Gospels, taking the Gospel narrative as it stands, and there one does find some things that do not seem to be very wise. For one thing, He certainly thought that His second coming would occur in clouds of glory before the death of all the people who were living at that time. There are a great many texts that prove that. He says, for instance, "Ye shall not have gone over the cities of Israel till the Son of Man be come." Then He says, "There are some standing here which shall not taste death till the Son of Man comes into His kingdom"; and there are a lot of places where it is quite clear that he believed that His second coming would happen during the lifetime of many then living. That was the belief of His earlier followers, and it was the basis of a good deal of His moral teaching. When He said, "Take no thought for the morrow," and things of that sort, it was very largely because He thought that the second coming was going to be very soon, and that all ordinary mundane affairs did not count. I have, as a matter of fact, known some Christians who did believe that the second coming was imminent. I knew a parson who frightened his congregation terribly by telling them that the second coming was very imminent indeed, but they were much consoled when they found that he was planting trees in his garden. The early Christians did really believe it, and they did abstain from such things as planting trees in their gardens, because they did accept from Christ the belief that the second coming was imminent. In that respect, clearly, He was not so wise as some other people have been, and He was certainly not superlatively wise.

2. *The Moral Problem* Then you come to moral questions. There is one very serious defect, to my mind, in Christ's moral character, and that is that He believed in hell. I do not myself feel that any person who is really profoundly humane can believe in everlasting punishment. Christ certainly as depicted in the Gospels did believe in everlasting punishment, and one does find repeatedly a vindictive fury against those people who would not listen to His preaching—an attitude which is not uncommon with preachers, but which does somewhat detract from superlative excellence. You do not, for instance, find that attitude in Socrates. You find him quite bland and urbane toward the people who would not listen to him; and it is, to my mind, far more worthy of a sage to take that line than to take the line of indignation. You probably all remember the sort of thing that Socrates was saying when he was dying, and the sort of things that he generally did say to people who did not agree with him.

You will find that in the Gospels Christ said, "Ye serpents, ye generation of vipers, how can ye escape the damnation of hell?" That was said to people who did not like His preaching. It is not really to my mind quite the best tone, and there are a great many of these things about hell. There is, of course, the familiar text about the sin against the Holy Ghost: "Whosoever speaketh against the Holy Ghost it shall not be forgiven him neither in this world nor in the world to come." That text has caused an unspeakable amount of misery in the world, for all sorts of people have imagined that they have committed the sin against the Holy Ghost, and thought that it would not be forgiven them either in this world or in the world to come. I really do not think that a person with a proper degree of kindliness in his nature would have put fears and terrors of that sort into the world.

Then Christ says, "The Son of Man shall send forth His angels, and they shall gather out of His kingdom all things that offend, and them which do iniquity, and shall cast them into a furnace of fire; there shall be wailing and gnashing of teeth"; and He goes on about the wailing and gnashing of teeth. It comes in one verse after another, and it is quite manifest to the reader that there is a certain pleasure in contemplating wailing and gnashing of teeth, or else it would not occur so often. Then you all, of course, remember about the sheep and the goats; how at the second coming He is going to divide the sheep from the goats, and He is going to say to the goats, "Depart from me, ye cursed, into everlasting fire." He continues, "And these shall go away into everlasting fire." Then He says again, "If thy hand offend thee, cut it off; it is better for thee to enter into life maimed, than having two hands to go into hell, into the fire that never shall be quenched; where the worm dieth not and the fire is not quenched." He repeats that again and again also. I must say that I think all this doctrine, that hell-fire is a punishment for sin, is a doctrine of cruelty. It is a doctrine that put cruelty into the world and gave the world generations of cruel torture; and the Christ of the Gospels, if you could take Him as His chroniclers represent Him, would certainly have to be considered partly responsible for that.

There are other things of less importance. There is the instance of the Gadarene swine, where it certainly was not very kind to the pigs to put the devils into them and make them rush down the hill to the sea. You must remember that He was omnipotent, and He could have made the devils simply go away; but He chose to send them into the pigs. Then there is the curious story of the fig tree, which always rather puzzled me. You remember what happened about the fig tree. "He was hungry; and seeing a fig tree afar off having leaves, He came if haply He might find anything thereon; and when He came to it He found nothing but leaves, for the time of figs was not yet. And Jesus answered and said unto it: 'No man eat fruit of thee hereafter for ever' ... and Peter ... saith unto Him: 'Master, behold the fig tree which thou cursedst is withered away.'" This is a very curious story, because it was not the right time of year for figs, and you really could not blame the tree. I cannot myself feel that either in the matter of wisdom or in the matter of virtue Christ stands quite as high as some other people known to history. I think I should put Buddha and Socrates above Him in those respects.

IV

The Emotional Factor

As I said before, I do not think that the real reason why people accept religion has anything to do with argumentation. They accept religion on emotional grounds. One is often told that it is a very wrong thing to attack religion, because religion makes men virtuous. So I am told; I have not noticed it. You know, of course, the parody of that argument in Samuel Butler's book, *Erewhon Revisited*. You will remember that in *Erewhon* there is a certain Higgs who arrives in a remote country, and after spending some time he escapes from that country in a balloon. Twenty years later he comes back to that country and finds a new religion in which he is worshiped under the name of the "Sun Child," and it is said that he ascended into heaven. He finds that the Feast of the Ascension is about to be celebrated, and he hears Professors Hanky and Panky say to each other that they never set eyes on the man

Higgs, and they hope they never will; but they are the high priests of the religion of the Sun Child. He is very indignant, and he comes up to them, and he says, "I am going to expose all this humbug and tell the people of Erewhon that it was only I, the man Higgs, and I went up in a balloon." He was told, "You must not do that, because all the morals of this country are bound round this myth, and if they once know that you did not ascend into heaven they will all become wicked"; and so he is persuaded of that and he goes quietly away.

That is the idea—that we should all be wicked if we did not hold to the Christian religion. It seems to me that the people who have held to it have been for the most part extremely wicked. You find this curious fact, that the more intense has been the religion of any period and the more profound has been the dogmatic belief, the greater has been the cruelty and the worse has been the state of affairs. In the so-called ages of faith, when men really did believe the Christian religion in all its completeness, there was the Inquisition, with its tortures; there were millions of unfortunate women burned as witches; and there was every kind of cruelty practiced upon all sorts of people in the name of religion.

You find as you look around the world that every single bit of progress in humane feeling, every improvement in the criminal law, every step toward the diminution of war, every step toward better treatment of the colored races, or every mitigation of slavery, every moral progress that there has been in the world, has been consistently opposed by the organized churches of the world. I say quite deliberately that the Christian religion, as organized in its churches, has been and still is the principal enemy of moral progress in the world.

How the Churches Have Retarded Progress

You may think that I am going too far when I say that that is still so. I do not think that I am. Take one fact. You will bear with me if I mention it. It is not a pleasant fact, but the churches compel one to mention facts that are not pleasant. Supposing that in this world that we live in today an inexperienced girl is married to a syphilitic man; in that case the Catholic Church says, "This is an indissoluble sacrament. You must endure celibacy or stay together. And if you stay together, you must not use birth control to prevent the birth of syphilitic children." Nobody whose natural sympathies have not been warped by dogma, or whose moral nature was not absolutely dead to all sense of suffering, could maintain that it is right and proper that that state of things should continue.

That is only an example. There are a great many ways in which, at the present moment, the church, by its insistence upon what it chooses to call morality, inflicts upon all sorts of people undeserved and unnecessary suffering. And of course, as we know, it is in its major part an opponent still of progress and of improvement in all the ways that diminish suffering in the world, because it has chosen to label as morality a certain narrow set of rules of conduct which have nothing to do with human happiness; and when you say that this or that ought to be done because it would make for human happiness, they think that has nothing to do with the matter at all. "What has human happiness to do with morals? The object of morals is not to make people happy."

Fear, the Foundation of Religion

Religion is based, I think, primarily and mainly upon fear. It is partly the terror of the unknown and partly, as I have said, the wish to feel that you have a kind of elder brother who will stand by you in all your troubles and disputes. Fear is the basis of the whole thing—fear of the mysterious, fear of defeat, fear of death. Fear is the parent of cruelty, and therefore it is no wonder if cruelty and religion have gone hand in hand. It is because fear is at the basis of those two things. In this world we can now begin a little to understand things, and a little to master them by help of science, which as forced its

way step by step against the Christian religion, against the churches, and against the opposition of all the old precepts. Science can help us to get over this craven fear in which mankind has lived for so many generations. Science can teach us, and I think our own hearts can teach us, no longer to look around for imaginary supports, no longer to invent allies in the sky, but rather to look to our own efforts here below to make this world a fit place to live in, instead of the sort of place that the churches in all these centuries have made it.

What We Must Do

We want to stand upon our own feet and look fair and square at the world—its good facts, its bad facts, its beauties, and its ugliness; see the world as it is and be not afraid of it. Conquer the world by intelligence and not merely by being slavishly subdued by the terror that comes from it. The whole conception of God is a conception derived from the ancient Oriental despotisms. It is a conception quite unworthy of free men. When you hear people in church debasing themselves and saying that they are miserable sinners, and all the rest of it, it seems contemptible and not worthy of self-respecting human beings. We ought to stand up and look the world frankly in the face. We ought to make the best we can of the world, and if it is not so good as we wish, after all it will still be better than what these others have made of it in all these ages. A good world needs knowledge, kindliness, and courage; it does not need a regretful hankering after the past or a fettering of the free intelligence by the words uttered long ago by ignorant men. It needs a fearless outlook and a free intelligence. It needs hope for the future, not looking back all the time toward a past that is dead, which we trust will be far surpassed by the future that our intelligence can create.

Study Questions

1. Is Russell accurate in his criticisms of Jesus?

2. Is belief in hell immoral?

3. What moral theory is Russell implicitly using?

Moral Dilemmas

- Mr. Beamish and his son are imprisoned in a concentration camp in Nazi Germany because they are Jewish. His son is sentenced to die for attempting to escape. The commandant of the camp orders the boy to stand against the wall without a blindfold. The officer then gives Mr. Beamish a gun with one bullet and orders him to kill his son. If he refuses, his son will die anyway and so will another innocent young man.

  What should the father do?

- Susan is a secretary for a well-known and loved television evangelist, the Reverend Taylor. One day, the minister's wife comes to Susan's apartment in a very depressed state and tells Susan that the reverend has committed adultery several times and has stolen millions of dollars from the church. If they go public with the information, millions of people will be hurt and many may leave the church for good. They confront the preacher, but he denies everything.

  What would you do if you were Susan?

- Mary met Omar, a graduate student from Iran, while studying at the university. They fell in love and married. After establishing themselves in their careers, they decided to have children. Mary, a devout Baptist, wants to raise the children as Christians and Omar, a devout Moslem, wants the children raised as Moslems. They decide to postpone having children until they resolve this disagreement.

  How would you resolve this dispute?

Suggested Readings

Bellah, Robert N. "Religious Evolution." *American Sociological Review* 29 (June 1964).

Carmody, Denise Lardner, and John T. Carmody. *How to Live Well: Ethics and the World Religions.* Belmont, Calif.: Wadsworth, 1988.

Finnis, John. *Natural Law and Natural Rights.* Oxford, England: Clarendon Press, 1980.

Kenny, Anthony, ed. *Aquinas.* New York: Anchor, 1969.

McCasland, S. Vernon, Grace E. Cairns, and David C. Yu. *Religions of the World.* New York: Random House, 1969.

Nielsen, Kai. "Ethics Without Religion." *Ohio Review* 6 (1964).

Westermarck, Edward. *The Origin and Development of the Moral Ideas,* Vol. 1–2, London: Macmillan, 1908.

Chapter Three

Morality and Reason

Because of the disagreements and bewildering proliferation of religions, philosophers have looked elsewhere to justify morality. The philosophical foundations for ethical principles have largely rested on human nature and rationality. These approaches seem promising because they offer the possibility of a universal basis for ethics since facts about human nature and the rules of reason are generally considered universal in a way that the religions of the world are not. The moral relativists, however, believe that not even these approaches will work and claim that ethics can never be a universal or objective body of knowledge.

Background

Ethics as the pursuit of a rational basis for morality essentially began with Socrates (470–399 B.C.) in the ancient Greek city of Athens. Most of our knowledge about Socrates comes from the writings of Plato (428–348 B.C.), his student. As a result, it is difficult to distinguish the ideas of Socrates from those of Plato. However, Plato's early dialogues are considered more representative of Socrates's views than Plato's later works. In the early dialogues, Socrates is concerned with the search for the definition of moral virtues such as 'justice,' 'piety,' and 'courage.' His search is a rational one that challenges the traditional beliefs of his society, including the belief that the gods are relevant in deciding moral questions. Though Socrates by no means left anything like a complete moral theory, his belief that moral goodness is based on knowledge, not tradition, faith, or the emotions, has been a recurring theme in moral philosophy.

Plato continued the search for a rational morality. Plato's ethic is intimately related to his general theory of reality, the Theory of Forms or Ideas. The *forms,* Plato argued, are nonmaterial, eternal, and unchanging structures that define ultimate reality, morality, and knowledge. The highest form is the form of the good, knowledge of which is essential to moral goodness. In this sense, Plato accepted Socrates's view that virtue is knowledge, which means, in part, that a good person is ruled by reason. A rational person is one whose soul is in harmony (i.e., a soul in which the four virtues, wisdom, courage, justice, and moderation, are present). These virtues are present to the degree that they truly reflect the eternal forms of these virtues. For Plato, unlike for his student Aristotle, goodness has an otherworldly basis.

In the period between the death of Aristotle and the birth of Christ, two major schools of moral philosophy developed, *Epicureanism* and *Stoicism.* The writings of Epicurus (341–270 B.C.) and Lucretius (99–55 B.C.) define the basic outlines of the Epicurean ethic. The highest good, as they saw it, consists in the avoidance of pain and the pursuit of moderate pleasures, especially those of the mind. The good life consists of ridding the mind of superstition and cultivating the intellect in the company of good friends. Stoics, such as Zeno of Citium (340–265 B.C.), Cleanthes (331–232 B.C.), Chrysippus (280–209 B.C.), Epictetus (A.D. 50–131), and Marcus Aurelius Antoninus (A.D. 121–180), recommended a life conducive to peace of mind, rational harmony with nature, and resignation and endurance of the evils of life. Stoicism stresses control of the emotions and indifference to pleasure and pain. Some of the later stoics believed in the universal moral equality of all persons, an idea that eventually became very influential in moral philosophy.

The spread of *Christianity* throughout Europe profoundly influenced moral philosophy. Christian moral philosophy was first fully and systematically proposed by St. Augustine (A.D. 354–430). His philosophical theology incorporated many ideas of the Greek philosophers (especially Plato) but added to them the belief in a personal God as ultimate reality who has communicated His wishes for mankind through His son, Jesus. Augustine taught that the morally highest life is one of faith and abstinence from bodily pleasures, especially sex (though he realized that not all are capable of living this moral ideal fully). The moral law is revealed to us by God in the Old Testament and through Jesus; moral goodness is not revealed by reason alone but requires faith in God. The purpose of life on earth is not to achieve happiness but to do our duty as commanded by God and to practice the theological virtues of faith, hope, and love; true happiness can only be experienced in the afterlife with God in heaven. Just as knowledge of the form of the good was the absolute for Plato, Augustine believed that love of God was the highest form and the source of all goodness.

Augustine was much impressed by the otherworldly ideas of Plato, just as Thomas Aquinas (A.D. 1225–1274) was impressed by Aristotle's more naturalistic approach to ethics. Aquinas's theory of natural law combines Aristotle's theory of human nature with Christian theology (see chapter 2). On this view, eternal law, an idea in the mind of God, rules the entire universe including humankind. God rules human beings, however, through their reason, and natural law is the moral theory that results from a rational reflection on human nature. Aquinas argues that the ultimate good of man is by nature happiness and, according to divine revelation, the beatific vision, or communion with God.

Christian ethical thinking is quite distinct from that of the ancient Greeks. The Christian belief that moral law is revealed by God (at least in part) moves morality toward the realm of faith and away from reason. This moral law is believed to be upheld by divine reward and punishment, especially in the afterlife, which creates moral problems when belief in the supernatural or the divine wanes. The downplaying of the importance of the natural world, a very restrictive sexual morality, and the exalting of spiritual and otherworldly values is typical of Christianity. Finally, an emphasis on humility, love of God and humankind, and obedience to church authority clearly distinguish Christian morality from that of the Greeks.

The Protestant Reformation, the spread of nationalism, and the growth of modern science reduced the power of the Christian Church. Fragmentation and disputes undermined its authority, and philosophers once again looked to reason to establish a moral system.

Relativism

Not all philosophers agreed, however, that morality could have a rational basis. The view that morality is not and can never be rational or objective or universal is called *moral relativism*. Philosophers who hold this view claim that ethical rules are not absolute and objective as science or math is but change relative to a particular society at a particular time. On this view, moral statements cannot be true or false for all time, but are simply a reflection of particular customs and traditions that change and that will in turn change the morality of that culture. Moral relativists do not simply postulate the obvious fact that different societies have different opinions about what is moral and immoral; history and anthropology have documented evidence that many cultures accept as moral such practices as cannibalism, human sacrifice, polygamy, incest, slavery, infanticide, and other acts that, in general, our own society does not consider to be moral. What relativists maintain is that, unlike scientific claims, such as that water boils at 100°C, a claim that can be empirically tested to see whether it is true or false by experiment and observation, moral claims such as 'Incest is wrong' cannot be tested. Ethical statements do not describe the way the world is, as science does, but the way the world ought to be. How do we determine whether these 'ought' statements are true? Scientific statements are true if they describe the way the world actually is, but moral statements don't seem to describe anything but rather prescribe certain kinds of behavior. If one society prescribes incest and another does not, how do we choose which is right? According to moral relativists, we cannot rationally choose between them.

William Graham Sumner

W. G. Sumner (1840–1910), a famous sociologist, defends moral relativism. His version of relativism is based on an understanding of how morals arise and develop within a culture. Sumner believes that in order to understand any society we must understand human nature. All persons have certain basic needs such as the survival need for food and shelter. In order to satisfy these needs, humankind relies on its knowledge of the world and its experience of pleasure and pain. If in the course of seeking to meet one's needs a certain way of interacting with the world brings us pain, we tend to avoid it in the future, and if it brings us pleasure and satisfies our needs, then we tend to repeat it. These experiences of pleasure and pain eventually develop into habits or general ways of living. Human beings are also social animals in that we need others to survive. It is also from others that we learn the ways and habits of our particular society.

These group ways of meeting needs Sumner calls *customs* or *folkways*. Folkways are group ways of meeting needs based on the group's interpretation of its collective experience. In time, these customs become entrenched within a society and thus become authoritative in that all members of the society are expected to follow them. Moral rules are simply part of customs, ways of living that arise out of the experience of a particular group at a particular time. 'Right' or 'good' simply means traditional or customary, and 'wrong' or 'evil' means contrary to custom and therefore taboo. A traditional ethic is simply the taboos and customs of a particular culture; it does not provide us with a universal or absolute morality. Morals change as the conditions of life change and as our experience and our understanding of that experience change. Our conscience, or inner sense of right and wrong, is a product of the society in which we were raised. Thus, people in different societies have different consciences.

Sumner points out that cultures sometimes interpret their experiences incorrectly and develop harmful customs based on 'false inference.' He considers the custom of burying people in the ancient pyramids of Egypt to be a very wasteful custom based on mistaken beliefs about the afterlife. If we take Sumner at his word, however, we can see a possible escape from the extreme relativism that he is advocating. He is, indirectly, admitting that we can rationally criticize a moral system by questioning the alleged facts on which the system is based.

That is, every moral system makes some assumptions about the way the world is—whether there is a god or a life after death, whether men and women are biologically equal, and the like. If any of these beliefs is false, then the moral rule based on it must be rejected. For example, if there is no life after death, then there is no point to the ancient Egyptian practice of burying servants and furniture with the pharaoh, since he cannot use them after he is dead. Similarly, if pork, for example, when properly cooked, is not harmful to eat, then the taboo against eating it could be abandoned as based on an interpretation of experience that is not applicable today. The point is that if we can show that certain traditional moral practices are based on falsehoods, then we have a starting point for building a more objective ethic.

Although Sumner is surely right about the widespread disagreement concerning what is moral, is there not some agreement as well? As suggested in chapter 1, principles against murder, lying, and stealing (specific rules do vary) are virtually universal. Can you envisage a society in which these acts were not considered immoral at least under some conditions? What kind of society would that be? Basic rules seem to be necessary for any society to exist if it is to be a society with some degree of order in which persons can meet their needs. The agreement that does exist does not in itself prove that moral relativism is false, but it suggests a way of arguing against it, as Aristotle does, by looking to certain universal traits of human nature as the basis of a universal ethic.

Aristotle

Aristotle (384–322 B.C.) is widely considered to be one of the greatest philosophers who ever lived. He sought to base ethics on human nature and the uniqueness of the human capacity to reason. Aristotle begins his discussion of ethics by pointing out that all persons live and act in order to meet their needs and so to achieve happiness; everything we do and seek is because we want to be happy. This is our ultimate 'good.' Unfortunately, not everyone agrees about the definition of happiness. Some say it is wealth, others say it is fame, and still others claim it is pleasure or virtue. The way to resolve

this dispute, Aristotle claims, is to ask ourselves what is unique to human nature and then to answer the question of what a good person is or what our happiness consists in. If we ask what a good knife is, the answer is that a good knife cuts well, for that is why knives exist, that is their function. It is what they do best. What does a human do better than any other animal? Aristotle's answer is "to reason." A person is a rational animal; that is his or her special capability. So, a good person is a rational person, one whose life is structured and guided by reason.

But what does it mean to be rational? To be rational is to live in accordance with human nature (i.e., in a way that will enable you to satisfy your needs throughout your life and so to achieve your goal, happiness). To satisfy your needs, you must have certain character traits because without them you will not be fully happy. These traits Aristotle calls 'virtues.' They are habits that help us to achieve and to maintain our happiness for as long as we live. Just as sharpness is a virtue in a knife because it enables it to perform its function well, so wisdom, courage, justice, and temperance are virtues for persons because they enable us to be rational and happy. Wisdom is a necessary virtue for Aristotle because he believed that one cannot be happy if one does not know himself or reality. To have wisdom is to have knowledge that gives us a kind of "map" of reality; if life is a journey through reality, then the need for wisdom is clear. Part of learning to live is learning to deal rationally with fear, hence the need for courage. Since we are social animals and need friends to be happy, we need to treat others fairly, hence the need for justice. And finally, a human is a creature who has many desires. We must learn to control these desires, or our lives will be ruined by excess alcohol, food, drugs, and so forth, hence the need for temperance or moderation.

Aristotle's ethic has been one of the most influential theories ever presented. His contribution toward building a universal morality based on the universality of human nature and man's pursuit for happiness has made an impact on those who are seeking to refute moral relativism. Still, some questions about this theory have been raised. Are the virtues that Aristotle lists the complete set of virtues? What of faith, hope, charity, humility, and loyalty? One definition of virtue that Aristotle gives is the mean between extremes as determined by a wise man; but how do we identify a wise man unless we are already wise, in which case we do not need one? How can we decide which virtues are necessary for happiness? Others claim that people are less rational and are more irrational. Is human nature universal, or do different cultures and environments shape and mold mankind so much as to greatly reduce the universality?

Immanuel Kant

Immanuel Kant (1724–1804) was a philosopher who, like Aristotle, looked to reason as the true basis of morality. Kant wanted morality to be universally true and certain for all people and all times. For him, the only way to achieve this kind of universality is to look to reason alone, for only reason, uncontaminated by the uncertainties of empirical observation and calculation, could provide it. Attempts to base ethics on ideas of human nature or happiness are not good enough for him because human nature is not universal throughout the universe and happiness is a vague concept that is hard to define. The only locus of certainty and universality is the mind itself. Kant believed morality must be grounded in how we reason about our contemplated actions and the logical structure of this reasoning and intention.

Kant argues that only one thing is absolutely good or good without qualification and that is the 'good will.' A good will is a will that acts from pure respect for the moral law. A will is good if it has a certain structure as dictated by what Kant calls the *categorical imperative.* The categorical imperative is the absolute rule of morality, which requires that we act only in such a manner that the logic of our intention could be a consistent universal law. The logic of our intention is what Kant calls a *maxim* (i.e., our intention expressed in a generalized form). That is, when we are thinking about doing something, we must ask ourselves, "What if everyone did this?" If everyone could not consistently do it, then it is immoral. What Kant is getting at here is that quite often the immoral act is that act that makes one the exception to a rule, an act that is parasitic on others and takes advantage of the fact

that others will not do as you are doing. So, for example, a liar may get away with lying because people normally tell the truth, a cheater can cheat on an exam because he or she can copy the work of someone who has studied, a thief can steal because others work and save, and so on. So for Kant, a moral act must be an instance of a universal law, a way of acting that is open to all of us under the same circumstances.

We may grant Kant that a moral act must be in some sense universalizable, but is that enough or sufficient to make something moral? One can surely universalize "Put on your left shoe before your right shoe," but this doesn't make it a normal duty. This may be why Kant formulated a second version of the categorical imperative. This second version requires that we treat persons as having *absolute value,* not as mere means for our ends. For Kant, persons, unlike inanimate objects, are entities of absolute value (i.e., they do not receive their value from others but have value simply because they are persons). Things like furniture, cars, and clothing are valuable because we need them; their value is relative to us, not absolute. But persons do not derive their value from things; their value must come either from themselves or from other persons. But if we get our value from other persons, from whom do these persons get their value? This line of reasoning leads to an infinite regress and gives no explanation for absolute value. Kant therefore concludes that we must say that persons are valuable simply because they are persons. This version of the categorical imperative gives more content to the purely formal first version of the imperative, thus giving us a better idea of what it means to be moral. Slavery, for example, means to use a person as a thing, and it is therefore immoral. Kant believes that to be moral means to treat all people with equal respect and dignity because we all have absolute value equally.

Kant's theory is a major contribution to moral philosophy and is widely regarded to this day. The equal and absolute value of persons and the need for universal rules are considered by many to be essential elements for any adequate moral theory. Some, however, fault Kant for apparently not including any moral protection for nonrational animals, which, some claim, also have rights. Others point out that Kant does not clarify what we should do when we have a conflict of duties. For example, suppose you found yourself in the time of Nazi Germany and a Jewish friend asked you to hide him in your house because the secret police wanted to take him to a concentration camp to be executed. If a Nazi officer came to your door and asked whether your friend were there, should you save his life? Most people would say that you should lie to save him because saving an innocent person is a higher moral duty that the duty not to lie. Kant believed one should never lie!

Still others think that Kant is too vague about what it means to use another person. When you go to a dentist, you use the dentist to help you, and the dentist uses you to earn an income. When exactly does using someone become immoral? Finally, others claim that Kant was too pessimistic about the possibility of basing ethics on the idea of happiness, which Mill believed was sufficiently clear to be the basis of his moral theory.

John Stuart Mill

J. S. Mill (1806–1873) is one of the major philosophers of the West. He made contributions to all branches of philosophy and was active in politics and social reform. Like Aristotle, he felt all persons finally seek only one thing and that is happiness. If we accept this as true, then all we do and how we order our politics and society should promote this goal. This includes morality. On this basis he further developed the theory of utilitarianism first introduced by another British philosopher, Jeremy Bentham (1748–1832).

Utilitarianism is a moral theory that has as its basic moral principle the *greatest happiness principle*. This principle states that actions are moral to the degree that they promote happiness or reduce pain. Happiness is defined as the presence of pleasure and the absence of pain. Pleasures, in turn are divided into the 'higher' and 'lower' pleasures. The lower pleasures are the pleasures of the body such as those of food, drink, and sex. The higher pleasures are those of the mind, such as knowledge, artistic appreciation, and the pleasures of friendship. Mill argued that persons must strive for the higher pleasures, for therein resides our long-lasting happiness.

Mill's theory is sometimes called *consequentialist* because he believed that the goodness of an action is based on the consequences it brings about in the world in terms of pleasure and pain. We must always act to maximize happiness and to minimize pain for all involved, not just ourselves. Unlike Kant, Mill was not so skeptical about what happiness or misery is. He believed that most human suffering is due to disease, poverty, ignorance, and lack of affection. To the degree that we reduce these, we are being moral.

Mill formulated this moral theory because he wanted to make ethics less mysterious and more objective than the religiously based systems then prevalent. Mill's contributions, including his belief in the importance of reducing human suffering and developing our capacity for higher pleasures, are significant. Some philosophers, however, are concerned that his theory doesn't give sufficient protection to human rights. For example, if we could frame an innocent person for a crime in order to prevent a riot in which many would be killed and much suffering produced, would Mill's theory allow it for the greatest good? Some think his theory would because he doesn't give persons the absolute value that Kant does. Others point out that a morality based on consequences is faulty in that we cannot know what all the consequences of an action are going to be. Thus, how can we measure the pleasure and pain produced by our actions?

Moral Perception of Facts

The history of ethics evolves in response to other significant developments. As mentioned in the discussions of moral relativism in chapters 1 and 2, the content of our moral beliefs is based partly on our understanding of what the 'facts' are (e.g., are women inferior in reasoning capacity by nature) and by our overall view of reality (e.g., a supernatural view such as those of Christianity and the major religions or a naturalistic philosophical view such as that of Aristotle). If the 'facts' change owing to the growth of modern science or to changes in religious belief, then moral beliefs will reflect this.

Changes in science, historical conditions, and religious belief affect some moral beliefs but not all of morality. What might be called the *core* of morality concerning murder, lying, theft, violence, and harm to others does not change very much. As suggested in chapter 1, the core morality cannot change significantly because it is based on fundamental human needs and human nature that do not change very much or very rapidly. According to Darwin, biological evolution is usually a very slow process. In addition, social coexistence, cooperation, and organization require that certain moral rules generally apply (e.g., rules against widespread lying and violence). Noncore morality can change as social circumstances change. For example, if the population became too large and starvation became a real possibility, moral attitudes about abortion and birth control could and probably would change (assuming certain flexibility in the religious or general worldview interpretations of what is moral). We should not be surprised to learn, therefore, that this moral core has been part of moral theories from the time of Aristotle through Christianity to modern times.

To the degree that moral theories differ then, they differ according to varying assessments of the 'facts' and the overall religious-philosophical contexts on which they function. They may also differ in how they rationally justify the core of morality. Aristotle, Kant, and Mill do not disagree essentially about the content of the core morality, but they disagree about how to justify it. Aristotle and Mill argue within a naturalistic and nonreligious context in which the fulfillment of human needs, desires, or preferences (i.e., human happiness) is the ultimate goal morality must serve. Here again the fundamental human desire or need for happiness is the foundation of the moral code. Kant at first rejects happiness as the foundation of morality because of its vagueness, but he nevertheless incorporates it in his ethic in at least three ways. First, he states that our own happiness is an indirect duty, for without it immorality is more likely. Thus, he indirectly concedes that happiness is not all that vague. Second, Kant tells us that when we universalize we must take into account possible future situations in which we might find ourselves. This is brought out clearly in the example of the rich and the poor in which Kant asks us whether one can universalize the maxim that the rich should not help the poor. He grants that one could consistently universalize such a maxim, but he believes that no one would will or desire such a law to be universal because one might find oneself poor in the future. Finally, Kant concedes elsewhere that, ultimately, happiness must be the reward for the moral life (How could morality make sense or have any followers if it made everyone miserable?) but that this may only take place in the afterlife and through God's actions. Here, the religious worldview of Kant explains some of his differences with Aristotle and Mill. If they did not disagree on this point, most other major disagreements among these moral theories would also be resolved.

Mores as Folkways

William Graham Sumner (1840–1910) Born in New Jersey, William Graham Sumner was one of the leading sociologists and economists of his time. Sumner taught at Yale University and was an Episcopalian minister.

William Graham Sumner

1. Definition and Mode of Origin of the Folkways.   If we put together all that we have

From *Folkways,* by William Graham Sumner, © copyright 1906 by William Graham Sumner. Published by Silver, Burdett & Ginn, Inc.

learned from anthropology and ethnography about primitive men and primitive society, we perceive that the first task of life is to live. Men begin with acts, not with thoughts. Every moment brings necessities which must be satisfied at once. Need was the first experience, and it was followed at once by a blundering effort to satisfy it. It is generally taken for granted that men inherited some guiding instincts from their beast ancestry, and it may be true, although it has never been proved. If there were such inheritances, they controlled and aided the first efforts to satisfy needs. Analogy makes it easy to assume that the ways of beasts had produced channels of habit and predisposition along which dexterities and other psychophysical activities would run easily. Experiments with newborn animals show that in the absence of any experience of the relation of means to ends, efforts to satisfy needs are clumsy and blundering. The method is that of trial and failure, which produces repeated pain, loss, and disappointments. Nevertheless, it is a method of rude experiment and selection. The earliest efforts of men were of this kind. Need was the impelling force. Pleasure and pain, on the one side and the other, were the rude constraints which defined the line on which efforts must proceed. The ability to distinguish between pleasure and pain is the only psychical power which is to be assumed. Thus ways of doing things were selected, which were expedient. They answered the purpose better than other ways, or with less toil and pain. Along the course on which efforts were compelled to go, habit, routine, and skill were developed. The struggle to maintain existence was carried on, not individually, but in groups. Each profited by the other's experience; hence there was concurrence towards that which proved to be most expedient. All at last adopted the same way for the same purpose; hence the ways turned into customs and became mass phenomena. Instincts were developed in connection with them. In this way folkways arise. The young learn them by tradition, imitation, and authority. The folkways, at a time, provide for all the needs of life then and there. They are uniform, universal in the group, imperative, and invariable. As time goes on, the folkways become more and more arbitrary, positive, and imperative. If asked why they

act in a certain way in certain cases, primitive people always answer that it is because they and their ancestors always have done so. A sanction also arises from ghost fear. The ghosts of ancestors would be angry if the living should change the ancient folkways. . . .

3. Folkways are Made Unconsciously.   It is of the first importance to notice that, from the first acts by which men try to satisfy needs, each act stands by itself, and looks no further than the immediate satisfaction. From recurrent needs arise habits for the individual and customs for the group, but these results are consequences which were never conscious, and never foreseen or intended. They are not noticed until they have long existed, and it is still longer before they are appreciated. Another long time must pass, and a higher stage of mental development must be reached, before they can be used as a basis from which to deduce rules for meeting, in the future, problems whose pressure can be foreseen. The folkways, therefore, are not creations of human purpose and wit. They are like products of natural forces which men unconsciously set in operation, or they are like the instinctive ways of animals, which are developed out of experience, which reach a final form of maximum adaptation to an interest, which are handed down by tradition and admit to no exception or variation, yet change to meet new conditions, still within the same limited methods, and without rational reflection or purpose. From this it results that all the life of human beings, in all ages and stages of culture, is primarily controlled by a vast mass of folkways handed down from the earliest existence of the race, having the nature of the ways of other animals, only the topmost layers of which are subject to change and control, and have been somewhat modified by human philosophy, ethics, and religion, or by other acts of intelligent reflection. We are told of savages that "It is difficult to exhaust the customs and small ceremonial usages of a savage people. Custom regulates the whole of a man's actions—his bathing, washing, cutting his hair, eating, drinking, and fasting. From his cradle to his grave he is the slave of ancient usage. In his life there is nothing free, nothing original, nothing spontaneous, no progress towards a higher and better life, and no attempt to improve his condition, mentally, morally, or spiritually." All men act in this way with only a little wider margin of voluntary variation....

28. Folkways Due to False Inference. Furthermore, folkways have been formed by accident, that is, by irrational and incongruous action, based on pseudo-knowledge. In Molembo a pestilence broke out soon after a Portuguese had died there. After that the natives took all possible measures not to allow any white man to die in their country. On the Nicobar islands some natives who had just begun to make pottery died. The art was given up and never again attempted. White men gave to one Bushman in a kraal a stick ornamented with buttons as a symbol of authority. The recipient died leaving the stick to his son. The son soon died. Then the Bushmen brought back the stick lest all should die. Until recently no building of incombustible materials could be built in any big town of the central province of Madagascar, on account of some ancient prejudice. A party of Eskimos met with no game. One of them returned to their sledges and got the ham of a dog to eat. As he returned with the ham bone in his hand he met and killed a seal. Ever afterwards he carried a ham bone in his hand when hunting. The Belenda women (peninsula of Malacca) stay as near to the house as possible during the period. Many keep the door closed. They know no reason for this custom. "It must be due to some now forgotten superstition." Soon after the Yakuts saw a camel for the first time smallpox broke out amongst them. They thought the camel to be the agent of the disease. A woman amongst the same people contracted an endogamous marriage. She soon afterwards became blind. This was thought to be on account of the violation of ancient customs. A very great number of such cases could be collected. In fact they represent the current mode of reasoning of nature people. It is their custom to reason that, if one thing follows another, it is due to it. A great number of customs are traceable to the notion of the evil eye, many more to ritual notions of uncleanness. No scientific investigation could discover

the origin of the folkways mentioned, if the origin had not chanced to become known to civilized men. We must believe that the known cases illustrate the irrational and incongruous origin of many folkways. In civilized history also we know that customs have owed their origin to "historical accident"—the vanity of a princess, the deformity of a king, the whim of a democracy, the love intrigue of a statesman or prelate. By the institutions of another age it may be provided that no one of these things can affect decisions, acts, or interests, but then the power to decide the ways may have passed to clubs, trades unions, trusts, commercial rivals, wire-pullers, politicians, and political fanatics. In these cases also the causes and origins may escape investigation.

29. Harmful Folkways. There are folkways which are positively harmful. Very often these are just the ones for which a definite reason can be given. The destruction of a man's goods at his death is a direct deduction from otherworldliness; the dead man is supposed to want in the other world just what he wanted here. The destruction of a man's goods at his death was a great waste of capital, and it must have had a disastrous effect on the interests of the living, and must have very seriously hindered the development of civilization. With this custom we must class all the expenditure of labor and capital on graves, temples, pyramids, rites, sacrifices, and support of priests, so far as these were supposed to benefit the dead. The faith in goblinism produced otherworldly interests which overruled ordinary worldly interests. Foods have often been forbidden which were plentiful, the prohibition of which injuriously lessened the food supply. There is a tribe of Bushmen who will eat no goat's flesh, although goats are the most numerous domestic animals in the district. Where totemism exists it is regularly accompanied by a taboo on eating the totem animal. Whatever may be the real principle in totemism, it overrules the interest in an abundant food supply. "The origin of the sacred regard paid to the cow must be sought in the primitive nomadic life of the Indo-European race," because it is common to Iranians and Indians of Hindostan. The Libyans ate oxen but not cows. The same was true of the Phœnicians and Egyptians. In some cases the sense of a food taboo is not to be learned. It may have been entirely capricious. Mohammed would not eat lizards, because he thought them the offspring of a metamorphosed clan of Israelites. On the other hand, the protective taboo which forbade killing crocodiles, pythons, cobras, and other animal enemies of man was harmful to his interests, whatever the motive. "It seems to be a fixed article of belief throughout southern India, that all who have willfully or accidentally killed a snake, especially a cobra, will certainly be punished, either in this life or the next, in one of three ways: either by childlessness, or by leprosy, or by ophthalmia." Where this faith exists man has a greater interest to spare a cobra than to kill it. India furnishes a great number of cases of harmful mores. "In India every tendency of humanity seems intensified and exaggerated. No country in the world is so conservative in its traditions, yet no country has undergone so many religious changes and vicissitudes." "Every year thousands perish of disease that might recover if they would take proper nourishment, and drink the medicine that science prescribes, but which they imagine that their religion forbids them to touch." "Men who can scarcely count beyond twenty, and know not the letters of the alphabet, would rather die than eat food which had been prepared by men of lower caste, unless it had been sanctified by being offered to an idol; and would kill their daughters rather than endure the disgrace of having unmarried girls at home beyond twelve or thirteen years of age." In the last case the rule of obligation and duty is set by the mores. The interest comes under vanity. The sanction of the caste rules is in a boycott by all members of the caste. The rules are often very harmful. "The authority of caste rests partly on written laws, partly on legendary fables or narratives, partly on the injunctions of instructors and priests, partly on custom and usage, and partly on the caprice and convenience of its votaries." The harm of caste rules is so great that of late they have been broken in some cases, especially in regard to travel over sea, which is a great advantage to Hindoos. The Hindoo folkways in regard to widows and child marriages must also be recognized as socially harmful.

30. How "True" and "Right" are Found.
If a savage puts his hand too near the fire, he suffers pain and draws it back. He knows nothing of the laws of the radiation of heat, but his instinctive action conforms to that law as if he did know it. If he wants to catch an animal for food, he must study its habits and prepare a device adjusted to those habits. If it fails, he must try again, until his observation is "true" and his device is "right." All the practical and direct element in the folkways seems to be due to common sense, natural reason, intuition, or some other original mental endowment. It seems rational (or rationalistic) and utilitarian. Often in the mythologies this ultimate rational element was ascribed to the teaching of a god or a culture hero. In modern mythology it is accounted for as "natural."

Although the ways adopted must always be really "true" and "right" in relation to facts, for otherwise they could not answer their purpose, such is not the primitive notion of true and right.

31. The Folkways are "Right." Rights. Morals.
The folkways are the "right" ways to satisfy all interests, because they are traditional, and exist in fact. They extend over the whole of life. There is a right way to catch game, to win a wife, to make one's self appear, to cure disease, to honor ghosts, to treat comrades or strangers, to behave when a child is born, on the warpath, in council, and so on in all cases which can arise. The ways are defined on the negative side, that is, by taboos. The "right" way is the way which the ancestors used and which has been handed down. The tradition is its own warrant. It is not held subject to verification by experience. The notion of right is in the folkways. It is not outside of them, of independent origin, and brought to them to test them. In the folkways, whatever is, is right. This is because they are traditional, and therefore contain in themselves the authority of the ancestral ghosts. When we come to the folkways we are at the end of our analysis. The notion of right and ought is the same in regard to all the folkways, but the degree of it varies with the importance of the interest at stake. The obligation of conformable and cooperative action is far greater under ghost fear and war than in other matters, and the

social sanctions are severer, because group interests are supposed to be at stake. Some usages contain only a slight element of right and ought. It may well be believed that notions of right and duty, and of social welfare, were first developed in connection with ghost fear and otherworldliness, and therefore that, in that field also, folkways were first raised to mores. "Rights" are the rules of mutual give and take in the competition of life which are imposed on comrades in the in-group, in order that the peace may prevail there which is essential to the group strength. Therefore rights can never be "natural" or "God-given," or absolute in any sense. The morality of a group at a time is the sum of the taboos and prescriptions in the folkways by which right conduct is defined. Therefore morals can never be intuitive. They are historical, institutional, and empirical.

World philosophy, life policy, right, rights, and morality are all products of the folkways. They are reflections on, and generalizations from, the experience of pleasure and pain which is won in efforts to carry on the struggle for existence under actual life conditions. The generalizations are very crude and vague in their germinal forms. They are all embodied in folklore, and all our philosophy and science have been developed out of them.

15. Ethnocentrism   is the technical name for this view of things in which one's own group is the center of everything, and all others are scaled and rated with reference to it. Folkways correspond to it to cover both the inner and the outer relation. Each group nourishes its own pride and vanity, boasts itself superior, exalts its own divinities, and looks with contempt on outsiders. Each group thinks its own folkways the only right ones, and if it observes that other groups have other folkways, these excite its scorn. Opprobrious epithets are derived from these differences. "Pig-eater," "cow-eater," "uncircumcised," "jabberers," are epithets of contempt and abomination. The Tupis called the Portuguese by a derisive epithet descriptive of birds which have feathers around their feet, on account of trousers.

For our present purpose the most important fact is that ethnocentrism leads a people to exaggerate and intensify everything in their own folkways which is peculiar and which differentiates them from others. It therefore strengthens the folkways.

16. Illustrations of Ethnocentrism.   The Papuans on New Guinea are broken up into village units which are kept separate by hostility, cannibalism, head hunting, and divergences of language and religion. Each village is integrated by its own language, religion, and interests. A group of villages is sometimes united into a limited unity by connubium. A wife taken inside of this group unit has full status; one taken outside of it has not. The petty group units are peace groups within and are hostile to all outsiders. The Mbayas of South America believed that their deity had bidden them live by making war on others, taking their wives and property, and killing their men.

17.   When Caribs were asked whence they came, they answered, "We alone are people." The meaning of the name Kiowa is "real or principal people." The Lapps call themselves "men," or "human beings." The Greenland Eskimo think that Europeans have been sent to Greenland to learn virtue and good manners from the Greenlanders. Their highest form of praise for a European is that he is, or soon will be, as good as a Greenlander. The Tunguses call themselves "men." As a rule it is found that nature peoples call themselves "men." Others are something else—perhaps not defined—but not real men. In myths the origin of their own tribe is that of the real human race. They do not account for the others. The Ainos derive their name from that of the first man, whom they worship as a god. Evidently the name of the god is derived from the tribe name. When the tribal name has another sense, it is always boastful or proud. The Ovambo name is a corruption of the name of the tribe for themselves, which means "the wealthy." Amongst the most remarkable people in the world for ethnocentrism are the Seri of Lower California. They observe an attitude of suspicion and hostility to all outsiders, and strictly forbid marriage with outsiders.

18. The Jews divided all mankind into themselves and Gentiles. They were the "chosen people." The Greeks and Romans called all outsiders "barbarians." In Euripides' tragedy of *Iphigenia in Aulis,* Iphigenia says that it is fitting that Greeks should rule over barbarians, but not contrariwise, because Greeks are free, and barbarians are slaves. The Arabs regarded themselves as the noblest nation and all others as more or less barbarous. In 1896, the Chinese minister of education and his counselors edited a manual in which this statement occurs: "How grand and glorious is the Empire of China, the middle kingdom! She is the largest and richest in the world. The grandest men in the world have all come from the middle empire." In all the literature of all the states equivalent statements occur, although they are not so naively expressed. In Russian books and newspapers the civilizing mission of Russia is talked about, just as, in the books and journals of France, Germany, and the United States, the civilizing mission of those countries is assumed and referred to as well understood. Each state now regards itself as the leader of civilization, the best, the freest, and the wisest, and all others are inferior. Within a few years our own man-on-the-curbstone has learned to class all foreigners of the Latin people as "dagos," and "dago" has become an epithet of contempt. These are all cases of ethnocentrism. . . .

34. Definition of the Mores.   When the elements of truth and right are developed into doctrines of welfare, the folkways are raised to another plane. They then become capable of producing inferences, developing into new forms, and extending their constructive influence over men and society. Then we call them the mores. The mores are the folkways, including the philosophical and ethical generalizations as to societal welfare which are suggested by them, and inherent in them, as they grow. . . .

42. Purpose of the Present Work.   "Ethology" would be a convenient term for the study of manners, customs, usages, and mores, including the study of the way in which they are formed, how they grow or decay, and how they affect the interests which it is their purpose to serve. The Greeks applied the term "ethos" to the sum of the characteristic usages, ideas, standards, and codes by which a group was differentiated and individualized in character from other groups. "Ethics" were things which pertained to the ethos and therefore the things which were the standard of right. The Romans used "mores" for customs in the broadest and richest sense of the word, including the notion that customs served welfare, and had traditional and mystic sanction, so that they were properly authoritative and sacred. It is a very surprising fact that modern nations should have lost these words and the significant suggestions which inhere in them. The English language has no derivative noun from "mores," and no equivalent for it. The French *mœurs* is trivial compared with "mores." The German *Sitte* renders "mores" but very imperfectly. The modern peoples have made morals and morality a separate domain, by the side of religion, philosophy, and politics. In that sense, morals is an impossible and unreal category. It has no existence, and can have none. The word "moral" means what belongs or appertains to the mores. Therefore the category of morals can never be defined without reference to something outside of itself. Ethics, having lost connection with the ethos of a people, is an attempt to systematize the current notions of right and wrong upon some basic principle, generally with the purpose of establishing morals on an absolute doctrine, so that it shall be universal, absolute, and everlasting. In a general way also, whenever a thing can be called moral, or connected with some ethical generality, it is thought to be "raised," and disputants whose method is to employ ethical generalities assume especial authority for themselves and their views. These methods of discussion are most employed in treating of social topics, and they are disastrous to sound study of facts. They help to hold the social sciences under the dominion of metaphysics. The abuse has been most developed in connection with political economy, which has been almost robbed of the character of a serious discipline by converting its discussions into ethical disquisitions.

43. *Why Use the Word Mores.* "Ethica," in the Greek sense, or "ethology," as above defined, would be good names for our present work. We aim to study the ethos of groups, in order to see how it arises, its power and influence, the modes of its operation on members of the group, and the various attributes of it (ethica). "Ethology" is a very unfamiliar word. It has been used for the mode of setting forth manners, customs, and mores in satirical comedy. The Latin word "mores" seems to be, on the whole, more practically convenient and available than any other for our purpose, as a name for the folkways with the connotations of right and truth in respect to welfare, embodied in them. The analysis and definition above given show that in the mores we must recognize a dominating force in history, constituting a condition as to what can be done, and as to the methods which can be employed.

44. *Mores are a Directive Force.* Of course the view which has been stated is antagonistic to the view that philosophy and ethics furnish creative and determining forces in society and history. That view comes down to us from the Greek philosophy and it has now prevailed so long that all current discussion conforms to it. Philosophy and ethics are pursued as independent disciplines, and the results are brought to the science of society and to statesmanship and legislation as authoritative dicta. We also have *Völkerpsychologie, Sozialpolitik,* and other intermediate forms which show the struggle of metaphysics to retain control of the science of society. The "historic sense," the *Zeitgeist,* and other terms of similar import are partial recognitions of the mores and their importance in the science of society. It can be seen also that philosophy and ethics are products of the folkways. They are taken out of the mores, but are never original and creative; they are secondary and derived. They often interfere in the second stage of the sequence—act, thought, act. Then they produce harm, but some ground is furnished for the claim that they are creative or at least regulative. In fact, the real process in great bodies of men is not one of deduction from any great principle of philosophy or ethics. It is one of minute efforts to live well under existing conditions, which

efforts are repeated indefinitely by great numbers, getting strength from habit and from the fellowship of united action. The resultant folkways become coercive. All are forced to conform, and the folkways dominate the societal life. Then they seem true and right, and arise into mores as the norm of welfare. Thence are produced faiths, ideas, doctrines, religions, and philosophies, according to the stage of civilization and the fashions of reflection and generalization.

61. *The Mores and Institutions.* Institutions and laws are produced out of mores. An institution consists of a concept (idea, notion, doctrine, interest) and a structure. The structure is a framework, or apparatus, or perhaps only a number of functionaries set to cooperate in prescribed ways at a certain conjuncture. The structure holds the concept and furnishes instrumentalities for bringing it into the world of facts and action in a way to serve the interests of men in society. Institutions are either crescive or enacted. They are crescive when they take shape in the mores, growing by the instinctive efforts by which the mores are produced. Then the efforts, through long use, become definite and specific. Property, marriage, and religion are the most primary institutions. They began in folkways. They became customs. They developed into mores by the addition of some philosophy of welfare, however crude. Then they were made more definite and specific as regards the rules, the prescribed acts, and the apparatus to be employed. This produced a structure and the institution was complete. Enacted institutions are products of rational invention and intention. They belong to high civilization. Banks are institutions of credit founded on usages which can be traced back to barbarism. There came a time when, guided by rational reflection on experience, men systematized and regulated the usages which had become current, and thus created positive institutions of credit, defined by law and sanctioned by the force of the state. Pure enacted institutions which are strong and prosperous are hard to find. It is too difficult to invent and create an institution, for a purpose, out of nothing. The electoral college in the constitution of the United States is an example. In that case the democratic mores of the people have seized upon the device and made of it something quite different from what the inventors planned. All institutions have come out of mores, although the rational element in them is sometimes so large that their origin in the mores is not to be ascertained except by an historical investigation (legislatures, courts, juries, joint stock companies, the stock exchange). Property, marriage, and religion are still almost entirely in the mores. Amongst nature men any man might capture and hold a woman at any time, if he could. He did it by superior force which was its own supreme justification. But his act brought his group and her group into war, and produced harm to his comrades. They forbade capture, or set conditions for it. Beyond the limits, the individual might still use force, but his comrades were no longer responsible. The glory to him, if he succeeded, might be all the greater. His control over his captive was absolute. Within the prescribed conditions, "capture" became technical and institutional, and rights grew out of it. The woman had a status which was defined by custom, and was very different from the status of a real captive. Marriage was the institutional relation, in the society and under its sanction, of a woman to a man, where the woman had been obtained in the prescribed way. She was then a "wife." What her rights and duties were defined by the mores, as they are to-day in all civilized society.

62. Laws.

Acts of legislation come out of the mores. In low civilization all societal regulations are customs and taboos, the origin of which is unknown. Positive laws are impossible until the stage of verification, reflection, and criticism is reached. Until that point is reached there is only customary law, or common law. The customary law may be codified and systematized with respect to some philosophical principles, and yet remain customary. The codes of Manu and Justinian are examples. Enactment is not possible until reverence for ancestors has been so much weakened that it is no longer thought wrong to interfere with traditional customs by positive enactment. Even then there is reluctance to make enactments, and there is a stage of transition during which traditional customs are extended

by interpretation to cover new cases and to prevent evils. Legislation, however, has to seek standing ground on the existing mores, and it soon becomes apparent that legislation, to be strong, must be consistent with the mores. Things which have been in the mores are put under police regulation and later under positive law. It is sometimes said that "public opinion" must ratify and approve police regulations, but this statement rests on an imperfect analysis. The regulations must conform to the mores, so that the public will not think them too lax or too strict. The mores of our urban and rural populations are not the same; consequently legislation about intoxicants which is made by one of these sections of the population does not succeed when applied to the other. The regulation of drinking places, gambling places, and disorderly houses has passed through

> *"The morality of a group at a time is the sum of the taboos and prescriptions in the folkways by which right conduct is defined."*

the above-mentioned stages. It is always a question of expediency whether to leave a subject under the mores, or to make a police regulation for it, or to put it into the criminal law. Betting, horse racing, dangerous sports, electric cars, and vehicles are cases now of things which seem to be passing under positive enactment and out of the unformulated control of the mores. When an enactment is made there is a sacrifice of the elasticity and automatic self-adaptation of custom, but an enactment is specific and is provided with sanctions. Enactments come into use when conscious purposes are formed, and it is believed that specific devices can be framed by which to realize such purposes in the society. Then also prohibitions take the place of taboos, and punishments are planned to be deterrent rather than revengeful. The mores of different societies, or of different ages, are characterized by greater or less readiness and confidence in regard to the use of positive enactments for the realization of societal purposes.

63. How Laws and Institutions Differ from Mores.
When folkways have become institutions or laws they have changed their character and are to be distinguished from the mores. The element of sentiment and faith inheres in the mores. Laws and institutions have a rational and practical character, and are more mechanical and utilitarian. The great difference is that institutions and laws have a positive character, while mores are unformulated and undefined. There is a philosophy implicit in the folkways; when it is made explicit it becomes technical philosophy. Objectively regarded, the mores are the customs which actually conduce to welfare under existing life conditions. Acts under the laws and institutions are conscious and voluntary; under the folkways they are always unconscious and involuntary, so that they have the character of natural necessity. Educated reflection and skepticism can disturb this spontaneous relation. The laws, being positive prescriptions, supersede the mores so far as they are adopted. It follows that the mores come into operation where laws and tribunals fail. The mores cover the great field of common life where there are no laws or police regulations. They cover an immense and undefined domain, and they break the way in new domains, not yet controlled at all. The mores, therefore, build up new laws and police regulations in time. . . .

83. Inertia and Rigidity of the Mores.
We see that we must conceive of the mores as a vast system of usages, covering the whole of life, and serving all its interests; also containing in themselves their own justification by tradition and use and wont, and approved by mystic sanctions until, by rational reflection, they develop their own philosophical and ethical generalizations, which are elevated into "principles" of truth and right. They coerce and restrict the newborn generation. They do not stimulate to thought, but the contrary. The thinking is already done and is embodied in the

mores. They never contain any provision for their own amendment. They are not questions, but answers, to the problem of life. They present themselves as final and unchangeable, because they present answers which are offered as "the truth." No world philosophy, until the modern scientific world philosophy, and that only within a generation or two, has ever presented itself as perhaps transitory, certainly incomplete, and liable to be set aside tomorrow by more knowledge. No popular world philosophy or life policy ever can present itself in that light. It would cost too great a mental strain. All the groups whose mores we consider far inferior to our own are quite as well satisfied with theirs as we are with ours. The goodness or badness of mores consists entirely in their adjustment to the life conditions and the interests of the time and place. . . . Therefore it is a sign of ease and welfare when no thought is given to the mores, but all cooperate in them instinctively. The nations of southeastern Asia show us the persistency of the mores, when the element of stability and rigidity in them becomes predominant. Ghost fear and ancestor worship tend to establish the persistency of the mores by dogmatic authority, strict taboo, and weighty sanctions. The mores then lose their naturalness and vitality. They are stereotyped. They lose all relation to expediency. They become an end in themselves. They are imposed by imperative authority without regard to interests or conditions (caste, child marriage, widows). When any society falls under the dominion of this disease in the mores it must disintegrate before it can live again. In that diseased state of the mores all learning consists in committing to memory the words of the sages of the past who established the formulæ of the mores. Such words are "sacred writings," a sentence of which is a rule of conduct to be obeyed quite independently of present interests, or of any rational considerations. . . .

232. Mores and Morals; Social Code.
For every one the mores give the notion of what ought to be. This includes the notion of what ought to be done, for all should cooperate to bring to pass, in the order of life, what ought to be. All notions of propriety, decency, chastity, politeness, order, duty,

right, rights, discipline, respect, reverence, cooperation, and fellowship, especially all things in regard to which good and ill depend entirely on the point at which the line is drawn, are in the mores. The mores can make things seem right and good to one group or one age which to another seem antagonistic to every instinct of human nature. The thirteenth century bred in every heart such a sentiment in regard to heretics that inquisitors had no more misgivings in their proceedings than men would have now if they should attempt to exterminate rattlesnakes. The sixteenth century gave to all such notions about witches that witch persecutors thought they were waging war on enemies of God and man. Of course the inquisitors and witch persecutors constantly developed the notions of heretics and witches. They exaggerated the notions and then gave them back again to the mores, in their expanded form, to inflame the hearts of men with terror and hate and to become, in the next stage, so much more fantastic and ferocious motives. Such is the reaction between the mores and the acts of the living generation. The world philosophy of the age is never anything but the reflection on the mental horizon, which is formed out of the mores, of the ruling ideas which are in the mores themselves. It is from a failure to recognize the to and fro in this reaction that the current notion arises that mores are produced by doctrines. The "morals" of an age are never anything but the consonance between what is done and what the mores of the age require. The whole revolves on itself, in the relation of the specific to the general, within the horizon formed by the mores. Every attempt to win an outside standpoint from which to reduce the whole to an absolute philosophy of truth and right, based on an unalterable principle, is a delusion. New elements are brought in only by new conquests of nature through science and art. The new conquests change the conditions of life and the interests of the members of the society. Then the mores change by adaptation to new conditions and interests. The philosophy and ethics then follow to account for and justify the changes in the mores; often, also, to claim that they have caused the changes. They never do anything but draw new lines of bearing between the parts of the mores and the horizon of thought within which they are inclosed, and which is a de-

duction from the mores. The horizon is widened by more knowledge, but for one age it is just as much a generalization from the mores as for another. It is always unreal. It is only a product of thought. The ethical philosophers select points on this horizon from which to take their bearings, and they think that they have won some authority for their systems when they travel back again from the generalization to the specific custom out of which it was deduced. The cases of the inquisitors and witch persecutors who toiled arduously and continually for their chosen ends, for little or no reward, show us the relation between mores on the one side and philosophy, ethics, and religion on the other. . . .

494. Honor, Seemliness, Common Sense, Conscience.   Honor, common sense, seemliness, and conscience seem to belong to the individual domain. They are reactions produced in the individual by the societal environment. Honor is the sentiment of what one owes to one's self. It is an individual prerogative, and an ultimate individual standard. Seemliness is conduct which befits one's character and standards. Common sense, in the current view, is a natural gift and universal outfit. As to honor and seemliness, the popular view seems to be that each one has a fountain of inspiration in himself to furnish him with guidance. Conscience might be added as another natural or supernatural "voice," intuition, and part of the original outfit of all human beings as such. If these notions could be verified, and if they proved true, no discussion of them would be in place here, but as to honor it is a well-known and undisputed fact that societies have set codes of honor and standards of it which were arbitrary, irrational, and both individually and socially inexpedient, as ample experiment has proved. These codes have been and are imperative, and they have been accepted and obeyed by great groups of men who, in their own judgment, did not believe them sound. Those codes came out of the folkways of the time and place. Then comes the question whether it is not always so. Is honor, in any case, anything but the code of one's duty to himself which he has accepted from the group in which he was educated? Family, class, religious sect, school, occupation, enter into the social environ-

ment. In every environment there is a standard of honor. When a man thinks that he is acting most independently, on his personal prerogative, he is at best only balancing against each other the different codes in which he has been educated, e.g., that of the trades union against that of the Sunday school, or of the school against that of the family. What we think "natural" and universal, and to which we attribute an objective reality, is the sum of traits whose origin is so remote, and which we share with so many, that we do not know when or how we took them up, and we can remember no rational selection by which we adopted them. The same is true of common sense. It is the stock of ways of looking at things which we acquired unconsciously by suggestion from the environment in which we grew up. Some have more common sense than others, because they are more docile to suggestion, or have been taught to make judgments by people who were strong and wise. Conscience also seems best explained as a sum of principles of action which have in one's character the most original, remote, undisputed, and authoritative position, and to which questions of doubt are habitually referred. If these views are accepted, we have in honor, common sense, and conscience other phenomena of the folkways, and the notions of eternal truths of philosophy or ethics, derived from somewhere outside of men and their struggles to live well under the conditions of earth, must be abandoned as myths....

438. Specification of the Subject. The ethnographers write of a tribe that the "morality" in it, especially of the women, is low or high, etc. This is the technical use of morality—as a thing pertaining to the sex relation only or especially, and the ethnographers make their propositions by applying our standards of sex behavior, and our form of the sex taboo, to judge the folkways of all people. All that they can properly say is that they find a great range and variety of usages, ideas, standards, and ideals, which differ greatly from ours. Some of them are far stricter than ours. Those we do not consider nobler than ours. We do not feel that we ought to adopt any ways because they are more strict than our traditional ones. We consider many to be excessive, silly, and harmful. A Roman senator was censured for impropriety because he kissed his wife in the presence of his daughter.

439. Meaning of "Immoral." When, therefore, the ethnographers apply condemnatory or depreciatory adjectives to the people whom they study, they beg the most important question which we want to investigate; that is, What are standards, codes, and ideas of chastity, decency, propriety, modesty, etc., and whence do they arise? The ethnographical facts contain the answer to this question.... "Immoral" never means anything but contrary to the mores of the time and place. Therefore the mores and the morality may move together, and there is no permanent or universal standard by which right and truth in regard to these matters can be established and different folkways compared and criticised.

Study Questions

1. Are there as many disagreements about morality as Sumner claims?

2. Will the human race eventually come to agree on one set of moral values?

3. If Sumner is right, how should we live our life in our own society?

The Nicomachean Ethics

Aristotle (384–322 B.C.) Aristotle was born in Greece. He was a student of Plato, tutor to Alexander the Great, and founder of a school, the Lyceum. He wrote on all major areas of philosophy and science.

Aristotle

Book I. The End.

1. Every art and every kind of inquiry, and likewise every act and purpose, seems to aim at some good: and so it has been well said that the good is that at which everything aims.

But a difference is observable among these aims or ends. What is aimed at is sometimes the exercise of a faculty, sometimes a certain result beyond that exercise. And where there is an end beyond the act, there the result is better than the exercise of the faculty.

Now since there are many kinds of actions and many arts and sciences, it follows that there are many ends also; *e.g.,* health is the end of medicine, ships of shipbuilding, victory of the art of war, and wealth of economy.

But when several of these are subordinated to some one art or science,—as the making of bridles and other trappings to the art of horsemanship, and this in turn, along with all else that the soldier does, to the art of war, and so on,—then the end of the master-art is always more desired than the ends of the subordinate arts, since these are pursued for its sake. And this is equally true whether the end in view be the mere exercise of a faculty or something beyond that, as in the above instances.

2. If then in what we do there be some end which we wish for on its own account, choosing all the others as means to this, but not every end with-

out exception as a means to something else (for so we should go on *ad infinitum,* and desire would be left void and objectless),—this evidently will be the good or the best of all things. And surely from a practical point of view it much concerns us to know this good; for then, like archers shooting at a definite mark, we shall be more likely to attain what we want.

If this be so, we must try to indicate roughly what it is, and first of all to which of the arts or sciences it belongs.

It would seem to belong to the supreme art or science, that one which most of all deserves the name of master-art or master-science.

Now Politics[1] seems to answer to this description. For it prescribes which of the sciences a state needs, and which each man shall study, and up to what point; and to it we see subordinated even the highest arts, such as economy, rhetoric, and the art of war.

Since then it makes use of the other practical sciences, and since it further ordains what men are to do and from what to refrain, its end must include the ends of the others, and must be the proper good of man.

---

1. To Aristotle, Politics is a much wider term than to us; it covers the whole field of human life, since man is essentially social; it has to determine (1) what is the good? and (2) what can law do to promote this good?

From *Nichomachean Ethics* by Aristotle, translated by F. H. Peters. Published by Routledge and Kegan Paul.

For though this good is the same for the individual and the state, yet the good of the state seems a grander and more perfect thing both to attain and to secure; and glad as one would be to do this service for a single individual, to do it for a people and for a number of states is nobler and more divine.

This then is the aim of the present inquiry, which is a sort of political inquiry.

3. We must be content if we can attain to so much precision in our statement as the subject before us admits of; for the same degree of accuracy is no more to be expected in all kinds of reasoning than in all kinds of handicraft.

Now the things that are noble and just (with which Politics deals) are so various and so uncertain, that some think these are merely conventional and not natural distinctions.

There is a similar uncertainty also about what is good, because good things often do people harm: men have before now been ruined by wealth, and have lost their lives through courage.

Our subject, then, and our data being of this nature, we must be content if we can indicate the truth roughly and in outline, and if, in dealing with matters that are not amenable to immutable laws, and reasoning from premises that are but probable, we can arrive at probable conclusions.[2]

The reader, on his part, should take each of my statements in the same spirit; for it is the mark of an educated man to require, in each kind of inquiry, just so much exactness as the subject admits of: it is equally absurd to accept probable reasoning from a mathematician, and to demand scientific proof from an orator.

But each man can form a judgment about what he knows, and is called "a good judge" of that—of any special matter when he has received a special education therein, "a good judge" (without any qualifying epithet) when he has received a universal education. And hence a young man is not qualified to be a student of Politics; for he lacks experience of the affairs of life, which form the data and the subjectmatter of Politics.

_____

2. The expression τὰ ὡς ἐπι τὸ πολύ covers both (1) what is generally thought not universally true and (2) what is probable though not certain.

Further, since he is apt to be swayed by his feelings, he will derive no benefit from a study whose aim is not speculative but practical.

But in this respect young in character counts the same as young in years; for the young man's disqualification is not a matter of time, but is due to the fact that feeling rules his life and directs all his desires. Men of this character turn the knowledge they get to no account in practice, as we see with those we call incontinent; but those who direct their desires and actions by reason will gain much profit from the knowledge of these matters.

So much then by way of preface as to the student, and the spirit in which he must accept what we say, and the object which we propose to ourselves.

4. Since—to resume—all knowledge and all purpose aims at some good, what is this which we say is the aim of Politics; or, in other words, what is the highest of all realizable goods?

As to its name, I suppose nearly all men are agreed; for the masses and the men of culture alike declare that it is happiness, and hold that to "live well" or to "do well" is the same as to be "happy."

But they differ as to what this happiness is, and the masses do not give the same account of it as the philosophers.

The former take it to be something palpable and plain, as pleasure or wealth or fame; one man holds it to be this, and another that, and often the same man is of different minds at different times,—after sickness it is health, and in poverty it is wealth; while when they are impressed with the consciousness of their ignorance, they admire most those who say grand things that are above their comprehension.

Some philosophers, on the other hand, have thought that, beside these several good things, there is an "absolute" good which is the cause of their goodness.

As it would hardly be worth while to review all the opinions that have been held, we will confine ourselves to those which are most popular, or which seem to have some foundation in reason.

5. Let us now take up the discussion at the point from which we digressed.

It seems that men not unreasonably take their notions of the good or happiness from the lives actually led, and that the masses who are the least refined suppose it to be pleasure, which is the reason why they aim at nothing higher than the life of enjoyment.

For the most conspicuous kinds of life are three: this life of enjoyment, the life of the statesman, and, thirdly, the contemplative life.

The mass of men show themselves utterly slavish in their preference for the life of brute beasts, but their views receive consideration because many of those in high places have the tastes of Sardanapălus.

Men of refinement with a practical turn prefer honour; for I suppose we may say that honour is the aim of the statesman's life.

But this seems too superficial to be the good we are seeking: for it appears to depend upon those who give rather than upon those who receive it; while we have a presentiment that the good is something that is peculiarly a man's own and can scarce be taken away from him.

Moreover, these men seem to pursue honour in order that they may be assured of their own excellence,—at least, they wish to be honoured by men of sense, and by those who know them, and on the ground of their virtue or excellence. It is plain, then, that in their view, at any rate, virtue or excellence is better than honour; and perhaps we should take this to be the end of the statesman's life, rather than honour.

But virtue or excellence also appears too incomplete to be what we want; for it seems that a man might have virtue and yet be asleep or be inactive all his life, and, moreover, might meet with the greatest disasters and misfortunes; and no one would maintain that such a man is happy, except for argument's sake. But we will not dwell on these matters now, for they are sufficiently discussed in the popular treatises.

The third kind of life is the life of contemplation: we will treat of it further on.

As for the money-making life, it is something quite contrary to nature; and wealth evidently is not the good of which we are in search, for it is merely useful as a means to something else. So we might rather take pleasure and virtue or excellence to be ends than wealth; for they are chosen on their own account. But it seems that not even they are the

end, though much breath has been wasted in attempts to show that they are.

6. Dismissing these views, then, we have now to consider the "universal good," and to state the difficulties which it presents; though such an inquiry is not a pleasant task in view of our friendship for the authors of the doctrine of ideas. But we venture to think that this is the right course, and that in the interests of truth we ought to sacrifice even what is nearest to us, especially as we call ourselves philosophers. Both are dear to us, but it is a sacred duty to give the preference to truth.

In the first place, the authors of this theory themselves did not assert a common idea in the case of things of which one is prior to the other; and for this reason they did not hold one common idea of numbers. Now the predicate good is applied to substances and also to qualities and relations. But that which has independent existence, what we call "substance," is logically prior to that which is relative; for the latter is an offshoot as it were, or [in logical language] an accident of a thing or substance. So [by their own showing] there cannot be one common idea of these goods.

Secondly, the term good is used in as many different ways as the term "is" or "being:" we apply the term to substances or independent existences, as God, reason; to qualities, as the virtues; to quantity, as the moderate or due amount; to relatives, as the useful; to time, as opportunity; to place, as habitation, and so on. It is evident, therefore, that the word good cannot stand for one and the same notion in all these various applications; for if it did, the term could not be applied in all the categories, but in one only.

Thirdly, if the notion were one, since there is but one science of all the things that come under one idea, there would be but one science of all goods; but as it is, there are many sciences even of the goods that come under one category; as, for instance, the science which deals with opportunity in war is strategy, but in disease is medicine; and the science of the due amount in the matter of food is medicine, but in the matter of exercise is the science of gymnastic.

Fourthly, one might ask what they mean by the "absolute": in "absolute man" and "man" the word "man" has one and the same sense; for in respect of manhood there will be no difference between them; and if so, neither will there be any difference in respect of goodness between "absolute good" and "good."

Fifthly, they do not make the good any more good by making it eternal; a white thing that lasts a long while is no whiter than what lasts but a day.

There seems to be more plausibility in the doctrine of the Pythagoreans, who [in their table of opposites] place the one on the same side with the good things [instead of reducing all goods to unity]; and even Speusippus[3] seems to follow them in this.

However, these points may be reserved for another occasion; but objection may be taken to what I have said on the ground that the Platonists do not speak in this way of all goods indiscriminately, but hold that those that are pursued and welcomed on their own account are called good by reference to one common form or type, while those things that tend to produce or preserve these goods, or to prevent their opposites, are called good only as means to these, and in a different sense.

It is evident that there will thus be two classes of goods: one good in themselves, the other good as means to the former. Let us separate then from the things that are merely useful those that are good in themselves, and inquire if they are called good by reference to one common idea or type.

Now what kind of things would one call "good in themselves"?

Surely those things that we pursue even apart from their consequences, such as wisdom and sight and certain pleasures and certain honours; for although we sometimes pursue these things as means, no one could refuse to rank them among the things that are good in themselves.

If these be excluded, nothing is good in itself except the idea; and then the type or form will be meaningless.[4]

If however, these are ranked among the things that are good in themselves, then it must be shown

that the goodness of all of them can be defined in the same terms, as white has the same meaning when applied to snow and to white lead.

But, in fact, we have to give a separate and different account of the goodness of honour and wisdom and pleasure.

Good, then, is not a term that is applied to all these things alike in the same sense or with reference to one common idea or form.

"The function of man, then, is exercise of his vital faculties [or soul] on one side in obedience to reason, and on the other side with reason."

But how then do these things come to be called good? for they do not appear to have received the same name by chance merely. Perhaps it is because they all proceed from one source, or all conduce to one end; or perhaps it is rather in virtue of some analogy, just as we call the reason the eye of the soul because it bears the same relation to the soul that the eye does to the body, and so on.

But we may dismiss these questions at present; for to discuss them in detail belongs more properly to another branch of philosophy.

And for the same reason we may dismiss the further consideration of the idea; for even granting that this term good, which is applied to all these different things, has one and the same meaning throughout, or that there is an absolute good apart from these particulars, it is evident that this good will not be anything that man can realize or attain: but it is a good of this kind that we are now seeking.

It might, perhaps, be thought that it would nevertheless be well to make ourselves acquainted with this universal good, with a view to the goods

---

3. Plato's nephew and successor.
4. For there is no meaning in a form which is a form of nothing, in a universal which has no particulars under it.

that are attainable and realizable. With this for a pattern, it may be said, we shall more readily discern our own good, and discerning achieve it.

There certainly is some plausibility in this argument, but it seems to be at variance with the existing sciences; for though they are all aiming at some good and striving to make up their deficiencies, they neglect to inquire about this universal good. And yet it is scarce likely that the professors of the several arts and sciences should not know, nor even look for, what would help them so much.

And indeed I am at a loss to know how the weaver or the carpenter would be furthered in his art by a knowledge of this absolute good, or how a man would be rendered more able to heal the sick or to command an army by contemplation of the pure form or idea. For it seems to me that the physician does not even seek for health in this abstract way, but seeks for the health of man, or rather of some particular man, for it is individuals that he has to heal.

7. Leaving these matters, then, let us return once more to the question, what this good can be of which we are in search.

It seems to be different in different kinds of action and in different arts,—one thing in medicine and another in war, and so on. What then is the good in each of these cases? Surely that for the sake of which all else is done. And that in medicine is health, in war is victory, in building is a house,—a different thing in each different case, but always, in whatever we do and in whatever we choose, the end. For it is always for the sake of the end that all else is done.

If then there be one end of all that man does, this end will be the realizable good,—or these ends, if there be more than one.

By this generalization our argument is brought to the same point as before. This point we must try to explain more clearly.

We see that there are many ends. But some of these are chosen only as means, as wealth, flutes, and the whole class of instruments. And so it is plain that not all ends are final.

But the best of all things must, we conceive, be something final.

If then there be only one final end, this will be what we are seeking,—or if there be more than one, then the most final of them.

Now that which is pursued as an end in itself is more final than that which is pursued as means to something else, and that which is never chosen as means than that which is chosen both as an end in itself and as means, and that is strictly final which is always chosen as an end in itself and never as means.

Happiness seems more than anything else to answer to this description: for we always choose it for itself, and never for the sake of something else; while honour and pleasure and reason, and all virtue or excellence, we choose partly indeed for themselves (for, apart from any result, we should choose each of them), but partly also for the sake of happiness, supposing that they will help to make us happy. But no one chooses happiness for the sake of these things, or as a means to anything else at all.

We seem to be led to the same conclusion when we start from the notion of self-sufficiency.

The final good is thought to be self-sufficing [or all-sufficing]. In applying this term we do not regard a man as an individual leading a solitary life, but we also take account of parents, children, wife, and, in short, friends and fellow-citizens generally, since man is naturally a social being. Some limit must indeed be set to this; for if you go on to parents and descendants and friends of friends, you will never come to a stop. But this we will consider further on: for the present we will take self-sufficing to mean what by itself makes life desirable and in want of nothing. And happiness is believed to answer to this description.

And further, happiness is believed to be the most desirable thing in the world, and that not merely as one among other good things; if it were merely one among other good things [so that other things could be added to it], it is plain that the addition of the least of other goods must make it more desirable; for the addition becomes a surplus of good, and of two goods the greater is always more desirable.

Thus it seems that happiness is something final and self-sufficing, and is the end of all that man does.

But perhaps the reader thinks that though no

one will dispute the statement that happiness is the best thing in the world, yet a still more precise definition of it is needed.

This will best be gained, I think, by asking, What is the function of man? For as the goodness and the excellence of a piper or a sculptor, or the practiser of any art, and generally of those who have any function or business to do, lies in that function, so man's good would seem to lie in his function, if he has one.

But can we suppose that, while a carpenter and a cobbler has a function and a business of his own, man has no business and no function assigned him by nature? Nay, surely as his several members, eye and hand and foot, plainly have each his own function, so we must suppose that man also has some function over and above all these.

What then is it?

Life evidently he has in common even with the plants, but we want that which is peculiar to him. We must exclude, therefore, the life of mere nutrition and growth.

Next to this comes the life of sense; but this too he plainly shares with horses and cattle and all kinds of animals.

There remains then the life whereby he acts—the life of his rational nature,[5] with its two sides or divisions, one rational as obeying reason, the other rational as having and exercising reason.

But as this expression is ambiguous,[6] we must be understood to mean thereby the life that consists in the exercise of the faculties; for this seems to be more properly entitled to the name.

The function of man, then, is exercise of his vital faculties [or soul] on one side in obedience to reason, and on the other side with reason.

But what is called the function of a man of any profession and the function of a man who is good in that profession are generically the same, *e.g.,* of a harper and of a good harper; and this holds in all cases without exception, only that in the case of the latter his superior excellence at his work is added; for we say a harper's function is to harp, and a good harper's to harp well.

(Man's function then being, as we say, a kind of life—that is to say, exercise of his faculties and action of various kinds with reason—the good man's function is to do this well and beautifully [or nobly]. But the function of anything is done well when it is done in accordance with the proper excellence of that thing.)

If this is be so the result is that the good of man is exercise of his faculties in accordance with excellence or virtue, or, if there be more than one, in accordance with the best and most complete virtue.[7]

But there must also be a full term of years for this exercise; for one swallow or one fine day does not make a spring, nor does one day or any small space of time make a blessed or happy man.

This, then, may be taken as a rough outline of the good; for this, I think, is the proper method,—first to sketch the outline, and then to fill in the details. But it would seem that, the outline once fairly drawn, any one can carry on the work and fit it the several items which time reveals to us or helps us to find. And this indeed is the way in which the arts and sciences have grown; for it requires no extraordinary genius to fill up the gaps.

We must bear in mind, however, what was said above, and not demand the same degree of accuracy in all branches of study, but in each case so much as the subject-matter admits of and as is proper to that kind of inquiry. The carpenter and the geometer both look for the right angle, but in different ways: the former only wants such an approximation to it as his work requires, but the latter wants to know what constitutes a right angle, or what is its special quality; his aim is to find out the truth. And so in other cases we must follow the same course, lest we spend more time on what is immaterial than on the real business in hand.

---

5. πρακτική τις τοῦ λόγον ἔχοντος Aristotle frequently uses the terms πρᾶξις, πρακτός, πρακτικός in this wide sense, covering all that man does, *i.e.,* all that part of man's life that is within the control of his will, or that is consciously directed to an end, including therefore speculation as well as action.

6. For it might mean either the mere possession of the vital faculties, or their exercise.

7. This "best and most complete excellence or virtue" is the trained faculty for philosophic speculation, and the contemplative life is man's highest happiness.

13. Since happiness is an exercise of the vital faculties in accordance with perfect virtue or excellence, we will now inquire about virtue or excellence; for this will probably help us in our inquiry about happiness.

Book II. Moral Virtue.

1. Excellence, then, being of these two kinds, intellectual and moral, intellectual excellence owes its birth and growth mainly to instruction, and so requires time and experience, while moral excellence is the result of habit or custom (ἔθος), and has accordingly in our language received a name formed by a slight change from ἔθlgos.[8]

From this it is plain that none of the moral excellences or virtues is implanted in us by nature; for that which is by nature cannot be altered by training. For instance, a stone naturally tends to fall downwards, and you could not train it to rise upwards, though you tried to do so by throwing it up ten thousand times, nor could you train fire to move downwards, nor accustom anything which naturally behaves in one way to behave in any other way.

The virtues,[9] then, come neither by nature nor against nature, but nature gives the capacity for acquiring them, and this is developed by training.

Again, where we do things by nature we get the power first, and put this power forth in act afterwards: as we plainly see in the case of the senses; for it is not by constantly seeing and hearing that we acquire those faculties, but, on the contrary, we had the power first and then used it, instead of acquiring the power by the use. But the virtues we acquire by doing the acts, as is the case with the arts too. We learn an art by doing that which we wish to do when we have learned it; we become builders by building, and harpers by harping. And so by doing just acts we become just, and by doing acts of temperance and courage we become temperate and courageous.

This is attested, too, by what occurs in states; for the legislators make their citizens good by training; *i.e.,* this is the wish of all legislators, and those who do not succeed in this miss their aim, and it is this that distinguishes a good from a bad constitution.

Again, both the moral virtues and the corresponding vices result from and are formed by the same acts; and this is the case with the arts also. It is by harping that good harpers and bad harpers alike are produced: and so with builders and the rest; by building well they will become good builders, and bad builders by building badly. Indeed, if it were not so, they would not want anybody to teach them, but would all be born either good or bad at their trades. And it is just the same with the virtues also. It is by our conduct in our intercourse with other men that we become just or unjust, and by acting in circumstances of danger, and training ourselves to feel fear or confidence, that we become courageous or cowardly. So, too, with our animal appetites and the passion of anger; for by behaving in this way or in that on the occasions with which these passions are concerned, some become temperate and gentle, and others profligate and ill-tempered. In a word, acts of any kind produce habits or characters of the same kind.

Hence we ought to make sure that our acts be of a certain kind; for the resulting character varies as they vary. It makes no small difference, therefore, whether a man be trained from his youth up in this way or in that, but a great difference, or rather all the difference.

5. We have next to inquire what excellence or virtue is.

A quality of the soul is either (1) a passion or emotion, or (2) a power or faculty, or (3) a habit or trained faculty; and so virtue must be one of these three. By (1) a passion or emotion we mean appetite, anger, fear, confidence, envy, joy, love, hate,

---

8. εθος, custom; ηθος, character; ηθικη αρετη, moral excellence: we have no similar sequence, but the Latin *mos, mores,* from which "morality" comes, covers both εθος and ηθος.

9. It is with the moral virtues that this and the three following books are exclusively concerned, the discussion of the intellectual virtues being postponed to Book VI. απεται is often used in these books, without any epithet, for "moral virtues," and perhaps is so used here.

longing, emulation, pity, or generally that which is accompanied by pleasure or pain; (2) a power or faculty is that in respect of which we are said to be capable of being affected in any of these ways, as, for instance, that in respect of which we are able to be angered or pained or to pity; and (3) a habit or trained faculty is that in respect of which we are well or ill regulated or disposed in the matter of our affections; as, for instance, in the matter of being angered, we are ill regulated if we are too violent or too slack, but if we are moderate in our anger we are well regulated. And so with the rest.

Now, the virtues are not emotions, nor are the vices—(1) because we are not called good or bad in respect of our emotions, but are called so in respect of our virtues or vices; (2) because we are neither praised nor blamed in respect of our emotions (a man is not praised for being afraid or angry, nor blamed for being angry simply, but for being angry in a particular way), but we are praised or blamed in respect of our virtues or vices; (3) because we may be angered or frightened without deliberate choice, but the virtues are a kind of deliberate choice, or at least are impossible without it; and (4) because in respect of our emotions we are said to be moved, but in respect of our virtues and vices we are not said to be moved, but to be regulated or disposed in this way or in that.

For these same reasons also they are not powers or faculties; for we are not called either good or bad for being merely capable of emotion, nor are we either praised or blamed for this. And further, while nature gives us our powers or faculties, she does not make us either good or bad. (This point, however, we have already treated.)

If, then, the virtues be neither emotions nor faculties, it only remains for them to be habits or trained faculties.

6. We have thus found the genus to which virtue belongs; but we want to know, not only that it is a trained faculty, but also what species of trained faculty it is.

We may safely assert that the virtue or excellence of a thing causes that thing both to be itself in good condition and to perform its function well. The excellence of the eye, for instance, makes both the eye and its work good; for it is by the excellence of the eye that we see well. So the proper excellence of the horse makes a horse what he should be, and makes him good at running, and carrying his rider, and standing a charge.

If, then, this holds good in all cases, the proper excellence or virtue of man will be the habit or trained faculty that makes a man good and makes him perform his function well.

How this is to be done we have already said, but we may exhibit the same conclusion in another way, by inquiring what the nature of this virtue is.

Now, if we have any quantity, whether continuous or discrete,[10] it is possible to take either a larger [or too large], or a smaller [or too small], or an equal [or fair] amount, and that either absolutely or relatively to our own needs.

By an equal or fair amount I understand a mean amount, or one that lies between excess and deficiency.

By the absolute mean, or mean relatively to the thing itself, I understand that which is equidistant from both extremes, and this is one and the same for all.

By the mean relatively to us I understand that which is neither too much nor too little for us; and this is not one and the same for all.

For instance, if ten be larger [or too large] and two be smaller [or too small], if we take six we take the mean relatively to the thing itself [or the arithmetical mean]; for it exceeds one extreme by the same amount by which it is exceeded by the other extreme: and this is the mean in arithmetical proportion.

But the mean relatively to us cannot be found in this way. If ten pounds of food is too much for a given man to eat, and two pounds too little, it does not follow that the trainer will order him six pounds: for that also may perhaps be too much for the man in question, or too little; too little for Milo, too much for the beginner. The same holds true in running and wrestling.

And so we may say generally that a master in any

---

10. A line (or a generous emotion)) is a "continuous equantity"; you can part it where you please: a rouleau of sovereigns is a "discrete quantity," made up of definite parts, and primarily separable into them.

art avoids what is too much and what is too little, and seeks for the mean and chooses it—not the absolute but the relative mean.

If, then, every art or science perfects its work in this way, looking to the mean and bringing its work up to this standard (so that people are wont to say of a good work that nothing could be taken from it or added to it, implying that excellence is destroyed by excess or deficiency, but secured by observing the mean; and good artists, as we say, do in fact keep their eyes fixed on this in all that they do), and if virtue, like nature, is more exact and better than any art, it follows that virtue also must aim at the mean—virtue of course meaning moral virtue or excellence; for it has to do with passions and actions, and it is these that admit of excess and deficiency and the mean. For instance, it is possible to feel fear, confidence, desire, anger, pity, and generally to be affected pleasantly and painfully, either too much or too little, in either case wrongly; but to be thus affected at the right times, and on the right occasions, and towards the right persons, and with the right object, and in the right fashion, is the mean course and the best course, and these are characteristics of virtue. And in the same way our outward acts also admit of excess and deficiency, and the mean or due amount.

Virtue, then, has to deal with feelings or passions and with outward acts, in which excess is wrong and deficiency also is blamed, but the mean amount is praised and is right—both of which are characteristics of virtue.

Virtue, then, is a kind of moderation (μεσότης τις),[11] inasmuch as it aims at the mean or moderate amount (τὸ μέσον).

Again, there are many ways of going wrong (for evil is infinite in nature, to use a Pythagorean figure, while good is finite), but only one way of going right; so that the one is easy and the other hard—easy to miss the mark and hard to hit. On this account also, then, excess and deficiency are characteristic of vice, hitting the mean is characteristic of virtue:

---

11. μεσότης, the abstract name for the quality, is untranslatable.

"Goodness is simple, ill takes any shape."

Virtue, then, is a habit or trained faculty of choice, the characteristic of which lies in moderation or observance of the mean relatively to the persons concerned, as determined by reason, *i.e.,* by the reason by which the prudent man would determine it. And it is a moderation, firstly, inasmuch as it comes in the middle or mean between two vices, one on the side of excess, the other on the side of defect; and, secondly, inasmuch as, while these vices fall short of or exceed the due measure in feeling and in action, it finds and chooses the mean, middling, or moderate amount.

Regarded in its essence, therefore, or according to the definition of its nature, virtue is a moderation or middle state, but viewed in its relation to what is best and right it is the extreme of perfection.

But it is not all actions nor all passions that admit of moderation; there are some whose very names imply badness, as malevolence, shamelessness, envy, and, among acts, adultery, theft, murder. These and all other like things are blamed as being bad in themselves, and not merely in their excess or deficiency. It is impossible therefore to go right in them; they are always wrong: rightness and wrongness in such things (*e.g.,* in adultery) does not depend upon whether it is the right person and occasion and manner, but the mere doing of any one of them is wrong.

It would be equally absurd to look for moderation or excess or deficiency in unjust cowardly or profligate conduct; for then there would be moderation in excess or deficiency, and excess in excess, and deficiency in deficiency.

The fact is that just as there can be no excess or deficiency in temperance or courage because the mean or moderate amount is, in a sense, an extreme, so in these kinds of conduct also there can be no moderation or excess or deficiency, but the acts are wrong however they be done. For, to put it generally, there cannot be moderation in excess or deficiency, nor excess or deficiency in moderation.

7. But it is not enough to make these general statements [about virtue and vice]: we must go on and apply them to particulars [*i.e.,* to the several virtues and vices]. For in reasoning about matters of conduct general statements are too vague,[12] and do not convey so much truth as particular propositions. It is with particulars that conduct is concerned:[13] our statements, therefore, when applied to these particulars, should be found to hold good.

These particulars then [*i.e.,* the several virtues and vices and the several acts and affections with which they deal], we will take from the following table.[14]

Moderation in the feelings of fear and confidence is courage: of those that exceed, he that exceeds in fearlessness has no name (as often happens), but he that exceeds in confidence is foolhardy, while he that exceeds in fear, but is deficient in confidence, is cowardly.

Moderation in respect of certain pleasures and also (though to a less extent) certain pains is temperance, while excess is profligacy. But defectiveness in the matter of these pleasures is hardly ever found, and so this sort of people also have as yet received no name: let us put them down as "void of sensibility."

In the matter of giving and taking money, moderation is liberality, excess and deficiency are prodigality and illiberality. But both vices exceed and fall short in giving and taking in contrary ways: the prodigal exceeds in spending, but falls short in taking; while the illiberal man exceeds in taking, but falls short in spending. (For the present we are but giving an outline or summary, and aim at nothing more; we shall afterwards treat these points in greater detail.)

But, besides these, there are other dispositions in the matter of money: there is a moderation which is called magnificence (for the magnificent is not the same as the liberal man: the former deals with large sums, the latter with small), and an excess which is called bad taste or vulgarity, and a deficiency which is called meanness; and these vices differ from those which are opposed to liberality: how they differ will be explained later.

With respect to honour and disgrace, there is a moderation which is high-mindedness, an excess which may be called vanity, and a deficiency which is little-mindedness.

But just as we said that liberality is related to magnificence, differing only in that it deals with small sums, so here there is a virtue related to high-mindedness, and differing only in that it is concerned with small instead of great honours. A man may have a due desire for honour, and also more or less than a due desire: he that carries this desire to excess is called ambitious, he that has not enough of it is called unambitious, but he that has the due amount has no name. There are also no abstract names for characters, except "ambition," corresponding to ambitious. And on this account those who occupy the extremes lay claim to the middle place. And in common parlance, too, the moderate man is sometimes called ambitious and sometimes unambitious, and sometimes the ambitious man is praised and sometimes the unambitious. Why this is we will explain afterwards; for the present we will follow out our plan and enumerate the other types of character.

In the matter of anger also we find excess and deficiency and moderation. The characters themselves hardly have recognized names, but as the moderate man is here called gentle, we will call his character gentleness; of those who go into extremes, we may take the term wrathful for him who exceeds, with wrathfulness for the vice, and wrathless for him who is deficient, with wrathlessness for his character.

Besides these, there are three kinds of moderation, bearing some resemblance to one another, and yet different. They all have to do with intercourse in speech and action, but they differ in that one has to do with the truthfulness of this intercourse, while the other two have to do with its pleasantness—one of the two with pleasantness in matters of amusement, the other with pleasantness

---

12. Or "cover more ground, but convey less truth than particular propositions," if we read κοινότεποι with most manuscripts.

13. In a twofold sense: my conduct cannot be virtuous except by exhibiting the particular virtues of justice, temperance, etc.; again, my conduct cannot be just except by being just in particular cases to particular persons.

14. The Greek seems to imply that this is a generally accepted list, but Aristotle repeatedly has to coin names.

in all the relations of life. We must therefore speak of these qualities also in order that we may the more plainly see how, in all cases, moderation is praiseworthy, while the extreme courses are neither right nor praiseworthy, but blamable.

In these cases also names are for the most part wanting, but we must try, here as elsewhere, to coin names ourselves, in order to make our argument clear and easy to follow.

In the matter of truth, then, let us call him who observes the mean a true [or truthful] person, and observance of the mean truth [or truthfulness]: pretence, when it exaggerates, may be called boasting, and the person a boaster; when it understates, let the names be irony and ironical.

With regard to pleasantness in amusement, he who observes the mean may be called witty, and his character wittiness; excess may be called buffoonery, and the man a buffoon; while boorish may stand for the person who is deficient, and boorishness for his character.

With regard to pleasantness in the other affairs of life, he who makes himself properly pleasant may be called friendly, and his moderation friendliness; he that exceeds may be called obsequious if he have no ulterior motive, but a flatterer if he has an eye to his own advantage; he that is deficient in this respect, and always makes himself disagreeable, may be called a quarrelsome or peevish fellow.

Moreover, in mere emotions[15] and in our conduct with regard to them, there are ways of observing the mean; for instance, shame (αἰδώς), is not a virtue, but yet the modest (αἰδήμων) man is praised. For in these matters also we speak of this man as observing the mean, of that man as going beyond it (as the shame-faced man whom the least thing makes shy), while he who is deficient in the feeling, or lacks it altogether, is called shameless; but the term modest (αἰδήμςν) is applied to him who observes the mean.

Righteous indignation, again, hits the mean between envy and malevolence. These have to do with feelings of pleasure and pain at what happens to our neighbours. A man is called righteously indignant when he feels pain at the sight of undeserved prosperity, but your envious man goes beyond him and is pained by the sight of any one in prosperity, while the malevolent man is so far from being pained that he actually exults in the misfortunes of his neighbours.

9. We have sufficiently explained, then, that moral virtue is moderation or observance of the mean, and in what sense, viz. (1) as holding a middle position between two vices, one on the side of excess, and the other on the side of deficiency, and (2) as aiming at the mean or moderate amount both in feeling and in action.

And on this account it is a hard thing to be good; for finding the middle or the mean in each case is a hard thing, just as finding the middle or centre of a circle is a thing that is not within the power of everybody, but only of him who has the requisite knowledge.

Book X. Pleasure and Happiness.

Conclusion.

6. Now that we have discussed the several kinds of virtue and friendship and pleasure, it remains to give a summary account of happiness, since we assume that it is the end of all that man does. And it will shorten our statement if we first recapitulate what we have said above.

We said that happiness is not a habitat or trained faculty. If it were, it would be within the reach of a man who slept all his days and lived the life of a vegetable, or of a man who met with the greatest misfortunes. As we cannot accept this conclusion, we must place happiness in some exercise of faculty, as we said before. But as the exercises of faculty are sometimes necessary (*i.e.,* desirable for the sake of something else), sometimes desirable in themselves, it is evident that happiness must be placed among those that are desirable in themselves, and not among those that are desirable for the sake of something else: for happiness lacks nothing; it is sufficient in itself.

Now, the exercise of faculty is desirable in itself when nothing is expected from it beyond itself.

---

15. That is, which do not issue in acts like those hitherto mentioned.

Of this nature are held to be (1) the manifestations of excellence; for to do what is noble and excellent must be counted desirable for itself: and (2) those amusements which please us; for they are not chosen for the sake of anything else—indeed, men are more apt to be injured than to be benefited by them, through neglect of their health and fortunes.

Now, most of those whom men call happy have recourse to pastimes of this sort. And on this account those who show a ready wit in such pastimes find favour with tyrants; for they make themselves pleasant in that which the tyrant wants, and what he wants is pastime. These amusements, then, are generally thought to be elements of happiness, because princes employ their leisure in them. But such persons, we may venture to say, are no criterion. For princely rank does not imply the possession of virtue or of reason, which are the sources of all excellent exercise of faculty. And if these men, never having tasted pure and refined pleasure, have recourse to the pleasures of the body, we should not on that account think these more desirable; for children also fancy that the things which they value are better than anything else. It is only natural, then, that as children differ from men in their estimate of what is valuable, so bad men should differ from good.

As we have often said, therefore, that is truly valuable and pleasant which is so to the perfect man. Now, the exercise of those trained faculties which are proper to him is what each man finds most desirable; what the perfect man finds most desirable, therefore, is the exercise of virtue.

Happiness, therefore, does not consist in amusement; and indeed it is absurd to suppose that the end is amusement, and that we toil and moil all our life long for the sake of amusing ourselves. We may say that we choose everything for the sake of something else, excepting only happiness; for it is the end. But to be serious and to labour for the sake of amusement seems silly and utterly childish; while to amuse ourselves is order that we may be serious, as Anacharsis says, seems to be right; for amusement is a sort of recreation, and we need recreation because we are unable to work continuously.

Recreation, then, cannot be the end; for it is taken as a means to the exercise of our faculties.

Again, the happy life is thought to be that which exhibits virtue; and such a life must be serious and cannot consist in amusement.

Again, it is held that things of serious importance[16] are better than laughable and amusing things, and that the better the organ or the man, the more important is the function; but we have already said that the function or exercise of that which is better is higher and more conducive to happiness.

Again, the enjoyment of bodily pleasures is within the reach of anybody, of a slave no less than the best of men; but no one supposes that a slave can participate in happiness, seeing that he cannot participate in the proper life of man. For indeed happiness does not consist in pastimes of this sort, but in the exercise of virtue, as we have already said.

7. But if happiness be the exercise of virtue, it is reasonable to suppose that it will be the exercise of the highest virtue; and that will be the virtue or excellence of the best part of us.

Now, that part or faculty—call it reason or what you will—which seems naturally to rule and take the lead, and to apprehend things noble and divine—whether it be itself divine, or only the divinest part of us—is the faculty the exercise of which, in its proper excellence, will be perfect happiness.

That this consists in speculation or contemplation we have already said.

This conclusion would seem to agree both with what we have said above, and with known truths.

This exercise of faculty must be the highest possible; for the reason is the highest of our faculties, and of all knowable things those that reason deals with are the highest.

Again, it is the most continuous; for speculation can be carried on more continuously than any kind of action whatsoever.

---

16. τὰ σπουδαῖα. It is impossible to convey in a translation the play upon the words σπουδή and σπουδαῖος: σπουδή is earnestness; σπουδαῖος usually = good: here, however, σπουδαῖος carries both senses, earnest or serious, and good.

We think too that pleasure ought to be one of the ingredients of happiness; but of all virtuous exercises it is allowed that the pleasantest is the exercise of wisdom.[17] At least philosophy[18] is thought to have pleasures that are admirable to purity and steadfastness; and it is reasonable to suppose that the time passes more pleasantly with those who possess, than with those who are seeking knowledge.

Again, what is called self-sufficiency will be most of all found in the speculative life. The necessaries of life, indeed, are needed by the wise men as well as by the just man and the rest; but, when these have been provided in due quantity, the just man further needs persons towards whom, and along with whom, he may act justly; and so does the temperate and the courageous man and the rest; while the wise man is able to speculate even by himself, and the wiser he is the more is he able to do this. He could speculate better, we may confess, if he had others to help him, but nevertheless he is more self-sufficient than anybody else.

Again, it would seem that this life alone is desired solely for its own sake; for it yields no result beyond the contemplation, but from the practical activities we get something more or less besides action.

Again, happiness is thought to imply leisure; for we toil in order that we may have leisure, as we make war in order that we may enjoy peace. Now, the practical virtues are exercised either in politics or in war; but these do not seem to be leisurely occupations:—

War, indeed, seems to be quite the reverse of leisurely; for no one chooses to fight for fighting's sake, or arranges a war for that purpose: he would be deemed a bloodthirsty villain who should set friends at enmity in order that battles and slaughter might ensue.

But the politician's life also is not a leisurely occupation, and, beside the practice of politics itself, it brings power and honours, or at least happiness, to himself and his fellow-citizens, which is something different from politics; for we [who are asking what happiness is] also ask what politics is, evidently implying that it is something different from happiness.

If, then, the life of the statesman and the soldier, though they surpass all other virtuous exercises in nobility and grandeur, are not leisurely occupations, and aim at some ulterior end, and are not desired merely for themselves, but the exercise of the reason seems to be superior in seriousness (since it contemplates truth), and to aim at no end beside itself, and to have its proper pleasure (which also helps to increase the exercise), and further to be self-sufficient, and leisurely, and inexhaustible (as far as anything human can be), and to have all the other characteristics that are ascribed to happiness, it follows that the exercise of reason will be the complete happiness of man, *i.e.*, when a complete term of days is added; for nothing incomplete can be admitted into our idea of happiness.

But a life which realized this idea would be something more than human; for it would not be the expression of man's nature, but of some divine element in that nature—the exercise of which is as far superior to the exercise of the other kind of virtue [*i.e.*, practical or moral virtue], as this divine element is superior to our compound human nature.[19]

If then reason be divine as compared with man, the life which consists in the exercise of reason will also be divine in comparison with human life. Nevertheless, instead of listening to those who advise us as men and mortals not to lift our thoughts above what is human and mortal, we ought rather, as far as possible, to put off our mortality and make every effort to live in the exercise of the highest of our faculties; for though it be but a small part of us, yet in power and value it far surpasses all the rest.

And indeed this part would even seem to constitute our true self, since it is the sovereign and the better part. It would be strange, then, if a man were to prefer the life of something else to the life of his true self.

Again, we may apply here what we said above—for every being that is best and pleasantest which is naturally proper to it. Since, then it is the reason

---

17. ἡ κατὰ τὴν σοφίαν ἐνέργεια, the contemplation of absolute truth.
18. The search for this truth.

19. That is, our nature as moral agents, as compounds of reason and desire.

that in the truest sense is the man, the life that consists in the exercise of the reason is the best and pleasantest for man—and therefore the happiest.

8. The life that consists in the exercise of the other kind of virtue is happy in a secondary sense; for the manifestations of moral virtue are emphatically human [not divine]. Justice, I mean, and courage, and the other moral virtues are displayed in our relations towards one another by the observance, in every case, of what is due in contracts and services, and all sorts of outward acts, as well as in our inward feelings. And all these seem to be emphatically human affairs.

Again, moral virtue seems, in some points, to be actually a result of physical constitution, and in many points to be closely connected with the passions.

Again, prudence is inseparably joined to moral virtue, and moral virtue to prudence, since the moral virtues determine the principles of prudence,[20] while prudence determines what is right in morals.

But the moral virtues, being bound up with the passions, must belong to our compound nature; and the virtues of the compound nature are emphatically human. Therefore the life which manifests them, and the happiness which consists in this, must be emphatically human.

But the happiness which consists in the exercise of the reason is separate from the lower nature. (So much we may be allowed to assert about it: a detailed discussion is beyond our present purpose.)

Further, this happiness would seem to need but a small supply of external goods, certainly less than the moral life needs. Both need the necessaries of life to the same extent, let us say; for though, in fact, the politician takes more care of his person than the philosopher, yet the difference will be quite inconsiderable. But in what they need for their activities there will be a great difference. Wealth will be needed by the liberal man, that he may act liberally; by the just man, that he may discharge his obligations (for a mere wish cannot be tested,—even unjust people

pretend a wish to act justly); the courageous man will need strength if he is to execute any deed of courage; and the temperate man liberty of indulgence,—for how else can he, or the possessor of any other virtue, show what he is?

Again, people dispute whether the purpose or the action be more essential to virtue, virtue being understood to imply both. It is plain, then, that both are necessary to completeness. But many things are needed for action, and the greater and nobler the action, the more is needed.

On the other hand, he who is engaged in speculation needs none of these things for his *work;* nay, it may even be said that they are a hindrance to speculation: but as a man living with other men, he chooses to act virtuously; and so he will need things of this sort to enable him to behave like a man.

That perfect happiness is some kind of speculative activity may also be shown in the following way:—

It is always supposed that the gods are, of all beings, the most blessed and happy; but what kind of actions shall we ascribe to them? Acts of justice? Surely it is ridiculous to conceive the gods engaged in trade and restoring deposits, and so on. Or the acts of the courageous character who endures fearful things and who faces danger because it is noble to do so? Or acts of liberality? But to whom are they to give? and is it not absurd to suppose that they have money or anything of that kind? And what could acts of temperance mean with them? Surely it would be an insult to praise them for having no evil desires. In short, if we were to go through the whole list, we should find that all action is petty and unworthy of the gods.

And yet it is universally supposed that they live, and therefore that they exert their powers; for we cannot suppose that they lie asleep like Endymion.

Now, if a being lives, and action cannot be ascribed to him, still less production, what remains but contemplation? It follows, then, that the divine life, which surpasses all others in blessedness, consists in contemplation.

Of all modes of human activity, therefore, that which is most akin to this will be capable of the greatest happiness.

---

20. That is, the principles of morals cannot be proved, but are accepted without proof by the man whose desires are properly trained.

And this is further confirmed by the fact that the other animals do not participate in happiness, being quite incapable of this kind of activity. For the life of the gods is entirely blessed, and the life of man is blessed just so far as he attains to some likeness of this kind of activity; but none of the other animals are happy, since they are quite incapable of contemplation.

Happiness, then, extends just so far as contemplation, and the more contemplation the more happiness is there in a life,—not accidentally, but as a necessary accompaniment of the contemplation; for contemplation is precious in itself.

Our conclusion, then, is that happiness is a kind of speculation or contemplation.

But as we are men we shall need external good fortune also: for our nature does not itself provide all that is necessary for contemplation; the body must be in health, and supplied with food, and otherwise cared for. We must not, however, suppose that because it is impossible to be happy without external good things, therefore a man who is to be happy will want many things or much. It is not the superabundance of good things that makes a man independent, or enables him to act; and a man may do noble deeds, though he be not ruler of land and sea. A moderate equipment may give you opportunity for virtuous action (as we may easily see, for private persons seem to do what is right not less, but rather more, than princes), and so much as gives this opportunity is enough; for that man's life will be happy who has virtue and exercises it.

Study Questions

1. Do you agree with Aristotle that rationality is what essentially distinguishes us from other animals?

2. Is Aristotle's list of virtues complete?

3. Can one be immoral and happy?

4. Does modern psychology support or question Aristotle's claim about happiness and morality?

Moral Worth

Immanuel Kant (1724–1804) Immanuel Kant was born in Konigsberg, Prussia. He was a professor of philosophy and the author of major works on knowledge, ethics, and art.

Immanuel Kant

Nothing can possibly be conceived in the world, or even out of it, which can be called good without qualification, except a *good will*. Intelligence, wit,

From Kant's *Foundations of the Metaphysics of Morals* (1787), trans. T. Abbott, published by Longman Group, Ltd.

judgment, and the other *talents* of the mind, however they may be named, or courage, resolution, perseverance, as qualities of temperament, are undoubtedly good and desirable in many respects; but these gifts of nature may also become extremely bad and mischievous if the will which is to make use of them, and which, therefore, constitutes what is called *character,* is not good. It is the same with the *gifts of fortune.* Power, riches, honor, even health, and the general well-being and contentment with one's condition which is called *happiness,* inspire pride, and often presumption, if there is not a good will to correct the influence of these on the mind, and with this also to rectify the whole principle of acting, and adapt it to its end. The sight of a being who is not adorned with a single feature of a pure and good will, enjoying unbroken prosperity, can never give pleasure to an impartial rational spectator. Thus a good will appears to constitute the indispensable condition even of being worthy of happiness.

There are even some qualities which are of service to this good will itself, and may facilitate its action, yet which have no intrinsic unconditional value, but always presuppose a good will, and this qualifies the esteem that we justly have for them, and does not permit us to regard them as absolutely good. Moderation in the affections and passions, self-control, and calm deliberation are not only good in many respects, but even seem to constitute part of the intrinsic worth of the person; but they are far from deserving to be called good without qualification, although they have been so unconditionally praised by the ancients. For without the principles of a good will, they may become extremely bad; and the coolness of a villain not only makes him far more dangerous, but also directly makes him more abominable in our eyes than he would have been without it.

A good will is good not because of what it performs or effects, not by its aptness for the attainment of some proposed end, but simply by virtue of the volition—that is, it is good in itself, and considered by itself is to be esteemed much higher than all that can be brought about by it in favor of any inclination, nay, even of the sum-total of all inclinations. Even if it should happen that, owing to special disfavor of fortune, or the niggardly provi-

sion of a step-motherly nature, this will should wholly lack power to accomplish its purpose, if with its greatest efforts it should yet achieve nothing, and there should remain only the good will (not, to be sure, a mere wish, but the summoning of all means in our power), then, like a jewel, it would still shine by its own light, as a thing which has its whole value in itself. Its usefulness or fruitlessness can neither add to nor take away anything from this value. It would be, as it were, only the setting to enable us to handle it the more conveniently in common commerce, or to attract to it the attention of those who are not yet connoisseurs, but not to recommend it to true connoisseurs, or to determine its value.

There is, however, something so strange in this idea of the absolute value of the mere will, in which no account is taken of its utility, that notwithstanding the thorough assent of even common reason to the idea, yet a suspicion must arise that may perhaps really be the product of mere high-flown fancy, and that we may have misunderstood the purpose of nature in assigning reason as the governor of our will. Therefore we will examine this idea from this point of view.

In the physical constitution of an organized being, that is, a being adapted suitably to the purposes of life, we assume it as a fundamental principle that no organ for any purpose will be found but what is also the fittest and best adapted for that purpose. Now in a being which has reason and a will, if the proper object of nature were its *conservation,* its *welfare,* in a word, its *happiness,* then nature would have hit upon a very bad arrangement in selecting the reason of the creature to carry out this purpose. For all the actions which the creature has to perform with a view to this purpose, and the whole rule of its conduct, would be far more surely prescribed to it by instinct, and that end would have been attained thereby much more certainly than it ever can be by reason. Should reason have been communicated to this favored creature over and above, it must only have served it to contemplate the happy constitution of its nature, to admire it, to congratulate itself thereon, and to feel thankful for it to the beneficent cause, but not that it should subject its desires to that weak and delusive guidance, and meddle bunglingly with the purpose of nature. In a word, nature would have taken care that reason should not break forth into *practical exercise,* nor have the presumption, with its weak insight, to think out for itself the plan of happiness and of the means of attaining it. Nature would not only have taken on herself the choice of the ends but also of the means, and with wise foresight would have entrusted both to instinct.

And, in fact, we find that the more a cultivated reason applies itself with deliberate purpose to the enjoyment of life and happiness, so much the more does the man fail of true satisfaction. And from this circumstance there arises in many, if they are candid enough to confess it, a certain degree in *misology,* that is, hatred of reason, especially in the case of those who are most experienced in the use of it, because after calculating all the advantages they derive—I do not say from the invention of all the arts of common luxury, but even from the sciences (which seem to them to be after all only a luxury of the understanding)—they find that they have, in fact, only brought more trouble on their shoulders rather than gained in happiness; and they end by envying rather than despising the more common stamp of men who keep closer to the guidance of mere instinct, and do not allow their reason much influence on their conduct. And this we must admit, that the judgment of those who would very much lower the lofty eulogies of the advantages which reason gives us in regard to the happiness and satisfaction of life, or who would even reduce them below zero, is by no means morose or ungrateful to the goodness with which the world is governed, but that there lies at the root of these judgments the idea that our existence has a different and far nobler end, for which, and not for happiness, reason is properly intended, and which must, therefore, be regarded as the supreme condition to which the private ends of man must, for the most part, be postponed.

For as reason is not competent to guide the will with certainty in regard to its objects and the satisfaction of all our wants (which it to some extent even multiplies), this being an end to which an implanted instinct would have led with much greater certainty; and since, nevertheless, reason is imparted to us as a practical faculty, that is, as one

which is to have influence on the *will,* therefore, admitting that nature generally in the distribution of her capacities has adapted the means to the end, its true destination must be to produce a *will,* not merely good as a *means* to something else, but *good in itself,* for which reason was absolutely necessary. This will then, though not indeed the sole and complete good, must be the supreme good and the condition of every other, even of the desire of happiness. Under these circumstances, there is nothing inconsistent with the wisdom of nature in the fact that the cultivation of the reason, which is requisite for the first and unconditional purpose, does in many ways interfere, at least in this life, with the attainment of the second, which is always conditional—namely, happiness. Nay, it may even reduce it to nothing, without nature thereby failing of her purpose. For reason recognizes the establishment of a good will as its highest practical destination, and in attaining this purpose is capable only of a satisfaction of its own proper kind, namely, that from the attainment of an end, which end again is determined by reason only, notwithstanding that this may involve many a disappointment to the ends of inclination.

We have then to develop the notion of a will which deserves to be highly esteemed for itself, and is good without a view to anything further, a notion which exists already in the sound natural understanding, required rather to be cleared up than to be taught, and which in estimating the value of our actions always takes the first place and constitutes the condition of all the rest. In order to do this, we will take the notion of duty, which includes that of a good will, although implying certain subjective restrictions and hindrances. These, however, far from concealing it or rendering it unrecognizable, rather bring it out by contrast and make it shine forth so much the brighter.

I omit here all actions which are already recognized as inconsistent with duty, although they may be useful for this or that purpose, for with these the question whether they are done *from duty* cannot arise at all, since they even conflict with it. I also set aside those actions which really conform to duty, but to which men have *no* direct *inclination,* performing them because they are impelled thereto by some other inclination. For in this case we can readily distinguish whether the action which agrees with duty is done *from duty* or from a selfish view. It is much harder to make this distinction when the action accords with duty, and the subject has besides a *direct* inclination to it. For example, it is always a matter of duty that a dealer should not overcharge an inexperienced purchaser; and wherever there is much commerce the prudent tradesman does not overcharge, but keeps a fixed price for everyone, so that a child buys of him as well as any other. Men are thus *honestly* served; but this is not enough to make us believe that the tradesman has so acted from duty and from principles of honesty; his own advantage required it; it is out of the question in this case to suppose that he might besides have a direct inclination in favor of the buyers, so that, as it were, from love he should give no advantage to one over another. Accordingly the action was done neither from duty nor from direct inclination, but merely with a selfish view.

On the other hand, it is a duty to maintain one's life; and, in addition, everyone has also a direct inclination to do so. But on this account the often anxious care which most men take for it has no intrinsic worth, and their maxim has no moral import. They preserve their life *as duty requires,* no doubt, but not *because duty requires.* On the other hand, if adversity and hopeless sorrow have completely taken away the relish for life, if the unfortunate one, strong in mind, indignant at his fate rather than desponding or dejected, wishes for death, and yet preserves his life without loving it—not from inclination or fear, but from duty—then his maxim has a moral worth.

To be beneficent when we can is a duty; and besides this, there are many minds so sympathetically constituted that, without any other motive of vanity or self-interest, they find a pleasure in spreading joy around them, and can take delight in the satisfaction of others so far as it is their own work. But I maintain that in such a case an action of this kind, however proper, however amiable it may be, has nevertheless no true moral worth, but is on a level with other inclinations, for example, the inclination to honor, which, if it is happily directed to that which is in fact of public utility and accordant with

duty, and consequently honorable, deserves praise and encouragement, but not esteem. For the maxim lacks the moral import, namely, that such actions be done *from duty,* not from inclination. Put the case that the mind of that philanthropist was clouded by sorrow of his own, extinguishing all sympathy with the lot of others, and that while he still has the power to benefit others in distress, he is not touched by their trouble because he is absorbed with his own; and now suppose that he tears himself out of this dead insensibility and performs the action without any inclination to it, but simply from duty, then first has his action its genuine moral worth. Further still, if nature has put little sympathy in the heart of this or that man, if he, supposed to be an upright man, is by temperament cold and indifferent to the sufferings of others, perhaps because in respect of his own he is provided with the special gift of patience and fortitude, and supposes, or even requires, that others should have the same—and such a man would certainly not be the meanest product of nature—but if nature had not specially framed him for a philanthropist, would he not still find in himself a source from whence to give himself a far higher worth than that of a good-natured temperament could be? Unquestionably. It is just in this that the moral worth of the character is brought out which is incomparably the highest of all, namely, that he is beneficent, not from inclination, but from duty.

To secure one's own happiness is a duty, at least indirectly; for discontent with one's condition, under a pressure of many anxieties and amidst unsatisfied wants, might easily become a great *temptation to transgression of duty.* But here again, without looking to duty, all men have already the strongest and most intimate inclination to happiness, because it is just in this idea that all inclinations are combined in one total. But the precept of happiness is often of such a sort that it greatly interferes with some inclinations, and yet a man cannot form any definite and certain conception of the sum of satisfaction of all of them which is called happiness. It is not then to be wondered at that a single inclination, definite both as to what it promises and as to the time within which it can be gratified, is often able to overcome such a fluctuating idea, and that a gouty patient, for instance, can choose to enjoy what he likes, and to suffer what he may, since, according to his calculation, on this occasion at least, he has [only] not sacrificed the enjoyment of the present moment to a possibly mistaken expectation of a happiness which is supposed to be found in health. But even in this case, if the general desire for happiness did not influence his will, and supposing that in his particular case health was not a necessary element in this calculation, there yet remains in this, as in all other cases, this law—namely, that he should promote his happiness not from inclination but from duty, and by this would his conduct first acquire true moral worth.

It is in this manner, undoubtedly, that we are to understand those passages of Scripture also in which we are commanded to love our neighbor, even our enemy. For love, as an affection, cannot be commanded, but beneficence for duty's sake may, even though we are not impelled to it by any inclination—nay, are even repelled by a natural and unconquerable aversion. This is *practical* love, and not *pathological*—a love which is seated in the will, and not in the propensions of sense—in principles of action and not of tender sympathy; and it is this love alone which can be commanded.

The second proposition is: That an action done from duty derives its moral worth; *not from the purpose* which is to be attained by it, but from the maxim by which it is determined, and therefore does not depend on the realization of the object of the action, but merely on the *principle of volition* by which the action has taken place, without regard to any object of desire. It is clear from what precedes that the purposes which we may have in view in our actions, or their effects regarded as ends and springs of the will, cannot give to actions any unconditional or moral worth. In what, then, can their worth lie if it is not to consist in the will and in reference to its expected effect? It cannot lie anywhere but in the *principle of the will* without regard to the ends which can be attained by the action. For the will stands between its *a priori* principle, which is formal, and its *a posteriori* spring, which is material, as between two roads, and as it must be determined by something, it follows that it must be determined by the formal principle of volition when an action is done from duty, in which case every material principle has been withdrawn from it.

The third proposition, which is a consequence of the two preceding, I would express thus: *Duty is the necessity of acting from respect for the law.* I may have *inclination* for an object as the effect of my proposed action, but I cannot have *respect* for it just for this reason that it is an effect and not an energy of will. Similarly, I cannot have respect for inclination, whether my own or another's; I can at most, if my own, approve it; if another's, sometimes even love it, that is, look on it as favorable to my own interest. It is only what is connected with my will as a principle, by no means as an effect—what does not subserve my inclination, but overpowers it, or at least in case of choice excludes it from its calculation—in other words, simply the law of itself, which can be an object of respect, and hence a command. Now an action done from duty must wholly exclude the influence of inclination, and with it every object of the will, so that nothing remains which can determine the will except objectively the *law,* and subjectively *pure respect* for this practical law, and consequently the maxim[1] that I should follow this law even to the thwarting of all my inclinations.

Thus the moral worth of an action does not lie in the effect expected from it, nor in any principle of action which requires to borrow its motive from this expected effect. For all these effects—agreeableness of one's condition, and even the promotion of the happiness of others—could have been also brought about by other causes, so that for this there would have been no need of the will of a rational being; whereas it is in this alone that the supreme and unconditional good can be found. The preeminent good which we call moral can therefore consist in nothing else than *the conception of law* in itself, *which certainly is only possible in a rational being,* is so far as this conception, and not the expected effect, determines the will. This is a

---

1. A *maxim* is the subjective principle of volition. The objective principle (i.e., that which would also serve subjectively as a practical principle to all rational beings if reason had full power over the faculty of desire) is the practical *law.*

good which is already present in the person who acts accordingly, and we have not to wait for it to appear first in the result.[2]

But what sort of law can that be the conception of which must determine the will, even without paying any regard to the effect expected from it, in order that this will may be called absolutely and without qualification? As I have deprived the will of every impulse which could arise to it from obedience to any law, there remains nothing but the universal conformity of its actions to law in general, which alone is to serve the will as a principle, that is, I am never to act otherwise than so *that I could also will that my maxim should become a universal law.* Here, now, it is the simple conformity to law

---

2. It might be here objected to me that I take refuge behind the word *respect* in an obscure feeling, instead of giving a distinct solution of the question by a concept of the reason. But although respect is a feeling, it is not a feeling *received* through influence, but is *self-wrought* by a rational concept, and, therefore, is specifically distinct from all feelings of the former kind, which may be referred either to inclination or fear. What I recognize immediately as a law for me, I recognize with respect. This merely signifies the consciousness that my will is *subordinate* to a law, without the intervention of other influences on my sense. The immediate determination of the will by the law, and the consciousness of this, is called *respect,* so that this regarded as an *effect* of the law on the subject, and not as the *cause* of it. Respect is properly the conception of a worth which thwarts my self-love. Accordingly it is something which is considered neither as an object of inclination nor of fear, although it has something analogous to both. The *object* of respect is the *law* only, that is, the law which we impose on *ourselves,* and yet recognize as necessary in itself. As a law, we are subjected to it without consulting self-love; as imposed by us on ourselves, it is a result of our will. In the former aspect it has an analogy to fear, in the latter to inclination. Respect for a person is properly only respect for the law (of honesty, etc.) of which he gives us an example. since we also look on the improvement of our talents as a duty, we consider that we see in a person of talents, as it were, the *example of a law* (viz., to become like him in this by exercise), and this constitutes our respect. All so-called moral *interest* consists simply in *respect* for the law.

in general, without assuming any particular law applicable to certain actions, that serves the will as its principle, and must so serve it if duty is not to be a vain delusion and a chimerical notion. The common reason of men in its practical judgments perfectly concides with this, and always has in view the principle here suggested. Let the question be, for example: May I when in distress make a promise with the intention not to keep it? I readily distinguish here between the two significations which the question may have: whether it is prudent or whether it is right to make a false promise? The former may undoubtedly often be the case. I see clearly indeed that it is not enough to extricate myself from a present difficulty by means of this subterfuge, but it must be well considered whether there may not hereafter spring from this lie much greater inconvenience than that from which I now free myself, and as, with all my supposed *cunning,* the consequences cannot be so easily foreseen but that credit once lost may be much more injurious to me than any mischief which I seek to avoid at present, it should be considered whether it would not be more *prudent* to act herein according to a universal maxim, and to make it a habit to promise nothing except with the intention of keeping it. But it soon clear to me that such a maxim will still only be based on the fear of consequences. Now it is a wholly different thing to be truthful from duty, and to be so from apprehension of injurious consequences. In the first, case, the very notion of the action already implies a law for me; in the second case, I must first look about elsewhere to see what results may be combined with it which would affect myself. For to deviate from the principle of duty is beyond all doubt wicked; but to be unfaithful to my maxim of prudence may often be very advantageous to me, although to abide by it is certainly safer. The shortest way, however, and an unerring one, to discover the answer to this question whether a lying promise is consistent with duty, is to ask myself, Should I be content that my maxim (to extricate myself from difficulty by a false promise) should hold good as a universal law, for myself as well as for others; and should I be able to say to myself, "Every one may make a deceitful promise when he finds himself in a difficulty from which he cannot otherwise extricate himself"? Then I presently become aware that, while I can will the lie, I can by no means will that lying should be a universal law. For with such a law there would be no promises at all, since it would be in vain to allege my intention in regard to my future actions to those who would not believe this allegation, or if they over-hastily did so, would pay me back in my own coin. Hence my maxim, as soon as it should be made a universal law, would necessarily destroy itself.

I do not, therefore, need any far-reaching penetration to discern what I have to do in order that my will may be morally good. Inexperienced in the course of the world, incapable of being prepared for all its contingencies, I only ask myself: Canst thou also will that thy maxim should be a universal law? If not, then it must be rejected, and that not because of a disadvantage accruing from it to myself or even to others, but because it cannot enter as a principle into a possible universal legislation, and reason extorts from me immediate respect for such legislation. I do not indeed as yet *discern* on what this respect is based (this the philosopher may inquire), but at least I understand this—that it is an estimation of the worth which far outweighs all worth of what is recommended by inclination, and that the necessity of acting from *pure* respect for the practical law is what constitutes duty, to which every other motive must give place because it is the condition of a will being good *in itself,* and the worth of such a will is above everything.

Thus, then, without quitting the moral knowledge of common human reason, we have arrived at its principle. And although, no doubt, common men do not conceive it in such an abstract and universal form, yet they always have it really before their eyes and use it as the standard of their decision. Here it would be easy to show how, with this compass in hand, men are well able to distinguish, in every case that occurs, what is good, what bad, conformably to duty or inconsistent with it, if, without in the least teaching them anything new, we only, like Socrates, direct their attention to the principle they themselves employ; and that, therefore, we do not need science and philosophy to know what we should do to be honest and good, yea, even wise and virtuous. Indeed we might well have conjectured beforehand that the knowledge of what every man is bound to do, and therefore also to know, would be within the reach of every man, even the commonest. Here we cannot forbear admiration when we see how great an advantage the practical judgment has over the theoretical in the common understanding of men. In the latter, if common reason ventures to depart from the laws of experience and from the perceptions of the senses, it falls into mere inconceivabilities and self-contradictions, at least into a chaos of uncertainty, obscurity, and instability. But in the practical sphere it is just when the common understanding excludes all sensible springs from practical laws that its power of judgment begins to show itself to advantage. It then becomes even subtle, whether it be that it chicanes with its own conscience or with other claims re-

> *"Act as if the maxim of thy action were to become by thy will a universal law of nature."*

specting what is to be called right, or whether it desires for its own instruction to determine honestly the worth of actions; and, in the latter case, it may even have as good a hope of hitting the mark as any philosopher whatever can promise himself. Nay, it is almost more sure of doing so, because the philosopher cannot have any other principle, while he may easily perplex his judgment by a multitude of considerations foreign to the matter, and so turn aside from the right way. Would it not therefore be wiser in moral concerns to acquiesce in the judgment of common reason, or at most only to call in philosophy for the purpose of rendering the system of morals more complete and intelligible, and its rules more convenient for use (especially for disputation), but not so as to draw off the common understanding from its happy simplicity, or to bring it by means of philosophy into a new path of inquiry and instruction?

Innocence is indeed a glorious thing; only, on the other hand, it is very sad that it cannot well maintain itself, and is easily seduced. On this account even wisdom—which otherwise consists more in conduct than in knowledge—yet has need of science, not in order to learn from it, but to secure for its precepts admission and permanence. Against all the commands of duty which reason represents to man as so deserving of respect, he feels in himself a powerful counterpoise in his wants and inclinations, the entire satisfaction of which he sums up under the name of happiness. Now reason issues its commands unyieldingly, without promising anything to the inclinations, and, as it were, with disregard and contempt for these claims, which are so impetuous and at the same time so plausible, and which will not allow themselves to be suppressed by any command. Hence there arises a natural *dialectic,* that is, a disposition to argue against these strict laws of duty and to question their validity, or at least their purity and strictness; and, if possible, to make them more accordant with our wishes and inclinations, that is to say, to corrupt them at their very source and entirely to destroy their worth—a thing which even common practical reason cannot ultimately call good. . . .

When we add further that, unless we deny that the notion of morality has any truth or reference to any possible object, we must admit that its law must be valid, not merely for men, but for all *rational creatures generally,* not merely under certain contingent conditions or with exceptions, but *with absolute necessity,* then it is clear that no experience could enable us to infer even the possibility of such apodictic laws. For with what right could we bring into unbounded respect as a universal precept for every rational nature that which perhaps holds only under the contingent conditions of humanity? Or how could laws of the determination of *our* will be regarded as laws of the determination of the will of rational beings generally, and for us only as such, if they were merely empirical and did not take their origin wholly *a priori* from pure but practical reason?

Nor could anything be more fatal to morality than that we should wish to derive it from examples. For every example of it that is set before me must be first itself tested by principles of morality, whether it is worthy to serve as an original example, that is, as a pattern, but by no means can it authoritatively furnish the conception of morality. Even the Holy One of the Gospels must first be compared with our ideal of moral perfection before we can recognize Him as such; and so He says of Himself, "Why call ye Me [whom you see] good; none is good [the model of good] but God only [whom ye do not see]?" But whence have we the conception of God as the supreme good? Simply from the *idea* of moral perfection, which reason frames *a priori* and connects inseparably with the notion of a free will. Imitation finds no place at all in morality, and examples serve only for encouragement, that is, they put beyond doubt the feasibility of what the law commands, they make visible that which the practical rule expresses more generally, but they can never authorize us to set aside the true original which lies in reason, and to guide ourselves by examples. . . .

From what has been said, it is clear that all moral conceptions have their seat and origin completely *a priori* in the reason, and that, moreover, in the commonest reason just as truly as in that which is in the highest degree speculative; that they cannot be obtained by abstraction from any empirical, and therefore merely contingent, knowledge; that it is just this purity of their origin that makes them worthy to serve as our supreme practical principle, and that just in proportion as we add anything empirical, we detract from their genuine influence and from the absolute value of actions; that it is not only of the greatest necessity, in a purely speculative point of view, but is also of the greatest practical importance, to derive these notions and laws from pure reason, to present them pure and unmixed, and even to determine the compass of this practical or more rational knowledge, that is, to determine the whole faculty of pure practical reason; and, in doing so, we must not make its principles dependent on the particular nature of human reason, though in speculative philosophy this may be permitted, or may even at times be necessary; but since moral laws ought to hold good for every rational creature, we must derive them from the general concept of a rational being. In this way, although for its *application* to man morality has need of anthropology, yet, in the first instance, we must treat it independently as pure philosophy, that is, as metaphysic, complete in itself (a thing which in such distinct branches of science is easily done); knowing well that, unless we are in possession of this, it would not only be vain to determine the moral element of duty in right actions for purposes of speculative criticism, but it would be impossible to base morals on their genuine principles, even for common practical purposes, especially of moral instruction, so as to produce pure moral dispositions, and to engraft them on men's minds to the promotion of the greatest possible good in the world.

But in order that in this study we may not merely advance by the natural steps from the common moral judgment (in this case very worthy of respect) to the philosophical, as has been already done, but also from a popular philosophy, which goes no further than it can reach by groping with the help of examples, to metaphysic (which does not allow itself to be checked by anything empirical and, as it must measure the whole extent of this kind of rational knowledge, goes as far as ideal conceptions, where even examples fail us), we must follow and clearly describe the practical faculty of reason, from the general rules of its determination to the point where the notion of duty springs from it.

Everything in nature works according to laws. Rational beings alone have the faculty of acting according *to the conception* of laws—that is, according to principles, that is, have a *will*. Since the deduction of actions from principles requires *reason*, the will is nothing but practical reason. If reason infallibly determines the will, then the actions of such a being which are recognized as objectively necessary are subjectively necessary also, that is, the will is a faculty to choose *that only* which reason independent of inclination recognizes as practically necessary, that is, as good. But if reason of itself does not sufficiently determine the will, if the latter is subject also to subjective conditions (particular impulses) which do not always coincide with the ob-

jective conditions, in a word, if the will does not *in itself* completely accord with reason (which is actually the case with men), then the actions which objectively are recognized as necessary are subjectively contingent, and the determination of such a will according to objective laws is *obligation,* that is to say, the relation of the objective laws to a will that is not thoroughly good is conceived as the determination of the will of a rational being by principles of reason, but which the will from its nature does not of necessity follow.

The conception of an objective principle, in so far as it is obligatory for a will, is called a command (of reason), and the formula of the command is called an Imperative.

All imperatives are expressed by the word *ought* [or *shall*], and thereby indicate the relation of an objective law of reason to a will which from its subjective constitution is not necessarily determined by it (an obligation). They say that something would be good to do or to forbear, but they say it to a will which does not always do a thing because it is conceived to be good to do it. That is practically *good,* however, which determines the will by means of the conceptions of reason, and consequently not from subjective causes, but objectively, that is, on principles which are valid for every rational being as such. It is distinguished from the *pleasant* as that which influences the will only by means of sensation from merely subjective causes, valid only for the sense of this or that one, and not as a principle of reason which holds for every one.

A perfectly good will would therefore be equally subject to objective laws (viz., laws of good), but could not be conceived as *obliged* thereby to act lawfully, because of itself from its subjective constitution it can only be determined by the conception of good. Therefore no imperatives hold for the Divine will, or in general for a *holy* will; *ought* is here out of place because the volition is already of itself necessarily in unison with the law. Therefore imperatives are only formulae to express the relation of objective laws of all volition to the subjective imperfection of the will of this or that rational being, for example, the human will.

Now all *imperatives* command either *hypothetically* or *categorically*. The former represent the practical necessity of a possible action as means to something else that is willed (or at least which one might possibly will). The categorical imperative would be that which represented an action as necessary of itself without reference to another end, that is, as objectively necessary.

Since every practical law represents a possible action as good, and on this account, for a subject who is practically determinable by reason as necessary, all imperatives are formulae determining an action which is necessary according to the principle of a will good in some respects. If now the action is good only as a means *to something else,* then the imperative is *hypothetical;* if it is conceived as good *in itself* and consequently as being necessarily the principle of a will which of itself conforms to reason, then it is *categorical.*

Thus the imperative declares what action possible by me would be good, and presents the practical rule in relation to a will which does not forthwith perform an action simply because it is good, whether because the subject does not always know that it is good, or because, even if it knows this, yet its maxims might be opposed to the objective principles of practical reason.

Accordingly the hypothetical imperative only says that the action is good for some purpose, *possible* or *actual.* In the first case it is a *problematical,* in the second an *assertorial* practical principle. The categorical imperative which declares an action to be objectively necessary in itself without reference to any purpose, that is, without any other end, is valid as an *apodictic* (practical) principle.

Whatever is possible only by the power of some rational being may also be conceived as a possible purpose of some will; and therefore the principles of action as regards the means necessary to attain some possible purpose are in fact infinitely numerous. All sciences have a practical part consisting of problems expressing that some end is possible for us, and of imperatives directing how it may be attained. These may, therefore, be called in general imperatives of *skill.* Here there is no question whether the end is rational and good, but only what one must do in order to attain it. The precepts for the physician to make his patient thoroughly healthy, and for a poisoner to ensure certain death, are of equal value in this respect, that each serves to effect its purpose perfectly. Since in early youth

it cannot be known what ends are likely to occur to us in the course of life, parents seek to have their children taught a *great many things,* and provide for their *skill* in the use of means for all sorts of arbitrary ends, of none of which can they determine whether it may not perhaps hereafter be an object to their pupil, but which it is at all events *possible* that he might aim at; and this anxiety is so great that they commonly neglect to form and correct their judgment on the value of the things which may be chosen as ends.

There is *one* end, however, which may be assumed to be actually such to all rational beings (so far as imperatives apply to them, viz., as dependent beings), and, therefore, one purpose which they not merely *may* have, but which we may with certainty assume that they all actually *have* by a natural necessity, and this is *happiness.* The hypothetical imperative which expresses the practical necessity of an action as means to the advancement of happiness is *assertorial.* We are not to present it as necessary for an uncertain and merely possible purpose, but for a purpose which we may presuppose with certainty and *a priori* in every man, because it belongs to his being. Now skill in the choice of means to his own greatest well-being may be called *prudence,* in the narrowest sense. And thus the imperative which refers to the choice of means to one's own happiness, that is, the precept of prudence, is still always *hypothetical;* the action is not commanded absolutely, but only as means to another purpose.

Finally, there is an imperative which commands a certain conduct immediately, without having as its condition any other purpose to be attained by it. This imperative is *categorical.* It concerns not the matter of the action, or its intended result, but its form and the principle of which it is itself a result; and what is essentially good in its consists in the mental disposition, let the consequence be what it may. This imperative may be called that of *morality.*

There is a marked distinction also between the volitions on these three sorts of principles in the *dissimilarity* of the obligation of the will. In order to mark this difference more clearly, I think they would be most suitably named in their order if we said they are either *rules* of skill, or *counsels* of prudence, or *commands (laws)* of morality. For it is *law* only that involves the conception of an *unconditional* and objective necessity, which is consequently universally valid; and commands are laws which must be obeyed, that is, must be followed, even in opposition to inclination. *Counsels,* indeed, involve necessity, but one which can only hold under a contingent subjective condition, viz., they depend on whether this or that man reckons this or that as part of his happiness; the categorical imperative, on the contrary, is not limited by any condition, and as being absolutely, although practically, necessary may be quite properly called a command. We might also call the first kind of imperatives *technical* (belonging to art), the second *pragmatic* (belonging to welfare), the third *moral* (belonging to free conduct generally, that is, to morals).

Now arises the question, how are all these imperatives possible? This question does not seek to know how we can conceive the accomplishment of the action which the imperative ordains, but merely how we can conceive the obligation of the will which the imperative expresses. No special explanation is needed to show how an imperative of skill is possible. Whoever wills the end wills also (so far as reason decides his conduct) the means in his power which are indispensably necessary thereto. This proposition is, as regards the volition, and analytical; for in willing an object as my effect there is already thought the causality of myself as an acting cause, that is to say, the use of the means; and the imperative educes from the conception of volition of an end the conception of actions necessary to this end. Synthetical propositions must no doubt be employed in defining the means to a proposed end; but they do not concern the principle, the act of the will, but the object and its realization. For example, that in order to bisect a line on an unerring principle I must draw from its extremities two intersecting arcs; this no doubt is taught by mathematics only in synthetical propositions; but if I know that it is only by this process that the intended operation can be performed, then to say that if I fully will the operation, I also will the action required for it, is an analytical proposition; for it is one and the same thing to conceive something as an effect which I can produce in a certain way, and to conceive myself as acting in this way.

If it were only equally easy to give a definite conception of happiness, the imperatives of prudence would correspond exactly with those of skill, and would likewise be analytical. For in this case as in that, it could be said whoever wills the end wills also (according to the dictate of reason necessarily) the indispensable means thereto which are in his power. But, unfortunately, the notion of happiness is so indefinite that although every man wishes to attain it, yet he never can say definitely and consistently what it is that he really wishes and wills. The reason of this is that all the elements which belong to the notion of happiness are altogether empirical, that is, they must be borrowed from experience, and nevertheless the idea of happiness requires an absolute whole, a maximum of welfare in my present and all future circumstances. Now it is impossible that the most clear-sighted and at the same time most powerful being (supposed finite) should frame to himself a definite conception of what he really wills in this. Does he will riches, how much anxiety, envy, and snares might he not thereby draw upon his shoulders? Does he will knowledge and discernment, perhaps it might prove to be only an eye so much the sharper to show him so much the more fearfully the evils that are now concealed from him and that cannot be avoided, or to impose more wants on his desires, which already give him concern enough. Would he have long life? Who guarantees to him that it would not be a long misery? Would he at least have health? How often has uneasiness of the body restrained from excesses into which perfect health would have allowed one to fall, and so on? In short, he is unable, on any principle, to determine with certainty what would make him truly happy; because to do so he would need to be omniscient. We cannot therefore act on any definite principles to secure happiness, but only on empirical counsels, for example, of regimen, frugality, courtesy, reserve, etc., which experience teaches do, on the average, most promote well-being. Hence it follows that the imperatives of prudence do not, strictly speaking, command at all, that is, they cannot present actions objectively as practically *necessary;* that they are rather to be regarded as counsels than precepts of reason, that the problem to determine certainly and universally what action would promote the happiness of a rational being is completely insoluble, and consequently no imperative respecting it is possible which should, in the strict sense, command to do what makes happy; because happiness is not an ideal of reason but of imagination, resting solely on empirical grounds, and it is vain to expect that these should define an action by which one could attain the totality of a series of consequences which is really endless. This imperative of prudence would, however, be an analytical proposition if we assume that the means to happiness could be certainly assigned; for it is distinguished from the imperative of skill only by this that in the latter the end is merely *possible,* in the former it is *given;* as, however, both only ordain the means to that which we suppose to be willed as an end, it follows that the imperative which ordains the willing of the means to him who wills the end is in both cases analytical. Thus there is no difficulty in regard to the possibility of an imperative of this kind either. . . .

When I conceive a hypothetical imperative, in general I do not know beforehand what it will contain until I am given the condition. But when I conceive a categorical imperative, I know at once what it contains. For as the imperative contains besides the law only the necessity that the maxims[3] shall conform to this law, while the law contains no conditions restricting it, there remains nothing but the general statement that the maxim of the action should conform to a universal law, and it is this conformity alone that the imperative properly represents as necessary.

There is therefore but one categorical imperative, namely, this: *Act only on that maxim whereby thou canst at the same time will that it should become a universal law.*

Now if all imperatives of duty can be deduced

---

3. A "maxim" is a subjective principle of action, and must be distinguished from the *objective principle,* namely, practical law. The former contains the practical rule set by reason according to the conditions of the subject (often its ignorance or its inclinations), so that it is the principle on which the subject *acts;* but the law is the objective principle valid for every rational being, and is the principle on which it *ought to act*—that is an imperative.

from this one imperative as from their principle, then, although it should remain undecided whether what is called duty is not merely a vain notion, yet at least we shall be able to show what we understand by it and what this notion means.

Since the universality of the law according to which effects are produced constitutes what is properly called *nature* in the most general sense (as to form)—that is, the existence of things so far as it is determined by general laws—the imperative of duty may be expressed thus: *Act as if the maxim of thy action were to become by thy will a universal law of nature.*

We will now enumerate a few duties, adopting the usual division of them into duties to ourselves and to others, and into perfect and imperfect duties.

1. A man reduced to despair by a series of misfortunes feels wearied of life, but is still to far in possession of his reason that he can ask himself whether it would not be contrary to his duty to himself to take his own life. Now he inquires whether the maxim of his action could become a universal law of nature. His maxim is: From self-love I adopt it as a principle to shorten my life when its longer duration is likely to bring more evil than satisfaction. It is asked then simply whether this principle founded on self-love can become a universal law of nature. Now we see at once that a system of nature of which it should be a low to destroy life by means of the very feeling whose special nature it is to impel to the improvement of life would contradict itself, and therefore could not exist as a system of nature; hence that maxim cannot possibly exist as a universal law of nature, and consequently would be wholly inconsistent with the supreme principle of all duty.

2. Another finds himself forced by necessity to borrow money. He knows that he will not be able to repay it, but sees also that nothing will be lent to him unless he promises stoutly to repay it in a definite time. He desires to make this promise, but he has still so much conscience as to ask himself: Is it not unlawful and inconsistent with duty to get out of a difficulty in this way? Suppose, however, that he resolves to do so, then the maxim of his action would be expressed thus: When I think myself in want of money, I will borrow money and promise to repay it, although I know that I never can do so. Now this principle of self-love or of one's own advantage may perhaps be consistent with my whole future welfare; but the question now is, Is it right? I change then the suggestion of self-love into a universal law, and state the question thus: How would it be if my maxim were a universal law? Then I see at once that it could never hold as a universal law of nature, but would necessarily contradict itself. For supposing it to be a universal law that everyone when he thinks himself in a difficulty should be able to promise whatever he pleases, with the purpose of not keeping his promise, the promise itself would become impossible, as well as the end that one might have in view in it, since no one would consider that anything was promised to him, but would ridicule all such statements as vain pretenses.

3. A third finds in himself a talent which with the help of some culture might make him a useful man in many respects. But he finds himself in comfortable circumstances and prefers to indulge in pleasure rather than to take pains in enlarging and improving his happy natural capacities. He asks, however, whether his maxim of neglect of his natural gifts, besides agreeing with his inclination to indulgence, agrees also with what is called duty. He sees then that a system of nature could indeed subsist with such a universal law, although men (like the South Sea islanders) should let their talents rest and resolve to devote their lives merely to idleness, amusement, and propagation of their species—in a word, to enjoyment; but he cannot possibly *will* that this should be a universal law of nature, or be implanted in us as such by a natural instinct. For, as a rational being, he necessarily wills that his faculties be developed, since they serve him, and have been given him, for all sorts of possible purposes.

4. A fourth, who is in prosperity, while he sees that others have to contend with great wretchedness and that he could help them, thinks: What concern is it of mine? Let everyone be as happy as Heaven pleases, or as he can make himself; I will take nothing from him nor even envy him, only I do not wish to contribute anything to his welfare or to his assistance in distress! Now now doubt, if such a mode of thinking were a universal law, the human race might very well subsist, and doubtless even

better than in a state in which everyone talks of sympathy and good-will, or even takes care occasionally to put it into practice, but, on the other side, also cheats when he can, betrays the rights of men, or otherwise violates them. But although it is possible that a universal law of nature might exist in accordance with that maxim, it is impossible to *will* that such a principle should have the universal validity of a law of nature. For a will which resolved this would contradict itself, inasmuch as many cases might occur in which one would have need of the love and sympathy of others, and in which, by such a law of nature, sprung from his own will, he would deprive himself of all hope of the aid he desires.

These are a few of the many actual duties, or at least what we regard as such, which obviously fall into two classes on the one principle that we have laid down. We must be *able to will* that a maxim of our action should be a universal law. This is the canon of the moral appreciation of the action generally. Some actions are of such a character that their maxim cannot without contradiction be even *conceived* as a universal law of nature, far from it being possible that we should *will* that it *should* be so. In others, this intrinsic impossibility is not found, but still it is impossible to *will* that their maxim should be raised to the universality of a law of nature, since such a will would contradict itself. It is easily seen that the former violate strict or rigorous (inflexible) duty; the latter only laxer (meritorious) duty. Thus it has been completely shown by these examples how all duties depend as regards the nature of the obligation (not the object of the action) on the same principle.

If now we attend to ourselves on occasion of any transgression of duty, we shall find that we in fact do not will that our maxim should be a universal law, for that is impossible for us; on the contrary, we will that the opposite should remain a universal law, only we assume the liberty of making an *exception* in our own favor or (just for this time only) in favor of our inclination. Consequently, if we considered all cases from one and the same point of view, namely, that of reason, we should find a contradiction in our own will, namely, that a certain principle should be objectively necessary as a universal law, and yet subjectively should not be universal, but admit of exceptions. As, however, we at one moment regard our action from the point of view of a will wholly conformed to reason, and then again look at the same action from the point of view of a will affected by inclination, there is not really any contradiction, but an antagonism of inclination to the precept of reason, whereby the universality of the principle is changed into a mere generality, so that the practical principle of reason shall meet the maxim half way. Now, although this cannot be justified in our own impartial judgment, yet it proves that we do really recognize the validity of the categorical imperative and (with all respect for it) only allow ourselves a few exceptions which we think unimportant and forced from us.

We have thus established at least this much—that if duty is a conception which is to have any import and real legislative authority for our actions, it can only be expressed in categorical, and not at all in hypothetical, imperatives. We have also, which is of great importance, exhibited clearly and definitely for every practical application the content of the categorical imperative, which must contain the principle of all duty if there is such a thing at all. We have not yet, however, advanced so far as to prove *a priori* that there actually is such an imperative, that there is a practical law which commands absolutely of itself and without any other impulse, and that the following of this law is duty.

With the view of attaining to this it is of extreme importance to remember that we must not allow ourselves to think of deducing the reality of this principle from the *particular attributes of human nature*. For duty is to be a practical, unconditional necessity of action; it must therefore hold for all rational beings (to whom an imperative can apply at all), and *for this reason only* be also a law for all human wills. On the contrary, whatever is deduced from certain feelings and propensions, nay, even, if possible, from any particular tendency proper to human reason, and which need not necessarily hold for the will of every rational being—this may indeed supply us with a maxim but not with a law; with a subjective principle on which we may have a propension and inclination to act, but not with an objective principle on which we should be *enjoined* to act, even though all our propensions, inclinations, and natural dispositions were opposed to

it. In fact, the sublimity and intrinsic dignity of the command in duty are so much the more evident, the less the subjective impulses favor it and the more they oppose it, without being able in the slightest degree to weaken the obligation of the law or to diminish its validity.

Here then we see philosophy brought to a critical position, since it has to be firmly fixed, notwithstanding that it has nothing to support it in heaven or earth. Here it must show its purity as absolute director of its own laws, not the herald of those which are whispered to it by an implanted sense or who knows what tutelary nature. Although these may be better than nothing, yet they can never afford principles dictated by reason, which must have their source wholly *a priori* and thence their commanding authority, expecting everything from the supremacy of the law and the due respect for it, nothing from inclination, or else condemning the man to self-contempt and inward abhorrence.

Thus every empirical element is not only quite incapable of being an aid to the principle of morality, but is even highly prejudicial to the purity of morals; for the proper and inestimable worth of an absolutely good will consists just in this that the principle of action is free from all influence of contingent grounds, which alone experience can furnish. We cannot too much or too often repeat our warning against this lax and even mean habit of thought which seeks for its principle among empirical motives and laws; for human reason in its weariness is glad to rest on this pillow, and in a dream of sweet illusions (in which, instead of Juno, it embraces a cloud) it substitutes for morality a bastard patched up from limbs of various derivation, which looks like anything one chooses to see in it; only not like virtue to one who has once beheld her in her true form.[4]

The question then is this: Is it a necessary law *for all rational beings* that they should always judge

---

4. To behold virtue in her proper form is nothing else but to contemplate morality stripped of all admixture of sensible things and of every spurious ornament of reward or self-love. How much she then eclipses everything else that appears charming to the affections, every one may readily perceive the least exertion of his reason, if it be not wholly spoiled for abstraction.

of their actions by maxims of which they can them-selves will that they should serve as universal laws? If it is so, then it must be connected (altogether *a priori*) with the very conception of the will of a rational being generally. But in order to discover this connection we must, however reluctantly, take a step into metaphysic, although into a domain of it which is distinct from speculative philosophy—namely, the metaphysic of morals. In a practical philosophy, where it is not the reasons of what *happens* that we have to ascertain, but the laws of what *ought to happen,* even although it never does, that is, objective practical laws, there it is not necessary to inquire into the reasons why anything pleases or displeases, how the pleasure of mere sensation differs from taste, and whether the latter is distinct from a general satisfaction of reason; on what the feeling of pleasure or pain rests, and how from it desires and inclinations arise, and from these again maxims by the cooperation of reason; for all this belongs to an empirical psychology, which would constitute the second part of physics, if we regard physics as the *philosophy* of nature, so far as it is based on *empirical laws.* But here we are concerned with objective practical laws, and consequently with the relation of the will to itself so far as it is determined by reason alone, in which case whatever has reference to anything empirical is necessarily excluded; since if *reason of itself alone* determines the conduct (and it is the possibility of this that we are now investigating), it must necessarily do so *a priori.*

The will is conceived as a faculty of determining oneself to action *in accordance with the conception of certain laws.* And such a faculty can be found only in rational beings. Now that which serves the will as the objective ground of its self-determination is the *end,* and if this is assigned by reason alone, it must hold for all rational beings. On the other hand, that which merely contains the ground of possibility of the action of which the effect is the end, this is called the *means.* The subjective ground of the desire is the *spring,* the objective ground of the volition is the *motive;* hence the distinction between subjective ends which rest on springs, and objective ends which depend on motives valid for every rational being. Practical principles are *formal*

when they abstract from all subjective ends; they are *material* when they assume these, and therefore particular, springs of action. The ends which a rational being proposes to himself at pleasure as *effects* of his actions (material ends) are all only relative, for it is only their relation to the particular desires of the subject that gives them their worth, which therefore cannot furnish principles universal and necessary for all rational beings and for every volition, that is to say, practical laws. Hence all these relative ends can give rise only to hypothetical imperatives.

Supposing, however, that there were something *whose existence* has *in itself* an absolute worth, something which, being *an end in itself,* could be a source of definite laws, then in this and this alone would lie the source of a possible categorical imperative, that is, a practical law.

Now I say: man and generally any rational being *exists* as an end in himself, *not merely as a means* to be arbitrarily used by this or that will, but in all his actions, whether they concern himself or other rational beings, must be always regarded at the same time as an end. All objects of the inclinations have only a conditional worth; for if the inclinations and the wants founded on them did not exist, then their object would be without value. But the inclinations themselves, being sources of want, are so far from having an absolute worth for which they should be desired that, on the contrary, it must be the universal wish of every rational being to be wholly free from them. Thus the worth of any object which is *to be acquired* by our action is always conditional. Beings whose existence depends not on our will but on nature's, have nevertheless, if they are nonrational beings, only a relative value as means, and are therefore called *things;* rational beings, on the contrary, are called *persons,* because their very nature points them out as ends in themselves, that is, as something which must not be used merely as means, and so far therefore restricts freedom of action (and is an object of respect). These, therefore, are not merely subjective ends whose existence has a worth *for us* as an effect of our action, but *objective ends,* that is, things whose existence is an end in itself—an end, moreover, for which no other can be substituted, which they should subserve *merely* as means, for otherwise nothing whatever would possess *absolute worth;* but if all worth were conditioned and therefore contingent, then there would be no supreme practical principle of reason whatever.

If then there is a supreme practical principle or, in respect of the human will, a categorical imperative, it must be one which, being drawn from the conception of that which is necessarily an end for everyone because it is *an end in itself,* constitutes an *objective* principle of will, and can therefore serve as a universal practical law. The foundation of this principle is: *rational nature exists as an end in itself.* Man necessarily conceives his own existence as being so; so far then this is a *subjective* principle of human actions. But every other rational being regards its existence similarly, just on the same rational principle that holds for me; so that it is at the same time an objective principle from which as a supreme practical law all laws of the will must be capable of being deduced. Accordingly the practical imperative will be as follows: *So act as to treat humanity, whether in thine own person or in that of any other, in every case as an end withal, never as means only.* We will now inquire whether this can be practically carried out.

To abide by the previous examples:

First, under the head of necessary duty to oneself: He who contemplates suicide should ask himself whether his action can be consistent with the idea of humanity *as an end in itself.* If he destroys himself in order to escape from painful circumstances, he uses a person merely as *a mean* to maintain a tolerable condition up to the end of life. But a man is not a thing, that is to say, something which can be used merely as means, but must in all his actions be always considered as an end in himself: I cannot, therefore, dispose in any way of a man in my own person so as to mutilate him, to damage or kill him. (It belongs to ethics proper to define this principle more precisely, so as to avoid all misunderstanding, for example, as to the amputation of the limbs in order to preserve myself; as to exposing my life to danger with a view to preserve it, etc. This question is therefore omitted here.)

Secondly, as regards necessary duties, or those of strict obligation, towards others: He who is thinking of making a lying promise to others will see at once that he would be using another man *merely as a mean,* without the latter containing at the same time the end in himself. For he whom I propose by such a promise to use for my own purposes cannot possibly assent to my mode of acting towards him, and therefore cannot himself contain the end of this action. This violation of the principle of humanity in other men is more obvious if we take in examples of attacks on the freedom and property of others. For then it is clear that he who transgresses the rights of men intends to use the person of others merely as means, without considering that as rational beings they ought always to be esteemed also as ends, that is, as beings who must be capable of containing in themselves the end of the very same action.

Thirdly, as regards contingent (meritorious) duties to oneself: It is not enough that the action does not violate humanity in our own person as an end in itself, it must also *harmonize with* it. Now there are in humanity capacities of greater perfection which belong to the end that nature has in view in regard to humanity in ourselves as the subject; to neglect these might perhaps be consistent with the *maintenance* of humanity as an end in itself, but not with the *advancement* of this end.

Fourthly, as regards meritorious duties towards others: The natural end which all men have is their own happiness. Now humanity might indeed subsist although no one should contribute anything to the happiness of others, provided he did not intentionally withdraw anything from it; but after all, this would only harmonize negatively, not positively, with *humanity as an end in itself,* if everyone does not also endeavor, as far as in him lies, to forward the ends of others. For the ends of any subject which is an end in himself ought as far as possible to be *my* ends also, if that conception is to have its *full* effect with me. . . .

1. Can one universalize an immoral maxim?

2. What would Kant say about torturing animals for our pleasure?

3. Is happiness as vague a concept as Kant thinks?

Utilitarianism

John Stuart Mill (1806–1873) John Stuart Mill was born in England and educated by his father, James Mill, who was also a philosopher. John Mill was a member of Parliament, a proponent of women's rights and labor unions, and the author of major philosophical works.

John Stuart Mill

Chapter I. General Remarks

There are few circumstances among those which make up the present condition of human knowledge more unlike what might have been expected, or more significant of the backward state in which speculation on the most important subjects still lingers, than the little progress which has been made in the decision of the controversy respecting the criterion of right and wrong. From the dawn of philosophy, the question concerning the *summum bonum,* or, what is the same thing, concerning the foundation of morality, has been accounted the main problem in speculative thought, has occupied the most gifted intellects and divided them into sects and schools, carrying on a vigorous warfare against one another. And after more than two thousand years the same discussions continue, philosophers are still ranged under the same contending banners, and neither thinkers nor mankind at large seem nearer to being unanimous on the subject than when the youth Socrates listened to the old Protagoras, and asserted (if Plato's dialogue be grounded on a real conversation) the theory of utilitarianism against the popular morality of the so-called sophist.

It is true that similar confusion and uncertainty and, in some cases, similar discordance exist respecting the first principles of all the sciences, not excepting that which is deemed the most certain of them—mathematics, without much impairing, generally indeed without impairing at all, the trustworthiness of the conclusions of those sciences. An apparent anomaly, the explanation of which is that the detailed doctrines of a science are not usually deduced from, nor depend for their evidence upon, what are called its first principles. Were it not so, there would be no science more precarious, or whose conclusions were more insufficiently made out, than algebra, which derives none of its certainty from what are commonly taught to learners as its elements, since these, as laid down by some of its most eminent teachers, are as full of fictions as English law, and of mysteries as theology. The truths which are ultimately accepted as the first principles of a science are really the last results of metaphysical analysis, practised on the elementary notions with which the science is conversant; and their relation to the science is not that of foundations to an edifice, but of roots to a tree, which may perform their office equally well though they be never dug down to and exposed to light. But though in science the particular truth precede the general theory, the contrary might be expected to be the case with a practical art, such as morals or legislation. All action is for the sake of some end, and rules of action, it seems natural to suppose, must take their whole character and color from the end to which they are subservient. When we engage in a pursuit, a clear and precise conception of what we are pursuing would seem to be the first thing we need, instead of the last we are to look forward to. A test of right and wrong must be the means, one would think, of ascertaining what is right or wrong, and not a consequence of having already ascertained it.

The difficulty is not avoided by having recourse to the popular theory of a natural faculty, a sense of instinct, informing us of right and wrong. For—besides that the existence of such a moral instinct is itself one of the matters in dispute—those believers in it who have any pretensions to philosophy have been obliged to abandon the idea that it discerns what is right or wrong in the particular case in hand, as our other senses discern the sight or sound actually present. Our moral faculty, according to all those of its interpreters who are entitled to the name of thinkers, supplies us only with the general principles of moral judgments; it is a branch of our reason, not of our sensitive faculty; and must be looked to for the abstract doctrines of morality, not for perception of it in the concrete. The intuitive, no less than what may be termed the inductive, school of ethics insists on the necessity of general

laws. They both agree that the morality of an individual action is not a question of direct perception, but of the application of a law to an individual case. They recognize also, to a great extent, the same moral laws, but differ as to their evidence and the source from which they derive their authority. According to the one opinion, the principles of morals are evident *a priori,* requiring nothing to command assent except that the meaning of the terms be understood. According to the other doctrine, right and wrong, as well as truth and falsehood, are questions of observation and experience. But both hold equally that morality must be deduced from principles; and the intuitive school affirm as strongly as the inductive that there is a science of morals. Yet they seldom attempt to make out a list of the *a priori* principles which are to serve as the premises of the science; still more rarely do they make any effort to reduce those various principles to one first principle, or common ground of obligation. They either assume the ordinary precepts of morals as of *a priori* authority, or they lay down as the common groundwork of those maxims, some generality much less obviously authoritative than the maxims themselves, and which has never succeeded in gaining popular acceptance. Yet to support their pretensions there ought either to be some one fundamental principle or law at the root of all morality, or, if there be several, there should be a determinate order of precedence among them; and the one principle, or the rule for deciding between the various principles when they conflict, ought to be self-evident.

To inquire how far the bad effects of this deficiency have been mitigated in practice, or to what extent the moral beliefs of mankind have been vitiated or made uncertain by the absence of any distinct recognition of an ultimate standard, would imply a complete survey and criticism of past and present ethical doctrine. It would, however, be easy to show that whatever steadiness or consistency these moral beliefs have attained has been mainly due to the tacit influence of a standard not recognized. Although the non-existence of an acknowledged first principle has made ethics not so much a guide as a consecration of men's actual sentiments, still, as men's sentiments, both in favor and of aversion, are greatly influenced by what they suppose to be the effect of things upon their happiness, the principle of utility, or, as Bentham latterly called it, the greatest happiness principle, has had a large share in forming the moral doctrines even of those who most scornfully reject its authority. Nor is there any school of thought which refuses to admit that the influence of actions on happiness is a most material and even predominant consideration in many of the details, of morals, however unwilling to acknowledge it as the fundamental principle of morality and the source of moral obligation. I might go much further and say that to all those *a priori* moralists who deem it necessary to argue at all, utilitarian arguments are indispensable. It is not my present purpose to criticize these thinkers; but I cannot help referring, for illustration, to a systematic treatise by one of the most illustrious of them, the *Metaphysics of Ethics* by Kant. This remarkable man, whose system of thought will long remain one of the landmarks in the history of philosophical speculation, does, in the treatise in question, lay down a universal first principle as the origin and ground of moral obligation; it is this: "So act that the rule on which thou actest would admit of being adopted as a law by all rational beings." But when he begins to deduce from this precept any of the actual duties of morality, he fails, almost grotesquely, to show that there would be any contradiction, any logical (not to say physical) impossibility, in the adoption by all rational beings of the most outrageously immoral rules of conduct. All he knows is that the *consequences* of their universal adoption would be such as no one would choose to incur.

On the present occasion, I shall, without further discussion of the other theories, attempt to contribute something towards the understanding and appreciation of the "utilitarian" or "happiness" theory, and towards such proof as it is susceptible of. It is evident that this cannot be proof in the ordinary and popular meaning of the term. Questions of ultimate ends are not amenable to direct proof. Whatever can be proved to be good must be so by being shown to be a means to something admitted to be good without proof. The medical art is proved to be good by its conducing to health; but how is it possible to prove that health is good? The art of

music is good, for the reason, among others, that it produces pleasure; but what proof is it possible to give that pleasure is good? If, then, it is asserted that there is a comprehensive formula, including all things which are in themselves good, and that whatever else is good is not so as an end but as a means, the formula may be accepted or rejected, but is not a subject of what is commonly understood by proof. We are not, however, to infer that its acceptance or rejection must depend on blind impulse, or arbitrary choice. There is a larger meaning of the word "proof," in which this question is as amenable to it as any other of the disputed questions of philosophy. The subject is within the cognizance of the rational faculty; and neither does that faculty deal with it solely in the way of intuition. Considerations may be presented capable of determining the intellect either to give or withhold its assent to the doctrine; and this equivalent to proof. . . .

Chapter II. What Utilitarianism Is

A passing remark is all that needs be given to the ignorant blunder of supposing that those who stand up for utility as the test of right and wrong use the term in that restricted and merely colloquial sense in which utility is opposed to pleasure. An apology is due to the philosophical opponents of utilitarianism, for even the momentary appearance of confounding them with anyone capable of so absurd a misconception; which is the more extraordinary, inasmuch as the contrary accusation, of referring everything to pleasure, and that, too, in its grossest form, is another of the common charges against utilitarianism: and, as has been pointedly remarked by an able writer, the same sort of persons, and often the very same persons, denounce the theory "as impracticably dry when the word 'utility' precedes the word 'pleasure,' and as too practically voluptuous when the word 'pleasure' precedes the word 'utility'." Those who know anything about the matter are aware that every writer, from Epicurus to Bentham, who maintained the theory of utility, meant by it, not something to be contradistinguished from pleasure, but pleasure itself, together with exemption from pain; and instead of opposing the useful to the agreeable or the ornamental, have always declared that the useful means these, among other things. Yet the common herd, including the herd of writers, not only in newspapers and periodicals, but in books of weight and pretension, are perpetually falling into this shallow mistake. Having caught up the word "utilitarian" while knowing nothing whatever about it but its sound they habitually express by it the rejection or the neglect of pleasure in some of its forms: of beauty, of ornament or of amusement. Nor is the term thus ignorantly misapplied solely in disparagement, but occasionally in compliment, as though it implied superiority to frivolity and the mere pleasures of the moment. And this perverted use is the only one in which the word is popularly known, and the one from which the new generation are acquiring their sole notion of its meaning. Those who introduced the word, but who had for many years discontinued it as a distinctive appellation, may well feel themselves called upon to resume it if by doing so they can hope to contribute anything towards rescuing it from this utter degradation.[1]

The creed which accepts as the foundation of morals "utility" or the "greatest happiness principle" holds that actions are right in proportion as they tend to promote happiness, wrong as they tend to produce the reverse of happiness. By happiness is intended pleasure, and the absence of pain; by unhappiness, pain, and the privation of pleasure. To give a clear view of the moral standard set up by the theory, much more requires to be said; in particular, what things it includes in the ideas of pain and pleasure; and to what extent this is left an open

_____

1. The author of this essay has reason for believing himself to be the first person who brought the word "utilitarian" into use. He did not invent it, but adopted it from a passing expression in Mr. Galt's *Annals of the Parish*. After using it as a designation for several years, he and others abandoned it from a growing dislike to anything resembling a badge or watchword of sectarian distinction. But as a name for one single opinion, not a set of opinions—to denote the recognition of utility as a standard, not any particular way of applying it—the term supplies a want in the language, and offers, in many cases, a convenient mode of avoiding tiresome circumlocution.

question. But these supplementary explanations do not affect the theory of life on which this theory of morality is grounded—namely, that pleasure and freedom from pain are the only things desirable as ends; and that all desirable things (which are as numerous in the utilitarian as in any other scheme) are desirable either for the pleasure inherent in themselves, or as means to the promotion of pleasure and the prevention of pain.

Now such a theory of life excites in many minds, and among them in some of the most estimable in feeling and purpose, inveterate dislike. To suppose that life has (as they express it) no higher end than pleasure—no better and nobler object of desire and pursuit—they designate as utterly mean and groveling; as a doctrine worthy only of swine, to whom the followers of Epicurus were, at a very early period, contemptuously likened; and modern holders of the doctrine are occasionally made the subject of equally polite comparisons by its German, French, and English assailants.

When thus attacked, the Epicureans have always answered that it is not they, but their accusers, who represent human nature in a degrading light, since the accusation supposes human beings to be capable of no pleasure except those of which swine are capable. If this supposition were true, the charge could not be gainsaid, but would then be no longer an imputation; for if the sources of pleasure were precisely the same to human beings and to swine, the rule of life which is good enough for the one would be good enough for the other. The comparison of the Epicurean life to that of beasts is felt as degrading, precisely because a beast's pleasures do not satisfy a human being's conceptions of happiness. Human beings have faculties more elevated than the animal appetites and, when once made conscious of them, do not regard anything as happiness which does not include their gratification. I do not, indeed, consider the Epicureans to have been by any means faultless in drawing out their scheme of consequences from the utilitarian principle. To do this in any sufficient manner, many Stoic, as well as Christian, elements require to be included. But there is no known Epicurean theory of life which does not assign to the pleasures of the intellect, of the feelings and imagination, and of the moral sentiments, a much higher value of pleasures than to those of mere sensation. It must be admitted, however, that utilitarian writers in general have placed the superiority of mental over bodily pleasures chiefly in the greater permanency, safety, uncostliness, etc., of the former—that is, in their circumstantial advantages rather than in their intrinsic nature. And on all these points utilitarians have fully proved their case; but they might have taken the other and, as it may be called, higher ground with entire consistency. It is quite compatible with the principle of utility to recognize the fact that some kinds of pleasure are more desirable and more valuable than others. It would be absurd that, while, in estimating all other things, quality is considered as well as quantity, the estimation of pleasures should be supposed to depend on quantity alone.

If I am asked what I mean by difference of quality in pleasures, or what makes one pleasure more valuable than another, merely as a pleasure, except its being greater in amount, there is but one possible answer. Of two pleasures, if there be one to which all or almost all who have experience of both give a decided preference, irrespective of a feeling of moral obligation to prefer it, that is the more desirable pleasure. If one of the two is, by those who are competently acquainted with both, placed so far above the other that they prefer it, even though knowing it to be attended with a greater amount of discontent, and would not resign it for any quantity of the other pleasure which their nature is capable of, we are justified in ascribing to the preferred enjoyment a superiority in quality so far outweighing quantity as to render it, in comparison, of small account.

Now it is an unquestionable fact that those who are equally acquainted with and equally capable of appreciating and enjoying both, do give a most marked preference to the manner of existence which employs their higher faculties. Few human creatures would consent to be changed into any of the lower animals for a promise of the fullest allowance of a beast's pleasures; no intelligent human being would consent to be a fool, no instructed person would be an ignoramus, no person of feeling and conscience would be selfish and base, even though they should be persuaded that the fool, the

dunce, or the rascal is better satisfied with his lot than they are with theirs. They would not resign what they possess more than he for the most complete satisfaction of all the desires which they have in common with him. If they ever fancy they would, it is only in cases of unhappiness so extreme that to escape from it they would exchange their lot for almost any other, however undesirable in their own eyes. A being of higher faculties requires more to make him happy, is capable probably of more acute suffering, and certainly accessible to it at more points, than one of an inferior type; but in spite of these liabilities, he can never really wish to sink into what he feels to be a lower grade of existence. We may give what explanation we please of this unwillingness; we may attribute it to pride, a name which is given indiscriminately to some of the most and to some of the least estimable feelings of which mankind are capable: we may refer it to the love of liberty and personal independence, an appeal to which was with the Stoics one of the most effective means for the inculcation of it; to the love of power or to the love of excitement, both of which do really enter into and contribute to it; but its most appropriate appellation is a sense of dignity, which all human beings possess in one form or other, and in some, though by no means in exact, proportion to their higher faculties, and which is so essential a part of the happiness of those in whom it is strong that nothing which conflicts with it could be otherwise than momentarily an object of desire to them. Whoever supposes that this preference takes place at a sacrifice of happiness—that the superior being, in anything like equal circumstances, is not happier than the inferior—confounds the two very different ideas of happiness and content. It is indisputable that the being whose capacities of enjoyment are low has the greatest chance of having them fully satisfied; and a highly endowed being will always feel that any happiness which he can look for, as the world is constituted, is imperfect. But he can learn to bear its imperfections, if they are at all bearable; and they will not make him envy the being who is indeed unconscious of the imperfections, but only because he feels not at all the good which those imperfections qualify. It is better to be a human being dissatisfied than a pig satisfied; better to be

Socrates dissatisfied than a fool satisfied. And if the fool, or the pig, are of a different opinion, it is because they only know their own side of the question. The other party to the comparison knows both sides.

It may be objected that many who are capable of the higher pleasures occasionally, under the influence of temptation, postpone them to the lower. But this is quite compatible with a full appreciation of the intrinsic superiority of the higher. Men often, from infirmity of character, make their election for the nearer good, though they know it to be the less valuable; and this no less when the choice is between two bodily pleasures than when it is between bodily and mental. They pursue sensual indulgences to the injury of health, though perfectly aware that health is the greater good. It may be further objected that many who begin with youthful enthusiasm for everything noble, as they advance in years, sink into indolence and selfishness. But I do not believe that those who undergo this very common change voluntarily choose the lower description of pleasures in preference to the higher. I believe that, before they devote themselves exclusively to the one, they have already become incapable of the other. Capacity for the nobler feelings is in most natures a very tender plant, easily killed, not only by hostile influences, but by mere want of sustenance; and in the majority of young persons it speedily dies away if the occupations to which their position in life has devoted them, and the society into which it has thrown them, are not favorable to keeping that higher capacity in exercise. Men lose their high aspirations as they lose their intellectual tastes, because they have not time or opportunity for indulging them; and they addict themselves to inferior pleasures, not because they deliberately prefer them, but because they are either the only ones to which they have access, or the only ones which they are any longer capable of enjoying. It may be questioned whether any one who has remained equally susceptible to both classes of pleasures, ever knowingly and calmly preferred the lower, though many, in all ages, have broken down in an ineffectual attempt to continue both.

From this verdict of the only competent judges, I apprehend there can be no appeal. On a question which is the best worth having of two pleasures, or which of two modes of existence is the most grateful to the feelings, apart from its moral attributes and from its consequences, the judgment of those who are qualified by knowledge of both, or, if they differ, that of the majority of them, must be admitted as final. And there needs be the less hesitation to accept this judgment respecting the quality of pleasures, since there is no other tribunal to be referred to even on the question of quantity. What means are there of determining which is the acutest of two pains, or the intensest of two pleasurable

> *". . . [H]appiness is the sole end of human action, and the promotion of it the test by which to judge of all human conduct; . . ."*

sensations, except the general suffrage of those who are familiar with both? Neither pains nor pleasures are homogeneous, and pain is always heterogeneous with pleasure. What is there to decide whether a particular pleasure is worth purchasing at the cost of a particular pain, except the feelings and judgment of the experienced? When, therefore, those feelings and judgment declare the pleasures derived from the higher faculties to be preferable *in kind,* apart from the question of intensity, to those of which the animal nature, disjoined from the higher faculties, is susceptible, they are entitled on this subject to the same regard.

I have dwelt on this point, as being a necessary part of a perfectly just conception of utility or happiness considered as the directive rule of human conduct. But it is by no means an indispensable condition to the acceptance of the utilitarian standard; for that standard is not the agent's own greatest happiness, but the greatest amount of happiness altogether; and if it may possibly be doubted whether a noble character is always the happier for its nobleness, there can be no doubt that it makes other people happier, and that the world in general is immensely a gainer by it. Utilitarianism, therefore, could only attain its end by the general cultivation of nobleness of character, even if each individual were only benefited by the nobleness of others, and his own, so far as happiness is concerned, where a sheer deduction from the benefit. . . .

Chapter IV. Of What Sort of Proof the Principle of Utility is Susceptible

It has already been remarked that questions of ultimate ends do not admit of proof, in the ordinary acceptation of the term. To be incapable of proof by reasoning is common to all first principles, to the first premises of our knowledge, as well as to those of our conduct. But the former, being matters of fact, may be the subject of a direct appeal to the faculties which judge of fact—namely, our senses and our internal consciousness. Can an appeal be made to the same faculties on questions of practical ends? Or by what other faculty is cognizance taken of them?

Questions about ends are, in other words, questions what things are desirable. The utilitarian doctrine is that happiness is desirable, and the only thing desirable, as an end; all other things being only desirable as means to that end. What ought to be required of this doctrine, what conditions is it requisite that the doctrine should fulfill—to make good its claim to be believed?

The only proof capable of being given that an object is visible is that people actually see it. The only proof that a sound is audible is that people hear it; and so of the other sources of our experience. In like manner, I apprehend, the sole evidence it is possible to produce that anything is desirable is that people do actually desire it. If the end which the utilitarian doctrine proposes to itself were not, in theory and in practice, acknowledged to be an end, nothing could ever convince any person that it was so. No reason can be given why the general happiness is desirable, except that each person, so far as he believes it to be attainable, desires

his own happiness. This, however, being a fact, we have not only all the proof which the case admits of, but all which it is possible to require, that happiness is a good; that each person's happiness is a good to that person, and the general happiness, therefore, a good to the aggregate of all persons. Happiness had made out its title as *one* of the ends of conduct, and consequently one of the criteria of morality.

But it has not, by this alone, proved itself to be the sole criterion. To do that, it would seem, by the same rule, necessary to show, not only that people desire happiness, but that they never desire anything else. Now it is palpable that they do desire things which, in common language, are decidedly distinguished from happiness. They desire, for example, virtue and the absence of vice, no less really than pleasure and the absence of pain. The desire of virtue is not as universal, but it is as authentic a fact as the desire of happiness. And hence the opponents of the utilitarian standard deem that they have a right to infer that there are other ends of human action besides happiness, and that happiness is not the standard of approbation and disapprobation.

But does the utilitarian doctrine deny that people desire virtue, or maintain that virtue is not a thing to be desired? The very reverse. It maintains not only that virtue is to be desired, but that it is to be desired disinterestedly, for itself. Whatever may be the opinion of utlitarian moralists as to the original conditions by which virtue is made virtue, however they may believe (as they do) that actions and dispositions are only virtuous because they promote another end than virtue, yet this being granted, and it having been decided, from considerations of this description, what *is* virtuous, they not only place virtue at the very head of the things which are good as means to the ultimate end, but they also recognize as a psychological fact the possibility of its being, to the individual, a good in itself, without looking to any end beyond it; and hold that the mind is not in a right state, not in a state conformable to utility, not in the state most conducive to the general happiness, unless it does love virtue in this manner—as a thing desirable in itself, even although, in the individual instance, it should not produce those other desirable consequences which it tends to produce, and on account of which it is held to be virtue. This opinion is not, in the smallest degree, a departure from the happiness principle. The ingredients of happiness are very various, and each of them is desirable in itself, and not merely when considered as swelling an aggregate. The principle of utility does not mean that any given pleasure, as music, for instance, or any given exemption from pain, as for example health, is to be looked upon as means to a collective something termed happiness, and to be desired on that account. They are desired and desirable in and for themselves; besides being means, they are a part of the end. Virtue, according to the utilitarian doctrine, is not naturally and originally part of the end, but it is capable of becoming so; and in those who love it disinterestedly it has become so, and is desired and cherished, not as a means to happiness, but as a part of their happiness.

To illustrate this further, we may remember that virtue is not the only thing originally a means, and which if it were not a means to anything else would be and remain indifferent, but which by association with what it is a means to comes to be desired for itself, and that too with the utmost intensity. What, for example, shall we say of the love of money? There is nothing originally more desirable about money than about any heap of glittering pebbles. Its worth is solely that of the things which it will buy; the desires for other things than itself, which it is a means of gratifying. Yet the love of money is not only one of the strongest moving forces of human life, but money is, in many cases, desired in and for itself; the desire to possess it is often stronger than the desire to use it, and goes on increasing when all the desires which point to ends beyond it, to be compassed by it, are falling off. It may, then, be said truly that money is desired not for the sake of an end, but as part of the end. From being a means to happiness, it has come to be itself a principal ingredient of the individual's conception of happiness. The same may be said of the majority of the great objects of human life: power, for example, or fame, except that to each of these there is a certain amount of immediate pleasure annexed, which has at least the semblance of being naturally inherent in them—a thing which cannot be said of money. Still,

however, the strongest natural attraction, both of power and of fame, is the immense aid they give to the attainment of our other wishes; and it is the strong association thus generated between them and all our objects of desire which gives to the direct desire of them the intensity it often assumes, so as in some characters to surpass in strength all other desires. In these cases the means have become a part of the end, and a more important part of it than any of the things which they are means to. What was once desired as an instrument for the attainment of happiness has come to be desired for its own sake. In being desired for its own sake it is, however, desired as *part* of happiness. The person is made, or thinks he would be made, happy by its mere possession; and is made unhappy by failure to obtain it. The desire of it is not a different thing from the desire of happiness any more than the love of music or the desire of health. They are included in happiness. They are some of the elements of which the desire of happiness is made up. Happiness is not an abstract idea but a concrete whole; and these are some of its parts. And the utilitarian standard sanctions and approves their being so. Life would be a poor thing, very ill provided with sources of happiness, if there were not this provision of nature by which things originally indifferent, but conducive to, or otherwise associated with, the satisfaction of our primitive desires, become in themselves sources of pleasure more valuable than the primitive pleasures, both in permanency, in the space of human existence that they are capable of covering, and even in intensity.

Virtue, according to the utilitarian conception, is a good of this description. There was no original desire of it, or motive to it, save its conduciveness to pleasure, and especially to protection from pain. But through the association thus formed it may be felt a good in itself, and desired as such with as great intensity as any other good; and with this difference between it and the love of money, of power, or of fame, that all of these may, and often do, render the individual noxious to the other members of the society to which he belongs, whereas there is nothing which makes him so much a blessing to them as the cultivation of the disinterested love of virtue. And consequently, the utilitarian standard, while it tolerates and approves those other acquired desires, up to the point beyond which they would be more injurious to the general happiness than promotive of it, enjoins and requires the cultivation of the love of virtue up to the greatest strength possible, as being above all things important to the general happiness.

It results from the preceding considerations that there is in reality nothing desired except happiness. Whatever is desired otherwise than as a means to some end beyond itself, and ultimately to happiness, is desired as itself a part of happiness, and is not desired for itself until it has become so. Those who desire virtue for its own sake desire it either because the consciousness of it is a pleasure, or because the consciousness of being without it is a pain, or for both reasons united; as in truth the pleasure and pain seldom exist separately, but almost always together—the same person feeling pleasure in the degree of virtue attained, and pain in not having attained more. If one of these gave him no pleasure, and the other no pain, he would not love or desire virtue, or would desire it only for the other benefits which it might produce to himself or to persons whom he cared for.

We have now, then, an answer to the question, of what sort of proof the principle of utility is susceptible. If the opinion which I have now stated is psychologically true—if human nature is so consti-

tuted as to desire nothing which is not either a part of happiness or a means of happiness, we can have no other proof, and we require no other, that these are the only things desirable. If so, happiness is the sole end of human action, and the promotion of it the test by which to judge of all human conduct; from whence it necessarily follows that it must be the criterion of morality, since a part is included in the whole.

And now to decide whether this is really so, whether mankind do desire nothing for itself but that which is a pleasure to them, or of which the absence is a pain, we have evidently arrived at a question of fact and experience, dependent, like all similar questions, upon evidence. It can only be determined by practised self-consciousness and self-observation, assisted by observation of others. I believe that these sources of evidence, impartially consulted, will declare that desiring a thing and finding it pleasant, aversion to it and thinking of it as painful, are phenomena entirely inseparable or rather two parts of the same phenomenon; in strictness of language, two different modes of naming the same psychological fact; that to think of an object as desirable (unless for the sake of its consequences) and to think of it as pleasant are one and the same thing; and that to desire anything except in proportion as the idea of it is pleasant, is a physical and metaphysical impossibility.

Study Questions

1. Would utilitarianism allow the killing of an innocent person to promote social harmony?

2. Do you agree with Mill that there are lower and higher pleasures? Can his theory support this distinction?

3. If different people feel pain and pleasure at varying degrees, how can we know we are maximizing pleasure when we act?

Moral Dilemmas

- During the Vietnam War, you drive into a town where you see two men about to be executed in front of a firing squad. You ask the captain why they are being shot. He tells you that some of his men were killed by some members of that village and that he wants to teach the villagers a lesson. He also tells you that, as far as he knows, these two men could be innocent. You express shock that he would kill innocent men. He gives you a gun with one bullet and tells you that if you kill one, he will let the other go free.

  What would you do?

- A ship capsizes, killing all but thirty survivors who crowd into a lifeboat meant to hold only ten. Captain Spike, who is also saved, takes control of the lifeboat. He tells the survivors that the lifeboat contains only enough food for ten. It will take them at least five days of hard rowing to get to land. If all stay on the boat, all will die, according to the captain. He says that he will pick the strongest to stay because they can row the hardest but that twenty persons have to be pushed overboard. Some of the survivors object, saying that for all to die would be better than to push twenty innocent persons into the shark-infested sea. Finally, the captain's wish is carried out—some jumping overboard willingly, and others being pushed. Two days later, the ten are rescued. The captain is indicted for murder.

  If you were on the jury that would judge Captain Spike, would you find him guilty of murder?

- Professor Worryd sees Karen cheating on an exam. He calls her into his office and confronts her with the cheating charge. She claims that cheating is not immoral because she and her friend Jessie had a mutual agreement to help each other during exams. Besides, she adds, cheating in this particular case isn't harming anyone, and how can anything be immoral if it doesn't harm anyone? Finally, she hints that if Professor Worryd does anything about this, she will spread a false rumor that the professor sexually harassed her and is simply punishing her now for refusing his proposition. Professor Worryd comes up for tenure next year.

  If you were the professor, what would you do?

Suggested Readings

Frankena, William. *Ethics.* Englewood Cliffs, N.J.: Prentice-Hall, 1973.

Hare, R. M. *Freedom and Reason.* Oxford, England: Oxford University Press, 1963.

Harris, John. "The Survival Lottery." *Philosophy* 50 (1975).

Hudson, W. D. *Modern Moral Philosophy.* New York: Anchor, 1970.

Kemp, John. *The Philosophy of Kant.* Oxford, England: Oxford University Press, 1968.

MacIntyre, Alasdair. *Against the Self-Images of the Age.* New York: Schocken, 1971.

Moore, G. E. *Principia Ethica*. New York: Cambridge, 1903.

Paton, H. J. *The Categorical Imperative*. London: Hutchinson, 1946.

Ross, W. D. *Aristotle*. New York: Barnes & Noble, 1964.

Wellman, Carl. *Morals and Ethics*. Englewood Cliffs, N.J.: Prentice-Hall, 1988.

Morality and Psychology

A re we born moral, or do we somehow acquire morality? Why are some people more moral than others? Can we teach morality in the same way we teach other subjects? Is morality a matter of reason, of emotion, or of religious faith?

Background

Philosophers such as Plato and Aristotle believed that for a person to be moral as an adult, he or she must have the proper moral training and education as a child. For these Greek philosophers and many others, morality is based in reason; being moral is part of being rational. By contrast, the mainstream Christian view, such as that of St. Augustine (A.D. 354–430), stresses the imperfection of humankind through original sin. For St. Augustine, being moral does not mean just being rational but also requires faith in God and membership in His church. More recently, the writings of Sigmund Freud (1856–1939) suggest that emotions, especially the sense of guilt, play a central role in morality. The research of Jean Piaget (1896–1980), a Swiss psychologist, however, claims that the moral development of children is largely a rational process moving from a heteronomous stage, during which parental rules are accepted out of fear, to the autonomous stage, where the acceptance of rules is a matter of personal choice. Piaget further contends that as children mature they tend to grow in their capacity for empathy (i.e., the ability to put oneself in another's place and to consider the other's interests). In assessing the morality of an action, Piaget found that older children consider not only the consequences of the act but also the intention of the agent. Lawrence Kohlberg's work is an extension and development of Piaget's.

Is morality a matter of reason as Plato, Aristotle, Maslow, Kohlberg, and Peck argued? Is it essentially an emotional reality as Freud believed? Or does morality presuppose faith and religion? Traditionally, the moral training of children has been the responsibility of the parents and the churches. Today, with the high rate of divorce, homes where both parents work, and what some believe to be the declining influence of religion in our society, where is the moral education of the children to occur? Should morality be taught in the schools? If so, should that morality be Protestant, Catholic, Jewish, or secular humanist?

Sigmund Freud

Sigmund Freud (1856–1939) developed the theory of psychoanalysis to explain human behavior. Psychoanalysis is based on the belief that the mind works according to laws of which we are usually unaware. He argued that to understand human psychology requires that we begin with the basic biological instincts of survival and sex. We are all born without any morality but with a capacity and desire for sexual pleasure. Our sexual expression, according to Freud, goes through distinct stages as we mature. This process of physical and psychological development usually includes the development of a *conscience,* or a moral sense. To a young child, parents appear to be all-powerful and almost divine. Consequently, in order to please them, the child eventually identifies with them. This identification is important in the development of a conscience. When the child identifies with the parent, he or she wishes to resemble that parent and to adopt the same values and morality. Freud called the conscience the *superego,* the part of the mind that controls the sexual instinct of the *id,* the pleasure principle. If parents are not present or are cruel or indifferent to their child during early childhood, the infant may grow into an adult with no conscience and may become psychopathic (i.e., may have no sense of right and wrong nor sympathy for others). In addition to the id and the superego, the third component of the psyche is the *ego,* or the reality principle, which is the sphere of rationality and the basis of interaction with the external world.

Many aspects and functions of the id, ego, and superego take place in the *unconscious* part of the mind, the realm of which we are unaware. Desires, usually of a sexual nature, that our society (hence the superego) finds morally unacceptable (such as incest) are repressed, or pushed into the unconscious, and can lead to the development of a neurosis, a personality disorder such as a phobia (an irrational fear), a psychosomatic illness, or a sexual abnormality. Freud's theory is based on the assumption that certain traumatic experiences, especially those in one's childhood, can live on in the unconscious and can detrimentally influence one's mental health. The purpose of psychoanalysis is to make these unconscious ideas conscious whereby they lose their ability to influence our behavior. The goal of psychoanalysis is a mentally healthy person who, according to Freud, has self-knowledge (i.e., is free from irrational, unconscious fear and guilt), can love another person, and can work or contribute to society.

A true morality for Freud is a morality based not on religion (Freud was an atheist) but on the scientific understanding of human nature and human needs. This includes an acceptance of men and women as sexual beings, although Freud did not believe in so-called "free love" or promiscuity. He argued that living in civilization requires the control of our sexual nature, but he believed the Western world had gone too far in repressing and restricting this natural sexuality. Repression produces excessive guilt in many unhappy individuals, according to Freud, and sexual satisfaction is necessary for most people's happiness. He also urged toleration of homosexuality.

Freud's theory has had an immense impact on Western attitudes toward sexuality, childhood, mental illness, and morality. Nevertheless, his ideas and methods have been criticized. Freud based his theories largely on what his patients said, but he never kept a verbatim record of these statements and often accepted them at face value without attempting to check them with the patient's parents, relatives, or friends. Many believe that his theory relies on incomplete evidence (his patients were mostly middle-class Austrians) and may not apply to all societies, nor to any non-Western societies. Many of his claims are difficult to prove scientifically. Still, Freud's thoughts have led many to pay closer attention to the importance of childhood experiences, and his ideas on the importance of self-knowledge and love recall the basic values of Aristotle and the Judeo-Christian ethic.

Lawrence Kohlberg

Unlike Freud, whose theory of morality was based primarily on reflections on his patients, Lawrence Kohlberg (1927–1987) made extensive scientific studies in many cultures on the development of moral beliefs in groups of varying ages, education, and wealth. His studies identified three levels of moral reasoning, each having two stages. (See the figure on page 000.) The first level is the *preconventional level* of most children under nine years of age. At stage one of this level, children behave morally only to avoid punishment from those in authority such as parents and teachers. At stage two of this level, children learn to recognize that other people have needs and that the right thing involves letting others meet their needs as well. At level one, moral rules are still external to the self and are not accepted as right in themselves.

The *conventional level* of morality is the level of most adolescents and adults in most societies. At this phase of development, the individual internalizes or accepts the rules of society and seeks to act accordingly. At stage three, the individual is motivated by the need to be accepted by others, and this is done by following the Golden Rule (Do unto others as you would have them do unto you) and behaving with trust, loyalty, and gratitude. At the second stage of the conventional level (stage four), the individual takes the perspective of the society and recognizes the need to contribute and maintain the social system as a whole. At this level, laws are to be upheld except perhaps in extreme cases when

a conflict with some other social rule occurs. Respecting authority and maintaining the status quo are important.

At the *postconventional level,* persons begin to make autonomous moral judgments (i.e., they act only on those principles that they believe to be right, even if the society disagrees). At stage five, the moral reasoning is of a utilitarian and contract orientation; right and wrong are determined by a sense of obligation to society at large and by what is the greatest good for the greatest number. At stage six, the highest stage of moral development, the individual achieves the belief that universal ethical principles exist such as the equal dignity of all persons, universal human rights, and justice. When one's society is in conflict with these self-chosen rational principles, the stage six person will follow his or her own principles. (Kohlberg interpreted Kant's moral theory as representative of stage six moral thinking.) Kohlberg's research indicates that individuals in all cultures go through the six stages, in the sequence he suggests, although not all individuals attain all the stages. Once a stage is reached, persons do not regress to a lower stage. Whether one attains the higher stage is closely associated with one's educational level, according to Kohlberg.

Empirical studies by others tend to support many of Kohlberg's claims. However, some critics contend that Kohlberg's theory uses a limited conception of morality that focuses on justice and human rights and ignores such moral concepts as nurturing and compassion.

Abraham Maslow

Abraham Maslow (1908–1970) was an American psychologist whose research suggests that concern for others is an integral element of human well-being. Maslow's theory claims that a universal human nature is the biological basis of our needs, capacities, and tendencies. In addition to these universal biological needs and capacities, individuals also have culturally specific needs and capacities. The healthy and fully human person is one who actualizes or develops his or her capacities and satisfies his or her needs. The immoral or sick person is one created by a society that does not allow for actualization of one's nature or the satisfaction of one's needs.

According to Maslow, human beings have several kinds of needs that exist in distinct relationship to one another. Human needs are ordered in a hierarchy so that when a need is satisfied, the next highest priority of need in the pyramid-like structure of needs can be satisfied. Physiological needs such as hunger and thirst are most basic and must be met before all others because our survival depends on it. Next, our security and safety needs become most pressing, as they are also closely related to survival. Once our physiological and safety needs are met, and the need for love, affection, and belonging will emerge. Maslow believes that much of human suffering and mental illness comes from isolation and the inability to love. Closely associated with the need to love is the need for self-esteem and recognition. This need is fulfilled by the genuine respect and appreciation of others for one's contribution and competence. Once all of these needs have been met, then the need for self-actualization is felt.

Self-actualization refers to the desire for self-fulfillment and development of one's potential. This desire, Maslow adds, is the desire to become a more unique and individual person. Those who actualize their potential achieve a high degree of psychological health and moral insight. Maslow studied the lives of such great self-actualizers as Abraham Lincoln, Thomas Jefferson, Henry David Thoreau, Ludwig van Beethoven, Eleanor Roosevelt, and Albert Einstein and concluded that they had some traits in common. They were all realistic in their understanding of the world and themselves, independent, creative, caring about others, involved in a deep and intimate relationship with at least one other person, autonomous in that they did not blindly conform to their own culture, had a spiritual or mystical experience, and most importantly, dedicated to the struggle for justice and a more humane world. Moral virtue, then, is an integral part of the self-actualized person. For Maslow, the psychologically healthy person is also a moral person who perceives reality more clearly, can meet his or her many needs more adequately, and can see the long-term consequences of actions.

M. Scott Peck

M. Scott Peck, like Freud, was trained as a psychiatrist. He sees life as a series of problems that we must solve through discipline. Those who lack discipline tend to avoid confronting the problems of life because of the pain involved in dealing with them. Peck points out that the avoidance of problems and pain as they occur in life merely causes us greater pain later in the forms of immaturity, lack of self-development, and mental illness.

According to Peck, discipline involves four components necessary for solving life's problems. These components are (1) delay of gratification, (2) acceptance of responsibility, (3) dedication to the truth, and (4) balancing. Delaying gratification means ordering the pains and pleasures of life so as to experience the pain first in order to enhance future happiness. Some persons are not able to postpone gratification because the lack self-esteem or a sense of being valuable. Lack of self-esteem is usually due to the lack of sufficient parental love in the early years of childhood. Without self-esteem, discipline is difficult because discipline assumes that we wish to take good care of ourselves, and this presupposes that we value ourselves.

Peck's second aspect of discipline is the acceptance of responsibility. Before we can solve our problems, we must recognize that we have them. This means accepting responsibility for them and acknowledging that we can make choices in dealing with our problems. Those who do not admit that they are at least partially responsible for their problems, often blame society, fate, or others just to avoid the pain of responsibility. This, Peck observes, can lead to a sense of helplessness and despair.

Peck looks at life as a journey through reality, and at truth as a map of that reality. To achieve the things we want in life, our map must be accurate, not clouded by falsehoods, misconceptions, or illusions. That is, we must have true beliefs about ourselves and the world. Without dedication to the truth, discipline is not possible. Dedication to the truth means the willingness to continually revise our map of reality to achieve a more accurate picture of reality. This requires an openness to the world, the maps of others, and a never-ending critical self-evaluation. To truthfully criticize oneself may involve pain, but unless we confront this pain, greater pain awaits us in the future.

Balancing, the fourth and final aspect of discipline, means ordering the many needs, goals, and obligations in life. To mature and be open to new experiences often requires us to give up old ways of behaving and living that were appropriate at a different time in our lives. Again, Peck points out that this can be painful but that maturity and growth is the reward for accepting suffering as part of life. For Peck, the most fully spiritual and human person is one who not only accepts his or her own suffering but also helps others to master their suffering through love.

Peck's views incorporate and suggest ideas we saw in Freud, Kohlberg, and Maslow. Peck agrees with Freud about the importance of the relations with parents in early childhood in developing self-esteem and the capacity to delay gratification. The capacities to love and to work were, for Freud as for Peck, the crucial characteristics of a mature and healthy person. A person at this level of psychological health would be at Kohlberg's stage six level, in which one displays a genuine concern for the dignity of all persons. Kohlberg's stage six individuals closely resemble Maslow's self-actualizers who are creative (work) and have a deep concern for others and for a more just world. If these psychologists are right, being moral is a necessary component of living a fully happy and human life. For them, as for Aristotle, to ask "Why should I be moral?" is to ask "Why should I be a truly human and happy person?"

"Civilized" Sexual Morality and Modern Nervousness

Sigmund Freud (1856–1939) Educated as a medical doctor, Sigmund Freud is best known as the founder of psychoanalysis. Freud lived most of his life in Austria and wrote on all aspects of psychology and mental illness.

Sigmund Freud

Our civilization is, generally speaking, founded on the suppression of instincts. Each individual has contributed some renunciation—of his sense of-dominating power, of the aggressive and vindictive tendencies of his personality. From these sources the common stock of the material and ideal wealth of civilization has been accumulated. Over and above the struggle for existence, it is chiefly family feeling, with its erotic roots, which has induced the individuals to make this renunciation. This re-

The Standard Edition of the Complete Psychological Works of Sigmund Freud. Edited and translated by James Strachey. By permission of Copyrights Ltd., The Institute of Psycho-Analysis and the Hogarth Press.

nunciation has been a progressive one in the evolution of civilization; the single steps in it were sanctioned by religion. The modicum of instinctual satisfaction from which each one had abstained was offered to the divinity as a sacrifice; and the communal benefit thus won was declared "holy." The man who in consequence of his unyielding nature cannot comply with the required suppression of his instincts, becomes a criminal, an outlaw, unless his social position or striking abilities enable him to hold his own as a great man, a "hero."

The sexual instinct—or, more correctly, the sexual instincts, since analytic investigation teaches us that the sexual instinct consists of many single component impulses—is probably more strongly developed in man than in most of the higher animals; it is certainly more constant, since it has almost entirely overcome the periodicity belonging to it in animals. It places an extraordinary amount of energy at the disposal of "cultural" activities; and this because of a particularly marked characteristic that it possesses, namely, the ability to displace its aim without materially losing in intensity. This ability to exchange the originally sexual aim for another which is no longer sexual but is psychically related, is called the capacity for sublimation. In contrast with this ability for displacement in which lies its value for civilization, the sexual instinct may also show a particularly obstinate tendency to fixation, which prevents it from being turned to account in this way, and occasionally leads to its degenerating into the so-called abnormalities. The original strength of the sexual instinct probably differs in each individual; certainly the capacity for sublimation is variable. We imagine that the original constitution pre-eminently decides how large a part of the sexual impulse of each individual can be sublimated and made use of. In addition to this, the forces of environment and of intellectual influence on the mental apparatus succeed in disposing of a further portion of it by sublimation. To extend this process of displacement illimitably is, however, certainly no more possible than with the transmutation of heat into mechanical power in the case of machines. A certain degree of direct sexual satisfaction appears to be absolutely necessary for by far the greater number of natures, and frustration of this variable individual need is avenged by manifestations which, on account of their injurious effect on functional activity and of their subjectively painful character, we must regard as illness.

Further aspects are opened up when we take into consideration the fact that the sexual instinct in man does not originally serve the purposes of procreation, but has as its aim the gain of particular kinds of pleasure. It manifests itself thus in infancy, when it attains its aim of pleasurable gratification not only in connection with the genitalia, but also in other parts of the body (erotogenic zones), and hence is in a position to disregard any other than these easily accessible objects. We call this stage that of auto-erotism, and assign to the child's training the task of circumscribing it, because its protracted continuance would render the sexual instinct later uncontrollable and unserviceable. In its development the sexual instinct passes on from auto-erotism to object-love, and from the autonomy of the erotogenic zones to the subordination of these under the primacy of the genitals, which come into the service of procreation. During this development a part of the self-obtained sexual excitation is checked, as being useless for the reproductive functions, and in favourable cases is diverted to sublimation. The energies available for "cultural" development are thus in great part won through suppression of the so-called perverse elements of sexual excitation.

> *"On the whole I have not gained the impression that sexual abstinence helps to shape energetic, self-reliant men of action, nor original thinkers, bold pioneers and reformers . . ."*

It would be possible to distinguish three stages in cultural development corresponding with this development in the sexual instinct: first, the stage in which the sexual impulse may be freely exercised in regard to aims which do not lead to procreation; a second stage, in which the whole of the sexual impulse is suppressed except that portion which subserves procreation; and a third stage, in which only *legitimate* procreation is allowed as a sexual aim. This third stage represents our current "civilized" sexual morality. . . .

In what relation [do] the possible injurious effects of . . . abstention stand to the benefit accruing to culture? . . .

Even he who admits the injurious results [neuroses] thus attributable to civilized sexual morality may reply that the cultural gain derived from the sexual restraint so generally practised probably more than balances these evils, which after all, in their more striking manifestations, affect only a minority. I own myself unable to balance gain and loss precisely: nevertheless I could advance a good many considerations as regards the loss. Returning to the theme of abstinence, already touched on, I must insist that yet other injurious effects besides the neuroses result therefrom, and that the neuroses themselves are not usually appraised at their full significance.

The retardation of sexual development and sexual activity at which our education and culture aim is certainly not injurious to begin with; it is seen to be a necessity, when one reflects at what a late age young people of the educated classes attain independence and begin to earn a living. Incidentally, one is reminded here of the intimate relations existing between all our civilized institutions, and of the difficulty of altering any part of them irrespective of the whole. But the benefit, for a young man, of abstinence continued much beyond his twentieth year, cannot any longer be taken for granted; it may lead to other injuries even when it does not lead to neurosis. It is indeed said that the struggle with such powerful instincts and the consequent strengthening of all ethical and aesthetic tendencies "steels" the character; and this, for some specially constituted natures, is true. The view may also be accepted that the differentiation of individual character, now so much in evidence, only becomes possible with sexual restraint. But in the great majority of cases the fight against sexuality absorbs the available energy of the character, and this at the very time when the young man is in need of all his powers to gain his share of worldly goods and his position in the community. The relation between possible sublimation and indispensable sexual activity naturally varies very much in different persons, and indeed with the various kinds of occupation. An abstinent artist is scarcely conceivable: an abstinent young intellectual is by no means a rarity. The young intellectual can by abstinence enhance his powers of concentration, whereas the production of the artist is probably powerfully stimulated by his sexual experience. On the whole I have not gained the impression that sexual abstinence helps to shape energetic, self-reliant men of action, nor original thinkers, bold pioneers and reformers; for more often it produces "good" weaklings who later become lost in the crowd that tends to follow painfully the initiative of strong characters.

Study Questions

1. Do you believe that our society is still sexually repressive?

2. Can civilization exist if sexuality is completely free?

3. Do you agree with Freud's theory that sexual repression leads to weak and unhappy individuals?

Moral Development: A Modern Statement of the Platonic View

Lawrence Kohlberg (1927–1987) Lawrence Kohlberg was a professor of education and social psychology at Harvard. His major contribution was the psychological study of morality most recently published as Essays on Moral Development.

Lawrence Kohlberg

When I called this essay a Platonic view I hoped it implied a paradox that was more than cute. It is surely a paradox that a modern psychologist should claim as his most relevant source not Freud, Skinner, or Piaget but the ancient believer in the ideal form of the good. Yet as I have tried to trace the stages of development of morality and to use these stages as the basis of a moral education program, I have realized more and more that its implication was the reassertion of the Platonic faith in the power of the rational good....

Because morally mature men are governed by the principle of justice rather than by a set of rules, there are not many moral virtues but one. Let us restate the argument in Plato's terms. Plato's argument is that what makes a virtuous action virtuous is that it is guided by knowledge of the good. A courageous action based on ignorance of danger is not courageous; a just act based on ignorance of justice is not just, etc. If virtuous action is based on knowledge of the good, then virtue is one, because knowledge of the good is one. We have already claimed that knowledge of the good is one because the good is justice. Let me briefly document these lofty claims by some lowly research findings. Using hypothetical moral situations, we have interviewed children and adults about right and wrong in the United States, Britain, Turkey, Taiwan, and Yucatan.

In all cultures we find the same forms of moral thinking. There are six forms of thinking and they constitute an invariant sequence of stages in each culture. These stages are summarized in the table on page 38 [page 120 in this text]. Why do I say existence of culturally universal stages means that knowledge of the good is one? First, because it implies that concepts of the good are culturally universal. Second, because an individual at a given level is pretty much the same in his thinking regardless of the situation he is presented with and regardless of the particular aspect of morality being tapped. There is a general factor of maturity of moral judgment much like the general factor of intelligence in cognitive tasks. If he knows one aspect of the good at a certain level, he knows other aspects of the good at that level. Third, because at each stage there is a single principle of the good, which only approaches a moral principle at the higher levels. At all levels, for instance, there is some reason for regard for law and some reason for regard of rights. Only at the highest stage, however, is regard for law a regard for universal moral law and regard for rights a regard for universal human rights. At this point, both regard for law and regard for human rights are grounded on a clear criterion of justice which was present in confused and obscure form at earlier stages.

Let me describe the stages in terms of the civil disobedience issue in a way that may clarify the argument I have just made. Here's a question we have asked: Before the Civil War, we had laws that allowed slavery. According to the law if a slave escaped, he had to be returned to his owner like a

Excerpted by permission of the publishers from *Moral Education: Five Lectures,* James M. Gustafson et al., Cambridge, Mass.: Harvard University Press, Copyright © 1970 by the President and Fellows of Harvard College.

runaway horse. Some people who didn't believe in slavery disobeyed the law and hid the runaway slaves and helped them to escape. Were they doing right or wrong?

A bright, middle-class boy, Johnny, answers the question this way when he is ten: "They were doing wrong because the slave ran away himself. They're being just like slaves themselves trying to keep 'em away." He is asked, "Is slavery right or wrong?" He answers, "Some wrong, but servants aren't so bad because they don't do all that heavy work."

Johnny's response is Stage 1: *Punishment and obedience orientation.* Breaking the law makes it wrong; indeed the badness of being a slave washes off on his rescuer.

Three years later he is asked the same question. His answer is mainly a Stage 2 *instrumental relativism.* He says: "They would help them escape because they were all against slavery. The South was for slavery because they had big plantations and the North was against it because they had big factories and they needed people to work and they'd pay. So the Northerners would think it was right but the Southerners wouldn't."

So early comes Marxist relativism. He goes on: "If a person is against slavery and maybe likes the slave or maybe dislikes the owner, it's OK for him to break the law if he likes, provided he doesn't get caught. If the slaves were in misery and one was a friend he'd do it. It would probably be right if it was someone you really loved."

At the end, his orientation to sympathy and love indicates the same Stage 3, *orientation to approval, affection, and helpfulness....*

At age nineteen, in college, Johnny is Stage 4: *Orientation to maintaining a social order of rules and rights.* He says: "They were right in my point of view. I hate the actual aspect of slavery, the imprisonment of one man ruling over another. They drive them too hard and they don't get anything in return. It's not right to disobey the law, no. Laws are made by the people. But you might do it because you feel it's wrong. If 50,000 people break the law, can you put them all in jail? Can 50,000 people be wrong?" → miss the point

Johnny here is oriented to the rightness and wrongness of slavery itself and of obedience to law. He doesn't see the wrongness of slavery in terms of equal human rights but in terms of an unfair economic relation, working hard and getting nothing in return. The same view of rights in terms of getting what you worked for leads Johnny to say about school integration: "A lot of colored people are now just living off of civil rights. You only get education as far as you want to learn, as far as you work for it, not being placed with someone else, you don't get it from someone else."

Johnny illustrates for us the distinction between virtue as the development of principles of justice and virtue as being unprejudiced. In one sense Johnny's development has involved increased recognition of the fellow-humanness of the slaves. For thinking of slaves as inferior and bad at age ten he thinks of them as having some sort of rights at age nineteen. He is still not just, however, because his only notions of right are that you should get what you earn, a conception easily used to justify a segregated society. In spite of a high school and college education, he has no real grasp of the conceptions of rights underlying the Constitution or the Supreme Court decisions involved. Johnny's lack of virtue is not that he doesn't want to associate with Negroes, it is that he is not capable of being a participating citizen of our society because he does not understand the principles on which our society is based. His failure to understand these principles cuts both ways. Not only does he fail to ground the rights of Negroes on principles but he fails to ground respect for law on this base. Respect for law is respect for the majority. But if 50,000 people break the law, can 50,000 be wrong? Whether the 50,000 people are breaking the law in the name of rights or of the Ku Klux Klan makes no difference in this line of thought.

It is to be hoped that Johnny may reach our next stage, Stage 5, *social contract legalism,* by his mid-twenties, since some of our subjects continue to develop up until this time. Instead of taking one of our research subjects, however, let us take some statements by Socrates as an example of Stage 5. Socrates is explaining to Crito why he refuses to save his life by taking advantage of the escape arrangements Crito has made:

Ought one to fulfill all one's agreements?, Socrates asks. Then consider the consequences. Suppose the laws and constitution of Athens were to

■ Table X   Levels and Stages in Moral Development

Levels	Basis of moral judgment	Stages of development
I	Moral value resides in external, quasi-physical happenings, in bad acts, or in quasi-physical needs rather than in persons and standards.	*Stage 1:* Obediences and punishment orientation. Egocentric deference to superior power or prestige, or a trouble-avoiding set. Objective responsibility.
		Stage 2: Naively egoistic orientation. Right action is that instrumentally satisfying the self's needs and occasionally others'. Awareness of relativism of value to each actor's needs and perspective. Naive egalitarianism and orientation to exchange and reciprocity.
II	Moral value resides in performing good or right roles, in maintaining the conventional order and the expectations of others.	*Stage 3:* Good-boy orientation. Orientation to approval and to pleasing and helping others. Conformity to sterotypical images of majority or natural role behavior, and judgment by intentions.
		Stage 4: Authority and social-order maintaining orientation. Orientation to "doing duty" and to showing respect for authority and maintaining the given social order for its own sake. Regard for earned expectations of others.
III	Moral value resides in conformity by the self to shared or sharable standards, rights, or duties.	*Stage 5:* Contractual legalistic orientation. Recognition of an arbitrary element or starting point in rules or expectations for the sake of agreement. Duty defined in terms of contract, general avoidance of violation of the will or rights of others, and majority will and welfare.
		Stage 6: Conscience or principle orientation. Orientation not only to actually ord[a]ined social rules but to principles of choice involving appeal to logical universality and consistency. Orientation to conscience as a directing agent and to mutual respect and trust.

[handwritten note near Stages 3–4:] Most people =

[handwritten note near Stage 6:] "The idea that slavery is Not fair." = personal conscience

confront us and ask, Socrates, can you deny that by this act you intend, so far as you have power, to destroy us. Do you image that a city can continue to exist if the legal judgments which are pronounced by it are nullified and destroyed by private persons? At an earlier time, you made a noble show of indifference to the possibility of dying. Now you show no respect for your earlier professions and no regard for us, the laws, trying to run away in spite of the contracts by which you agreed to live as a member of our state. Are we not speaking the truth when we say that you have undertaken in deed, if not in word, to live your life as a citizen in obedience to us? It is a fact, then, that you are breaking convenants made with us under no compulsion or misunderstanding. You had seventy years in which you could have left the country if you were not satisfied with us or felt that the agreements were unfair.

As an example of Stage 6, *orientation to universal moral principles,* let me cite Martin Luther King's letter from a Birmingham jail.

There is a type of constructive non-violent tension which is necessary for growth. Just as Socrates felt it was necessary to create a tension in the mind so that individuals could rise from the bondage of half-truths, so must we see the need for nonviolent gadflies to create the kind of tension in society that will help men rise from the dark depths of prejudice and racism.

One may well ask, "How can you advocate breaking some laws and obeying others?" The answer lies in the fact that there are two types of laws, just and unjust. One has not only a legal but a moral responsibility to obey just laws. One has a moral responsibility to disobey unjust laws. An unjust law is a human law that is not rooted in eternal law and natural law. Any law that uplifts human personality is just, any law that degrades human personality is unjust. An unjust law is a code that a numerical or power majority group compels a minority group to obey but does not make binding on itself. This is difference made legal.

I do not advocate evading or defying the law as would the rabid segregationist. That would lead to anarchy. One who breaks an unjust law must do so openly, lovingly, and with a willingness to accept the penalty. An individual who breaks a law that conscience tells him is unjust, and willingly accepts the penalty of imprisonment in order to arouse the conscience of the community over its injustice, is in reality expressing the highest respect for law.

King makes it clear that moral disobedience of the law must spring from the same root as moral obedience to law, out of respect for justice. We respect the law because it is based on rights, both in the sense that the law is designed to protect the rights of all and because the law is made by the principle of equal political rights. If civil disobedience is to be Stage 6, it must recognize the contractual respect for law of Stage 5, even to accepting imprisonment. That is why Stage 5 is a way of thinking about the laws which are imposed upon all, while a morality of justice which claims to judge the law can never be anything but a free, personal ideal. It must accept the idea of being put in jail by its enemies, not of putting its enemies in jail. While we

classified Socrates' statements to Crito as Stage 5, his statement of his civilly disobedient role as a moral educator quoted earlier was Stage 6, at least in spirit.

Both logic and empirical study indicate there is no shortcut to autonomous morality, no Stage 6 without a previous Stage 5.

We have claimed that knowledge of the moral good is one. We now will try to show that virtue in action is knowledge of the good, as Plato claimed ... Knowledge of the good in terms of what Plato calls opinion or conventional belief is not virtue. An individual may believe that cheating is very bad but that does not predict that he will resist cheating in real life. Espousal of unprejudiced attitudes toward Negroes does not predict action to assure civil rights in an atmosphere where others have some

> *"If virtuous action is based on knowledge of the good, then virtue is one, because knowledge of the good is one."*

prejudice; however, true knowledge, knowledge of principles of justice, does predict virtuous action. With regard to cheating, the essential elements of justice are understood by both our Stage 5 and our Stage 6 subjects. In cheating, the critical issue is recognition of the element of contract and agreement implicit in the situation, and the recognition that while it doesn't seem so bad if one person cheats, what holds for all must hold for one. In a recent study, 100 sixth-grade children were given experimental cheating tests and our moral judgment interview. The majority of the children were below the principled level in moral judgment; they were at our first four moral stages. Seventy-five percent of these children cheated. In contrast, only 20 percent of the principled subjects, that is, Stage 5 or 6, cheated. In another study conducted at the college level, only 11 percent of the principled subjects cheated, in contrast to 42 percent of the students at lower levels of moral judgment. In the case of cheating, justice and the expectations of conventional authority both dictate the same behavior. What happens when justice and authority are opposed?

An experimental study of Stanley Milgram involved such an opposition. Under the guise of a learning experiment, undergraduate subjects were ordered by an experimenter to administer increasingly more severe electric shock punishment to a stooge victim. In this case, the principles of justice involved in the Stage 5 social contract orientation do not clearly prescribe a decision. The victim had voluntarily agreed to participate in the experiment, and the subject himself had contractually committed himself to perform the experiment. Only Stage 6 thinking clearly defined the situation as one in which the experimenter did not have the moral right to ask them to inflict pain on another person. Accordingly, 75 percent of those at Stage 6 quit or refused to shock the victim, as compared to only 13 percent of all the subjects at lower stages.

A study of Berkeley students carries the issue into political civil disobedience. Berkeley students were faced with a decision to sit in the Administration building in the name of political freedom of communication. Haan and Smith administered moral judgment interviews to over 200 of these students. The situation was like that in Milgram's study. A Stage 5 social contract interpretation of justice, which was that held by the University administration, could take the position that a student who came to Berkeley came with foreknowledge of the rules and could go elsewhere if he did not like them. About 50 percent of the Stage 5 subjects sat in. For Stage 6 students, the issue was clear cut, and 80 percent of them sat in. For students at the conventional levels, Stages 3 and 4, the issue was also clear cut, and only 10 percent of them sat in. These results will sound very heartwarming to those who have engaged in protest activities. Protesting is a sure sign of being at the most mature moral level; however, there was another group [that] was almost as disposed to sit in as the Stage 6 students. These

were our Stage 2 instrumental relativists, of whom about 60 percent sat in. From our longitudinal studies, we know that most Stage 2 college students are in a state of confusion. In high school most were at the conventional level, and in college they kick conventional morality, searching for their thing, for self-chosen values, but cannot tell an autonomous morality of justice from one of egoistic relativism, exchange, and revenge. Our longitudinal studies indicate that all of our middle-class Stage 2 college students grow out of it to become principled adults. If the pressures are greater and you are a Stokely Carmichael,[1] things may take a different course.

I make the point to indicate that protest activities, like other acts, are neither virtuous nor vicious, it is only the knowledge of the good which lies behind them which can give them virtue. As an example, I would take it that a Stage 6 sense of justice would have been rather unlikely to find the Dow Chemical sit-in virtuous.[2] The rules being disobeyed by the protesters were not unjust rules, and the sit-in was depriving individuals of rights, not trying to protect individual rights. Principled civil disobedience is not illegitimate propaganda for worthy political causes, it is the just questioning of injustice.

I hope this last example will indicate the complexity of the behaviors by which knowledge of justice may be manifested and that no trait of virtue in the ordinary sense will describe the behavior of the principled or just man. Having, I hope, shown the validity of the Platonic view of virtue, I will take the little time left to consider the sense in which it may be taught. The Platonic view implies that, in a sense,

---

1. Stokely Carmichael, elected head of the SNCC (Student Nonviolent Coordinating Committee) in 1966, parted camp with Martin Luther King, Jr. by advocating "Black Power" and self-defense. Frustrated with the lack of progress in the civil rights movement, Carmichael believed that blacks had to establish their own institutions in order to be free from white oppression.
2. In February of 1967, students at the University of Wisconsin sat-in at the office of the Dow Chemical Company to protest the manufacture and sale of napalm (a jelly that sticks to and burns anything it touches) by the company to the U.S. military for use in the Vietnam War.

knowledge of the good is always within but needs to be drawn out like geometric knowledge in Meno's slave.[3] In a series of experimental studies, we have found that children and adolescents rank as "best" the highest level of moral reasoning they can comprehend. Children comprehend all lower stages than their own, and often comprehend the stage one higher than their own and occasionally two stages higher, though they cannot actively express these higher stages of thought. If they comprehend the stage one higher than their own, they tend to prefer it to their own. This fact is basic to moral leadership in our society. While the majority of adults in American society are at a conventional level, Stages 3 and 4, leadership in our society has usually been expressed at the level of Stages 5 and 6, as our example of Martin Luther King suggests. While it may be felt as dangerous, the moral leadership of the Platonic philosopher-ruler is nonetheless naturally felt.

Returning to the teaching of virtue as a drawing out, the child's preference for the next level of thought shows that it is greeted as already familiar, that it is felt to be a more adequate expression of that already within, of that latent in the child's own thought. If the child were responding to fine words and external prestige he would not pick the next stage continuous with his own, but something else.

Let me now suggest a different example in the sense in which moral teaching must be a drawing out of that already within. At the age of four my son joined the pacifist and vegetarian movement and refused to eat meat, because as he said, "it's bad to kill animals." In spite of lengthy Hawk argumentation by his parents about the difference between justified and unjustified killing, he remained a vegetarian for six months. Like most Doves, however, his principles recognized occasions for just or legitimate killing. One night I read to him a book of Eskimo life involving a seal-killing expedition. He got angry during the story and said, "You know, there is one kind of meat I would eat, Eskimo meat. It's bad to kill animals so it's all right to eat Eskimos."

For reasons I won't detail, this eye for an eye,

---

3. From the dialogue "Meno" by Plato.

tooth for a tooth concept of justice is Stage 1. You will recognize, however, that it is a very genuine though four-year-old sense of justice and that it contains within it the Stage 6 sense of justice in shadowy form. The problem is to draw the child's perceptions of justice from the shadows of the cave step by step toward the light of justice as an ideal form. This last example indicates another Platonic truth, which is that the child who turns from the dark images of the cave toward the light is at first still convinced that his dark images best represent the truth. Like Meno's slave, the child is initially quite confident of his moral knowledge, of the rationality and efficacy of his moral principles. The notion that the child feels ignorant and is eager to absorb the wisdom of adult authority in the moral domain is one which any teacher or parent will know is nonsense. Let me give another example. Following a developmental timetable, my son moved to an expedient Stage 2 orientation when he was six. He told me at that time, "You know the reason people don't steal is because they're afraid of the police. If there were no police around everyone would steal." Of course I told him that I and most people didn't steal because we thought it wrong, because we wouldn't want other people to take things from us, and so on. My son's reply was, "I just don't see it, it's sort of crazy not to steal if there are no police."

The story indicates, that like most ordinary fathers, I had no great skill in teaching true virtue. My son, of course, has always been virtuous in the conventional sense. Even when he saw no rational reason for being honest, he received the highest marks on his report card on the basis of the bag of virtues of obedience, responsibility, and respect for property. Contrary to what we usually think, it is quite easy to teach conventionally virtuous behavior but very difficult to teach true knowledge of the good.

The first step in teaching virtue, then, is the Socratic step of creating dissatisfaction in the student about his present knowledge of the good. This we do experimentally by exposing the student to moral conflict situations for which his principles have no ready solution. Second, we expose him to disagreement and argument about these situations with his peers. Our Platonic view holds that if we inspire cognitive conflict in the student and point the way to the next step up the divided line, he will tend to see things previously invisible to him.

In practice, then, our experimental efforts at moral education have involved getting students at one level, say Stage 2, to argue with those at the next level, say Stage 3. The teacher would support and clarify the Stage 3 arguments. Then he would pit the Stage 3 students against the Stage 4 students on a new dilemma. Initial results with this method with a junior high school group indicated that 50 percent of the students moved up one stage and 10 percent moved up two stages. In comparison, only 10 percent of a control group moved up one stage in the four-month period involved.

Obviously, the small procedures I have described are only a way station to genuine moral education.... [A] more complete approach implies full student participation in a school in which justice is a living matter. Let me sketch out one Platonic republic with this aim, a boarding school I recently visited. The heart of this school is described in its brochure somewhat as follows:

> The sense of community is most strongly felt in the weekly Meeting, consisting of faculty, their families and students. Decisions are made by consensus rather than by majority rule. This places responsibility on each member to struggle to see through his own desires to the higher needs of others and the community, while wit-

nessing the deepest concerns of his conscience. The results of these decisions are not rules in the traditional sense, but agreements entered into by everyone and recorded as minutes.

The brochure goes on to quote a letter by one of its graduation students:

> The School is an entity surrounded by the rest of the world in which each individual struggles against that which restrains him—himself. It has been said that the School gives too much freedom to its young, often rebellious students. But a film will darken to a useless mass of chemical if it's not developed in time. People change early, too. If they meet a loving atmosphere, they are affected by it profoundly. Growing up is a lonely thing to be doing, but at the Meeting School, it is also a beautiful thing.

All schools need not and cannot be self-contained little Republics in which knowledge of the good is to be brought out through love and community as well as through participation in a just institution. Such schools do stand as a challenge to an educational establishment which makes a pious bow to the bag of virtues while teaching that true goodness is tested on the College Boards. The Platonic view I've been espousing suggests something still revolutionary and frightening to me if not to you, that the schools would be radically different places if they took seriously the teaching of real knowledge of the good.

Study Questions

1. What do you think accounts for the similar pattern of moral development across many cultures?

2. Are educated people generally more moral than the uneducated?

The Good Life of the Self-Actualizing Person

Abraham Maslow (1908–1970) A psychologist, Abraham Maslow studied the relation of human nature to psychology and happiness. He authored Motivation and Personality *and* The Farther Reaches of Human Nature *among other writings.*

A. H. Maslow

Self-actualizing people are gratified in all their basic needs embracing affection, respect, and self-esteem. They have a feeling of belongingness and rootedness. They are satisfied in their love needs, because they have friends, feel loved and love-worthy. They have status, place in life, and respect from other people, and they have a reasonable feeling of worth and self-respect.

Self-actualizing people do not for any length of time feel anxiety-ridden, insecure, unsafe; do not feel alone, ostracized, rootless, or isolated; do not feel unlovable, rejected, or unwanted; do not feel despised and looked down upon; and do not feel unworthy nor do they have crippling feelings of inferiority or worthlessness.

Since the basic needs had been assumed to be the only motivations for human beings, it was possible, and in certain contexts useful, to say of self-actualizing people that they were "unmotivated." This aligned these people with the Eastern philosophical view of health as the transcendence of striving or desiring or wanting.

It is also possible to say and to describe self-actualizing people as expressing rather than coping. They are spontaneous, natural, and more easily themselves than other people.

What motivates the self-actualizing person? What are the psychodynamics in self-actualization? What makes him move and act and struggle? What drives or pulls such a person? What attracts him? For what

does he hope? What makes him angry, or dedicated, or self-sacrificing? What does he feel loyal to? Devoted to? What does he aspire to and yearn for? What would he die or live for?

These questions ask for an answer to the question: What are the motivations of self-actualizing people? Clearly we must make an immediate distinction between the ordinary motives of those people who are below the level of self-actualization and motivated by the basic needs, and the motivations of people who are sufficiently gratified in all their basic needs and are no longer primarily motivated by them. For convenience, call these motives and needs of self-actualizing persons "meta-needs." This also differentiates the category of motivation from the category of "meta-motivation."

Examining self-actualizing people, I find that they are dedicated people, devoted to some task outside themselves, some vocation, or duty, or job. Generally the devotion and dedication is so marked that one can correctly use the old words vocation, calling, or mission to describe their passionate, selfless, and profound feeling for their "work." We could even use the words destiny or fate in the sense of biological or temperamental or constitutional destiny or fate. Sometimes I have gone so far as to speak of oblation in the religious sense of dedicating oneself upon some altar for a particular task, some cause outside oneself and bigger than oneself, something not merely selfish, something impersonal. This is one way of putting into adequate words the feeling that one gets when one listens to self-actualizing people talking about their work or task. One gets the feeling of a beloved job,

This article first appeared in *The Humanist* issue of July/August 1967 and is reprinted by permission.

and further, of something for which the person is "a natural," that he is suited for, that is right for him, even something for which he was born.

In this kind of situation, it is easy to sense something like a preestablished harmony or a good match like a perfect love affair in which it seems that people belong to each other and were meant for each other. In the best instances the person and his job fit together and belong together perfectly like a key and a lock, or resonate together like a sung note which sets into sympathetic resonance a particular string in the piano keyboard.

Often I get the feeling that I can tease apart two kinds of determinants from this fusion which has created a unity out of a duality, and that these two sets of determinants can, and sometimes do, vary independently. One can be spoken of as the responses to forces relatively within the person: e.g., "I love babies (or painting, or research, or political power) more than anything in the world." "It fascinates me." "I am inexorably drawn to . . ." "I need to . . ." This we may call "inner requiredness" and it is felt as a kind of self-indulgence rather than as a duty. It is different from and separable from "external requiredness," which is felt as a response to what the environment, the situation, the problem, or the external world calls for and requires of the person. A fire "calls for" putting out, or a helpless baby demands that one take care of it, or some obvious injustice calls for righting. Here one feels more the element of duty, of obligation, of responsibility, of being compelled helplessly to respond no matter what one was planning to do, or wished to do. It is more "I must," "I have to," "I am compelled" than "I want to."

In the ideal instance, "I want to" coincides with "I must." There is a good matching of inner with outer requirements. The observer is overawed by the degree of compellingness, of inexorability, or preordained destiny, necessity, and harmony that he perceives. Furthermore, the observer, as well as the person involved, feels not only that "it has to be" but also that "it ought to be, it is right, it is suitable, appropriate, fitting, and proper." I have often felt a gestaltlike quality about this kind of belonging together, the formation of a "one" out of "two." I hesitate to call this simply "purposefulness" because

that may imply that it happens only out of will, purpose, decision, or calculation; the word doesn't give enough weight to the subjective feeling of being swept along, of willing and eager surrender, or yielding to fate and happily embracing it at the same time. Ideally, one discovers one's fate; it is not made or constructed or decided upon. It is recognized as if one had been unwittingly waiting for it. Perhaps the better phrase would be "Spinozistic" or "Taoistic" choice or decision or purpose.

The best way to explain these feelings is to use the example of "falling in love." It is clearly different from doing one's duty, or doing what is sensible or logical. Also "will," if mentioned at all, is used in a very special sense. When two people fall in love with each other fully, each one knows what it feels like to be a magnet and what it feels like to be iron filings and what it feels like to be both simultaneously. Very useful, also, is the parallel with the happy abandon of the ideal sexual situation. Here people resist and delay the inevitable climax, in a kind of fond self- and other-teasing, holding off as long as possible. Suddenly, in a single instant they can change to the opposite course of embracing eagerly and totally the end which they were moments ago delaying, as the tides suddenly change from going north to going south.

This example also helps convey what is difficult to communicate in words; the lovers' sense of good fortune, of luck, of gratuitous grace, of gratitude, of awe that this miracle should have occurred, of wonder that they should have been chosen, and of the peculiar mixture of pride fused with humility, of arrogance shot through with the pity-for-the-less-fortunate that one finds in lovers.

It can be said of the self-actualizing person that he is being his own kind of person, or being himself, or actualizing his real self. Observation would lead one to understand that "This person is the best one in the whole world for this particular job, and this particular job is the best job in the whole world for this particular person and his talents, capacities, and tastes. He was meant for it, and it was meant for him."

Accepting this premise, we move into another realm of discourse—the realm of being, of transcendence. Now we can speak meaningfully only in the language of being (the "B-language," communication at the mystical level described in my book *Toward a Psychology of Being*). It is quite obvious with such people that the ordinary or conventional dichotomy between work and play is transcended totally. Such a person's work is his play and his play is his work. If a person loves his work and enjoys it more than any other activity in the whole world and is eager to get to it, to get back to it, after any interruption, then how can we speak about "labor" in the sense of something one is forced to do against one's wishes?

What sense, for instance, is left to the concept "vacation"? For such individuals is it often observed that during the periods in which they are totally free to choose whatever they wish to do and in which they have no external obligations to anyone else, they devote themselves happily and totally to their "work." What does it mean "to have some fun"? What is the meaning of the word "entertainment"? How does such a person "rest"? What are his "duties," responsibilities, obligations?

What sense does money or pay or salary make in such a situation? Obviously the most beautiful fate, the most wonderful good luck, the most marvelous good fortune that can happen to any human being is to be paid for doing that which he passionately loves to do. This is exactly the situation, or almost the situation, with many self-actualizing persons. Of course, money is welcome, and in certain amounts is even needed. It is certainly not the finality, the end, the goal, however. The check such a man gets is only a small part of his "pay." Self-actualizing work or B-work, being its own intrinsic reward, transforms the money or paycheck into a by-product, an epiphenomenon. This is different from the situation of less fortunate human beings who do something that they do not want to do in order to get money, which they then use to get what they really want. The role of money in the realm of being is certainly different from the role of money in the realm of deficiencies.

These are scientific questions, and can be investigated in scientific ways. They have been investigated in monkeys and apes to a degree. The most obvious example, of course, is the rich research literature on monkey curiosity and other precursors of the human yearning for and satisfaction with the truth. But it will be just as easy in principle to explore the aesthetic choices of these and other animals under conditions of fear and of lack of fear, by healthy specimens or by unhealthy ones, under good choice conditions or bad ones, etc.

If one asks the fortunate, work-loving, self-actualizing person, "Who are you?" or "What are you?" he tends to answer in terms of his "call" . . . "I am a lawyer." "I am a mother." "I am a psychiatrist." "I am an artist." He tells you that he identifies his call with his identity, his Self. It is a label for the whole of him and it becomes a defining characteristic of the person.

If one confronts him with the question, "Supposing you were not a scientist (or a teacher, or a pi-

> *". . . [I]n self-actualizing subjects, their beloved calling tends to be perceived as a defining characteristic of the self, to be identified with, incorporated, introjected."*

lot), then what would you be?" or "Supposing you were not a psychologist, then what?" his response is apt to be one of puzzlement, thoughtfulness. He does not have a ready answer. Or the response can be one of amusement. It strikes him funny. In effect, the answer is, "If I were not a mother (lover, anthropologist, industrialist) then I wouldn't be *me*. I would be someone else, and I can't imagine being someone else."

A tentative conclusion is, then, that in self-actualizing subjects, their beloved calling tends to be perceived as a defining characteristic of the self, to be identified with, incorporated, introjected. It becomes an inextricable aspect of one's Being.

When asked why they love their work, which are the moments of higher satisfaction in their work, which moments of reward make all the necessary chores worthwhile or acceptable, which are the peak-experiences, self-actualizing people give many specific and *ad hoc* answers which to them are intrinsic reinforcers.

As I classified these moments of reward, it became apparent that the best and most natural categories of classification were mostly or entirely values of an ultimate and irreducible kind! Call them "B-values": truth, goodness, beauty, unity, aliveness, uniqueness, perfection, completion, justice, simplicity, totality, effortlessness, playfulness, self-sufficiency, meaningfulness.

For these people the profession seems to be not functionally autonomous, but to be a carrier of ultimate values. I could say, if I were not afraid of being misunderstood, that for example, the profession of law, is a means to the end of justice, and not a law to itself in which justice might get lost. For one man the law is loved because it is justice, while another man, the pure value-free technologist, might love the law simply as an intrinsically lovable set of rules, precedents, procedures without regard to the ends or products of their use.

B-values or meta-motives are not only intrapsychic or organismic. They are equally inner and outer. The meta-needs, insofar as they are inner, and the requiredness of all that is outside the person are each stimulus and response to each other. And they move toward becoming indistinguishable, toward fusion.

This means that the distinction between self and not-self has broken down or has been transcended. There is less differentiation between the world and the person because he has incorporated into himself part of the world and defines himself thereby. He becomes an enlarged self. If justice or truth or lawfulness have now become so important to him that he identifies his self with them, then where are they? Inside his skin or outside his skin? This distinction comes close to being meaningless at this point because his self no longer has his skin as its boundary.

Certainly simple selfishness is transcended here and has to be defined at higher levels. For instance, we know that it is possible for a person to get more pleasure out of food through having his child eat it than through eating it with his own mouth. His self has enlarged enough to include his child. Hurt his child and you hurt him. Clearly the self can no longer be identified with the biological entity which is supplied with blood from his heart along his blood vessels. The psychological self can obviously be bigger than his own body.

Just as beloved people can be incorporated into the self, thereby becoming defining characteristics of it, so also can causes and values be similarly incorporated into a person's self. Many people are so passionately identified with trying to prevent war, racial injustices, slums, or poverty that they are quite willing to make great sacrifices, even to the point of risking death. Very clearly, they do not mean justice for their own biological bodies alone. They mean justice as a general value, justice for everyone, justice as a principle.

There are other important consequences of this incorporation of values into the self. For instance, you can love justice and truth in the world or in a person out there. You can be made happier as your friends move toward truth and justice, and sadder as they move away from it. That's easy to understand. However, suppose you see yourself moving successfully toward truth, justice, beauty, and virtue? Then you may find that, in a peculiar kind of detachment and objectivity toward oneself, for which our culture has no place, you will be loving and admiring yourself in the kind of healthy self-love that Fromm has described. You can respect yourself, admire yourself, take tender care of yourself, reward yourself, feel virtuous, love-worthy, respect-worthy. You may then treat yourself with the responsibility and otherness that a pregnant woman does whose self now has to be defined to overlap with not-self. So may a person with a great talent protect it and himself as if he were a carrier of something which is simultaneously himself and not himself. He may become his own friend.

These people, although concretely working for, motivated by, and loyal to some conventional category of work, are transparently motivated by the intrinsic or ultimate values or aspects of reality for which the profession is only a vehicle.

This is my impression from observing them, interviewing them, and asking them why they like doctoring, or just which are the most rewarding moments in running a home, or chairing a committee, or having a baby, or writing. They may meaningfully be said to be working for truth, for beauty, for goodness, for law and for order, for justice, for perfection, if I boil down to a dozen or so intrinsic values (or values of Being) all the hundreds of specific reports of what is yearned for, what gratifies, what is valued, what they work for from day to day, and why they work.

It is at this point in my theory that, quite fairly, both methodology and validity can be called into question. I have not deliberately worked with an *ad hoc* control group of non-self-actualizing people. I could say that most of humanity is a control group. I have a considerable fund of experience with the attitudes toward work of average people, immature people, neurotic and borderline people, psychopaths, and others. There is no question that their attitudes cluster around money, basic-need gratification rather than B-values, sheer habit, stimulus-binding, convention, and the inertia of the unexamined and nonquestioned life, and from doing what other people expect or demand. However, this intuitive or naturalistic conclusion is susceptible to more careful and more controlled and predesigned examination.

Secondly, it is my strong impression that there is not a sharp line between my subjects chosen as self-actualizing and other people. I believe that each self-actualizing subject more or less fits the description I have given, but it seems also true that some percentage of other, less healthy people are meta-motivated by the B-values also; especially individuals with special talents and people placed in especially fortunate circumstances. Perhaps all people are meta-motivated to some degree.

The conventional categories of career, profession, or work may serve as channels of many other kinds of motivations, not to mention sheer habit or convention or functional autonomy. They may satisfy or seek vainly to satisfy any or all of the basic needs as well as various neurotic needs. They may be a channel for "acting out" or for "defensive" activities rather than for real gratifications.

My guess, supported by both my "empirical" impressions and by general psychodynamic theory,

is that we will find it ultimately most true and most useful to say that all these various habits, determinants, motives, and meta-motives are acting simultaneously in a very complex pattern which is centered more toward one kind of motivation or determinedness than the others.

If we can try to define the deepest, most authentic, most constitutionally based aspects of the real self, of the identity, or of the authentic person, we find that in order to be comprehensive, we must include not only the person's constitution and temperament, not only anatomy, physiology, neurology, and endocrinology, not only his capacities, his biological style, not only his basic instinctoid needs, but also *the* B-values which are also *his* B-values. They are equally a part of his "nature," or definition, or essence, along with his "lower" needs. They must be included in any definition of the human being, or of full-humanness, or of a person. It is true that they are not fully evident or actualized in most people. Yet, so far as I can see at this time, they are not excluded as potentials in any human being born into the world.

Thus, a fully inclusive definition of a fully developed self or person includes a value system by which he is meta-motivated.

What all of this means is that the so-called spiritual or "higher" life is on the same continuum (is the same kind of quality or thing) with the life of the flesh, or of the body, i.e., the animal life, the "lower" life. The spiritual life is part of our biological life. It is the "highest" part of it, but yet part of it. The spiritual life is part of the human essence. It is a defining-characteristic of human nature, without which human nature is not full human nature. It is part of the real self, of one's identity, of one's inner core, or one's specieshood, of full-humanness.

To the extent that pure expressing of oneself, or pure spontaneity is possible, to that extent will the meta-needs be expressed. "Uncovering" or Taoistic therapeutic or "Ontogogic" techniques should uncover and strengthen the meta-needs as well as the basic needs. Depth-diagnostic and therapeutic techniques should ultimately also uncover these same meta-needs because, paradoxically, our highest nature is also our deepest nature. They are not in two separate realms as most religions and philosophies have assumed, and as classical science has also assumed. The spiritual life (the contemplative, "religious," philosophical, or value-life) is within the jurisdiction of human thought and is attainable in principle by man's own efforts. Even though it has been cast out of the realm of reality by the classical, value-free science which models itself upon physics, it is now being reclaimed as an object of study and technology by humanistic science. Such an expanded science will consider the eternal verities, the ultimate truths, the final values, to be "real" and natural, fact-based rather than wish-based, legitimate scientific problems calling for research.

The so-called spiritual, transcendent, or axiological life is clearly rooted in the biological nature of the species. It is a kind of "higher" animality whose precondition is a healthy "lower" animality and the two are hierarchically integrated rather than mutually exclusive. However, the higher, spiritual "animality" is timid and weak. It is so easily lost, easily crushed by stronger cultural forces, that it can become widely actualized *only* in a culture which approves of human nature and, therefore, fosters its fullest growth.

Study Questions

1. Can a person be immoral and happy?

2. Do you know anyone who is self-actualized but unlike the individuals described by Maslow?

3. Is Maslow's theory more reminiscent of the ethics of Aristotle, Kant, Mill, Jesus, Buddha, or Muhammad? Explain why.

The Road Less Traveled

M. Scott Peck is a practicing psychiatrist who has written several books, including People of the Lie.

M. Scott Peck

Problems and Pain

Life is difficult.

This is a great truth, one of the greatest truths.[1] It is a great truth because once we truly see this truth,

we transcend it. Once we truly know that life is difficult—once we truly understand and accept it—then life is no longer difficult. Because once it is ac-

---

1. The first of the "Four Noble Truths" that Buddha taught was "Life is suffering."

cepted, the fact that life is difficult no longer matters.

Most do not fully see this truth that life is difficult. Instead they moan more or less incessantly, noisily or subtly, about the enormity of their problems, their burdens, and their difficulties as if life were generally easy, as if life *should* be easy. They voice their belief, noisily or subtly, that their difficulties represent a unique kind of affliction that should not be and that has somehow been especially visited upon them, or else upon their families, their tribe, their class, their nation, their race or even their species, and not upon others. I know about this moaning because I have done my share.

Life is a series of problems. Do we want to moan about them or solve them? Do we want to teach our children to solve them?

Discipline is the basic set of tools we require to solve life's problems. Without discipline we can solve nothing. With only some discipline we can solve only some problems. With total discipline we can solve all problems.

What makes life difficult is that the process of confronting and solving problems is a painful one. Problems, depending upon their nature, evoke in us frustration or grief or sadness or loneliness or guilt or regret or anger or fear or anxiety or anguish or despair. These are uncomfortable feelings, often very uncomfortable, often as painful as any kind of physical pain, sometimes equaling the very worst kind of physical pain. Indeed, it is *because* of the pain that events or conflicts engender in us that we call them problems. And since life poses an endless series of problems, life is always difficult and is full of pain as well as joy.

Yet it is in this whole process of meeting and solving problems that life has its meaning. Problems are the cutting edge that distinguishes between success and failure. Problems call forth our courage and our wisdom; indeed, they create our courage and our wisdom. It is only because of problems that we grow mentally and spiritually. When we desire to encourage the growth of the human spirit, we challenge and encourage the human capacity to solve problems, just as in school we deliberately set problems for our children to solve. It is through the pain of confronting and resolving problems that we learn. As Benjamin Franklin said, "Those things

that hurt, instruct." It is for this reason that wise people learn not to dread but actually to welcome problems and actually to welcome the pain of problems.

Most of us are not so wise. Fearing the pain involved, almost all of us, to a greater or lesser degree, attempt to avoid problems. We procrastinate, hoping that they will go away. We ignore them, forget them, pretend they do not exist. We even take drugs to assist us in ignoring them, so that by deadening ourselves to the pain we can forget the problems that cause the pain. We attempt to skirt around problems rather than meet them head on. We attempt to get out of them rather than suffer through them.

This tendency to avoid problems and the emotional suffering inherent in them is the primary basis of all human mental illness. Since most of us have this tendency to a greater or lesser degree, most of us are mentally ill to a greater or lesser degree, lacking complete mental health. Some of us will go to quite extraordinary lengths to avoid our problems and the suffering they cause, proceeding far afield from all that is clearly good and sensible in order to try to find an easy way out, building the most elaborate fantasies in which to live, sometimes to the total exclusion of reality. In the succinctly elegant words of Carl Jung, "Neurosis is always a substitute for legitimate suffering."[2]

But the substitute itself ultimately becomes more painful than the legitimate suffering it was designed to avoid. The neurosis itself becomes the biggest problem. True to form, many will then attempt to avoid this pain and this problem in turn, building layer upon layer of neurosis. Fortunately, however, some possess the courage to face their neuroses and begin—usually with the help of psychotherapy—to learn how to experience legitimate suffering. In any case, when we avoid the legitimate suffering that results from dealing with problems, we also avoid the growth that problems demand from us. It is for this reason that in chronic mental illness we stop growing, we become stuck. And without healing, the human spirit begins to shrivel.

---

2. *Collected Works of C. G. Jung,* Bollengen Ser., No. 20, 2d ed. (Princeton, N.J.: Princeton Univ. Press, 1973), trans. R. F. C. Hull, Vol. II, *Psychology and Religion: West and East,* 75.

Therefore let us inculcate in ourselves and in our children the means of achieving mental and spiritual health. By this I mean let us teach ourselves and our children the necessity for suffering and the value thereof, the need to face problems directly and to experience the pain involved. I have stated that discipline is the basic set of tools we require to solve life's problems. It will become clear that these tools are techniques of suffering, means by which we experience the pain of problems in such a way as to work them through and solve them successfully, learning and growing in the process. When we teach ourselves and our children discipline, we are teaching them and ourselves how to suffer and also how to grow.

What are these tools, these techniques of suffering, these means of experiencing the pain of problems constructively that I call discipline? There are four: delaying of gratification, acceptance of responsibility, dedication to truth, and balancing. As will be evident, these are not complex tools whose application demands extensive training. To the contrary, they are simple tools, and almost all children are adept in their use by the age of ten. Yet presidents and kings will often forget to use them, to their own downfall. The problem lies not in the complexity of these tools but in the will to use them. For they are tools with which pain is confronted rather than avoided, and if one seeks to avoid legitimate suffering, then one will avoid the use of these tools. Therefore, after analyzing each of these tools, we shall in the next section examine the will to use them, which is love.

Delaying Gratification

. . . . In summary, for children to develop the capacity to delay gratification, it is necessary for them to have self-disciplined role models, a sense of self-worth, and a degree of trust in the safety of their existence. These "possessions" are ideally acquired through the self-discipline and consistent, genuine caring of their parents; they are the most precious gifts of themselves that mothers and fathers can bequeath. When these gifts have not been proffered by one's parents, it is possible to acquire them from other sources, but in that case the process of their

acquisition is invariably an uphill struggle, often of lifelong duration and often unsuccessful. . . .

Responsibility

We cannot solve life's problems except by solving them. This statement may seem idiotically tautological or self-evident, yet it is seemingly beyond the comprehension of much of the human race. This is because we must accept responsibility for a problem before we can solve it. We cannot solve a problem by saying "It's not my problem." We cannot solve a problem by hoping that someone else will solve it for us. I can solve a problem only when I say "This is *my* problem and it's up to me to solve it." But many, so many, seek to avoid the pain of their problems by saying to themselves: "This problem was caused me by other people, or by social circumstances beyond my control, and therefore it is up to other people or society to solve this problem for me. It is not really my personal problem."

Neuroses and Character Disorders

Most people who come to see a psychiatrist are suffering from what is called either a neurosis or a character disorder. Put most simply, these two conditions are disorders of responsibility, and as such they are opposite styles of relating to the world and its problems. The neurotic assumes too much responsibility; the person with a character disorder not enough. When neurotics are in conflict with the world they automatically assume that they are at fault. When those with character disorders are in conflict with the world they automatically assume that the world is at fault.

Even the speech patterns of neurotics and those with character disorders are different. The speech of the neurotic is notable for such expressions as "I ought to," "I should," and "I shouldn't," indicating the individual's self-image as an inferior man or woman, always falling short of the mark, always making the wrong choices. The speech of a person with a character disorder, however, relies heavily on "I can't," "I couldn't," "I have to," and "I had to," demonstrating a self-image of a being who has no power of choice, whose behavior is completely directed by external forces totally beyond his or her control. As might be imagined, neurotics, compared with character-disordered people, are easy to work with in psychotherapy because they assume responsibility for their difficulties and therefore see themselves as having problems. Those with character disorders are much more difficult, if not impossible, to work with because they don't see themselves as the source of their problems; they see the world rather than themselves as being in need of change and therefore fail to recognize the necessity for self-examination. In actuality, many individuals have both a neurosis and a character disorder and are referred to as "character neurotics," indicating that in some areas of their lives they are guilt-ridden by virtue of having assumed responsibility that is not really theirs, while in other areas of their lives they fail to take realistic responsibility for themselves. Fortunately, once having established the faith and trust of such individuals in the psychotherapy process through helping them with the neurotic part of their personalities, it is often possible then to engage them in examining and correcting their unwillingness to assume responsibility where appropriate.

Few of us can escape being neurotic or character disordered to at lest some degree (which is why essentially everyone can benefit from psychotherapy if he or she is seriously willing to participate in the process). The reason for this is that the problem of distinguishing what we are and what we are not responsible for in this life is one of the greatest problems of human existence. It is never completely solved; for the entirety of our lives we must continually assess and reassess where our responsibilities lie in the everchanging course of events. Nor is this assessment and reassessment painless if performed adequately and conscientiously. To perform either process adequately we must possess the willingness and the capacity to suffer continual self-examination. And such capacity or willingness is not inherent in any of us. In a sense all children have character disorders, in that their instinctual tendency is to deny their responsibility for many conflicts in which they find themselves. Thus two siblings fighting will always blame each other for initiating the fight and each will totally deny that he or she may have been the culprit. Similarly, all children have neuroses, in

that they will instinctually assume responsibility for certain deprivations that they experience but do not yet understand. Thus the child who is not loved by his parents will always assume himself or herself to be unlovable rather than see the parents as deficient in their capacity to love. Or early adolescents who are not yet successful at dating or at sports will see themselves as seriously deficient human beings rather than the late or even average but perfectly adequate bloomers they usually are. It is only through a vast amount of experience and a lengthy and successful maturation that we gain the capacity to see the world and our place in it realistically, and thus are enabled to realistically assess our responsibility for ourselves and the world.

Escape from Freedom

When a psychiatrist makes the diagnosis of a character disorder, it is because the pattern of avoidance of responsibility is relatively gross in the diagnosed individual. Yet almost all of us from time to time seek to avoid—in ways that can be quite subtle—the pain of assuming responsibility for our own problems. Whenever we seek to avoid the responsibility for our own behavior, we do so by attempting to give that responsibility to some other individual or organization or entity. But this means we then give away our power to that entity, be it "fate" or "society" or the government or the corporation or our boss. It is for this reason that Erich Fromm so aptly titled his study of Nazism and authoritarianism *Escape from Freedom*. In attempting to avoid the pain of responsibility, millions and even billions daily attempt to escape from freedom.

One of the roots of this "sense of impotence" in the majority of patients is some desire to partially or totally escape the pain of freedom, and, therefore, some failure, partial or total, to accept responsibility for their problems and their lives. They fell impotent because they have, in fact, given their power away. Sooner or later, if they are to be healed, they must learn that the entirety of one's adult life is a series of personal choices, decisions. If they can accept this totally, then they become free people. To the extent that they do not accept this they will forever feel themselves victims.

Dedication to Reality

The third tool of discipline or technique of dealing with the pain of problem-solving, which must continually be employed if our lives are to be healthy and our spirits are to grow, is dedication to the truth. Superficially, this should be obvious. For truth is reality. That which is false is unreal. The more clearly we see the reality of the world, the better equipped we are to deal with the world. The less clearly we see the reality of the world—the more our minds are befuddled by falsehood, misperceptions and illusions—the less able we will be to determine correct courses of action and make wise decisions. Our view of reality is like a map with which to negotiate the terrain of life. If the map is true and accurate, we will generally know where we are, and if we have decided where we want to go, we will generally know how to get there. If the map is false and inaccurate, we generally will be lost.

While this is obvious, it is something that most people to a greater or lesser degree choose to ignore. They ignore it because our route to reality is not easy. First of all, we are not born with maps; we have to make them, and the making requires effort. The more effort we make to appreciate and perceive reality, the larger and more accurate our maps will be. But many do not want to make this effort. Some stop making it by the end of adolescence. Their maps are small and sketchy, their views of the world narrow and misleading. By the end of middle age most people have given up the effort. They feel certain that their maps are complete and their Weltanschauung is correct (indeed, even sacrosanct), and they are no longer interested in new information. It is as if they are tired. Only a relative and fortunate few continue until the moment of death exploring the mystery of reality, ever enlarging and refining and redefining their understanding of the world and what is true.

But the biggest problem of map-making is not that we have to start from scratch, but that if our maps are to be accurate we have to continually revise them. The world itself is constantly changing. Glaciers come, glaciers go. Cultures come, cultures go. There is too little technology, there is too much technology. Even more dramatically, the vantage point from which we view the world is constantly and quite rapidly changing. When we are children we are dependent, powerless. As adults we may be powerful. Yet in illness or an infirm old age we may become powerless and dependent again. When we have children to care for, the world looks different from when we have none; when we are raising infants, the world seems different from when we are raising adolescents. When we are poor, the world looks different from when we are rich. We are daily bombarded with new information as to the nature of reality. If we are to incorporate this information, we must continually revise our maps, and sometimes when enough new information has accumulated, we must make very major revisions. The process of making revisions, particularly major revisions, is painful, sometimes excruciatingly painful. And herein lies the major source of many of the ills of mankind.

What happens when one has striven long and hard to develop a working view of the world, a seemingly useful, workable map, and then is confronted with new information suggesting that that view is wrong and the map needs to be largely redrawn? The painful effort required seems frightening, almost overwhelming. What we do more often than not, and usually unconsciously, is to ignore the new information. Often this act of ignoring is much more than passive. We may denounce the new information as false, dangerous, heretical, the work of the devil. We may actually crusade against it, and even attempt to manipulate the world so as to make it conform to our view of reality. Rather than try to change the map, an individual may try to destroy the new reality. Sadly, such a person may expend much more energy ultimately in defending an outmoded view of the world than would have been required to revise and correct it in the first place. . . .

Openness to Challenge

What does a life of total dedication to the truth mean? It means, first of all, a life of continuous and never-ending stringent self-examination. We know the world only through our relationship to it.

Therefore, to know the world, we must not only examine it but we must simultaneously examine the examiner....

A life of total dedication to the truth also means a life of willingness to be personally challenged. The only way that we can be certain that our map of reality is valid is to expose it to the criticism and challenge of other map-makers. Otherwise we live in a closed system—within a bell jar, to use Sylvia Plath's analogy, rebreathing only our own fetid air, more and more subject to delusion. Yet, because of the pain inherent in the process of revising our map of reality, we mostly seek to avoid or ward off any challenges to its validity. To our children we say, "Don't talk back to me, I'm your parent." To our spouse we give the message, "Let's live and let live. If you criticize me, I'll be a bitch to live with, and you'll regret it." To their families and the world the elderly give the message, "I am old and fragile. If you challenge me I may die or at least you will bear upon your head the responsibility for making my last days on earth miserable." To our employees we communicate, "If you are bold enough to challenge me at all, you had best do so very circumspectly indeed or else you'll find yourself looking for another job."

The tendency to avoid challenge is so omnipresent in human beings that it can properly be considered a characteristic of human nature. But calling it natural does not mean it is essential or beneficial or unchangeable behavior. It is also natural to defecate in our pants and never brush our teeth. Yet we teach ourselves to do the unnatural until the unnatural becomes itself second nature. Indeed, all self-discipline might be defined as teaching ourselves to do the unnatural. Another characteristic of human nature—perhaps the one that makes us most human—is our capacity to do the unnatural, to transcend and hence transform our own nature.

We lie, of course, not only to others but also to ourselves. The challenges to our adjustment—our maps—from our own consciences and our own realistic perceptions may be every bit as legitimate

and painful as any challenge from the public. Of the myriad lies that people often tell themselves, two of the most common, potent and destructive are "We really love our children" and "Our parents really loved us." It may be that our parents did love us and we do love our children, but when it is not the case, people often go to extraordinary lengths to avoid the realization. I frequently refer to psychotherapy as the "truth game" or the "honesty game" because its business is among other things to help patients confront such lies. One of the roots of mental illness is invariably an interlocking system of lies we have been told and lies we have told ourselves. These roots can be uncovered and excised only in an atmosphere of utter honesty. To create this atmosphere it is essential for therapists to bring to their relationships with patients a total capacity for openness and truthfulness. How can a patient be expected to endure the pain of confronting reality unless we bear the same pain? We can lead only insofar as we go before.

What rules, then, can one follow if one is dedicated to the truth? First, never speak falsehood. Second, bear in mind that the act of withholding the truth is always potentially a lie, and that in each instance in which the truth is withheld a significant moral decision is required. Third, the decision to withhold the truth should never be based on personal needs, such as a need for power, a need to be liked or a need to protect one's map from challenge. Fourth, and conversely, the decision to withhold the truth must always be based entirely upon the needs of the person or people from whom the truth is being withheld. Fifth, the assessment of another's needs is an act of responsibility which is so complex that it can only be executed wisely when one operates with genuine love for the other. Sixth, the primary factor in the assessment of another's needs is the assessment of that person's capacity to utilize the truth for his or her own spiritual growth. Finally, in assessing the capacity of another to utilize the truth for personal spiritual growth, it should be borne in mind that our tendency is generally to underestimate rather than overestimate this capacity.

All this might seem like an extraordinary task,

impossible to ever perfectly complete, a chronic and never-ending burden, a real drag. And it is indeed a never-ending burden of self-discipline, which is why most people opt for a life of very limited honesty and openness and relative closedness, hiding themselves and their maps from the world. It is easier that way. Yet the rewards of the difficult life of honesty and dedication to the truth are more than commensurate with the demands. By virtue of the fact that their maps are continually being challenged, open people are continually growing people. Through their openness they can establish and maintain intimate relationships far more effectively than more closed people. Because they never speak falsely they can be secure and proud in the knowledge that they have done nothing to contribute to the confusion of the world, but have served as

> *"Discipline is the basic set of tools we require to solve life's problems."*

sources of illumination and clarification. Finally, they are totally free to be. They are not burdened by any need to hide. They do not have to slink around in the shadows. They do not have to construct new lies to hide old ones. They need waste no effort covering tracks or maintaining disguises. And ultimately they find that the energy required for the self-discipline of honesty is far less than the energy required for secretiveness. The more honest one is, the easier it is to continue being honest, just as the more lies one has told, the more necessary it is to lie again. By their openness, people dedicated to the truth live in the open, and through the exercise of their courage to live in the open, they become free from fear.

Balancing

By this time I hope it is becoming clear that the exercise of discipline is not only a demanding but also a complex task, requiring both flexibility and judgment. Courageous people must continually push themselves to be completely honest, yet must also possess the capacity to withhold the whole truth when appropriate. To be free people we must assume total responsibility for ourselves, but in doing so must possess the capacity to reject responsibility that is not truly ours. To be organized and efficient, to live wisely, we must daily delay gratification and keep an eye on the future; yet to live joyously we must also possess the capacity, when it is not destructive, to live in the present and act spontaneously. In other words, discipline itself must be disciplined. The type of discipline required to discipline discipline is what I call balancing, and it is the fourth and final type that I would like to discuss here.

Balancing is the discipline that gives us flexibility. Extraordinary flexibility is required for successful living in all spheres of activity. . . .

Mature mental health demands, then, an extraordinary capacity to flexibly strike and continually restrike a delicate balance between conflicting needs, goals, duties, responsibilities, directions, et cetera. The essence of this discipline of balancing is "giving up." I remember first being taught this one summer morning in my ninth year. I had recently learned to ride a bike and was joyously exploring the dimensions of my new skill. About a mile from our house the road went down a steep hill and turned sharply at the bottom. Coasting down the hill on my bike that morning I felt my gathering speed to be ecstatic. To give up this ecstacy by the application of brakes seemed an absurd self-punishment. So I resolved to simultaneously retain my speed and negotiate the corner at the bottom. My ecstasy ended seconds later when I was propelled a dozen feet off the road into the woods. I was badly scratched and bleeding and the front wheel of my new bike was twisted beyond use from its impact against a tree. I had lost my balance.

Balancing is a discipline precisely because the act of giving something up is painful. In this instance I had been unwilling to suffer the pain of giving up my ecstatic speed in the interest of maintaining my balance around the corner. I learned, however, that the loss of balance is ultimately more painful than the giving up required to maintain balance. In one way or another it is a lesson I have continually had to relearn throughout my life. As must everyone, for as we negotiate the curves and corners of our lives, we must continually give up parts of ourselves. The only alternative to this giving up is not to travel at all on the journey of life.

Although an entire book could be written about each one, let me simply list, roughly in order of their occurrence, some of the major conditions, desires and attitudes that must be given up in the course of a wholly successful evolving lifetime:

The state of infancy, in which no external demands need be responded to

The fantasy of omnipotence

The desire for total (including sexual) possession of one's parent(s)

The dependency of childhood

Distorted images of one's parents

The omnipotentiality of adolescence

The "freedom" of uncommitment

The agility of youth

The sexual attractiveness and/or potency of youth

The fantasy of immortality

Authority over one's children

Various forms of temporal power

The independence of physical health

And, ultimately, the self and life itself.

Renunciation and Rebirth

In regard to the last of the above, it may seem to many that the ultimate requirement—to give up one's self and one's life—represents a kind of cruelty on the part of God or fate, which makes our existence a sort of bad joke and which can never be completely accepted. This attitude is particularly true in present-day Western culture, in which the self is held sacred and death is considered an unspeakable insult. Yet the exact opposite is the reality. It is in the giving up of self that human beings can find the most ecstatic and lasting, solid, durable joy of life. And it is death that provides life with all

its meaning. This "secret" is the central wisdom of religion.

The process of giving up the self (which is related to the phenomenon of love, as will be discussed in the next section of this book) is for most of us a gradual process which we get into by a series of fits and starts. One form of temporary giving up of the self deserves special mention because its practice is an absolute requirement for significant learning during adulthood, and therefore for significant growth of the human spirit. I am referring to a subtype of the discipline of balancing which I call "bracketing." Bracketing is essentially the act of balancing the need for stability and assertion of the self with the need for new knowledge and greater understanding by temporarily giving up one's self—putting one's self aside, so to speak—so as to make room for the incorporation of new material into the self. . . .

The discipline of bracketing illustrates the most consequential fact of giving up and of discipline in general: namely, that for all that is given up even more is gained. Self-discipline is a self-enlarging process. The pain of giving up is the pain of death, but death of the old is birth of the new. The pain of death is the pain of birth, and the pain of birth is the pain of death. For us to develop a new and better idea, concept, theory or understanding means that an old idea, concept, theory or understanding must die. . . .

Since birth and death seem to be but different sides of the same coin, it is really not at all unreasonable to pay closer heed than we usually do in the West to the concept of reincarnation. But whether or not we are willing to entertain seriously the possibility of some kind of rebirth occurring simultaneously with our physical death, it is abundantly clear that *this* lifetime is a series of simultaneous deaths and births. "Throughout the whole of life one must continue to learn to live," said Senaca two millennia ago, "and what will amaze you even more, throughout life one must learn to die."[3] It is also clear that the farther one travels on the journey of life, the more births one will experience, and therefore the more deaths—the more joy and the more pain.

---

3. Quoted in Erich Fromm, *The Same Society* (New York: Rinehart, 1955).

This raises the question of whether it is ever possible to become free from emotional pain in this life. Or, putting it more mildly, is it possible to spiritually evolve to a level of consciousness at which the pain of living is at least diminished? The answer is yes and no. The answer is yes, because once suffering is completely accepted, it ceases in a sense to be suffering. It is also yes because the unceasing practice of discipline leads to mastery, and the spiritually evolved person is masterful in the same sense that the adult is masterful in relation to the child. Matters that present great problems for the child and cause it great pain may be of no consequence to the adult at all. Finally, the answer is yes because the spiritually evolved individual is, as will be elaborated in the next section, an extraordinarily loving individual, and with his or her extraordinary love comes extraordinary joy.

The answer is no, however, because there is a vacuum of competence in the world which must be filled. In a world crying out in desperate need for competence, an extraordinarily competent and loving person can no more withhold his or her competence than such a person could deny food to a hungry infant. Spiritually evolved people, by virtue of their discipline, mastery and love, are people of extraordinary competence, and in their competence they are called on to serve the world, and in their love they answer the call. They are inevitably, therefore, people of great power, although the world may generally behold them as quite ordinary people, since more often than not they will exercise their power in quiet or even hidden ways. Nonetheless, exercise power they do, and in this exercise they suffer greatly, even dreadfully. For to exercise power is to make decisions, and the process of making decisions with total awareness is often infinitely more painful than making decisions with limited or blunted awareness (which is the way most decisions are made and why they are ultimately proved wrong). Imagine two generals, each having to decide whether or not to commit a division of ten thousand men to battle. To one the division is but a thing, a unit of personnel, an instrument of strategy and nothing more. To the other it is these things, but he is also aware of each and every one of the ten thousand lives and the lives of the fami-

lies of each of the ten thousand. For whom is the decision easier? It is easier for the general who has blunted his awareness precisely because he cannot tolerate the pain of a more nearly complete awareness: It may be tempting to say, "Ah, but a spiritually evolved man would never become a general in the first place." But the same issue is involved in being a corporation president, a physician, a teacher, a parent. Decisions affecting the lives of others must always be made. The best decision-makers are those who are willing to suffer the most over their decisions but still retain their ability to be decisive. One measure—and perhaps the best measure—of a person's greatness is the capacity for suffering. Yet the great are also joyful. This, then, is the paradox. Buddhists tend to ignore the Buddha's suffering and Christians forget Christ's joy. Buddha and Christ were not different men. The suffering of Christ letting go on the cross and the joy of Buddha letting go under the bo tree are one.

So if your goal is to avoid pain and escape suffering, I would not advise you to seek higher levels of consciousness or spiritual evolution. First, you cannot achieve them without suffering, and second, insofar as you do achieve them, you are likely to be called on to serve in ways more painful to you, or at least demanding of you, than you can now imagine. Then why desire to evolve at all, you may ask. If you ask this question, perhaps you do not know enough of joy. Perhaps you may find an answer in the remainder of this book; perhaps you will not.

A final word on the discipline of balancing and its essence of giving up: you must have something in order to give it up. You cannot give up anything you have not already gotten. If you give up winning without ever having won, you are where you were at the beginning: a loser. You must forge for yourself an identity before you can give it up. You must develop an ego before you can lose it. This may seem incredibly elementary, but I think it is necessary to say it, since there are many people I know who possess a vision of evolution yet seem to lack the will for it. They want, and believe it is possible, to skip over the discipline, to find an easy shortcut to sainthood. Often they attempt to attain it by simply imitating the superficialities of saints, retiring to the desert or taking up carpentry. Some even believe that by such imitation they have really become saints and prophets, and are unable to acknowledge that they are still children and face the painful fact that they must start at the beginning and go through the middle.

Discipline has been defined as a system of techniques of dealing constructively with the pain of problem-solving—instead of avoiding that pain—in such a way that all of life's problems can be solved. Four basic techniques have been distinguished and elaborated: delaying gratification, assumption of responsibility, dedication to the truth or reality, and balancing. Discipline is a *system* of techniques, because these techniques are very much interrelated. In a single act one may utilize two, three or even all of the techniques at the same time and in such a way that they may be indistinguishable from each other. The strength, energy and willingness to use these techniques are provided by love, as will be elaborated in the next section. This analysis of discipline has not been intended to be exhaustive, and it is possible that I have neglected one or more additional basic techniques, although I suspect not. It is also reasonable to ask whether such processes as biofeedback, meditation, yoga, and psychotherapy itself are not techniques of discipline, but to this I would reply that, to my way of thinking, they are technical aids rather than basic techniques. As such they may be very useful but are not essential. On the other hand, the basic techniques herein described, if practiced unceasingly and genuinely, are alone sufficient to enable the practitioner of discipline, or "disciple," to evolve to spiritually higher levels.

Study Questions

1. How is Peck's theory similar to Aristotle's?

2. Do you agree that postponing gratification or pleasure is important in life?

3. Compare Peck's ideas to those of Freud, Kohlberg, and Maslow.

Moral Dilemmas

- In 1970, Laud Humphreys, a sociologist, published a book based on his research concerning sexual encounters between men in public restrooms. After observing the men perform sexual acts in the restrooms, Humphreys copied the license plate numbers of their cars. He used these numbers to find their names and addresses. He then disguised himself and posed as someone conducting a survey on social health. He visited these men in their homes and told them they were randomly selected to participate in the survey. While filling out the survey Humphreys secretly noted their appearance, house furnishings, neighborhood and general life style.

He found out that about half of these men were married; some had children. He also discovered that many were middle class and appeared quite conventional and respectable.

Critics questioned Humphreys's methods. His

disguise and deceptive motives were pointed out. It was also mentioned that these men could have been blackmailed had this private information been available to others.

Humphreys defended himself by arguing that there was no other way to obtain this kind of information since most of these men would have denied they were engaged in any such activity. He pointed out that the sciences of sociology and psychology had benefitted by his research; without deception, this information would never have been uncovered.

What do you think?

■ While on a leisurely boat trip, your mother and a world-famous heart surgeon fall overboard. Neither can swim and you have time to save only one. Your mother is old and needs constant medical care, while the doctor is young and can save many lives.

Whom do you save?

■ Dr. Cluesoh, a psychiatrist, has been counseling Sam, a student at a nearby college, for six

months. Sam has been with Buffy for over a year but their relationship is stormy. Sam is in love with Buffy and cannot bear the idea of her seeing other men.

One day Sam storms into Dr. Cluesoh's office, enraged. He tells his therapist that Buffy left him for his best friend with whom she says she has been sleeping for over a month. Sam feels he has been made a fool. He vows to kill them both and runs out of the office.

Dr. Cluesoh knows that Sam is capable of violence and is a gun collector. He's afraid Sam might do as he says but as a therapist, he is bound by his code of ethics that requires confidentiality and privacy between doctor and patient. This confidentiality is essential if the patient is to trust the doctor and be completely open and honest about his or her problems.

Should Dr. Cluesoh call the police so they can warn Buffy or should he keep Sam's comments confidential? After all, he really doesn't know whether Sam was serious.

Suggested Readings

Feuer, Lewis. *Psychoanalysis and Ethics.* Springfield, Ill.: Charles C. Thomas, 1955.

Flanagan, Owen, and Kathryn Jackson. "Justice, Care and Gender: The Kohlberg-Gilligan Debate Revisited." *Ethics* 97 (April 1987).

Freud, Sigmund. *Five Lectures on Psychoanalysis.* New York: Norton, 1977; and *Civilisation and Its Discontents.* New York: Norton, 1978.

Gay, Peter. *Freud: A Life for Our Time.* New York: Norton, 1988.

Gibbs, John C., and Keith Widaman. *Social Intelligence.* Englewood Cliffs, N.J.: Prentice-Hall, 1982.

Kohlberg, Lawrence. *Essays on Moral Development.* Vol. 1, San Francisco: Harper and Row, 1981.

Snarey, John R. "Cross-Cultural Universality of Social-Moral Development: A Critical Review of Kohlbergian Research." *Psychological Bulletin* 97 (no. 2, 1985).

Morality and
the Law

All societies have laws that set guidelines for what persons can and cannot do. In most societies, murder, theft, and various other kinds of violence are both immoral and illegal, yet some things are illegal in some societies and legal in others. Some countries allow prostitution, pornography, and capital punishment, but others do not. It is also true that most societies distinguish between morality and the law in that not all immoral acts are illegal. For example, it would generally be considered immoral for someone to stand by and do nothing when someone else is drowning, yet in many countries this would not be illegal. Similarly, one may lie to a friend, but most such lies cannot be punished by the law. The philosophical issue is, which immoralities should be illegal and which should not? How much of morality should be translated into laws and enforced by the police and the courts?

Background

As far as we are able to judge, the earliest humans saw law as divine in its origin. Most of these primitive communities did not distinguish among their customs, traditions, morality, and law. All laws and standards for behavior were the expression of divine will, and no conflict could exist within it. As human society evolved and became more complex, conflict between the moral law and positive (human-made) law began to occur. Ancient Greek philosophers and playwrights addressed this problem of individual conscience in opposition to the state and positive law. For example, the dramatist Sophocles (496–406 B.C.), in his play *Antigone,* tells the story of a sister who wishes to bury her dead brother as morality dictates in opposition to her king, who forbids it. Plato and Aristotle believed that an absolute morality exists based on human nature and reason that positive law must aspire to imitate.

Aristotle stressed the need for the rule of law for the common good. However, Western society has moved out of that ancient state in which there was general agreement about a 'common good' into a pluralistic and individualistic world in which deep disagreements occur about whether such a good exists or what its meaning consists in. Even as early as the thirteenth century, St. Thomas Aquinas argued that, although a just system of human law must not contradict the moral law, not everything immoral should be illegal. Human positive law, Aquinas suggested, concerns only the most basic moral duties such as the avoidance of murder and violence (heresy, too!)—the rest of morality is to be enforced by the church and ultimately by God.

One widely debated principle that specifies what should be illegal is the *harm principle*. This principle states that only behavior that harms another must be illegal and punishable. Such acts as murder, rape, and theft that harm others physically or economically must be restricted. Others favor the principle of *legal paternalism,* which includes preventing behavior that harms only the person performing the act. For example, laws that require the wearing of seat belts or motorcycle helmets seek to prevent us from harming ourselves. Still others favor the principle of *legal moralism,* which seeks to prevent immoral behavior even when the behavior does not involve physical harm. Laws against gambling, prostitution, homosexuality, and pornography are sometimes justified on this basis. And finally, some philosophers favor the *offense principle,* which intends to prevent acts that offend or embarrass others. This would prohibit public nudity, public sex, and perhaps even pornography.

Liberal Position: John Stuart Mill

J. S. Mill (1806–1873) was born in England and contributed to many branches of philosophy. In his political philosophy, he defended the harm principle as the proper limit to what kinds of laws we should have. As defined above, the harm principle holds that the only justification for limiting an adult's liberty is to prevent harm to others. That is, government should outlaw only those actions that harm other people, or other-regarding acts, not those actions that harm only the person doing it, what Mill called self-regarding acts. However, the harm principle applies only to rational adults, not to the insane, to the irrational, or to children. The reason the principle does not apply to these kinds of persons, according to Mill, is because these persons do not know what is in their best interest. Rational adults, on the other hand, do know best what they want and need, and therefore their liberty of speech, individuality, and life-style should not be limited if they do not harm others. Harm includes death or physical injury, theft or damage to property, restriction of liberty, damage to reputation, or causing pain of a physical or psychological nature.

Mill believed that the harm principle should determine where we draw the line between morality and the law. To draw the line anywhere else could lead to what he called the "tyranny of the majority" (i.e., the majority imposing its will and way of life on the minority or the individual). Excessive loss of freedom would cause suffering and prohibit social progress. Suffering would ensue because the freedom to be a free individual and to lead the kind of life one wants is, for Mill, an essential part of happiness. Mill was convinced that people are different and that they need to express their differences in the development of worthwhile lives. For a society to restrict individual liberty is for that society to assume that it has all of the truth and that no new ideas or ways of living can be developed that are better; this is why Mill claimed that to restrict human liberty hinders social progress, for progress can only exist if a society is willing to accept the possibility that it could be wrong and is open to new and better ideas. Fallibility, or the possibility that one could be mistaken, is a basic assumption of Mill's philosophy.

Mill's defense of the harm principle has been widely regarded as a basic element of a free society. Nevertheless, his critics question some of the basic assumptions of his theory. Mill seems to assume that people know what is in their best interest and this assumes that people are rational, but are they? Haven't we all seen people behave in emotional and irrational ways, such as using drugs, alcohol, or cigarettes, driving without wearing seat belts, racing cars, and the like? Are people more prisoners of emotion than rational masters of their own destinies? If human beings are not basically rational, then freedom does not lead to happiness or utility but rather to the opposite. Another criticism of Mill is that his view would lead to widespread indifference to the welfare of others, which would produce a cold and impersonal society. Would Mill's view allow people to be nude and perform sex acts in public, since these acts wouldn't physically harm anyone? Mill considers many of these objections in his full discussion in *On Liberty*. In general, Mill concluded that freedom will lead to happiness only if it is a freedom fully informed by education and rationality.

Conservative Position: Patrick Devlin

Mill's point of view has been criticized by Patrick Devlin, a British judge who defends *legal moralism*. He argues that a society is a community of ideas including customs and morals and that it has a right to protect itself and its way of life. Moral ideas are an essential component of a society's identity and existence, and therefore Devlin claims that it has a right to protect its morality even through laws and punishment. A society, then, has a right to enforce its morality even when some immoral actions do not harm any other person, because they may harm the fabric of society.

One can determine the content of a society's morality, according to Devlin, by asking the "reasonable man" in that society. A reasonable man is the average person in the street who decides morality usually on the basis of deeply held feelings. Behavior between consenting adults in private, such as homosexuality, can be illegal if the average person is disgusted by it. Devlin believes that sexual "immorality" is caused by human weakness and that if not controlled, it will lead to the disintegration of society. In this way, immorality is similar to treason, for both can destroy a society's way of life.

H. L. A. Hart

H. L. A. Hart, a contemporary philosopher of law, takes exception to Devlin's position. Hart believes that to assume that a society's morality should be determined by strong emotions of the ordinary citizen is dangerous. Moral judgment should be rationally based on a critical and objective assessment of the importance of various moral rules to the fabric of society. If a lawmaker believes the moral views of a society are based on ignorance and superstition, he or she should not use it as a guide for drafting laws. To compare immorality with treason is ridiculous, Hart argues, because those who engage in what may be considered immorality do not intend the destruction of their society, nor do such acts usually result in society's destruction. Rather, they may influence a society's moral views to begin to change and evolve, which is quite distinct from treason, the violent overthrow of a government. Hart claims that Devlin's view could justify racism, sexism, slavery, the burning of heretics, and other repugnant practices based on the disgust and strong feelings of the people when such practices are sanctioned by the majority. Hart warns that democracy as majority rule does not mean that the minority has no rights.

Paternalism: Joel Feinberg

Legal paternalism is the view that government may restrict the liberty of adults even if they harm only themselves. Joel Feinberg distinguishes between *weak* and *strong paternalism*. Weak paternalism is justified if the actions in question are basically harmful to the agent or are nonvoluntary (coerced, not fully informed or rational, or performed under great emotional stress). Strong paternalism restricts harmful behavior even when the person is fully informed and rational. Feinberg's distinction and support for weak paternalism are based on the belief that adults can be irrational at times, and consequently government can limit their liberty for their own good. Feinberg's view suggests that only voluntary, rational actions are actions of the true self, and consequently only they must be protected from interference by individuals and the state.

Strong paternalism would allow the prohibition of drinking alcohol, smoking cigarettes, eating fried food because all are unhealthy, especially if taken in excess. Feinberg would not ban these activities and products; however, to insure that the risks are voluntarily assumed by those who do indulge in their use, he would hold that government must inform the users of the risks involved. Government may elect to tax these activities and products heavily, but

to outlaw them would be tyrannical. Weak paternalism would not allow the selling of oneself into slavery, or freely being able to purchase deadly and addictive drugs, or committing suicide in most cases. Thus, Feinberg's view echoes Mill's belief that general and individual happiness will result only if freedom is joined by rationality and education.

Finding the Proper Relationship

The proper relationship of morality and the law is an issue that requires certain other questions to be answered. What is the purpose of government? Is it to make us good or to protect our freedom? What is the nature and source of rational morality? Is it God, human nature, reason, or something else? What rights do persons have, and how are they to be justified? Only after resolving these questions would Mill, Devlin, and the others move closer to an agreement.

On Liberty

John Stuart Mill

John Stuart Mill (1806–1873) John Stuart Mill was born in England and educated by his father, James Mill, who was also a philosopher. John Mill was a member of Parliament, a proponent of women's rights and labor unions, and the author of major philosophical works.

The subject of this essay is not the so-called liberty of the will, so unfortunately opposed to the misnamed doctrine of philosophical necessity; but civil, or social liberty: the nature and limits of the power which can be legitimately exercised by society over the individual. A question seldom stated and hardly

From *On Liberty* by John Stuart Mill, first published in 1859. Reprinted by permission from J. M. Dent & Sons, Ltd.

ever discussed in general terms, but which profoundly influences the practical controversies of the age by its latent presence, and is likely soon to make itself recognized as the vital question of the future. It is so far from being new, that, in a certain sense, it has divided mankind almost from the remotest ages; but in the stage of progress into which the more civilized portions of the species have now entered, it presents itself under new conditions, and requires a different and more fundamental treatment.

The struggle between liberty and authority is the most conspicuous feature in the portions of history with which we are earliest familiar, particularly in that of Greece, Rome, and England. But in old times this contest was between subjects, or some classes of subjects, and the government. By liberty, was meant protection against the tyranny of the political rulers. The rulers were conceived (except in some of the popular governments of Greece) as in a necessarily antagonistic position to the people whom they ruled. They consisted of a governing One, or a governing tribe or caste, who derived their authority from inheritance or conquest, who, at all events, did not hold it at the pleasure of the governed, and whose supremacy men did not venture, perhaps did not desire, to contest, whatever precautions might be taken against its oppressive exercise. Their power was regarded as necessary, but also as highly dangerous; as a weapon which they would attempt to use against their subjects, no less than against external enemies. To prevent the weaker members of the community from being preyed upon by innumerable vultures, it was needful that there should be an animal of prey stronger than the rest, commissioned to keep them down. But as the king of the vultures would be no less bent upon preying on the flock than any of the minor harpies, it was indispensable to be in a perpetual attitude of defense against his beak and claws. The aim, therefore, of patriots was to set limits to the power which the ruler should be suffered to exercise over the community; and this limitation was what they meant by liberty. It was attempted in two ways. First, by obtaining a recognition of certain immunities, called political liberties or rights, which it was to be regarded as a breach of duty in the ruler to infringe, and which if he did infringe, specific resistance, or general rebellion, was held to be justifiable. A second, and generally a later expedient, was the establishment of constitutional checks, by which the consent of the community, or of a body of some sort, supposed to represent its interests, was made a necessary condition to some of the more important acts of the governing power. To the first of these modes of limitation, the ruling power, in most European countries, was compelled, more or less, to submit. It was not so with the second; and,

to attain this, or when already in some degree possessed, to attain it more completely, became everywhere the principal object of the lovers of liberty. And so long as mankind were content to combat one enemy by another, and to be ruled by a master, on condition of being guaranteed more or less efficaciously against his tyranny, they did not carry their aspirations beyond this point.

A time, however, came, in the progress of human affairs, when men ceased to think it a necessity of nature that their governors should be an independent power, opposed in interest to themselves. It appeared to them much better that the various magistrates of the State should be their tenants or delegates, revocable at their pleasure. In that way alone, it seemed, could they have complete security that the powers of government would never be abused to their disadvantage. By degrees this new demand for elective and temporary rulers became the prominent object of the exertions of the popular party, wherever any such party existed; and superseded, to a considerable extent, the previous efforts to limit the power of rulers. As the struggle proceeded for making the ruling power emanate from the periodical choice of the ruled, some persons began to think that too much importance had been attached to the limitation of the power itself. *That* (it might seem) was a resource against rulers whose interests were habitually opposed to those of the people. What was now wanted was, that the rulers should be identified with the people; that their interest and will should be the interest and will of the nation. The nation did not need to be protected against its own will. There was no fear of its tyrannizing over itself. Let the rulers be effectually responsible to it, promptly removable by it, and it could afford to trust them with power of which it could itself dictate the use to be made. Their power was but the nation's own power, concentrated, and in a form convenient for exercise. This mode of thought, or rather perhaps of feeling, was common among the last generation of European liberalism, in the Continental section of which it still apparently predominates. Those who admit any limit to what a government may do, except in the case of such governments as they think ought not to exist, stand out as brilliant exceptions among the political thinkers of the Continent. A similar tone of sentiment might by this time have been prevalent in our own country, if the circumstances which for a time encouraged it had continued unaltered.

But in political and philosophical theories, as well as in persons, success discloses faults and infirmities which failure might have concealed from observation. The notion that the people have no need to limit their power over themselves, might seem axiomatic when popular government was a thing only dreamed about, or read of as having existed at some distant period of the past. Neither was that notion necessarily disturbed by such temporary aberrations as those of the French Revolution, the worst of which were the work of a usurping few, and which, in any case, belonged not to the permanent working of popular institutions, but to a sudden and convulsive outbreak against monarchical and aristocratic despotism. In time, however, a democratic republic came to occupy a large portion of the earth's surface, and made itself felt as one of the most powerful members of the community of nations; and elective and responsible government became subject to the observations and criticism which wait upon a great existing fact. It was now perceived that such phrases as "self-government," and the "power of the people over themselves," do not express the true state of the case. The "people" who exercise the power are not always the same people with those over whom it is exercised; and the "self-government" spoken of is not the government of each by himself, but of each by all the rest. The will of the people, moreover, practically means the will of the most numerous or the most active *part* of the people; the majority, or those who succeed in making themselves accepted as the majority: the people, consequently *may* desire to oppress a part of their number, and precautions are as much needed against this as against any other abuse of power. The limitation, therefore, of the power of government over individuals loses none of its importance when the holders of power are regularly accountable to the community, that is, to the strongest party therein. This view of things, recommending itself equally to the intelligence of thinkers and to the inclination of those important classes in European society to whose real or supposed interests democracy is adverse, has had no difficulty in establishing itself; and in political speculations "the tyranny of the majority" is now generally included among the evils against which society requires to be on its guard.

Like other tyrannies, the tyranny of the majority was at first, and is still vulgarly, held in dread chiefly as operating through the acts of the public authorities. But reflecting persons perceived that when society is itself the tyrant—society collectively over the separate individuals who compose it—its means of tyrannizing are not restricted to the acts which it may do by the hands of its political functionaries. Society can and does execute its own mandates; and if it issues wrong mandates instead of right, or any mandates at all in things with which it ought not to meddle, it practices a social tyranny more formidable than many kinds of political oppression, since, though not usually upheld by such extreme penalties, it leaves fewer means of escape, penetrating much more deeply into the details of life, and enslaving the soul itself. Protection, therefore, against the tyranny of the magistrate is not enough: there needs protection also against the tyranny of the prevailing opinion and feeling; against the tendency of society to impose, by other means than civil penalties, its own ideas and practices as rules of conduct on those who dissent from them; to fetter the development, and if possible, prevent the formation, of any individuality not in harmony with its ways, and compels all characters to fashion themselves upon the model of its own. There is a limit to the legitimate interference of collective opinion with individual independence; and to find that limit, and maintain it against encroachment, is as indispensable to a good condition of human affairs, as protection against political despotism.

But though this proposition is not likely to be contested in general terms, the practical question, where to place the limit—how to make the fitting adjustment between individual independence and social control—is a subject on which nearly everything remains to be done. All that makes existence valuable to anyone, depends on the enforcement of restraints upon the actions of other people. Some rules of conduct, therefore, must be imposed, by law in the first place, and by opinion on many things which are not fit subjects for the operation of law. What these rules should be is the principal question in human affairs; but if we except a few of the most obvious cases, it is one of those which least progress has been made in resolving. No two ages, and scarcely any two countries, have decided it alike; and the decision of one age or country is a wonder to another. Yet the people of any given age and country no more suspect any difficulty in it, than if it were a subject on which mankind had always been agreed. The rules which obtain among themselves appear to them self-evident and self-justifying. This all but universal illusion is one of the examples of the magical influence of custom, which is not only, as the proverb says, a second nature, but is continually mistaken for the first. The effect of custom in preventing any misgiving respecting the rules of conduct which mankind impose on one another, is all the more complete because the subject is one on which it is not generally considered necessary that reasons should be given, either by one person to others or by each to himself. People are accustomed to believe, and have been encouraged in the belief by some who aspire to the character of philosophers, that their feelings, on subjects of this nature, are better than reasons, and render reasons unnecessary. The practical principle which guides them to their opinions on the regulation of human conduct, is the feeling in each person's mind that everybody should be required to act as he, and those with whom he sympathizes, would like them to act. No one, indeed, acknowledges to himself that his standard of judgment is his own liking; but an opinion on a point of conduct, not supported by reasons, can only count as one person's preference; and if the reasons, when given, are a mere appeal to a similar preference felt by the other people, it is still only many people's liking instead of one. To an ordinary man, however, his own preference, thus supported, is not only a perfectly satisfactory reason, but the only one he generally has for any of his notions of morality, taste, or propriety, which are not expressly written in his religious creed; and his chief guide in the interpretation even of that. Men's opinions, accordingly, on what is laudable or blamable, are affected by all the multifarious causes which influence their wishes in regard to the conduct of others, and which are as numerous as those which determine their wishes on any other subject. Sometimes their reason, at other times their prejudices or superstitions; often their social affections, not seldom their antisocial ones, their envy or jealousy, their arrogance or contemptuousness: but most commonly their desires or fears for themselves—their legitimate or illegitimate self-interest. Wherever there is an ascendant class, a large portion of the morality of the country emanates from its class interests, and its feelings of class superiority. The morality between Spartans and Helots, between planters and Negroes, between princes and subjects, between nobles and roturiers, between men and women, has been for the most part of the creation of these class interests and feelings; and the sentiments thus generated react in turn upon the moral feelings of the members of the ascendant class, in their relations among themselves. Where, on the other hand, a class, formerly ascendant, has lost its ascendancy, or where its ascendancy is unpopular, the prevailing moral sentiments frequently bear the impress of an impatient dislike of superiority. Another grand determining principle of the rules of conduct, both in act and forbearance, which have been enforced by law or opinion, has been the servility of mankind towards the supposed preferences or aversions of their temporal masters or of their gods. This servility, though essentially selfish, is not hypocrisy; it gives rise to perfectly genuine sentiments of abhorrence; it made men burn magicians and heretics. Among so many baser influences, the general and obvious interests of society have of course had a share, and a large one, in the direction of the moral sentiments; less, however, as a matter of reason, and on their own account, than as a consequence of the sympathies and antipathies which grew out of them; and sympathies and antipathies which had little or nothing to do with the interests of society, have made themselves felt in the establishment of moralities with quite as great force.

The likings and dislikings of society, or of some powerful portion of it, are thus the main thing which has practically determined the rules laid down for general observance, under the penalties of law or opinion. And in general, those who have been in advance of society in thought and feeling, have left this condition of things unassailed in principle, however they may have come into conflict with it in some of its details. They have occupied themselves rather in inquiring what things society ought to like or dislike, than in questioning whether its likings or dislikings should be a law to individuals. They preferred endeavoring to alter the feelings of mankind on the particular points on which they were themselves heretical, rather than make common cause in defense of freedom, with heretics generally.... The great writers of whom the world owes what religious liberty it possesses, have mostly asserted freedom of conscience as an indefeasible right, and denied absolutely that a human being is accountable to others for his religious belief. Yet so natural to mankind is intolerance in whatever they really care about, that religious freedom has hardly anywhere been practically realized, except where religious indifference, which dislikes to have its peace disturbed by theological quarrels, has added its weight to the scale. In the minds of almost all religious persons, even in the most tolerant countries, the duty of toleration is admitted with tacit reserves. One person will bear with dissent in matters of church government, but not of dogma; another can tolerate everybody, short of a Papist or a Unitarian; another everyone who believes in revealed religion; a few extend their charity a little further, but stop at the belief in a God and in a future state. Wherever the sentiment of the majority is still genuine and intense, it is found to have abated little of its claim to be obeyed....

The object of this essay is to assert one very simple principle, as entitled to govern absolutely the dealings of society with the individual in the way of compulsion and control, whether the means used by physical force in the form of legal penalties, or the moral coercion of public opinion. That principle is, that the sole end for which mankind are warranted, individually or collectively, in interfering with the liberty of action of any of their number, is self-protection. That the only purpose for which power can be rightfully exercised over any member of a civilized community, against his will, is to prevent harm to others. His own good, either physical or moral, is not a sufficient warrant. He cannot rightfully be compelled to do or forbear because it will be better for him to do so, because it will

make him happier, because, in the opinions of others, to do so would be wise, or even right. These are good reasons for remonstrating with him, or reasoning with him, or persuading him, or entreating him, but not for compelling him, or visiting him with any evil in case he do otherwise. To justify that, the conduct from which it is desired to deter him must be calculated to produce evil to someone else. The only part of the conduct of anyone, for which he is amenable to society, is that which concerns others. In the part which merely concerns himself, his independence is, of right, absolute. Over himself, over his own body and mind, the individual is sovereign.

> "... [T]he sole end for which mankind are warranted, individually or collectively, in interfering with the liberty of action of any of their number, is self-protection."

It is perhaps hardly necessary to say that this doctrine is meant to apply only to human beings in the maturity of their faculties.... Those who are still in a state to require being taken care of by others, must be protected against their own actions as well as against external injury.... Liberty, as a principle, has no application to any state of things anterior to the time when mankind have become capable of being improved by free and equal discussion. Until then, there is nothing for them but implicit obedience to an Akbar or a Charlemagne, if they are so fortunate as to find one. But as soon as mankind have attained the capacity of being guided to their own improvement by conviction or persuasion..., compulsion, either in the direct form or in that of pains and penalties for noncompliance, is no longer admissible as a means to their own good, and justifiable only for the security of others.

It is proper to state that I forego any advantage which could be derived to my argument from the idea of abstract right, as a thing independent of utility. I regard utility as the ultimate appeal on all ethical questions; but it must be utility in the largest sense, grounded on the permanent interests of a man as a progressive being. Those interests, I contend, authorized the subjection of individual spontaneity to external control, only in respect to those actions of each which concern the interest of other people. If anyone does an act hurtful to others, there is a *prima facie* case for punishing him, by law, or, where legal penalties are not safely applicable, by general disapprobation. There are also many positive acts for the benefit of others, which he may rightfully be compelled to perform: such as to give evidence in a court of justice; to bear his fair share in the common defense, or in any other joint work necessary to the interest of the society of which he enjoys the protection; and to perform certain acts of individual beneficence, such as saving a fellow-creature's life, or interposing to protect the defenseless against ill-usage, things which whenever it is obviously a man's duty to do, he may rightfully be made responsible to society for not doing. A person may cause evil to others not only by his actions but by his inaction, and in either case he is justly accountable to them for the injury. The latter case, it is true, requires a much more cautious exercise of compulsion than the former. To make anyone answerable for doing evil to others is the rule; to make him answerable for not preventing evil is comparatively speaking, the exception. Yet there are many cases clear enough and grave enough to justify that exception. In all things which regard the external relations of the individual, he is *de jure* amenable to those whose interests are concerned, and, if need be, to society as their protector. There are often good reasons for not holding him to the responsibility; but these reasons must arise from the special expediencies of the case; either because it is a kind of case in which he is on the whole likely to act better, when left to his own discretion, than when controlled in any way in which society have it in their power to control him; or because the attempt to exercise control would produce other evils, greater than those which it would prevent. When such reasons as these preclude the enforce-

ment of responsibility, the conscience of the agent himself should step into the vacant judgment seat, and protect those interests of others which have no external protection; judging himself all the more rigidly, because the case does not admit of his being made accountable to the judgment of his fellow-creatures.

But there is a sphere of action in which society, as distinguished from the individual, has, if any, only an indirect interest; comprehending all that portion of a person's life and conduct which affects only himself, or if it also affects others, only with their free, voluntary, and undeceived consent and participation. When I say only himself, I mean directly, and in the first instance; for whatever affects himself, may affect others through himself; and the objection which may be grounded on this contingency, will receive consideration in the sequel. This, then, is the appropriate region of human liberty. It comprises, *first,* the inward domain of consciousness; demanding liberty of conscience in the most comprehensive sense; liberty of thought and feeling; absolute freedom of opinion and sentiment on all subjects, practical or speculative, scientific, moral, or theological. The liberty of expressing and publishing opinions may seem to fall under a different principle, since it belongs to that part of the conduct of an individual which concerns other people; but, being almost of as much importance as the liberty of thought itself, and resting in great part on the same reasons, is practically inseparable from it. *Secondly,* the principle requires liberty of tastes and pursuits; of framing the plan of our life to suit our own character; of doing as we like, subject to such consequences as may follow: without impediment from our fellow-creatures, so long as what we do does not harm them, even though they should think our conduct foolish, perverse, or wrong. *Thirdly,* from this liberty of each individual, follows the liberty, within the same limits, of combination among individuals; freedom to unite for any purpose not involving harm to others: the persons combining being supposed to be of full age, and not forced or deceived.

No society in which these liberties are not, on the whole, respected, is free, whatever may be its form of government; and none is completely free in which they do not exist absolute and unqualified.

The only freedom which deserves the name, is that of pursuing our own good in our own way, so long as we do not attempt to deprive others of theirs, or impede their efforts to obtain it. Each is the proper guardian of his own health, whether bodily, or mental and spiritual. Mankind are greater gainers by suffering each other to live as seems good to themselves, than by compelling each to live as seems good to the rest. . . .

The time, it is to be hoped, is gone by, when any defence would be necessary of the "liberty of the press" as one of the securities against corrupt or tyrannical government. No argument, we may suppose, can now be needed, against permitting a legislature or an executive, not identified in interest with the people, to prescribe opinions to them, and determine what doctrines or what arguments they shall be allowed to hear. This aspect of the question, besides, has been so often and so triumphantly enforced by preceding writers, that it need not be specially insisted on in this place. Though the law of England, on the subject of the press, is as servile to this day as it was in the time of the Tudors, there is little danger of its being actually put in force against political discussion, except during some temporary panic, when fear of insurrection drives ministers and judges from their propriety; and, speaking generally, it is not, in constitutional countries, to be apprehended, that the government, whether completely responsible to the people or not, will often attempt to control the expression of opinion, except when in doing so it makes itself the organ of the general intolerance of the public. Let us suppose, therefore, that the government is entirely at one with the people, and never thinks of exerting any power of coercion unless in agreement with what it conceives to be their voice. But I deny the right of the people to exercise such coercion, either by themselves or by their government. The power itself is illegitimate. The best government has no more title to it than the worst. It is as noxious, or more noxious, when exerted in accordance with public opinion, than when in opposition to it. If all mankind minus one, were of one opinion, and only one person were of the contrary opinion, mankind would be no more justified in silencing that one person, than he, if he had the power, would be justified in silencing mankind. Were an opinion a per-

sonal possession of no value except to the owner; if to be obstructed in the enjoyment of it were simply a private injury, it would make some difference whether the injury was inflicted only on a few persons or on many. But the peculiar evil of silencing the expression of an opinion is, that it is robbing the human race; posterity as well as the existing generation; those who dissent from the opinion, still more than those who hold it. If the opinion is right, they are deprived of the opportunity of exchanging error for truth: if wrong, they lose, what is almost as great a benefit, the clearer perception and livelier impression of truth, produced by its collision with error. . . .

As it is useful that while mankind are imperfect there should be different opinions, so is it that there should be different experiments of living; that free scope should be given to varieties of character, short of injury to others; and that the worth of different modes of life should be proved practically, when any one thinks fit to try them. It is desirable, in short, that in things which do not primarily concern others, individuality should assert itself. Where, not the person's own character, but the traditions or customs of other people are the rule of conduct, there is wanting one of the principal ingredients of human happiness, and quite the chief ingredient of individual and social progress.

In maintaining this principle, the greatest difficulty to be encountered does not lie in the appreciation of means towards an acknowledged end, but in the indifference of persons in general to the end itself. If it were felt that the free development of individuality is one of the leading essentials of wellbeing; that it is not only a co-ordinate element with all like that is designated by the terms civilization, instruction, education, culture, but is itself a necessary part and condition of all those things; there would be no danger that liberty should be undervalued, and the adjustment of the boundaries between it and social control would present no extraordinary difficulty. But the evil is, that individual spontaneity is hardly recognized by the common modes of thinking, as having any intrinsic worth, or deserving any regard on its own account. . . .

He who lets the world, or his own portion of it, choose his plan of life for him, has no need of any other faculty than the ape-like one of imitation. He who chooses his plan for himself, employs all his faculties. He must use observation to see, reasoning and judgment to foresee, activity to gather materials for decision, discrimination to decide, and when he has decided, firmness and self-control to hold to his deliberate decision. And these qualities he requires and exercises exactly in proportion as the part of his conduct which he determines according to his own judgment and feelings is a large one. It is possible that he might be guided in some good path, and kept out of harm's way, without any of these things. But what will be his comparative worth as a human being? It really is of importance, not only what men do, but also what manner of men they are that do it. Among the works of man, which human life is rightly employed in perfecting and beautifying, the first in importance surely is man himself. Supposing it were possible to get houses built, corn grown, battles fought, causes tried, and even churches erected and prayers said, by machinery—by automatons in human form—it would be a considerable loss to exchange for these automatons even the men and women who at present inhabit the more civilized parts of the world, and who assuredly are but starved specimens of what nature can and will produce. Human nature is not a machine to be built after a model, and set to do exactly the work prescribed for it, but a tree, which requires to grow and develop itself on all sides, according to the tendency of the inward forces which make it a living thing. . . .

Study Questions

1. Does liberty lead to happiness?
2. Are human beings basically rational?
3. Would Mill allow public nudity?

The Enforcement of Morals

Patrick Devlin is a contemporary British judge. In addition to The Enforcement of Morals, *he has authored* Too Proud to Fight: Woodrow Wilson's Neutrality.

Lord Patrick Devlin

. . . In jurisprudence, as I have said, everything is thrown open to discussion and, in the belief

that they cover the whole field, I have framed three interrogatories addressed to myself to answer:

1. Has society the right to pass judgement at all on matters of morals? Ought there, in other words,

to be a public morality, or are morals always a matter for private judgement?

2. If society has the right to pass judgement, has it also the right to use the weapon of the law to enforce it?

3. If so, ought it to use that weapon in all cases or only in some; and if only in some, on what principles should it distinguish?

I shall begin with the first interrogatory and consider what is meant by the right of society to pass a moral judgement, that is, a judgement about what is good and what is evil. . . . What makes a society of any sort is community of ideas, not only political ideas but also ideas about the way its members should behave and govern their lives; these latter ideas are its morals. Every society has a moral structure as well as a political one: or rather, since that might suggest two independent systems, I should say that the structure of every society is made up both of politics and morals. Take, for example, the institution of marriage. Whether a man should be allowed to take more than one wife is something about which every society has to make up its mind one way or the other. In England we believe in the Christian idea of marriage and therefore adopt monogamy as a moral principle. Consequently the Christian institution of marriage has become the basis of family life and so part of the structure of our society. It is there not because it is Christian. It has got there because it is Christian, but it remains there because it is built into the house in which we live and could not be removed without bringing it down. The great majority of those who live in this country accept it because it is the Christian idea of marriage and for them the only true one. But a non-Christian is bound by it, not because it is part of Christianity but because, rightly or wrongly, it has been adopted by the society in which he lives. It would be useless for him to stage a debate designed to prove that polygamy was theologically more correct and socially preferable; if he wants to live in the house, he must accept it as built in the way in which it is.

We see this more clearly if we think of ideas or institutions that are purely political. Society cannot tolerate rebellion; it will not allow argument about the rightness of the cause. Historians a century later may say that the rebels were right and the Government was wrong and a percipient and conscientious subject of the State may think so at the time. But it is not a matter which can be left to individual judgement.

The institution of marriage is a good example for my purpose because it bridges the division, if there is one, between politics and morals. Marriage is part of the structure of our society and it is also the basis of a moral code which condemns fornication and adultery. The institution of marriage would be gravely threatened if individual judgements were permitted about the morality of adultery; on these points there must be a public morality. But public morality is not to be confined to those moral principles which support institutions such as marriage. People do not think of monogamy as something which has to be supported because our society has chosen to organize itself upon it; they think of it as something that is good in itself and offering a good way of life and that it is for that reason that our society has adopted it. I return to the statement that I have already made, that society means a community of ideas; without shared ideas on politics, morals, and ethics no society can exist. Each one of us has ideas about what is good and what is evil; they cannot be kept private from the society in which we live. If men and women try to create a society in which there is no fundamental agreement about good and evil they will fail; if, having based it on common agreement, the agreement goes, the society will disintegrate. For society is not something that is kept together physically; it is held by the invisible bonds of common thought. If the bonds were too far relaxed the members would drift apart. A common morality is part of the bondage. The bondage is part of the price of society; and mankind, which needs society, must pay its price. . . .

You may think that I have taken far too long in contending that there is such a thing as public morality, a proposition which most people would readily accept, and may have left myself too little time to discuss the next question which to many minds may cause greater difficulty: to what extent should society use the law to enforce its moral judgements? But I believe that the answer to the first question determines the way in which the second should be approached and may indeed very nearly dictate the answer to the second question. If society has no right to make judgements on morals, the law must find some special justification for entering the field of morality: if homosexuality and prostitution are not in themselves wrong, then the onus is very clearly on the lawgiver who wants to frame a law against certain aspects of them to justify the exceptional treatment. But if society has the right to make a judgement and has it on the basis that a recognized morality is as necessary to society as, say, a recognized government, then society may use the law to preserve morality in the same way as it uses it to safeguard anything else that is essential to its existence. If therefore the first proposition is securely established with all its implications, society has a prima facie right to legislate against immorality as such. . . .

I think, . . . that it is not possible to set theoretical limits to the power of the State to legislate against immorality. It is not possible to settle in advance exceptions to the general rule or to define inflexibly areas of morality into which the law is in no circumstances to be allowed to enter. Society is entitled by means of its law to protect itself from dangers, whether from within or without. Here again I think that the political parallel is legitimate. The law of treason is directed against aiding the king's enemies and against sedition from within. The justification of this is that established government is necessary for the existence of society and therefore its safety against violent overthrow must be secured. But an established morality is as necessary as good government to the welfare of society. Societies disintegrate from within more frequently than they are broken up by external pressures. There is disintegration when no common morality is observed and history shows that the loosening of moral bonds is often the first stage of disintegration, so that society is justified in taking the same steps to preserve its moral code as it does to preserve its government and other essential institutions. The suppression of vice is as much the law's business as the suppression of subversive activities; it is no more possible to define a sphere of private morality than it is to define one of private subversive activity. It is wrong to talk of private morality or of the law not being concerned with immorality as such or to try to set rigid bounds to the part which the law

may play in the suppression of vice. There are no theoretical limits to the power of the State to legislate against treason and sedition, and likewise I think there can be no theoretical limits to legislation against immorality. You may argue that if a man's sins affect only himself it cannot be the concern of society. If he chooses to get drunk every night in the privacy of his own home, is any one except himself the worse for it? But suppose a quarter or a half of the population got drunk every night, what sort of society would it be? You cannot set a theoretical limit to the number of people who can get drunk before society is entitled to legislate against drunkenness. The same may be said of gambling. . . .

In what circumstances the State should exercise its power is the third of the interrogatories I have framed. But before I get to it I must raise a point which might have been brought up in any one of the three. How are the moral judgements of society to be ascertained? By leaving it until now, I can ask it in the more limited form that is now sufficient for my purpose. How is the law-maker to ascertain the moral judgements of society? It is surely not enough that they should be reached by the opinion of the majority; it would be too much to require the individual assent of every citizen. English law has evolved and regularly uses a standard which does not depend on the counting of heads. It is that of the reasonable man. He is not to be confused with the rational man. He is not expected to reason about anything and his judgement may be largely a matter of feeling. It is the viewpoint of the man in the street—or to use an archaism familiar to all lawyers—the man in the Clapham omnibus. He might also be called the right-minded man. For my purpose I should like to call him the man in the jury box, for the moral judgement of society must be something about which any twelve men or women drawn at random might after discussion be expected to be unanimous. This was the standard the judges applied in the days before Parliament was as active as it is now and when they laid down rules of public policy. They did not think of themselves as making law but simply as stating principles which every right-minded person would accept as valid. It is what Pollock called 'practical morality,' which is based not on theological or philosophical foundations but 'in the mass of continuous experience half-consciously or unconsciously accumulated and embodied in the morality of common sense.' He called it also 'a certain way of thinking on questions of morality which we expect to find in a reasonable civilized man or a reasonable Englishman, taken at random.'[1]

Immorality then, for the purpose of the law, is what every right-minded person is presumed to consider to be immoral. Any immorality is capable of affecting society injuriously and in effect to a greater or lesser extent it usually does; this is what gives the law its *locus standi*. It cannot be shut out. But—and this brings me to the third question—the individual has a *locus standi* too; he cannot be ex-

> *"... [S]ociety means a community of ideas; without shared ideas on politics, morals, and ethics no society can exist."*

pected to surrender to the judgement of society the whole conduct of his life. It is the old and familiar question of striking a balance between the rights and interests of society and those of the individual. This is something which the law is constantly doing in matters large and small. To take a very down-to-earth example, let me consider the right of the individual whose house adjoins the highway to have access to it; that means in these days the right to have vehicles stationary in the highway, sometimes for a considerable time if there is a lot of loading or unloading. There are many cases in which the courts have had to balance the private right of access against the public right to use the highway without obstruction. It cannot be done by carving up the highway into public and private areas. It is done by

1. *Essays in Jurisprudence and Ethics* (1882), Macmillan, pp. 278 and 353.

recognizing that each have rights over the whole; that if each were to exercise their rights to the full, they would come into conflict; and therefore that the rights of each must be curtailed so as to ensure as far as possible that the essential needs of each are safeguarded.

I do not think that one can talk sensibly of a public and private morality any more than one can of a public or private highway. Morality is a sphere in which there is a public interest and a private interest, often in conflict, and the problem is to reconcile the two. This does not mean that it is impossible to put forward any general statements about how in our society the balance ought to be struck. Such statements cannot of their nature be rigid or precise; they would not be designed to circumscribe the operation of the law-making power but to guide those who have to apply it. While every decision which a court of law makes when it balances the public against the private interest is an *ad hoc* decision, the cases contain statements of principle to which the court should have regard when it reaches its decision. In the same way it is possible to make general statements of principle which it may be thought the legislature should bear in mind when it is considering the enactment of laws enforcing morals.

I believe that most people would agree upon the chief of these elastic principles. There must be toleration of the maximum individual freedom that is consistent with the integrity of society.... The principle appears to me to be peculiarly appropriate to all questions of morals. Nothing should be punished by the law that does not lie beyond the limits of tolerance. It is not nearly enough to say that a majority dislike a practice; there must be a real feeling of reprobation.... We should ask ourselves in the first instance whether, looking at it calmly and dispassionately, we regard it as a vice so abominable that its mere presence is an offense. If that is the genuine feeling of the society in which we live, I do not see how society can be denied the right to eradicate it. Our feeling may not be so intense as that. We may feel about it that, if confined, it is tolerable, but that if spread it might be gravely injurious; it is in this way that most societies look upon fornication, seeing it as a natural weakness which must be kept within bounds but which cannot be rooted out. It becomes then a question of balance, the danger to society in one scale and the extent of the restriction in the other....

The limits of tolerance shift. This is supplementary to what I have been saying but of sufficient importance in itself to deserve statement as a separate principle which law-makers have to bear in mind.... It may be that over-all tolerance is always increasing. The pressure of the human mind, always seeking greater freedom of thought, is outwards against the bonds of society forcing their gradual relaxation. It may be that history is a tale of contraction and expansion and that all developed societies are on their way to dissolution. I must not speak of things I do not know; and anyway as a practical matter no society is willing to make provision for its own decay. I return therefore to the simple and observable fact that in matters of morals the limits of tolerance shift. Laws, especially those which are based on morals, are less easily moved. It follows as another good working principle that in any new matter of morals the law should be slow to act. By the next generation the swell of indignation may have abated and the law be left without the strong backing which it needs. But it is then difficult to alter the law without giving the impression that moral judgement is being weakened....

A third elastic principle must be advanced more tentatively. It is that as far as possible privacy should be respected. This is not an idea that has ever been made explicit in the criminal law. Acts or words done or said in public or in private are all brought within its scope without distinction in principle. But there goes with this a strong reluctance on the part of judges and legislators to sanction invasions of privacy in the detection of crime. The police have no more right to trespass than the ordinary citizen has; there is no general right of search; to this extent an Englishman's home is still his castle. The Government is extremely careful in the exercise even of those powers which it claims to be undisputed. Telephone tapping and interference with the mails afford a good illustration of this....

This indicates a general sentiment that the right to privacy is something to be put in the balance against the enforcement of the law. Ought the same sort of consideration to play any part in the formation of the law? Clearly only in a very limited number of cases. When the help of the law is invoked by an injured citizen, privacy must be irrelevant; the individual cannot ask that his right to privacy should be measured against injury criminally done to another. But when all who are involved in the deed are consenting parties and the injury is done to morals, the public interest in the moral order can be balanced against the claims of privacy....

Study Questions

1. Is immorality the same as treason?

2. Is morality a matter of deeply held feelings?

3. Does every society have a right to exist?

4. Will Devlin's view lead to the tyranny of the majority?

Immorality and Treason

Formerly professor of law at Oxford University, H. L. A. Hart is the author of The Concept of Law *and other writings on the philosophy of law.*

H. L. A. Hart

The most remarkable feature of Sir Patrick's lecture is his view of the nature of morality—the morality which the criminal law may enforce. Most previous thinkers who have repudiated the liberal point of view have done so because they thought that morality consisted either of divine commands or of rational principles of human conduct discoverable by human reason. Since morality for them had this elevated divine or rational status as the law of God or reason, it seemed obvious that the state should enforce it, and that the function of human law should not be merely to provide men with the opportunity for leading a good life, but actually to see that they lead it. Sir Patrick does not rest his repudiation of the liberal point of view on these religious or rationalist conceptions. Indeed much that he writes reads like an abjuration of the notion that reasoning or thinking has much to do with morality. English popular morality has no doubt its historical connexion with the Christian religion: 'That,' says Sir Patrick, 'is how it got there.' But it does not owe its present status or social significance to religion any more than to reason.

What, then, is it? According to Sir Patrick it is primarily a matter of feeling. 'Every moral judgment,' he says, 'is a feeling that no right-minded man could act in any other way without admitting that he was doing wrong.' Who then must feel this way if we are to have what Sir Patrick calls a public morality? He tells us that it is 'the man in the street,'

"Immorality and Treason" originally appeared in *The Listener* (July 30, 1959), pp. 162–163, and it is reprinted here by permission of the author.

'the man in the jury box,' or (to use the phrase so familiar to English lawyers) 'the man on the Clapham omnibus.' For the moral judgments of society so far as the law is concerned are to be ascertained by the standards of the reasonable man, and he is not to be confused with the rational man. Indeed, Sir Patrick says 'he is not expected to reason about anything and his judgment may be largely a matter of feeling.'

Intolerance, Indignation, and Disgust

But what precisely are the relevant feelings, the feelings which may justify use of the criminal law? Here the argument becomes a little complex. Widespread dislike of a practice is not enough. There must, says Sir Patrick, be 'a real feeling of reprobation.' Disgust is not enough either. What is crucial is a combination of intolerance, indignation, and disgust. These three are the forces behind the moral law, without which it is not 'weighty enough to deprive the individual of freedom of choice.' Hence there is, in Sir Patrick's outlook, a crucial difference between the mere adverse moral judgment of society and one which is inspired by feeling raised to the concert pitch of intolerance, indignation, and disgust.

This distinction is novel and also very important. For on it depends the weight to be given to the fact that when morality is enforced individual liberty is necessarily cut down. Though Sir Patrick's abstract formulation of his views on this point is hard to follow, his examples make his position fairly clear. We can see it best in the contrasting things he says about fornication and homosexuality. In regard to fornication, public feeling in most societies is not now of the concert-pitch intensity. We may feel that it is tolerable if confined: only its spread might be gravely injurious. In such cases the question whether individual liberty should be restricted is for Sir Patrick a question of balance between the danger to society in the one scale, and the restriction of the individual in the other. But if, as may be the case with homosexuality, public feeling is up to concert pitch, if it expresses a 'deliberate judgment' that a practice as such is injurious to society, if there is 'a genuine feeling that it is a vice so abominable that its mere presence is an offence,' then it is beyond the limits of tolerance, and society may eradicate it. In this case, it seems, no further balancing of the claims of individual liberty is to be done, though as a matter of prudence the legislator should remember that the popular limits of tolerance may shift: the concert pitch feeling may subside. This may produce a dilemma for the law; for the law may then be left without the full moral backing that it needs, yet it cannot be altered without giving the impression that the moral judgment is being weakened.

A Shared Morality

If this is what morality is—a compound of indignation, intolerance, and disgust—we may well ask what justification there is for taking it, and turning it as such, into criminal law with all the misery which criminal punishment entails. Here Sir Patrick's answer is very clear and simple. A collection of individuals is not a society; what makes them into a society is among other things a shared or public morality. This is as necessary to its existence as an organized government. So society may use the law to preserve its morality like anything else essential to it. 'The suppression of vice is as much the law's business as the suppression of subversive activities.' The liberal point of view which denies this is guilty of 'an error in jurisprudence': for it is no more possible to define an area of private morality than an area of private subversive activity. There can be no

'theoretical limits' to legislation against immorality just as there are no such limits to the power of the state to legislate against treason and sedition.

Surely all this, ingenious as it is, is misleading. Mills' formulation of the liberal point of view may well be too simple. The grounds for interfering with human liberty are more various than the single criterion of 'harm to others' suggests: cruelty to animals or organizing prostitution for gain do not, as Mill himself saw, fall easily under the description of harm to others. Conversely, even where there is harm to others in the most literal sense, there may well be other principles limiting the extent to which harmful activities should be repressed by law. So there are multiple criteria, not a single criterion, determining when human liberty may be restricted. Perhaps this is what Sir Patrick means by a curious distinction which he often stresses between theoretical and practical limits. But with all its simplicities the liberal point of view is a better guide than Sir Patrick to clear thought on the proper relation of morality to the criminal law: for it stresses what he obscures—namely, the points at which thought is needed before we turn popular morality into criminal law.

Society and Moral Opinion

No doubt we would all agree that a consensus of moral opinion on certain matters is essential if society is to be worth living in. Laws against murder, theft, and much else would be of little use if they were not supported by a widely diffused conviction that what these laws forbid is also immoral. So much is obvious. But it does not follow that everything to which the moral vetoes of accepted morality attach is of equal importance to society; nor is there the slightest reason for thinking of morality as a seamless web: one which will fall to pieces carrying society with it, unless all its emphatic vetoes are enforced by law. Surely even in the face of the moral feeling that is up to concert pitch—the trio of intolerance, indignation, and disgust—we must pause to think. We must ask a question at two different levels which Sir Patrick never clearly enough identifies or separates. First, we must ask whether a practice which offends moral feeling is harmful, independently of its repercussion on the general moral code. Secondly, what about repercussion on the moral code? Is it really true that failure to translate this item of general morality into criminal law will jeopardize the whole fabric of morality and so of society?

We cannot escape thinking about these two different questions merely by repeating to ourselves the vague nostrum: 'This is part of public morality and public morality must be preserved if society is to exist.' Sometimes Sir Patrick seems to admit this, for he says in words which both Mill and the Wolfenden Report might have used, that there must be the maximum respect for individual liberty consistent with the integrity of society. Yet this, as his contrasting examples of fornication and homosexuality show, turns out to mean only that the immorality which the law may punish must be generally felt to be intolerable. This plainly is no adequate substitute for a reasoned estimate of the damage to the fabric of society likely to ensue if it is not suppressed.

Nothing perhaps shows more clearly the inadequacy of Sir Patrick's approach to this problem than his comparison between the suppression of sexual immorality and the suppression of treason or subversive activity. Private subversive activity is, of course, a contradiction in terms because 'subversion' means overthrowing government, which is a public thing. But it is grotesque, even where moral feeling against homosexuality is up to concert pitch, to think of the homosexual behaviour of two adults in private as in any way like treason or sedition either in intention or effect. We can make it *seem* like treason only if we assume that deviation from a general moral code is bound to affect that code, and to lead not merely to its modification but to its destruction. The analogy could begin to be plausible only if it was clear that offending against this item of morality was likely to jeopardize the whole structure. But we have ample evidence for believing that people will not abandon morality, will not think any better of murder, cruelty, and dishonesty, merely because some private sexual practice which they abominate is not punished by the law.

Because this is so the analogy with treason is absurd. Of course 'No man is an island': what one man does in private, if it is known, may affect others in many different ways. Indeed it may be that deviation from general sexual morality by those whose lives, like the lives of many homosexuals, are noble ones and in all other ways exemplary will lead to what Sir Patrick calls the shifting of the limits of tolerance. But if this has any analogy in the sphere of government it is not the overthrow of ordered government, but a peaceful change in its form. So we may listen to the promptings of common sense and of logic, and say that though there could not logically be a sphere of private treason there is a sphere of private morality and immorality.

Sir Patrick's doctrine is also open to a wider, perhaps a deeper, criticism. In his reaction against a rationalist morality and his stress on feeling, he has I think thrown out the baby and kept the bath

"Certainly there is a special risk in a democracy that the majority may dictate how all should live."

water; and the bath water may turn out to be very dirty indeed. When Sir Patrick's lecture was first delivered *The Times* greeted it with these words: 'There is a moving and welcome humility in the conception that society should not be asked to give its reason for refusing to tolerate what in its heart it feels intolerable.' This drew from a correspondent in Cambridge the retort: 'I am afraid that we are less humble than we used to be. We once burnt old women because, without giving our reasons, we felt in our hearts that witchcraft was intolerable.'

This retort is a bitter one, yet its bitterness is salutary. We are not, I suppose, likely, in England, to take again to the burning of old women for witch-craft or to punishing people for associating with those of a different race or colour, or to punishing people again for adultery. Yet if these things were viewed with intolerance, indignation, and disgust, as the second of them still is in some countries, it seems that on Sir Patrick's principles no rational criticism could be opposed to the claim that they should be punished by law. We could only pray, in his words, that the limits of tolerance might shift.

Curious Logic

It is impossible to see what curious logic has led Sir Patrick to this result. For him a practice is immoral if the thought of it makes the man on the Clapham omnibus sick. So be it. Still, why should we not summon all the resources of our reason, sympa-thetic understanding, as well as critical intelligence, and insist that before general moral feeling is turned into criminal law it is submitted to scrutiny of a different kind from Sir Patrick's? Surely, the legislator should ask whether the general morality is based on ignorance, superstition, or misunder-standing; whether there is a false conception that those who practise what it condemns are in other ways dangerous or hostile to society; and whether the misery to many parties, the blackmail and the other evil consequences of criminal punishment, es-

pecially for sexual offences, are well understood. It is surely extraordinary that among the things which Sir Patrick says are to be considered before we leg-islate against immorality these appear nowhere; not even as 'practical considerations,' let alone 'theoreti-cal limits.' To any theory which, like this one, asserts that the criminal law may be used on the vague ground that the preservation of morality is es-sential to society and yet omits to stress the need for critical scrutiny, our reply should be: 'Morality, what crimes may be committed in thy name!'

As Mill saw, and de Tocqueville showed in detail long ago in his critical but sympathetic study of de-mocracy, it is fatally easy to confuse the democratic principle that power should be in the hands of the majority with the utterly different claim that the ma-jority, with power in their hands, need respect no limits. Certainly there is a special risk in a democ-racy that the majority may dictate how all should live. This is the risk we run, and should gladly run; for it is the price of all that is so good in demo-cratic rule. But loyalty to democratic principles does not require us to maximize this risk: yet this is what we shall do if we mount the man in the street on the top of the Clapham omnibus and tell him that if only he feels sick enough about what other people do in private to demand its suppression by law no theoretical criticism can be made of his demand.

Study Questions

1. Would Devlin's view allow for slavery and racism?

2. If a society's moral views are based on ignorance and superstition, should the lawmaker ignore them?

Legal Paternalism

Joel Feinberg is a professor of philosophy at the University of Arizona and author of several books on social philosophy, most recently The Moral Limits of the Criminal Law.

Joel Feinberg

The principle of legal paternalism justifies state coercion to protect individuals from self-inflicted harm or, in its extreme version, to guide them, whether they like it or not, toward their own good. Parents can be expected to justify their interference in the lives of their children (e.g., telling them what they must eat and when they must sleep) on the ground that "We know best." Legal paternalism seems to imply that since the state often can know the interests of individual citizens better than the citizens know them themselves, it stands as a permanent guardian of those interests *in loco parentis.* Put in this blunt way, paternalism seems a preposterous doctrine. If adults are treated as children they will come in time to be like children. Deprived of the right to choose for themselves, they will soon lose the power of rational judgment and decision. Even children, after a certain point, had better not be treated as children; otherwise they will never acquire the outlook and capability of responsible adults.

Yet if we reject paternalism entirely, and deny that a person's own good is *ever* a valid ground for coercion, we seem to fly in the face of both common sense and our long established customs and laws. In the criminal law, for example, a prospective victim's freely granted consent is no defense to the charge of mayhem or homicide. The state simply refuses to permit people to agree to their own dis-

Joel Feinberg, "Legal Paternalism," *Canadian Journal of Philosophy,* 1, no. 1, pp. 106–24. Copyright © 1971 by the Canadian Association for Publishing in Philosophy. Reprinted with permission.

ablement or killing. The law of contracts, similarly, refuses to recognize as valid contracts to sell oneself into slavery, or to become a mistress, or to enter a bigamous marriage. Any ordinary citizen is legally justified in using reasonable force to prevent another's self-mutilation or suicide. No one is allowed to purchase certain drugs, even for therapeutic purposes, without a physician's prescription ("Doctor knows best"). The use of other drugs, such as heroin, merely for pleasure is permitted under no circumstances whatever. It is hard to find any plausible rationale for such restrictions apart from the arguments that beatings, mutilations, and death, concubinage, slavery, and bigamy are always bad for a person, whether he or she knows it or not, and that antibiotics are too dangerous for any non-expert, and heroin for anyone at all, to take on his or her own initiative.

The trick to stopping short once we undertake this path, unless we wish to ban whiskey, cigarettes, and fried foods, which tend to be bad for people too, whether they know it or not. The problem is to reconcile somehow our general repugnance for paternalism with the apparent necessity, or at least the reasonableness, of some paternalistic regulations. My method of dealing with this problem will not be particularly ideological. Rather, I shall try to organize our elementary intuitions by finding a principle that will render them consistent. Let us begin, then, by rejecting the views both that the protection of people from themselves is *always* a valid ground for interference in their affairs, and that it is *never* a valid ground. It follows that it is a valid ground only under certain conditions, and we must now try to state those conditions.[1]

I

It will be useful to make some preliminary distinctions. The first distinction is between harms or likely harms that are produced directly by people upon themselves and those produced by the actions of another person to which the first party has consented. Committing suicide would be an example of self-inflicted harm; arranging for a person to put one out of one's misery would be an example of a harm inflicted by the action of another to which one has consented. There is a venerable legal maxim traceable to Roman Law, *"Volenti non fit injuria,"* that is sometimes translated misleadingly as: "To one who consents no harm is done." I suppose that the notion of consent applies, strictly speaking, only to the actions of another person that affect oneself. If so, then, consent to one's *own* actions is a kind of metaphor. Indeed, to say that I consented to my own actions seems just a colorful way of saying that I acted voluntarily. My involuntary actions, after all, are, from the moral point of view, no different from the actions of someone else to which I have not had an opportunity to consent. In any case, it seems plainly false to say that people cannot be *harmed* by actions, whether their own or those of another, to which they have consented. People who quite voluntarily eat an amount that is in fact too much cause themselves to suffer from indiges-

tion; and women who consent to advances sometimes become pregnant.

One way of interpreting the *Volenti* maxim is to take it as a kind of presumptive principle. People do not generally consent to what they believe will be, on balance, harmful to themselves and, by and large, individuals are in a better position to appraise risks to themselves than are outsiders. Given these data, and considering convenience in the administration of the law, the *Volenti* maxim might be understood to say that for the purposes of the law (whatever the actual facts might be) nothing is to count as harm to a given person that he or she has freely consented to. If this presumption is held to be conclusive, then the *Volenti* maxim becomes a kind of "legal fiction" when applied to cases of undeniable harm resulting from behavior to which the harmed one freely consented. A much more likely interpretation, however, takes the *Volenti* maxim to say nothing at all, literal or fictional, about *harms.* Rather, it is about what used to be called injuries, that is, injustices or wrongs. To one who freely consents to a thing no *wrong* is done, no matter how harmful to him the consequences may be. "He cannot waive his right," says Salmond, "and then complain of its infringement."[2] If the *Volenti* maxim is simply an expression of Salmond's insight, it is not a presumptive or fictional principle about harms, but rather an absolute principle about wrongs.

The *Volenti* maxim (or something very like it) plays a key role in the argument for John Stuart Mill's doctrine about liberty. Characteristically, Mill seems to employ the maxim in both of its interpretations, as it suits his purposes, without noticing the distinction between them. On the one hand, Mill's argument purports to be an elaborate application of the calculus of harms and benefits to the problem of political liberty. The state can rightly restrain those who wish to harm others. Why then can it not restrain those who wish to harm themselves? After all, a harm is a harm whatever its cause and if our sole concern is to minimize harms all round, why should we distinguish between origins of harm?

---

1. The discussion that follows has two important unstated and undefended presuppositions. The first is that in some societies and at some times, a line can be drawn (as Mill claimed it could be in Victorian England) between other-regarding behavior and behavior that is primarily and directly self-regarding and only indirectly and remotely, therefore trivially, other-regarding. If this assumption is false, there is no interesting problem concerning legal paternalism since all paternalistic restrictions could be defended as necessary to protect persons other than those restricted, and hence would not be wholly paternalistic. The second presupposition is that the spontaneous repugnance toward paternalism (which I assume the reader shares with me) is well-grounded and supportable.

2. See Glanville Williams, ed., *Salmond on Jurisprudence,* 11th ed. (London: Sweet & Maxwell, 1957), p. 531.

One way Mill answers this question is to employ the *Volenti* maxim in its first interpretation. For the purposes of his argument, he will presume conclusively that "to one who consents no *harm* is done." Self-inflicted or consented-to harm simply is not to count as harm at all; and the reasons for this are that the coercion required to prevent such harm is itself a harm of such gravity that it is likely in the overwhelming proportion of cases to outweigh any good it can produce for the one coerced; moreover, individuals themselves, in the overwhelming proportion of cases, can know their own true interests better than any outsiders can, so that outside coercion is almost certain to be self-defeating.

But as Gerald Dworkin has pointed out,[3] arguments of this merely statistical kind create at best a strong but rebuttable presumption against coercion of people in their own interests. Yet Mill purports to be arguing for an absolute prohibition. Absolute prohibitions are hard to defend on purely utilitarian grounds, so Mill, when his confidence wanes, tends to move to the second interpretation of the *Volenti* maxim. People can be harmed by what they consent to, but they cannot be wronged; and Mill's "harm principle," reinterpreted accordingly, is designed to protect people only from wrongful invasions of their interest. Moreover, when the state intervenes on any ground, its own intervention is a wrongful invasion. What justifies the absolute prohibition of interference in primarily self-regarding affairs is *not* that such interference is self-defeating and likely (merely likely) to cause more harm than it prevents, but rather that it would itself be an injustice, a wrong, a violation of the private sanctuary which is every person's self; and this is so whatever the calculus of harms and benefits might show.[4]

The second distinction is between those cases in which people directly produce harm to themselves, where the harm is the certain upshot of their conduct and its desired end, on the one hand, and those cases in which people simply create a *risk* of harm to themselves in the course of activities directed toward other ends. The woman who knowingly swallows a lethal dose of arsenic will certainly die, and death must be imputed to her as her goal in acting. A man is offended by the sight of his left hand, so he grasps an ax in his right hand and chops off his left hand. He does not thereby "endanger" his interest in the physical integrity of his limbs or "risk" the loss of his hand. He brings about the loss directly and deliberately. On the other hand, to smoke cigarettes or to drive at excessive speeds is not to harm oneself directly, but rather to increase beyond a normal level the probability that harm to oneself will result.

The third distinction is between reasonable and unreasonable risks. There is no form of activity (or inactivity either for that matter) that does not involve some risks. On some occasions we have a choice between more and less risky actions and prudence dictates that we take the less dangerous course; but what is called "prudence" is not always reasonable. Sometimes it is more reasonable to assume a great risk for a great gain than to play it safe and forfeit a unique opportunity. Thus it is not nec-

---

3. See his excellent article, "Paternalism," in *Morality and the Law,* ed. R. A. Wasserstrom (Belmont, CA: Wadsworth Publishing Co., 1971).

4. Mill's rhetoric often supports this second interpretation of his argument. He is especially fond of such political metaphors as independence, legitimate rule, dominion, and sovereignty. The state must respect the status of the individual as an independent entity whose "*sovereignty* over himself" (in Mill's phrase), like Britain's over its territory, is absolute. In self-regarding affairs, a person's individuality ought to

"*reign* uncontrolled from the outside" (another phrase of Mill's). Interference in those affairs, whether successful or self-defeating, is a violation of *legitimate boundaries,* like trespass in law, or aggression between states. Even self-mutilation and suicide are permissible if the individual truly chooses them, and other interests are not directly affected. Individual persons have an absolute right to choose for themselves, to be wrong, to go to hell on their own, and it is nobody else's proper *business* or *office* to interfere. Individuals *own* (not merely possess) their lives; they have *title* to them. They alone are *arbiters* of their own lives and deaths. See how legalistic and un-utilitarian these terms are! The great wonder is that Mill could claim to have foregone any benefit in argument from the notion of an abstract right. Mill's intentions abide, however, I can not conceal my own preference for this second interpretation of his argument.

essarily more reasonable for a coronary patient to increase life expectancy by living a life of quiet inactivity than to continue working hard at a career in the hope of achieving something important even at the risk of a sudden fatal heart attack at any moment. There is no simple mathematical formula to guide one in making such decisions or in judging them "reasonable" or "unreasonable." On the other hand, there are other decisions that are manifestly unreasonable. It is unreasonable to drive at sixty miles an hour through a twenty-mile-an-hour zone in order to arrive at a party on time, but may be reasonable to drive fifty miles an hour to get a seriously ill person to the hospital. It is foolish to resist an armed robber in an effort to protect one's wallet, but it may be worth a desperate lunge to protect one's very life, or the life of a loved one.

In all these cases a number of distinct considerations are involved.[5] If there is time to deliberate one should consider: (1) the degree of probability that harm to oneself will result from a given course of action; (2) the seriousness of the harm being risked, i.e., the value or importance of that which is exposed to the risk; (3) the degree of probability that the goal inclining one to shoulder the risk will in fact result from the course of action; (4) the value or importance of achieving that goal, that is, just how worthwhile it is to one (this is the intimately personal factor, requiring a decision about one's own preferences, that makes the reasonableness of a risk-assessment on the whole so difficult for the *outsider* to make); and (5) the necessity of the risk, that is, the availability or absence of alternative, less risky, means to the desired goal. Certain judgments about the reasonableness of risk-assumptions are quite uncontroversial. We can say, for example, that the *greater* the probability of harm to self (1) and the magnitude of the harm risked (2), the *less* reasonable the risk; and the *greater* the probability the desired goal will result (3), the importance of the goal to the doer (4), and the necessity of the means (5), the *more* reasonable the risk. But in a given difficult case, even where questions of probability are

---

5. The distinctions in this paragraph are borrowed from: Henry T. Terry, "Negligence," *Harvard Law Review* 29, 1915.

meaningful and beyond dispute, and where all the relevant facts are known, the risk-decision may defy objective assessment because of its component personal value judgments. In any case, if the state is to be given the right to prevent individuals from risking harm to themselves (and only themselves) this must be not only on the ground that the prohibited action is highly risky, but also on the ground that, in respect to its objectively assessable components, it is manifestly unreasonable. There are, sometimes, very good reasons for regarding even a person's judgment of personal worthwhileness (consideration 4) to be "manifestly unreasonable," but it remains to be seen whether (or when) that kind of unreasonableness can be sufficient grounds for interference.

The fourth and final distinction is between fully voluntary and not fully voluntary assumptions of a risk. One assumes a risk in a fully voluntary way when one shoulders it while fully informed of all relevant facts and contingencies, with one's eyes wide open, so to speak, and in the absence of all coercive pressure. There must be calmness and deliberateness, no distracting or unsettling emotions, no neurotic compulsion, no misunderstanding. To whatever extent there is compulsion, misinformation, excitement or impetuousness, clouded judgment (as from alcohol), or immature or defective faculties of reasoning, to that extent the choice falls short of perfect voluntariness. Voluntariness then is a matter of degree. One's "choice" is *completely involuntary* when it is no choice at all, properly speaking—when one lacks all muscular control of one's movements; or when one is knocked down, or pushed, or sent reeling by a blow, or a wind, or an explosion; or when through ignorance one chooses something other than what one means to choose, as when one thinks the arsenic powder is table salt, and thus chooses to sprinkle it on one's scrambled eggs. Most harmful choices, like most choices generally, fall somewhere between the extremes of perfect voluntariness and complete involuntariness.

The terms voluntary and involuntary have a variety of disparate but overlapping uses in philosophy, law, and ordinary life, and some of them are not altogether clear. I should point out here that my usage does not correspond with that of Aristotle, who allowed that infants, animals, drunkards, and people in a towering rage might yet act voluntarily if only they are undeceived and not overwhelmed by external physical force. What I call a voluntary assumption of risk corresponds more closely to what Aristotle called "deliberate choice." Impulsive and emotional actions, and those of animals and infants are voluntary in Aristotle's sense, but they are not *chosen.* Chosen actions are those that are decided upon by *deliberation,* and that is a process that requires time, information, a clear head, and highly developed rational faculties. When I use such phrases as "voluntary act," "free and genuine consent," and so on, I refer to acts that are more than "voluntary" in the Aristotlelian sense, acts that Aristotle himself would call "deliberately chosen." Such acts not only have their origin "in the agent," they also represent the agent faithfully in some important way: they express his or her settled values and preferences. In the fullest sense, therefore, they are actions for which the agent can take responsibility.

II

The central thesis of John Stuart Mill and other individualists about paternalism is that the fully voluntary choice or consent of a mature and rational human being concerning matters that affect only the individual's own interests is such a precious thing that no one else (and certainly not the state) has a right to interfere with it simply for the person's "own good." No doubt this thesis was also meant to apply to almost-but-not-quite fully voluntary choices as well, and probably also even to some substantially nonvoluntary ones (e.g., a neurotic person's choice of a wife who will satisfy his neurotic needs but only at the price of great unhappiness, eventual divorce, and exacerbated guilt); but it is not probable that the individualist thesis was meant to apply to choices near the bottom of the scale of voluntariness, and Mill himself left no doubt that he did *not* intend it to apply to completely involuntary "choices." Nor should we *expect* anti-paternalistic individualism to deny people protection from their own nonvoluntary choices, for insofar as the choices are not voluntary they are just as alien to the individual as the choices of someone else.

Thus Mill would permit the state to protect people from their own ignorance at least in circumstances that create a strong presumption that their uninformed or misinformed choice would not correspond to their eventual one.

If either a public officer or anyone else saw a person attempting to cross a bridge which had been ascertained to be unsafe, and there were no time to warn him of his danger, they might seize him and turn him back, without any real infringement of his liberty; for liberty consists in doing what one desires, and he does not desire to fall into the river.[6]

Of course, for all the public officer may know, the man on the bridge does desire to fall into the river, or to take the risk of falling for other purposes. If the person is then fully warned of the danger and wishes to proceed anyway, then, Mill argues, that is his business alone; but because most people do *not* wish to run such risks, there was a solid presumption, in advance of checking, that this person did not wish to run the risk either. Hence the officer was justified, Mill would argue, in his original interference.

On other occasions a person may need to be protected not from ignorance but from some other condition that may render an informed choice substantially less than voluntary. The individual may be "a child, or delirious, or in some state of excitement or absorption incompatible with the full use of the reflecting faculty."[7] Mill would not permit any such person to cross an objectively unsafe bridge. On the other hand, there is no reason why a child, or an excited person, or a drunkard, or a mentally ill person should not be allowed to proceed home across a perfectly safe thoroughfare. Even substantially nonvoluntary choices deserve protection unless there is good reason to judge them dangerous.

It may be the case, for all we can know, that the behavior of a drunk or an emotionally upset person would be exactly the same even if the individual were sober and calm. But when the behavior seems patently self-damaging and is of a sort that most calm and normal persons would not engage in,

---

6. John Stuart Mill, *On Liberty* (New York: Liberal Arts Press, 1956), p. 117.

7. *Ibid.*

then there are strong grounds, if only a statistical sort, for inferring that it would not be the same; and these grounds, on Mill's principle, would justify interference. It may be that there is no action of which it can be said, "No mentally competent adult in a calm, attentive mood, fully informed, etc., would ever choose (or consent to) *that*." Nevertheless, there are actions that create a powerful *presumption* that any given actor, if he were in his right mind, would not choose them. The point of calling this hypothesis a "presumption" is to require that it be completely overridden before giving legal permission to a person who has already been interfered with to go on as before. For example, if a police officer (or anyone else) sees John Doe about to chop off his hand with an ax, the person is perfectly justified in using force to prevent him, because of the presumption that no one could voluntarily choose to do such a thing. The presumption, however, should always be taken as rebuttable in principle; and now it will be up to Doe to prove before an official tribunal that he is calm, competent, and free, and that he still wishes to chop off his hand. Perhaps this is too great a burden to expect Doe himself to "prove," but the tribunal should require that the presumption against voluntariness be overturned by evidence from some source or other. The existence of the presumption should require that an objective determination be made, whether by the usual adversary procedures of law courts, or simply by a collective investigation by the tribunal into the available facts. The greater the presumption to be overridden, the more elaborate and fastidious should be the legal paraphernalia required, and the stricter the standards of evidence. (The law of wills might prove a model for this.) The point of the procedure would not be to evaluate the wisdom or worthiness of a person's choice, but rather to determine whether the choice really is his.

This seems to lead us to a form of paternalism that is so weak and innocuous that it could be accepted even by Mill, namely, that the state has the right to prevent self-regarding harmful conduct when but only when it is substantially nonvoluntary or when temporary intervention is necessary to establish whether it is voluntary or not. A strong presumption that no normal person would voluntarily choose or consent to the kind of conduct in ques-

tion should be a proper ground for detaining the person until the voluntary character of the choice can be established. We can use the phrase "the standard of voluntariness" as a label for the considerations that mediate the application of the principle that a person may properly be protected from his own folly. (Still another ground for forcible delay and inquiry that is perfectly compatible with Mill's individualism is the possibility that important third-party interests might be involved. Perhaps a man's wife and family should be heard before he is permitted to commit suicide—or even to chop off his hand.)

III

Working out the details of the voluntariness standard is far too difficult to undertake here, but some of the complexities can be illustrated by a consideration of some typical hard cases. Consider first of all the problem of harmful drugs. Suppose Mary Roe requests a prescription of drug X from Dr. Doe, and the following discussion ensues:

Dr. Doe: I cannot prescribe drug X to you because it will do you physical harm.
Mary Roe: But you are mistaken. It will not cause me physical harm.

In a case like this, the state, of course, backs the doctor. The state deems medical questions to be technical matters subject to expert opinions. This means that nonexpert laypeople are not the best judge of their own medical interests. If a layperson disagrees with a physician on a question of medical fact the layperson can be presumed wrong, and if she nevertheless chooses to act on her factually mistaken belief, her action will be substantially less than fully voluntary in the sense explained above. That is to say that the action of *ingesting a substance which will in fact harm her* is not the action she voluntarily chooses. Hence the state intervenes to protect her not from her own free and voluntary choices, but from her own ignorance.

Suppose however that the exchange goes as follows:

Dr. Doe: I cannot prescribe drug X to you because it will do you physical harm.
Mary Roe: Exactly. That's just what I want. I want to harm myself.

In this case Roe *is* properly apprised of the facts. She suffers from no delusions or misconceptions. Yet her choice is so odd that there exists a reasonable presumption that she has been deprived somehow of the "full use of [her] reflecting faculty." It is because we know that the overwhelming majority of choices to inflict injury for its own sake on oneself are not fully voluntary that we are entitled to presume that the present choice too is not fully voluntary. If no further evidence of derangement, illness, severe depression, or unsettling excitation can be discovered, however, and the patient can convince an objective panel that the choice is voluntary (unlikely event!) and further if there are no third-party interests, for example, those of spouse or family, that require protection, then our "voluntariness standard" would permit no further state constraint.

Now consider the third possibility:

Dr. Doe: I cannot prescribe drug X to you because it is very likely to do you physical harm.

Mary Roe: I don't care if it causes me physical harm. I'll get a lot of pleasure first, so much pleasure in fact, that it is well worth running the risk of physical harm. If I must pay a price for my pleasure I am willing to do so.

This is perhaps the most troublesome case. Roe's choice is not patently irrational on its face. A well thought-out philosophical hedonism may be one of her profoundest convictions. She may have made a fundamental decision of principle commiting herself to the intensely pleasurable, even if brief, life. If no third-party interests are directly involved, the state can hardly be permitted to declare these philosophical convictions unsound or "sick" and prevent her from practicing them without assuming powers that it will inevitably misuse disastrously.

On the other hand, this example may be very little different from the preceding one, depending, of course, on what the exact facts are. If the drug is known to give only an hour's mild euphoria and then to cause an immediate violently painful death, the risks incurred appear so unreasonable as to create a powerful presumption of nonvoluntariness. The desire to commit suicide must always be presumed to be both nonvoluntary and harmful to others until shown otherwise. (Of course, in some cases it *can* be shown otherwise.) On the other hand, drug X may be harmful in the way nicotine is now known to be harmful; twenty or thirty years of heavy use may create a grave risk of lung cancer or heart disease. Using the drug merely for pleasure, when the risks are of this kind may be to run unreasonable risks, but that is not strong evidence of nonvoluntariness. Many perfectly normal, rational persons voluntarily choose to run precisely these risks for whatever pleasures they find in smoking.[8] The way the state can assure itself that such practices are truly voluntary is to confront smokers continually with the ugly medical facts so that there is no escaping the knowledge of exactly what the medical risks to health are. Constant reminders of the hazards should be at every hand and with no softening of the gory details. The state might even be justified in using its taxing, regulatory, and persuasive powers to make smoking (and similar drug usage) more difficult or less attractive; but to prohibit it outright for everyone would be to tell voluntary risk-takers that even their informed judgments of what is worthwhile are less reasonable than those of the state, and that, therefore, they may not act on them. This is paternalism of the strong kind, unmediated by the voluntariness standard. As a principle of public policy, it has an acrid moral flavor, and creates serious risks of governmental tyranny.

IV

Another class of difficult cases are those involving contracts in which one party agrees to restrict his own liberty in some respect. The most extreme case is that in which one party freely sells himself into slavery to another, perhaps in exchange for some benefit that is to be consumed before the period of slavery begins or perhaps for some reward to be bestowed upon some third party. Our point of de-

---

8. Perfectly rational individuals can have "unreasonable desires" as judged by other perfectly rational individuals, just as perfectly rational people (e.g., great philosophers) can hold "unreasonable beliefs" or doctrines as judged by other perfectly rational people. Particular unreasonableness, then, can hardly be strong evidence of general irrationality.

parture will be Mill's classic treatment of the subject:

> In this and most other civilized countries .... an engagement by which a person should sell himself, or allow himself to be sold, as a slave, would be null and void; neither enforced by law nor by opinion. The ground for *thus limiting his power of voluntarily disposing of his own lot in life* [italics mine] is apparent, and is very clearly seen in this extreme case. The reason for not interfering, unless for the sake of others, with a person's voluntary acts is consideration for his liberty. His voluntary choice is evidence that what he so chooses is desirable, or at the least endurable, to him, and his good is on the whole best provided for by allowing him to take his own means of pursuing it. But by selling himself for a slave, he abdicates his liberty; he foregoes any future use of it beyond the single act. He therefore defeats, in his own case, the very purpose which is the justification of allowing him to dispose of himself. He is no longer free; but is thenceforth in a position which has no longer the presumption in its favor, that would be afforded by his voluntarily remaining in it. The principle of freedom cannot require that he should be free not to be free.[9]

It seems plain to me that Mill, in this one extreme case, has been driven to embrace the principle of paternalism. The "harm-to-others principle," as mediated by the *Volenti* maxim[10] would permit competent, fully informed adults, who are capable of rational reflection and free of undue pressure, to be themselves the judge of their own interests, no matter how queer or perverse their judgments may seem to others. There is, of course, always the presumption, and a very strong one indeed, that those who elect to "sell" themselves into slavery are either incompetent, unfree, or misinformed. Hence the state should require very strong evidence of

voluntariness—elaborate tests, swearings, psychiatric testifying, waiting periods, public witnessing, and the like—before validating such contracts. Similar forms of official "making sure" are involved in marriages and wills, and slavery is an even more serious thing, not to be rashly undertaken. Undoubtedly, very few slavery contracts would survive such procedures, perhaps even none at all. It may be literally true that "no one in his right mind would sell himself into slavery," but if this is a truth it is not an *a priori* one but rather one that must be tested anew in each case by the application of independent, noncircular criteria of mental illness.

> *"The state has the right to prevent self-regarding harmful conduct when but only when it is substantially nonvoluntary or when temporary intervention is necessary to establish whether it is voluntary or not."*

The supposition is at least possible, therefore, that every now and then a normal person in full possession of her or his faculties would voluntarily consent to permanent slavery. We can imagine any number of intelligible (if not attractive) motives for doing such a thing. A person might agree to become a slave in exchange for a million dollars to be delivered in advance to a loved one or to a worthy cause, or out of a religious conviction requiring a life of humility or penitence, or in payment for the prior enjoyment of some supreme benefit, as in the *Faust* legend. Mill, in the passage quoted earlier, would disallow such a contract no matter how certain it is that the agreement is fully voluntary, apparently on the ground that the permanent and irrev-

---

9. Mill, *On Liberty,* p. 125.
10. That is, the principle that prevention of harm to others is the sole ground for legal coercion, and that what is freely consented to is not to count as harm. These are Mill's primary normative principles in *On Liberty.*

ocable loss of freedom is such a great evil, and slavery so harmful a condition, that no one ought ever to be allowed to choose it, even voluntarily. Any person who thinks to gain, in the end, from such an agreement, Mill implies, is simply wrong whatever the reasons, and the individual can be known *a priori* to be wrong. Mill's earlier argument, if I understand it correctly, implies that people should be permitted to mutilate their bodies, take harmful drugs, or commit suicide, provided that the decision to do these things is voluntary and no other person will be directly and seriously harmed. But voluntarily acceding to slavery is too much for Mill to stomach. Here is an evil of another order, he seems to say; so the "harm to others" principle and the *Volenti* maxim come to their limiting point here, and paternalism in the strong sense (unmediated by the voluntariness test) must be invoked, if only for this one kind of case.

There are, of course, other ways of justifying the refusal to enforce slavery contracts. Some of these are derived from principles not acknowledged in Mill's moral philosophy but which at least have the merit of being non-paternalistic. One might argue that what is odious in "harsh and unconscionable" contracts, even when they are voluntary on both sides, is not that people should suffer the harm they freely risk, but rather that another party should "exploit" or take advantage of them. What is to be prevented, according to this line argument, is one person exploiting the weakness, foolishness, or recklessness of another. If a weak, foolish, or reckless person freely chooses or risks self-harm, that is all right, but that is no reason why another should be a party to it, or be permitted to benefit at the first person's expense. (This principle, however, can only apply to extreme cases, else it will ban all competition). Applied to voluntary slavery, the principle of nonexploitation might say that it isn't aimed at preventing one person from being a slave so much as preventing the other from being a slave-owner. The basic principle of argument here is a form of legal moralism. To own another human being, as one might own a table or a horse, is to be in a relation to that person that is inherently immoral, and therefore properly forbidden by law. That, of course, is a line of argument that would be uncongenial to Mill, as would also be the Kantian argument that there is something in every human being that is not his or hers to alienate or dispose of: the "humanity" that we are enjoined to "respect, whether in our own person or that of another."

There are still other ways of arguing against the recognition of slavery contracts, however, that are neither paternalistic (in the strong sense) nor inconsistent with Mill's primary principles. One might argue, for example, that weakening respect for human dignity (which is weak enough to begin with) can lead in the long run to harm of the most serious kind to nonconsenting parties. Or one might use a variant of the "public charge" argument commonly used in the nineteenth century against permitting even those without dependents to assume the risk of penury, illness, and starvation. We could let people gamble recklessly with their lives, and then adopt inflexibly unsympathetic attitudes toward the losers. "They made their beds," we might say in the manner of some proper Victorians, "now let them sleep in them." But this would be to render the whole national character cold and hard. It would encourage a general insensitivity and impose an unfair economic penalty on those who possess the socially useful virtue of benevolence. Realistically, we just can't let people wither and die right in front of our eyes; and if we intervene to help, as we inevitably must, it will cost us a lot of money. There are certain risks then of an *apparently* self-regarding kind that people cannot be permitted to run, if only for the sake of others who must either pay the bill or turn their backs on intolerable misery. This kind of argument, which can be applied equally well to the slavery case, is at least not *very* paternalistic.

Finally, a non-paternalistic opponent of voluntary slavery might argue (and this is the argument to which I wish to give the most emphasis) that while exclusively self-regarding and fully voluntary slavery contracts are unobjectionable in principle, the legal machinery for testing voluntariness would be so cumbersome and expensive as to be impractical. Such procedures, after all, would have to be paid for out of tax revenues, the payment of which is mandatory for taxpayers. (And psychiatric consultant fees, among other things, are very high.) Even expensive legal machinery might be so fallible that there could be no sure way of determining voluntariness, so that some mentally ill people, for example, might become enslaved. Given the uncertain quality of evidence on these matters, and the enormous general presumption of nonvoluntariness, the state might be justified simply in *presuming nonvoluntariness conclusively in every case as the least risky course.* Some rational bargain-makers might be unfairly restrained under this policy, but under the alternative policy, perhaps even more people would become unjustly (mistakenly) enslaved, so that the evil prevented by the absolute prohibition would be greater than the occasional evil permitted. The principles involved in this argument are of two kinds: (1) It is better that one hundred people be wrongly denied permission to be enslaved than that one be wrongly permitted, and (2) If we allow the institution of voluntary slavery at all, then no matter how stringent our tests of voluntariness are, it is likely that a good many persons *will* be wrongly permitted.

V

Mills' argument that leads to a strong paternalistic conclusion in this one case (slavery) employs only calculations of harms and benefits and the presumptive interpretation of *Volenti non fit injuria.* The notion of the inviolable sovereignty of individual persons over their own lives does not appear in the argument. Liberty, he seems to tell us, is one good or benefit (though an extremely important one) among many, and its loss is one evil or harm (though an extremely serious one) among many types of harm. Since the aim of the law is to prevent harms of all kinds and from all sources, the law must take a very negative attitude toward forfeitures of liberty. Still, by and large, legal paternalism is an unacceptable policy because, in attempting to impose upon people at external conception of their own good, it is very likely to be self-defeating. "His voluntary choice is *evidence* [italics mine] that what he so chooses is desirable, or at least endurable to him, and his good is *on the whole* [italics mine] best provided for by allowing him to take his own means of pursuing it."

On the whole, then, the harm of coercion will outweigh any good it can produce for the person coerced. But when the person chooses slavery, the scales are clearly and necessarily tipped the other way, and the normal case against intervention is defeated. The ultimate appeal in this argument of Mill's is to the prevention of personal harms, so that permitting people to sell their freedom voluntarily would be to permit them to be "free not to be free," that is, free to inflict an *undeniable* harm upon themselves, and this (Mill would say) is as paradoxical as permitting a legislature to vote by a majority to abolish majority rule. If, on the other hand, our ultimate principle expresses respect for a person's voluntary choice *as such,* even when it is the choice of a loss of freedom, we can remain adamantly opposed to paternalism even in the most extreme cases of self-harm, for we shall be committed to the view that there is something even more important than the avoidance of harm. The principle that shuts and locks the door leading to strong paternalism is that every human being has a right to "voluntarily dispose of his or her own lot in life" whatever the effect on the net balance of benefits (including "freedom") and harms.

What does Mill say about less extreme cases of contracting away liberty? His next sentence (but one) is revealing: "These reasons, the force of which is so conspicuous in this particular case [slavery], are evidently of far wider application, yet a limit is everywhere set to them by the necessities of life, which continually require, not indeed that we should resign our freedom, but that we should consent to this and the other limitation of it."[11] Mill seems to say here that the same reasons that justify preventing the total and irrevocable relinquishment of freedom also militate against agreements to relinquish lesser amounts for lesser periods, but that unfortunately such agreements are sometimes rendered necessary by practical considerations. I would prefer to argue in the very opposite way, from the obvious permissibility of limited resignations of freedom to the permissibility in principle of even extreme forfeitures, except that in the case of slavery the "necessities of life"—administrative compli-

---

11. Mill, *On Liberty,* p. 125.

cations in determining voluntariness, high expenses, and so on—forbid it.

Many perfectly reasonable employment contracts involve an agreement by the employees virtually to abandon their liberty to do as they please for a daily period, and even to do (within obvious limits) whatever their boss tells them, in exchange for a salary that the employer, in turn, is not at liberty to withhold. Sometimes, of course, the terms of such agreements are quite unfavorable to one of the parties, but when the agreements have been fairly bargained, with no undue pressure or deception (i.e., when they are fully voluntary), the courts enforce them even though lopsided in their distribution of benefits. Employment contracts, of course, are relatively easily broken; in that respect they are altogether different from slavery contracts. Perhaps better examples for our purposes are contractual forfeitures of some extensive liberty for long periods of time or even forever. Certain contracts "in restraint of trade" are good examples. Consider contracts for the sale of the "good will" of a business.

> Manifestly, the buyer of a shop or of a practice will not be satisfied with what he buys unless he can persuade the seller to contract that he will not immediately set up a competing business next door and draw back most of his old clients or customers. Hence the buyer will usually request the seller to agree not to enter into competition with him. . . . Clauses of this kind are [also] often found in written contracts of employment, the employer requiring his employee to agree that he will not work for a competing employer after he leaves his present work.[12]

There are limits, both spatial and temporal, to the amount of liberty the courts will permit to be relinquished in such contracts. In general, it is considered reasonable for a seller to agree not to reopen a business in the same neighborhood or even the same city for several years, but not reasonable to agree not to re-enter the trade in a distant city, or for a period of fifty years. The courts insist that the agreed-to self restraint be no wider "than is reasonably necessary to protect the buyer's purchase;"[13]

but where the buyer's interests are very large the restraints may cover a great deal of space and time:

> For instance, in the leading case on the subject, a company which bought an armaments business for the colossal sum of £287,000 was held justified in taking a contract from the seller that he would not enter into competition with this business anywhere in the world for a period of twenty-five years. In view of the fact that the business was world-wide in its operations, and that its customers were mainly governments, any attempt by the seller to re-enter the armament business anywhere in the world might easily have affected the value of the buyer's purchase.[14]

The courts then do permit people to contract away extensive liberties for extensive periods of time in exchange for other benefits in reasonable bargains. Persons are even permitted to forfeit their future liberties in exchange for cash. Sometimes such transactions are perfectly reasonable, promoting the interests of both parties. Hence there would appear to be no good reason why they should be prohibited. Selling oneself into slavery is forfeiting *all* one's liberty for the rest of one's life in exchange for some prized benefit, and thus is only the extreme case of contracting away liberty, but not altogether different in principle. Mill's argument that liberty is not the sort of good that by its very nature can properly be traded does not seem a convincing way of arguing against voluntary slavery.

On the other hand, a court does permit the seller of a business to forfeit freely any more liberty than is reasonable or necessary, and reserves to *itself* the right to determine the question of reasonableness. This restrictive policy *could* be an expression of paternalism designed to protect contractors from their own foolishness; but in fact it is based on an entirely different ground—the public interest in maintaining a competitive system of free trade. The consumer's interest in having prices determined by a competitive marketplace rather than by uncontrolled monopolies requires that the state make it difficult for wealthy business people to buy off their competitors. Reasonable contracts "in restraint of trade" are a limited class of exceptions to a general policy designed to protect the economic

---

12. P.S. Atiyah, *An Introduction to the Law of Contracts* (Oxford: Clarendon Press, 1961), p. 176.

13. *Ibid.,* p. 176–77.

14. *Ibid.,* p. 177.

interests of third parties (consumers) rather than the expression of an independent paternalistic policy of protecting free bargainers from their own mistakes.

There is still a final class of cases that deserves mention. These too are instances of persons voluntarily relinquishing liberties for other benefits; but they occur under such circumstances that prohibitions against them could not be plausibly justified except on paternalistic grounds, and usually not even on those grounds. I have in mind examples of persons who voluntarily "put themselves under the protection of rules" that deprive them and others of liberties, when those liberties are unrewarding and burdensome. Suppose all upperclass undergraduates are given the option by their college to live either in private apartment buildings entirely unrestricted or else in college dormitories subject to the usual curfew and parietal rules. If one chooses the latter, he or she must be in after a certain hour, be quiet after a certain time, and so on, subject to certain sanctions. In "exchange" for these forfeitures, of course, one is assured that the other students too must be predictable in their habits, orderly, and quiet. The net gain for one's interests as a student over the "freer" private life could be considerable. Moreover, the curfew rule can be a great convenience for a girl who wishes to date boys often, but who also wishes: (a) to get enough sleep for good health, (b) to remain efficient in her work, and (c) to be free of tension and quarrels when on dates over the question of when it is time to return home. If the rule requires a return at a certain time then neither the girl nor the boy has any choice in the matter, and what a boon that can be! To invoke these considerations is *not* to resort to paternalism unless they are employed in support of a prohibition. It is paternalism to *forbid* students to live in a private apartment "for their own good" or "their own safety." It is not paternalism to *permit* them to live under the governance of coercive rules when they freely choose to do so, and the other alternative is kept open to them. In fact it would be paternalism to deny people the liberty of trading liberties for other benefits when they voluntarily choose to do so.

VI

In summary: Thee are weak and strong versions of legal paternalism. The weak version is hardly an independent principle and can be entirely acceptable to the philosopher who, like Mill, is committed only to the "harm to others" principle as mediated by the *Volenti* maxim, where the latter is more than a mere presumption derived from generalizations about the causes of harm. According to the strong version of legal paternalism, the state is justified in protecting people against their will, from the harmful consequences even of their fully voluntary choices and undertakings. Strong paternalism is a departure from the "harm to others" principle and the strictly interpreted *Volenti* maxim that Mill should not, or need not, have taken in his discussion of contractual forfeitures of liberty. According to the weaker version of legal paternalism, people can rightly be prevented from harming themselves (when other interests are not directly involved) only if their intended action is substantially nonvoluntary or can be presumed to be so in the absence of evidence to the contrary. The "harm to others" principle, after all, permits us to protect individuals from the choices of other people; weak paternalism would permit us to protect people from "nonvoluntary choices," which, being the choices of no one at all, are no less foreign to them.

Study Questions

1. Should drugs like marijuana and cocaine be illegal?
2. Should suicide be illegal?

3. Are seat-belt laws and motorcycle helmet laws based on strong or weak paternalism?

■ A life-long friend of yours confesses to you one night that he killed the man who raped and murdered his wife. Your friend was never caught for this, and the police knew nothing about it. A few days later, you discover that an innocent man has been arrested and charged with the murder of your friend's wife. You ask your friend to give himself up, but he refuses and reminds you of your promise not to tell anyone about what he did.

What should you do?

■ Mr. Francis Robinson made his last will and testament in which he left a part of his large estate to his grandson, Andrew Robinson, then nineteen years old. Sometime thereafter, Andrew begins to suspect that his grandfather will change his will and totally exclude Andrew from any inheritance. To prevent this from happening, Andrew kills his grandfather. After his arrest and conviction, Andrew is sentenced to life imprisonment without possibility of parole.

When the issue of the will comes to court, Andrew argues that he should get his share of the estate as originally provided for in the will because a legal document properly drawn up should be enforced. Andrew wants to give his share of the estate, if the court rules in his favor, to his girlfriend Jennie so that she can buy a restaurant. The lawyer for the other beneficiaries of the will argues that the state should not recognize the will as valid because, if it did, the state would be allowing a criminal to profit from his criminal act.

If you were on the jury, how would you vote?

■ A man widely suspected of being involved in organized crime wishes to donate five million dollars to Olib College, a small but distinguished school. The college badly needs the money to survive and to give scholarships to poor but gifted students. The benefactor, who is rumored to have acquired his money mostly from the sale of illegal drugs like cocaine, wants a building named after him as recognition for his generosity.

If you had to vote on whether to accept the offer, how would you vote?

■ You discover that your roommate is selling cocaine. You know her to be an excellent student and a fine human being otherwise. You ask her about this. She tells you that as far as she is concerned, drugs should be legal and the laws against drugs are unjust. Besides, she tells you that she needs the money to support herself and her sick mother who lives alone.

What should you do about your roommate?

■ You go shopping with your friend Kevin one day. As you go down the aisles of a large department store, you notice that Kevin is switching labels on products, putting the lower-priced tags on more expensive items, which he then puts in his cart. After you leave the store, you ask Kevin about this. He tells you that the large corporations rip off everybody anyway and that no one is really harmed by what he is doing.

What do you think?

Suggested Readings

Feinberg, Joel. *Social Philosophy*. Englewood Cliffs, N.J.: Prentice-Hall, 1973.

Golding, Martin. *Philosophy of Law*. Englewood Cliffs, N.J.: Prentice-Hall, 1975.

Grey, Thomas C. *The Legal Enforcement of Morality*. New York: Knopf, 1983.

Hart, H. L. A. *Law, Liberty and Morality*. Stanford: Stanford University Press, 1963.

Pennock, J. Roland, and John W. Chapman, eds. *Religion, Morality and the Law*. New York: New York University Press, 1988.

Sartorius, Rolf, ed. *Paternalism*. Minneapolis: University of Minnesota Press, 1983.

Vice and Virtue

Morality is concerned with the question of what constitutes a good character. We know from our everyday experience that some people are honest, trustworthy, and kind and that others are not. Those who have a good character not only know in most cases what the moral course of action is but also are willing to take that course; they have a character trait or tendency to act in a way that we would call *virtuous.* The opposite of virtue is *vice,* a character trait that leads people to act in an immoral way. Various cultures in history have proposed various habitual ways of acting as either virtuous or vicious, but does a universally correct set of virtues exist? Are virtues good in themselves or good only as a means to something else? Is morality properly understood as having the right set of virtues or the right set of principles and rules? Is a morality of virtues such as that of Aristotle compatible with a morality of principles such as that of Kant and Mill?

Background

In his great work, *The Republic,* Plato discusses the four basic, or cardinal, virtues (wisdom, justice, courage, and moderation) as essential to moral goodness. A person of virtue, according to Plato, is a person of inner harmony and rational living. Aristotle defined virtue as the mean between extremes. Courage, for example, is a virtue between the extremes of foolhardiness (irrational disregard of danger) and cowardice (irrational exaggeration of danger). Aristotle agreed that Plato's four virtues were essential for achieving what we all seek, happiness. Plato and Aristotle believed these virtues were universally necessary for everyone and not merely relative to their culture and their time. Later thinkers such as the stoic philosopher Marcus Aurelius Antoninus (A.D. 121–180) argued that all virtue can be reduced to the calm acceptance of reality and life in conformity to nature.

Christianity introduced a new understanding of virtue. Thomas Aquinas (A.D. 1225–1274), a major philosopher in the Christian tradition, accepted the four virtues of Plato and Aristotle and added to them the three theological virtues: faith, hope, and love. These virtues have intrinsic value but also serve as a means to achieving our ultimate goal, salvation and eternal life with God. These seven virtues are opposed by what Christianity calls the seven deadly sins: pride, lust, anger, gluttony, envy, greed, and laziness. Aquinas added to Aristotle's naturalistic framework a supernatural reality that takes precedence and requires an expanded conception of virtue to properly situate humanity in the new cosmology.

The rise of modern science, starting at about the sixteenth century, brought increased skepticism to bear on the worldview of Aquinas and religion in general. With the growth of capitalism, the expansion of the industrial revolution, and the emergence of Protestantism, a new stress on the value of work, savings, and the entrepreneurial drive appeared. Making a profit and lending money at an interest were no longer vices, and poverty was no longer a virtue. Philosophers such as Mill and Kant sought to base morality on reason alone, not on religion. With this new emphasis on reason came a greater attention to new principles over some traditional virtues. Can one solve the problems of abortion, capital punishment, mercy killing, and other controversial issues through the application of the virtues alone, or does one need rational principles? Yet, what good are principles without the virtues that give us the desire to apply them?

Alasdair MacIntyre

Even though the definitions of virtues change from society to society, virtues are necessary in every society for the development of human potential and excellence, according to Alasdair MacIntyre. In the Greek society at the time of Homer (about 800 B.C.), the virtue of courage was extolled not just as an ex-

cellent individual character trait but also as socially useful in the protection of the family and community from foreign attack. Courageous individuals were rewarded by the community with *kudos,* or glory. Courage was valued because a courageous individual is reliable and trustworthy, hence courage is an important element in a true friend. Friendship was also valued because it includes fidelity, or faithfulness, and endurance through tough times. Moral traits were those that promoted the particular social structure of that time. An individual in Homer's time defined himself or herself through roles in the community; father, warrior, craftsperson, and so on. To be honorable in Homer's time meant to accept one's society as well as life itself with its inevitable dangers and death.

MacIntyre's view is important, for it shows that what is considered moral or virtuous is at least partly defined by the culture in which we live. A Christian community, for example, might stress love over the Homeric virtue of courage. Still, one might want to ask whether particular virtues are necessary for the existence of any community. Can a culture exist in which lying or laziness is a virtue? Shouldn't moral theory enable us to criticize and to evaluate our culture, not just to accept it?

Charles Fried

According to Charles Fried, to lie is to intentionally cause someone to have a false belief. To be a free and rational person, however, means to have the truth and to know the way the world really is. When someone lies to us, he or she is controlling us and thus denying us due respect as persons. When we lie, we undermine the freedom and independence of those we deceive. Language and communication are based on the assumption of truth; without truth-telling, language itself would be impossible. For Fried, lies are wrong because they attempt to manipulate and to control another in a way that reduces his or her right to dignity and respect.

Immanuel Kant

All of us have opinions about ourselves—our abilities, strengths, and weaknesses. Kant (1724–1804) points out that we come to have a certain opinion of ourselves either by comparing ourselves to others or by comparing ourselves with some standard of perfection. If we compare ourselves with others and find that the others are better in some respect than we are, we may become jealous. Even though Kant concedes that jealousy is natural to a degree, he does not believe that it should be encouraged in children. If we desire the failure and unhappiness of others, we suffer from envy. The envious person not only wants to be happy, he or she wants to be the only happy person in the world. This person would destroy the happiness of others, which would clearly be immoral for Kant.

When others offer us a benefit or gift, we become obligated to the giver in some ways. To those who are proud, this is painful and often leads to ingratitude. If ingratitude became widespread, no one would do a good deed for others. Some persons are so corrupt that they enjoy seeing others suffer—this is malice. All of these vices, Kant points out, are in conflict with human compassion, which differentiates us from animals and is an integral part of a truly moral person.

Kant is a keen observer of human nature and moral weakness. He suggests that proper upbringing on the part of parents can reduce jealousy, envy, and malice. What would this upbringing be like? Do you agree with Kant that humankind is not by nature evil? If so, how does a person become immoral?

Lawrence Blum

Many philosophers including Lawrence Blum believe that morality would not be possible were persons not naturally compassionate toward others. Blum argues that compassion is an emotion that is oriented toward helping others in pain or distress. To have compassion means to understand the suffering of others and to imaginatively put ourselves in their place. Compassion is based on our belief in our common humanity and equality. It is not merely a brief and fleeting emotion but an enduring concern for the welfare of others that spurs us to take action and help when we can.

Blum believes that compassion is essential to morality but that it too can be misplaced. If a person feels compassion but misunderstands the situation, he or she may act wrongly. But, a key question that Blum does not address is, how do we make people more compassionate? Why do some people such as Gandhi or Mother Teresa seem to be full of compassion and others seem to lack it totally?

What one takes to be a virtue or a vice depends on what one believes is the nature and purpose of human existence. If one believes, as many Christians, Moslems, and Jews do, that our final destiny lies in an otherworldly and spiritual realm with God, then this world is a preparation for that existence and requires us to live accordingly. If, on the other hand, one takes a naturalistic perspective such as that of Aristotle, this life is the only one there is and we must make the best of it. Again, as in virtually every moral question, one's general *weltanschauung,* or worldview, will influence or determine what virtue is.

The Virtues in Heroic Societies

Alasdair MacIntyre is a professor of philosophy at the University of Notre Dame. He is also author of After Virtue *and many other writings on ethics and social philosophy.*

Alasdair MacIntyre

The word *aretê,* which later comes to be translated as 'virtue,' is in the Homeric poems used for excel-

From *After Virtue: A Study in Moral Philosophy* by Alasdair MacIntyre. Copyright © 1981, by University of Notre Dame Press, Notre Dame, Indiana 46556. Reprinted by permission.

lence of any kind; a fast runner displays the *aretê* of his feet (*Iliad* 20.411) and a son excels in his father in every kind of *aretê*—as athlete, as soldier and in mind (*Iliad* 15. 642). This concept of virtue or excellence is more alien to us than we are apt at first to recognise. It is not difficult for us to recognise the central place that strength will have in such a conception of human excellence or the way in which courage will be one of the central virtues, perhaps the central virtue. What is alien to our conception of virtue is the intimate connection in heroic society between the concept of courage and its allied virtues on the other hand and the concepts of friendship, fate and death on the other.

Courage is important, not simply as a quality of individuals, but as the quality necessary to sustain a household and a community. *Kudos,* glory, belongs to the individual who excels in battle or in contest as a mark of recognition by his household and his community. Other qualities linked to courage also merit public recognition because of the part they play in sustaining the public order. In the Homeric poems cunning is such a quality because cunning may have its achievements where courage is lacking or courage fails. In the Icelandic sagas a wry sense of humour is closely bound up with courage. In the saga account of the battle of Clontarf in 1014, where Brian Boru defeated a Viking army, one of the norsemen, Thorstein, did not flee when the rest of his army broke and ran, but remained where he was, tying his shoestring. An Irish leader, Kerthialfad, asked him why he was not running. 'I couldn't get home tonight,' said Thorstein. 'I live in Iceland.' Because of the joke, Kerthialfad spared his life.

To be courageous is to be someone on whom reliance can be placed. Hence courage is an important ingredient in friendship. The bonds of friendship in heroic societies are modelled on those of kinship. Sometimes friendship is formally vowed, so that by the vow the duties of brothers are mutually incurred. Who my friends are and who my enemies, is as clearly defined as who my kinsmen are. The other ingredient of friendship is fidelity. My friend's courage assures me of his power to aid me and my household; my friend's fidelity assures me of his will. My household's fidelity is the basic guarantee of its unity. So in women, who constitute the crucial relationships within the household, fidelity is the

key virtue. Andromache and Hector, Penelope and Odysseus are friends (*philos*) as much as are Achilles and Patroclus.

What I hope this account makes clear already is the way in which any adequate account of the virtues in heroic society would be impossible which divorced them from their context in its social structure, just as no adequate account of the social structure of heroic society would be possible which did not include an account of the heroic virtues. But to put it this way is to understate the crucial point: morality and social structure are in fact one and the same in heroic society. There is only one set of social bonds. Morality as something distinct does not yet exist. Evaluative questions *are* questions of social fact. It is for this reason that Homer speaks always of *knowledge* of what to do and how to judge. Nor are such questions difficult to answer, except in exceptional cases. For the given rules which assign men their place in the social order and with it their identity also prescribe what they owe and what is owed to them and how they are to be treated and regarded if they fail and how they are to treat and regard others if those others fail.

Without such a place in the social order, a man would not only be incapable of receiving recognition and response from others; not only would others not know, but he would not himself know who he was. It is precisely because of this that heroic societies commonly have a well-defined status to which any stranger who arrives in the society from outside can be assigned. In Greek the word for 'alien' and the word for 'guest' are the same word. A stranger has to be received with hospitality, limited but well-defined. When Odysseus encounters the Cyclopes the question as to whether they possess *themis* (the Homeric concept of *themis* is the concept of customary law shared by all civilised peoples) is to be answered by discovering how they treat strangers. In fact they eat them—that is, for them strangers have no recognised human identity.

We might thus expect to find in heroic societies an emphasis upon the contrast between the expectations of the man who not only possesses courage and its allied virtues, but who also has kinsmen and friends on the one hand and the man lacking all these on the other. Yet one central theme of heroic societies is also that death waits for both alike. Life is fragile, men are vulnerable and it is of the essence of the human situation that they are such. For in heroic societies life is the standard of value. If someone kills you, my friend or brother, I owe you their death and when I have paid my debt to you their friend or brother owes them my death. The more extended my system of kinsmen and friends, the more liabilities I shall incur of a kind that may end in my death.

Moreover there are powers in the world which no one can control. Human life is invaded by passions which appear sometimes as impersonal forces, sometimes as gods. Achilles' wrath disrupts Achilles as well as his relationship to the other Greeks. These forces and the rules of kinship and friendship together constitute patterns of an ineluctable kind. Neither willing nor cunning will enable anyone to evade them. Fate is a social reality and the descrying of fate an important social role. It is no accident that the prophet or the seer flourishes equally in Homeric Greece, in saga Iceland and in pagan Ireland.

The man therefore who does what he ought moves steadily towards his fate and his death. It is defeat and not victory that lies at the end. To understand this is itself a virtue; indeed it is a necessary part of courage to understand this. But what is involved in such understanding? What would have been understood if the connections between courage, friendship, fidelity, the household, fate and death had been grasped? Surely that human life has a determinate form, the form of a certain kind of story. It is not just that poems and sagas narrate what happens to men and women, but that in their narrative form poems and sagas capture a form that was already present in the lives which they relate.

'What is character but the determination of incident?' wrote Henry James. 'What is incident but the illustration of character?' But in heroic society character of the relevant kind can only be exhibited in a succession of incidents and the succession itself must exemplify certain patterns. Where heroic society agrees with James is that character and incident cannot be characterised independently of each other. So to understand courage as a virtue is not just to understand how it may be exhibited in character, but also what place it can have in a certain kind of enacted story. For courage in heroic society

is a capacity not just to face particular harms and dangers but to face a particular kind of pattern of harms and dangers, a pattern in which individual lives find their place and which such lives in turn exemplify.

What epic and saga then portray is a society which already embodies the form of epic or saga. Its poetry articulates its form of individual and social life. To say this is still to leave open the question of whether there ever were such societies; but it does suggest that if there were such societies they could only be adequately understood through their poetry. Yet epic and saga are certainly not simple mirror images of the society they profess to portray. For it is quite clear that the poet or the saga writer claims for himself a kind of understanding which is denied to the characters about whom he writes. The

> *". . . [M]orality and social structure are in fact one and the same in heroic society."*

poet does not suffer from the limitations which define the essential condition of his characters. Consider especially the *Iliad*.

As I said earlier of heroic society in general, the heroes in the *Iliad* do not find it difficult to know what they owe one another, they feel *aidôs*—a proper sense of shame—when confronted with the possibility of wrongdoing, and if that is not sufficient, other people are always at hand to drive home the accepted view. Honour is conferred by one's peers and without honour a man is without worth. There is indeed in the vocabulary available to Homer's characters no way for them to view their own culture and society as if from the outside. The evaluative expressions which they employ are mutually interdefined and each has to be explained in terms of the others.

Let me use a dangerous, but illuminating analogy. The rules which govern both action and evaluative judgment in the *Iliad* resemble the rules and the precepts of a game such as chess. It is a question of fact whether a man is a good chess player, whether he is good at devising end-game strategies, whether a move is the right move to make in a particular situation. The game of chess presupposes, indeed is partially constituted by, agreement on how to play chess. Within the vocabulary of chess it makes no sense to say 'That was the one and only move which would achieve checkmate, but was it the right move to make?' And therefore someone who said this and understood what he was saying would have to be employing some notion of 'right' which receives its definition from outside chess, as someone might ask this whose purpose in playing chess was to amuse a small child rather than to win.

One reason why the analogy is dangerous is that we do play games such as chess for a variety of purposes. But there is nothing to be made of the question: for what purpose do the characters in the *Iliad* observe the rules that they observe and honour the precepts which they honour? It is rather the case that it is only within their framework of rules and precepts that they are able to frame purposes at all; and just because of this the analogy breaks down in another way, too. All questions of choice arise within the framework; the framework itself therefore cannot be chosen.

There is thus the sharpest of contrasts between the emotivist self of modernity and the self of the heroic age. The self of the heroic age lacks precisely that characteristic which we have already seen that some modern moral philosophers take to be an essential characteristic of human selfhood: the capacity to detach oneself from any particular standpoint or point of view, to step backwards, as it were, and view and judge that standpoint or point of view from the outside. In heroic society there is no 'outside' except that of the stranger. A man who tried to withdraw himself from his given position in heroic society would be engaged in the enterprise of trying to make himself disappear.

Identity in heroic society involves particularity and accountability. I am answerable for doing or failing to do what anyone who occupies my role owes to others and this accountability terminates only with death. I have until my death to do what I have to do. Moreover this accountability is particular. It is to, for and with specific individuals that I must do what I ought, and it is to these same and other individuals, members of the same local community, that I am accountable. The heroic self does not itself aspire to universality even although in retrospect we may recognise universal worth in the achievements of that self.

The exercise of the heroic virtues thus requires both a particular kind of human being and a particular kind of social structure. Just because this is so, an inspection of the heroic virtues may at first sight appear irrelevant to any general enquiry into moral theory and practice. If the heroic virtues require for their exercise the presence of a kind of social structure which is now irrevocably lost—as they do—what relevance can they possess for us? Nobody now can be a Hector or a Gisli. The answer is that perhaps what we have to learn from heroic societies is twofold: first that all morality is always to some degree tied to the socially local and particular and that the aspirations of the morality of modernity to a universality freed from all particularity is an illusion; and secondly that there is no way to possess the virtues except as part of a tradition in which we inherit them and our understanding of them from a series of predecessors in which series heroic societies hold first place. . . .

Study Questions

1. Can something be a virtue in one society and a vice in another?

2. To what extent do historical, scientific, and economic conditions determine what is considered vice and virtue?

Jealousy, Envy, and Spite

Immanuel Kant (1724–1804) Immanuel Kant was born in Konigsberg, Prussia. He was a professor of philosophy and the author of major works on knowledge, ethics, and art.

Immanuel Kant

There are two methods by which men arrive at an opinion of their worth: by comparing themselves with the idea of perfection and by comparing themselves with others. The first of these methods is sound; the second is not, and it frequently even leads to a result diametrically opposed to the first. The Idea of perfection is a proper standard, and if we measure our worth by it, we find that we fall short of it and feel that we must exert ourselves to come nearer to it; but if we compare ourselves with others, much depends upon who those others are and how they are constituted, and we can easily believe ourselves to be of great worth if those with whom we set up comparison are rogues. Men love to compare themselves with others, for by that method they can always arrive at a result favourable to themselves. They choose as a rule the worst and not the best of the class with which they set up comparison; in this way their own excellence shines out. If they choose those of greater worth the result of the comparison is, of course, unfavourable to them.

When I compare myself with another who is better than I, there are but two ways by which I can bridge the gap between us. I can either do my best to attain to his perfections, or else I can seek to depreciate his good qualities. I either increase my own worth, or else I diminish his so that I can always regard myself as superior to him. It is easier to depreciate another than to emulate him, and men prefer the easier course. They adopt it, and

From *Lectures On Ethics,* translated by Louis Infield. Published by Methuen & Co. (U.K.) Ltd., London.

this is the origin of jealousy. When a man compares himself with another and finds that the other has many more good points, he becomes jealous of each and every good point he discovers in the other, and tries to depreciate it so that his own good points may stand out. This kind of jealousy may be called grudging. The other species of the genus jealousy, which makes us try to add to our good points so as to compare well with another, may be called emulating jealousy. The jealousy of emulation is, as we have stated, more difficult than the jealousy of grudge and so is much the less frequent of the two.

Parents ought not, therefore, when teaching their children to be good, to urge them to model themselves on other children and try to emulate them, for by so doing they simply make them jealous. If I tell my son, 'Look, how good and industrious John is,' the result will be that my son will bear John a grudge. He will think to himself that, but for John, he himself would be the best, because there would be no comparison. By setting up John as a pattern for imitation I anger my son, make him feel a grudge against this so-called paragon, and I instil jealousy in him. My son, might, of course, try to emulate John, but not finding it easy, he will bear John ill-will. Besides, just as I can say to my son, 'Look, how good John is,' so can he reply: 'Yes, he is better than I, but are there not many who are far worse? Why do you compare me with those who are better? Why not with those who are worse than I?' Goodness must, therefore, be commended to children in and for itself. Whether other children are better or worse has no bearing on the point. If the comparison were in the child's favour, he would lose all ground of impulse to improve his own conduct. To ask our children to model themselves on others is to adopt a faulty method of upbringing, and as time goes on the fault will strike its roots deep. It is jealousy that parents are training and presupposing in their children when they set other children before them as patterns. Otherwise, the children would be quite indifferent to the qualities of others. They will find it easier to belittle the good qualities of their patterns than to emulate them, so they will choose the easier path and learn to show a grudging disposition. It is true that jealousy is natural, but that is no excuse for cultivating it. It is only a motive, a reserve in case of need. While the maxims of reason are still undeveloped in us, the proper course is to use reason to keep it within bounds. For jealousy is only one of the many motives, such as ambition, which are implanted in us because we are designed for a life of activity. But so soon as reason is enthroned, we must cease to seek perfection in emulation of others and must covet it in and for itself. Motives must abdicate and let reason bear rule in their place.

Persons of the same station and occupation in life are particularly prone to be jealous of each other. Many business-men are jealous of each other; so are many scholars, particularly in the same line of scholarship; and women are liable to be jealous of each other regarding men.

Grudge is the displeasure we feel when another has an advantage; his advantage makes us feel unduly small and we grudge it him. But to grudge a man his share of happiness is envy. To be envious is to desire the failure and unhappiness of another not for the purpose of advancing our own success and happiness but because we might then ourselves be perfect and happy as we are. An envious man is not happy unless all around him are unhappy; his aim is to stand alone in the enjoyment of his happiness. Such is envy, and we shall learn below that it is satanic. Grudge, although it too should not be countenanced, is natural. Even a good-natured person may at times be grudging. Such a one may, for instance, begrudge those around him their jollity when he himself happens to be sorrowful; for it is hard to bear one's sorrow when all around are joyful. When I see everybody enjoying a good meal

and I alone must content myself with inferior fare, it upsets me and I feel a grudge; but if we are all in the same boat I am content. We find the thought of death bearable, because we know that all must die; but if everybody were immortal and I alone had to die, I should feel aggrieved. It is not things themselves that affect us, but things in their relation to ourselves. We are grudging because others are happier than we. But when a good-natured man feels happy and cheerful, he wishes that every one else in the world were as happy as he and shared his joy; he begrudges no one his happiness.

When a man would not grant to another even that for which he himself has no need, he is spiteful. Spite is a maliciousness of spirit which is not the same thing as envy. I may not feel inclined to give to another something which belongs to me, even though I myself have no use for it, but it does not follow that I grudge him his own possessions, that I want to be the only one who has anything and wish him to have nothing at all. There is a deal of grudge in human nature which could develop into envy but which is not itself envy. We feel pleasure in gossiping about the minor misadventures of other people; we are not averse, although we may express no pleasure thereat, to hearing of the fall of some rich man; we may enjoy in stormy weather, when comfortably seated in our warm, cosy parlour, speaking of those at sea, for it heightens our own feeling of comfort and happiness; there is grudge in all this, but it is not envy.

The three vices which are the essence of vileness and wickedness are ingratitude, envy, and malice. When these reach their full degree they are devilish.

Men are shamed by favours. If I receive a favour, I am placed under an obligation to the giver; he has a call upon me because I am indebted to him. We all blush to be obliged. Noble-minded men accordingly refuse to accept favours in order not to put themselves under an obligation. But this attitude predisposes the mind to ingratitude. If the man who adopts it is noble-minded, well and good; but if he be proud and selfish and has perchance received a favour, the feeling that he is beholden to his benefactor hurts his pride and, being selfish, he cannot accommodate himself to the idea that he owes his benefactor anything. He becomes defiant and ungrateful. His ingratitude might even conceivably assume such dimensions that he cannot bear his benefactor and becomes his enemy. Such ingratitude is of the devil; it is out of all keeping with human nature. It is inhuman to hate and persecute one from whom we have reaped a benefit, and if such conduct were the rule it would cause untold harm. Men would then be afraid to do good to anyone lest they should receive evil in return for their good. They would become misanthropic.

The second devilish vice is envy. Envy is in the highest degree detestable. The envious man does not merely want to be happy; he wants to be the only happy person in the world; he is really contented only when he sees nothing but misery around him. Such an intolerable creature would gladly destroy every source of joy and happiness in the world.

Malice is the third kind of viciousness which is of the devil. It consists in taking a direct pleasure in the misfortunes of others. Men prone to this vice will seek, for instance, to make mischief between husband and wife, or between friends, and then enjoy the misery they have produced. In these matters we should make it a rule never to repeat to a person anything that we may have heard to his disadvantage from another, unless our silence would injure him. Otherwise we start an enmity and disturb his peace of mind, which our silence would have avoided, and in addition we break faith with our informant. The defence against such mischief-makers is upright conduct. Not by words but by our lives we should confute them. As Socrates said: We ought so to conduct ourselves that people will not credit anything spoken in disparagement of us.

These three vices—ingratitude (*ingratitudo qualificata*), envy, and malice—are devilish because they imply a direct inclination to evil. There are in man certain indirect tendencies to wickedness which are human and not unnatural. The miser wants everything for himself, but it is no satisfaction to him to see that his neighbour is destitute. The evilness of a vice may thus be either direct or indirect. In these three vices it is direct.

We may ask whether there is in the human mind an immediate inclination to wickedness, an inclination to the devilish vices. Heaven stands for the acme of happiness, hell for all that is bad, and the earth stands midway between these two extremes; and just as goodness which transcends anything which might be expected of a human being is spoken of as being angelic, so also do we speak of devilish wickedness when the wickedness oversteps the limits of human nature and becomes inhuman. We may take it for granted that the human mind has no immediate inclination to wickedness, but is only indirectly wicked. Man cannot be so ungrateful that he simply must hate his neighbour; he may be too proud to show his gratitude and so avoid him, but he wishes him well. Again, our pleasure in the misfortune of another is not direct. We may rejoice, for example, in a man's misfortunes, because he was haughty, rich and selfish; for man loves to preserve equality. We have thus no direct inclination towards evil as evil, but only an indirect one. But how are we to explain the fact that even young children have the spirit of mischief strongly developed? For a joke, a boy will stick a pin in an unsuspecting playmate, but it is only for fun. He has no thought of the pain the other must feel on all such occasions. In the same spirit he will torture animals; twisting the cat's tail or the dog's. Such tendencies must be nipped in the bud, for it is easy to see where they will lead. They are, in fact, something animal, something of the beast of prey which is in us all, which we cannot overcome, and the source of which we cannot explain. There certainly are in human nature characteristics for which we can assign no reason. There are animals too who steal anything that comes their way, though it is quite useless to them; and it seems as if man had retained this animal tendency in his nature.

Ingratitude calls for some further observations here. To help a man in distress is charity; to help him in less urgent needs is benevolence; to help him in the amenities of life is courtesy. We may be the recipients of a charity which has not cost the giver much and our gratitude is commensurate with the degree of good-will which moved him to the action. We are grateful not only for what we have received but also for the good intention which prompted it, and the greater the effort it has cost our benefactor, the greater our gratitude.

Gratitude may be either from duty or from inclination. If an act of kindness does not greatly move us, but if we nevertheless feel that it is right and proper that we should show gratitude, our gratitude is merely prompted by a sense of duty. Our heart is not grateful, but we have principles of gratitude. If, however, our heart goes out to our benefactor, we are grateful from inclination. There is a weakness of the understanding which we often have cause to recognize. It consists in taking the conditions of our understanding as conditions of the thing understood. We can estimate force only in terms of the obstacles it overcomes. Similarly, we can only estimate the degree of good-will in terms of the obstacles it has to surmount. In consequence we cannot comprehend the love and goodwill of a being for whom there are no obstacles. If God has been good to me, I am liable to think that after all it has cost God no trouble, and that gratitude to God would be mere fawning on my part. Such thoughts are not at all unnatural. It is easy to fear God, but not nearly so easy to love God from inclination because of our consciousness that God is a being whose

> "Men love to compare themselves with others, for by that method they can always arrive at a result favourable to themselves."

goodness is unbounded but to whom it is no trouble to shower kindness upon us. This is not to say that such should be our mental attitude; merely that when we examine our hearts, we find that this is how we actually think. It also explains why to many races God appeared to be a jealous God, seeing that it cost Him nothing to be more bountiful with His goodness; it explains why many nations thought that their gods were sparing of their benefits and that they required propitiating with prayers and sacrifices. This is the attitude of man's heart; but when we call reason to our aid we see that God's goodness must be of a high order if He is to be good to a being so unworthy of His goodness. This solves our difficulty. The gratitude we owe to God is not gratitude from inclination, but from duty, for God is

not a creature like ourselves, and can be no object of our inclinations.

We ought not to accept favours unless we are either forced to do so by dire necessity or have implicit confidence in our benefactor (for he ceases to be our friend and becomes our benefactor) that he will not regard it as placing us under an obligation to him. To accept favours indiscriminately and to be constantly seeking them is ignoble and the sign of a mean soul which does not mind placing itself under obligations. Unless we are driven by such dire necessity that it compels us to sacrifice our own worth, or unless we are convinced that our benefactor will not account it to us as a debt, we ought rather to suffer deprivation than accept favours, for a favour is a debt which can never be extinguished. For even if I repay my benefactor tenfold, I am still not even with him, because he has done me a kindness which he did not owe. He was the first in the field, and even if I return his gift tenfold I do so only as repayment. He will always be the one who was the first to show kindness and I can never be beforehand with him.

The man who bestows favours can do so either in order to make the recipient indebted to him or as an expression of his duty. If he makes the recipient feel a sense of indebtedness, he wounds his pride and diminishes his sense of gratitude. If he wishes to avoid this he must regard the favours he bestows as the discharge of a duty he owes to mankind, and he must not give the recipient the impression that it is a debt to be repaid. On the other hand, the recipient of the favour must still consider himself under an obligation to his benefactor and must be grateful to him. Under these conditions there can be benefactors and beneficiaries. A right-thinking man will not accept kindnesses, let alone favours. A grateful disposition is a touching thing and brings tears to our eyes on the stage, but a generous disposition is lovelier still. Ingratitude we detest to a surprising degree; even though we are not ourselves the victims of it, it angers us to such an extent that we feel inclined to intervene. But this is due to the fact that ingratitude decreases generosity.

Envy does not consist in wishing to be more happy than others—that is grudge—but in wishing to be the only one to be happy. It is this feeling which makes envy so evil. Why should not others be happy along with me? Envy shows itself also in relation to things which are scarce. Thus the Dutch, who as a nation are rather envious, once valued tulips at several hundreds of florins apiece. A rich merchant, who had one of the finest and rarest specimens, heard that another had a similar specimen. He thereupon bought it from him for 2,000 florins and trampled it underfoot, saying that he had no use for it, as he already possessed a specimen, and that he only wished that no one else should share that distinction with him. So it is also in the matter of happiness.

Malice is different. A malicious man is pleased when others suffer, he can laugh when others weep. An act which wilfully brings unhappiness is cruel; when it produces physical pain it is bloodthirsty. Inhumanity is all these together, just as humanity consists in sympathy and pity, since these differentiate man from the beasts. It is difficult to explain what gives rise to a cruel disposition. It may arise when a man considers another so evilly disposed that he hates him. A man who believes himself hated by another, hates him in return, although the former may have good reason to hate him. For if a man is hated because he is selfish and has other vices, and he knows that he is hated for these reasons, he hates those who hate him although these latter do him no injustice. Thus kings who know that they are hated by their subjects become even more cruel. Equally, when a man has done a good deed to another, he knows that the other loves him, and so he loves him in return, knowing that he himself is loved. Just as love is reciprocated, so also is hate. We must for our own sakes guard against being hated by others lest we be affected by that hatred and reciprocate it. The hater is more disturbed by his hatred than is the hated.

Study Questions

1. To what extent is jealousy and envy a part of human nature?

2. Is humankind by nature good or evil?

3. Is there a way to raise children to make them more moral as adults?

The Evil of Lying

Charles Fried was a professor of law at Harvard before becoming Solicitor General of the United States in the Department of Justice where he argues the government's case before the U.S. Supreme Court.

Charles Fried

The evil of lying is as hard to pin down as it is strongly felt. Is lying wrong or is it merely something bad? If it is bad, why is it bad—is it bad in

Reprinted by permission of the publishers from *Right and Wrong* by Charles Fried, Cambridge, Mass.: Harvard University Press, copyright © 1978 by the President and Fellows of Harvard College.

itself or because of some tendency associated with it? Compare lying to physical harm. Harm is a state of the world and so it can only be classified as bad; the wrong I argued for was the *intentional doing* of harm. Lying, on the other hand, can be wrong, since it is an action. But the fact that lying is an action does not mean that it *must* be wrong rather than bad. It might be that the action of lying should be judged as just another state of the world—a time-extended state, to be sure, but there is no problem about that—and as such it would count as a negative element in any set of circumstances in which it occurred. Furthermore, if lying is judged to be bad it can be bad in itself, like something ugly or painful, or it can be bad only because of its tendency to produce results that are bad in themselves.

If lying were bad, not wrong, this would mean only that, other things being equal, we should avoid lies. And if lying were bad not in itself but merely because of its tendencies, we would have to avoid lies only when those tendencies were in fact likely to be realized. In either case lying would be permissible to produce a net benefit, including the prevention of more or worse lies. By contrast the categorical norm "Do not lie" does not evaluate states of affairs but is addressed to moral agents, forbidding lies. Now if lying is wrong it is also bad in itself, for the category of the intrinsically bad is weaker and more inclusive than the category of the wrong. And accordingly, many states of the world are intrinsically bad (such as destruction of valuable property) but intentional acts bringing them about are not necessarily wrong.

Bentham plainly believed that lying is neither wrong nor even intrinsically bad: "Falsehood, take it by itself, consider it as not being accompanied by any other material circumstances, nor therefore productive of any material effects, can never, upon the principle of utility, constitute any offense at all" (*An Introduction to the Principles of Morals and Legislation,* ch. 16, sec. 24). By contrast, Kant and Augustine argued at length that lying is wrong. Indeed, they held that lying is not only wrong *unless* excused or justified in defined ways (which is my view) but that lying is always wrong. Augustine sees lying as a kind of defilement, the liar being tainted by the lie, quite apart from any consequences of the lie. Kant's views are more complex. He argues at

one point that lying undermines confidence and trust among men generally: "Although by making a false statement I do no wrong to him who unjustly compels me to speak, yet I do wrong to men in general ... I cause that declarations in general find no credit, and hence all rights founded on contract should lose their force; and this is a wrong to mankind" ("On a Supposed Right to Tell Lies from Benevolent Motives," in *Kant's Critique of Practical Reason and Other Works,* translated by T. K. Abbott [London: Longmans, Green, 1973]). This would seem to be a consequentialist argument, according to which lying is bad only insofar as it produces these bad results. But elsewhere he makes plain that he believes these bad consequences to be necessarily, perhaps even conceptually linked to lying. In this more rigoristic vein, he asserts that lying is a perversion of one's uniquely human capacities irrespective of any consequences of the lie, and thus lying is not only intrinsically bad but wrong.[1]

---

1. "The greatest violation of man's duty to himself merely as a moral being (to humanity in his own person) is ... the lie. In the doctrine of Law an intentional wrong is called a lie only if it infringes on another's right. But ... in ethics ... every deliberate untruth deserves this harsh name. By a lie a man makes himself contemptible ... and violates the dignity of humanity in his own person. And so, since the harm that can come to others from it is not the characteristic property of this vice (for it if were, the vice would consist only in violating one's duty to others), we do not take this harm into account here ... By a lie man throws away and, as it were, annihilates his dignity as a man. A man [who lies] ... has even less worth than if he were a mere thing. For a thing, as something real and given, has the property of being serviceable ... But the man who communicates his thoughts to someone in words which yet (intentionally) contain the contrary of what he thinks on the subject has a purpose directly opposed to the natural purposiveness of the power of communicating one's thoughts and therefore renounces his personality and makes himself a mere deceptive appearance of man, not man himself.

"A lie (in the ethical sense of the term), as an intentional untruth as such, need not be harmful to others in order to be pronounced reprehensible; for then it would be a violation of the rights of others ... A lie requires a second person whom

Finally, a number of writers have taken what looks like an intermediate position: the evil of lying is indeed identified with its consequences, but the connection between lying and those consequences, while not a necessary connection, is close and persistent, and the consequences themselves are pervasive and profound. Consider this passage from a recent work by G. F. Warnock:

> I do not necessarily do you any harm at all by deed or word if I induce you to believe what is not in fact the case; I may even do you good, possibly by way, for example, of consolation or flattery. Nevertheless, though deception is not thus necessarily directly damaging it is easy to see how crucially important it is that the natural inclination to have recourse to it should be counteracted. It is, one might say, not the implanting of false beliefs that is damaging, but rather the generation of the suspicion that they may be being implanted. For this undermines trust; and, to the extent that trust is undermined, all cooperative undertakings, in which what one person can do or has reason to do is dependent on what others have done, are doing, or are going to do, must tend to break down. . . . There is no sense in my asking you for your opinion on some point, if I do not suppose that your answer will actually express your opinion (verbal communication is doubtless the most important of all our co-operative undertakings). (*The Object of Morality* [London: Methuen, 1971], p. 84.)

Warnock does not quite say that truth-telling is good in itself or that lying is wrong, yet the moral quality of truth-telling and lying is not so simply instrumental as it is, for instance, for Bentham. Rather, truth-telling seems to bear a fundamental, pervasive relation to the human enterprise, just as lying appears to be fundamentally subversive of that enterprise. What exactly is the nature of this relation? How does truth-telling bear to human goods a relation which is more than instrumental but less than necessary?

The very definition of lying makes plain that consequences are crucial, for lying is intentional and the intent is an intent to produce a consequence: false belief. But how can I then resist the consequentialist analysis of lying? Lying is an attempt to produce a certain effect on another, and if that effect (consequence) is not bad, how can lying be wrong? I shall have to argue, therefore, that to lie is to intend to produce an effect which always has something bad about it, an effect moreover of the special sort that it is wrong to produce it intentionally. To lay that groundwork for my argument about lying, I must consider first the moral value of truth.

Truth and Rationality

A statement is true when the world is the way the statement says it is.[2] Utilitarians insist (as in the quotation from Bentham above) that truth, like everything else, has value just exactly as it produces value—pleasure, plain, the satisfaction or frustration of desire. And of course it is easy to show that truth (like keeping faith, not harming the innocent, respecting rights) does not always lead to the net satisfactions of desire, to the production of utility. It may *tend* to do so, but that tendency explains only why we should discriminate between occasions when truth does and when it does not have value—

---

one intends to deceive, and intentionally to deceive oneself seems to contain a contradiction.

"Man as a moral being (*homo noumenon*), cannot use his natural being (*homo phaenomenon*) as a mere means (a speaking machine), as if it were not bound to its intrinsic end (the communication of thought)." (*Tugendlehre* [428–430], translated by Mary J. Gregor, *The Doctrine of Virtue*, Philadelphia: University of Pennsylvania Press, 1964.)

2. This definition is derived from Alfred Tarski via Donald Davidson, "Meaning and Truth," in Jay F. Rosenberg and Charles Travis, eds., *Reading in the Philosophy of Language* (Englewood Cliffs, N.J.: Prentice-Hall, 1971). See also Gottlob Frege, "The Thought: A Logical Inquiry," and Michael Dummett, "Truth," both in Peter Strawson, ed., *Philosophical Logic* (Oxford: Oxford University Press, 1967). The difficulties in arriving at a satisfactory conception of truth do not touch the moral issues that I discuss in this chapter. Indeed, I suppose that any of a large class of definitions might be substituted for the one I used in the text and my substantive argument would go through without a hitch.

an old story. It is an old story, for truth—like justice, respect, and self-respect—has a value which consequentialist analyses (utilitarian or any other) do not capture. Truth, like respect, is a foundational value.

The morality of right and wrong does not count the satisfaction of desire as the overriding value. Rather, the integrity of persons, as agents and as the objects of the intentional agency of others, has priority over the attainment of the goals which agents choose to attain. I have sought to show how respect for physical integrity is related to respect for the person. The person, I argued, is not just a locus of potential pleasure and pain but an entity with determinate characteristics. The person is, among other things, necessarily an incorporated, a physical, not an abstract entity. In relation to truth we touch another necessary aspect of moral personality: the capacity for judgment, and thus for choice. It is that aspect which Kant used to ground his moral theory, arguing that freedom and rationality are the basis for moral personality. John Rawls makes the same point, arguing that "moral personality and not the capacity for pleasure and pain ... [is] the fundamental aspect of the self ... The essential unity of the self is ... provided by the concept of right" (*A Theory of Justice* [Cambridge, Mass.: Harvard University Press, 1971], p. 563). The concept of the self is prior to the goods which the self chooses, and these goods gather their moral significance from the fact that they have been chosen by moral beings— beings capable of understanding and acting on moral principles.

In this view freedom and rationality are complementary capacities, or aspects of the same capacity, which is moral capacity. A man is free insofar as he is able to act on a judgment because he perceives it to be correct; he is free insofar as he may be moved to action by the judgments his reason offers to him. This is the very opposite of the Humean conception of reason as the slave of the passions. There is no slavery here. The man who follows the steps of a mathematical argument to its conclusion because he judges them to be correct is free indeed. To the extent that we choose our ends we are free; and as to objectively valuable ends which we choose because we see their value, we are still free.

Now, rational judgment is true judgment, and so the moral capacity for rational choice implies the capacity to recognize the matter on which choice is to act and to recognize the kind of result our choices will produce. This applies to judgments about other selves and to judgments in which one locates himself as a person among persons, a self among selves. These judgments are not just arbitrary suppositions: *they are judged to be true of the world.* For consider what the self would be like if these judgments were not supposed to be true. Maybe one might be content to be happy in the manner of the fool of Athens who believed all the ships in the harbor to be his. But what of our perceptions of other people? Would we be content to have those whom we love and trust the mere figments of our imaginations? The foundational values of freedom and rationality imply the foundational value of truth, for the rational man is the one who judges aright, that is, truly. Truth is not the same as judgment, as rationality; it is rather the proper subject of judgment. If we did not seek to judge truly, and if we did not believe we could judge truly, the act of judgment would not be what we know it to be at all.

Judgment and thus truth are *part* of a structure which as a whole makes up the concept of self. A person's relation to his body and the fact of being an incorporated self are another part of that structure. These two parts are related. The bodily senses provide matter for judgments of truth, and the body includes the physical organs of judgment.

The Wrong of Lying

So our capacity for judgment is foundational and truth is the proper object of that capacity, but how do we get to the badness of lying, much less its categorical wrongness? The crucial step to be supplied has to do not with the value of truth but with the evil of lying. We must show that to lie to someone is to injure him in a way that particularly touches his moral personality. From that, the passage is indeed easy to the conclusion that to inflict such injury intentionally (remember that all lying is by hypothesis intentional) is not only bad but wrong. It is this first, crucial step which is difficult. After all, a person's capacity for true judgment is not necessarily impaired by inducing in him a particular false belief. Nor would it seem that a person suffers a greater injury in respect to that capacity when he is induced to believe a falsity than when we intentionally prevent him from discovering the truth, yet only in the first case do we lie. Do we really do injury to a person's moral personality when we persuade him falsely that it rained yesterday in Bangkok—a fact in which he has no interest? And do we do him more injury than when we fail to answer his request for yesterday's football scores, in which he is mildly interested? Must we not calculate the injury by the *other* harm it does: disappointed expectations, lost property, missed opportunities, physical harm? In this view, lying would be a way of injuring a person in his various substantive interests—a way of stealing from him, hurting his feelings, perhaps poisoning him—but then the evil of lying would be purely instrumental, not wrong at all.

All truth, however irrelevant or trivial, has value, even though we may cheerfully ignore most truths, forget them, erase them as encumbrances from our memories. The value of every truth is shown just in the judgment that the only thing we must not do is falsify truth. Truths are like other people's property, which we can care nothing about but may not use for our own purposes. It is as if the truth were not ours (even truth we have discovered and which is known only to us), and so we may not exercise an unlimited dominion over it. Our relations to other people have a similar structure: we may perhaps have no duty to them, we may be free to put them out of our minds to make room for others whom we care about more, but we may not harm them. And so we may not falsify truth. But enough of metaphors—what does it mean to say that the truth is not ours?

The capacity for true judgment is the capacity to arrive at judgments which are in fact true of the world as it exists apart from our desires, our choices, our values. It is the world presented to us by true judgments—including true judgments about ourselves—which we then make the subject of our choices, our valuation. Now, if we treat the truth as our own, it must be according to desire or valuation. But for rational beings these activities are supposed to depend on truth; we are supposed to depend and choose according to the world as it is. To choose that something not be the case when it is in fact the case is very nearly self-contradictory—for choice is not *of* truth but *on the basis of* truth. To deliberate about whether to believe a truth (not whether it is indeed true—another story altogether) is like deciding whether to cheat at solitaire. All this is obvious. In fact I suppose one cannot even coherently talk about choosing to believe something one believes to be false. And this holds equally for all truths—big and little, useful, useless, and downright inconvenient. But we do and must calculate *about* (and not just *with*) truths all the time as we decide what truths to acquire, what to forget. We decide all the time not to pursue some inquiry because it is not worth it. Such calculations surely must go forward on the basis of what truths are useful, given one's plans and desires. Even when we pursue truth for its own sake, we distinguish between interesting and boring truths.

"When I lie, I lay claim to your mind."

Considering what truth to acquire or retain differs, however, from deliberately acquiring false beliefs. All truths are acquired as propositions correctly (truly) corresponding to the world, and in this respect, all truths are equal. A lie, however, has the form and occupies the role of truth in that it too purports to be a proposition about the world; only the world does not correspond to it. So the choice of a lie is not like a choice among truths, for the choice of a lie is a choice to affirm as the basis for judgment a proposition which does not correspond to the world. So, when I say that truth is foundational, that truth precedes choice, what I mean is *not* that this or that truth is foundational but that judging according to the facts is foundational to judging at all. A scientist may deliberate about which subject to study and, having chosen his subject, about the data worth acquiring, but he cannot even deliberate as a scientist about whether to acquire false data. Clearly, then, there is something funny (wrong?) about lying to oneself, but how do we go from there to the proposition that it is wrong to lie to someone else? After all, much of the peculiarity about lying to oneself consists in the fact that it seems not so much bad as downright self-contradictory, logically impossible, but that does not support the judgment that it is wrong to lie to another. I cannot marry myself, but that hardly makes it wrong to marry someone else.

Let us imagine a case in which you come as close as you can to lying to yourself: You arrange some operation, some fiddling with your brain that has no effect other than to cause you to believe a proposition you know to be false and also to forget entirely the prior history of how you came to believe that proposition. It seems to me that you do indeed harm yourself in such an operation. This is because a free and rational person wishes to have a certain relation to reality: as nearly perfect as possible. He wishes to build his conception of himself and the world and his conception of the good on the basis of truth. Now if he affirms that the truth is available for fiddling in order to accommodate either his picture of the world or his conception of the good, then this affirms that reality is dependent on what one wants, rather than what one wants being fundamentally constrained by what there is. Rationality is the respect for this fundamental constraint of truth. This is just another way of saying that the truth is prior to our plans and prospects and must be respected whatever our plans might be. What if the truth we "destroy" by this operation is a very trivial and irrelevant truth—the state of the weather in Bangkok on some particular day? There is still an injury to self, because the fiddler must have some purpose in his fiddling. If it is a substantive purpose, then the truth is in fact relevant to that purpose, and my argument holds. If it is just to show it can be done, then he is only trying to show he can do violence to his rationality—a kind of moral blasphemy. Well, what if it is a very *little* truth? Why, then, it is a very little injury he does himself—but that does not undermine my point.[3]

Now, when I lie to you, I do to you what you cannot actually do to yourself—brain-fiddling being only an approximation. The nature of the injury I would do to myself, if I could, explains why lying to you is to do you harm, indeed why it is wrong. The lie is an injury because it produces an effect (or seeks to) which a person as a moral agent should not wish to have produced in him, and thus it is as much an injury as any other effect which a moral agent would not wish to have produced upon his person. To be sure, some people may want to be lied to. That is a special problem; they are like people who want to suffer (not just are willing to risk) physical injury. In general, then, I do not want you to lie to me in the same way that as a rational man I would not lie to myself if I could. But why does this make lying wrong and not merely bad?[4]

Lying is wrong because when I lie I set up a relation which is essentially exploitative. It violates the principle of respect, for I must affirm that the mind of another person is available to me in a way in which I cannot agree my mind would be available to him—for if I do so agree, then I would not expect my lie to be believed. When I lie, I am like a counterfeiter: I do not want the market flooded with counterfeit currency; I do not want to get back my own counterfeit bill. Moreover, in lying to you, I affirm such an unfairly unilateral principle in respect to an interest and capacity which is crucial, as crucial as physical integrity: your freedom and your rationality. When I do intentional physical harm, I say that your body, your person, is available for my purposes. When I lie, I lay claim to your mind.

Lying violates respect and is wrong, as is any breach of trust. Every lie is a broken promise, and

---

3. Distinguish from this the frequent and important instances where one refuses to receive certain

truths: the man of honor who will not read scandalous accusations about another's private life, the judge who will not receive unauthorized information about a matter before him. These do not involve deliberate espousals of falsity. There is, after all, a proper domain of secret, private truths and of things which are none of our business.

4. It may be the case that every instance of any intentional injury to another person constitutes a wrongful relation (is wrong), but I am not prepared to argue that. I would rather examine the circumstances of this one kind of injury, lying, and show how that is wrong.

the only reason this seems strained is that in lying the promise is made and broken at the same moment. Every lie necessarily implies—as does every assertion—an assurance, a warranty of its truth. The fact that the breach accompanies the making should, however, only strengthen the conclusion that this is wrong. If promise-breaking is wrong, then a lie must be wrong, since there cannot be the supervening factor of changed circumstances which may excuse breaches of promises to perform in the future.

The final one of the convergent strands that make up the wrong of lying is the shared, communal nature of language. This is what I think Kant had in mind when he argued that a lie does wrong "to men in general." If whether people stood behind their statements depended wholly on the particular circumstances of the utterance, then the whole point of communication would be undermined. For every utterance would simply be the occasion for an analysis of the total circumstances (speaker's and hearer's) in order to determine what, if anything, to make of the utterance. And though we do often wonder and calculate whether a person is telling the truth, we do so from a baseline, a presumption that people do stand behind their statements. After all, the speaker surely depends on such a baseline. He wants us to think that he is telling the truth. Speech is a paradigm of communication, and all human relations are based on some form of communication. Our very ability to think, to conceptualize, is related to speech. Speech allows the social to penetrate the intimately personal. Perhaps that is why Kant's dicta seem to vacillate between two positions: lying as a social offense, and lying as an offense against oneself; the requirement of an intent to deceive another, and the insistence that the essence of the wrong is not injury to

another but to humanity. Every lie violates the basic commitment to truth which stands behind the social fact of language.

I have already argued that bodily integrity bears a necessary relation to moral integrity, so that an attack upon bodily integrity is wrong, not just bad. The intimate *and* social nature of truth make the argument about lying stronger. For not only is the target aspect of the victim crucial to him as a moral agent but, by lying, we attack that target by a means which itself offends his moral nature; the means of attack are social means which can be said to belong as much to the victim as to his assailant. There is not only the attack at his moral vitals, but an attack with a weapon which belongs to him. Lying is, thus, a kind of treachery. (*Kind of* treachery? Why not treachery pure and simple?) It is as if we not only robbed a man of his treasure but in doing so used his own servants or family as our agents. That speech is our *common* property, that it belongs to the liar, his victim and all of us makes the matter if anything far worse.

So this is why lying is not only bad (a hurt), but wrong, why lying is wrong apart from or in addition to any other injury it does, and why lying seems at once an offense against the victim and against mankind in general, an offense against the liar himself, and against the abstract entity, truth. Whom do you injure when you pass a counterfeit bill?

What about little pointless lies? Do I really mean they are wrong? Well, yes, even a little lie is wrong, *if* it is a true piece of communication, an assertion of its own truth and not just a conventional way of asserting nothing at all or something else (as in the case of polite or diplomatic formulas). A little lie is a little wrong, but it is still something you must not do.

Study Questions

1. Is lying always wrong?
2. If one had to choose, should one make someone happy and lie or tell the truth and cause someone unhappiness?

3. Why do you feel the way you do when you find out that someone has lied to you?

Compassion

Lawrence Blum is a professor of philosophy at the
University of Massachusetts, Boston, and author of
Friendship, Altruism and Morality.

Lawrence Blum

This paper offers an account of compassion as a
moral phenomenon. I regard compassion as a kind
of emotion or emotional attitude; though it differs
from paradigmatic emotions such as fear, anger, distress, love, it has, I will argue, an irreducible affective dimension.

Compassion is one among a number of attitudes,
emotions, or virtues which can be called "altruistic"
in that they involve a regard for the good of other
persons. Some others are pity, helpfulness, well-
wishing. Such phenomena and the distinctions between them have been given insufficient attention
in current moral philosophy. By distinguishing compassion from some of these other altruistic phenomena I want to bring out compassion's particular
moral value, as well as some of its limitations.[1]

My context for this inquiry is an interest in developing an alternative to Kantianism, in particular
to its minimization of the role of emotion in morality and its exclusive emphasis on duty and rationality. I am influenced here by Schopenhauer's critique of Kant's ethics and by his view of compassion
as central to morality.[2] But discussion of the specific
views of these two philosophers will be peripheral
to my task here.

The Objects of Compassion

How must a compassionate person view someone
in order to have compassion for him?[3] Compassion
seems restricted to beings capable of feeling or

From *Explaining Emotions,* ed. Amelie O. Rorty; pp.
507–17. Reprinted by permission of the publisher,
University of California Press. © 1980 The Regents of
the University of California.

being harmed. Bypassing the question of compassion for plants, animals, institutions, I will focus on
persons as objects of compassion. A person in a
negative condition, suffering some harm, difficulty,
danger (past, present, or future) is the appropriate
object of compassion. But there are many negative
conditions and not all are possible objects of compassion. The inconvenience and irritation of a short
detour for a driver on his way to a casual visit are
not compassion-grounding conditions.[4] The negative
condition must be relatively central to a person's
life and well-being, describable as pain, misery,

---

1. Compassion has a particular cultural history: its
   sources are Christian, it was further developed by
   Romanticism, especially by the German Romantics.
   Though I do not focus on this history explicitly,
   my emphasis on compassion as a particular moral
   emotion among others should leave room for the
   results of such a historical account.
2. Arthur Schopenhauer, *On the Basis of Morality*
   (New York: Bobbs-Merrill, 1965).
3. In general I will use feminine pronouns to refer to
   the person having compassion (the "subject") and
   masculine pronouns to refer to the person for
   whom she has compassion (the "object").
4. I am making a conceptual rather than a moral
   point. The compassionate person cannot regard
   the object of her compassion as merely irritated or
   discomforted; but of course a genuinely
   compassionate person might mistakenly take an
   inconvenience to be a serious harm. To say that
   compassion is "appropriate" in this context is,
   then, simply to say that the object actually
   possesses the compassion-grounding feature which
   the subject takes him to possess. I do not discuss
   the further issue of when compassion is *morally*
   appropriate or inappropriate.

hardship, suffering, affliction, and the like. Although it is the person and not merely the negative condition which is the object of compassion, the focus of compassion is the condition.

Compassion can be part of a complex attitude toward its object; it is possible to have compassion for someone in a difficult or miserable situation without judging his overall condition to be difficult or miserable. It is therefore necessary to distinguish the conditions for someone being an appropriate object of compassion from the conditions for compassion being the appropriate dominant response to the person. One might predominantly admire and take pleasure in the happiness of a blind person who has gotten through college, found a rewarding job, made close friends—someone whose life is generally happy and who does not dwell on what he misses by being blind. Nevertheless one can also feel compassion for him because his life is deficient and damaged by his blindness.

It is not necessary that the object of compassion be aware of his condition; he might be deceiving himself with regard to it. Nor, as in the case of the happy blind man, need he think of it as a substantial affliction, even if he is aware of it as a deficiency.

That compassion is limited to grave or serious negative conditions does not exclude other altruistic emotions from being entirely appropriate to less serious states. One can feel sorry for, commiserate with, or feel sympathy for a person's irritation, discomfort, inconvenience, displeasure. Nor are all altruistic attitudes primarily directed to particular persons: they can be directed to classes of persons (the blind) or to general conditions (poverty). In addition, there are altruistic virtues not so clearly involving emotions, which come into play in regard to less serious negative conditions: considerateness, thoughtfulness, helpfulness. It would be considerate or thoughtful to warn an acquaintance of an unexpected detour so that he could avoid needless inconvenience and irritation. Such virtues as these, while not necessarily involving emotion or feeling, do involve attention to another's situation and a genuine regard for the other's good, even when more self-regarding attitudes are conjointly brought into play.

Not all altruistic emotions are focused on nega-

tive states. Someone might take delight in giving pleasure to others. Though this altruistic attitude shares with compassion a regard for the good of others, compassion focuses on pain, suffering, and damage, whereas this other attitude focuses on pleasure. The capacity for one altruistic attitude is no assurance of the capacity for others. It is quite possible for a compassionate person to be insensitive to the pleasures of others. A focus on misery and suffering in the absence of regard for others' joys and pleasures constitutes a limitation in the moral consciousness of the merely compassionate person.[5]

The Emotional Attitude of Compassion

The compassionate person does not merely believe that the object suffers some serious harm or injury; such a belief is compatible with indifference, malicious delight in his suffering, or intense intellectual interest, for example of a novelist or psychologist for whom the suffering is primarily material for contemplation or investigation. Even a genuine interest in relieving someone's suffering can stem from meeting an intellectual or professional challenge rather than from compassion.

Compassion is not a simple feeling-state but a complex emotional attitude toward another, characteristically involving imaginative dwelling on the condition of the other person, an active regard for his good, a view of him as a fellow human being, and emotional responses of a certain degree of intensity.

Imaginatively reconstructing someone's condition is distinct from several sorts of "identification" with the other person. For instance, it does not involve an identity confusion in which the compassionate person fails to distinguish his feelings and situation from the other person's.[6] Such a pathologi-

---

5. Nietzsche saw this focus on misery and suffering as a kind of morbidity in the compassionate consciousness; this view formed part of this critique of compassion.
6. Philip Mercer, *Sympathy and Ethics* (Oxford: Clarendon Press, 1972), and Max Scheler, *The Nature of Sympathy,* trans. Werner Stark (London: Routledge & Kegan Paul, 1965).

cal condition actually precludes genuine compassion because it blurs the distinction between subject and object.

In a second type of identification the subject "identifies" with the object because of having had an experience similar to his, the memory of which his experience evokes. ("I can identify with what you are going through, since I've suffered from the same problem myself.") Here no identity confusion is involved. While such identification can promote compassion and imaginative understanding it is not required for it. For compassion does not require even that its subject have experienced the sort of suffering that occasions it. We can commiserate with someone who has lost a child in a fire, even if we do not have a child or have never lost someone we love. The reason for this is that the imaginative reconstruction involved in compassion consists in imagining what the other person, given his character, beliefs, and values is undergoing, rather than what we ourselves would feel in his situation. For example I might regard my son's decision to work for the CIA with distress, while someone with different beliefs and values might regard such a decision with pride; yet this other person may well be able to understand my reaction and to feel compassion for me in regard to it.

The degree of imaginative reconstruction need not be great. The friend in the previous example might find it difficult to reconstruct for herself the outlook and set of values within which my son's decision is viewed with distress. But to have compassion she must at least dwell in her imagination on the fact that I am distressed. So some imaginative representation is a necessary condition for compassion, though the degree can be minimal. Certainly a detailed and rich understanding of another person's outlook and consciousness, of the sort available only to persons of exceptional powers of imagination, is not required for compassion.

Nevertheless, as a matter of empirical fact, we often do come to understand someone's condition by imagining what our own reactions would be. So expanding our powers of imagination expands our capacity for compassion. And conversely the limits of a person's capacities for imaginative reconstruction set limits on her capacity for compassion. Finding another person's experience opaque may well

get in the way of compassion. Persons who are in general quite poor at imagining the experiences of others who are different from themselves, may well be less likely to have compassion for them. Yet this failure of imagination is typically not a purely intellectual or cognitive failure; for it can itself be part of a more general failure to regard the other as fully human, or to take that humanity sufficiently seriously. That a white colonialist in Africa does not imagine to himself the cares and sufferings of the blacks whom he rules cannot be separated from the fact that he does not see them as fully human.

A second constituent of compassion is concern for or regard for the object's good. It is not enough that we imaginatively reconstruct someone's suffering; for, like belief, such imagining is compatible with malice and mere intellectual curiosity. (In fact it is likely to be a component of them.) In addition we must care about that suffering and desire its alleviation. Suppose a neighbor's house burns down, though no one is hurt. Compassion would involve not only imagining what it is like for the neighbor to be homeless but also concerned responses such as the following: being upset, distressed, regretting the different aspects of his plight (his homelessness, his loss of prized possessions, his terror when inside the burning house, etc.); wishing the tragedy had not happened; giving thought to what might be done to alleviate the neighbor's situation; worrying whether he will be able to find another place to live; hoping that he will obtain a decent settlement from the insurance company; hoping and desiring that, in general, his suffering will be no greater than necessary.

The relation between concern for another person's good and these thoughts, feelings, hopes, desires is a necessary or conceptual one; compassionate concern would not be attributed to someone who lacked them (or at least most of them). This concern is not merely tacked on to the imaginative reconstruction as a totally independent component of compassion. Rather the manner in which we dwell on the other's plight expresses the concern for his good.

These concerned reactions must be directed toward the other's plight and not merely caused by it. The distress that is part of compassion cannot take as its focus the vivid realization that I might be afflicted with a like misfortune; for it would then be self-regarding rather than altruistic.

Compassion also involves viewing the other person and his suffering in a certain way. I can put this by saying that compassion involves a sense of shared humanity, of regarding the other as a fellow human being. This means that the other person's suffering (though not necessarily their particular afflicting condition) is seen as the kind of thing that could happen to anyone, including oneself insofar as one is a human being.[7]

This way of viewing the other person contrasts with the attitude characteristic of pity, in which one holds oneself apart from the afflicted person and from their suffering thinking of it as something that defines that person as fundamentally different from oneself. In this way the other person's condition is taken as given whereas in compassion the person's affliction is seen as deviating from the general conditions of human flourishing. That is why pity (unlike compassion) involves a kind of condescension, and why compassion is morally superior to pity.

Because compassion involves a sense of shared humanity, it promotes the *experience* of equality, even when accompanied by an acknowledgement of actual social inequality. Compassion forbids regarding social inequality as establishing human inequality. This is part of the moral force of compassion: by transcending the recognition of social inequality, it promotes the sensed experience of equality in common humanity.

Sometimes the reason we feel pity rather than compassion is that we feel that the object has in some way brought the suffering on himself or deserved it, or in any case that he has allowed himself to be humiliated or degraded by it. But such ways of regarding the objects do not necessarily under-

mine compassion, and they are not incompatible with it. It would be a mistake to see the essential difference between pity and compassion in such differing beliefs about the object's condition. No matter how pitiful or self-degraded one regards another human being, it is possible (and not necessarily unwarranted) to feel compassion and concern for him, simply because he is suffering.

Nietzsche's use of the term *Mitleid* does not distinguish between compassion and pity. Because Mitleid is focused on the negative states of others, Nietzsche saw it as life-denying and without positive value. But insofar as compassion involves a genuine concern for the good of others and a "living sense of another's worth,"[8] it is, unlike pity, fundamentally life-affirming and positive.

A fourth aspect of compassion is its strength and duration. If the distress, sorrow, hopes, and desires of an altruistic attitude were merely passing reactions or twinges of feeling, they would be insufficient for the level of concern, the imaginative reconstruction, and the disposition to beneficent action required for compassion. Though there are degrees of compassion, the threshold of emotional strength required from compassion (in contrast with other altruistic attitudes) is relatively high and enduring. Because well-wishing and pity can be more episodic and less action-guiding, they are morally inferior to compassion. As the etymology of the word suggests, compassion involves "feeling with" the other person, sharing his feelings. In one sense this means that the subject and the object have the same feeling-type: distress, sorrow, desire for relief. But in a more important sense the feelings are not the same; for the relation between their subjects and their objects are different. The focus of my neighbor's distress is *his own* homelessness; the focus of my distress in having compassion for him is *my neighbor's* homelessness (or his distress at his homelessness). This can partly be expressed as a matter of degree. My neighbor suffers; in "suffering with" him there is a sense in which I suffer too, but my suffering is much less than his.

---

7. This way of viewing the other's plight differs from fundamentally self-regarding sentiment in which the person's plight is regarded as a symbol of what could happen to oneself. It is not actually necessary that one believe that the afflicting condition *could* happen to oneself: one might have compassion for someone suffering napalm burns without believing that there is any possibility of oneself being in that condition.

---

8. Nicolai Hartmann, *Ethics* (London: George Allen and Unwin, 1932), II, 273.

Compassion and Beneficent Action

When it is possible for her to relieve another person's suffering without undue demands on her time, energy, and priorities, the compassionate person is disposed to attempt to help. We would hardly attribute compassion to X if she were to saunter by on a spring day and, seeing an elderly man fall on the sidewalk, walk right by, perhaps with a sad shudder of dismay, leaving the old man lying alone.

Characteristically, then, compassion requires the disposition to perform beneficent actions, and to perform them because the agent has had a certain sort of imaginative reconstruction of someone's condition and has a concern for his good. The steps that the person takes to ameliorate the condition are guided by and prompted by that imaginative reconstruction and concern. So the beneficent action of a compassionate person has a specific sort of causal history, which distinguishes it from an equally beneficent action that might be prompted by other sorts of attitudes and emotions.

We saw that concern exists at different degrees of strength in different altruistic emotions and attitudes. Hence its corresponding disposition to beneficence exists at different levels of strength also. The stronger the disposition the more one is willing to go out of one's way, to act contrary to inclination and interest, in order to help the other person.[9] That compassion as a motive can and often does withstand contrary inclination begins to address the Kantian charge that emotions, including compassion, are unreliable as motives to beneficent action.[10] As a motive to beneficence, compassion can

have the strength, stability, and reliability that Kant thought only the sense of duty could have. As a trait of character compassion can be as stable and consistent in its prompting of appropriate beneficent action as a conscientious adherence to principles of beneficence.

Though compassion is a type of emotion or emotional attitude, it is not like a Kantian "inclination." Acting from compassion does not typically involve doing what one is in the mood to do, or feels like doing. On the contrary the regard for the other's good which compassion implies means that one's compassionate acts often involve acting very much contrary to one's moods and inclinations. Compassion is fundamentally other-regarding rather than self-regarding; its affective nature in no way detracts from this.

Compassionate action may extinguish or diminish compassion itself, most obviously when its ob-

> *"Compassion is not a simple feeling-state but a complex emotional attitude toward another...."*

ject is relieved of the negative condition by the action. But even merely *engaging* in action may involve a shift in the subject's consciousness from the imaginative reconstruction of the object's condition to a focus on the expected relief of that condition, thereby diminishing the compassion (though not the regard for the other's good and hence not the moral value of the attitude or state of mind).

Compassion, however, is not always linked so directly to the prompting of beneficent actions. For in many situations it is impossible (without extraordinary disruption of one's life and priorities) for the

---

9. Aristotle recognizes differences in the strength of the disposition to beneficence in his discussion of *eunoia* ("well-wishing" or "good will" in Thompson's translation). Of persons who have eunoia toward others, Aristotle says, "All they wish is the good of those for whom they have a kindness; they would not actively help them to attain it, nor would they put themselves out for their sake." Aristotle, *Nichomachean Ethics,* b. IX (Baltimore: Penguin Books, 1955), 269.

10. For this Kantian view, see Kant, *Fundamental Principles of the Metaphysics of Morals,* trans.

Beck (New York: Bobbs-Merrill, 1960), 6, 14, 28; and *Critique of Practical Reason,* trans. Beck (New York: Bobbs-Merrill, 1956), 75, 122.

compassionate person herself to improve the sufferer's condition (for instance, when one is concerned for the welfare of distant flood victims). In other situations the beneficence might be inappropriate, as when intervention might jeopardize the sufferer's autonomy. Compassionate concern, in such cases, involves hope and desire for the relief of the condition by those in a position to provide it. It does not involve an active setting oneself in readiness to perform beneficent acts, once one firmly believes such acts to be impossible or inappropriate.

In the cases so far discussed a link exists between compassion and beneficent action, through the desire that action be taken by someone to relieve the sufferer's condition. But compassion is also appropriate in situations in which nothing whatever can be done to alleviate the affliction, as for instance when someone is suffering from incurable blindness or painful terminal cancer. In such situations compassionate concern involves sorrowing for the person, hoping that the condition might—all expectations to the contrary—be mitigated or compensated, being pleased or grateful if this occurs, and similar responses.

Because being compassionate involves actively giving thought to the relief of the sufferer's condition, a compassionate person may discover the possibility of beneficent action when it seemed unclear whether any existed. Compassion often involves resisting regarding situations as absolutely irremediable. On the other hand the compassionate person may for this reason fail to see and hence to face up to the hopelessness of the sufferer's situation.

That compassion is often appropriate when there is little or no scope for the subject's disposition to beneficence indicates that compassion's sole significance does not lie in its role as motive to beneficence. Even when nothing can be done by the compassionate person to improve the sufferer's condition, simply being aware that one is an object or recipient of compassion can be an important human good. The compassionate person's expression of concern and shared sorrow can be valuable to the sufferer for its own sake, independently of its instrumental value in improving his condition. Nor does the good of recognizing oneself to be an ob-

ject of compassion depend on the compassionate person wanting to convey his attitude, though the recipient can in addition value the intention to communicate.

The compassionate attitude is a good to the recipient, not only because it signifies that the subject would help if she could but because we are glad to receive the concern of others, glad of the sense of equality that it promotes. Yet it is morally good to be compassionate even when—as often happens—the object of compassion is unaware of it. For any concern for the welfare of others, especially when it promotes the sense of equality, is (*ceteris paribus*) morally good. In this, compassion contrasts with attitudes and feelings such as infatuation or admiration which may convey goods to their recipients but which are without moral value because they do not essentially involve a regard for their recipient's good. The moral significance of compassion is not exhausted by the various types of goods it confers on its recipients.

Compassion can hurt its recipient. It may, for instance, cause him to concentrate too much on his plight, or to think that people around him see him primarily in terms of that plight. But these dangers and burdens of compassion can be mitigated to the extent that a person recognizes that compassion is not the sole or the dominant attitude with which one is regarded.

Compassion can also be misguided, grounded in superficial understanding of a situation. Compassion is not necessarily wise or appropriate. The compassionate person may even end up doing more harm than good. True compassion must be allied with knowledge and understanding if it is to serve adequately as a guide to action: there is nothing inherent in the character of compassion that would prevent—and much that would encourage—its alliance with rational calculation. Because compassion involves an active and objective interest in another person's welfare, it is characteristically a spur to a deeper understanding of a situation than rationality alone could ensure. A person who is compassionate by character is in principle committed to as rational and as intelligent a course of action as possible.

Study Questions

1. Is morality more a matter of emotion or of reason?

2. Why are some people more compassionate toward others?

3. Is it possible to make people more sensitive to the feelings of others? Will this make them more moral?

Moral Dilemmas

■ You and another person are shipwrecked on a deserted island. One day you both find a chestful of gold worth millions of dollars. Your friend becomes ill and is dying. Just as he is about to die, he asks you to promise him that, if you are rescued, you will give his half of the money to his only son, David. You make this promise, and he dies.

A few days later, you are rescued and proceed to look for your friend's son. You find his son, but you also find that he is a rich drug dealer and murderer.

Would you give him the five million dollars and keep your promise, or would you give the money to a charity and break your promise?

■ The University of Middle America, a large midwestern school, is offered a million dollars by a private citizen. The gift giver has only one condition; that the university hire his son Dr. Gypsy as a professor. The university administrators approve the deal but give the final word to the department in which the man's son would be teaching.

The department holds a meeting to debate the offer. Professor Laurel argues for the offer, pointing out that (1) Dr. Gypsy is qualified because he has a Ph.D. from an accredited university and (2) paying him on the basis of the income from the gift would be equivalent to having someone freely donate his services to the department.

Dr. Hardy argues against the offer, saying that (1) to hire Dr. Gypsy would be in effect to accept a bribe and (2) no one should be hired to teach unless he or she is the most qualified as determined from a pool of applicants who apply after the job is fully advertised.

If you were in the department, how would you vote?

■ A neighbor asks you for a recommendation for a job that he needs very badly in order to support his family. You don't think he is qualified for this job.

Would you recommend him and lie or refuse to write the letter?

■ Dr. Helen Garvey determines that an eighteen year old has a terminal illness. She tells his parents, who beg her not to tell the teenager until absolutely necessary.

What should Dr. Garvey do?

Suggested Readings

Auxter, Thomas. *Kant's Moral Teleology,* Macon, GA.: Mercer University Press, 1982.

Foot, Philippa. *Virtues and Vices and Other Essays in Moral Philosophy.* Berkeley: University of California Press, 1978.

Geach, Peter. *The Virtues.* Cambridge, England: Cambridge University Press, 1977.

Kruschwitz, Robert B., and Robert C. Roberts, eds. *The Virtues.* Belmont, Calif.: Wadsworth, 1987.

Pieper, Josef. *The Four Cardinal Virtues.* Notre Dame, Ind.: Notre Dame University Press, 1966

Sex and Love

I s sex outside of marriage immoral? Is the traditional family the best way to raise children? Is homosexuality immoral? Does everyone have the right to marry and have children? These are some of the central issues of sexual morality.

Background

When a baby is born, the first question usually is: "Is it a boy or a girl?" This suggests how much importance our society places on sexual identity. Because our culture and thinking are so thoroughly permeated by sexual categories, we may forget how complex a phenomenon sexuality really is. The biological dimension of sex includes the hormonal and physical process that affect one's sexual development from conception to the end of life. How one relates to others, one's emotional states, one's identity as male or female, and even one's sense of self-worth are part of the psychological aspect of sex. The cultural influence on sex involves conventions, taboos, and attitudes toward sexual behavior. Cultural customs concerning marriage, pre- and extra-marital sex, incest, sexual deviance, and the like vary among different cultures and different periods in history. Finally, the ethical dimension of sexuality is concerned with determining the appropriate rules and standards for sexual interaction.

Information about human sexual behavior is virtually nonexistent prior to about 1000 B.C. Anthropological research shows that incest was forbidden in most cultures and that women were treated as property of a sexual and child-bearing nature. The inferior political, economic, and social status of women was almost universal until this century. This male domination usually translated into a double standard concerning sexual behavior where men were allowed to be promiscuous before (and often after) marriage, but women were generally not allowed the same freedom. In fact, some cultures placed "chastity belts" or performed infibulation (the sewing up of the vagina) to ensure the woman's virginity or fidelity.

Documents of all major religions include moral precepts concerning sex. The Old Testament of Judaism generally forbids adultery and homosexuality, but the Song of Songs, a book of the Old Testament, presents sex not only as procreational but also as recreational and to be enjoyed. Eastern cultures have been generally less puritanical about sexuality; some sects of Hinduism (those practicing tantric yoga) go so far as to see sexual intercourse as sacred and holy, independent of its possible reproductive value. The *Kama Sutra,* an ancient Hindu sex manual, and many writings of the ancient Greeks are more liberal concerning sex as recreation and more tolerant of certain forms of homosexuality. Christianity introduced a new attitude toward human sexuality. St. Augustine, for example, believed that sexual desire was the result of original sin and nothing more than a sign of human weakness. This antisexual attitude, especially in early Christianity, led to the praise of celibacy and virginity as the ideal; marriage was a concession to human imperfection.

The scientific study of human sexuality did not begin seriously until the nineteenth century. At first, these "studies" merely reflected the prevalent negative cultural attitudes toward sex outside of marriage. For example they labeled masturbation a disorder that would lead to mental illness, and considered women to be essentially without sexual desire. The studies of Sigmund Freud (1856–1939), Havelock Ellis (1859–1939), Alfred Kinsey (1894–1956), and Masters and Johnson have expanded our understanding of the importance and diversity of human sexuality. Their findings, the large-scale movement of the population due to the industrial revolution from small, traditional, tightly-knit com-

munities into large urban centers, the decline in the social power of organized religion, the growth of the women's rights movement, and the development of the contraceptive pill in 1960 have generally promoted a more liberal and tolerant attitude toward human sexual behavior.

Conservative Position: Catholic Church

Traditional Christian sexual morality teaches that sex is morally acceptable only in marriage. The purpose of sex on this view is to procreate and to raise children in a stable, monogamous family. Consequently, all sexual expression that is outside marriage and not open to reproduction, such as homosexuality, masturbation, adultery, and promiscuity, is considered immoral. This is the official position of the Roman Catholic church as explained in the Vatican Declaration. This moral theory is based on their understanding of human nature and the teachings of Jesus. The church believes that God created all of nature, including human nature, and that human nature is therefore basically good. All moral behavior must be within the parameters of human nature. According to the church, we understand what the function of sex is when we understand that the sex organs are uniquely constructed to procreate; any other use is against nature, or unnatural. Homosexuality, therefore, is immoral, and so is all nonmarital and extramarital sex since children need a stable family environment in order to develop normally.

Homosexuality: Burton M. Leiser

The morality of homosexuality is the focus of Burton M. Leiser's article, "Homosexuality and the 'Unnaturalness Argument.'" What does it mean to say that something is unnatural? It could not mean that it does not exist in nature, for homosexuality obviously does exist. If it means that something is uncommon, why should that make it evil? Saints and geniuses are uncommon, but they are clearly good and beneficial to society. If it means artificial or humanmade, then why are other artificial things (such as clothing, houses, or medicine) not bad? If unnatural means using an organ in a way that is contrary to its function, then the question becomes, "What is the function of some organ?" Leiser admits that sex organs can be used for procreation, but they may have more than one function. They can be used to experience and give pleasure and to express love. Why, Leiser asks, should we restrict the sex organs to procreation? How we use our organs should be a matter of personal choice and individual need.

Conservatives are not satisfied with Leiser's argument. They believe that the immorality of homosexuals is shown by their promiscuity, which they assume to be wrong. Homosexuals, they claim, are immature and unable to form long-term, stable, and loving relationships. They further claim that widespread homosexuality would undermine the institution of the family, the foundation of all civilization.

Here, as in all moral controversies, rational discussion requires an accurate assessment of the facts. To this end, psychologists and anthropologists have undertaken the study of homosexuality. The available historical evidence shows that most cultures have had homosexual individuals or have accepted some version of homosexual expression. Alfred Kinsey made a major study of sexual behavior in the United States and argued that human sexuality is too complex to divide evenly into two exclusive categories of homosexuality and heterosexuality. He argued that human sexual desire is expressed on a continuum between exclusive heterosexuality on one end and exclusive homosexuality on the other. Most people behave sexually somewhere between the two extremes. Those who fall roughly in the middle are bisexual, equally attracted to both sexes. Kinsey's research and other studies estimate that the number of exclusive male homosexuals in the population varies between six to ten percent and that the percentage of lesbians is somewhat less. Other studies have shown that many creative and talented people have been homosexual. The causes of homosexuality are still disputed, but evidence points to a combination of hormonal, genetic, and familial-environmental causes.

Many who oppose gay rights do so because they believe that homosexuality is a mental disease. But what is a disease? Most doctors agree that a disease is something that interferes with a satisfying life. Mentally ill individuals cannot function in society,

keep a job, or relate well with others. They are not able to properly understand the world around them. They lack self-understanding and often cannot control their own behavior. On the basis of this understanding of health and disease, the American Psychiatric Association, the major professional organization of psychiatrists, decided in 1973 that homosexuality is not necessarily a mental illness in those individuals who are well adjusted and who accept themselves as such. This was a major victory for the gay rights movement.

Bowers v. Hardwick

In *Bowers v. Hardwick* (1986), the U.S. Supreme Court ruled in a five-to-four decision that the Constitution does not protect the right to practice homosexuality even by consenting adults in private. Justice Byron R. White argued that just because some conduct occurs in the privacy of someone's home between consenting adults does not make it legal, as evidenced by valid laws against incest, drug dealing, and so forth. Justice Warren Burger concurred, adding that laws against homosexuality have a long history in Western civilization and in Judeo-Christian morality, a tradition that must be upheld by law. The Court ruled that the states may, if they choose, legally prohibit homosexual conduct.

Justice Harry A. Blackmun and three other justices disagreed with the majority on this question. Blackmun argued that the constitutional right to privacy protects consenting adults who engage in homosexual activity in their homes. He defended the right to privacy and sexual intimacy as essential to the dignity of persons and said that it must be protected. He found Burger's appeal to the long history of antisodomy laws irrelevant; the fact that a law is old doesn't mean that it is right. Furthermore, Blackmun maintained that to impose society's view of moral sexual behavior on a minority is a form of tyranny of the majority, which the Constitution was meant to prevent. The fact that the Judeo-Christian moral system traditionally opposes sodomy cannot be used to argue for the legitimacy of a law in a society such as ours that believes in the separation of church and state.

Liberal Position: Raymond A. Belliotti

Raymond A. Belliotti defends a very liberal and non-religious view of sexual morality. His starting point is Kant's moral philosophy. According to Kant's categorical imperative, to use another person as a mere thing or tool for your own satisfaction is wrong. Persons have absolute value; their freedom or autonomy over their own bodies must be respected. That is why all moral sexual relations must be based on the voluntary consent between the adults involved.

Sex is immoral only if it involves using another against his or her will, breaking a promise, or lying. On this view, rape is clearly immoral because it does not involve the consent of the other; so also is bestiality and usually necrophilia for the same reason. Adultery is immoral if two individuals have promised to each other that they will not have sex with others but moral if they have not made such a promise.

Belliotti is careful to point out that the morality of an action is not the only criterion we should use when deciding whether to do it. Promiscuity and incest may be moral, yet one may choose not to commit these acts for reasons of self-interest such as to avoid contracting disease or to avoid losing the respect of others. A prudent person may restrict sexual expression to further his or her long-term happiness and welfare. Some might see this last point as an indication that Belliotti's theory of sex is incomplete, for how can something be moral yet contrary to our happiness? Are morality and happiness opposites? Should incest be allowed if the children are old enough and consent? Is the institution of the family threatened by incest? Is necrophilia moral if the deceased had consented prior to death to having his or her corpse used in that way, or is it a disease?

Moderate Position: John Hunter

John Hunter believes that impersonal or promiscuous sexual relations can be moral, but he does not consider them ideal. A personal relationship involves caring about the other as a complete person, not just liking his or her talents, characteristics, or appearance. A personal relationship includes mutual trust and total acceptance of the other, and personal intimacy means sharing one's body and innermost thoughts with someone else. Hunter argues that most people want a personal and intimate relationship because in such a relationship we escape our loneliness and satisfy the need to communicate, which we all feel. In an intimate association, we come to know ourselves more fully and can explore our own individual uniqueness in an open and trusting environment. Sex without personal intimacy or love can be pleasurable, but it can often be mixed with regret and a kind of emptiness. This emptiness arises from our unmet needs for intimacy.

Sex Outside of Marriage

Liberals such as Belliotti believe that premarital sex is not necessarily wrong. They stress that to delay sexual intercourse until marriage is too long because many people marry later today than was once common owing to the need to acquire an advanced education in order to function in an increasingly complex society. They argue that sexual expression is a pleasurable activity conducive to mental and physical health. It enhances our self-esteem and reduces stress. Premarital sex improves sexual functioning in marriage and adds excitement to life. Liberals also believe that a less repressive sexual morality would reduce the incidence of sexual problems and perversions. They add that it might reduce the prevalence of pornography, prostitution, and sex crimes, all symptoms of a sexually intolerant society.

The conservative view, such as that held by the Catholic church, argues against premarital sex. Conservatives contend that the possibility of disease and pregnancy are strong reasons to wait until marriage to have sex. The possibility of being deceived and used by a sex partner who is essentially a stranger is very real. Finally, they believe that sexual promiscuity before marriage will make fidelity in marriage more difficult and may lead to divorce and broken homes.

Individuals such as Hunter who hold a position between the extremes of liberalism and conservatism would agree with elements of both. They believe that sex before marriage can be moral if it involves trust and commitment in a long-term relationship, the essential components of love. A loving relationship can deal with the negative elements cited by conservatives while incorporating the positive elements of the liberal position.

Hunter's approach and psychological studies suggest that personal intimacy and romantic love involve at least three components: sexual attraction, intimacy, and commitment. Love includes the sexual desire to be physically close and have intercourse with the beloved. Intimacy adds to this the willingness to communicate our most private thoughts and feelings with the beloved. Commitment involves the realization and the desire that the love relationship be long term. Commitment and intimacy require reciprocal trust, which increases our sense of self-esteem and the meaningfulness of our lives.

Vatican Declaration on Some Questions of Sexual Ethics

Pope Paul VI (1897–1978) Pope Paul VI, formerly the Archbishop of Milan, Italy, became Pope of the Catholic Church in 1963.

Pope Paul VI

Introduction

Importance of Sexuality

1. The human person, according to the scientific disciplines of our day, is so deeply influenced by his sexuality that this latter must be regarded as one of the basic factors shaping human life. The person's sex is the source of the biological, psychological and spiritual characteristics which make the person male or female, and thus are extremely important and influential in the maturation and socialization of the individual. It is easy to understand, therefore, why matters pertaining to sex are frequently and openly discussed in books, periodicals, newspapers and other communications media.

Reprinted with permission from *The Pope Speaks,* vol. 21, no. 1 (1976), pp. 60–68. Copyright © Publications Office, United States Catholic Conference, Washington, D.C.

Meanwhile, moral corruption is on the increase. One of the most serious signs of this is the boundless exaltation of sex. In addition, with the help of the mass media and the various forms of entertainment, sex has even invaded the field of education and infected the public mind.

In this situation, some educators, teachers and moralists have been able to contribute to a better understanding and vital integration of the special values and qualities proper to each sex. Others, however, have defended views and ways of acting which are in conflict with the true moral requirements of man, and have even opened the door to a licentious hedonism.

The result is that, within a few years' time, teachings, moral norms and habits of life hitherto faithfully preserved have been called into doubt, even by Christians. Many today are asking what they are to regard as true when so many current views are at odds with what they learned from the Church.

Occasion for This Declaration

2. In the face of this intellectual confusion and moral corruption the Church cannot stand by and do nothing. The issue here is too important in the life both of the individual and of contemporary society.[1]

Bishops see each day the ever increasing difficulties of the faithful in acquiring sound moral teaching, especially in sexual matters, and of pastors in effectively explaining that teaching. The bishops know it is their pastoral duty to come to the aid of the faithful in such a serious matter. Indeed, some outstanding documents have been published on the subject by some bishops and some episcopal conferences. But, since erroneous views and the deviations they produce continue to be broadcast everywhere, the Sacred Congregation for the Doctrine of the Faith in accordance with its role in the universal Church[2] and by mandate of the Supreme Pontiff, has thought it necessary to issue this Declaration.

I. General Considerations

The Sources of Moral Knowledge

3. The men of our day are increasingly persuaded that their dignity and calling as human beings requires them to use their minds to discover the values and powers inherent in their nature, to develop these without ceasing and to translate them into action, so that they may make daily greater progress.

When it comes to judgments on moral matters, however, man may not proceed simply as he thinks fit. "Deep within, man detects the law of conscience—a law which is not self-imposed but which holds him to obedience.... For man has in his heart a law written by God. To obey it is the very dignity of man; according to it he will be judged."[3]

To us Christians, moreover, God has revealed his plan of salvation and has given us Christ, the Savior and sanctifier, as the supreme and immutable norm of life through his teaching and example. Christ himself has said: "I am the light of the world. No follower of mine shall ever walk in darkness; no, he shall possess the light of life."[4]

The authentic dignity of man cannot be promoted, therefore, except through adherence to the order which is essential to his nature. There is no denying, of course, that in the history of civilization many of the concrete conditions and relationships of human life have changed and will change again in the future but every moral evolution and every manner of life must respect the limits set by the immutable principles which are grounded in the constitutive elements and essential relations proper to the human person. These elements and relations are not subject to historical contingency.

The basic principles in question can be grasped by man's reason. They are contained in "the divine law—eternal, objective and universal—whereby God orders, directs and governs the entire universe and all the ways of the human community by a plan conceived in wisdom and love. God has made man a participant in this law, with the result that, under the gentle disposition of divine Providence, he can come to perceive ever more fully the truth that is unchanging."[5] This divine law is something we can know.

The Principles of Morality Are Perennial

4. Wrongly, therefore, do many today deny that either human nature or revealed law furnishes any absolute and changeless norm for particular actions except the general law of love and respect for human dignity. To justify this position, they argue that both the so-called norms of the natural law and the precepts of Sacred Scripture are simply products of a particular human culture and its expressions at a certain point in history.

But divine revelation and, in its own order, natural human wisdom show us genuine exigencies of human nature and, as a direct and necessary conse-

---

1. See Vatican II, *Pastoral Constitution on the Church in the World of Today*, no. 47: *Acta Apostolicae Sedis* 58 (1966) 1067 [*The Pope Speaks* XI, 289–290].

2. See the Apostolic Constitution *Regimini Ecclesiae universae* (August 15, 1967), no. 29: *AAS* 59 (1967) 897 [*TPS* XII, 401–402].

3. *Pastoral Constitution on the Church in the World of Today*, no. 16: *AAS* 58 (1966) 1037 [*TPS* XI, 268].

4. *Jn* 8, 12.

5. *Declaration on Religious Freedom*, no. 3: *AAS* 58 (1966) 931 [*TPS* XI, 86].

quence, immutable laws which are grounded in the constitutive elements of human nature and show themselves the same in all rational beings.

Furthermore, the Church was established by Christ to be "the pillar and bulwark of truth."[6] With the help of the Holy Spirit she keeps a sleepless watch over the truths of morality and transmits them without falsification. She provides the authentic interpretation not only of the revealed positive law but also of "those principles of the moral order which have their origin in human nature itself"[7] and which relate to man's full development and sanctification. Throughout her history the Church has constantly maintained that certain precepts of the natural law bind immutably and without qualification, and that the violation of them contradicts the spirit and teaching of the Gospel.

The Fundamental Principles of Sexual Morality

5. Since sexual morality has to do with values which are basic to human and Christian life, the general doctrine we have been presenting applies to it. In this area there are principles and norms which the Church has always unhesitatingly transmitted as part of her teaching, however opposed they might be to the mentality and ways of the world. These principles and norms have their origin, not in a particular culture, but in knowledge of the divine law and human nature. Consequently, it is impossible for them to lose their binding force or to be called into doubt on the grounds of cultural change.

These principles guided Vatican Council II when it provided advice and directives for the establishment of the kind of social life in which the equal dignity of man and woman will be respected, even while the differences between them also are preserved.[8]

In speaking of the sexual nature of the human being and of the human generative powers, the Council observes that these are "remarkably superior to those found in lower grades of life."[9] Then it deals in detail with the principles and norms which apply to human sexuality in the married state and are based on the finality of the function proper to marriage.

In this context the Council asserts that the moral goodness of the actions proper to married life, when ordered as man's true dignity requires, "does not depend only on a sincere intention and the evaluating of motives, but must be judged by objective standards. These are drawn from the nature of the human person and of his acts, and have regard for the whole meaning of mutual self-giving and human procreation in the context of true love."[10]

These last words are a brief summation of the Council's teaching (previously set forth at length in the same document[11]) on the finality of the sexual act and on the chief norm governing its morality. It is respect for this finality which guarantees the moral goodness of the act.

The same principle, which the Church derives from divine revelation and from her authentic interpretation of the natural law, is also the source of her traditional teaching that the exercise of the sexual function has its true meaning and is morally good only in legitimate marriage.[12]

---

6. *I TM* 3, 15.

7. *Declaration on Religious Freedom,* no. 14: *AAS* 58 (1966) 940 [*TPS* XI, 93]. See also Pius XI, Encyclical *Casti Connubii* (December 31, 1930): *AAS* 22 (1930) 579–580; Pius XII, Address of November 2, 1954 *AAS* 46 (1954) 671–672 [*TPS* 1, 380–381]; John XXIII, Encyclical *Mater et Magistra* (May 25, 1961), no. 239: *AAS* 53 (1961) 457 [*TPS* VII, 388]; Paul VI, Encyclical *Humanae Vitae* (July 25, 1968), no. 4, *AAS* 60 (1968) 483 [*TPS* XIII, 331–332].

8. See Vatican II, *Declaration on Christian Education,* nos. 1 and 8: *AAS* 58 (1966) 729–730, 734–736 [*TPS* XI, 201–202, 206–207]; *Pastoral Constitution on the Church in the World of Today,* nos. 29, 60, 67: *AAS* 58 (1966) 1048–1049, 1080–1081, 1088–1089 [*TPS* XI, 276–277, 299–300, 304–305].

9. *Pastoral Constitution on the Church in the World of Today,* no. 51: *AAS* 58 (1966) 1072 [*TPS* XI, 293].

10. *Loc. cit.;* see also no. 49: *AAS* 58 (1966) 1069–1070 [*TPS* XI, 291–292].

11. See *Pastoral Constitution on the Church in the World of Today,* nos. 49–50: *AAS* 58 (1966) 1069–1072 [*TPS* XI, 291–293].

12. The present Declaration does not review all the moral norms for the use of sex, since they have already been set forth in the encyclicals *Casti Connubii* and *Humanae Vitae.*

Limits of this Declaration

6. It is not the intention of this declaration to treat all abuses of the sexual powers nor to deal with all that is involved in the practice of chastity but rather to recall the Church's norms on certain specific points, since there is a crying need of opposing certain serious errors and deviant forms of behavior.

II. Specific Applications

Premarital Relations

7. Many individuals at the present time are claiming the right to sexual union before marriage, at least when there is a firm intention of marrying and when a love which both partners think of as already conjugal demands this further step which seems to them connatural. They consider this further step justified especially when external circumstances prevent the formal entry into marriage or when intimate union seems necessary if love is to be kept alive.

This view is opposed to the Christian teaching that any human genital act whatsoever may be placed only within the framework of marriage. For, however firm the intention of those who pledge themselves to each other in such premature unions, these unions cannot guarantee the sincerity and fidelity of the relationship between man and woman, and, above all, cannot protect the relationship against the changeableness of desire and determination.

Yet, Christ the Lord willed that the union be a stable one and he restored it to its original condition as founded in the difference between the sexes. "Have you not read that at the beginning the Creator made them male and female and declared, 'For this reason a man shall leave his father and mother and cling to his wife and the two shall become as one'? Thus they are no longer two but one flesh. Therefore, let no man separate what God has joined."[13]

St. Paul is even more explicit when he teaches that if unmarried people or widows cannot be continent, they have no alternative but to enter into a stable marital union: "It is better to marry than to

___
13. *Mt* 19, 4–6.

be on fire."[14] For, through marriage the love of the spouses is taken up into the irrevocable love of Christ for his Church,[15] whereas unchaste bodily union[16] defiles the temple of the Holy Spirit which the Christian has become. Fleshly union is illicit, therefore, unless a permanent community of life has been established between man and woman.

Such has always been the Church's understanding of and teaching on the exercise of the sexual function.[17] She finds, moreover, that natural human wisdom and the lessons of history are in profound agreement with her.

> *"The authentic dignity of man cannot be promoted, therefore, except through adherence to the order which is essential to his nature."*

Experience teaches that if sexual union is truly to satisfy the requirements of its own finality and of human dignity, love must be safeguarded by the stability marriage gives. These requirements necessitate a contract which is sanctioned and protected by society; the contract gives rise to a new state of life and is of exceptional importance for the exclusive union of man and woman as well as for the good of their family and the whole of human society. Premarital relations, on the other hand, most often ex-

___
14. *1 Cor* 7, 9.
15. See *Eph* 5, 25–32.
16. Extramarital intercourse is expressly condemned in *1 Cor* 5, 1; 6, 9; 7, 2; 10, 8; *Eph* 5, 5–7; *1 Tm* 1, 10; *Heb* 13, 4; there are explicit arguments given in *1 Cor* 6, 12–20.
17. See Innocent IV, Letter *Sub Catholicae professione* (March 6, 1254) (*DS* 835); Pius II, Letter *Cum sicut accepimus* (November 14, 1459) (*DS* 1367); Decrees of the Holy Office on September 24, 1665 (*DS* 2045) and March 2, 1679 (*DS* 2148); Pius XI, Encyclical *Casti Connubii* (December 31, 1930); *AAS* 22 (1930) 538–539.

clude any prospect of children. Such love claims in vain to be conjugal since it cannot, as it certainly should, grow into a maternal and paternal love; or, if the pair do become parents, it will be to the detriment of the children, who are deprived of a stable environment in which they can grow up in a proper fashion and find the way and means of entering into the larger society of men.

Therefore, the consent of those entering into marriage must be externally manifested, and this in such a way as to render it binding in the eyes of society. The faithful, for their part, must follow the laws of the Church in declaring their marital consent; it is this consent that makes their marriage a sacrament of Christ.

Homosexuality

8. Contrary to the perennial teaching of the Church and the moral sense of the Christian people, some individuals today have, on psychological grounds, begun to judge indulgently or even simply to excuse homosexual relations for certain people.

They make a distinction which has indeed some foundation: between homosexuals whose bent derives from improper education or a failure of sexual maturation or habit or bad example or some similar cause and is only temporary or at least is not incurable; and homosexuals who are permanently such because of some innate drive or a pathological condition which is considered incurable.

The propensity of those in the latter class is—it is argued—so natural that it should be regarded as justifying homosexual relations within a sincere and loving communion of life which is comparable to marriage inasmuch as those involved in it deem it impossible for them to live a solitary life.

Objective Evil of Such Acts

As far as pastoral care is concerned, such homosexuals are certainly to be treated with understanding and encouraged to hope that they can some day overcome their difficulties and their inability to fit into society in a normal fashion. Prudence, too, must be exercised in judging their guilt. However, no pastoral approach may be taken which would consider these individuals morally justified on the grounds that such acts are in accordance with their

nature. For, according to the objective moral order homosexual relations are acts deprived of the essential ordination they ought to have.

In Sacred Scripture such acts are condemned as serious deviations and are even considered to be the lamentable effect of rejecting God.[18] This judgment on the part of the divinely inspired Scriptures does not justify us in saying that all who suffer from this anomaly are guilty of personal sin but it does show that homosexual acts are disordered by their very nature and can never be approved.

Masturbation

9. Frequently today we find doubt or open rejection of the traditional Catholic teaching that masturbation is a serious moral disorder. Psychology and sociology (it is claimed) show that masturbation, especially in adolescents, is a normal phase in the process of sexual maturation and is, therefore, not gravely sinful unless the individual deliberately cultivates a solitary pleasure that is turned in upon itself ("ipsation"). In this last case, the act would be radically opposed to that loving community between persons of different sexes which (according to some) is the principal goal to be sought in the use of the sexual powers.

This opinion is contrary to the teaching and pastoral practice of the Catholic Church. Whatever be the validity of certain arguments of a biological and philosophical kind which theologians sometimes use, both the magisterium of the Church (following a constant tradition) and the moral sense of the faithful have unhesitatingly asserted that masturba-

---

18. *Rom* 1:24–27: "In consequence, God delivered them up in their lusts to unclean practices; they engaged in the mutual degradation of their bodies, these men who exchanged the truth of God for a lie and worshipped and served the creature rather than the Creator—blessed be he forever, amen! God therefore delivered them to disgraceful passions. Their women exchanged natural intercourse for unnatural, and the men gave up natural intercourse with women and burned with lust for one another. Men did shameful things with men, and thus received in their own persons the penalty for their perversity." See also what St. Paul says of sodomy in *1 Cor* 6, 9; *1 Tm* 1, 10.

tion is an intrinsically and seriously disordered act.[19] The chief reason for this stand is that, whatever the motive, the deliberate use of the sexual faculty outside of normal conjugal relations essentially contradicts its finality. In such an act there is lacking the sexual relationship which the moral order requires, the kind of relationship in which "the whole meaning of mutual self-giving and human procreation" is made concretely real "in the context of true love."[20] Only within such a relationship may the sexual powers be deliberately exercised.

Even if it cannot be established that Sacred Scripture condemns this sin under a specific name, the Church's tradition rightly understands it to be condemned in the New Testament when the latter speaks of "uncleanness" or "unchasteness" or the other vices contrary to chastity and continence.

Sociological research can show the relative frequency of this disorder according to places, types of people and various circumstances which may be taken into account. It thus provides an array of facts. But facts provide no norm for judging the morality of human acts.[21] The frequency of the act here in ques-

tion is connected with innate human weakness deriving from original sin, but also with the loss of the sense of God, with the moral corruption fostered by the commercialization of vice, with the unbridled license to be found in so many books and forms of public entertainment and with the forgetfulness of modesty, which is the safeguard of chastity.

In dealing with masturbation, modern psychology provides a number of valid and useful insights which enable us to judge more equitably of moral responsibility. They can also help us understand how adolescent immaturity (sometimes prolonged beyond the adolescent years) or a lack of psychological balance or habits can affect behavior, since they may make an action less deliberate and not always a subjectively serious sin. But the lack of serious responsibility should not be generally presumed; if it is, there is simply a failure to recognize man's ability to act in a moral way.

In the pastoral ministry, in order to reach a balanced judgment in individual cases account must be taken of the overall habitual manner in which the person acts, not only in regard to charity and justice, but also in regard to the care with which he observes the precept of chastity in particular. Special heed must be paid to whether he uses the necessary natural and supernatural helps which Christian asceticism recommends, in the light of long experience, for mastering the passions and attaining virtue. . . .

---

19. See Leo IX, Letter *Ad splendidum nitentes* (1054) (*DS* 687–688); Decree of the Holy Office on March 2, 1679 (*DS* 2149); Pius XII, Addresses of October 8, 1953: *AAS* 45 (1953) 677–678, and May 19, 1956: *AAS* 48 (1956) 472–473.

20. *Pastoral Constitution on the Church in the World of Today,* no. 51: *AAS* 58 (1966) 1072 [*TPS* XI, 293].

21. See Paul VI, Apostolic Exhortation *Quinque iam anni* (December 8, 1970): *AAS* 63 (1971) 102 [*TPS* XV, 329]: "If sociological surveys are useful for better discovering the thought patterns of the people of a particular place, the anxieties and needs of those to whom we proclaim the world

---

of God, and also the oppositions made to it by modern reasoning through the widespread notion that outside science there exists no legitimate form of knowledge, still the conclusions drawn from such surveys could not of themselves constitute a determining criterion of truth."

Study Questions

1. Is sex primarily for procreation or for recreation?

2. If you agree with the Vatican, should homosexuals be celibate for their entire lives?

3. Has modern science made the Vatican's position stronger or weaker?

4. Is celibacy more unnatural than homosexuality? Why does the Catholic church require its priests and nuns to be celibate?

Homosexuality and the "Unnaturalness Argument"

Burton M. Leiser is a contemporary professor of philosophy at Pace University in New York City.

Burton M. Leiser

[The alleged "unnaturalness" of homosexuality] raises the question of the meaning of *nature, natural,* and similar terms. Theologians and other moralists have said that … [homosexual acts] violate the "natural law," and that they are therefore immoral and ought to be prohibited by the state.

The word *nature* has a built-in ambiguity that can lead to serious misunderstandings. When something is said to be "natural" or in conformity with "natural law" or the "law of nature," this may mean either (1) that it is in conformity with the descriptive laws of nature, or (2) that it is not artificial, that man has not imposed his will or his devices upon events or conditions as they exist or would have existed without such interference.

1   The Descriptive Laws of Nature

The laws of nature, as these are understood by the scientist, differ from the laws of man. The former are purely descriptive, whereas the latter are prescriptive. When a scientist says that water boils at 212° Fahrenheit or that the volume of a gas varies directly with the heat that is applied to it and inversely with the pressure, he means merely that as a matter of recorded and observable fact, pure water under standard conditions always boils at precisely 212° Fahrenheit and that as a matter of observed fact, the volume of a gas rises as it is heated and falls as pressure is applied to it. These "laws" merely *describe* the manner in which physical sub-

stances *actually behave.* They differ from municipal and federal laws in that they *do not prescribe behavior.* Unlike manmade laws, natural laws are not passed by any legislator or group of legislators; they are not proclaimed or announced; they impose no obligation upon anyone or anything; their "violation" entails no penalty, and there is no reward for "following" them or "abiding by" them. When a scientist says that the air in a tire "obeys" the laws of nature that "govern" gases, he does *not* mean that the air, having been informed that it *ought* to behave in a certain way, behaves appropriately under the right conditions. He means, rather, that as a matter of fact, the air in a tire *will* behave like all other gases. In saying that Boyle's law "governs" the behavior of gases, he means merely that gases do, as a matter of fact, behave in accordance with Boyle's law, and that Boyle's law enables one to predict accurately what will happen to a given quantity of a gas as its pressure is raised; he does *not* mean to suggest that some heavenly voice has proclaimed that all gases should henceforth behave in accordance with the terms of Boyle's law and that a ghostly policeman patrols the world, ready to mete out punishments to any gases that "violate" the heavenly decree. In fact, according to the scientist, it does not make sense to speak of a natural law being violated. For if there were a true exception to a so-called law of nature, the exception would require a change in the description of those phenomena, and the "law" would have been shown to be no law at all. The laws of nature are revised as scientists discover new phenomena that require new refinements in their descriptions of the way things actually happen. In this respect they differ fundamentally from human laws, which are revised periodically by legislators who are not so interested in *describing* human behavior as they are in *prescribing* what human behavior *should* be.

2 The Artificial as a Form of the Unnatural

On occasion when we say that something is not natural, we mean that it is a product of human artifice. My typewriter is not a natural object, in this sense, for the substances of which it is composed have been removed from their natural state—the state in which they existed before men came along—and have been transformed by a series of chemical and physical and mechanical processes into other substances. They have been rearranged into a whole that is quite different from anything found in nature. In short, my typewriter is an artificial object. In this sense, the clothing that I wear as I lecture before my students is not natural, for it has been transformed considerably from the state in which it was found in nature; and my wearing of clothing as I lecture before my students is also not natural, in this sense, for in my natural state, before the application of anything artificial, before any human interference with things as they are, I am quite naked. Human laws, being artificial conventions designed to exercise a degree of control over the natural inclinations and propensities of men, may in this sense be considered to be unnatural.

Now when theologians and moralists speak of homosexuality, contraception, abortion, and other forms of human behavior as being unnatural, and say that for that reason such behavior must be considered to be wrong, in what sense are they using the word *unnatural?* Are they saying that homosexual behavior and the use of contraceptives are contrary to the scientific laws of nature, are they saying that they are artificial forms of behavior, or are they using the terms *natural* and *unnatural* in some third sense?

They cannot mean that homosexual behavior (to stick to the subject presently under discussion) violates the laws of nature in the first sense, for, as we have pointed out, in *that* sense it is impossible to violate the laws of nature. Those laws, being merely descriptive of what actually does happen, would have to *include* homosexual behavior if such behavior does actually take place. Even if the defenders of the theological view that homosexuality is unnatural were to appeal to a statistical analysis by pointing out that such behavior is not normal from a statistical point of view, and therefore not what the laws of nature require, it would be open to their critics to reply that any descriptive law of nature must account for and incorporate all statistical deviations, and that the laws of nature, in this sense, do not *require anything*. These critics might also note that the best statistics available reveal that about half of all American males engage in homosexual activity at some time in their lives, and that a very large percentage of American males have exclusively homosexual relations for a fairly extensive period of time; from which it would follow that such behavior is natural, for them, at any rate, in this sense of the word *natural*.

If those who say that homosexual behavior is unnatural are using the term *unnatural* in the second sense, it is difficult to see why they should be fussing over it. Certainly nothing is intrinsically wrong with going against nature (if that is how it should be put) in this sense. That which is artificial is often far better than what is natural. Artificial homes seem, at any rate, to be more suited to human habitation and more conducive to longer life and better health than caves and other natural shelters. There are distinct advantages to the use of such unnatural (i.e., artificial) amenities as clothes, furniture, and books. Although we may dream of an idyllic return to nature in our more wistful moments, we would soon discover, as Thoreau did in his attempt to escape from the artificiality of civilization, that needles and thread, knives and matches, ploughs and nails, and countless other products of human artifice are essential to human life. We would discover, as Plato pointed out in the *Republic,* that no man can be truly self-sufficient. Some of the by-products of industry are less than desirable; but neither industry itself, nor the products of industry, are intrinsically evil, even though both are unnatural in this sense of the word.

Interference with nature is not evil in itself. Nature, as some writers have put it, must be tamed. In some respects man must look upon it as an enemy to be conquered. If nature were left to its own devices, without the intervention of human artifice, men would be consumed with disease, they would be plagued by insects, they would be chained to the places where they were born with no means of swift communication or transport, and they would suffer the discomforts and the torments of wind and weather and flood and fire with no practical means of combating any of them. Interfering with nature, doing battle with nature, using human will and reason and skill to thwart what might otherwise follow from the conditions that prevail in the world, is a peculiarly human enterprise, one that can hardly be condemned merely because it does what is not natural.

Homosexual behavior can hardly be considered to be unnatural in this sense. There is nothing "artificial" about such behavior. On the contrary, it is quite natural, in this sense, to those who engage in it. And even if it were not, even if it were quite artificial, this is not in itself a ground for condemning it.

It would seem, then, that those who condemn homosexuality as an unnatural form of behavior must mean something else by the word *unnatural*, something not covered by either of the preceding definitions. A third possibility is this:

3 Anything Uncommon or Abnormal Is Unnatural

If this what is meant by those who condemn homosexuality on the ground that it is unnatural, it is quite obvious that their condemnation cannot be accepted without further argument. For the fact that a given form of behavior is uncommon provides no justification for condemning it. Playing viola in a string quartet is no doubt an uncommon form of human behavior. I do not know what percentage of the human race engages in such behavior, or what percentage of his life any given violist devotes to such behavior, but I suspect that the number of such people must be very small indeed, and that the total number of manhours spent in such activity would justify our calling that form of activity uncommon, abnormal (in the sense that it is statistically not the kind of thing that people are ordinarily inclined to do), and therefore unnatural, in this

sense of the word. Yet there is no reason to suppose that such uncommon, abnormal behavior is, by virtue of its uncommonness, deserving of condemnation or ethically or morally wrong. On the contrary, many forms of behavior are praised precisely because they are so uncommon. Great artists, poets, musicians, and scientists are "abnormal" in this sense; but clearly the world is better off for having them, and it would be absurd to condemn them on their activities for their failure to be common and normal. If homosexual behavior is wrong, then, it must be for some reason other than its "unnaturalness" in this sense of the word.

4 Any Use of an Organ or an Instrument That Is Contrary to Its Principal Purpose or Function Is Unnatural

Every organ and every instrument—perhaps even every creature—has a function to perform, one for which it is particularly designed. Any use of those instruments and organs that is consonant with their purposes is natural and proper, but any use that is inconsistent with their principal functions is unnatural and improper, and to that extent, evil or harmful. Human teeth, for example, are admirably designed for their principal functions—biting and chewing the kinds of food suitable for human consumption. But they are not particularly well suited for prying the caps from beer bottles. If they are used for the latter purpose, which is not natural to them, they are liable to crack or break under the strain. The abuse of one's teeth leads to their destruction and to a consequent deterioration in one's overall health. If they are used only for their proper function, however, they may continue to serve well for many years. Similarly, a given drug may have a proper function. If used in the furtherance of that end, it can preserve life and restore health. But if it is abused, and employed for purposes for which it was never intended, it may cause serious harm and even death. The natural uses of things are good and proper, but their unnatural uses are bad and harmful.

What we must do, then, is to find the proper use, or the true purpose, of each organ in our bodies. Once we have discovered that, we will know what constitutes the natural use of each organ, and what constitutes an unnatural, abusive, and potentially harmful employment of the various parts of our bodies. If we are rational, we will be careful to confine our behavior to our proper functions and to refrain from unnatural behavior. According to those philosophers that follow this line of reasoning, the way to discover the "proper" use of any organ is to determine what it is peculiarly suited to do. The eye is suited for seeing, the ear for hearing, the nerves for transmitting impulses from one part of the body to another, and so on.

What are the sex organs peculiarly suited to do? Obviously, they are peculiarly suited to enable men and women to reproduce their own kind. No other organ in the body is capable of fulfilling that function. It follows, according to those who follow the natural-law line, that the "proper" or "natural" function of the sex organs is reproduction, and that strictly speaking, any use of those organs for other purposes is unnatural, abusive, potentially harmful, and therefore wrong. The sex organs have been given to us in order to enable us to maintain the continued existence of mankind on this earth. All perversions—including masturbation, homosexual behavior, and heterosexual intercourse that deliberately frustrates the design of the sexual organs—are unnatural and bad. As Pope Pius XI once said, "Private individuals have no other power over the members of their bodies than that which pertains to their natural ends."

But the problem is not so easily resolved. Is it true that every organ has one and only one proper function? A hammer may have been designed to pound nails, and it may perform that particular job best. But it is not sinful to employ a hammer to crack nuts if I have no other more suitable tool immediately available. The hammer, being a relatively versatile tool, may be employed in a number of ways. It has no one "proper" or "natural" function. A woman's eyes are well adapted to seeing, it is true. But they seem also to be well adapted to flirting. Is a woman's use of her eyes for the latter purpose sinful merely because she is not using them, at that moment, for their "primary" purpose of seeing? Our sexual organs are uniquely adapted for procreation, but that is obviously not the only function

for which they are adapted. Human beings may—and do—use those organs for a great many other purposes, and it is difficult to see why any *one* use should be considered to be the only proper one. The sex organs, for one thing, seem to be particularly well adapted to give their owners and others intense sensations of pleasure. Unless one believes that pleasure itself is bad, there seems to be little reason to believe that the use of the sex organs for the production of pleasure in oneself or in others is evil. In view of the peculiar design of these organs, with their great concentration of nerve endings, it would seem that they were designed (if they *were* designed) with that very goal in mind, and that their use for such purposes would be no more unnatural than their use for the purpose of procreation.

> *"Those who oppose homosexuality and other sexual 'perversions' on the ground that they are 'unnatural' are saying that there is some objectively identifiable quality in such behavior that is unnatural...."*

Nor should we overlook the fact that human sex organs may be and are used to express, in the deepest and most intimate way open to man, the love of one person for another. Even the most ardent opponents of "unfruitful" intercourse admit that sex does serve this function. They have accordingly conceded that a man and his wife may have intercourse even though she is pregnant, or past the age of child bearing, or in the infertile period of her menstrual cycle.

Human beings are remarkably complex and adaptable creatures. Neither they nor their organs can properly be compared to hammers or to other tools. The analogy quickly breaks down. The generalization that a given organ or instrument has one and only one proper function does not hold up, even with regard to the simplest manufactured tools, for, as we have seen, a tool may be used for more than one purpose—less effectively than one especially designed for a given task, perhaps, but "properly" and certainly not *sinfully*. A woman may use her eyes not only to see and to flirt, but also to earn money—if she is, for example, an actress or a model. Though neither of the latter functions seems to have been a part of the original "design," if one may speak sensibly of *design* in this context, of the eye, it is difficult to see why such a use of the eyes of a woman should be considered sinful, perverse, or unnatural. Her sex organs have the unique capacity of producing ova and nurturing human embryos, under the right conditions; but why should any other use of these organs, including their use to bring pleasure to their owner or to someone else, or to manifest love to another person, or even, perhaps, to earn money, be regarded as perverse, sinful, or unnatural? Similarly, a man's sexual organs possess the unique capacity of causing the generation of another human being, but if a man chooses to use them for pleasure, or for the expression of love, or for some other purpose—so long as he does not interfere with the rights of some other person—the fact that his sex organs do have their unique capabilities does not constitute a convincing justification for condemning their other uses as being perverse, sinful, unnatural, or criminal. If a man "perverts" himself by wiggling his ears for the entertainment of his neighbors instead of using them exclusively for their "natural" function of hearing, no one thinks of consigning him to prison. If he abuses his teeth by using them to pull staples from memos—a function for which teeth were clearly not designed—he is not accused of being immoral, degraded, and degenerate. The fact that people *are* condemned for using their sex organs for their own pleasure or profit, or for that of others, may be more revealing about the prejudices and taboos of our society than it is about our perception of the true nature or purpose or "end" (whatever that might be) of our bodies.

To sum up, then, the proposition that any use of an organ that is contrary to its principal purpose or function is unnatural assumes that organs *have* a principal purpose or function, but this may be de-

nied on the ground that the purpose or function of a given organ may vary according to the needs or desires of its owner. It may be denied on the ground that a given organ may have more than one principal purpose or function, and any attempt to call one use or another the only natural one seems to be arbitrary, if not questionbegging. Also, the proposition suggests that what is unnatural is evil or depraved. This goes beyond the pure description of things, and enters into the problem of the evaluation of human behavior, which leads to the fifth meaning of "natural."

5 That Which Is Natural Is Good, and Whatever Is Unnatural Is Bad

When one condemns homosexuality or masturbation or the use of contraceptives on the ground that it is unnatural, one implies that whatever is unnatural is bad, wrongful, or perverse. But as we have seen, in some senses of the word, the unnatural (i.e., the artificial) is often very good, whereas that which is natural (i.e., that which has not been subjected to human artifice or improvement) may be very bad indeed. Of course, interference with nature may be bad. Ecologists have made us more aware than we have ever been of the dangers of unplanned and uninformed interference with nature. But this is not to say that *all* interference with nature is bad. Every time a man cuts down a tree to make room for a home for himself, or catches a fish to feed himself or his family, he is interfering with nature. If men did not interfere with nature, they would have no homes, they could eat no fish, and, in fact, they could not survive. What, then, can be meant by those who say that whatever is natural is good and whatever is unnatural is bad? Clearly they cannot have intended merely to reduce the word *natural* to a synonym of *good, right,* and *proper,* and *unnatural* to a synonym of *evil, wrong, improper, corrupt,* and *depraved.* If that were all they had intended to do, there would be very little to discuss as to whether a given form of behavior might be proper even though it is not in strict conformity with someone's views of what is natural; for *good* and *natural* being synonyms, it would follow inevitably that whatever is good must be natural, and vice versa, by definition. This is certainly not what the opponents of homosexuality have been saying when they claim that homosexuality, being unnatural, is evil. For if it were, their claim would be quite empty. They would be saying merely that homosexuality, being evil, is evil—a redundancy that could as easily be reduced to the simpler assertion that homosexuality is evil. This assertion, however, is not an argument. Those who oppose homosexuality and other sexual "perversions" on the ground that they are "unnatural" are saying that there is some objectively identifiable quality in such behavior that is unnatural; and that that quality, once it has been identified by some kind of scientific observation, can be seen to be detrimental to those who engage in such behavior, or to those around them; and that *because* of the harm (physical, mental, moral, or spiritual) that results from engaging in any behavior possessing the attribute of unnaturalness, such behavior must be considered to be wrongful, and should be discouraged by society. "Unnaturalness" and "wrongfulness" are not synonyms, then, but different concepts. The problem with which we are wrestling is that we are unable to find a meaning for *unnatural* that enables us to arrive at the conclusion that homosexuality is unnatural or that if homosexuality is unnatural, it is therefore wrongful behavior. We have examined four common meanings of *natural* and *unnatural*, and have seen that none of them performs the task that it must perform if the advocates of this argument are to prevail. Without some more satisfactory explanation of the connection between the wrongfulness of homosexuality and its alleged unnaturalness, the argument must be rejected.

Study Questions

1. Is homosexuality a disease? If so, should it be illegal?
2. Are homosexuals more promiscuous than heterosexuals? What importance does this have morally?
3. How does AIDS affect the morality or legality of homosexuality?

Bowers v. Hardwick

A graduate of Yale Law School, Byron White became Associate Justice of the U.S. Supreme Court in 1962.

Harry A. Blackmun was graduated from Harvard Law School. He became Associate Justice of the U.S. Supreme Court in 1970.

Justice White delivered the opinion of the Court.

In August 1982, respondent was charged with violating the Georgia statute criminalizing sodomy[1] by

1. Ga.Code Ann. § 16-6-2 (1984) provides, in pertinent part, as follows: "(a) A person commits

From an opinion delivered by the U.S. Supreme Court, 106 S.Ct. 2841 [, 2842–56] (1986).

committing that act with another adult male in the bedroom of respondent's home. After a preliminary hearing, the District Attorney decided not to present the matter to the grand jury unless further evidence developed.

Respondent then brought suit in the Federal District Court, challenging the constitutionality of the statute insofar as it criminalized consensual sodomy.[2] He asserted that he was a practicing homosexual, that the Georgia sodomy statute, as administered by the defendants, placed him in imminent danger of arrest, and that the statute for several reasons violates the Federal Constitution. The District Court granted the defendants' motion to dismiss for failure to state a claim. . . .

A divided panel of the Court of Appeals for the Eleventh Court reversed. . . . [T]he court [held] that the Georgia statute violated respondent's fundamental rights because his homosexual activity is a private and intimate association that is beyond the reach of state regulation by reason of the Ninth Amendment and the Due Process Clause of the Fourteenth Amendment. The case was remanded for trial, at which, to prevail, the State would have to prove that the statute is supported by a compelling interest and is the most narrowly drawn means of achieving that end.

[1] Because other Courts of Appeals have arrived at judgments contrary to that of the Eleventh

---

the offense of sodomy when he performs or submits to any sexual act involving the sex organs of one person and the mouth or anus of another. . . . (b) A person convicted of the offense of sodomy shall be punished by imprisonment for not less than one nor more than 20 years. . . ."

2. John and Mary Doe were also plaintiffs in the action. They alleged that they wished to engage in sexual activity proscribed by § 16-6-2 in the privacy of their home, App. 3, and that they had been "chilled and deterred" from engaging in such activity by both the existence of the statute and Hardwick's arrest. . . . The District Court held, however, that because they had neither sustained, nor were in immediate danger of sustaining, any direct injury from the enforcement of the statute, they did not have proper standing to maintain the action. . . . The Court of Appeals affirmed the District Court's judgment dismissing the Does' claim for lack of standing, . . . and the Does do not challenge that holding in this Court. . . .

Circuit in this case, . . . we granted the State's petition for certiorari questioning the holding that if sodomy statute violates the fundamental rights of homosexuals. We agree with the State that the Court of Appeals erred, and hence reverse its judgment. . . .

[2] This case does not require a judgment on whether laws against sodomy between consenting adults in general, or between homosexuals in particular, are wise or desirable. It raises no question about the right or propriety of state legislative decisions to repeal their laws that criminalize homosexual sodomy, or of state court decisions invalidating those laws on state constitutional grounds. The issue presented is whether the Federal Constitution confers a fundamental right upon homosexuals to engage in sodomy and hence invalidates the laws of the many States that still make such conduct illegal and have done so for a very long time. The case also calls for some judgment about the limits of the Court's role in carrying out its constitutional mandate.

We first register our disagreement with the Court of Appeals and with respondent that the Court's prior cases have construed the Constitution to confer a right of privacy that extends to homosexual sodomy and for all intents and purposes have decided this case. . . .

[T]hree cases were interpreted as construing the Due Process Clause of the Fourteenth Amendment to confer a fundamental individual right to decide whether or not to beget or bear a child. . . .

Accepting the decisions in these cases and the above description of them, we think it evident that none of the rights announced in those cases bears any resemblance to the claimed constitutional right of homosexuals to engage in acts of sodomy that is asserted in this case. No connection between family, marriage, or procreation on the one hand and homosexual activity on the other has been demonstrated, either by the Court of Appeals or by respondent. Moreover, any claim that these cases nevertheless stand for the proposition that any kind of private sexual conduct between consenting adults is constitutionally insulated from state proscription is unsupportable. . . .

Precedent aside, however, respondent would have us announce, as the Court of Appeals did, a fundamental right to engage in homosexual sodomy. This we are quite unwilling to do. It is true that despite the language of the Due Process Clauses of the Fifth and Fourteenth Amendments, which appears to focus only on the processes by which life, liberty, or property is taken, the cases are legion in which those Clauses have been interpreted to have substantive content, subsuming rights that to a great extent are immune from federal or state regulation or proscription. Among such cases are those recognizing rights that have little or no textual support in the constitutional language....

Striving to assure itself and the public that announcing rights not readily identifiable in the Constitution's text involves much more than the imposition of the Justices' own choice of values on the States and the Federal Government, the Court has sought to identify the nature of the rights qualifying for heightened judicial protection. In *Palko* v. *Connecticut,* 302 U.S. 319, 325, 326 ... (1937), it was said that this category includes those fundamental liberties that are "implicit in the concept of ordered liberty," such that "neither liberty nor justice would exist if [they] were sacrificed." A different description of fundamental liberties appeared in *Moore* v. *East Cleveland,* 431 U.S. 494, 503 ... (1977) (opinion of Powell, J.), where they are characterized as those liberties that are "deeply rooted in this Nation's history and tradition." *Id.,* at 503....

It is obvious to us that neither of these formulations would extend a fundamental right to homosexuals to engage in acts of consensual sodomy. Proscriptions against that conduct have ancient roots.... Sodomy was a criminal offense at common law and was forbidden by the laws of the original thirteen States when they ratified the Bill of Rights.... In 1868, when the Fourteenth Amendment was ratified, all but 5 of the 37 States in the Union had criminal sodomy laws.... In fact, until 1961, ... all 50 States outlawed sodomy, and today, 24 States and the District of Columbia continue to provide criminal penalties for sodomy performed in private and between consenting adults.... Against this background, to claim that a right to engage in such conduct is "deeply rooted in this Nation's history and tradition" or "implicit in the concept of ordered liberty" is, at best, facetious.

[3] Nor are we inclined to take a more expansive view of our authority to discover new fundamental rights imbedded in the Due Process Clause. The Court is most vulnerable and comes nearest to illegitimacy when it deals with judge-made constitutional law having little or no cognizable roots in the language or design of the Constitution.... There should be, therefore, great resistance to expand the substantive reach of those Clauses, particularly if it requires redefining the category of rights deemed to be fundamental. Otherwise, the Judiciary necessarily takes to itself further authority to govern the country without express constitutional authority. The claimed right pressed on us today falls far short of overcoming this resistance.

Respondent, however, asserts that the result should be different where the homosexual conduct occurs in the privacy of the home. He relies on *Stanley* v. *Georgia,* 394 U.S. 557 ... (1969), where the Court held that the First Amendment prevents conviction for possessing and reading obscene material in the privacy of his home. "If the First Amendment means anything, it means that a State has no business telling a man, sitting alone in his house, what books he may read or what films he may watch." *Id.,* at 565....

Stanley did protect conduct that would not have been protected outside the home, and it partially prevented the enforcement of state obscenity laws; but the decision was firmly grounded in the First Amendment. The right pressed upon us here has no similar support in the text of the Constitution, and it does not qualify for recognition under the prevailing principles for construing the Fourteenth Amendment. Its limits are also difficult to discern. Plainly enough, otherwise illegal conduct is not always immunized whenever it occurs in the home. Victimless crimes, such as the possession and use of illegal drugs, do not escape the law where they are committed at home. *Stanley* itself recognized that its holding offered no protection for the possession in the home of drugs, firearms, or stolen goods.... And if respondent's submission is limited to the voluntary sexual conduct between consenting adults, it would be difficult, except by fiat, to limit the claimed right to homosexual conduct while leaving exposed to prosecution adultery, incest, and other sexual crimes even though they are committed in the home. We are unwilling to start down that road.

[4] Even if the conduct at issue here is not a fundamental right, respondent asserts that there must be a rational basis for the law and that there is none in this case other than the presumed belief of a majority of the electorate in Georgia that homosexual sodomy is immoral and unacceptable. This is said to be an inadequate rationale to support the law. The law, however, is constantly based on notions of morality, and if all laws representing essentially moral choices are to be invalidated under the Due Process Clause, the courts will be very busy indeed. Even respondent makes no such claim, but insists that majority sentiments about the morality of homosexuality should be declared inadequate. We do not agree, and are unpersuaded that the sodomy laws of some 25 States should be invalidated on this basis. . . .

Accordingly, the judgment of the Court of Appeals is

Reversed.

Chief Justice Burger, concurring.

I join the Court's opinion, but I write separately to underscore my view that in constitutional terms there is no such thing as a fundamental right to commit homosexual sodomy.

As the Court notes, . . . the proscriptions against sodomy have very "ancient roots." Decisions of individuals relating to homosexual conduct have been subject to state intervention throughout the history of Western Civilization. Condemnation of those practices is firmly rooted in Judaeo-Christian moral and ethical standards. Homosexual sodomy was a capital crime under Roman law. See Code Theod. 9.7.6; Code Just. 9.9.31. See also D. Bailey, *Homosexuality in the Western Christian Tradition* 70–81 (1975). During the English Reformation when powers of the ecclesiastical courts were transferred to the King's Courts, the first English statute criminalizing sodomy was passed. 25 Hen. VIII, c. 6. Blackstone described "the infamous crime against nature" as an offense of "deeper malignity" than rape, an heinous act "the very mention of which is a disgrace to human nature," and "a crime not fit to be named." Blackstone's Commentaries *215. The common law of England, including its prohibition of sodomy, became the received law of Georgia and the other Colonies. In 1816 the Georgia Legislature passed the statute at issue here, and that statute has been continuously in force in one form or another since that time. To hold that the act of homosexual sodomy is somehow protected as a fundamental right would be to cast aside millennia of moral teaching.

> *"To hold that the act of homosexual sodomy is somehow protected as a fundamental right would be to cast aside millennia of moral teaching."*

This is essentially not a question of personal "preferences" but rather of the legislative authority of the State. I find nothing in the Constitution depriving a State of the power to enact the statute challenged here. . . .

Justice Blackmun, with whom Justice Brennan, Justice Marshall, and Justice Stevens join, dissenting.

This case is no more about "a fundamental right to engage in homosexual sodomy," as the Court purports to declare, . . . than *Stanley* v. *Georgia*, 394 U.S. 557 . . . (1969), was about a fundamental right to watch obscene movies, or *Katz* v. *United States*, 389 U.S. 347 . . . (1967), was about a fundamental right to place interstate bets from a telephone booth. Rather, this case is about "the most comprehensive of rights and the right most valued by civilized men," namely, "the right to be let alone." *Olmstead* v. *United States*, 277 U.S. 438 . . . (1928) (Brandeis, J., dissenting).

The statute at issue, Ga.Code Ann. § 16-6-2, denies individuals the right to decide for themselves whether to engage in particular forms of private, consensual sexual activity. The Court concludes that § 16-6-2 is valid essentially because "the laws of . . . many States . . . still make such conduct illegal and have done so for a very long time." . . . But the fact that the moral judgments expressed by statutes like § 16-6-2 may be "natural and familiar . . . ought not to conclude our judgment upon the question whether statutes embodying them conflict with the Constitution of the United States." *Roe* v. *Wade,* 410 U.S. 113 . . . (1973). . . . Like Justice Holmes, I believe that "[i]t is revolting to have no better reason for a rule of law than that so it was laid down in the time of Henry IV. It is still more revolting if the grounds upon which it was laid down have vanished long since, and the rule simply persists from blind imitation of the past." Holmes, "The Path of the Law," 10 *Harv.L.Rev.* 457, 469 (1897). I believe we must analyze respondent's claim in the light of the values that underlie the constitutional right to privacy. If that right means anything, it means that, before Georgia can prosecute its citizens for making choices about the most intimate aspects of their lives, it must do more than assert that the choice they have made is an " 'abominable crime not fit to be named among Christians.' " *Herring* v. *State,* 119 Ga. 709, 721 . . . (1904).

I

In its haste to reverse the Court of Appeals and hold that the Constitution does not "confe[r] a fundamental right upon homosexuals to engage in sodomy," . . . the Court relegates the actual statute being challenged to a footnote and ignores the procedural posture of the case before it. A fair reading of the statute and of the complaint clearly reveals that the majority has distorted the question this case presents.

First, the Court's almost obsessive focus on homosexual activity is particularly hard to justify in light of the broad language Georgia has used. Unlike the Court, the Georgia Legislature has not proceeded on the assumption that homosexuals are so different from other citizens that their lives may be controlled in a way that would not be tolerated if it limited the choices of those other citizens. . . .
Rather, Georgia has provided that "[a] person commits the offense of sodomy when he performs or submits to any sexual act involving the sex organs of one person and the mouth or anus of another." Ga. Code Ann. § 16-6-2(a). The sex or status of the persons who engage in the act is irrelevant as a matter of state law. In fact, to the extent I can discern a legislative purpose for Georgia's 1968 enactment of § 16-6-2, that purpose seems to have been to broaden the coverage of the law to reach heterosexual as well as homosexual activity. . . . I therefore see no basis for the Court's decision to treat this case as an "as applied" challenge to § 16-6-2, see *ante,* at 2842, n. 2, or for Georgia's attempt, both in its brief and at oral argument, to defend § 16-6-2 solely on the grounds that it prohibits homosexual activity. Michael Hardwick's standing may rest in significant part on Georgia's apparent willingness to enforce against homosexuals a law it seems not to have any desire to enforce against heterosexuals . . . But his claim that § 16-6-2 involves an unconstitutional intrusion into his privacy and his right of intimate association does not depend in any way on his sexual orientation. . . .

II

"Our cases long have recognized that the Constitution embodies a promise that a certain private sphere of individual liberty will be kept largely beyond the reach of government." *Thornburgh* v. *American Coll. of Obst. & Gyn.,* . . . 106 S.Ct. 2169, 2184 . . . (1986). In construing the right to privacy, the Court has proceeded along two somewhat distinct, albeit complementary, lines. First, it has recognized a privacy interest with reference to certain *decisions* that are properly for the individual to make. . . . Second, it has recognized a privacy interest with reference to certain *places* without regard for the particular activities in which the individuals who occupy them are engaged. . . . The case before us implicates both the decisional and the spatial aspects of the right to privacy.

A. The Court concludes today that none of our prior cases dealing with various decisions that individuals are entitled to make free of governmental interference "bears any resemblance to the claimed constitutional right of homosexuals to engage in acts of sodomy that is asserted in this case." . . .

While it is true that these cases may be characterized by their connection to protection of the family, ... the Court's conclusion that they extend no further than this boundary ignores the warning in *Moore* v. *East Cleveland*, 431 U.S. 494, 501 ... (1977) (plurality opinion), against "clos[ing] our eyes to the basic reasons why certain rights associated with the family have been accorded shelter under the Fourteenth Amendment's Due Process Clause." We protect those rights not because they contribute, in some direct and material way, to the general public welfare, but because they form so central a part of an individual's life. "[T]he concept of privacy embodies the 'moral fact that a person belongs to himself and not others nor to society as a whole.'" *Thornburgh* v. *American Coll. of Obst. & Gyn.,* ... 106 S.Ct., at 2187, n. 5 (Stevens, J., concurring), quoting Fried, Correspondence, 6 Phil. & Pub. Affairs 288–289 (1977). And so we protect the decision whether to marry precisely because marriage "is an association that promotes a way of life, not causes; a harmony in living, not political faiths; a bilateral loyalty, not commercial or social projects." *Griswold* v. *Connecticut,* 381 U.S., at 486.... We protect the decision whether to have a child because parenthood alters so dramatically an individual's self-definition, not because of demographic considerations or the Bible's command to be fruitful and multiply.... And we protect the family because it contributes so powerfully to the happiness of individuals, not because of a preference for stereotypical households.... The Court recognized in *Roberts,* 468 U.S., at 619 ..., that the "ability independently to define one's identity that is central to any concept of liberty" cannot truly be exercised in a vacuum; we all depend on the "emotional enrichment of close ties with others." *Ibid.*

Only the most willful blindness could obscure the fact that sexual intimacy is "a sensitive, key relationship of human existence, central to family life, community welfare, and the development of human personality," *Paris Adult Theatre I* v. *Slaton,* 413 U.S. 49, 63 ... (1973).... The fact that individuals define themselves in a significant way through their intimate sexual relationships with others suggests, in a Nation as diverse as ours, that there may be many "right" ways of conducting those relationships, and

that much of the richness of a relationship will come from the freedom an individual has to *choose* the form and nature of these intensely personal bonds....

In a variety of circumstances we have recognized that a necessary corollary of giving individuals freedom to choose how to conduct their lives is acceptance of the fact that different individuals will make different choices.... "A way of life that is odd or even erratic but interferes with no rights or interests of others is not to be condemned because it is different." *Wisconsin* v. *Yoder,* 406 U.S. 205, 223–24 ... (1972). The Court claims that its decision today merely refuses to recognize a fundamental right to engage in homosexual sodomy; what the Court really has refused to recognize is the fundamental interest all individuals have in controlling the nature of their intimate associations with others....

III

... First, petitioner asserts that the acts made criminal by the statute may have serious adverse consequences for "the general public health and welfare," such as spreading communicable diseases or fostering other criminal activity.... Inasmuch as this case was dismissed by the District Court on the pleadings, it is not surprising that the record before us is barren of any evidence to support petitioner's claim.[3]... Nothing in the record before the Court provides any justification for finding the activity for-

---

3. Even if a court faced with a challenge to § 16-6-2 were to apply simple rational-basis scrutiny to the statute, Georgia would be required to show an actual connection between the forbidden acts and the ill effects it seeks to prevent. The connection between the acts prohibited by § 16-6-2 and the harms identified by petitioner in his brief before this Court is a subject of hot dispute, hardly amenable to dismissal under Federal Rule or Civil Procedure 12(b)(6). Compare ... Brief for Petitioner 36–37 and Brief for David Robinson, Jr., as *Amicus Curiae* 23–28, on the one hand, with *People* v. *Onofre,* 51 N.Y.2d 476, 489, ... (1980); Brief for the Attorney General of the State of New York, joined by the Attorney General of the State of California, as *Amici Curiae* 11–14; and Brief for the American Psychological Association and American Public Health Association as *Amici Curiae* 19–27, on the other.

bidden by § 16-6-2 to be physically dangerous, either to the person engaged in it or to others.[4]

The core of petitioner's defense of § 16-6-2, however, is that respondent and others who engage in the conduct prohibited by § 16-6-2 interfere with Georgia's exercise of the "'right of the Nation and of the States to maintain a decent society,'" *Paris Adult Theatre I* v. *Slaton,* 413 U.S., at 59–60.... Essentially, petitioner argues, and the Court agrees, that the fact that the acts described in § 16-6-2 "for hundreds of years, if not thousands, have been uniformly condemned as immoral" is a sufficient reason to permit a State to ban them today....

I cannot agree that either the length of time a majority has held its convictions or the passions with which it defends them can withdraw legislation from this Court's scrutiny.... As Justice Jackson wrote so eloquently for the Court in *West Virginia Board of Education* v. *Barnette,* 319 U.S. 624, 641–42 ... (1943), "we apply the limitations of the Constitution with no fear that freedom to be intellectually and spiritually diverse or even

---

4. Although I do not think it necessary to decide today issues that are not even remotely before us, it does seem to me that a court could find simple, analytically sound distinctions between certain private, consensual sexual conduct, on the one hand, and adultery and incest (the only two vaguely specific "sexual crimes" to which the majority points ...), on the other. For example, marriage, in addition to its spiritual aspects, is a civil contract that entitles the contracting parties to a variety of governmentally provided benefits. A State might define the contractual commitment necessary to become eligible for these benefits to include a commitment of fidelity and then punish individuals for breaching that contract. Moreover, a State might conclude that adultery is likely to injure third persons, in particular, spouses and children of persons who engage in extramarital affairs. With respect to incest, a court might well agree with respondent that the nature of familial relationships renders true consent to incestuous activity sufficiently problematical that a blanket prohibition of such activity is warranted.... Notably, the Court makes no effort to explain why it has chosen to group private, consensual homosexual activity with adultery and incest rather than with private, consensual heterosexual activity by unmarried persons or, indeed, with oral or anal sex within marriage.

contrary will disintegrate the social organization.... [F]reedom to differ is not limited to things that do not matter much. That would be a mere shadow of freedom. The test of its substance is the right to differ as to things that touch the heart of the existing order." ... It is precisely because the issue raised by this case touches the heart of what makes individuals what they are that we should be especially sensitive to the rights of those whose choices upset the majority.

The assertion that "traditional Judaeo-Christian values proscribe" the conduct involved ... cannot provide an adequate justification for § 16-6-2. That certain, but by no means all, religious groups condemn the behavior at issue gives the State no license to impose their judgments on the entire citizenry. The legitimacy of secular legislation depends instead on whether the State can advance some justification for its law beyond its conformity to religious doctrine.... Thus, far from buttressing his case, petitioner's invocation of Leviticus, Romans, St. Thomas Aquinas, and sodomy's heretical status during the Middle Ages undermines his suggestion that § 16-6-2 represents a legitimate use of secular coercive power.... A State can no more punish private behavior because of religious intolerance than it can punish such behavior because of racial animus. "The Constitution cannot control such prejudices, but neither can it tolerate them. Private biases may be outside the reach of the law, but the law cannot, directly or indirectly, give them effect." *Palmore* v. *Sidoti,* 466 U.S. 429, 433 ... (1984). No matter how uncomfortable a certain group may make the majority of this Court, we have held that "[m]ere public intolerance or animosity cannot constitutionally justify the deprivation of a person's physical liberty." *O'Connor* v. *Donaldson,* 422 U.S. 563, 575 ... (1975)....

Nor can § 16-6-2 be justified as a "morally neutral" exercise of Georgia's power to "protect the public environment," *Paris Adult Theatre I,* 413 U.S., at 68–69.... Certainly, some private behavior can affect the fabric of society as a whole. Reasonable people may differ about whether particular sexual acts are moral or immoral, but "we have ample evidence for believing that people will not abandon morality, will not think any better of murder, cruelty, and dishonesty, merely because some private sexual practice which they abominate is not punished by the law." H. L. A. Hart, "Immorality and Treason," reprinted in *The Law as Literature* 220, 225 (L. Blom-Cooper, ed., 1961). Petitioner and the Court fail to see the difference between laws that protect public sensibilities and those that enforce private morality. Statutes banning public sexual activity are entirely consistent with protecting the individual's liberty interest in decisions concerning sexual relations: The same recognition that those decisions are intensely private, which justifies protecting them from governmental interference, can justify protecting individuals from unwilling exposure to the sexual activities of others. But the mere fact that intimate behavior may be punished when it takes place in public cannot dictate how States can regulate intimate behavior that occurs in intimate places....

This case involves no real interference with the rights of others, for the mere knowledge that other individuals do not adhere to one's value system cannot be a legally cognizable interest, ... let alone an interest that can justify invading the houses, hearts, and minds of citizens who choose to live their lives differently.

IV

It took but three years for the Court to see the error in its analysis in *Minersville School District* v. *Gobitis,* 310 U.S. 586 ... (1940), and to recognize that the threat to national cohesion posed by a refusal to salute the flag was vastly outweighed by the threat to those same values posed by compelling such a salute.... I can only hope that here, too, the Court soon will reconsider its analysis and conclude that depriving individuals of the right to choose for themselves how to conduct their intimate relationships poses a far greater threat to the values most deeply rooted in our Nation's history than tolerance of nonconformity could ever do. Because I think the Court today betrays those values, I dissent.

Study Questions

1. Does the right to privacy include the right of consenting adults to practice homosexuality in their homes?

2. If homosexuality is legalized, will incest have to be legalized also?

A Philosophical Analysis of Sexual Ethics

Raymond A. Belliotti is a professor of philosophy at the State University of New York at Fredonia. He received his J.D. from Harvard Law School.

Raymond A. Belliotti

I shall advance and defend what can be labeled a secular analysis of sexual ethics. As a secular analy-

Reprinted with permission of Raymond A. Belliotti, and the publisher of the *Journal of Social Philosophy,* vol. X, no. 3 (September 1979), pp. 8–11.

sis it shall make no appeal to religious considerations; it shall, in fact, consider religious factors irrelevant to the analysis. In doing so it should be obvious that the account will seem unsatisfactory to fervent religious believers.

I

I begin with what I take to be a fundamental ethical maxim: it is morally wrong for someone to treat another merely as a means to his own ends. Immanuel Kant first formulated the maxim in this way,[1] but I think it can be considered uncontroversially true by most, if not all, moral thinkers. We often speak disparagingly of a person who "uses" or "exploits" another. What do we mean by this? It seems that we are suggesting that the former is morally culpable because he has treated the latter in a way that is morally wrong for one human to treat another. The culpable individual has "objectified" his victim; he has treated the other as an object to be manipulated and used, much as we might utilize a tool. One of the worst things that one person can do to another is to recognize the other as something less than human or as something less than the other really is: to recognize the other, not as an end in himself, but rather as an object to be used merely as a means to the user's ends. If we believe, and I think we do, that each person has an intrinsic worth and value which demands that we treat all others as subjects of experience and as being as fully human as ourselves, then we are following the general pattern of Kant's ethical maxim.

Notice that the maxim does not state that we cannot treat others as a means to our ends. It only states that we cannot *merely* treat the other in this way. We often need others to fulfill our goals, but immorality occurs only if we treat them merely as a means to these goals and not as an equal subject of experience.

So in all our human interactions we have a moral obligation to treat others as more than just means to our ends. This obligation becomes even more important when considering sexual interac-

tions since very important feelings, desires, and drives are involved.

The second stage of the argument concerns the nature of sexual interactions. I contend that the nature of these interactions is contractual and involves the important notion of reciprocity. When two people voluntarily consent to interact sexually they create obligations to each other based on their needs and expectations. Every sexual encounter has as its base the needs, desires, and drives of the individuals involved. That we choose to interact sexually is an acknowledgement that none of us is totally self-sufficient. We interact with others in order to fulfill certain desires which we cannot fulfill by ourselves. This suggests that the basis of the sexual encounter is contractual; i.e., it is a voluntary agreement on the part of both parties to satisfy the expectations of the other.

Some might recoil at the coldness of such an analysis. Is the sexual encounter as business-like a contract as the relationship between two corporations or the agreements one makes with his insurance agent? Of course it is not. Very important feelings of intimacy are involved which make the consenting parties emotionally vulnerable. But all this shows is that the sexual contract may well be the most important agreement that one makes from an emotional standpoint; it does not show that the interaction itself is not contractual. The contractual basis of the sexual interaction involves the notion of a voluntary agreement founded on the expectations of fulfillment of reciprocal needs.

The final stage of the argument consists of two acknowledgements: (1) That voluntary contracts are such that the parties are under a moral obligation, other things being equal, to fulfill that which they agreed upon, and (2) that promise-breaking and deception are, other things equal, immoral actions. The acknowledgement of the second makes the recognition of the first redundant, since the non-fulfillment of one's contractual duties is a species of promise-breaking. Ordinarily we feel that promise-breaking and deception are paradigm cases of immoral actions, since they involve violations of moral duties, and often, explicit or implicit lying. If it is true that sexual interactions entail contractual rela-

---

1. Immanuel Kant, *Foundations of the Metaphysics of Morals*, L. W. Beck, trans. (Indianapolis, Indiana: Library of Liberal Arts Press), p. 87.

tionships then any violation of that which one has voluntarily consented to perform is morally wrong, since it involves promise-breaking and the non-fulfillment of the moral duty to honor one's voluntary agreements.

It is clear, then, that both parties must perform that which they voluntarily contracted to do for the other, unless the other agrees to the non-performance of the originally agreed upon action. Although sexual contracts are not as formal or explicit as corporation agreements, the rule of thumb should be the concept of reasonable expectation. If a woman smiles at me and agrees to have a drink I cannot reasonably assume, at least at this point, that she has agreed to spend the weekend with me. On the other hand if she did agree to share a room

> *"... [S]ex is immoral if and only if it involves deception, promise-breaking, and/or the treatment of the other merely as a means to one's own ends."*

and bed with me for the weekend I could reasonably assume that she had agreed to have sexual intercourse with me. Although all examples are not clearcut, in general, the notion of reasonable expectation should guide us here. If there is any doubt concerning whether or not someone has agreed to perform a certain sexual act with another, I would suggest that the doubting party simply ask the other and make the contract more explicit. In lieu of this, prudence dictates that we be cautious in assuming what the other has offered, and when in doubt assume nothing until a more explicit overture has been made.

The conclusion of the argument is that sex is immoral if and only if it involves deception, promise-

breaking, and/or the treatment of the other merely as a means to one's own ends.

II

The results of this analysis can now be applied to various sexual activities.

(1) *Rape* is intrinsically immoral because it involves the involuntary participation of one of the parties. Since the basis of the sexual encounter is contractual it should be clear that any coercion or force renders the interaction immoral; contracts are not validly consummated if one of the parties is compelled to agree by force or fraud. An interesting question concerns whether it is possible for a husband to rape his wife. I tend to think that this is possible. Some contend that the marriage contract allows both parties unrestricted sexual access to the other, and that, therefore, rape cannot occur in a marital situation. Others define rape as a sexual interaction which occurs when one individual forcibly uses another and the parties are not married to each other. But I think of rape as any case of forcibly using another in a sexual encounter without the other's consent. Under this definition it would be possible for a man to rape his wife, and in doing so commit an immoral act.

(2) *Bestiality* is intrinsically immoral because it too involves the involuntary participation of one of the parties. No non-human animal is capable of entering into a valid sexual contract with a human; as such all cases of bestiality can be considered instances of animal rape. A critic might argue that bestiality is only a form of sex with an object since only a non-human animal is involved. Kant, himself, felt that animals could be used merely as a means to the ends of humans.[2] But this is mistaken from a moral point of view. Animals, unlike objects, have interests, desires, and are capable of experiencing pleasure and pain; i.e., they are sentient beings. As sentient beings their interests ought to be taken into account. As it seems clear that the interests of non-human animals are not advanced by being used as sexual objects by humans, it also seems clear that to do so cannot be morally justified. The differences

---

2. *Ibid.*

between mere objects, which can be legitimately used merely as means to human ends, and nonhuman animals, who are sentient beings, are obvious. To use or totally objectify the latter is morally wrong; although probably less wrong than the use or objectification of other human beings.[3]

(3) *Necrophilia* is immoral since it also involves the involuntary participation of one of the parties. The corpse cannot voluntarily enter into a contract with a living human; hence cases of necrophilia can be considered instances of the rape of dead humans. Now it may seem that corpses *are* mere objects; certainly they cannot feel pleasure and pain. But are they mere objects in the sense that rocks, stones, and desks are objects? The corpse was once a sentient being and it may still be the case that even as a corpse it has interests. This may seem absurd at first glance. But we really acknowledge this very fact by honoring death bed promises made to the dying, by taking care when handling and displaying the bodies of the dead, and by being careful not to defame maliciously the reputations of dead people. Don't we feel that there is a difference between being buried with dignity and being hung and mutilated after we die?[4] Wouldn't we prefer the former? And the reason we would involves the fact that no *mere* object is involved, but rather a human corpse.

There are imaginable instances in which necrophilia would not be immoral. Suppose the will of man X contains a clause stipulating that "anyone wishing to use my corpse for sexual purposes between the hours of 7–9 P.M. on Thursdays at the Greenmount Cemetery may do so." As long as X made the stipulation rationally and sincerely[5] my

analysis would consider sexual acts performed on the appointed day and time as not immoral; the law, however, might take a dimmer view of this activity.

(4) *Incest* is immoral when it involves a child who cannot be considered capable of entering into a contractual relationship. Children cannot know the ramifications of a sexual interaction with their parent(s); hence they cannot be thought of as fully responsible agents. Any contract, sexual or otherwise, can only be legitimately consummated with fully responsible parties.

Incest would also be immoral if the parties knowingly conceived a child with the likelihood of genetic defect, since this is an act which would contribute to the needless misery of another.

But there are times when incest is not immoral. Suppose a 50 year old father and his 30 year old daughter voluntarily agree, rationally and sincerely, to a sexual interaction. Both parties are fully responsible agents knowing the ramifications of their actions, and employ proper birth control methods to eliminate the possibility of conceiving a defective child, or engage in a sexual act in which no child could possibly be conceived. This, repugnant though it may seem, would not be an immoral act.

(5) *Promiscuity* and *adultery* are immoral only if they involve promise-breaking, deceit, or exploitation. Promise-breaking and deceit can occur in a number of ways: one party may deceive another concerning his real feelings for the other; he may break promises to his spouse in order that he might be with the other; he may explicitly lie in order to sustain the two relationships. In romantic triangles of this nature, immorality can occur from the actions of any of the parties in relation to the two other parties.

Some would argue that the nature of the marriage contract itself entails that *any* extramarital encounter on the part of either party is immoral (i.e., it involves promise-breaking) since one provision of the marriage contract is sexual exclusivity. But under my analysis the parties to the marriage contract may legitimately amend the contract at any time,

---

3. This raises the interesting issue of whether other ways that humans treat animals are morally justified. A strong case can be made that eating meat and using animals for clothes are immoral.

4. This was in fact the reason that Italian partisans thought that subjecting Mussolini to degradation after he was dead was in a sense *harming* Mussolini. They assumed that he still possessed certain interests which could be harmed by the indignities they inflicted upon him.

5. By "rationally" and "sincerely" I only mean that the individual is not under the influence of hallucinogens and is not joking. The individual

must be of sound mind. I do not mean by "rationally" that the individual is making the best decision, all things considered.

and an extramarital sexual encounter need not be immoral as long as both marital partners agree prior to the encounter that it is permissible. If the marriage relationship is construed as a voluntary reciprocal contract the partners are free to amend its provisions insofar as they can both agree on the alterations involved.

III

The religious argument against many of the aforementioned sexual activities is often straightforward:

(A) If an action is a violation of God's law then it is immoral.

(B) X breaks the law of God.
X is an immoral action.

Substitute the acts in question for X and we see the essence of the religious argument against these acts. For the believer a supernatural being, possessing certain qualities, has created us and set down a variety of laws. To transgress these laws is to violate morality, since the ultimate lawgiver has set forth the basis for morality in these laws. All the believer need do is point to the relevant biblical scripture or the relevant source of these laws to show that certain acts are immoral. These acts are seen as *intrinsically* immoral, regardless of whether promise-breaking, deception, or exploitation are involved. Surely these latter factors are viewed as immoral, but even if they do not occur the action in question is still immoral because it violates the law of God. Violating the law of God is considered a sufficient condition for an act to be immoral by the religious believer.

Of course to someone who does not believe in any supernatural being or to one who believes in a supernatural being of a radically different nature from the Christian God, this argument is not convincing. Without a religious conviction premise (A) is vacuous.

Yet it is true that many nonbelievers share the believer's convictions regarding the immorality of certain of the sexual practices we have considered. Why is this so? I think that an important reason is that many religious convictions about practical moral issues have become imbedded into our considered moral judgments. Because of the influence and historical power of Christianity throughout the ages certain beliefs about the immorality of particular actions became an integral part of our moral education and customs. Hence many nonbelievers still think that adultery, promiscuity, etc. are morally prenicious even though they deny the existence of the Christian God. Under my analysis, however, these actions are not immoral (presupposing no promise-breaking, deception, or exploitation) once belief in the Christian God is abrogated. Once sexual interactions are viewed as being contractual and reciprocal we have a basis for judging their morality independent of any reliance upon the laws of a supernatural being.

IV

The results of my analysis are in certain cases more liberal than conventional moralists (e.g., adultery, promiscuity, necrophilia, and incest are not immoral if certain conditions pertain), and in other cases more conservative (e.g., "teasing" without the intention to fulfill that which the other reasonably can be expected to think was offered is immoral, since it involves the nonfulfillment of that which the other could reasonably be expected to think was agreed upon).

It must be pointed out that to state that a certain act is not immoral does not entail that it is advisable to pursue. I have argued that under certain conditions these acts are not immoral, but I would certainly advise against most, if not all, of these actions. Often these actions still are offensive to our tastes, not in our best long term interests, and may be psychologically harmful. Because our most important feelings and emotions are involved in sexual interactions we must be cautious about engaging in certain acts which may be damaging in the long run. Just as we should be careful in agreeing to *any* voluntary contract involving a reciprocal exchange of goods and services, we should be most careful before agreeing upon what may be our most important kind of contract. The sexual contract is one in which our most valuable intangible commodities are at stake; in fact our self-esteem may well be on the line. And although we may freely enter into certain sexual contracts it is important to know the ramifications and long range effects of our own interests and the interests of others.

The purpose of this essay, then, is not to endorse or encourage certain of the sexual practices mentioned, but rather to show that the basis of our secular aversion to them often cannot be the notion of morality.

Study Questions

1. Is there anything morally wrong with promiscuity?

2. Are bestiality and necrophilia immoral?

3. Can something be immoral if no physical or psychological harm results from it?

Sex and Personal Intimacy

John Hunter is a professor of philosophy at the University of Toronto, Canada.

John Hunter

... While our sex lives are matters of proper moral concern in many ways and cases, sexual activity is not immoral nearly so often as some people would have us believe.... It will be suggested that there is more than one mode of evaluation of behavior in general and sexual behavior in particular: not all defects are moral imperfections, and not all perfections moral virtues. The specific mode of evaluation with which we will be concerned here is that of personal intimacy. What we will call "personal intimacy" is not something commonly known by that or any other name; but it will be argued that it is something about which many people do care, and which could be recommended to those who so far have not learned to care about it.

From *Thinking About Sex and Love,* pp. 80–109. Reprinted by permission of St. Martin's Press, Inc.

Before explaining the concept of personal intimacy, it will be useful to make as clear as possible the idea, and the implications of the idea, that there are various modes of evaluation of behavior, not all of them moral. That will be the task of this introduction.

We may praise or criticize human behavior on moral, aesthetic and intellectual grounds, to name some of the most obvious. People are admired for achieving high standards, and criticized for failing to do so, but the admiration and criticism are of a different kind from case to case. Except in special cases, it is not immoral to paint a picture amateurishly or sing a tune off key. We would criticize but not deplore these things, and certainly not chastise or imprison the person who did them.

We admire people who are witty, perceptive, friendly or warm, and criticize them for being humorless or obtuse or insensitive; but except in special cases, the former are not moral virtues and the latter not moral vices. It is not saintly of a person to be an entertaining conversationalist or a shrewd observer; it is possible for thieves, liars and cowards to be perceptive or witty and for honest, brave and generous people to be dull, gauche or unfriendly. . . .

[This distinction] opens the possibility that some of our sexual activities may be regrettable without being immoral; but if anything is substandard in some nonmoral way, its avoidance will not be something we have a right to require of people, but will be a matter of preference, recommendation, encouragement. We will perhaps teach people to appreciate the preferred way of managing things, in much the way we cultivate taste in architecture or music. The preferred way will be recommended, not as a concession to other people, but primarily as something personally rewarding; and it will be treated as sad, rather than unacceptable, when anyone is slow to learn such things.

What Is Personal Intimacy?

There are at least three distinguishable ways in which personal relations can be better or worse, and it will be the aim of this section to concentrate on one of these, delineating it as clearly as possible and distinguishing it from the other two.

We might call the first point of view from which our relations with people can be evaluated that of *congeniality*. If two people bore or annoy one another, then given that they have a relationship—for example, if they work at the same place or are members of the same family—it is a poor or unsatisfactory one; while if each finds the other amusing, interesting or merely agreeable, they have a satisfactory or congenial relationship. If they are uncongenial they may also be nasty or deceitful, and then their relationship will involve questions of morality; but an uncongenial relationship is not in itself immoral, nor is a congenial one in itself virtuous. We can be uncongenial without being nasty, and congenial without being helpful or considerate. There is, of course, the case in which it is because someone is immoral in some way that he is uncongenial; but even here there is a distinction between the person

interesting enough to be congenial, if he were not so malicious, and the person who would be boring even if he were saintly.

Secondly, a person can be morally upright in his dealings with people, without finding those persons congenial or being found so by them. Indeed, we might say that it is the mark of a virtuous person to be honest, generous and so on toward others regardless of whether they are congenial. A person who is fair or considerate only toward people he likes is to that extent morally defective.

Congeniality and morality are then two of our three ways in which personal relationships can be better or worse; and their distinctness from one another is shown by their independent variability, by the fact that one of them can exist without the other.

The third dimension we will call *personal intimacy*. That expression has no clear ordinary use, nor do we have much else in the way of a standard vocabulary for talking about this quality sometimes found in our relations with people; however, if we describe some examples of its presence and its absence, most of us will recognize something that we care a good deal about; that we rejoice in when it exists and regret when it does not exist.

If two people see a good deal of one another, talk animatedly and enjoy doing things together, each may yet remain somewhat of a mystery to the other. An amusing remark about a serious subject may leave the other person wondering whether the remark was made with no serious intent and merely because it was amusing, or whether it expressed a cynical or skeptical attitude. If questions like that somehow just cannot be raised between them, their relationship may be felt to be defective in being, although extremely congenial, quite superficial.

Similarly, if two people have been on friendly terms and one of them moves to another city for a time and does not write, but resumes the amicable relationship on his return, it may be unclear whether in the interval he missed or thought about his friend, or whether the friendship had no deeper basis than the pleasure of the moment. If that question could somehow not be raised, then although these two people may entirely enjoy one another, and although there need be no deception, unkindness or other moral fault, something is missing.

It is the same thing as is missing sometimes between persons who meet and have a convivial time at a party. They may regard party conversation as a kind of game at which one can be skilled, the object of which is to take on any topic someone raises and make it the subject of a fine display of wit and discernment. Part of the fun is in being able to do something with whatever topic comes up, and poor players are people who are stumped by too many topics. One may very much enjoy this game, and be delighted to meet someone who plays it well, but go away knowing little about the other person, not interested in how he gets along with his wife, what he does on weekends or whether he fears death, and not inclined to help him fix his washing machine or to drop by his place on a Saturday just to say hello. It is not that in party conversation such personal topics as the fear of death are avoided, but they are treated in a way that leaves it unclear what lies behind the display of wit and discernment: whether the good conversationalist has the same thoughts when he is alone at night as he is now offering for our amusement.

We might say that in such cases what is missing is interest in the person. There is interest, not in the person, but in the output: in various capacities that we may find amusing or congenial or useful. We may want good company or good conversation or skill at chess or tennis or lovemaking, and it may not matter who possesses these desired qualities.

We see the same lack of personal interest in commercial relationships, although in these cases it does not usually strike anyone as regrettable. A plumber comes and fixes the water tank; we pay him and he rushes on to his next job. There is perhaps time for a joke or for him to admire the garden, but there is little question of his staying for supper. We are interested in him only in his capacity as a fixer of pipes. This is not because of snobbishness about plumbers: it would be the same with lawyers or doctors. There is just no time in our lives for more than a few close personal relationships.

We should not let the examples of the plumber or the party-goer lead us to think that it is a question of *how many* of a person's capacities we are interested in. Two people may be married and find

one another satisfactory mates. They may usually sort out their differences amicably, be proud of one another in public, have interesting conversations about friends, films and books, and enjoy one another in bed—and yet be quite capable of parting with no greater sense of loss than derives from the rarity of such a congenial arrangement. If one mate could immediately be replaced by another equally congenial and there was no sense of a particular personal loss, then there was not an attachment to just this person. Each person was interested, not in the other person, but in that person's conversation, taste, cheerfulness, cooking ability or sexual compatibility.

This extreme case brings out an important point about the concept of being interested in specific persons. As long as we limit ourselves to cases in which we are interested in some one or some few qualities in a person, it can look as if what is missing is just breadth of appreciation: if we were interested in a person not only as an enjoyable lover or a competent plumber or an agreeable conversationalist, but in most of his other qualities and abilities as well, that would be what it is to be interested in him as a person. But in the case of the couple who are entirely pleased with one another, there are no other qualities to be appreciated. Hence the question arises, what is it to be interested in a person? What can there be, over and above all the qualities we are supposing these two people appreciate, in which they might be interested? It would surely be absurd to say that we are interested in something that never shows, something underlying all such things as high spirits and courage and gentleness and wit.

If we seem here to be on the verge of having to suppose that there is something mysterious or hidden that we can appreciate or fail to appreciate, it is perhaps because we are predisposed to think that being interested in a person is a matter of appreciating some good quality or another. Given that supposition, on the one hand, we must find some quality to be appreciated, and on the other, in the case of the couple who like most everything about one another, we can find no ordinary quality to fill the slot, and we have no option but to look for some mysterious or hidden quality. But if being interested in someone is not a matter of appreciating qualities, we will not find ourselves in that peculiar fix.

What then *is* being interested in a person? If we suppose that there is nothing mysterious about it, it ought to be accessible to perceptive observation. As a prelude to trying to say what it is, let us review some significant differences we can notice between personal and impersonal relationships. To do this we can either set before ourselves some extreme cases, or construct a composite out of tendencies noticeable in various moderate cases.

1. The conversation of people whose relation is impersonal will have a kind of showiness about it, as if they were always playing to an audience; and the topics of conversation will either run to matters of little or no personal involvement, such as films, books, news items, puzzles and scientific curiosities, or, if they extend to such things as the hopes, fears, joys and tribulations of the parties themselves, will be handled in such a way as to conceal attitudes. A person will perhaps be amusing or scientific about his fears, and one will be left wondering whether he is amused by them when they are upon him, and if so what kind of fears they can be.

2. In an impersonal relation, each person's appreciation of the other will run noticeably to concentration on the output, as we have put it: on the joke or the interesting story, for example, rather than on who made the joke or told the story. It is the difference between "What a good joke!" and "How funny you are!" Each will rejoice in the interest of the performance, and it will seem incidental who is performing.

3. In an impersonal relation, tensions, disagreements and disappointments will tend immediately to threaten the connection. If we are interested only in the quality of the output, enthusiasm will diminish to the extent that the quality deteriorates. The attitude will be like the average person's feeling for his car: delighted with it as long as it looks good and performs well, willing to put up with it when it develops faults as long as no other is readily available and able to part with it without a sigh when something better becomes available.

4. By contrast, we tend to dote even on the imper-fections of someone in whom our interest is personal. The peculiar plainness of a face or a peculiar awkwardness of manner are welcomed, not as being in general admirable qualities, but just as being so characteristic of a person for whom we care.

5. While people who are impersonally related may stimulate each other to better than average displays of their capabilities, when a relation is personal we draw each other out, reveal ourselves. We express ourselves unreservedly to one another, and if there is uncertainty as to the other person's attitudes or feelings, it is not because they are kept back, but just because there has not happened to be an occasion to express them.

From these observations we might construct the following generalizations:

(a) A test of whether a relationship is personal or not is whether anyone else having the same or comparable good qualities would do as well. A commercial relationship is usually impersonal, and there it makes no difference, as between honest and competent practitioners, whom we employ; and similarly in our friendships if we can move without a sigh from one person to another who is equally congenial, our relationship is impersonal.

(b) The application of this test is complicated somewhat by the fact that it may pain us to lose a friend, not because of a particular attachment to that person, but only because congenial connections can be somewhat rare, or because we have been particularly fortunate in a certain friendship. Then we will experience a sense of loss, and it may not be clear whether that is because there was a particular attachment, or because of the difficulty of finding a replacement. The test may still be useful, however, either in the case in which we are fortunate in replacing one friend by another, or in the case in which, although we enjoyed a friendship and it was not replaced by another, no loss was felt. In other cases, we may have to apply other tests.

(c) There is, paradoxically perhaps, a sense in which a personal relation is objective, and an impersonal one subjective: in the latter case it is just to the extent that I find a person's qualities agreeable or congenial that I am interested, whereas in the former case I care about a person's tastes or hopes or fears *whatever they may be,* just because they are the person's. There is thus a quality of total acceptance about a relationship that is personal, a readiness to let the chips fall where they may.

(d) There are two related character traits that make for personal intimacy, one a disposition to trust other people, so that one will not fear to reveal oneself, and the other a tendency to inspire trust. Conversely, a disposition to fear other people and a tendency to inspire fear will make for such self-concealing behavior as hiding behind a wall of banter and wit, or avoiding such closeness as would create pressures to show oneself.

Being interested in a person, then, is not a matter of appreciating something in addition to various charms and abilities, but of relating to someone in a certain way—a way that is outgoing and trusting, that is not contingent on maintaining any particular standard of attractiveness or agreeability, and that tends to find personal qualities interesting independent of their charm, just because they are the qualities of a given person.

To make perfectly clear that personal intimacy is a quality of human relationships quite distinct from morality or congeniality, we need to show that it varies independently of them, that whatever connections there may be, it is possible to have one without the other.

In the case of congeniality, there is a connection with personal intimacy in that we are not likely to have a very close relationship with someone who is quite uncongenial; but on the other hand, (i) the person with an aptitude for personal intimacy will be undemanding with regard to congeniality, will not always be reviewing friendships as to whether they are sufficiently rewarding; and (ii) clearly there is congeniality without personal intimacy in our cases of the party-goers or the couple who find one another altogether agreeable.

In the case of morality, it seems clear in the first place that there need be nothing morally wrong with a relationship that is impersonal. Take, as the hardest case, the man who engages the services of a prostitute: there need be nothing deceitful, cruel, unfair, selfish or cowardly about such an episode,

and hence except in special cases his action, although impersonal, is not immoral. There can, of course, be immorality in such cases, for example, if he is cruel or gratuitously insulting to the woman, or does not pay her, or if he later has sexual contact with someone else without knowing whether he has contracted venereal disease, or if he pretends to deplore the practice of prostitution. But none of these faults must exist, and when they do not it is difficult to see on what ground it could be represented as immoral to use the services of a prostitute. Yet the relationship is normally lacking in personal warmth.

(There is something to be said for the argument that, since it is almost certainly harmful to a person, at least over any length of time, to be a prostitute, anyone employing her services contributes to the degradation of a human being. To do that is certainly immoral; but since prostitutes will generally continue their activities regardless of whether any particular person employs them, it is not perfectly clear whether each customer contributes to their degradation. But even if that is true, it is not because the relationship is impersonal that something immoral is done, but because the life of a prostitute is so afflicted with cruelty, harassment and disease.)

Take a less extreme case: there are people who do not much care for other people, but greatly enjoy the excitement of sex. They may seek out others who are like-minded, and who when called upon most any time will eagerly make love. If these people conscientiously avoid sexual involvement with anyone who shows signs of being in love, or of regarding sexual activity as anything more than a pleasure, and if they are careful not to mislead another person as to their own attitude, there would be nothing dishonest, cruel, harmful or unfair about their practice, and therefore no ground for saying it is immoral. However, such relationships are clearly impersonal.

This is not to say, of course, that no purely sexual relationship is ever immoral, but only that it is not immoral just because it is purely sexual. If there is deception or cruelty, or carelessness about contraception, there will be moral defect; but those faults are independent of the impersonal character of the relationship, and by no means typical of such relationships.

At the other extreme from our first case is the example of our broadly congenial couple whose relation is impersonal. It is obvious here that in spite of the impersonal character of their relationship, there is nothing immoral about it. They may be as fair, honest, generous and considerate as anyone could ask, without revealing themselves to one another, or having any greater attachment than is dictated by the quality of the other person's charms.

Yet there are two reasons why, in spite of the above arguments, some people might hesitate to accept the contention that morality varies independently of personal intimacy:

1. Morality is often (and probably correctly) represented as being at least in part a matter of respect for persons, of treating other people, as Kant put it, "never merely as means, but always also as ends in themselves"; but personal intimacy appears from what we have seen to require the same attitude. How then is it possible for them to vary independently?

The answer is that the ethical way of treating people as ends in themselves is different from the personal intimacy way. A typical ethical application of the principle might be that if something one considers doing will adversely affect another person, then that fact alone demands to be taken account of in our ethical thinking. The ethical attitude is that it does not matter whether the person in question is a friend or a stranger, rich or poor, saintly or sinful. All we need to know is that a human being would be adversely affected. To have that attitude is to have respect for persons. If I delude someone, even into doing something that is to his advantage, I have not treated him with the kind of respect due to a person: I have not allowed him to decide in a free and well-informed way what he will do. In these cases, it is just because it is a human being we are dealing with that we act in certain ways, not because it is a specific person. It may be a boring and annoying fact that his interests would be adversely affected. We need not be intrigued by it or probe into it; and our actions can be affected by it without there being any personal contact whatever, without the other person knowing that we have changed our plans because of the way they might affect his interests. He can be someone we know of only indirectly; and even where there is personal contact,

the transaction need involve none of the colorful interplay between persons that is characteristic of personal intimacy.

In the moral application of the principle, whether we are interested in a person or not, we treat him with respect; whereas the application in the case of personal intimacy is a matter of taking an interest. The interest we take is itself the burden of the principle. We take that interest, not with a view to being able to behave well toward other people, but with a view to appreciating them more, and to having a warmer and richer relationship.

2. It is sometimes said that a person is morally defective if he does right by other people merely from principle, and not out of any kind of affection or personal concern. If this is true, then personal intimacy would perhaps have to be regarded as part of morality, and they could not vary independently; but surely it is not true. A wife may be disappointed if her husband is faithful and considerate, not out of enthusiasm for her, but out of duty, but she can hardly say it is morally defective of him. She is right in thinking that it would be more rewarding if he rejoiced in her as a person, but wrong in thinking it would be morally better. She has not made the distinction we have been trying to draw between two fundamentally different types or scales of evaluation.

Morality requires that we do right by people regardless of whether we know or like them, and therefore it must vary independently of personal intimacy. The quality of life would deteriorate radically if we were expected to be fair or generous only to our friends.

There are, however, relations between the personal and the ethical. Although it is possible to treat another person fairly and with consideration when one feels no personal attachment or enthusiasm, it requires a particular effort and a higher level of concern than is common in the human race. On the other hand, it comes naturally to us to be fair and considerate to someone we rejoice in as a person, because when we care for a person, we become involved in their interests as if they were our own.

In such relations as these between the personal and the moral lies the great strength of any moral perspective in which love has a central place; for example, Christianity. It is easy and natural to do right by someone you love; and one might say that Christianity, recognizing this, chooses to say little about just how to do right, but instead tries to encourage love, which may, if we independently have some understanding of moral virtue, motivate us to do what we know to be right. The weaknesses of such an approach are chiefly two: (i) it tends not to face up to the fact that, while we must do right by everyone, we deceive ourselves if we think we can or do love everyone, and (ii) it offers little guidance as to how to do right, and thus both leaves us ill equipped for the finer questions of right behavior toward those we do love, and quite unprepared for virtuous treatment of people we do not love. It also encourages us to believe that we love people whom we do not love, and so to believe that we are doing right by them when we are not.

If we are right in concluding that it is not a moral question whether our relations with other people are impersonal ... impersonal relationships are not something we have a right to complain of, and personal intimacy is not something we have right to insist on. If I choose to avoid people who, however amusing they may be, do not reveal themselves and take no personal interest in me, I am expressing a personal preference. I should not despise or deplore such people, and there should be no question of their being penalized or refused entry into the country, as there might be if they were deemed immoral.

If it is not a moral question what kind of personal relationships we have, but a matter of personal preference, is it as much a matter of taste as whether one likes strawberry jam, or are there non-moral considerations that make one kind of relationship preferable to another?

To put the question just this way suggests falsely that personal intimacy can be achieved at will, that it is as much under our control as what we eat or what we do with our leisure time. There are at least two reasons why this is not true: (i) it is a mutual thing, and depends very much on the reactions and attitudes of the other person, and (ii) one has to have or to cultivate a certain disposition before it is possible, and when one has that disposition, close personal relationships *happen,* rather than being artfully brought about. One cannot turn on the trust, the demonstrativeness or the kind of "objec-

tive" interest in people that we described earlier. If it is turned on, either its artificiality shows, defeating one's purpose, or in any case it *is* artificial, and a falsity in the relationship emerges.

Yet it may be possible over a period of time to cultivate these qualities in oneself; and for that reason it is worth asking what sorts of personal relations are preferable. As with most questions of personal preference, the considerations making something advisable or otherwise will relate to individual tastes, capacities and situations, and therefore the wisest and best advised will not necessarily all make the same choice. Some people may be constitutionally ill equipped for close personal relations, and may be happier emphasizing other forms of so-

"... [W]hile sex is not likely to be positively distasteful just through being impersonal, our pleasure in it may be mixed with regrets and dissatisfactions."

cial relationship. However, since we are all capable of changing, it is difficult to be sure what one's taste or capacity is. Just as a person who initially dislikes chess or mathematics may become an enthusiast, so we may initially derive little satisfaction from friendships until perhaps some exceptional person breaks through the barriers of reserve and awkwardness and shows us capacities we did not know we had.

What kind of personal relations are preferable is perhaps basically a question of whether one finds a certain picture of oneself acceptable. One can live for a long time without self-examination, but when attention is drawn to the fact that in a sense one's life is perfectly solitary, that other people are nothing but sources of pleasure or annoyance, it is a question whether that fact is disturbing.

It is important here to keep moral considerations out of it. It is not a question of selfishness. It is possible to be quite generous and considerate of other people while taking no interest in them as persons. We should focus on the solitude and egoism of someone of as much moral rectitude as one could wish, who however takes no interest in people except insofar as either duty requires or fancy dictates.

We must all decide for ourselves whether we can live with such a picture of ourselves; but it is evident that many people neither want it for themselves nor like it in other people. This shows in their dismay at the coldness of someone who, however entertainingly, talks at them rather than to them, who loses interest if he is not entertained in return, who shows no curiosity about their hopes and anxieties, and with whom friendship seems a very fragile thing, entirely dependent on maintaining a sufficiently amusing output. It shows also in the desire of many people to reveal themselves: to be demonstrative in the expression of feeling, to share their dreams, discuss their problems or make known their virtues and faults.

We are in many ways afraid of other people, afraid of boring them or appearing foolish, afraid of establishing relationships that may overwhelm or hurt us, and so we withdraw behind facades of manners and safe behavior. But at the same time many of us yearn for warmer and more open personal relationships, and find it immensely gratifying if, with some few persons, this can be achieved.

It might be possible to see more clearly why personal intimacy can be gratifying if we paused here to replace a possible misconception as to its nature with a more revealing understanding of it. We sometimes want very much to be close to another person: to trust, to understand, to share secrets, to know that nothing is held back, and to be confident that if we express ourselves freely, what we say and do will be rejoiced in. While many of us want this, for some of us its achievement is a rare turn of fortune, and most of the time with most people we feel a lack of such intimacy. We are unsure whether we enjoy the confidence of another person, wonder what that person's real thoughts or feelings are, hesitate to let ourselves go for fear of doing or saying unwelcome things.

At such times another person may seem a mystery to us, something concealed behind actions and words, deep inside. It can seem that it is this inner person that we yearn to know; and when we reflect that we can never see behind a person's actions and words, we can come to feel unbearably alone in the world. The inner person is there, we think, but can never be known. Yet the idea of knowing the inner person does not cease to attract us. Any kind of closeness seems to be an approach to it, and it can even seem disappointing that by gazing into someone's eyes we cannot see the soul that lies behind them. Sexual intimacy similarly seems a way of getting close, and this may be one source of the intensity of our interest in sex; but again it is maddening that even here the hidden person is still not revealed.

It can seem to us that people's natures are very imperfectly shown by the way they smile, the things they say, the things that make them angry or sad or jubilant. We are impatient with the (as it seems) crude indications of the real person that we find in smiles and jokes and fits of temper, and we wish we could see right into a person. We of course do not want to see the inner things a surgeon sees, but rather the contents of another person's consciousness. We reckon that a person's true thoughts, desires, hopes and fears appear undisguised on the inner stage of consciousness, and it is for that show that we would like to have tickets.

Yet when we think of it, it should strike us that we do not know *ourselves* the way we would like to know another person. If we concentrate our attention just on what we are conscious of over any randomly chosen interval of time, the show is disappointing: perhaps some feelings of heat or cold, a twinge of pain in the shoulder, a sensation in the throat as we breathe, a slight feeling of weariness, a stray thought here and there about a problem that worries us or a plan we have. Nothing very significant or very revealing. If we could chronicle accurately what we are conscious of over any period of time, even the time when we are doing something that leaves another person mystified, it would be an uninteresting catalogue, and would scarcely satisfy anyone's desire to know the person behind our words and deeds. The fact, however, that the contents of anyone's consciousness are uninteresting does not show that we are all uninteresting people. A person may deliver himself of all sorts of ingenious suggestions, shrewd observations, beguiling fancies and comical remarks, and be most unusual in the things that excite or sadden him, without his conscious states being interesting to know of. The dullest and most interesting people will not likely differ greatly in the true reports they make of their conscious states.

If this seems surprising to you, perhaps this is because you think that everything of which a person delivers himself first appears on the inner stage; that only some of the things that so appear are in fact delivered; and that often what appears inwardly differs from what is delivered, owing either to some want of skill in expressing thoughts, feelings and attitudes, or to some reserve or some deviousness that makes us falsify what we say about ourselves.

If that were the case, there would be much more on the inner stage than is ever revealed outwardly, and in knowing the happenings on the inner stage one would be knowing a person as he is and not as he pretends to be or, through ineptitude, falsely appears to be. Yet are there always two things going on, what we think and what we say; and is it the case that these two things sometimes (perhaps ideally) agree, but all too often differ, either in that we say much less than we think, or in that we say something different from what we think?

Catch yourself in a lively and friendly conversation with someone and you will find that for the most part you just say things: you do not first think them and then say them, but interesting, funny or instructive remarks come forth directly. What you say is, even for you, all there is to your part of the conversation. It does not even *seem* as if something inward showed you what to say, and then you said it.

If the conversation is about a difficult or unfamiliar topic, the flow may not be so smooth. You may have to stop and struggle to find words. You may experience a sense of tension and effort, and may inwardly formulate something to say and decide against saying it because it is not quite true or not sufficiently clear; but if you find the right thing to say you will not generally say it to yourself first, and then aloud; after a time, words will come, and when you have said them you may or may not be pleased with the result of your struggle.

If a conversation is delicate and requires diplo-

macy, you may find yourself saying something different from what you think; but what you think is not necessarily or even generally spoken inwardly prior to or alongside of what you say: it is just that if you asked yourself whether what you said was quite frank, you would have to say no. What you said aloud is different, not from what you said inwardly, but from what you would have said had you not been moved by diplomatic considerations.

Is this diplomacy at least something that went on inwardly, concealed from the other person—something that, had he seen it in the flow of your consciousness, he would have found revealing or disappointing? Perhaps some people think out their diplomatic stratagems explicitly, saying to themselves, for example, "I had better say something complimentary to this chap, because he is so sensitive"; but generally a diplomatic person acts instinctively. The artful things he says are not premeditated, but are a direct or prime expression of his sensitivity to another person's fears or foibles. Diplomacy then is not a secret process but a personal trait of certain individuals that is usually quite apparent.

Sometimes a person who knows a great deal about some subject, when talking to a beginner, will say much less than he knows; but the things he knows and does not say are not things that run through his head at such times and are not made public, but rather things he has learned and now could say, if he were talking to someone to whom they would be intelligible or useful.

Through these various cases, we can see that there is something right about the idea that what a person says may be the same as or different from what he thinks; but we go wrong if we imagine that what he thinks is something that goes on prior to or alongside of what he says, and that therefore it would be useful to be able to see into his consciousness. When a person is being frank, he indeed says what he thinks, but that just means that he is not being diplomatic or devious, that he would say the same to his diary or anyone else. When a person is being diplomatic he may say something different from what he thinks, but that just means that what he would write in his diary or say to someone else would not square with what he diplomatically said. When a person explains something to a beginner he tells less than he knows, but that just means that if he were writing a book, he would without further research have a great deal more to say. What is more than or different from what people say is not something that is there but hidden, something that would be fully revealed if only we could see into people's minds, but something they might have said, or done, had circumstances been different.

The things we might do or say, the things we are capable of, the poems we could write, the fun we might concoct, the sympathy or courage we might show, are in a sense hidden all right, but hidden from ourselves as much as from other people. They are not there under wraps: they have not yet been created. We gain access to them, not by somehow going behind behavior, but by letting ourselves go—by behaving more freely. This happens when situations are created in which we are encouraged to be what we are capable of being, situations of trust and mutual appreciation, in which two people draw one another out. When those situations occur, the deeper person we are in search of will be right there in the wistful smiles or imaginative inventions, and will be revealed in what we do as much to ourselves as to anyone else.

That is how two people achieve closeness: when each has the confidence of the other, and each stimulates the other to the inventive things of which we are capable but seldom deliver.

Personal intimacy is thus a rich and unreserved interaction with another person, and therefore even if people's unexpressed thoughts and attitudes were there in their consciousness, and we had some device by means of which we could experience the mental states of other people, personal intimacy would still not prevail. We would not be interacting richly with another person, but rather observing like spectators their conscious processes. Whenever there was any need for the device, that itself would show that there was not intimacy. The way to closeness with and enjoyment of another person is not by coming to know what lies behind the outward shell, but by eliciting from other people the best of which they are capable. For some people and with some people, that is often quite difficult, but it is at least possible; whereas it is neither possible nor what one really wants, to come to know the sup-

posed person behind the smiles and jokes and questions and fits of rage that often seem mere outward show.

An important feature of the picture of personal intimacy we have just sketched is that people appear as sources of creativity that are often dammed up, and that this creativity can be released in some kinds of personal interaction, in which fear and distrust are reduced, self-confidence is generated, and the development and exercise of abilities is stimulated. Creativity here is primarily not a matter of painting pictures, writing books or decorating rooms, but of doing things with another person that are rich and various in their interest and that, unlike party conversation that is designed for universal consumption, expresses the particular interest that two people take in one another.

Here, to return to our earlier question, "What is good about personal intimacy?" we can now see that wherever it prevails, it releases us from constraints of caution and distrust, which are both thwarting in themselves and tend to make our lives arid. The intimate relationship enriches our lives, both by releasing a creativity of personal interaction that has been inhibited, and by eliciting it from another person.

This, however, still puts it too egocentrically, as if we were talking about an unsuspected way in which another person can be used for maximizing the satisfaction we can get from life. Anyone who approached personal intimacy from this egocentric point of view would not achieve it, because he is not yet so constituted as to find this special kind of relationship good in itself. The slightly paradoxical situation appears to be that the rewards accrue only if one does not aim at them; but this is common to a great many things in life. If we concentrate just on doing something well, the pleasure of so doing it accrues; but if our eye is on the pleasure, our performance will likely be substandard, and whatever enjoyment we derive will not be the satisfaction of a task well performed.

Why Not Sex Without Personal Intimacy?

So far we have concentrated on explaining the notion of personal intimacy. In doing so it was assumed that this is not an entirely new notion, and that many people care about it, but that it was in need of clarification, both as to what it is and as to what is good about it. Up to this point, except incidentally, we have said nothing as to the bearing of personal intimacy on our sex lives.

In this part of our deliberations it will save a lot of verbiage if we can use expressions like "a purely sexual relationship" or "an impersonal relationship" to mean anything that tends in those directions. Even when sex is put on a commercial basis, it may not always be quite devoid of personal intimacy; and not many of the people who make love casually with near strangers on a Saturday night will be altogether lacking in personal interest in their sex partners. Still, there will not often be much depth of personal interest in such cases, and it would be cumbersome always to construct an expression that allowed for various possible shades and degrees of such interest.

While many people would not want sex without personal intimacy, probably few of those same people, if they had no moral qualms about it, would find sex positively unpleasant just because it lacked personal warmth; and probably many others would not knowingly want and therefore not miss personal intimacy.

It is quite possible to regard sex as essentially a pleasurable activity that happens to require the participation of another person, like dancing. As with dancing, the participants can display skill and style, but it need not matter with whom one is performing, as long as the participants function well together. It would be folly to say that sex, when similarly regarded, need be in any way unrewarding. On the contrary, since it is both a more natural and a more intense pleasure, it is likely to be very much more gratifying than any other activity requiring the participation of someone else.

Yet while sex is not likely to be positively distasteful just through being impersonal, our pleasure in it may be mixed with regrets and dissatisfactions. Whether foolishly or not, many of us are deeply disposed to regard sexual caresses as an expression of affection and enthusiasm for the person who receives them; but when sex is impersonal, caresses come out as an expression of enthusiasm for caressing. If one does not know or care whether the

other person is lonely, reads Dickens, likes cats or believes in God, caresses lose their character as expressions of affection. Then there is an emptiness in lovemaking that may be disturbing; and in the case in which one does know and does not like such things about a person, caresses take on the character of falsity.

The disposition to regard sexual tenderness as an expression of affection is not, of course, universal or incurable; but in our culture any other disposition is rare, and it will require either insensitivity or sophistication, when a relationship is primarily sexual, not to wish for personal warmth as well, or to wish one were with someone else with whom there could be such warmth.

From this point of view, when there is personal intimacy between people who make love, they have much the best of it. They want just the person they are with, and have a full relationship with the person they want. There is genuine tenderness in their caresses, which are therefore not only just as pleasant as those of the couple whose lovemaking is mainly sexual, but satisfying to the deep human wish to demonstrate interest and affection.

Hence it may seem much to be recommended that one adopt a policy of making love only with persons for whom one can wholeheartedly express tenderness. Yet while we might admire and commend the sensitivity and concern about personal relationships of anyone who so resolved, it is not clear whether anything else would be foolish, or would show a regrettable want of sensitivity or of concern about personal relationships. It might be that this is the analogue of what in moral contexts is sometimes called supererogatory conduct: acts of conspicuous heroism or extreme generosity, for example. Although these are altogether admirable, failure to perform them is not regarded as a defect.

Not everyone has any talent or taste for close personal relationships, and those who do will not always find others to share themselves with in an intimate way. Our cultural climate tends to make us so cautious, hurried and pragmatic that close friendships do not develop easily. Hence, although we are passionate fairly constantly, we are on close terms with a suitable person only sometimes; and this can make it seem the better part of wisdom to make love as and when we can, and hope that we will be so fortunate as sometimes to fall into a relationship in which there is also the joy of personal intimacy.

People differ so much, not only in how passionate they are, but in how much they want close friendships and in their aptitude for them, that the answer to the question what is best here will be different from person to person. If one has no interest in personal intimacy there will be no problem, except possibly the question whether one might be turning a blind eye on one of life's joys.

If one does care about the quality of personal relationships, and also requires personal intimacy in one's sex life, then for all but the most outgoing and attractive people, the result will almost certainly be some reduction in the amount of sexual activity one enjoys. However, one may be compensated by the assurance that one's sex life will be rich in the qualities of joy, affection and respect attendant on people's rejoicing in one another as persons.

People who demand personal intimacy in their sex lives may find that having this kind of ideal makes them too self-conscious. They may always be asking themselves, "Is this it? Will my principles permit this?" Not only could these questions be hard to answer with any assurance, the very concern about them could strain the free development of a good relationship. Moreover, the cherished expectation that making love would be particularly splendid might interfere with its spontaneity and cause disappointment.

While not many people would be so deliberate as to encounter this sort of difficulty, perhaps the only general remedy would be the evolution of a cultural climate in which most couples would not make love unless they were on quite special terms, but in which this would not be an ideal that they would list as one of their convictions, or something that was urged upon them by parents and school teachers, but rather something that simply did not happen amongst people who had lived in that climate for any length of time. The thought of making love would perhaps occur to people only when there was an especially warm relationship, or if it occurred to them at other times, it would strike them as a strange or unpleasant idea. Such a cultural climate is not likely to exist soon, but it is perhaps not impossible. Short of that, it is perhaps possible for a person to adopt this attitude deliberately,

but over a period of time to make it so much part of the way he functions that it is no longer a principle to which he strives to conform, but instead has become an instinct.

The hardest question is as to the workability of the plan according to which one makes love as fancy dictates or opportunity allows, and hopes that sometimes it will be with someone about whom one cares personally. Clearly this way one might have the best of both worlds: all the sexual satisfaction one wants or fortune provides, some of it under conditions one regards as ideal.

The question as to its workability is whether we can successfully make the switch from one perception of sexual activity to the other; for example, from regarding caresses as a pleasure requiring the participation of another person, to seeing them as an expression of affection and mutual delight. The significance that we can attach to sexual activity ... is a magic and a fragile thing. It is easy to sustain its reality when it is the only way we perceive sexual intimacies, but the danger is that if we sometimes make love when there is no affection or personal delight being expressed, then even when we are with someone for whom we care, the spell may be broken and our intimacies may remain private pleasures happening to require the cooperation of another person. In that case we will have tried to have the best of both worlds and lost. What we lose is something magic and intangible, which not everyone will miss; and since sex will surely still remain extremely pleasant, it is not a loss which leaves us destitute; but still something splendid will have gone from our lives.

Since it is not a moral issue how we handle these matters, it is acceptable that we should all decide for ourselves about them. We differ widely, both in how much we care about what is at stake, and probably also in how readily we can switch back and forth from one perception of sexual activity to another. If we do not care very much about personal intimacy we will perhaps find the risk in trying to have it both ways well worth taking, while if we care intensely even a slight risk may well seem too great.

What we have called personal intimacy is a dimension of human relations to which many people attach importance, and of whose value many others might be persuaded. It is partly out of concern about personal intimacy that many people deplore sexual promiscuity, and many parents worry about whether their children, in their eagerness to experiment with sex, might not be very particular as to whether there is a good personal relationship between them and their sexual partners, and therefore whether they may grow up insensitive to the possibility and the value of personal intimacy.

What has been suggested is that personal intimacy is indeed an excellent thing, deserving of concern and much to be cherished and promoted, but that we make a mistake if we treat it as a matter of moral concern—except in a way that will be indicated shortly. Personal intimacy is therefore not something on which we have a right to insist. It may be regrettable but it is not sinful to relate to people in a generally impersonal way; and it may

be excellent but it is not saintly to be caring, interested in and responsive to people in the way described. Possibly people of the latter disposition are more likely also to be morally virtuous, but their moral virtue is a distinct attribute; and it is both possible and common for people of the other disposition to be as honest, generous, fair and courageous as one could wish.

It is no doubt immoral to do anything likely to destroy or adversely affect a good personal relationship, and morally commendable to further and create such relationships. In this one respect, personal intimacy *is* a matter of moral concern; but it is similarly a matter of moral concern whether what I do adversely affects a person's ability to play the violin, although having that ability is not itself a moral virtue.

Study Questions

1. Is personal intimacy necessary for human happiness?

2. Is promiscuity immoral?

3. Can love between two people be immoral?

Moral Dilemmas

■ Jane becomes pregnant when she is seventeen. When she finds out, she drops out of high school and decides to have the baby. She had dated Scott, whom she claims is the father, for a couple of months. Scott has already gone away to school, but she gets in touch with him and tells him that she wants to marry him. He tells her that he does not love her but agrees to drop out of college and marry her. In the meantime, Jane receives a call from a man who claims to have been Scott's lover. The man tells her that he and Scott have had a long-standing homosexual affair. Jane is shocked and confronts Scott with the accusation. Scott concedes that he does have homosexual tendencies, but he wants to marry anyway.

Should Jane marry Scott?

Is what Scott did immoral?

■ Bob is a forty-five-year-old executive in an advertising firm in a small midwestern town. One day he tells his therapist: "I'm gay and have been for as long as I can remember. I have tried to change, but I just can't. I'm afraid that if anyone who works with me finds out, I will lose my job. I'm lonely and miserable. I can't go on like this. Please help me."

If you were Bob's therapist, what would you tell Bob? What should Bob do?

■ After a year-long affair, Nancy breaks up with Jim and doesn't hear from him for six months. Out of the blue, he sends her an expensive watch with a note suggesting that he would like to see her again. Nancy is involved with another man whom she likes very much.

Should Nancy keep the watch?

■ Arthur and Jade have been living together as lovers for two years. Jade becomes interested in another man. Arthur threatens to commit suicide if Jade leaves him. Jade knows that Arthur has had a history of emotional instability.

What should Jade do?

■ Betty and Sam, both college students, have been together for six months. They decide to get married after they learn that Betty is pregnant. In order to marry, they must take a blood test, which they do. The test reveals that Sam has AIDS. He claims that he got it by sharing hypodermic needles with his heroin-addict friends. Betty is shocked but is also relieved that she doesn't have the incurable and deadly disease. They call the wedding off. She leaves Sam, and goes to live with her parents.

A few weeks later, she learns from a friend that Sam has been sleeping with every woman he can find without telling them about his disease.

What should Betty do?

Suggested Readings

Baker, Robert, and Frederick Elliston, eds. *Philosophy and Sex.* Buffalo: Prometheus Press, 1984.

Ehman, Robert. "Personal Love." In *Occasions or Philosophy,* edited by James C. Edwards. Englewood Cliffs, N.J.: Prentice-Hall, 1979.

Ellis, Albert. "Rationality in Sexual Morality." *The Humanist* (September/October 1969).

Grcic, Joseph. "The Right to Privacy: Behavior as Property." *The Journal of Value Inquiry.* 20 (1986).

Leone, Bruno, and M. Teresa O'Neill, eds. *Sexual Values.* St. Paul: Greenhaven Press, 1983.

Sternberg, Robert J. "A Triangular Theory of Love." *Psychological Review* 93, no. 2 (1986).

Thomas, Laurence. "Friendship." *Synthese* 72 (1987).

Marriage

I s the traditional family the best way to meet the needs of men, women, and children? Is the sexual nature of a human being such that it can be satisfied with one life-long partner? Is the traditional family the best way to raise children to be free and healthy individuals?

Background

Many types and varieties of marriages have existed throughout human history. However, it is possible to give a general definition of marriage that will fit most forms of this institution. Marriage is a more or less lasting relationship between at least one male and one female that extends beyond the conception and bearing of children (if, indeed, there are children). This definition covers most historical instances of marriage (with the exception of homosexual marriages, which are a recent phenomenon). The most common form of marriage today is that of *monogamy*: one male and one female living together to support each other and their offspring, if they have any. The monogamous family unit performs many functions. It satisfies the sexual needs of the adults; it offers protection and support for the female during her pregnancy and for the offspring once they are born; and it provides an environment within which the children are socialized (i.e., educated to be members of their community and to adopt its language, customs, beliefs, and values). The family as an institution then, has sexual, procreative, economic, and educational functions.

Monogamy is the most common form of marriage practiced today, but other arrangements have existed and continue to be practiced in many parts of the world. *Polygamy* allows a spouse of either sex to have more than one mate at the same time. For a husband to have more than one wife is called *polygyny,* and for a wife to have more than one husband is *polyandry.* Often, these arrangements developed in cultures that experienced a scarcity of one or the other sex so that one-on-one pairing was not possible. Some Mormons of the United States and some Moslems still practice polygamy.

Monogamous and polygamous marriages may be either *nuclear,* in which the household consists of only husbands, wives, and children, or *extended,* in which the household includes grandparents, aunts and uncles, or other family members. Another type of extended marriage arrangement is the *communal* marriage, in which many men and women form a kind of extended or open marriage and collectively raise their children. Rules concerning sexual exclusivity and adultery (i.e., whether either marriage partner may have other sexual partners) vary among the different types of marriage arrangements and from family to family.

A central issue in marriage concerns the equality of husband and wife. In many societies where marriages are arranged by parents, not by the free choice of the partners, a man usually has more freedom in choosing his wife than a woman does in choosing her husband. In these situations, a man has more freedom in every aspect of their marriage, including death. This inequality is dramatically shown by the now generally abandoned Hindu custom of sati where the widow must join her dead husband on his funeral pyre and be burned alive. Once they are married, the question of equal rights and responsibilities in raising children and pursuing careers arises. Throughout history, women have been denied the same moral and political rights that men have enjoyed for generations. The practice of the double standard in sexual morality has been almost universal and always in favor of male freedom. In the United States, women did not get the right to vote until 1920 and are still engaged in the struggle for greater economic rights. Women are still underrepresented in many professions and still have much lower incomes, as a rule, than most men.

Some conservatives believe that the social inferiority of women is based on the biological differences that exist between men and women. According to this view, women are by nature more passive and emotional than men, who are more rational and aggressive. If this is true, women would naturally be more skilled at mothering and taking care of the household and men would be more adept at dealing with the outside world of work, war, and politics, which require more aggressiveness. Conservatives point out that women have lower levels of the hormone testosterone, which has been associated with aggressiveness, which in turn has been associated with success in the world of work and politics. Why, they ask, do women account for only about five percent of the prison population if not because crime is a form of violence based on the greater aggressive drive of the male?

Liberals and feminists maintain that the social inferiority of women is based not on biology but on cultural training, or socialization. Women are raised and educated to be passive in many societies and hence often do not achieve positions of power in business and politics. Liberals believe that men and women should be raised freely to achieve their individual potentials rather than to take on either traditional "feminine" or traditional "masculine" personalities. Feminists cite the historical models of Joan of Arc, Eleanor Roosevelt, Queen Elizabeth, Indira Gandhi, Queen Victoria, Golda Meir, and more recently, Corazon Aquino and Margaret Thatcher as evidence of what women can achieve in the political sphere.

The institution of marriage and the family concerns not only the rights of husbands and wives but also the rights of children. Until recently, the right to conceive and raise children has been assumed without question, but philosophers have now begun to question whether all couples should be permitted to have children. The debate focuses not only on population control (as in China where couples are by law allowed to have only one child) but also on the rights of the children themselves. Hugh LaFollette contends that people have no right to have children unless they can ensure a genetically normal infant who will be adequately nourished and cared for.

Historically, parents have had the right to make decisions regarding the education of their children. But how far does this right extend? Do parents have the right to indoctrinate their child into their own beliefs and values to the degree that the child's future autonomy is destroyed? Autonomy implies self-determination and moral independence, not mindless imitation of the beliefs, values, and opinions of others. Autonomy cannot exist unless the child has been educated with sufficient rationality and has the ability to critically evaluate parental beliefs and values. Does the present institution of the family allow for this, or are children treated like property, molded in the moral image of their parents?

Liberal Position: John McMurtry

John McMurtry analyzes marriage as it exists in our society, and the only socially accepted form of marriage in the United States today is monogamy. Monogamy means marriage between one man and one woman as specified by a state-approved contract. It requires that neither shall have sex with anyone else for the duration of the marriage. This arrangement, some believe, is commanded by God; others believe that monogamous marriage is necessary to control sex and to provide a stable family within which to bring up children. McMurtry believes that this traditional form of marriage is outmoded and should be replaced. He thinks that monogamy unnecessarily limits the freedom of husbands and wives and that the exclusion of sex outside the marriage promotes frustration, prostitution, deception, and tension between the couple. Children are not served well in such an atmosphere but are deprived of other possible sources of affection and nurturing. Monogamy, McMurtry believes, is based on the idea of private property and asserts that partners own each other. It further supports capitalism by channeling sexual frustration into work and the accumulation of material goods.

Moderate Position: Michael D. Bayles

Michael D. Bayles takes exception to many of Mc-Murtry's points. He argues that many criticisms of the family are based on a belief in a vulgar hedonism, or pleasure-seeking, that greatly exaggerates the importance of sex in life. He agrees that some people are not fit for marriage or marry for the wrong reasons and that nonheterosexual and non-monogamous marriages should be allowed legally. However, monogamous marriage will continue to survive, according to Bayles, because it is an expression of a universal need for companionship and intimate relationships that we all feel. Intimate and loving relationships (which often involve sexual intercourse) usually do not extend to many persons at the same time, but to one. The monogamous family also provides a loving context for the rearing of children that is essential for their psychological well-being. He also disagrees with McMurtry that monogamy restricts the affection that children can get, for it simply does not prevent others from sharing in their upbringing. Bayles suggests that parenting can be a dangerous occupation and that further restrictions should be placed on it.

Rebecca West

Although marriages are widespread phenomena, divorces are almost as common in our culture. Rebecca West (1892–1982) points out the disadvantages of divorce, among which most importantly is the harm done to the psychological well-being of the children. Children need both parents in order to grow into healthy adulthood, according to West. After a divorce, the children may become resentful and may find forming loving relationships later in life difficult. Nevertheless, West believes that divorce should be allowed for several reasons. First, children will not be happy in a marriage in which the partners are unloving and vicious to each other and their offspring. Second, the denial of the right to divorce will lead to a double standard that permits adultery on the part of the husband but not on the part of the wife. Denial of divorce can also lead to prostitution, which spreads disease and generally erodes the value of the marriage.

Hugh LaFollette

The problems West raises concerning marriage, divorce, and the rights of children are the kinds of issues that Hugh LaFollette believes require society to restrict who can or cannot have children. LaFollette points out that every society restricts activities that may be harmful to others. For example, poor driving can obviously cause harm to many people, and so the state requires us to have sufficient skill in driving to prevent harm to others. Once we have achieved this skill and have passed a test to prove it, the state gives us a license, or permission, to drive the car on public roads. Statistics on child abuse prove to LaFollette that inappropriate child rearing can be harmful to children. He therefore recommends that married couples should pass a test to prove that they are psychologically fit to be parents before they have children.

Monogamy: A Critique

John McMurtry is a professor of philosophy at the University of Guelph, Canada.

John McMurtry

"Remove away that black'ning church
Remove away that marriage hearse
Remove away that man of blood
You'll quite remove the ancient curse."

William Blake

I

Almost all of us have entered or will one day enter a specifically standardized form of monogamous marriage. This cultural requirement is so very basic to our existence that we accept it for most part as a kind of intractable given: dictated by the laws of God, Nature, Government and Good Sense all at once. Though it is perhaps unusual for a social practice to be so promiscuously underwritten, we generally find comfort rather than curiosity in this fact and seldom wonder how something could be divinely inspired, biologically determined, coerced and reasoned out all at the same time. We simply take for granted.

Those in society who are officially charged with the thinking function with regard to such matters

are no less responsible for this uncritical acceptance than the man on the street. The psychoanalyst traditionally regards our form of marriage as a necessary restraint on the anarchic id and no more to be queried than civilization itself. The lawyer is as undisposed to questioning the practice as he is to criticizing the principle of private property (this is appropriate, as I shall later point out). The churchman formally perceives the relationship between man and wife to be as inviolable and insusceptible to question as the relationship between the institution he works for and the Christ. The sociologist standardly accepts the formalized bonding of heterosexual pairs as the indispensable basis of social order and perhaps a societal universal. The politician is as incapable of challenging it as he is in the virtue of his own continued holding of office. And the philosopher (at least the English-speaking philosopher), as with most issues of socially controversial or sexual dimensions, ignores the question almost altogether.

Even those irreverent adulterers and unmarried couples who would seem to be challenging the institution in the most basic possible way, in practice,

Reprinted from *The Monist,* Vol. 56, No. 4, with the permission of the author and the publisher.

tend merely to mimic its basic structure in unofficial form. The coverings of sanctity, taboo and cultural habit continue to hold them with the grip of public clothes.

II

"Monogamy" means, literally, "one marriage." But it would be wrong to suppose that this phrase tells us much about our particular species of official wedlock. The greatest obstacle to the adequate understanding of our monogamy institution has been the failure to identify clearly and systematically the full complex of principles it involves. There are four such principles, each carrying enormous restrictive force and together constituting a massive social control mechanism that has never, so far as I know, been fully schematized.

To come straight to the point, the four principles in question are as follows:

1. *The partners are required to enter a formal contractual relation:* (*a*) whose establishment demands a specific official participant, certain conditions of the contractors (legal age, no blood ties, etc.) and a standard set of procedures; (*b*) whose governing terms are uniform for all and exactly prescribed by law; and (*c*) whose dissolution may only be legally effected by the decision of state representatives.

The ways in which this elaborate principle of contractual requirement are importantly restrictive are obvious. One may not enter into a marriage union without entering into a contract presided over by a state-investured official.[1] One may not set any of the terms of the contractual relationship by which one is bound for life. And one cannot dissolve the contract without legal action and costs, court proceedings and in many places actual legislation. (The one and only contract in all English-speaking law that is not dissoluble by the consent of the contracting parties.) The extent of control here—over the most intimate and putatively "loving" relationships in all social intercourse—is so

great as to be difficult to catalogue without exciting in oneself a sense of disbelief.

Lest it be thought there is always the real option of entering a common law relationship free of such encumbrances, it should be noted that: (*a*) these relationships themselves are subject to state regulation, though of a less imposing sort; and (much more important) (*b*) there are very formidable selective pressures against common law partnerships such as employment and job discrimination, exclusion from housing and lodging facilities, special legal disablements,[2] loss of social and moral status (consider such phrases as "living in sin," "make her an honest woman," etc.), family shame and embarrassment, and so on.

2. *The number of partners involved in the marriage must be two and only two* (as opposed to three, four, five or any of the almost countless other possibilities of intimate union).

This second principle of our specific form of monogamy (the concept of "one marriage," it should be pointed out, is consistent with any number of participating partners) is perhaps the most important and restrictive of the four principles we are considering. Not only does it confine us to just *one* possibility out of an enormous range, but it confines us to that single possibility which involves the *least* number of people, two. It is difficult to conceive of a more thoroughgoing mechanism for limiting extended social union and intimacy. The fact that this monolithic restriction seems so "natural" to us (if it were truly "natural" of course, there would be no need for its rigorous cultural prescription by everything from severe criminal law[3] to

---

1. Any person who presides over a marriage and is not authorized by law to do so is guilty of a criminal offense and is subject to several years imprisonment (e.g., Canadian Criminal Code, Sec. 258).

2. For example, offspring are illegitimate, neither wife nor children are legal heirs, and husband has no right of access or custody should separation occur.

3. "Any kind of conjugal union with more than one person at the same time, whether or not it is by law recognized as a binding form of marriage is guilty of an indictable offence and is liable to imprisonment for five years" (Canadian Criminal Code, Sec. 257, [1][a][ii]). Part 2 of the same section adds: "Where an accused is charged with an offence under this section, no averment or proof of the method by which the alleged relationship was entered into, agreed to or consented to is necessary in the indictment or

ubiquitous housing regulations) simply indicates the extent to which its hold is implanted in our social structure. It is the institutional basis of what I will call the "binary frame of sexual consciousness," a frame through which all our heterosexual relationships are typically viewed ("two's company, three's a crowd") and in light of which all larger circles of intimacy seem almost inconceivable.[4]

3. *No person may participate in more than one marriage at a time or during a lifetime* (unless the previous marriage has been officially dissolved by, normally, one partner's death or successful divorce).

Violation of this principle is, of course, a criminal offence (bigamy) which is punishable by a considerable term in prison. Of various general regulations of our marriage institution it has experienced the most significant modification: not indeed in principle, but in the extent of flexibility of its "escape hatch" of divorce. The case with which this escape hatch is open has increased considerably in the past few years (the grounds for divorce being more permissive than previously) and it is in this regard most of all that the principles of our marriage institution have undergone formal alteration. That is, in plumbing rather than in substance.

---

upon the trial of the accused, nor is it necessary upon the trial to prove that the persons who are alleged to have entered into the relationship had or intended to have sexual intercourse."

(Here and elsewhere, I draw examples from Canadian criminal law. There is no reason to suspect the Canadian code is eccentric in these instances.)

4. Even the sexual revolutionary Wilhelm Reich seems constrained within the limits of this "binary frame." Thus he says (my emphasis): "Nobody has the right to prohibit his or her partner from entering a temporary or lasting sexual relationship with someone else. He has only the right *either to withdraw or to win the partner back.*" (Wilhelm Reich, *The Sexual Revolution,* trans. by T. P. Wolfe [New York: Farrar, Strauss & Giroux, 1970], p. 28.) The possibility of sexual partners extending their union to include the other loved party as opposed to one partner having either to "win" against this third party or to "withdraw" altogether,) does not seem even to occur to Reich.

4. *No married person may engage in any sexual relationship with any person whatever other than the marriage partner.*

Although a consummated sexual act with another person alone constitutes an act of adultery, lesser forms of sexual and erotic relationships[5] may also constitute grounds for divorce (i.e., cruelty) and are generally proscribed as well by informal social convention and taboo. In other words, the fourth and final principle of our marriage institution involves not only a prohibition of sexual intercourse per se outside one's wedlock (this term deserves pause) but a prohibition of all one's erotic relations whatever outside this bond. The penalties for violation here are as various as they are severe, ranging from permanent loss of spouse, children, chattel, and income to job dismissal and social ostracism. In this way, possibly the most compelling natural force towards expanded intimate relations with others[6] is strictly confined within the narrowest possible circle for (barring delinquency) the whole of adult life. The sheer weight and totality of this restriction is surely one of the great wonders of all historical institutional control.

III

With all established institutions, apologetics for perpetuation are never wanting. Thus it is with our form of monogamous marriage.

Perhaps the most celebrated justification over the years has proceeded from a belief in a Supreme Deity who secretly utters sexual and other commands to privileged human representatives. Almost as well known a line of defence has issued from a conviction, similarly confident, that the need for some social regulation of sexuality demonstrates the need for our specific type of two-person wedlock. Although these have been important justifications in the sense of being very widely supported, they are

---

5. I will be using "sexual" and "erotic" interchangeably throughout the paper.

6. It is worth noting here that: (*a*) man has by nature the most "open" sexual instinct—year-round operativeness and variety of stimuli—of all the species (except perhaps the dolphin); and (*b*) it is a principle of human needs in general that maximum satisfaction involves regular variation in the form of the need-object.

not—having other grounds than reasons—susceptible to treatment here.

If we put aside such arguments, we are left I think with two major claims. The first is that our form of monogamous marriage promotes a profound affection between the partners which is not only of great worth in itself but invaluable as a sanctuary from the pressures of outside society. Since, however, there are no secure grounds whatever for supposing that such "profound affection" is not at least as easily achievable by any number of *other* marriage forms (i.e., forms which differ in one or more of the four principles), this justification conspicuously fails to perform the task required of it.

"Marriage is simply a form of private property."

The second major claim for the defence is that monogamy provides a specially loving context for child upbringing. However here again there are no grounds at all for concluding that it does so as, or any more, effectively than other possible forms of marriage (the only alternative type of upbringing to which it has apparently been shown to be superior is nonfamily institutional upbringing, which of course is not relevant to the present discussion). Furthermore, the fact that at least half the span of a normal monogamous marriage *involves no child-upbringing at all* is disastrously overlooked here, as is the reinforcing fact that there is no reference to or mention of the quality of child-upbringing in any of the prescriptions connected with it.

In brief, the second major justification of our particular type of wedlock scents somewhat too strongly of red herring to pursue further.

There is, it seems, little to recommend the view that monogamy specially promotes "profound affection" between the partners or a "loving context" for child-upbringing. Such claims are simply without force. On the other hand, there are several aspects

to the logic and operation of the four principles of this institution which suggest that it actually *inhibits* the achievement of these desiderata. Far from uniquely abetting the latter, it militates against them. In these ways:

(1) Centralized official control of marriage (which the Church gradually achieved through the mechanism of Canon Law after the Fall of the Roman Empire[7] in one of the greatest seizures of social power in history) necessarily alienates the partners from full responsibility for and freedom in their relationship. "Profound closeness" between the partners—or least an area of it—is thereby expropriated rather than promoted, and "sanctuary" from the pressures of outside society prohibited rather than fostered.

(2) Limitation of the marriage bond to two people necessarily restricts, in perhaps the most unilateral possible way consistent with offspring survival, the number of adult sources of affection, interest, material support and instruction for the young. The "loving context for child-upbringing" is thereby dessicated rather than nourished: providing the structural conditions for such notorious and far-reaching problems as (*a*) sibling rivalry for scarce adult attention,[8] and (*b*) parental oppression through exclusive monopoly of the child's means of life.[9]

(3) Formal exclusion of all others from erotic contact with the marriage partner systematically pro-

---

7. "Roman Law had no power of intervening in the formation of marriages and there was no legal form of marriage.... Marriage was a matter of simple private agreement and divorce was a private transaction" (Havelock Ellis, *Studies in the Psychology of Sex* [New York: Random House, 1963], Vol. II, Part 3, p. 429).

8. The dramatic reduction of sibling rivalry through an increased number of adults in the house is a phenomenon which is well known in contemporary domestic communes.

9. One of the few other historical social relationships I can think of in which persons hold thoroughly exclusive monopoly over other persons' means of life is slavery. Thus, as with another's slave, it is a criminal offence "to receive" or "harbour" another's child without "right of possession" (Canadian Criminal Code, Sec. 250).

motes conjugal insecurity, jealousy and alienation by:

(*a*) Officially underwriting a literally totalitarian expectation of sexual confinement on the part of one's husband or wife: which expectation is, *ceteris paribus,* inevitably more subject to anxiety and disappointment than one less extreme in its demand and/or cultural-juridical backing;[10]

(*b*) Requiring so complete a sexual isolation of the marriage partners that should one violate the fidelity code the other is left alone and susceptible to a sense of fundamental deprivation and resentment;

(*c*) Stipulating such a strict restraint of sexual energies that there are habitual violations of the regulation: which violations *qua* violations are frequently if not always attended by (i) willful deception and reciprocal suspicion about the occurrence of quality of the extramarital relationship, (ii) anxiety and fear on both sides of permanent estrangement from partner and family, and/or (iii) overt and covert antagonism over the prohibited act in both offender (who feels "trapped") and offended (who feels "betrayed").

The disadvantages of the four principles of monogamous marriage do not, however, end with inhibiting the very effects they are said to promote. There are further shortcomings:

(1) The restriction of marriage union to two partners necessarily prevents the strengths of larger groupings. Such advantages as the following are thereby usually ruled out.

(*a*) The security, range and power of larger socioeconomic units;

(*b*) The epistemological and emotional substance, variety and scope of more pluralist interactions;

(*c*) The possibility of extra-domestic freedom founded on more adult providers and upbringers as well as more broadly based circles of intimacy.

(2) The sexual containment and isolation which the four principles together require variously stimulates such social malaises as:

(*a*) Destructive aggression (which notoriously results from sexual frustration);

(*b*) Apathy, frustration and dependence within the marriage bond;

(*c*) Lack of spontaneity, bad faith and distance in relationships without the marriage bond;

(*d*) Sexual phantasizing, perversion, fetishism, prostitution and pornography in the adult population as a whole.[11]

Taking such things into consideration, it seems difficult to lend credence to the view that the four principles of our form of monogamous marriage constitute a structure beneficial either to the marriage partners themselves or to their offspring (or indeed to anyone else). One is moved to seek for some other ground of the institution, some ground that lurks beneath the reach of our conventional apprehensions.

IV

The ground of our marriage institution, the essential principle that underwrites all four restrictions, is this: *the maintenance by one man or woman of the effective right to exclude indefinitely all others from erotic access to the conjugal partner.*

The first restriction creates, elaborates on, and provides for the enforcement of this right to exclude. And the second, third and fourth restrictions together ensure that the said right to exclude is— respectively—not cooperative, not simultaneously or sequentially distributed, and not permissive of even casual exception.

In other words, the four restrictions of our form of monogamous marriage together constitute a state-regulated, indefinite and exclusive ownership

---

10. Certain cultures, for example, permit extramarital sexuality by married persons with friends, guests, or in-laws with no reported consequences of jealousy. From such evidence, one is led to speculate that the intensity and extent of jealousy at a partner's extramarital sexual involvement is in direct proportion to the severity of the accepted cultural regulations against such involvements. In short such regulations do not prevent jealousy so much as effectively engender it.

---

11. It should not be forgotten that at the same time marriage excludes marital partners from sexual contact with others, it necessarily excludes those others from sexual contact with marital partners. Walls face two ways.

by two individuals of one another's sexual powers. Marriage is simply a form of private property.[12]

That our form of monogamous marriage is when the confusing layers of sanctity, apologetic and taboo are cleared away another species of private property should not surprise us.[13] The history of the institution is so full of suggestive indicators—dowries, inheritance, property alliances, daughter sales (of which women's wedding rings are a carryover) bride exchanges, legitimacy and illegitimacy—that it is difficult not to see some intimate connections between marital and ownership ties. We are better able still to apprehend the ownership essence of our marriage institution, when in addition we consider:

(*a*) That until recently almost the only way to secure official dissolution of consummated marriage was to be able to demonstrate violation of one or both partner's sexual ownership (i.e., adultery);

(*b*) That the imperative of premarital chastity is tantamount to a demand for retrospective sexual ownership by the eventual marriage partner;

(*c*) That successful sexual involvement with a married person is prosecutable as an expropriation of ownership—"alienation of affections"—which is restituted by cash payment;

(*d*) That the incest taboo is an iron mechanism which protects the conjugal ownership of sexual properties: both the husband's and wife's from the access of affectionate offspring and the offsprings' (who themselves are future marriage partners) from access of siblings and parents;[14]

(*e*) That the language of the marriage ceremony is the language of exclusive possession ("take," "to have and to hold," "forsaking all others and keeping you only unto him/her," etc.), not to mention the proprietary locutions associated with the marital relationship (e.g., "he's mine," "she belongs to him," "keep to your own husband," "wife stealer," "possessive husband," etc.).

V

Of course, it would be remarkable if marriage in our society was not a relationship akin to private property. In our socioeconomic system we relate to virtually everything of value by individual ownership: by, that is, the effective right to exclude others from the thing concerned.[15] That we do so as well with perhaps the most highly valued thing of all—the sexual partners' sexuality—is only to be expected. Indeed it would probably be an intolerable strain on our entire social structure if we did otherwise.

This line of thought deserves pursuit. The real secret of our form of monogamous marriage is not that it functionally provides for the needs of adults

---

12. Those aspects of marriage law which seem to fall outside the pale of sexual property holding—for example, provisions for divorce if the husband fails to provide or is convicted of a felony or is an alcoholic—may themselves be seen as simply prescriptive characterizations of the sort of sexual property which the marriage partner must remain to retain satisfactory conjugal status: a kind of permanent warranty of the "good working order" of the sexual possession.

    What constitutes the "good working order" of the conjugal possession is, of course, different in the case of the husband and in the case of the wife: an *asymmetry* within the marriage institution which, I gather, women's liberation movements are anxious to eradicate.

13. I think it is instructive to think of even the nonlegal aspects of marriage, for example, its sentiments as essentially private property structured. Thus the preoccupation of those experiencing conjugal sentiments with expressing how much "my very own," "my precious," the other is: with expressing, that is, how valuable and inviolable the ownership is and will remain.

14. I think the secret to the long mysterious incest taboo may well be the fact that in all its forms it protects sexual property: not only conjugal (as indicated above) but paternal and tribal as well. This crucial line of thought, however, requires extended separate treatment.

15. Sometimes—as with political patronage, criminal possession, *de facto* privileges and so forth—a *power* to exclude others exists with no corresponding "right" (just as sometimes a right to exclude exists with no corresponding power). Properly speaking, thus, I should here use the phrase "power to exclude," which covers "effective right to exclude" as well as all nonjuridical enablements of this sort.

who love one another or the children they give birth to, but that it serves the maintenance of our present social system. It is an institution which is indispensable to the persistence of the capitalist order,[16] in the following ways:

(1) A basic principle of current social relations is that some people legally acquire the use of other people's personal powers from which they may exclude other members of society. This system operates in the workplace (owners and hirers of all types contractually acquire for their exclusive use workers' regular labour powers) and in the family (husbands and wives contractually acquire for their exclusive use their partner's sexual properties). A conflict between the structures of these primary relations—as would obtain were there a suspension of the restrictions governing our form of monogamous marriage—might well undermine the systemic coherence of present social intercourse.

(2) The fundamental relation between individuals and things which satisfy their needs is, in our present society, that each individual has or does not have the effective right to exclude other people from the thing in question.[17] A rudimentary need is that for sexual relationship(s). Therefore the object of this need must be related to the one who needs it as owner or not owner (i.e., via marriage or not-marriage, or approximations thereto) if people's present relationship to what they need is to retain—again—systemic coherence.

(3) A necessary condition for the continued existence of the present social formation is that its members feel powerful motivation to gain favorable positions in it. But such social ambition is heavily dependent on the preservation of exclusive monogamy in that:

(a) The latter confines the discharge of primordial sexual energies to a single unalterable partner and thus typically compels the said energies to seek alternative outlet, such as business or professional success;[18]

(b) The exclusive marriage necessarily reduces the sexual relationships available to any one person to absolute (nonzero) minimum, a unilateral promotion of sexual shortage which in practice renders hierarchial achievement essential as an economic and "display" means for securing scarce partners.[19]

(4) Because the exclusive marriage necessarily and dramatically reduces the possibilities of sexual-love relationships, it thereby promotes the existing economic system by:

(a) Rendering extreme economic self-interest—the motivational basis of the capitalistic process—less vulnerable to altruistic subversion;

(b) Disciplining society's members into the habitual repression of natural impulse required for long-term performance of repetitive and arduous work tasks;

(c) Developing a complex of suppressed sexual desires to which sales techniques may effectively apply in creating those new consumer wants which provide indispensable outlets for ever-increasing capital funds.

---

16. It is no doubt indispensable as well—in some form or other—to any private property order. Probably (if we take the history of Western society as our data base) the more thoroughgoing and developed the private property formation is, the more total the sexual ownership prescribed by the marriage institution.

17. Things in unlimited supply—like, presently, oxygen—are not of course related to people in this way.

18. This is, of course, a Freudian or quasi-Freudian claim. "Observation of daily life shows us," says Freud, "that most persons direct a very tangible part of their sexual motive powers to their professional or business activities" (Sigmund Freud, *Dictionary of Psychoanalysis,* ed. by Nandor Fodor and Frank Gaynor [New York: Fawcett Publications, Premier Paperbook, 1966], p. 139).

19. It might be argued that exclusive marriage also protects those physically less attractive persons who—in an "open" situation—might be unable to secure any sexual partnership at all. The force of this claim depends, I think, on improperly continuing to posit the very principle of exclusiveness which the "open" situation rules out (e.g., in the latter situations, x might be less attractive to y than z is and yet z not be rejected, any more than at present an intimate friend is rejected who is less talented than another intimate friend).

(5) The present form of marriage is of fundamental importance to:

(*a*) The continued relative powerlessness of the individual family: which, with larger numbers would constitute a correspondingly increased command of social power;

(*b*) The continued high demand for homes, commodities and services: which, with the considerable economies of scale that extended unions would permit, would otherwise falter;

(*c*) The continued strict necessity for adult males to sell their labour power and adult women to remain at home (or vice versa): which strict necessity would diminish as the economic base of the family unit extended;

(*d*) The continued immense pool of unsatisfied sexual desires and energies in the population at large: without which powerful interests and institutions would lose much of their conventional appeal and force;[20]

(*e*) the continued profitable involvement of lawyers, priests and state officials in the jurisdiction of marriage and divorce and the myriad official practices and proceedings connected thereto.[21]

---

20. The sexual undercurrents of corporate advertisements, religious systems, racial propaganda and so on is too familiar to dwell on here.

21. It is also possible that exclusive marriage protects the adult youth power structure in the manner outlined on p. 281.

VI

If our marriage institution is a linchpin of our present social structure, then a breakdown in this institution would seem to indicate a breakdown in our social structure. On the face of it, the marriage institution is breaking down—enormously increased divorce rates, nonmarital sexual relationships, wife-swapping, the Playboy philosophy, and communes. Therefore one might be led by the appearance of things to anticipate a profound alteration in the social system.

But it would be a mistake to underestimate the tenacity of an established order or to overestimate the extent of change in our marriage institution. Increased divorce rates merely indicate the widening of a traditional escape hatch. Nonmarital relationships imitate and culminate in the marital mold. Wife-swapping presupposes ownership, as the phrase suggests. The Playboy philosophy is merely the view that if one has the money one has the right to be titillated, the commercial call to more fully exploit a dynamic sector of capital investment. And communes—the most hopeful phenomenon—almost nowhere offer a *praxis* challenge to private property in sexuality. It may be changing. But history, as the old man puts it, weighs like a nightmare on the brains of the living.

Study Questions

1. Is the institution of marriage that presently exists in the United States the best way to meet the needs of men, women, and children?

2. How, if at all, should the family change to promote the welfare of children?

Marriage, Love, and Procreation

Michael D. Bayles is a professor of philosophy at Florida State University and author of Professional Ethics, Reproductive Ethics, Principles of Law, *other books, and numerous articles.*

Michael D. Bayles

The current era is one of that vulgar form of hedonism rejected by philosophical hedonists such as Epicurus and John Stuart Mill.[1] Apologists thinly disguise the tawdriness of a hedonism of biological pleasures by appeals to individual rights and autonomy. Far too frequently these appeals merely mask a refusal to accept responsibility. This failure to accept personal responsibility is periodically atoned for by ritualistic and ill-conceived attempts to help the poor and underprivileged people of the world.

One of the central focuses of the current vulgar hedonism has been sexual liberation. Premarital intercourse, gay liberation, no-fault divorce, open marriage (read, "open adultery"), polygamy, and orgies all have their advocates. About the only forms of sexual behavior yet to have strong advocates are pedophilia and bestiality. Any day now one may expect grade-school children to assert their right to happiness through pedophilia and animal lovers to argue that disapproval of bestiality is unfair to little lambs.

The result, especially in Western society, is an emphasis on sex that is out of all proportion to its significance for a eudaemonistic life—that is, a life worth living, including elements besides pleasure. The only ultimate test for the value of a life is whether at its end it is found to have been worth living. It is difficult to conceive of a person's thinking his life significant because it was a second-rate approximation to the sexual achievements of the notorious rabbit. However, many people seem to think such a life offers the highest ideal of a "truly human" existence, forgetting Aristotle's insight that reproduction is characteristic of all living things, not just humans.[2] Consequently, the institution of marriage has been attacked for hindering the achievement of this vulgar hedonistic ideal.

Attacks on Marriage

Not all attacks on the institution of marriage have been based solely on the vulgar hedonistic ideal. A more broad ranging, although no more plausible, attack has recently been made by John McMurtry. His attack is directed not against marriage per se but against that form of it found in Western society—monogamy. McMurtry does not merely find that monogamous marriage hinders the achievement of the vulgar hedonistic ideal. He also claims it is at least one of the causes of the following social ills: (1) Central official control of marriage "*necessarily* alienates the partners from full responsibil-

---

1. Epicurus, "Letter to Menoeceus," in *The Stoic and Epicurean Philosophers,* ed. Whitney J. Oates (New York: Modern Library, 1957), p. 31. Epicurus even wrote, "Sexual intercourse has never done a man good, and he is lucky if it has not harmed him" (Fragment 8 in *The Stoic and Epicurean Philosophers*). John Stuart Mill, *Utilitarianism,* chap. 2, especially paragraphs 1–9.
2. *De Anima* 2. 4.

ity for and freedom in their relationship."[3] (2) Monogamy restricts the sources of adult affection and support available to children.[4] (3) It "systematically promotes conjugal insecurity, jealousy, and alienation...."[5] (4) It "prevents the strengths of larger groupings."[6] (5) It stimulates aggression, apathy, frustration, lack of spontaneity, perversion, fetishism, prostitution, and pornography.[7] (6) It serves to maintain the status quo and capitalism.[8] (7) It supports the powerlessness of the individual family by keeping it small.[9] (8) By promoting many small families it creates a high demand for homes and consumer goods and services.[10] (9) It makes it necessary for many more males to sell their labor than would be necessary if monogamy were not practices.[11] (10) By limiting opportunities for sexual satisfaction it channels unsatisfied desire into support for various institutions and interests.[12] (11) Finally, it promotes financial profit for lawyers, priests, and so forth, in marriage and divorce proceedings.[13] Such a catalog of evils omits only a few social problems such as political corruption and environmental deterioration, although even they are hinted at in numbers 8 and 11.

Many people have hoped that the simple-mindedness that attributes all or most or even many of society's ills to a single factor would disappear. At one time private ownership of the means of production was the *bête noir* for society.[14] Recently it has been replaced in that role by unlimited population growth.[15] Both of these beasts have been slain by the St. George of reasonableness.[16] McMurtry has called forth yet another single-factor beast. There is no reason to suppose this one to be any more powerful than its predecessors.

No attempt will be made in this essay to examine in detail McMurtry's criticisms of monogamous marriage. In general they are characterized by a lack of historical and sociological perspective. It is unclear whether he is attacking the ideal of monogamous marriage as it perhaps existed a hundred years ago or as it exists today. Yet this difference is crucial. A century ago divorce was not widely recognized or accepted; today that is not true. When divorce was not recognized, concubinage and prostitution were quite prevalent, as was simply abandoning one's family. Such practices certainly mitigated the effect of the strict social rules that McMurtry discusses. Also, he criticizes monogamy for limiting the access of children to adult affection and support, since they must rely upon their parents alone for care. But in the extended family, which existed until the urbanization of society, that limitation was considerably less common than it may be at present.

McMurtry seems to be unaware of the social realities of modern society. He emphasizes the law as it is written rather than the law in action. It is generally recognized that despite the wording of statutes, marriages can in practice now be dissolved by mutual consent.[17] Nor is adultery usually prose-

3. Monogamy: A Critique," *The Monist* 56 (1972); reprinted herein, pp. 277–287. This quote appears on page 281 of this volume (italics added). Subsequent references to McMurtry's essay are to pages in this volume.
4. Ibid., p. 281.
5. Ibid.
6. Ibid.
7. Ibid., p. 282.
8. Ibid., p. 283.
9. Ibid., p. 284.
10. Ibid.
11. Ibid.
12. Ibid., p. 284.
13. Ibid., p. 284.
14. Karl Marx and Friedrich Engels, "Manifesto of the Communist Party," in *Basic Writings on Politics and Philosophy*, ed. Lewis S. Feuer (Garden City, N.Y.: Doubleday, Anchor Books, 1959), especially p. 24.
15. Paul R. Ehrlich, *The Population Bomb* (New York: Ballantine Books, 1968).
16. Even new Marxists perceive other sources of problems. See Milovan Djilas, *The New Class* (New York: Praeger, 1964); and, more generally, Richard T. De George, *The New Marxism* (New York: Pegasus, 1968), chapt. 2. The importance of population for pollution, with which it is most frequently connected, has been contested by Barry Commoner, *The Closing Circle* (New York: Knopf, 1971), pp. 133–35. Ehrlich now clearly recognizes that various causal factors are important, although he still disagrees with Commoner on the importance of population growth; see Paul R. Ehrlich et al., *Human Ecology* (San Francisco: W. H. Freeman and Company, 1973), chap. 7, esp. pp. 206, 213–15, 221.
17. Max Rheinstein, *Marriage Stability, Divorce, and the Law* (Chicago: University of Chicago Press, 1972), p. 251.

cuted in those states in which it is still a crime. Nor does McMurtry present any sociological evidence for the various effects that he claims monogamous marriage has. Sometimes the evidence may well be against him. For example, he claims that monogamy supports the high demand for homes. Yet, for a century in Ireland monogamy coincided with a low demand for new homes. Couples simply postponed marriage until the male inherited the home of his parents, and those who did not inherit often did not marry.[18]

Underlying McMurtry's view of monogamous marriage is the Kantian conception of the marriage contract. According to Kant, marriage "is the Union of two Persons of different sex for life-long reciprocal possession of their sexual faculties."[19] McMurtry takes the following principle to be the essential ground of monogamous marriage: "the maintenance by one man or woman of the effective right to exclude indefinitely all others from erotic access to the conjugal partner."[20] Since by "possession" Kant meant legal ownership and the consequent right to exclude others, these two views come to the same thing. They both view marriage as chiefly concerned with private ownership of the means to sexual gratification, thus combining capitalism with vulgar hedonism (although Kant was not a hedonist).

Such a view of marriage is pure nonsense. However, it has more plausibility in today's era of vulgar hedonism than it did in Kant's time. Historically, the official aims of marriage, according to the Catholic Church—which was the only church during a period of the establishment of monogamous marriage in Western society—were procreation and companionship. There was also a tendency to view it as a legitimate outlet for man's sinful nature.[21] It is this latter element that Kant and McMurtry have taken as the chief one.

In addition to the avowed purposes of marriage there were the actual social functions that it performed. The family unit was the basic social unit, not only for the education of children (that is, socialization, not formal schooling—which has only become widespread during the past century), but also for the production of necessities, including food and clothing, and for recreation. These historical functions of the extended-family unit based on monogamous marriage have been undermined by the development of industrial, urban society.[22] Consequently, the moral and legal status and functions of marriage require reexamination in the light of current social conditions.

Before undertaking such a reexamination it is necessary to distinguish between rules of marriage and attendant social rules. They are mixed together in the traditional social institution of monogamous marriage, but there is no necessity for this mix and it is probably unjustified. In particular one must distinguish between penal laws prohibiting various forms of sexual union—homosexual, premarital, adulterous—and private arranging laws granting legal recognition to the marital relationship.[23] Private arranging laws do not prescribe punishment for offenses; instead, they enable people to carry out their desires. People are not punished for improperly made marriages; instead, the marriages are invalid and unenforceable. Laws against fornication, prostitution, cohabitation, and homosexuality are almost always penal. Objections to them cannot be transferred directly to the marriage relationship. All of these penal laws could be abolished and monogamous marriage could still be retained.

It may be claimed that despite their nonpenal form, marriage laws do in fact penalize those who prefer other forms of relationship. If homosexual and polygamous relationships are not legally recognized as "marriages," then persons desiring these forms of relationship are being deprived of some degree of freedom. When considering freedom one

---

18. Edwin D. Driver, "Population Policies of State Governments in the United States: Some Preliminary Observations," *Villanova Law Review* 15 (1970): 846–47.
19. Immanuel Kant, *The Philosophy of Law,* trans. W. Hastie (Edinburgh: T. & T. Clark, 1887), p. 110.
20. McMurtry, "Monogamy," p. 282; italics in original omitted.
21. See John T. Noonan, Jr., *Contraception* (Cambridge, Mass.: Harvard University Press, 1966), pp. 312–14.

22. Keith G. McWalter, "Marriage as Contract: Towards a Functional Redefinition of the Marital Status," *Columbia Journal of Law and Social Problems* 9 (1973): 615.
23. Robert S. Summers, "The Technique Element of Law," *California Law Review* 59 (1971): 736–37, 741–45.

must be clear about what one is or is not free to do. Consider, for example, the case of gambling. One must distinguish between laws that forbid gambling and the absence of laws that recognize gambling debts. The latter does not deprive people of the freedom to contract gambling debts; it simply does not allow the use of legal enforcement to collect them. Similarly, the absence of laws recognizing polygamous and homosexual marriages does not deprive people of the freedom to enter polygamous and homosexual unions. Instead, it merely fails to provide legal recourse to enforce the agreements of the parties to such unions. The absence of laws recognizing such marriages does not deprive people of a freedom they previously had, for they were never able to have such agreements legally enforced. Nor have people been deprived of a freedom they would have if there were no legal system, for in the absence of a legal system no agreements can be legally enforced. If there is a ground for complaint, then, it must be one of inequality—that one type of relationship is legally recognized but others are not. However, a charge of inequality is warranted only if there are no relevant reasonable grounds for distinguishing between relationships. To settle that issue one must be clear about the state's or society's interests in marriage.

The rest of this essay is concerned with the purposes or functions of the marriage relationship in which society has a legitimate interest. It is not possible here to set out and to justify the purposes for which governments may legislate. It is assumed that the state may act to facilitate citizens' engaging in activities that they find desirable and to protect the welfare and equality of all citizens, including future ones. Government has an especially strong responsibility for the welfare of children. Of course, these legitimate governmental or social interests and responsibilities must be balanced against other interests and values of citizens, including those of privacy and freedom from interference.

There is no attempt or intention to justify penal laws prohibiting forms of relationship other than monogamous marriage. Indeed, it is generally assumed that they ought not be prohibited and that more people will enter into them than has been the case. In such a context, monogamous marriage

would become a more specialized form of relationship, entered into by a smaller proportion of the population than previously. Underlying this assumption are the general beliefs that many people are unqualified or unfit for a marital relationship and ought never to enter one and that many people marry for the wrong reasons. If true, these beliefs may explain why both marriage and divorce rates have been steadily rising in most Western countries during this century.[24]

Promoting Interpersonal Relationships

Alienation from others and loss of community are perceived by many to be among the most serious ills of modern, mass society. In such a situation it seems unlikely that many would deny the need for intimate interpersonal relationships of affection. The importance of such relationships for a good or *eudaemonistic* life have been recognized by philosophers as diverse as Aristotle and G. E. Moore.[25] In considering such interpersonal relationships to be among the most valuable elements of a good life, one must distinguish between the value of a good and the strength of the desire for it. Many people have a stronger desire for life than for such interpersonal relationships, but they may still recognize such relationships as more valuable than mere life. Life itself is of little value, but it is a necessary condition for most other things of value.

Among the most valuable forms of interpersonal relationship are love, friendship, and trust. These relationships are limited with respect to the number of persons with whom one can have them. Classically, there has been a distinction between agapeic and erotic love. Agapeic love is the love of all man-

---

24. Burton M. Leiser, *Liberty, Justice and Morals* (New York: Macmillan Co., (1973), p. 126; R[oland] Pressat, *Population,* trans. Robert and Danielle Atkinson (Baltimore: Penguin Books, 1970), pp. 84, 86; U.S. Commission on Population Growth and the American Future, *Population and the American Future* (New York: Signet, New American Library, 1972), pp. 102–03.

25. Aristotle, *Nicomachean Ethics* 9, 9–12; George Edward Moore, *Principia Ethica* (Cambridge, At the University Press, 1903), p. 188, 203–05.

kind—general benevolence. The concept of erotic love is more limited. In today's world erotic love is apt to be confused with sexual desire and intercourse. But there can be and always has been sex without love and love without sex. Personal love is more restricted than either agapeic love or sexual desire. It implies a concern for another that is greater than that for most people. Hence, it cannot be had for an unlimited number of other people.[26] Similar distinctions must be drawn between friendship and acquaintance, trust of a political candidate and that of a friend.

Such interpersonal relationships require intimacy. Intimacy involves a sharing of information about one another that is not shared with others. Moreover, it often involves seclusion from others—being in private where others cannot observe.[27] In some societies where physical privacy is not possible, psychological privacy—shutting out the awareness of the presence of others—substitutes. Consequently, these valuable interpersonal relationships require intimacy and usually physical privacy from others, and at the very least nonintrusion upon the relationship.

Moreover, these forms of interpersonal relationship require acts expressing the concern felt for the other person. In most societies acts of sexual intercourse have been such expressions of love and concern. It is not physically or psychologically necessary that sexual intercourse have this quasi-symbolic function, but it is a natural function of sexual intercourse. All that is here meant by "natural" is that in most societies sexual intercourse has this function, for which there is some psychological basis even though it is not contrary to scientific laws for it to be otherwise. Intercourse usually involves an ele-

ment of giving of oneself, and one's sexual identity is frequently a central element of one's self-image. It is not, however, sexual intercourse that is intrinsically valuable but the feelings and attitudes, the underlying interpersonal relationship, that it expresses. Nonsexual acts also currently express such relationships, but sexual intercourse is still one of the most important ways of doing so. If sexual intercourse ceases to have this function in society, some other act will undoubtedly replace it in this function. Moreover, sexual intercourse will have lost much of its value.

If these interpersonal relationships of personal love and trust are of major value, it is reasonable for the state to seek to protect and foster them by according legal recognition to them in marriage. The specific forms of this recognition cannot be fully discussed. However, there is some basis for treating the partners to a marriage as one person. Historically, of course, the doctrine that the parties to a marriage are one person has supported the subjugation of women in all sorts of ways, for example, in their disability from owning property. But there is an underlying rationale for joint responsibility. Two people who, without a special reason such as taxes, keep separate accounts of income and expenditures do not have the love and trust of a couple who find such an accounting unnecessary. Moreover, in such a joint economic venture there is no point to allowing one party to sue the other. Only the advent of insurance, whereby neither spouse, but a third party, pays, makes such suits seem profitable. Another recognition of these relationships—albeit one not frequently invoked—is that one is not forced to testify against his or her spouse. More important is that neither party is encouraged to violate the trust and intimacy of the relationship, for example, by encouraging one to inform authorities about bedroom comments of his or her spouse.[28]

---

26. It is thus misleading for McMurtry to write of monogamous marriage excluding "almost *countless* other possibilities of *intimate* union" with any number of persons (p. 279; my italics). On the limited nature of personal love or friendship see also Aristotle, *Nicomachean Ethics* 9. 10.

27. For a discussion of these relationships and the need for privacy, see Charles Fried, "Privacy," in *Law, Reason, and Justice,* ed. Graham Hughes (New York: New York University Press, 1969), pp. 45–69.

28. See the discussion (in another context) of such a case in Nazi Germany by H. L. A. Hart, "Positivism and the Separation of Law and Morals," *Harvard Law Review* 71 (1958): 618–20; and Lon L. Fuller, "Positivism and Fidelity to Law—A Reply to Professor Hart," *Harvard Law Review* 71 (1958): 652–55.

The character of these valuable forms of interpersonal relationship provides an argument against according marriages of definite duration legal recognition equal to that accorded those that are intentionally of indefinite duration. For it to be "intentionally of indefinite duration," neither partner may, when entering the marriage, intend it to be for a specific period of time, for example, five years, nor may the marriage contract specify such a period. The following argument is not to show that marriages for a definite duration should not be recognized, but merely to show that they should not have equal standing with those intentionally of indefinite duration. The basic reason for unequal recognition is that interpersonal relationships that are not intentionally of indefinite duration are less valuable than those that are.

Suppose one were to form a friendship with a colleague, but the two mutually agree to be friends for only three years, with an option to renew the friendship at that time. Such an agreement would indicate a misunderstanding of friendship. Such agreements make sense for what Aristotle called friendships of utility, but in the modern world these friendships are business partnerships.[29] While there is nothing wrong with business friendships, they do not have the intrinsic value of personal friendships. In becoming close personal friends with someone, one establishes a concern and trust that would be seriously weakened or destroyed by setting a time limit to the friendship. It is sometimes claimed that time limits may be set because people will only be together for a while. But one need not see a person every day or even every year to remain friends. However, extended separation usually brings about a withering away of the friendship.

Similarly, the personal relationship of love and trust in marriage is of lesser value if it is intentionally for only a definite period of time. Moreover, the entering into a relationship that is intentionally of indefinite duration and legally recognized symbolizes a strength of commitment not found in other types of relationships. While two unmarried

---

29. *Nicomachean Ethics* 8. 3. The vulgar hedonists treat marriage as a form of friendship for pleasure, but that is not the highest form of friendship.

people may claim that there is no definite limit to their mutual commitment, their commitment is always questionable. Entering into a marital relationship assures the commitment more than does a mere verbal avowal.

There are two common objections to this argument. First, it is sometimes said that there may be special reasons for making marriages of short, definite duration, for example, if one partner will only live in the area for a while. But a personal love that is not strong enough to overcome difficulties of moving to another area and possible sacrifices of

> *"The only ultimate test for the value of a life is whether at its end it is found to have been worth living."*

employment is not as close and strong as a love that can. Many married couples make such compromises and sacrifices. Second, it is sometimes claimed that commitment is in fact stronger when not legally reinforced, when one does not need the law to support the relationship. However, this claim overlooks the fact that when a married couple's relationship rests substantially upon their legal obligations, their relationship has already begun to deteriorate. The strength of commitment is established by the willingness to enter into a legal relationship that cannot be broken simply, without any difficulties. A person who is not willing to undertake the risk of the legal involvement in divorce should he desire to terminate the relationship is probably unsure of his commitment. Moreover, the legal relationship provides security against a sudden and unexpected change in one's life—the breakup of the social aspects will take some time, giving one a chance to prepare for a new style of life. Even then the change is often very difficult.

Hence, if marriage is for the purpose of providing legal recognition of some of the most valuable interpersonal relationships, it should grant more protection and recognition to those intentionally of indefinite duration than to others. Such a conclusion does not imply that divorce should be impossible or exceedingly difficult. Friendships frequently do not last forever despite their not being intended for a limited period of time. The same may happen to a marital relationship. So while this argument supports not according legal recognition to relationships intended to be of definite duration equal to that accorded those intended to be of indefinite duration, it does not support restrictions on divorce in the latter case. Moreover, the average length of time of marriages has increased considerably since the seventeenth century. When a couple married then, one of them was likely to die within twenty years. With today's increased life expectancy, both parties may live close to fifty years after they marry.[30] Obviously, with such an increased possible length of marriage, there is a greater chance for marital breakdown and divorce. One may expect more divorces in marriages that have lasted twenty to twenty-five years simply because there are more such marriages. Nevertheless, such marriages are intentionally of indefinite duration—for life.

Protecting the Welfare of Children

Another area of pervasive social interest that has historically centered in marriage concerns the procreation and raising of children. Society has an interest not only in the number of children born but their quality of life. This fact is in deep conflict with the current emphasis on the freedom of individuals to make reproductive decisions unfettered by social rules and restrictions. Moreover, it is an area in which social control has traditionally been weak. Child abuse is widespread, and efforts to prevent it are mediocre at best. There are few general legal qualifications or tests for becoming a parent. Yet parenthood is one of the most potentially dangerous relationships that one person can have with another. If one is a poor college teacher, then at worst a few students do not receive a bit of education they might have. But as a parent one potentially can ruin completely the lives of one's children. At the least, they may develop into psychological misfits incapable of leading responsible and rewarding lives.

Essentially, there are three areas of social interest and responsibility with respect to procreation and the raising of children. First, there is a social interest in the sheer number of children born. The current emphasis on population control makes this interest abundantly clear.[31] Second, there is a social interest in the potentialities of children. This area includes concern for genetic and congenital birth defects and abnormalities. Over 5 percent of all children born have a genetic defect. The possibility of genetic control of those who are born will soon take on major significance. Already, approximately sixty genetic diseases as well as almost all chromosomal abnormalities can be detected *in utero,* and adult carriers of about eighty genetic defects can be identified.[32] Given the possibility of genetic control, society can no longer risk having genetically disadvantaged children by leaving the decision of whether to have children to the unregulated judgment of individual couples. Some social regulations with respect to genetic screening and, perhaps, eugenic sterilization are needed. While potential parents have interests of privacy and freedom in reproductive decisions, the social interests in preventing the suffering and inequality of possibly defective children may outweigh them in certain types of cases.

Third, the care and development of those who are born is a social interest and responsibility. This interest has been recognized for some time in the form of children's homes and compulsory education. However, increasing knowledge about childhood development extends the area in which social interests and responsibility may be reasonably involved. To give an example at the most elementary level, the nutritional diet of children during their first three years is crucial for their future development. So also is their psychological support. The welfare of future generations is not a private but a

---

30. Pressat, *Population,* p. 52.

31. For a more complete discussion see my "Limits to a Right to Procreate," in *Ethics and Population,* ed. Michael D. Bayles (Cambridge, Mass.: Schenkman Publishing Company, 1975).

32. Daniel Callahan, *The Tyranny of Survival* (New York: Macmillan Co., 1973), p. 219.

social matter. It is a proper task of society, acting through its government, to ensure that the members of the next generation are not physical or psychological cripples due to the ignorance, negligence, or even indifference of parents.

Historically, society has attempted to control procreation through the institution of marriage. Society's means were primarily to stigmatize children born out of wedlock and to encourage the having of many children. It is now recognized that no useful purpose is served by stigmatizing children born out of wedlock as illegitimate. (However, some useful purpose may be served by not according children born out of wedlock all the rights of those born in wedlock, for example, inheritance without parental recognition.) The emphasis on having as many children as one can has also disappeared. It is not this historical concern with procreation that is misplaced in modern society but the forms that the concern has taken.

If society has the responsibility to protect the welfare of children, then some social regulation and control of human reproduction and development is justified. Such regulation and control need not be effected by penal laws. For example, social concern has traditionally been expressed in adoptions through regulations to ensure that those who adopt children are fit to care for them. That some regulations have been inappropriate and not reasonably related to the welfare of children is not in question. Rather, the point is that there has been regulation without penal laws, or at least without resorting primarily to penal laws. Nor can social regulation and control be solely by legislation. Legislation alone is usually ineffective; it must be supported by informal social rules and expectations.

Not only has modern biomedicine made sex possible without procreation; it has also made procreation possible without sex. The techniques of artificial insemination and fertilization, embryo transfer, ova donation, ectogenesis, and cloning now, or soon will, make it possible for people to reproduce without sexual intercourse.[33] Hence, not only may

one have sex for pleasure, but one may reproduce for pleasure without sexual intercourse. Not only may people reproduce outside marriage; they are not even biologically required to have intercourse. Thus, sex and marriage may become dissociated from reproduction.

However, there are strong reasons for restricting procreation primarily to marriages of indefinite duration, which does not imply that such marriages should be restricted to procreation. Marriage has traditionally been the central social institution concerned with procreation. Consequently, if society is to exercise some control over procreation in the future, it would involve the least change in conditions to do so through marriage. Moreover, there is considerable evidence that the disruption of family life contributes to juvenile delinquency. Whether divorce or marital breakdown (with or without divorce) is a prime cause of such delinquency does not matter. The point is that the disruption of home life does seriously affect the development of children.[34] The chance of such disruption outside of a marriage that is intentionally of indefinite duration is higher than for that within. Moreover, there is some reason to believe that the presence of both mother and father is instrumental in the psychological development of children. In any case, the presence of two people rather than one provides the security that there will be someone to care for the children should one of the parents die. Generally, children are better off being with one parent than in a state orphanage, but better off still with both parents. Hence, for the welfare of children it seems best that procreation and child rearing primarily occur within the context of marriages intentially of indefinite duration.

---

33. For a good general survey of these techniques and some suggestions for social controls, see George A. Hudock, "Gene Therapy and Genetic Engineering: Frankenstein Is Still a Myth, But It

Should Be Reread Periodically," *Indiana Law Journal* 48 (1973): 533–58. Various ethical issues are discussed in Joseph Fletcher, *The Ethics of Genetic Control* (Garden City, N.Y.: Doubleday, Anchor Books, 1974). Successful human embryo implantation and growth to term after *in vitro* fertilization has been reported in Britain (see *Time,* July 29, 1974, p. 58–59; and *Newsweek,* July 29, 1974, p. 70).

34. President's Commission on Law Enforcement and Administration of Justice, *The Challenge of Crime in a Free Society* (New York: Avon Books, 1968), pp. 184–89.

While society has a responsibility for the care and development of children, this general responsibility is best carried out if specific adults have obligations to care for specific children. In the past, the biological parent-child relation has reinforced the allocation of responsibility for specific children and has been a major factor in monogamy.[35] The separation of reproduction and sexual intercourse threatens disruption of this assignment. For example, if gestation occurs in an artificial womb in a laboratory, there may be no "parents," only a specific research group. More realistically, if a woman has an embryo from ova and sperm donors transferred to her uterus, it is unclear who are the child's parents. However, if there is to be optimal care for children, specific adults must have obligations for specific children. It cannot be left to somebody in general, for then nobody in particular is likely to do it. "Let George do it" is too prevalent and careless an attitude to allow with regard to children.

McMurtry's contention that monogamy restricts the care for children is not well founded.[36] First, if there are no specific adults responsible for children, they may become "lost" in large groups and victims of the "it's not my job" syndrome. Second, monogamy per se does not cut children off from the support and care of others. One must distinguish the marital relationship from living arrangements. It is the isolated situation of the family that deprives children of such support. In many married-student housing complexes children have access to other adults. Even in general-residential neighborhoods with separate family housing units, such support is available if there is a sense of community in the neighborhood.

Given the social interests in and responsibility for the procreation and development of children, some more effective controls of parenthood appear desirable. If the primary locus of reproduction is to be within marriages of intentionally indefinite duration, then the easiest way to institute controls is to add requirements for people to enter such marriages. A few requirements such as blood tests are already generally prevalent. Alternatively, one might have a separate licensing procedure for procreation. Nonmarried couples and single people might also qualify for such licenses. Moreover, couples who want to marry but not have children would not have to meet requirements. However, the only requirements suggested below that might bar marriages are almost as important for those couples who do not have children as for those who do. If the requirements were tied to marriage they would be easier to administer. The only drawback is that unmarried people would not have to meet them. However, such requirements can and should be part of the medical practice of the "artificial" techniques of reproduction—artificial insemination and embryo transfer. And there are few if any effective methods, except generally accepted social rules, to control procreation outside of marriage.

One obvious requirement would be genetic screening. With modern medical techniques genetic problems do not imply that couples cannot become married, but they might be expected not to have children who are their genetic offspring. Artificial insemination and embryo transfer make it possible for almost everyone to have children, even though the children might not be genetically theirs. A general distinction between biological and social parenthood should be made, with legal emphasis on the latter.

More important, perhaps, is some general expectation of psychological fitness for family life and the raising of children. The difficulty with such an expectation is the absence of any clear criteria for fitness and reliable methods for determining who meets them. Perhaps, however, some formal instruction in family relations and child rearing would be appropriate. The Commission on Population Growth and the American Future has already called for an expansion of education for parenthood.[37] It is only a bit further to require some sort of minimal family education for marriage. Probably the easiest method for ensuring such education would be to make it a required subject in secondary schools. If

---

35. Daniel Callahan, "New Beginnings in Life: A Philosopher's Response," in *The New Genetics and the Future of Man,* ed. Michael P. Hamilton (Grand Rapids, Mich.: William B. Eerdmans Publishing Company, 1972), pp. 102–03.

36 "Monogamy," p. 281.

---

37. *Population and the American Future,* pp. 126–33, esp. 133.

that were done, few people would have difficulty meeting this requirement for marriage.

There should not be any financial or property qualifications for marriage.[38] Society's interest in and responsibility for the welfare of the population in general is such that governments should ensure an adequate standard of living for all persons. Were that to be done there would be no reason to impose any financial restrictions on marriage. Nonetheless, prospective parents should have more concern for their financial situation than is now frequently the case. The adequate care of children is an expensive task, financially as well as psychologically and temporally.

Conclusion

It may be objected that neither the argument from interpersonal relations nor that from the welfare of children specifically supports monogamous marriage. While loving relationships cannot extend to an indefinite number of people, they can extend to more than one other person. Also, a polygamous union may provide a reasonable environment for procreation. Hence, neither of the arguments supports monogamous marriage per se.

Logically, the objection is quite correct. But it is a misunderstanding of social philosophy to expect arguments showing that a certain arrangement is always best under all circumstances. The most that can be shown is that usually, or as a rule, one social arrangement is preferable to another. Practically, polygamous marriage patterns will probably never be prevalent.[39] For centuries they have been gradually disappearing throughout the world. If a disproportionate sex distribution of the population occurs in some areas or age groups (such as the elderly), then they may increase in significance. Unless that

occurs, most people will probably continue to prefer marital monogamy.

More important, the burden of this paper has not been to defend the traditional idea of marital union or even the current practice. Many of the traditional rules of marriage have been unjust, for example, the inequality between the sexes, both legally and in terms of social roles. Instead, it has been to defend social recognition of marriage of intentionally indefinite duration as a unique and socially valuable institution that society has interests in promoting and regulating. In particular, society has interests in and responsibility for promoting a certain form of valuable interpersonal relationship and protecting the welfare of children. Both of these purposes can be well served by monogamous marriage.

The image, then, is of a society with various forms of living together, but one in which marriage of intentionally indefinite duration would have a distinctive though lessened role as a special kind of socially and legally recognized relationship. There would not be laws prohibiting nonmarital forms of cohabitation. Divorce would be based on factual marital breakdown or mutual consent, with due regard for the welfare of children. Monogamous marriage would recognize a special form of personal relationship in which reproduction and child rearing primarily occur. Given the social interest in decreasing procreation, many people might marry but not have children, and others might not marry at all. Details of the legal marital relationship have not been specified, nor could they be in this brief essay except with respect to the main social interests. Questions of inheritance, legal residence and name, social-security benefits, and so on, have not been specified. Changes in laws with respect to many of these matters can be made without affecting the arguments for the value of, social responsibility for, and interests in marriage. Above all, it is an image in which sexual intercourse plays a much smaller role in the conception of marriage and the good life in general, a society in which vulgar hedonism has at least been replaced by a broader-based *eudaemonism*.

---

38. For some suggested financial requirements as well as others, see Jack Parsons, *Population versus Liberty* (Buffalo, N.Y.: Prometheus Books, 1971), p. 349.

39. Even McMurtry appears to recognize this fact, see "Monogamy," p. 278.

1. Does our society exaggerate the importance of sex?

2. Can one love equally more than one person at a time?

3. If some people are unfit to be parents, what should society do?

Divorce

Rebecca West (1892–1982) Rebecca West was a writer of fiction, history, and criticism.

Rebecca West

The way one looks at divorce depends on the way one looks at a much broader question.

Is the mental state of humanity so low that it is best to lay down invariable rules for it which have been found to lead to the greatest happiness of the greatest number, and insist that everyone keep them in spite of the hardship necessarily inflicted on certain special cases, thus dragooning the majority into compulsory happiness? Or is it so high that it is safe to lay down rules which will admit of variation for different people in different circumstances, when it seems to them these variations can secure their happiness?

If one agrees with the first view, then one is bound to disapprove altogether of divorce. If one agrees with the second, then one is bound to approve of legislation which enables unhappily married persons to separate and remarry.

Though I have the kind of temperament that hates to own failure and would never wish to break a marriage I had made, I regard divorce laws as a necessary part of the arrangements in a civilized State. This is the result of my experience of life in countries where there is practically no divorce, and in countries where divorce is permissible on grounds of varying latitude.

Superficially the case against divorce is overwhelming: and indeed it should never be forgotten, least of all by those who approve of divorce as a possibility. Getting a divorce is nearly always as cheerful and useful an occupation as breaking very valuable china. The divorce of married people with children is nearly always an unspeakable calamity. It is only just being understood, in the light of modern psychological research, how much a child de-

From *The London Daily Express,* 1930. Reprinted by permission of Express Newspapers, PLC (London).

pends for its healthy growth on the presence in the home of both its parents. This is not a matter of its attitude to morals; if divorce did nothing more than make it accustomed to the idea of divorce, then no great harm would be done. The point is that if a child is deprived of either its father or its mother it feels that it has been cheated out of a right. It cannot be reasoned out of this attitude, for children are illogical, especially where their affections are concerned, to an even greater degree than ourselves. A child who suffers from this resentment suffers much more than grief: he is liable to an obscuring of his vision, to a warping of his character. He may turn against the parent to whom the courts have given him, and regard him or her as responsible for the expulsion of the other from the home. He may try to compensate himself for what he misses by snatching everything else he can get out of life, and become selfish and even thievish. He may, through yearning for the unattainable parent, get himself into a permanent mood of discontent, which will last his life long and make him waste every opportunity of love and happiness that comes to him later.

If either parent remarries, the child may feel agonies of jealousy. What is this intruder coming in and taking affection when already there is not as much as there ought to be? This is an emotion that is felt by children even in the case of fathers and mothers who have lost their partners by death: as witness the innumerable cases of children who come up before the Juvenile Courts and prove on examination to have committed their offences as acts of defiance against perfectly inoffensive and kindly step-parents. It is felt far more acutely in the case of parents whose relationships have been voluntarily severed, who have no excuse of widowhood or widowerhood to justify the introduction of a new partner. This, of course, need not always happen. One of the happiest homes I can think of is the second venture of a man and a woman who both divorced their first partners as a result of conduct that poisoned not only their lives but their children's: it is one of the most cheerful sights I know to see their combined family of four children realizing with joy and surprise that actually they can have a family life like other people. But that man

and that woman are not only kindly people, they are clever people. They handle the children with extreme sensitiveness to the issues involved. More commonly the situation for the child is not completely salved.

In fact, people with children who divorce husbands or wives because they are troublesome are likely to find themselves saddled with rather more discontent than they hoped to escape. And the new trouble is of a radiating kind, likely to travel down and down through the generations, such as few would care to have on their consciences.

As for the divorce of childless married couples, there is of course a matter of infinitely less social significance. If it is regarded too lightly it cheats a lot of them out of their one chance of happiness. A man and woman marry each other because they represent to each other the types they have always found attractive and about which they have spun innumerable romantic dreams. They then grow disappointed with each other because they insist on being themselves, the human beings they happened to be born, instead of the dreamed-of types. If they stay together it may in time penetrate to each that the other may not have the qualities of the imagined one, but may have real and valuable virtues which are much more useful; and a very kindly feeling of attachment may develop. But if a couple break up during the first shock of disappointment they are certain to go off and immediately find other people who resemble the dreamed-of types, marry them, and go through the same process of disillusionment, ending another separation. Thus a whole group of people will be involved in sterile and inharmonious excitements which will waste the very short time we are given to establish ourselves in fruitful and harmonious relationships.

Against these considerations, of course, we have to reckon that although the consequences of being the child of divorced parents are heavy, they are sometimes not so heavy as the consequences of being a child brought up in close propinquity and at the mercy of a brutal and vicious parent. We have also to admit that in the case of a childless couple there may be reasons why a divorce may become as essential to a human being's continued existence as food or air. There is infidelity, there is drunkenness, there is, above all, cruelty, not only of the body but of the mind. No one who has not been through it can know the full horror of being tied to a man who craves war instead of peace, whose love is indistinguishable from hate. The day that is poisoned from its dawn by petty rages about nothing, by a deliberate destruction of everything pleasant: the night that is full of fear, because it is certain that no one can suffer all this without going mad, and if one goes mad there will be nobody to be kind; these are things to which no human being should have a life sentence.

But brutal and vicious parents are in a minority. Human nature is not so bad as all that. The opponents of divorce are therefore justified when they ask if it is not dangerous to give the victims of this minority the power to free themselves from these burdens that cannot be borne, when that power will inevitably be available to those who want to free themselves from burdens that they only think cannot be borne. For human beings are stupid; they do not know what is best for them, they certainly will not use that power wisely. If the majority is to suffer unnecessarily from these facilities for divorce, would it not be better to withdraw and let the minority fend for itself?

I do not think so. Because there is another element involved; and that is the general attitude of the community toward sex. That seems to be invariably less sane where there is no divorce than where there is. What makes humanity stupid is that it will act on certain mad fairy-tales about life which it refuses to outgrow, and its attitude to sex determines all these mad fairy-tales.

The lack of divorce corrupts the community's attitude to sex for several reasons. First of all, it deprives marriage of all standards. If one cannot be penalized for failure in an activity, and the prizes for success in it are of a highly rarefied and spiritual nature, the baser man will regard it as a go-as-you-please affair. The man who knows that he cannot commit adultery without the slightest check from society will have to be a very high type if he does not come to the conclusion that, since society is so indifferent to it, adultery must be a trivial matter. But his natural jealousy will not permit him to think like that of his wife's adultery. That he will

punish in all of the very existence ways which are open to him through his economic power.

Thus there starts the fictitious system of morality which, instead of regarding sexual conduct as a means to an end, and that end the continuance of the species in the most harmonious conditions, places purely arbitrary values on different sexual entities and plays a game with them like Mah-Jong. Since a man's adultery does not matter and a woman's adultery does, it follows that a man's whole sexual life is without moral significance, and a woman's sexual life is portentous with it. Whenever

> *"Whenever you have no divorce laws you must have the double standard of morality."*

you have no divorce laws you must have the double standard of morality. Consequently a large part of the male sex, as much as is not controlled by idealism, roves about the world trying with complete impunity to persuade the female sex to a course of action which, should the female comply, leads them to disaster. The seducer, it must be noted, has an enormous advantage in countries where there is no divorce. Even in England, we sometimes come across a Don Juan who has the luck to have a wife who will not divorce him, and note how useful he finds this in persuading ladies that he loves them. He can so safely say that he would marry them if he could, without danger that his bluff will be called. Every Don Juan enjoys this advantage in a country where there is no divorce. Illegitimate births follow which—because of the arbitrary distinction between the sexes—are not robbed of their sting as they are in the countries where divorce is possible by laws that guarantee the offspring its maintenance, but result in the persecution of mother and child.

In fact, sex is associated with cruelty in countries where there is no divorce, as it is in the institution of prostitution: this also flourishes wherever there is this double standard of morality. No illicit love affair, where both parties are exercising free choice, can possibly do the community as much harm as the traffic between the prostitute and her client. That a woman should be held in contempt for submitting to the same physical relationship that is the core of marriage degrades marriage, and all women, and all men; and the greater the contempt she is held in the more she becomes genuinely contemptible. For as she sinks lower she becomes more and more a source of disease, and more and more a brutalized machine. It is in countries where there is no divorce that the prostitute is most firmly established as the object of extra-marital adventures and is most deeply despised.

One can test this by its converse if one goes to a library and turns up old comic papers and plays, particularly farces. As the law and society began to sanction divorce, and impressed on the public a sense of moral obligation, this ceased to be the case.

It is one of the most important things in the world that people should have a sane and kindly outlook on sex; that it should not be associated with squalor and cruelty. Because divorce makes it clear to the ordinary man and woman that they must behave well in the married state or run the risk of losing its advantages, it does impress on them some rudiments of a sane attitude towards sex. It therefore lifts up the community to a level where happy marriages, in which the problem of our human disposition to cruelty and jealousy is satisfactorily solved, are much more likely to occur.

Study Questions

1. Is divorce moral if children are involved?
2. How can we reduce the frequency of divorce in our society?

Licensing Parents

Hugh LaFollette is a professor of philosophy at East Tennessee State University and is author of the forthcoming book, Just Good Friends.

Hugh LaFollette

In this essay I shall argue that the state should require all parents to be licensed. My main goal is to demonstrate that the licensing of parents is theoreti-

Hugh LaFollette, "Licensing Parents," *Philosophy & Public Affairs* 9, no. 2 Reprinted with permission of Princeton University Press (Winter 1980). © 1980 by Princeton University Press.

cally desirable, though I shall also argue that a workable and just licensing program actually could be established.

My strategy is simple. After developing the basic rationale for the licensing of parents, I shall consider several objections to the proposal and argue that these objections fail to undermine it. I shall then isolate some striking similarities between this licensing program and our present policies on the adoption of children. If we retain these adoption policies—as we surely should—then, I argue, a general licensing program should also be established. Finally, I shall briefly suggest that the reason many people object to licensing is that they think parents, particularly biological parents, own or have natural sovereignty over their children.

Regulating Potentially Harmful Activities

Our society normally regulates a certain range of activities; it is illegal to perform these activities unless one has received prior permission to do so. We require automobile operators to have licenses. We forbid people from practicing medicine, law, pharmacy, or psychiatry unless they have satisfied certain licensing requirements.

Society's decision to regulate just these activities is not ad hoc. The decision to restrict admission to certain vocations and to forbid some people from driving is based on an eminently plausible, though not often explicitly formulated, rationale. We require drivers to be licensed because driving an auto is an activity which is potentially harmful to others, safe performance of the activity requires a certain competence, and we have a moderately reliable procedure for determining that competence. The potential harm is obvious: incompetent drivers can and do maim and kill people. The best way we have of limiting this harm without sacrificing the benefits of automobile travel is to require that all drivers demonstrate at least minimal competence. We likewise license doctors, lawyers, and psychologists because they perform activities which can harm others. Obviously they must be proficient if they are to perform these activities properly, and we have moderately reliable procedures for determining proficiency.[1] Imagine a world in which everyone could legally drive a car, in which everyone could legally perform surgery, prescribe medications, dispense drugs, or offer legal advice. Such a world would hardly be desirable.

Consequently, any activity that is potentially harmful to others and requires certain demonstrated competence for its safe performance, is subject to regulation—that is, it is theoretically desirable that we regulate it. If we also have a reliable procedure for determining whether someone has the requisite competence, then the action is not only subject to regulation but ought, all things considered, to be regulated.

It is particularly significant that we license these hazardous activities, even though denying a license to someone can severely inconvenience and even harm that person. Furthermore, available competency tests are not 100 percent accurate. Denying someone a driver's license in our society, for example, would inconvenience that person acutely. In effect that person would be prohibited from working, shopping, or visiting in places reachable only by car. Similarly, people denied vocational licenses are inconvenienced, even devastated. We have all heard of individuals who had the "life-long dream" of becoming physicians or lawyers, yet were denied that dream. However, the realization that some people are disappointed or inconvenienced does not diminish our conviction that we must regulate occupations or activities that are potentially dangerous to others. Innocent people must be protected even if it means that others cannot pursue activities they deem highly desirable.

Furthermore, we maintain licensing procedures even though our competency tests are sometimes

---

1. "When practice of a profession or calling requires special knowledge or skill and intimately affects public health, morals, order or safety, or general welfare, legislature may prescribe reasonable qualifications for persons desiring to pursue such professions or calling and require them to demonstrate possession of such qualifications by examination on subjects with which such profession or calling has to deal as a condition precedent to right to follow that profession or calling." 50 SE and 735 (1949). Also see 199 U.S. 306, 318 (1905) and 123 U.S. 623, 661 (1887).

inaccurate. Some people competent to perform the licensed activity (for example, driving a car) will be unable to demonstrate competence (they freeze up on the driver's test). Others may be incompetent, yet pass the test (they are lucky or certain aspects of competence—for example, the sense of responsibility—are not tested). We recognize clearly—or should recognize clearly—that no test will pick out all and only competent drivers, physicians, lawyers, and so on. Mistakes are inevitable. This does not mean we should forget that innocent people may be harmed by faulty regulatory procedures. In fact, if the procedures are sufficiently faulty, we should cease regulating that activity entirely until more reliable tests are available. I only want to emphasize here that tests need not be perfect. Where moderately reliable tests are available, licensing procedures should be used to protect innocent people from incompetents.[2]

These general criteria for regulatory licensing can certainly be applied to parents. First, parenting is an activity potentially very harmful to children. The potential for harm is apparent: each year more than half a million children are physically abused or neglected by their parents.[3] Many millions more are psychologically abused or neglected—not given love, respect, or a sense of self-worth. The results of this maltreatment are obvious. Abused children bear the physical and psychological scars of maltreatment throughout their lives. Far too often they turn to

crime.[4] They are far more likely than others to abuse their own children.[5] Even if these maltreated children never harm anyone, they will probably never be well-adjusted, happy adults. Therefore, parenting clearly satisfies the first criterion of activities subject to regulation.

The second criterion is also incontestably satisfied. A parent must be competent if he is to avoid harming his children; even greater competence is required if he is to do the "job" well. But not everyone has this minimal competence. Many people lack the knowledge needed to rear children adequately. Many others lack the requisite energy, temperament, or stability. Therefore, child-rearing manifestly satisfies both criteria of activities subject to regulation. In fact, I dare say that parenting is a paradigm of such activities since the potential for harm is so great (both in the extent of harm any one person can suffer and in the number of people potentially harmed) and the need for competence is so evident. Consequently, there is good reason to believe that all parents should be licensed. The only ways to avoid this conclusion are to deny the need for licensing *any* potentially harmful activity; to deny that I have identified the standard criteria of activities which should be regulated; to deny that

---

2. What counts as a moderately reliable test for these purposes will vary from circumstance to circumstance. For example, if the activity could cause a relatively small amount of harm, yet regulating that activity would place extensive constraints on people regulated, then any tests should be extremely accurate. On the other hand, if the activity could be exceedingly harmful but the constraints on the regulated person are minor, then the test can be considerably less reliable.

3. The statistics on the incidence of child abuse vary. Probably the most recent detailed study (Saad Nagi, *Child Maltreatment in the United States,* Columbia University Press, 1977) suggests that between 400,000 and 1,000,000 children are abused or neglected each year. Other experts claim the incidence is considerably higher.

4. According to the National Committee for the Prevention of Child Abuse, more than 80 percent of incarcerated criminals were, as children, abused by their parents. In addition, a study in the *Journal of the American Medical Association* 168, no. 3: 1755–1758, reported that first-degree murderers from middle-class homes and who have "no history of addiction to drugs, alcoholism, organic disease of the brain, or epilepsy" were frequently found to have been subject to "remorseless physical brutality at the hands of the parents."

5. "A review of the literature points out that abusive parents were raised in the same style that they have recreated in the pattern of rearing children.... An individual who was raised by parents who used physical force to train their children and who grew up in a violent household has had as a role model the use of force and violence as a means of family problem solving." R. J. Gelles, "Child Abuse as Psychopathology—a Sociological Critique and Reformulation," *American Journal of Orthopsychiatry* 43, no. 4 (1973): 618–19.

parenting satisfies the standard criteria; to show that even though parenting satisfies the standard criteria there are special reasons why licensing parents is not theoretically desirable; or to show that there is no reliable and just procedure for implementing this program.

While developing my argument for licensing I have already identified the standard criteria for activities that should be regulated, and I have shown that they can properly be applied to parenting. One could deny the legitimacy of regulation by licensing, but in doing so one would condemn not only the regulation of parenting, but also the regulation of drivers, physicians, druggists, and doctors. Furthermore, regulation of hazardous activities appears to be a fundamental task of any stable society.

Thus only two objections remain. In the next section I shall see if there are any special reasons why licensing parents is not theoretically desirable. Then, in the following section, I shall examine several practical objections designed to demonstrate that even if licensing were theoretically desirable, it could not be justly implemented.

Theoretical Objections to Licensing

Licensing is unacceptable, someone might say, since people have a right to have children, just as they have rights to free speech and free religious expression. They do not need a license to speak freely or to worship as they wish. Why? Because they have a right to engage in these activities. Similarly, since people have a right to have children, any attempt to license parents would be unjust.

This is an important objection since many people find it plausible, if not self-evident. However, it is not as convincing as it appears. The specific rights appealed to in this analogy are not without limitations. Both slander and human sacrifice are prohibited by law; both could result from the unrestricted exercise of freedom of speech and freedom of religion. Thus, even if people have these rights, they may sometimes be limited in order to protect innocent people. Consequently, even if people had a right to have children, that right might also be lim-

ited in order to protect innocent people, in this case children. Secondly, the phrase "right to have children" is ambiguous; hence, it is important to isolate its most plausible meaning in this context. Two possible interpretations are not credible and can be dismissed summarily. It is implausible to claim either that infertile people have rights to be *given* children or that people have rights to intentionally create children biologically without incurring any subsequent responsibility to them.

A third interpretation, however, is more plausible, particularly when coupled with observations about the degree of intrusion into one's life that the licensing scheme represents. On this interpretation people have a right to rear children if they make good-faith efforts to rear procreated children the best way they see fit. One might defend this claim on the ground that licensing would require too much intrusion into the lives of sincere applicants.

Undoubtedly one should be wary of unnecessary governmental intervention into individuals' lives. In this case, though, the intrusion would not often be substantial, and when it is, it would be warranted. Those granted licenses would face merely minor intervention; only those denied licenses would encounter marked intrusion. This encroachment, however, is a necessary side-effect of licensing parents—just as it is for automobile and vocational licensing. In addition, as I shall argue in more detail later, the degree of intrusion arising from a general licensing program would be no more than, and probably less than, the present (and presumably justifiable) encroachment into the lives of people who apply to adopt children. Furthermore, since some people hold unacceptable views about what is best for children (they think children should be abused regularly), people do not automatically have rights to rear children just because they will rear them in a way they deem appropriate.[6]

---

6. Some people might question if any parents actually believe they should beat their children. However, that does appear to be the sincere view of many abusing parents. See, for example, case descriptions in *A Silent Tragedy* by Peter and Judith DeCourcy (Sherman Oaks, CA.: Alfred Publishing Co., 1973).

Consequently, we come to a somewhat weaker interpretation of this right claim: a person has a right to rear children if he meets certain minimal standards of child rearing. Parents must not abuse or neglect their children and must also provide for the basic needs of the children. This claim of right is certainly more credible than the previously canvassed alternatives, though some people might still reject this claim in situations where exercise of the right would lead to negative consequences, for example, to overpopulation. More to the point, though, this conditional right is compatible with licensing. On this interpretation one has a right to have children only if one is not going to abuse or neglect them. Of course the very purpose of licensing is just to determine whether people *are* going to abuse or neglect their children. If the determination is made that someone will maltreat children, then that person is subject to the limitations of the right to have children and can legitimately be denied a parenting license.

In fact, this conditional way of formulating the right to have children provides a model for formulating all alleged rights to engage in hazardous activities. Consider, for example, the right to drive a car. People do not have an unconditional right to drive, although they do have a right to drive if they are competent. Similarly, people do not have an unconditional right to practice medicine; they have a right only if they are demonstrably competent. Hence, denying a driver's or physician's license to someone who has not demonstrated the requisite competence does not deny that person's rights. Likewise, on this model, denying a parenting license to someone who is not competent does not violate that person's rights.

Of course someone might object that the right is conditional on actually being a person who will abuse or neglect children, whereas my proposal only picks out those we can reasonably predict will abuse children. Hence, this conditional right *would* be incompatible with licensing.

There are two ways to interpret this objection and it is important to distinguish these divergent formulations. First, the objection could be a way of questioning our ability to predict reasonably and accurately whether people would maltreat their own children. This is an important practical objection, but I will defer discussion of it until the next section. Second, this objection could be a way of expressing doubt about the moral propriety of the prior restraint licensing requires. A parental licensing program would deny licenses to applicants judged to be incompetent even though they had never maltreated any children. This practice would be in tension with our normal skepticism about the propriety of prior restraint.

> "... [T]here is good reason to believe that all parents should be licensed."

Despite this healthy skepticism, we do sometimes use prior restraint. In extreme circumstances we may hospitalize or imprison people judged insane, even though they are not legally guilty of any crime, simply because we predict they are likely to harm others. More typically, though, prior restraint is used only if the restriction is not terribly onerous and the restricted activity is one which could lead easily to serious harm. Most types of licensing (for example, those for doctors, drivers, and druggists) fall into this latter category. They require prior restraint to prevent serious harm, and generally the restraint is minor—though it is important to remember that some individuals will find it oppressive. The same is true of parental licensing. The purpose of licensing is to prevent serious harm to children. Moreover, the prior restraint required by licensing would not be terribly onerous for many people. Certainly the restraint would be far less extensive than the presumably justifiable prior restraint of, say, insane criminals. Criminals preventively detained and mentally ill people forceably hospitalized are denied most basic liberties, while those denied parental licenses would be denied only that one specific opportunity. They could still vote, work for political candidates, speak on controversial topics, and so on. Doubtless some individuals would find the restraint onerous. But when compared to other types of restraint currently practiced, and when judged in light of the severity of harm maltreated children suffer, the restraint appears *relatively* minor.

Furthermore, we could make certain, as we do with most licensing programs, that individuals denied licenses are given the opportunity to reapply easily and repeatedly for a license. Thus, many people correctly denied licenses (because they are incompetent) would choose (perhaps it would be provided) to take counseling or therapy to improve their chances of passing the next test. On the other hand, most of those mistakenly denied licenses would probably be able to demonstrate in a later test that they would be competent parents.

Consequently, even though one needs to be wary of prior restraint, if the potential for harm is great and the restraint is minor relative to the harm we are trying to prevent—as it would be with parental licensing—then such restraint is justified. This objection, like all the theoretical objections reviewed, has failed.

Practical Objections to Licensing

I shall now consider five practical objections to licensing. Each objection focuses on the problems or difficulties of implementing this proposal. According to these objections, licensing is (or may be) theoretically desirable; nevertheless, it cannot be efficiently and justly implemented.

The first objection is that there may not be, or we may not be able to discover, adequate criteria of "a good parent." We simply do not have the knowledge, and it is unlikely that we could ever obtain the knowledge, that would enable us to distinguish adequate from inadequate parents.

Clearly there is some force to this objection. It is highly improbable that we can formulate criteria that would distinguish precisely between good and less than good parents. There is too much we do not know about child development and adult psychology. My proposal, however, does not demand that we make these fine distinctions. It does not demand that we license only the best parents; rather it

is designed to exclude only the very bad ones.[7] This is not just a semantic difference, but a substantive one. Although we do not have infallible criteria for picking out good parents, we undoubtedly can identify bad ones—those who will abuse or neglect their children. Even though we could have a lively debate about the range of freedom a child should be given or the appropriateness of corporal punishment, we do not wonder if a parent who severely beats or neglects a child is adequate. We know that person isn't. Consequently, we do have reliable and useable criteria for determining who is a bad parent; we have the criteria necessary to make a licensing program work.

The second practical objection to licensing is that there is no reliable way to predict who will maltreat their children. Without an accurate predictive test, licensing would be not only unjust, but also a waste of time. Now I recognize that as a philosopher (and not a psychologist, sociologist, or social worker), I am on shaky ground if I make sweeping claims about the present or future abilities of professionals to produce such predictive tests. Nevertheless, there are some relevant observations I can offer.

Initially, we need to be certain that the demands on predictive tests are not unreasonable. For example, it would be improper to require that tests be 100 percent accurate. Procedures for licensing drivers, physicians, lawyers, druggists, etc., plainly are not 100 percent (or anywhere near 100 percent) accurate. Presumably we recognize these deficiencies yet embrace the procedures anyway. Consequently, it would be imprudent to demand considerably more exacting standards for the tests used in licensing parents.

In addition, from what I can piece together, the practical possibilities for constructing a reliable predictive test are not all that gloomy. Since my pro-

---

7. I suppose I might be for licensing only good parents if I knew there were reasonable criteria and some plausible way of deciding if a potential parent satisfied these criteria. However, since I don't think we have those criteria or that method, nor can I seriously envision that we will discover those criteria and that method, I haven't seriously entertained the stronger proposal.

posal does not require that we make fine line distinctions between good and less than good parents, but rather that we weed out those who are potentially very bad, we can use existing tests that claim to isolate relevant predictive characteristics—whether a person is violence-prone, easily frustrated, or unduly self-centered. In fact, researchers at Nashville General Hospital have developed a brief interview questionnaire which seems to have significant predictive value. Based on their data, the researchers identified 20 percent of the interviewees as a "risk group"—those having great potential for serious problems. After one year they found "the incidence of major breakdown in parent-child interaction in the risk group was approximately four to five times as great as in the low risk group."[8] We also know that parents who maltreat children often have certain identifiable experiences, for example, most of them were themselves maltreated as children. Consequently, if we combined our information about these parents with certain psychological test results, we would probably be able to predict with reasonable accuracy which people will maltreat their children.

However, my point is not to argue about the precise reliability of present tests. I cannot say emphatically that we now have accurate predictive tests. Nevertheless, even if such tests are not available, we could undoubtedly develop them. For example, we could begin a longitudinal study in which all potential parents would be required to take a specified battery of tests. Then these parents could be "followed" to discover which ones abused or neglected their children. By correlating test scores with information on maltreatment, a usable, accurate test could be fashioned. Therefore, I do not think that the present unavailability of such tests

(if they are unavailable) would count against the legitimacy of licensing parents.

The third practical objection is that even if a reliable test for ascertaining who would be an acceptable parent were available, administrators would unintentionally misuse that test. These unintentional mistakes would clearly harm innocent individuals. Therefore, so the argument goes, this proposal ought to be scrapped. This objection can be dispensed with fairly easily unless one assumes there is some special reason to believe that more mistakes will be made in administering parenting licenses than in other regulatory activities. No matter how reliable our proceedings are, there will always be mistakes. We may license a physician who, through incompetence, would cause the death of a patient; or we may mistakenly deny a physician's license to someone who would be competent. But the fact that mistakes are made does not and should not lead us to abandon attempts to determine competence. The harm done in these cases could be far worse than the harm of mistakenly denying a person a parenting license. As far as I can tell, there is no reason to believe that more mistakes will be made here than elsewhere.

The fourth proposed practical objection claims that any testing procedure will be intentionally abused. People administering the process will disqualify people they dislike, or people who espouse views they dislike, from rearing children.

The response to this objection is parallel to the response to the previous objection, namely, that there is no reason to believe that the licensing of parents is more likely to be abused than driver's license tests or other regulatory procedures. In addition, individuals can be protected from prejudicial treatment by pursuing appeals available to them. Since the licensing test can be taken on numerous occasions, the likelihood of the applicant's working with different administrative personnel increases and therefore the likelihood decreases that intentional abuse could ultimately stop a qualified person from rearing children. Consequently, since the probability of such abuse is not more than, and may even be less than, the intentional abuse of judicial and other regulatory authority, this objection does

---

8. The research gathered by Altemeir was reported by Ray Helfer in "Review of the Concepts and a Sampling of the Research Relating to Screening for the Potential to Abuse and/or Neglect One's Child." Helfer's paper was presented at a workshop sponsored by the National Committee for the Prevention of Child Abuse, 3–6 December 1978.

not give us any reason to reject the licensing of parents.

The fifth objection is that we could never adequately, reasonably, and fairly enforce such a program. That is, even if we could establish a reasonable and fair way of determining which people would be inadequate parents, it would be difficult, if not impossible, to enforce the program. How would one deal with violators and what could we do with babies so conceived? There are difficult problems here, no doubt, but they are not insurmountable. We might not punish parents at all—we might just remove the children and put them up for adoption. However, even if we are presently uncertain about the precise way to establish a just and effective form of enforcement, I do not see why this should undermine my licensing proposal. If it is important enough to protect children from being maltreated by parents, then surely a reasonable enforcement procedure can be secured. At least we should assume one can be unless someone shows that it cannot.

An Analogy With Adoption

So far I have argued that parents should be licensed. Undoubtedly many readers find this claim extremely radical. It is revealing to notice, however, that this program is not as radical as it seems. Our moral and legal systems already recognize that not everyone is capable of rearing children well. In fact, well-entrenched laws require adoptive parents to be investigated—in much the same ways and for much the same reasons as in the general licensing program advocated here. For example, we do not allow just anyone to adopt a child; nor do we let someone adopt without first estimating the likelihood of the person's being a good parent. In fact, the adoptive process is far more rigorous than the general licensing procedures I envision. Prior to adoption the candidates must first formally apply to adopt a child. The applicants are then subjected to an exacting home study to determine whether they really want to have children and whether they are capable of caring for and rearing them adequately. No one is allowed to adopt a child until the administrators

can reasonably predict that the person will be an adequate parent. The results of these procedures are impressive. Despite the trauma children often face before they are finally adopted, they are five times less likely to be abused than children reared by their biological parents.[9]

Nevertheless we recognize, or should recognize, that these demanding procedures exclude some people who would be adequate parents. The selection criteria may be inadequate; the testing procedures may be somewhat unreliable. We may make mistakes. Probably there is some intentional abuse of the system. Adoption procedures intrude directly in the applicants' lives. Yet we continue the present adoption policies because we think it better to mistakenly deny some people the opportunity to adopt than to let just anyone adopt.

Once these features of our adoption policies are clearly identified, it becomes quite apparent that there are striking parallels between the general licensing program I have advocated and our present adoption system. Both programs have the same aim—protecting children. Both have the same drawbacks and are subject to the same abuses. The only obvious dissimilarity is that the adoption requirements are *more* rigorous than those proposed for the general licensing program. Consequently, if we think it is so important to protect adopted children, even though people who want to adopt are less likely than biological parents to maltreat their children, then we should likewise afford the same pro-

---

9. According to a study published by the Child Welfare League of America, at least 51 percent of the adopted children had suffered, prior to adoption, more than minimal emotional deprivation. See *A Follow-up Study of Adoptions: Post Placement Functioning of Adoption Families,* Elizabeth A. Lawder et al., New York 1969.

According to a study by David Gill (*Violence Against Children,* Cambridge: Harvard University Press, 1970) only .4 percent of abused children were abused by adoptive parents. Since at least 2 percent of the children in the United States are adopted (*Encyclopedia of Social Work,* National Association of Social Workers, New York, 1977), that means the rate of abuse by biological parents is five time[s] that of adoptive parents.

tection to children reared by their biological parents.

I suspect, though, that many people will think the cases are not analogous. The cases are relevantly different, some might retort, because biological parents have a natural affection for their children and the strength of this affection makes it unlikely that parents would maltreat their biologically produced children.

Even if it were generally true that parents have special natural affections for their biological offspring, that does not mean that all parents have enough affection to keep them from maltreating their children. This should be apparent given the number of children abused each year by their biological parents. Therefore, even if there is generally such a bond, that does not explain why we should not have licensing procedures to protect children of parents who do not have a sufficiently strong bond. Consequently, if we continue our practice of regulating the adoption of children, and certainly we should, we are rationally compelled to establish a licensing program for all parents.

However, I am not wedded to a strict form of licensing. It may well be that there are alternative ways of regulating parents which would achieve the desired results—the protection of children—without strictly prohibiting nonlicensed people from rearing children. For example, a system of tax incentives for licensed parents, and protective services scrutiny of nonlicensed parents, might adequately protect children. If it would, I would endorse the less drastic measure. My principal concern is to protect children from maltreatment by parents. I begin by advocating the more strict form of licensing since that is the standard method of regulating hazardous activities.

I have argued that all parents should be licensed by the state. This licensing program is attractive, not because state intrusion is inherently judicious and efficacious, but simply because it seems to be the best way to prevent children from being reared by incompetent parents. Nonetheless, even after considering the previous arguments, many people will find the proposal a useless academic exercise, probably silly, and possibly even morally perverse. But why? Why do most of us find this proposal unpalatable, particularly when the arguments supporting it are good and the objections to it are philosophically flimsy?

I suspect the answer is found in a long-held, deeply ingrained attitude toward children, repeatedly reaffirmed in recent court decisions, and present, at least to some degree, in almost all of us. The belief is that parents own, or at least have natural sovereignty over, their children.[10] It does not matter precisely how this belief is described, since on both views parents legitimately exercise extensive and virtually unlimited control over their children. Others can properly interfere with or criticize parental decisions only in unusual and tightly prescribed circumstances—for example, when parents severely and repeatedly abuse their children. In all other cases, the parents reign supreme.

This belief is abhorrent and needs to be supplanted with a more child-centered view. Why? Briefly put, this attitude has adverse effects on children and on the adults these children will become. Parents who hold this view may well maltreat their children. If these parents happen to treat their children well, it is only because they want to, not because they think their children deserve or have a right to good treatment. Moreover, this belief is manifestly at odds with the conviction that parents

10. We can see this belief in a court case chronicled by DeCourcy and DeCourcy in *A Silent Tragedy.* The judge ruled that three children, severely and regularly beaten, burned, and cut by their father, should be placed back with their father since he was only "trying to do what is right." If the court did not adopt this belief would it even be tempted to so excuse such abusive behavior? This attitude also emerges in the all-too-frequent court rulings (see S. Katz, *When Parents Fail,* Boston: Beacon Press, 1971) giving custody of children back to their biological parents even though the parents had abandoned them for years, and even though the children expressed a strong desire to stay with foster parents.

In "The Child, the Law, and the State" (*Children's Rights: Toward the Liberation of the Child,* Leila Berg et al., New York: Praeger Publishers, 1971), Nan Berger persuasively argues that our adoption and foster care laws are comprehensible only if children are regarded as the property of their parents.

should prepare children for life as adults. Children subject to parents who perceive children in this way are likely to be adequately prepared for adulthood. Hence, to prepare children for life as adults and to protect them from maltreatment, this attitude toward children must be dislodged. As I have argued, licensing is a viable way to protect children. Furthermore, it would increase the likelihood that more children will be adequately prepared for life as adults than is now the case....

Study Questions

1. Should the right to have children be restricted by the state?

2. If having children required a license, how would the state prevent nonlicensed people from having children?

3. Can we protect children in the present family institution?

Moral Dilemmas

- Mary had fallen in love with and married Mike before she finished college. After having two children, she discovers that her husband is having an affair with another woman. He admits to her that he is having an affair but refuses to end the relationship. Mike tells Mary that she can do the same if she wants to. Mary is in her late thirties, has no marketable skills, and is afraid of being on her own. The idea of having affairs and still being married seems like hypocrisy to her. Besides, she is worried about what the children will think.

  What should Mary do?
  Is what Mike doing immoral?

- Mr. and Mrs. Jones are very happy with their year-old child Jason. One day they find that a mistake had been made at the hospital and that they have the wrong child. The other couple is willing to switch. Mr. Jones wants to give Jason back, but Mrs. Jones is not sure.

  What should they do?

- Mr. and Mrs. Brown, both in their thirties, have been together for ten years. They deeply want a child but cannot have one because Mrs. Brown is infertile. Their neighbor, Mrs. Smith, has two healthy children and offers to be a surrogate mother for them for the fee of five thousand dollars plus all the expenses. Mr. and Mrs. Brown are delighted, and Mrs. Smith is artificially inseminated with sperm from Mr. Brown.

  When Mrs. Smith finally gives birth to a healthy baby, she changes her mind and refuses to part with the baby. The Browns remind her of her contract and promise, but Mrs. Smith refuses the five thousand dollars and wants to pay the expenses herself. She feels that to keep the contract is to engage in baby selling, which is immoral. The Browns claim that she should keep her word since they will provide a loving environment for the baby. They believe that the situation is essentially similar to an adoption, which is moral.

Who do you think is right? Why?

- You have been dating someone for two years. Your partner proposes marriage, and you accept. A month later you find out that your fiancé(e) has a life-long, disabling illness.

Would you still want to get married?

Suggested Readings

Abbott, Philip. *The Family on Trial.* University Park, Pa.: Pennsylvania State University Press, 1981.

Bettelheim, Bruno. *The Children of the Dream.* New York: MacMillan, 1969.

Blustein, Jeffrey. *Parents and Children.* Oxford, England: Oxford University Press, 1982.

Fishkin, James S. *Justice, Equal Opportunity and the Family.* New Haven, Conn.: Yale University Press, 1983.

Libby, Roger W., and Robert N. Whitehurst, eds. *Marriage and Alternatives.* London: Scott, Foresman & Co., 1977.

O'Neill, Onora, and William Ruddick, eds. *Having Children.* New York: Oxford University Press, 1979.

Skolnick, Arlene and Jerome eds. *Intimacy, Family and Society.* Boston: Little, Brown & Co., 1974.

Abortion

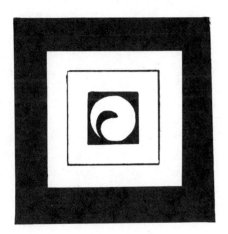

W hat is a person? When does human life begin? Is a fetus a person? What are our duties to other persons? Does a potential person have actual rights? Is it ever right to kill an innocent person? These and other questions are part of the abortion debate. The way one answers these questions will determine how one views the morality of abortion.

Background

Abortion can be defined as the destruction of a fetus, the unborn entity, before natural birth. Abortions can be *spontaneous,* as in miscarriage, when the fetus dies of natural causes and is ejected, or *induced,* i.e., caused by action of the woman or some third party. About ten to twenty percent of all pregnancies result in miscarriages, and about ninety percent of miscarriages occur before the twelfth week of pregnancy, sometimes before the woman realizes that she is pregnant. Induced abortions may be *therapeutic* (to save the life or health of a woman) or *nontherapeutic* (for nonmedical reasons such as rape, incest, or birth control). The development of new medical technology, especially amniocentesis, a prenatal test that can determine whether the fetus will be born genetically deformed, has contributed to the increased number of abortions. Well over a million abortions take place in the United States each year. Of the women who have abortions, approximately two-thirds are unmarried.

Abortion has existed since ancient times and has been practiced primarily as a means of controlling population growth. Early abortion techniques included drinking various potions or receiving sharp blows to the stomach. Sometimes abortion was performed to avoid the embarrassment of a child born out of wedlock or to avoid having a child too soon after marriage. In some primitive cultures, abortion was resorted to by unmarried women to avoid the penalty for fornication, which in some cases was death. However, Hippocrates (c. 460–377 B.C.), the father of modern medicine and author of the oath that all doctors take, believed that abortion was immoral. In the United States, laws against abortion were enacted beginning primarily in the nineteenth century, partly because the procedure was not medically safe at that time. At the beginning of the twentieth century, due to improved medical technology, the rise in world population, the dangers of illegal abortions, and the women's rights movement, abortion became more legally acceptable.

Part of the controversy over abortion has to do with the very gradual development of the fetus. Pregnancy begins at *conception* when a sperm combines with an ovum and the process of biological development begins. At about two months, fetal brain waves become detectable. At about the third month, *quickening* occurs—the point at which the mother begins to feel movements of the fetus. *Viability* usually occurs at seven months, the point at which the fetus can survive outside of the womb with special medical care. At what point do we have a person? At conception, the gene structure is determined for life. Is that when human life begins? Or does it begin at viability or at birth?

Roe v. Wade

The Supreme Court of the United States tried to answer some of these questions. In the famous *Roe v. Wade* (1973) decision, the Court ruled that a woman has a right to an abortion up through the first six months of pregnancy and possibly beyond. Justice Harry A. Blackmun argued for the majority view that there is a right to privacy implied in the Constitution's Bill of Rights. Liberty cannot be protected, according to Blackmun, without a right to privacy that includes rights relating to marriage, procreation, contraception, and child rearing. A woman's decision whether or not to terminate her pregnancy is a private decision protected by the Constitution.

The majority conceded that it could not determine whether the fetus is a person. Nevertheless, the state has a legitimate interest in protecting the potential life of the fetus and the health of the woman. Because modern medical science has progressed to such a degree, an abortion in the first trimester (three months) is safer than childbirth and therefore allowed. During the second trimester, the state has the right to regulate the abortion to protect the health of the woman. In the third trimester, when the fetus reaches viability, individual states may prohibit abortions to protect the potential life of the fetus.

Justice Blackmun and the majority sought to resolve the question of abortion by balancing certain values. They wanted to protect a woman's right to control her own body and her right to privacy, but at the same time they wanted to protect the potential human life of the fetus when it reaches viability. Questions were immediately raised about viability. Clearly, as medical science progresses, the viability of the fetus outside of the womb will be pushed increasingly earlier in the pregnancy. One day artificial wombs may be created; will this mean that abortion will not be allowed?

Justices Byron R. White and William Rehnquist disagreed with the majority in *Roe v. Wade*. The minority argued that to allow a woman to have an abortion for any reason she wishes at the expense of the life of the fetus puts a greater value on a woman's convenience than on a human life. Furthermore, White and Rehnquist argued that no right to privacy exists in the Constitution. They concluded that it would be more democratic for the individual states to decide the issue for themselves rather than to have the Court's view imposed on them.

Conservative Position: John T. Noonan, Jr.

John T. Noonan defends the conservative position on abortion. He believes that the central issue here is whether the fetus is a person. For him, the best theory about the personhood of the fetus is that it is a person from the moment of conception. He believes this theory is supported by the biological fact that the fetus is genetically human (because it has human parents) and that most conceptions (about eighty percent) result in the birth of a person unless an abortion is performed.

Noonan surveys all the other views on when a fetus becomes a person and rejects all as inadequate and inferior to the conception theory. He rejects the viability theory because viability varies with available technology. He rejects the others (experience, the sentiments of adults, sensation by parents, social visibility) as either too narrow or too broad definitions of personhood. If the fetus threatens the life of the woman, then an abortion is justified, based on the *principle of double effect*. This principle is a rule used by Roman Catholics and others to determine when a person may perform an action that has both good and bad consequences. When a pregnancy threatens the life of a woman, the abortion has a good consequence (saving the woman's life) and a bad consequence (the death of the fetus). In such a case, the abortion would be allowed according to this principle because the bad consequence is foreseen but not intended or desired. The principle allows for such *indirect abortions* but strictly forbids *direct abortions*.

Noonan's conservative position has been criticized in many ways. Critics question whether self-defense is the only justification for abortion. More liberal philosophers such as Jane English believe that other, less serious threats can justify abortion, including mental and economic hardships. Noonan also does not seem to allow for abortion in cases of incest or rape. Furthermore, Noonan's view, that the fetus is a person from conception, is not consistent with our cultural practice of dealing with miscarriages, for which no funerals or death certificates are required. What if the fetus is severely deformed and will have a short and painful life? Should it be allowed to come to term?

Liberal Position: Mary Ann Warren

Mary Anne Warren argues that the fetus is not a person with rights, and therefore abortion is moral. According to her, for something to be a person and have rights, it must have at least two characteristics: consciousness and rationality. A fetus has neither of these traits. The fact that the fetus has these potentially is somewhat significant for Warren, but it does not outweigh the actual rights of the woman to have an abortion at any time. She goes so far as to say that even infanticide is not murder, although to practice it would be wrong in most cases because of the value our society places on children and because unwanted infants can be adopted.

Warren's position has been questioned by those who hold a more conservative view. One must ask why Warren believes that a person must have consciousness and rationality in order to have the rights of a person. An Alzheimer's patient may not have rationality. Does that mean that we can kill the person at will? Warren's belief that infanticide is not murder may lead some to argue that her definition of personhood is too narrow and is designed to give the result she wants.

Moderate Position: Jane English

Jane English (1947–1978) believes that the conservative and liberal views are both too extreme and defends the moderate position. She rejects the conservative position that the fetus is a person from conception because she believes that our ideas of what a person is are too unclear. Our language is not precise in the gray outer edges of many basic concepts. Even if the fetus is a person as the conservatives claim, abortion is justified in self-defense and to prevent other kinds of economic and psychological harm, especially in the early stages of pregnancy. Liberals are also wrong when they say that because the fetus is not a person, one can have an abortion for whatever reason and at any time. English points out that animals are not persons, yet we shouldn't kill or torture them without good reason. Corpses are not persons either, yet to mutilate them is wrong. English reminds us that we cannot ignore the fact that our morality is partly based on our capacity for sympathy for others, especially those that resemble persons; hence, the similarity in appearance of the fetus in the later stages to that of a baby is important in deciding the morality of abortion. English concludes that, whether the fetus is a person or not, a woman has a right to an abortion in the early stages of pregnancy even if only to avoid minor harm, whereas a late pregnancy should not be aborted except to avoid severe injury or death to the woman.

Abortion and Morality

The abortion controversy goes to the very heart of the nature of morality. This debate essentially involves two competing values; the freedom of the woman to control her own body and life, and the potential or actual personhood of the fetus. Conservatives argue that human life and personhood start at conception, making abortion murder in all cases except to save the life of the woman. They further contend that the legalization of abortion will lead down the slippery slope to a general decrease in the value of life that might ultimately end up in

the killing of old, senile, disabled, and retarded individuals. If the woman does not want the child, they recommend adoption.

Liberals claim that the right to life of the fetus starts at birth or shortly before. They stress the right of the woman to control her own body and her right to privacy. Liberals also remind us that unwanted and deformed children may have a right not to be born if they cannot be assured a good life. Finally, they disagree that the slippery slope will in fact lead to those consequences that the conservatives mention.

Moderates such as Jane English seek a compromise between the two extreme positions. English balances the opposing values by conceding some points to each side. Regardless of how one chooses to deal with abortion, the central questions of what a person is and what rights persons have recur in virtually every moral debate.

Majority Opinion in *Roe v. Wade*

Harry A. Blackmun was graduated from Harvard Law School. He became Associate Justice of the U.S. Supreme Court in 1970.

Justice Harry A. Blackmun

It is ... apparent that at common law, at the time of the adoption of our Constitution, and throughout the major portion of the 19th century, abortion was viewed with less disfavor than under most American statutes currently in effect. Phrasing it another way, a woman enjoyed a substantially broader right to terminate a pregnancy than she does in most States today. At least with respect to the early stage of pregnancy, and very possibly without such a limita-

tion, the opportunity to make this choice was present in this country well into the 19th century. Even later, the law continued for some time to treat less punitively an abortion procured in early pregnancy....

Three reasons have been advanced to explain historically the enactment of criminal abortion laws in the 19th century and to justify their continued existence.

It has been argued occasionally that these laws were the product of a Victorian social concern to

U.S. Supreme Court, 410 U.S. 113 (1973).

discourage illicit sexual conduct. Texas, however, does not advance this justification in the present case, and it appears that no court or commentator has taken the argument seriously. . . .

A second reason is concerned with abortion as a medical procedure. When most criminal abortion laws were first enacted, the procedure was a hazardous one for the woman. This was particularly true prior to the development of antisepsis. Antiseptic techniques, of course, were based on discoveries by Lister, Pasteur, and others first announced in 1867, but were not generally accepted and employed until about the turn of the century. Abortion mortality was high. Even after 1900, and perhaps until as late as the development of antibiotics in the 1940s, standard modern techniques such as dilatation and curettage were not nearly so safe as they are today. Thus it has been argued that a State's real concern in enacting a criminal abortion law was to protect the pregnant woman, that is, to restrain her from submitting to a procedure that placed her life in serious jeopardy.

Modern medical techniques have altered this situation. Appellants and various *amici* refer to medical data indicating that abortion in early pregnancy, that is, prior to the end of first trimester, although not without its risk, is now relatively safe. Mortality rates for women undergoing early abortions, where the procedure is legal, appear to be as low as or lower than the rates for normal childbirth. Consequently, any interest of the State in protecting the woman from an inherently hazardous procedure, except when it would be equally dangerous for her to forgo it, has largely disappeared. Of course, important state interests in the area of health and medical standards do remain. The State has a legitimate interest in seeing to it that abortion, like any other medical procedure, is performed under circumstances that insure maximum safety for the patient. This interest obviously extends at least to the performing physician and his staff, to the facilities involved, to the availability of after-care, and to adequate provision for any complication or emergency that might arise. The prevalence of high mortality rates at illegal "abortion mills" strengthens, rather than weakens, the State's interest in regulating the conditions under which abortions are performed.

Moreover, the risk to the woman increases as her pregnancy continues. Thus the State retains a definite interest in protecting the woman's own health and safety when an abortion is performed at a late stage of pregnancy.

> *"This right of privacy . . . is broad enough to encompass a woman's decision whether or not to terminate her pregnancy. . . ."*

The third reason is the State's interest—some phrase it in terms of duty—in protecting prenatal life. Some of the argument for this justification rests on the theory that a new human life is present from the moment of conception. The State's interest and general obligation to protect life then extends, it is argued, to prenatal life. Only when the life of the pregnant mother herself is at stake, balanced against the life she carries within her, should the interest of the embryo or fetus not prevail. Logically, of course, a legitimate state interest in this area need not stand or fall on acceptance of the belief that life begins at conception or at some other point prior to live birth. In assessing the State's interest, recognition may be given to the less rigid claim that as long as at least *potential* life is involved, the State may assert interests beyond the protection of the pregnant woman alone.

Parties challenging state abortion laws have sharply disputed in some courts the contention that a purpose of these laws, when enacted, was to protect prenatal life. Pointing to the absence of legislative history to support the contention, they claim that most state laws were designed solely to protect the woman. Because medical advances have lessened this concern, at least with respect to abortion in early pregnancy, they argue that with respect to such abortions the laws can no longer be justified by any state interest. There is some scholarly support for this view of original purpose. The few state courts called upon to interpret their laws in the late 19th and early 20th centuries did focus on the State's interest in protecting the woman's health rather than in preserving the embryo and fetus....

The Constitution does not explicitly mention any right of privacy. In a line of decisions, however, going back perhaps as far as *Union Pacific R. Co. v. Botsford* (1891), the Court has recognized that a right of personal privacy, or a guarantee of certain areas or zones of privacy, does exist under the Constitution. In varying contexts the Court or individual Justices have indeed found at least the roots of that right in the First Amendment, ... in the Fourth and Fifth Amendments ... in the penumbras of the Bill of Rights ... in the Ninth Amendment ... or in the concept of liberty guaranteed by the first section of the Fourteenth Amendment.... These decisions make it clear that only personal rights that can be deemed "fundamental" or "implicit in the concept of ordered liberty," ... are included in this guarantee of personal privacy. They also make it clear that the right has some extension to activities relating to marriage, ... procreation, ... contraception, ... family relationships, ... and child rearing and education....

This right of privacy, whether it be founded in the Fourteenth Amendment's concept of personal liberty and restrictions upon state action, as we feel it is, or, as the District Court determined, in the Ninth Amendment's reservation of rights to the people, is broad enough to encompass a woman's decision whether or not to terminate her pregnancy....

... [A]ppellants and some *amici* argue that the woman's right is absolute and that she is entitled to terminate her pregnancy at whatever time, in whatever way, and for whatever reason she alone chooses. With this we do not agree. Appellants' arguments that Texas either has no valid interest at all in regulating the abortion decision, or no interest strong enough to support any limitation upon the woman's sole determination, is unpersuasive. The Court's decisions recognizing a right of privacy also acknowledge that some state regulation in areas

protected by that right is appropriate. As noted above, a state may properly assert important interests in safe-guarding health, in maintaining medical standards, and in protecting potential life. At some point in pregnancy, these respective interests become sufficiently compelling to sustain regulation of the factors that govern the abortion decision. The privacy right involved, therefore, cannot be said to be absolute....

We therefore conclude that the right of personal privacy includes the abortion decision, but that this right is not unqualified and must be considered against important state interests in regulation.

We note that those federal and state courts that have recently considered abortion law challenges have reached the same conclusion....

Although the results are divided, most of these courts have agreed that the right of privacy, however based, is broad enough to cover the abortion decision; that the right, nonetheless, is not absolute and is subject to some limitations; and that at some point the state interests as to protection of health, medical standards, and prenatal life, become dominant. We agree with this approach....

The appellee and certain *amici* argue that the fetus is a "person" within the language and meaning of the Fourteenth Amendment. In support of this they outline at length and in detail the well-known facts of fetal development. If this suggestion of personhood is established, the appellant's case, of course, collapses, for the fetus' right to life is then guaranteed specifically by the Amendment. The appellant conceded as much on reargument. On the other hand, the appellee conceded on reargument that no case could be cited that holds that a fetus is a person within the meaning of the Fourteenth Amendment....

All this, together with our observation, *supra,* that throughout the major portion of the 19th century prevailing legal abortion practices were far freer than they are today, persuades us that the word "person," as used in the Fourteenth Amendment, does not include the unborn.... Indeed, our decision in *United States v. Vuitch* (1971) inferentially is to the same effect, for we there would not have indulged in statutory interpretation favorable to abortion in specified circumstances if the necessary consequence was the termination of life entitled to Fourteenth Amendment protection.

... As we have intimated above, it is reasonable and appropriate for a State to decide that at some point in time another interest, that of health of the mother or that of potential human life, becomes significantly involved. The woman's privacy is no longer sole and any right of privacy she possesses must be measured accordingly.

Texas urges that, apart from the Fourteenth Amendment, life begins at conception and is present throughout pregnancy, and that, therefore, the State has a compelling interest in protecting that life from and after conception. We need not resolve the difficult question of when life begins. When those trained in the respective disciplines of medicine, philosophy, and theology are unable to arrive at any consensus, the judiciary, at this point in the development of man's knowledge, is not in a position to speculate as to the answer.

It should be sufficient to note briefly the wide divergence of thinking on this most sensitive and difficult question. There has always been strong support for the view that life does not begin until live birth. This was the belief of the Stoics. It appears to be the predominant, though not the unanimous, attitude of the Jewish faith. It may be taken to represent also the position of a large segment of the Protestant community, insofar as that can be ascertained; organized groups that have taken a formal position on the abortion issue have generally regarded abortion as a matter for the conscience of the individual and her family. As we have noted, the common law found greater significance in quickening. Physicians and their scientific colleagues have regarded that event with less interest and have tended to focus either upon conception or upon live birth or upon the interim point at which the fetus becomes "viable," that is, potentially able to live outside the mother's womb, albeit with artificial aid. Viability is usually placed at about seven months (28 weeks) but may occur earlier, even at 24 weeks....

In areas other than criminal abortion the law has been reluctant to endorse any theory that life, as we recognize it, begins before live birth or to accord legal rights to the unborn except in narrowly defined situations and except when the rights are contingent upon live birth.... In short, the unborn have never been recognized in the law as persons in the whole sense.

In view of all this, we do not agree that, by adopting one theory of life, Texas may override the rights of the pregnant woman that are at stake. We repeat, however, that the State does have an important and legitimate interest in preserving and protecting the health of the pregnant woman, whether she be a resident of the State or a nonresident who seeks medical consultation and treatment there, and that it has still *another* important and legitimate interest in protecting the potentiality of human life. These interests are separate and distinct. Each grows in substantiality as the woman approaches term and, at a point during pregnancy, each becomes "compelling."

With respect to the State's important and legitimate interest in the health of the mother, the "compelling" point, in the light of present medical knowledge, is at approximately the end of the first trimester. This is so because of the now established medical fact ... that until the end of the first trimester mortality in abortion is less than mortality in normal childbirth. It follows that, from and after this point, a State may regulate the abortion procedure to the extent that the regulation reasonably relates to the preservation and protection of maternal health. Examples of permissible state regulation in this area are requirements as to the qualifications of the person who is to perform the abortion; as to the licensure of that person; as to the facility in which the procedure is to be performed, that is, whether it must be a hospital or may be a clinic or some other place of less-than-hospital status; as to the licensing of the facility; and the like.

This means, on the other hand, that, for the period of pregnancy prior to this "compelling" point, the attending physician, in consultation with his patient, is free to determine, without regulation by the State, that in his medical judgment the patient's pregnancy should be terminated. If that decision is reached, the judgment may be effectuated by an abortion free of interference by the State.

With respect to the State's important and legitimate interest in potential life, the "compelling" point is at viability. This is so because the fetus then presumably has the capability of meaningful life outside the mother's womb. State regulation protective of fetal life after viability thus has both logical and biological justifications. If the State is interested in protecting fetal life after viability, it may go so far as to proscribe abortion during that period except when it is necessary to preserve the life or health of the mother....

To summarize and repeat:

1. A state criminal abortion statute for the current Texas type, that excepts from criminality only a *life saving* procedure on behalf of the mother, without regard to pregnancy stage and without recognition of the other interests involved, is violative of the Due Process Clause of the Fourteenth Amendment.

(a) For the stage prior to approximately the end of the first trimester, the abortion decision and its effectuation must be left to the medical judgment of the pregnant woman's attending physician.

(b) For the stage subsequent to approximately the end of the first trimester, the State, in promoting its interest in the health of the mother, may, if it chooses, regulate the abortion procedure in ways that are reasonably related to maternal health.

(c) For the stage subsequent to viability the State, in promoting its interest in the potentiality of human life, may, if it chooses, regulate, and even proscribe, abortion except where it is necessary, in appropriate medical judgment, for the preservation of the life or health of the mother.

2. The State may define the term "physician," as it has been employed [here], to mean only a physician currently licensed by the State, and may proscribe any abortion by a person who is not a physician as so defined.

... The decision leaves the State free to place increasing restrictions on abortion as the period of pregnancy lengthens, so long as those restrictions are tailored to the recognized state interests. The decision vindicates the right of the physician to administer medical treatment according to his professional judgment up to the points where important state interests provide compelling justifications for intervention. Up to those points the abortion decision in all its aspects is inherently, and primarily, a medical decision, and basic responsibility for it must rest with the physician. If an individual practitioner abuses the privilege of exercising proper medical judgment, the usual remedies, judicial and intraprofessional, are available....

Study Questions

1. Is viability a good point at which to protect potential life? Do potential persons have actual rights?

2. Do persons have a right to privacy? If so, how is it justified?

3. Has the legalization of abortion caused a general loss of respect for the value of human life?

Dissenting Opinion in *Roe v. Wade*

A graduate of Yale Law School, Byron R. White became Associate Justice of the U.S. Supreme Court in 1962.

Justice Byron R. White

At the heart of the controversy in these cases are those recurring pregnancies that pose no danger whatsoever to the life or health of the mother but are nevertheless unwanted for any one or more of a variety of reasons—convenience, family planning, economics, dislike of children, the embarrassment of illegitimacy, etc. The common claim before us is that for any one of such reasons, or for no reason at all, and without asserting or claiming any threat to life or health, any woman is entitled to an abortion at her request if she is able to find a medical advisor willing to undertake the procedure.

The Court for the most part sustains this position: During the period prior to the time the fetus becomes viable, the Constitution of the United States values the convenience, whim or caprice of the putative mother more than the life or potential life of the fetus; the Constitution, therefore, guarantees the right to an abortion as against any state law or policy seeking to protect the fetus from an abortion not prompted by more compelling reasons of the mother.

With all due respect, I dissent. I find nothing in the language or history of the Constitution to support the Court's judgment. The Court simply fashions and announces a new constitutional right for pregnant mothers and, with scarcely any reason or authority for its action, invests that right with sufficient substance to override most existing state abortion statutes. The upshot is that the people and the

U.S. Supreme Court, 410 U.S. 113 (1973).

legislatures of the 50 States are constitutionally disentitled to weigh the relative importance of the continued existence and development of the fetus on the one hand against a spectrum of possible impacts on the mother on the other hand. As an exercise of raw judicial power, the Court perhaps has authority to do what it does today; but in my view its judgment is an improvident and extravagant exercise of the power of judicial review which the Constitution extends to this Court.

The Court apparently values the convenience of the pregnant mother more than the continued existence and development of the life or potential life which she carries. Whether or not I might agree with that marshalling of values, I can in no event join the Court's judgment because I find no constitutional warrant for imposing such an order of priorities on the people and legislatures of the States. In a sensitive area such as this, involving as it does issues over which reasonable men may easily and heatedly differ, I cannot accept the Court's exercise of its clear power of choice by interposing a constitutional barrier to state efforts to protect human life and by investing mothers and doctors with the constitutionally protected right to exterminate it. This issue, for the most part, should be left with the people and to the political processes the people have devised to govern their affairs.

It is my view, therefore, that the Texas statute is not constitutionally infirm because it denies abortions to those who seek to serve only their convenience rather than to protect their life or health....

1. Was the Court wrong in deciding the abortion question? If so, who should decide?

2. Did the majority prefer the rights of the woman over those of the fetus? If so, is this right?

An Almost Absolute Value in History

A Roman Catholic, John T. Noonan, Jr. is a professor of law at the University of California, Berkeley.

John T. Noonan, Jr.

The most fundamental question involved in the long history of thought on abortion is: How do you determine the humanity of a being? To phrase the question that way is to put in comprehensive humanistic terms what the theologians either dealt with as an explicitly theological question under the heading of "ensoulment" or dealt with implicitly in their treatment of abortion. The Christian position as it originated did not depend on a narrow theological or philosophical concept. It had no relation to theories of infant baptism. It appealed to no special theory of instantaneous ensoulment. It took the world's view on ensoulment as that view changed from Aristotle to Zacchia. There was, indeed, theological influence affecting the theory of ensoulment finally adopted, and, of course, ensoulment itself was a theological concept, so that the position was always explained in theological terms. But the theo-logical notion of ensoulment could easily be translated into humanistic language by substituting "human" for "rational soul"; the problem of knowing when a man is a man is common to theology and humanism.

If one steps outside the specific categories used by the theologians, the answer they gave can be analyzed as a refusal to discriminate among human beings on the basis of their varying potentialities. Once conceived, the being was recognized as man because he had man's potential. The criterion for humanity, thus, was simple and all-embracing: if you are conceived by human parents, you are human.

The strength of this position may be tested by a review of some of the other distinctions offered in the contemporary controversy over legalizing abortion. Perhaps the most popular distinction is in terms of viability. Before an age of so many months, the fetus is not viable, that is, it cannot be removed from the mother's womb and live apart from her. To that extent, the life of the fetus is absolutely dependent on the life of the mother. This dependence is made the basis of denying recognition to its humanity.

There are difficulties with this distinction. One is that the perfection of artificial incubation may make the fetus viable at any time: it may be removed and artificially sustained. Experiments with animals already show that such a procedure is possible. This hypothetical extreme case relates to an actual difficulty: there is considerable elasticity to the idea of viability. Mere length of life is not an exact measure. The viability of the fetus depends on the extent of its anatomical and functional development. The weight and length of the fetus are better guides to the state of its development than age, but weight and length vary. Moreover, different racial groups have different ages at which their fetuses are viable. Some evidence, for example, suggests that Negro fetuses mature more quickly than white fetuses. If viability is the norm, the standard would vary with race and with many individual circumstances.

The most important objection to this approach is that dependence is not ended by viability. The fetus is still absolutely dependent on someone's care in order to continue existence; indeed a child of one or three or even five years of age is absolutely dependent on another's care for existence; uncared for, the older fetus or the younger child will die as surely as the early fetus detached from the mother. The unsubstantial lessening in dependence at viability does not seem to signify any special acquisition of humanity.

A second distinction has been attempted in terms of experience. A being who has had experience, has lived and suffered, who possesses memories, is more human than one who has not. Humanity depends on formation by experience. The fetus is thus "unformed" in the most basic human sense.

This distinction is not serviceable for the embryo which is already experiencing and reacting. The embryo is responsive to touch after eight weeks and at least at that point is experiencing. At an earlier stage the zygote is certainly alive and responding to its environment. The distinction may also be challenged by the rare case where aphasia has erased adult memory: has it erased humanity? More fundamentally, this distinction leaves even the older fetus or the younger child to be treated as an unformed inhuman thing. Finally, it is not clear why experience as such confers humanity. It could be argued that certain central experiences such as loving or

learning are necessary to make a man human. But then human beings who have failed to love or to learn might be excluded from the class called man.

A third distinction is made by appeal to the sentiments of adults. If a fetus dies, the grief of the parents is not the grief they would have for a living child. The fetus is an unnamed "it" till birth, and is not perceived as personality until at least the fourth month of existence when movements in the womb manifest a vigorous presence demanding joyful recognition by the parents.

"A being with a human genetic code is man."

Yet feeling is notoriously an unsure guide to the humanity of others. Many groups of humans have had difficulty in feeling that persons of another tongue, color, religion, sex, are as human as they. Apart from reactions to alien groups, we mourn the loss of a ten-year-old boy more than the loss of his one-day-old brother or his 90-year-old grandfather. The difference felt and the grief expressed vary with the potentialities extinguished, or the experience wiped out; they do not seem to point to any substantial difference in the humanity of baby, boy, or grandfather.

Distinctions are also made in terms of sensation by the parents. The embryo is felt within the womb only after about the fourth month. The embryo is seen only at birth. What can be neither seen nor felt is different from what is tangible. If the fetus cannot be seen or touched at all, it cannot be perceived as man.

Yet experience shows that sight is even more untrustworthy than feeling in determining humanity. By sight, color became an appropriate index for saying who was a man, and the evil of racial discrimination was given foundation. Nor can touch provide the test; a being confined by sickness, "out of touch" with others, does not thereby seem to lose his humanity. To the extent that touch still has appeal as a criterion, it appears to be a survival of the old English idea of "quickening"—a possible mistranslation of the Latin *animatus* used in the canon law. To that extent touch as a criterion seems to be dependent on the Aristotelian notion of ensoulment, and to fall when this notion is discarded.

Finally, a distinction is sought in social visibility. The fetus is not socially perceived as human. It cannot communicate with others. Thus, both subjectively and objectively, it is not a member of society. As moral rules are rules for the behavior of members of society to each other, they cannot be made for behavior toward what is not yet a member. Excluded from the society of men, the fetus is excluded from the humanity of men.

By force of the argument from the consequences, this distinction is to be rejected. It is more subtle than that founded on an appeal to physical sensation, but it is equally dangerous in its implications. If humanity depends on social recognition, individuals or whole groups may be dehumanized by being denied any status in their society. Such a fate is fictionally portrayed in *1984* and has actually been the lot of many men in many societies. In the Roman empire, for example, condemnation to slavery meant the practical denial of most human rights; in the Chinese Communist world, landlords have been classified as enemies of the people and so treated as nonpersons by the state. Humanity does not depend on social recognition, though often the failure of society to recognize the prisoner, the alien, the heterodox as human has led to the destruction of human beings. Anyone conceived by a man and a woman is human. Recognition of this condition by society follows a real event in the objective order, however imperfect and halting the recognition. Any attempt to limit humanity to exclude some group runs the risk of furnishing authority and precedent for excluding other groups in the name of the consciousness or perception of the controlling group in the society.

A philosopher may reject the appeal to the humanity of the fetus because he views "humanity" as a secular view of the soul and because he doubts the existence of anything real and objective which can be identified as humanity. One answer to such a philosopher is to ask how he reasons about moral questions without supposing that there is a sense in which he and the others of whom he speaks are

human. Whatever group is taken as the society which determines who may be killed is thereby taken as human. A second answer is to ask if he does not believe that there is a right and wrong way of deciding moral questions. If there is such a difference, experience may be appealed to: to decide who is human on the basis of the sentiment of a given society has led to consequences which rational men would characterize as monstrous.

The rejection of the attempted distinctions based on viability and visibility, experience and feeling, may be buttressed by the following considerations: Moral judgments often rest on distinctions, but if the distinctions are not to appear arbitrary fiat, they should relate to some real difference in probabilities. There is a kind of continuity in all life, but the earlier stages of the elements of human life possess tiny probabilities of development. Consider for example, the spermatozoa in any normal ejaculate: There are about 200,000,000 in any single ejaculate, of which one has a chance of developing into a zygote. Consider the oocytes which may become ova: there are 100,0000 to 1,000,000 oocytes in a female infant, of which a maximum of 390 are ovulated. But once spermatozoon and ovum meet and the conceptus is formed, such studies as have been made show that roughly in only 20 percent of the cases will spontaneous abortion occur. In other words, the chances are about 4 out of 5 that this new being will develop. At this stage in the life of the being there is a sharp shift in probabilities, an immense jump in potentialities. To make a distinction between the rights of spermatozoa and the rights of the fertilized ovum is to respond to an enormous shift in possibilities. For about twenty days after conception the egg may split to form twins or combine with another egg to form a chimera, but the probability of either event happening is very small.

It may be asked, What does a change in biological probabilities have to do with establishing humanity? The argument from probabilities is not aimed at establishing humanity but at establishing an objective discontinuity which may be taken into account in moral discourse. As life itself is a matter of probabilities, as most moral reasoning is an estimate of probabilities, so it seems in accord with the structure of reality and the nature of moral thought to found a moral judgment on the change in probabilities at conception. The appeal to probabilities is the most commonsensical of arguments, to a greater or smaller degree all of us base our actions on probabilities, and in morals, as in law, prudence and negligence are often measured by the account one has taken of the probabilities. If the chance is 200,000,000 to 1 that the movement in the bushes into which you shoot is a man's, I doubt if many persons would hold you careless in shooting; but if the chances are 4 out of 5 that the movement is a human being's, few would acquit you of blame. Would the argument be different if only one out of ten children conceived came to term? Of course this argument would be different. This argument is an appeal to probabilities that actually exist, not to any and all states of affairs which may be imagined.

The probabilities as they do exist do not show the humanity of the embryo in the sense of a demonstration in logic any more than the probabilities of the movement in the bush being a man demonstrate beyond all doubt that the being is a man. The appeal is a "buttressing" consideration, showing the plausibility of the standard adopted. The argument focuses on the decisional factor in any moral judgment and assumes that part of the business of a moralist is drawing lines. One evidence of the nonarbitrary character of the line drawn is the difference of probabilities on either side of it. If a spermatozoon is destroyed, one destroys a being which had a chance of far less than 1 in 200 million of developing into a reasoning being, possessed of the genetic code, a heart and other organs, and capable of pain. If a fetus is destroyed, one destroys a being already possessed of the genetic code, organs, and sensitivity to pain, and one which had an 80 percent chance of developing further into a baby outside the womb who, in time, would reason.

The positive argument for conception as the decisive moment of humanization is that at conception the new being receives the genetic code. It is this genetic information which determines his characteristics, which is the biological carrier of the possibility of human wisdom, which makes him a self-evolving being. A being with a human genetic code is man.

This review of current controversy over the humanity of the fetus emphasizes what a fundamental question the theologians resolved in asserting the inviolability of the fetus. To regard the fetus as possessed of equal rights with other humans was not, however, to decide every case where abortion might be employed. It did decide the case where the argument was that the fetus should be aborted for its own good. To say a being was human was to say it had a destiny to decide for itself which could not be taken from it by another man's decision. But human beings with equal rights often come in conflict with each other, and some decision must be made as whose claims are to prevail. Cases of conflict involving the fetus are different only in two respects: the total inability of the fetus to speak for itself and the fact that the right of the fetus regularly at stake is the right to life itself.

The approach taken by the theologians to these conflicts was articulated in terms of "direct" and "indirect." Again, to look at what they were doing from outside their categories, they may be said to have been drawing lines or "balancing values." "Direct" and "indirect" are spatial metaphors; "line-drawing" is another. "To weigh" or "to balance" values is a metaphor of a more complicated mathematical sort hinting at the process which goes on in moral judgments. All the metaphors suggest that, in the moral judgments made, comparisons were necessary, that no value completely controlled. The principle of double effect was no doctrine fallen from heaven, but a method of analysis appropriate where two relative values were being compared. In Catholic moral theology, as it developed, life even of the innocent was not taken as an absolute. Judgments on acts affecting life issued from a process of weighing. In the weighing, the fetus was always given a value greater than zero, always a value separate and independent from its parents. This valuation was crucial and fundamental in all Christian thought on the subject and marked it off from any approach which considered that only the parents' interests needed to be considered.

Even with the fetus weighed as human, one interest could be weighed as equal or superior: that of the mother in her own life. The casuists between 1450 and 1895 were willing to weigh this interest as superior. Since 1895, that interest was given decisive weight only in the two special cases of the cancerous uterus and the ectopic pregnancy. In both of these cases the fetus itself had little chance of survival even if the abortion were not performed. As the balance was once struck in favor of the mother whenever her life was endangered, it could be so struck again. The balance reached between 1895 and 1930 attempted prudentially and pastorally to forestall a multitude of exceptions for interests less than life.

The perception of the humanity of the fetus and the weighing of fetal rights against other human rights constituted the work of the moral analysts. But what spirit animated their abstract judgments? For the Christian community it was the injunction of Scripture to love your neighbor as yourself. The fetus as human was a neighbor; his life had parity with one's own. The commandment gave life to what otherwise would have been only rational calculation.

The commandment could be put in humanistic as well as theological terms: Do not injure your fellow man without reason. In these terms, once the humanity of the fetus is perceived, abortion is never right except in self-defense. When life must be taken to save life, reason alone cannot say that a mother must prefer a child's life to her own. With this exception, now of great rarity, abortion violates the rational humanist tenet of the equality of human lives.

For Christians the commandment to love had received a special imprint in that the exemplar proposed of love was the love of the Lord for his disciples. In the light given by this example, self-sacrifice carried to the point of death seemed in the extreme situations not without meaning. In the less extreme cases, preference for one's own interests to the life of another seemed to express cruelty or selfishness irreconcilable with the demands of love.

Study Questions

1. What would Noonan say about someone who became pregnant through rape or incest and wanted an abortion?

2. If the fetus is a person from conception, why is there no funeral (birth certificate, or name) for a miscarriage?

On the Moral and Legal Status of Abortion

Mary Anne Warren is a feminist and a professor of philosophy at San Francisco State University.

Mary Anne Warren

The question which we must answer in order to produce a satisfactory solution to the problem of the moral status of abortion is this: How are we to define the moral community, the set of beings with

Reprinted by permission of *The Monist*, vol. 57, no. 1 (January 1973). "Postscript on Infanticide" reprinted with permission of the author from Richard Wasserstrom, ed., *Today's Moral Problems* (New York: Macmillan Publishing Co., 1975).

full and equal moral rights, such that we can decide whether a human fetus is a member of this community or not? What sort of entity, exactly, has the inalienable rights to life, liberty, and the pursuit of happiness? Jefferson attributed these rights to all *men,* and it may or may not be fair to suggest that he intended to attribute them *only* to men. Perhaps he ought to have attributed them to all human beings. If so, then we arrive, first, at Noonan's problem of defining what makes a being human, and, second, at the equally vital question which Noonan does not consider, namely, What reason is there for identifying the moral community with the set of all human beings, in whatever way we have chosen to define that term?

1. On the Definition of "Human"

One reason why this vital second question is so frequently overlooked in the debate over the moral status of abortion is that the term "human" has two distinct, but not often distinguished, senses. This fact results in a slide of meaning, which serves to conceal the fallaciousness of the traditional argument that since (1) it is wrong to kill innocent human beings, and (2) fetuses are innocent human beings, then (3) it is wrong to kill fetuses. For if "human" is used in the same sense in both (1) and (2) then, whichever of the two senses is meant, one of these premises is question-begging. And if it is used in two different senses then of course the conclusion doesn't follow.

Thus, (1) is a self-evident moral truth,[1] and avoids begging the question about abortion, only if "human being" is used to mean something like "a full-fledged member of the moral community." (It may or may not also be meant to refer exclusively to members of the species *Homo sapiens.*) We may call this the *moral* sense of "human." It is not to be confused with what we will call the *genetic* sense, i.e., the sense in which *any* member of the species is a human being, and no member of any other

species could be. If (1) is acceptable only if the moral sense is intended, (2) is non-question-begging only if what is intended is the genetic sense.

In "Deciding Who Is Human," Noonan argues for the classification of fetuses with human beings by pointing to the presence of the full genetic code, and the potential capacity for rational thought.[2] It is clear that what he needs to show, for his version of the traditional argument to be valid, is that fetuses are human in the moral sense, the sense in which it is analytically true that all human beings have full moral rights. But, in the absence of any argument showing that whatever is genetically human is also morally human, and he gives none, nothing more than genetic humanity can be demonstrated by the presence of the human genetic code. And, as we will see, the *potential* capacity for rational thought can at most show that an entity has the potential for *becoming* human in the moral sense.

2. Defining the Moral Community

Can it be established that genetic humanity is sufficient for moral humanity? I think that there are very good reasons for not defining the moral community in this way. I would like to suggest an alternative way of defining the moral community, which I will argue for only to the extent of explaining why it is, or should be, self-evident. The suggestion is simply that the moral community consists of all and only *people,* rather than all and only human beings;[3] and probably the best way of demonstrating its self-evidence is by considering the concept of personhood, to see what sorts of entity are and are not persons, and what the decision that a being is or is not a person implies about its moral rights.

What characteristics entitle an entity to be considered a person? This is obviously not the place to attempt a complete analysis of the concept of personhood, but we do not need such a fully adequate

---

1. Of course, the principle that it is (always) wrong to kill innocent human beings is in need of many other modifications, e.g., that it may be permissible to do so to save a greater number of other innocent human beings, but we may safely ignore these complications here.

2. John Noonan, "Deciding Who is Human," *Natural Law Forum,* 13 (1968), 135.

3. From here on, we will use "human" to mean genetically human, since the moral sense seems closely connected to, and perhaps derived from, the assumption that genetic humanity is sufficient for membership in the moral community.

analysis just to determine whether and why a fetus is or isn't a person. All we need is a rough and approximate list of the most basic criteria of personhood, and some idea of which, or how many, of these an entity must satisfy in order to properly be considered a person.

In searching for such criteria, it is useful to look beyond the set of people with whom we are acquainted, and ask how we would decide whether a totally alien being was a person or not. (For we have not right to assume that genetic humanity is necessary for personhood.) Imagine a space traveler who lands on an unknown planet and encounters a race of beings utterly unlike any he has ever seen or heard of. If he wants to be sure of behaving morally toward these beings, he has to somehow decide whether they are people, and hence have full moral rights, or whether they are the sort of thing which he need not feel guilty about treating as, for example, a source of food.

How should he go about making this decision? If he has some anthropological background, he might look for such things as religion, art, and the manufacturing of tools, weapons, or shelters, since these factors have been used to distinguish our human from our prehuman ancestors, in what seems to be closer to the moral than the genetic sense of "human." And no doubt he would be right to consider the presence of such factors as good evidence that the alien beings were people, and morally human. It would, however, be overly anthropocentric of him to take the absence of these things as adequate evidence that they were not, since we can imagine people who have progressed beyond, or evolved without ever developing, these cultural characteristics.

I suggest that the traits which are most central to the concept of personhood, or humanity in the moral sense, are, very roughly, the following:

1. consciousness (of objects and events external and/or internal to the being), and in particular the capacity to feel pain;
2. reasoning (the *developed* capacity to solve new and relatively complex problems);
3. self-motivated activity (activity which is relatively independent of either genetic or direct external control);

4. the capacity to communicate, by whatever means, messages of an indefinite variety of types, that is, not just with an indefinite number of possible contents, but on indefinitely many possible topics;
5. the presence of self-concepts, and self-awareness, either individual or racial, or both.

Admittedly, there are apt to be a great many problems involved in formulating precise definitions of these criteria, let alone in developing universally valid behavioral criteria for deciding when they apply. But I will assume that both we and our explorer know approximately what (1)–(5) mean, and that he is also able to determine whether or not they apply. How, then, should he use his findings to decide whether or not the alien beings are people? We needn't suppose that an entity must have *all* of these attributes to be properly considered a person; (1) and (2) alone may well be sufficient for personhood, and quite probably (1)–(3) are sufficient. Neither do we need to insist that any one of these criteria is *necessary* for personhood, although once again (1) and (2) look like fairly good candidates for necessary conditions, as does (3), if "activity" is construed so as to include the activity of reasoning.

All we need to claim, to demonstrate that a fetus is not a person, is that any being which satisfies *none* of (1)–(5) is certainly not a person. I consider this claim to be so obvious that I think anyone who denied it, and claimed that a being which satisfied none of (1)–(5) was a person all the same, would thereby demonstrate that he had no notion at all of what a person is—perhaps because he had confused the concept of a person with that of genetic humanity. If the opponents of abortion were to deny the appropriateness of these five criteria, I do not know what further arguments would convince them. We would probably have to admit that our conceptional schemes were indeed irreconcilably different, and that our dispute could not be settled objectively.

I do not expect this to happen, however, since I think that the concept of a person is one which is very nearly universal (to people), and that it is common to both proabortionists and antiabortionists, even though neither group has fully realized the relevance of this concept to the resolution of their dispute. Furthermore, I think that on reflection even the antiabortionists ought to agree not only that (1)–(5) are central to the concept of personhood, but also that it is a part of this concept that all and only people have full moral rights. The concept of a person is in part a moral concept; once we have admitted that *x* is a person we have recognized, even if we have not agreed to respect, *x*'s right to be treated as a member of the moral community. It is true that the claim that *x* is a *human being* is more commonly voiced as part of an appeal to treat *x* decently than is the claim that *x* is a person, but this is either because "human being" is here used in the sense which implies personhood, or because the genetic and moral senses of "human" have been confused.

Now if (1)–(5) are indeed the primary criteria of personhood, then it is clear that genetic humanity is neither necessary nor sufficient for establishing that an entity is a person. Some human beings are not people, and there may well be people who are not human beings. A man or woman whose consciousness has been permanently obliterated but who remains alive is a human being which is no longer a person; defective human beings, with no appreciable mental capacity, are not and presumably never will be people; and a fetus is a human being which is not yet a person, and which therefore cannot coherently be said to have full moral rights. Citizens of the next century should be prepared to recognize highly advanced, self-aware robots or computers, should such be developed, and intelligent inhabitants of other worlds, should such be found, as people in the fullest sense, and to respect their moral rights. But to ascribe full moral rights to an entity which is not a person is as absurd as to ascribe moral obligations and responsibilities to such an entity.

3. Fetal Development and The Right to Life

Two problems arise in the application of these suggestions for the definition of the moral community to the determination of the precise moral status of a human fetus. Given that the paradigm example of a person is a normal adult human being, then (1) How like this paradigm, in particular how far advanced since conception, does a human being need to be before it begins to have a right to life by virtue, not of being fully a person as of yet, but of being *like* a person? and (2) To what extent, if any, does the fact that a fetus has the *potential* for becoming a person endow it with some of the same rights? Each of these questions requires some comment.

"... [I]nfanticide is wrong for reasons analogous to those which make it wrong to wantonly destroy natural resources, or great works of art."

In answering the first question, we need not attempt a detailed consideration of the moral rights of organisms which are not developed enough, aware enough, intelligent enough, etc., to be considered people, but which resemble people in some respects. It does seem reasonable to suggest that the more like a person, in the relevant respects, a being is, the stronger is the case for regarding it as having a right to life, and indeed the stronger its right to life is. Thus we ought to take seriously the suggestion that, insofar as "the human individual develops biologically in a continuous fashion ... the rights of a human person might develop in the same way."[4] But we must keep in mind that the attributes which are relevant in determining whether or not an entity is enough like a person to be regarded as having some of the same moral rights are

---

4. Thomas L. Hayes, "A Biological View," *Commonweal*, 85 (March 17, 1967), 677–78; quoted by Daniel Callahan, in *Abortion: Law, Choice and Morality* (London: Macmillan & Co., 1970).

no different from those which are relevant to determining whether or not it is fully a person—i.e., are no different from (1)–(5)—and that being genetically human, or having recognizably human facial and other physical features, or detectable brain activity, or the capacity to survive outside the uterus, are simply not among these relevant attributes.

Thus it is clear that even though a seven- or eight-month fetus has features which make it apt to arouse in us almost the same powerful protective instinct as is commonly aroused by a small infant, nevertheless it is not significantly more personlike than is a very small embryo. It is *somewhat* more personlike; it can apparently feel and respond to pain, and it may even have a rudimentary form of consciousness, insofar as its brain is quite active. Nevertheless, it seems safe to say that it is not fully conscious, in the way that an infant of a few months is, and that it cannot reason, or communicate messages of indefinitely many sorts, does not engage in self-motivated activity, and has no self-awareness. Thus, in the *relevant* respects, a fetus, even a fully developed one, is considerably less personlike than is the average mature mammal, indeed the average fish. And I think that a rational person must conclude that if the right to life of a fetus is to be based upon its resemblance to a person, then it cannot be said to have any more right to life than, let us say, a newborn guppy (which also seems to be capable of feeling pain), and that a right of that magnitude could never override a woman's right to obtain an abortion, at any stage of her pregnancy.

There may, of course, be other arguments in favor of placing legal limits upon the stage of pregnancy in which an abortion may be performed. Given the relative safety of the new techniques of artificially inducing labor during the third trimester, the danger to the woman's life or health is no longer such an argument. Neither is the fact that people tend to respond to the thought of abortion in the later stages of pregnancy with emotional repulsion, since mere emotional responses cannot take the place of moral reasoning in determining what ought to be permitted. Nor, finally, is the frequently heard argument that legalizing abortion, especially late in the pregnancy, may erode the level of respect for human life, leading, perhaps, to an increase in unjustified euthanasia and other crimes. For this threat, if it is a threat, can be better met by educating people to the kinds of moral distinctions which we are making here than by limiting access to abortion (which limitation may, in its disregard for the rights of women, be just as damaging to the level of respect for human rights).

Thus, since the fact that even a fully developed fetus is not personlike enough to have any significant right to life on the basis of its personlikeness shows that no legal restrictions upon the stage of pregnancy in which an abortion may be performed can be justified on the grounds that we should protect the rights of the older fetus, and since there is no other apparent justification for such restrictions, we may conclude that they are entirely unjustified. Whether or not it would be *indecent* (whatever that means) for a woman in her seventh month to obtain an abortion just to avoid having to postpone a trip to Europe, it would not, in itself, be *immoral,* and therefore it ought to be permitted.

4. Potential Personhood and The Right to Life

We have seen that a fetus does not resemble a person in any way which can support the claim that it has even some of the same rights. But what about its *potential,* the fact that if nurtured and allowed to develop naturally it will very probably become a person? Doesn't that alone give it at least some right to life? It is hard to deny that the fact that an entity is a potential person is a strong prima facie reason for not destroying it; but we need not conclude from this that a potential person has a right to life, by virtue of that potential. It may be that our feeling that it is better, other things being equal, not to destroy a potential person is better explained by the fact that potential people are still (felt to be) an invaluable resource, not to be lightly squandered. Surely, if every speck of dust were a potential person, we would be much less apt to conclude that every potential person has a right to become actual.

Still, we do not need to insist that a potential person has no right to life whatever. There may well be something immoral, and not just imprudent, about wantonly destroying potential people, when doing so isn't necessary to protect anyone's rights. But even if a potential person does have some prima facie right to life, such a right could not possibly outweigh the right of a woman to obtain an abortion, since the rights of any actual person invariably outweigh those of any potential person, whenever the two conflict. Since this may not be immediately obvious in the case of a human fetus, let us look at another case.

Suppose that our space explorer falls into the hands of an alien culture, whose scientists decide to create a few hundred thousand or more human beings, by breaking his body into its component cells, and using these to create fully developed human beings, with, of course, his genetic code. We may imagine that each of these newly created men will have all of the original man's abilities, skills, knowledge, and so on, and also have an individual self-concept, in short that each of them will be a bona fide (though hardly unique) person. Imagine that the whole project will take only seconds, and that its chances of success are extremely high, and that our explorer knows all of this, and also knows that these people will be treated fairly. I maintain that in such a situation he would have every right to escape if he could, and thus to deprive all of these potential people of their potential lives; for his right to life outweighs all of theirs together, in spite of the fact that they are all genetically human, all innocent, and all have a very high probability of becoming people very soon, if only he refrains from acting.

Indeed, I think he would have a right to escape even if it were not his life which the alien scientists planned to take, but only a year of his freedom, or, indeed, only a day. Nor would he be obligated to stay if he had gotten captured (thus bringing all these people-potentials into existence) because of his own carelessness, or even if he had done so deliberately, knowing the consequences. Regardless of how he got captured, he is not morally obligated to remain in captivity for *any* period of time for the sake of permitting any number of potential people to come into actuality, so great is the margin by which one actual person's right to liberty outweighs whatever right to life even a hundred thousand potential people have. And it seems reasonable to conclude that the rights of a woman will outweigh by a similar margin whatever right to life a fetus may have by virtue of its potential personhood.

Thus, neither a fetus's resemblance to a person, nor its potential for becoming a person provides any basis whatever for the claim that it has any significant right to life. Consequently, a woman's right to protect her health, happiness, freedom, and even her life,[5] by terminating an unwanted pregnancy, will always override whatever right to life it may be appropriate to ascribe to a fetus, even a fully developed one. And thus, in the absence of any overwhelming social need for every possible child, the laws which restrict the right to obtain an abortion, or limit the period of pregnancy during which an abortion may be performed, are a wholly unjustified violation of a woman's most basic moral and constitutional rights.[6]

Postscript on Infanticide

Since the publication of this article, many people have written to point out that my argument appears to justify not only abortion, but infanticide as well. For a newborn infant is not significantly more personlike than an advanced fetus, and consequently it would seem that if the destruction of the latter is permissible so too must be that of the former. Inasmuch as most people, regardless of how they feel about the morality of abortion, consider infanticide a form of murder, this might appear to represent a serious flaw in my argument.

Now, if I am right in holding that it is only people who have a full-fledged right to life, and who can be murdered, and if the criteria of personhood are as I have described them, then it obviously follows that killing a new-born infant isn't murder. It does *not* follow, however, that infanticide is permissible, for two reasons. In the first place, it would be wrong, at least in this country and in this period of

5. That is, insofar as the death rate, for the woman, is higher for childbirth than for early abortion.
6. My thanks to the following people, who were kind enough to read and criticize an earlier version of this paper: Herbert Gold, Gene Glass, Anne Lauterbach, Judith Thomson, Mary Mothersill, and Timothy Binkley.

history, and other things being equal, to kill a new-born infant, because even if its parents do not want it and would not suffer from its destruction, there are other people who would like to have it, and would, in all probability, be deprived of a great deal of pleasure by its destruction. Thus, infanticide is wrong for reasons analogous to those which make it wrong to wantonly destroy natural resources, or great works of art.

Secondly, most people, at least in this country, value infants and would much prefer that they be preserved, even if foster parents are not immediately available. Most of us would rather be taxed to support orphanages than allow unwanted infants to be destroyed. So long as there are people who want an infant preserved, and who are willing and able to provide the means of caring for it, under reasonably humane conditions, it is *ceteris paribus,* wrong to destroy it.

But, it might be replied, if this argument shows that infanticide is wrong, at least at this time and in this country, doesn't it also show that abortion is wrong? After all, many people value fetuses, are disturbed by their destruction, and would much prefer that they be preserved, even at some cost to themselves. Furthermore, as a potential source of pleasure to some foster family, a fetus is just as valuable as an infant. There is, however, a crucial difference between the two cases: so long as the fetus is unborn, its preservation, contrary to the wishes of the pregnant woman, violates her rights to freedom, happiness, and self-determination. Her rights override the rights of those who would like the fetus preserved, just as if someone's life or limb is threatened by a wild animal, his right to protect himself by destroying the animal overrides the rights of those who would prefer that the animal not be harmed.

The minute the infant is born, however, its preservation no longer violates any of its mother's rights, even if she wants it destroyed, because she is free to put it up for adoption. Consequently, while the moment of birth does not mark any sharp discontinuity in the degree to which an infant possesses the right to life, it does mark the end of its mother's right to determine its fate. Indeed, if abortion could be performed without killing the fetus, she would never possess the right to have the fetus destroyed, for the same reasons that she has no right to have an infant destroyed.

On the other hand, it follows from my argument that when an unwanted or defective infant is born into a society which cannot afford and/or is not willing to care for it, then its destruction is permissible. This conclusion will, no doubt, strike many people as heartless and immoral; but remember that the very existence of people who feel this way, and who are willing and able to provide care for unwanted infants, is reason enough to conclude that they should be preserved.

Study Questions

1. Do potential persons have actual rights?

2. Is infanticide immoral?

3. Is Warren's example about the space explorer relevant to the abortion issue?

4. Is Warren's definition of personhood biased? If so, how?

Abortion and the Concept of a Person

Jane English (1947–1978) Jane English was a professor of philosophy at the University of North Carolina, Chapel Hill.

Jane English

The abortion debate rages on. Yet the two most popular positions seem to be clearly mistaken. Conservatives maintain that a human life begins at conception and that therefore abortion must be wrong because it is murder. But not all killings of humans are murders. Most notably, self defense may justify even the killing of an innocent person.

Liberals, on the other hand, are just as mistaken in their argument that since a fetus does not become a person until birth, a woman may do whatever she pleases in and to her own body. First, you cannot do as you please with your own body if it affects other people adversely.[1] Second, if a fetus is not a person, that does not imply that you can do to it anything you wish. Animals, for example, are not persons, yet to kill or torture them for no reason at all is wrong.

At the center of the storm has been the issue of just when it is between ovulation and adulthood that a person appears on the scene. Conservatives draw the line at conception, liberals at birth. In this paper I first examine our concept of a person and conclude that no single criterion can capture the concept of a person and no sharp line can be drawn. Next I argue that if a fetus is a person, abortion is still justifiable in many cases; and if a fetus is not a person, killing it is still wrong in many cases. To a large extent, these two solutions are in agreement. I conclude that our concept of a person can-

Reprinted with the permission of the editors from the *Canadian Journal of Philosophy,* Vol. V, No. 2, Oct. 1975.

not and need not bear the weight that the abortion controversy has thrust upon it.

I

The several factions in the abortion argument have drawn battle lines around various proposed criteria for determining what is and what is not a person. For example, Mary Ann Warren[2] lists five features (capacities for reasoning, self-awareness, complex communication, etc.) as her criteria for personhood and argues for the permissibility of abortion because a fetus falls outside this concept. Baruch Brody[3] uses brain waves. Michael Tooley[4] picks having-a-concept-of-self as his criterion and concludes that infanticide and abortion are justifiable, while the killing of adult animals is not. On the other side, Paul Ramsey[5] claims a certain gene structure is

---

1. We also have paternalistic laws which keep us from harming our own bodies even when no one else is affected. Ironically, antiabortion laws were originally designed to protect pregnant women from a dangerous but tempting procedure.
2. Mary Anne Warren, "On the Moral and Legal Status of Abortion," *Monist* 57 (1973), p. 55.
3. Baruch Brody, "Fetal Humanity and the Theory of Essentialism," in Robert Baker and Frederick Elliston, eds., *Philosophy and Sex* (Buffalo, N.Y., 1975).
4. Michael Tooley, "Abortion and Infanticide," *Philosophy and Public Affairs* 2 (1971).
5. Paul Ramsey, "The Morality of Abortion," in James Rachels, ed., *Moral Problems* (New York, 1971).

the defining characteristic. John Noonan[6] prefers conceived-of-humans and presents counterexamples to various other candidate criteria. For instance, he argues against viability as the criterion because the newborn and infirm would then be non-persons, since they cannot live without the aid of others. He rejects any criterion that calls upon the sorts of sentiments a being can evoke in adults on the grounds that this would allow us to exclude other races as non-persons if we could just view them sufficiently unsentimentally.

These approaches are typical: foes of abortion propose sufficient conditions for personhood which fetuses satisfy, while friends of abortion counter with necessary conditions for personhood which fetuses lack. But these both presuppose that the concept of a person can be captured in a strait jacket of necessary and/or sufficient conditions.[7] Rather, "person" is a cluster of features, of which rationality, having a self concept and being conceived of humans are only part.

What is typical of persons? Within our concept of a person we include, first, certain biological factors: descended from humans, having a certain genetic makeup, having a head, hands, arms, eyes, capable of locomotion, breathing, eating, sleeping. There are psychological factors: sentience, perception, having a concept of self and of one's own interests and desires, the ability to use tools, the ability to use language or symbol systems, the ability to joke, to be angry, to doubt. There are rationality factors: the ability to reason and draw conclusions, the ability to generalize and to learn from past experience, the ability to sacrifice present interests for greater gains in the future. There are social factors: the ability to work in groups and respond to peer pressures, the ability to recognize and consider as valuable the interests of others, seeing oneself as one among "other minds," the ability to sympathize, encourage, love, the ability to evoke from others the responses of sympathy, encouragement, love, the ability to

work with others for mutual advantage. Then there are legal factors: being subject to the law and protected by it, having the ability to sue and enter contracts, being counted in the census, having a name and citizenship, the ability to own property, inherit, and so forth.

Now the point is not that this list is incomplete, or that you can find counterinstances to each of its points. People typically exhibit rationality, for instance, but someone who was irrational would not thereby fail to qualify as a person. On the other hand, something could exhibit the majority of these features and still fail to be a person, as an advanced robot might. There is no single core of necessary and sufficient features which we can draw upon with the assurance that they constitute what really makes a person; there are only features that are more or less typical.

This is not to say that no necessary or sufficient conditions can be given. Being alive is a necessary condition for being a person, and being a U.S. Senator is sufficient. But rather than falling inside a sufficient condition or outside a necessary one, a fetus lies in the penumbra region where our concept of a person is not so simple. For this reason I think a conclusive answer to the question whether a fetus is a person is unattainable.

Here we might note a family of simple fallacies that proceed by stating a necessary condition for personhood and showing that a fetus has that characteristic. This is a form of the fallacy of affirming the consequent. For example, some have mistakenly reasoned from the premise that a fetus is human (after all, it is a human fetus rather than, say, a canine fetus), to the conclusion that it is *a* human. Adding an equivocation on "being," we get the fallacious argument that since a fetus is something both living and human, it is a human being.

Nonetheless, it does seem clear that a fetus has very few of the above family of characteristics, whereas a newborn baby exhibits a much larger proportion of them—and a two-year-old has even more. Note that one traditional anti-abortion argument has centered on pointing out the many ways in which a fetus resembles a baby. They emphasize its development ("It already has ten fingers....") without mentioning its dissimilarities to adults (it

---

6. John Noonan, "Abortion and the Catholic Church: A Summary History," *Natural Law Forum* 12 (1967), pp. 125–131.

7. Wittgenstein has argued against the possibility of so capturing the concept of a game, *Philosophical Investigations* (New York, 1958), §66–71.

still has gills and a tail). They also try to evoke the sort of sympathy on our part that we only feel toward other persons ("Never to laugh ... or feel the sunshine?"). This all seems to be a relevant way to argue, since its purpose is to persuade us that a fetus satisfies so many of the important features on the list that it ought to be treated as a person. Also note that a fetus near the time of birth satisfies many more of these factors than a fetus in the early months of development. This could provide reason for making distinctions among the different stages of pregnancy, as the U.S. Supreme Court has done.[8]

Historically, the time at which a person has been said to come into existence has varied widely. Muslims date personhood from fourteen days after conception. Some medievals followed Aristotle in placing ensoulment at forty days after conception for a male fetus and eighty days for a female fetus.[9] In European common law since the Seventeenth Century, abortion was considered the killing of a person only after quickening, the time when a pregnant woman first feels the fetus move on its own. Nor is this variety of opinions surprising. Biologically, a human being develops gradually. We shouldn't expect there to be any specific time or sharp dividing point when a person appears on the scene.

For these reasons I believe our concept of a person is not sharp or decisive enough to bear the weight of a solution to the abortion controversy. To use it to solve that problem is to clarify *obscurum per obscurius.*

II

Next let us consider what follows if a fetus is a person after all. Judith Jarvis Thomson's landmark article, "A Defense of Abortion,"[10] correctly points out

---

8. Not because the fetus is partly a person and so has some of the rights of persons, but rather because of the rights of person-like non-persons. This I discuss in part III below.

9. Aristotle himself was concerned, however, with the different question of when the soul takes form. For historical data, see Jimmye Kimmey, "How the Abortion Laws Happened," *Ms.* 1 (April, 1973), pp. 48ff, and John Noonan, *loc. cit.*

10. J. J. Thomson, "A Defense of Abortion," *Philosophy and Public Affairs* 1 (1971).

that some additional argumentation is needed at this point in the conservative argument to bridge the gap between the premise that a fetus is an innocent person and the conclusion that killing it is always wrong. To arrive at this conclusion, we would need the additional premise that killing an innocent person is always wrong. But killing an innocent person is sometimes permissible, most notably in self defense. Some examples may help draw out our intuitions or ordinary judgments about self defense.

Suppose a mad scientist, for instance, hypnotized innocent people to jump out of the bushes and attack innocent passers-by with knives. If you are so attacked, we agree you have a right to kill the attacker in self defense, if killing him is the only way to protect your life or to save yourself from serious injury. It does not seem to matter here that the attacker is not malicious but himself an innocent pawn, for your killing of him is not done in a spirit of retribution but only in self defense.

How severe an injury may you inflict in self defense? In part this depends upon the severity of the injury to be avoided: you may not shoot someone merely to avoid having your clothes torn. This might lead one to the mistaken conclusion that the defense may only equal the threatened injury in severity; that to avoid death you may kill, but to avoid a black eye you may only inflict a black eye or the equivalent. Rather, our laws and customs seem to say that you may create an injury somewhat, but not enormously, greater than the injury to be avoided. To fend off an attack whose outcome would be as serious as rape, a severe beating or the loss of a finger, you may shoot; to avoid having your clothes torn, you may blacken an eye.

Aside from this, the injury you may inflict should only be the minimum necessary to deter or incapacitate the attacker. Even if you know he intends to kill you, you are not justified in shooting him if you could equally well save yourself by the simple expedient of running away. Self defense is for the purpose of avoiding harms rather than equalizing harms.

Some cases of pregnancy present a parallel situation. Though the fetus is itself innocent, it may pose a threat to the pregnant woman's well-being, life prospects or health, mental or physical. If the pregnancy presents a slight threat to her interests, it seems self defense cannot justify abortion. But if the threat is on a par with a serious beating or the loss of a finger, she may kill the fetus that poses such a threat, even if it is an innocent person. If a lesser harm to the fetus could have the same defensive effect, killing it would not be justified. It is unfortunate that the only way to free the woman from the pregnancy entails the death of the fetus (except in very late stages of pregnancy). Thus a self defense model supports Thomson's point that the woman has a right only to be freed from the fetus, not a right to demand its death.[11]

The self defense model is most helpful when we take the pregnant woman's point of view. In the pre-Thomson literature, abortion is often framed as a question for a third party: do you, a doctor, have a right to choose between the life of the woman and that of the fetus? Some have claimed that if you were a passer-by who witnessed a struggle between the innocent hypnotized attacker and his equally innocent victim, you would have no reason to kill either in defense of the other. They have concluded that the self defense model implies that a woman may attempt to abort herself, but that a doctor should not assist her. I think the position of the third party is somewhat more complex. We do feel some inclination to intervene on behalf of the victim rather than the attacker, other things equal. But if both parties are innocent, other factors come into consideration. You would rush to the aid of your husband whether he was attacker or attackee. If a hypnotized famous violinist were attacking a skid row bum, we would try to save the individual who is of more value to society. These considerations would tend to support abortion in some cases.

But suppose you are a frail senior citizen who wishes to avoid being knifed by one of these innocent hypnotics, so you have hired a bodyguard to accompany you. If you are attacked, it is clear we believe that the bodyguard, acting as your agent, has a right to kill the attacker to save you from a serious beating. Your rights of self defense are transferred to your agent. I suggest that we should similarly view the doctor as the pregnant woman's agent

in carrying out a defense she is physically incapable of accomplishing herself.

Thanks to modern technology, the cases are rare in which pregnancy poses as clear a threat to a woman's bodily health as an attacker brandishing a switchblade. How does self defense fare when more subtle, complex and long-range harms are involved?

> *"There is no single core of necessary and sufficient features which we can draw upon with the assurance that they constitute what really makes a person...."*

To consider a somewhat fanciful example, suppose you are a highly trained surgeon when you are kidnapped by the hypnotic attacker. He says he does not intend to harm you but to take you back to the mad scientist who, it turns out, plans to hypnotize you to have a permanent mental block against all your knowledge of medicine. This would automatically destroy your career which would in turn have a serious adverse impact on your family, your personal relationships and your happiness. It seems to me that if the only way you can avoid this outcome is to shoot the innocent attacker, you are justified in so doing. You are defending yourself from a drastic injury to your life prospects. I think it is no exaggeration to claim that unwanted pregnancies (most obviously among teenagers) often have such adverse life-long consequences as the surgeon's loss of livelihood.

Several parallels arise between various views on abortion and the self defense model. Let's suppose further that these hypnotized attackers only operate at night, so that it is well known that they can be avoided completely by the considerable inconvenience of never leaving your house after dark. One

11. *Ibid.*, p. 52.

view is that since you could stay home at night, therefore if you go out and are selected by one of these hypnotized people, you have no right to defend yourself. This parallels the view that abstinence is the only acceptable way to avoid pregnancy. Others might hold that you ought to take along some defense such as Mace which will deter the hypnotized person without killing him, but that if this defense fails, you are obliged to submit to the resulting injury, no matter how severe it is. This parallels the view that contraception is all right but abortion is always wrong, even in cases of contraceptive failure.

A third view is that you may kill the hypnotized person only if he will actually kill you, but not if he will only injure you. This is like the position that abortion is permissible only if it is required to save a woman's life. Finally we have the view that it is all right to kill the attacker, even if only to avoid a very slight inconvenience to yourself and even if you knowingly walked down the very street where all these incidents have been taking place without taking along any Mace or protective escort. If we assume that a fetus is a person, this is the analogue of the view that abortion is always justifiable, "on demand."

The self defense model allows us to see an important difference that exists between abortion and infanticide, even if a fetus is a person from conception. Many have argued that the only way to justify abortion without justifying infanticide would be to find some characteristic of personhood that is acquired at birth. Michael Tooley, for one, claims infanticide is justifiable because the really significant characteristics of person are acquired some time after birth. But all such approaches look to characteristics of the developing human and ignore the relation between the fetus and the woman. What if, after birth, the presence of an infant or the need to support it posed a grave threat to the woman's sanity or life prospects? She could escape this threat by the simple expedient of running away. So a solution that does not entail the death of the infant is available. Before birth, such solutions are not available because of the biological dependence of the fetus on the woman. Birth is the crucial point not because of any characteristics the fetus gains, but because after birth the woman can defend herself by a means less drastic than killing the infant. Hence self defense can be used to justify abortion without necessarily thereby justifying infanticide.

III

On the other hand, supposing a fetus is not after all a person, would abortion always be morally permissible? Some opponents of abortion seem worried that if a fetus is not a full-fledged person, then we are justified in treating it in any way at all. However, this does not follow. Non-persons do get some consideration in our moral code, though of course they do not have the same rights as persons have (and in general they do not have moral responsibilities), and though their interests may be overridden by the interests of persons. Still, we cannot just treat them in any way at all.

Treatment of animals is a case in point. It is wrong to torture dogs for fun or to kill wild birds for no reason at all. It is wrong Period, even though dogs and birds do not have the same rights persons do. However, few people think it is wrong to use dogs as experimental animals, causing them considerable suffering in some cases, provided that the resulting research will probably bring discoveries of great benefit to people. And most of us think it all right to kill birds for food or to protect our crops. People's rights are different from the consideration we give to animals, then, for it is wrong to experiment on people, even if others might later benefit a great deal as a result of their suffering. You might volunteer to be a subject, but this would be supererogatory; you certainly have a right to refuse to be a medical guinea pig.

But how do we decide what you may or may not do to non-persons? This is a difficult problem, one for which I believe no adequate account exists. You do not want to say, for instance, that torturing dogs is all right whenever the sum of its effects on people is good—when it doesn't warp the sensibilities of the torturer so much that he mistreats people. If that were the case, it would be all right to torture dogs if you did it in private, or if the torturer lived on a desert island or died soon afterward, so that his actions had no effect on people. This is an inadequate account, because whatever moral consideration animals get, it has to be indefeasible, too. It will have to be a general proscription of certain actions, not merely a weighing of the impact on people on a case-by-case basis.

Rather, we need to distinguish two levels on which consequences of actions can be taken into account in moral reasoning. The traditional objections to Utilitarianism focus on the fact that it operates solely on the first level, taking all the consequences into account in particular cases only. Thus Utilitarianism is open to "desert island" and "lifeboat" counterexamples because these cases are rigged to make the consequences of actions severely limited.

Rawls' theory could be described as a teleological sort of theory, but with teleology operating on a higher level.[12] In choosing the principles to regulate society from the original position, his hypothetical choosers make their decision on the basis of the total consequences of various systems. Furthermore, they are constrained to choose a general set of rules which people can readily learn and apply. An ethical theory must operate by generating a set of sympathies and attitudes toward others which reinforces the functioning of that set of moral principles. Our prohibition against killing people operates by means of certain moral sentiments including sympathy, compassion and guilt. But if these attitudes are to form a coherent set, they carry us further; we tend to perform supererogatory actions, and we tend to feel similar compassion toward person-like non-persons.

It is crucial that psychological facts play a role here. Our psychological constitution makes it the case that for our ethical theory to work, it must prohibit certain treatment of non-persons which are significantly person-like. If our moral rules allowed people to treat some person-like non-persons in ways we do not want people to be treated, this would undermine the system of sympathies and attitudes that makes the ethical system work. For this reason, we would choose in the original position to make mistreatment of some sorts of animals wrong in general (not just wrong in the cases with public impact), even though animals are not themselves parties in the original position. Thus it makes sense that it is those animals whose appearance and behavior are most like those of people that get the most consideration in our moral scheme.

It is because of "coherence of attitudes," I think, that the similarity of a fetus to a baby is very significant. A fetus one week before birth is so much like a newborn baby in our psychological space that we cannot allow any cavalier treatment of the former while expecting full sympathy and nurturative support for the latter. Thus, I think that anti-abortion forces are indeed giving their strongest arguments when they point to the similarities between a fetus and a baby, and when they try to evoke our emotional attachment to and sympathy for the fetus. An early horror story from New York about nurses who were expected to alternate between caring for six-week premature infants and disposing of viable 24-week aborted fetuses is just that—a horror story. These beings are so much alike that no one can be asked to draw a distinction and treat them so very differently.

Remember, however, that in the early weeks after conception, a fetus is very much unlike a person. It is hard to develop these feelings for a set of genes which doesn't yet have a head, hands, beating heart, response to touch or the ability to move by itself. Thus it seems to me that the alleged "slippery slope" between conception and birth is not so very slippery. In the early stages of pregnancy, abortion can hardly be compared to murder for psychological reasons, but in the latest stages it is psychologically akin to murder.

Another source of similarity is the bodily continuity between fetus and adult. Bodies play a surprisingly central role in our attitudes toward persons. One has only to think of the philosophical literature on how far physical identity suffices for personal identity or Wittgenstein's remark that the best picture of the human soul is the human body. Even after death, when all agree the body is no longer a person, we still observe elaborate customs of respect for the human body; like people who torture dogs, necrophiliacs are not to be trusted with people.[13] So it is appropriate that we show re-

---

12. John Rawls, *A Theory of Justice* (Cambridge, Mass., 1971), §3–4.

13. On the other hand, if they can be trusted with people, then our moral customs are mistaken. It all depends on the facts of psychology.

spect to a fetus as the body continuous with the body of a person. This is a degree of resemblance to persons that animals cannot rival.

Michael Tooley also utilizes a parallel with animals. He claims that it is always permissible to drown newborn kittens and draws conclusions about infanticide.[14] But it is only permissible to drown kittens when their survival would cause some hardship. Perhaps it would be a burden to feed and house six more cats or to find other homes for them. The alternative of letting them starve produces even more suffering than the drowning. Since the kittens get their rights second-hand, so to speak, *via* the need for coherence in our attitudes, their interests are often overridden by the interests of full-fledged persons. But if their survival would be no inconvenience to people at all, then it is wrong to drown them, *contra* Tooley.

Tooley's conclusions about abortion are wrong for the same reason. Even if a fetus is not a person, abortion is not always permissible, because of the resemblance of a fetus to a person. I agree with Thomson that it would be wrong for a woman who is seven months pregnant to have an abortion just to avoid having to postpone a trip to Europe. In the early months of pregnancy when the fetus hardly resembles a baby at all, then, abortion is permissi-

---

14. *Op. cit.*, pp. 40, 60–61.

ble whenever it is in the interests of the pregnant woman or her family. The reasons would only need to outweigh the pain and inconvenience of the abortion itself. In the middle months, when the fetus comes to resemble a person, abortion would be justifiable only when the continuation of the pregnancy or the birth of the child would cause harms—physical, psychological, economic or social—to the woman. In the late months of pregnancy, even on our current assumption that a fetus is not a person, abortion seems to be wrong except to save a woman from significant injury or death.

The Supreme Court has recognized similar gradations in the alleged slippery slope stretching between conception and birth. To this point, the present paper has been a discussion of the moral status of abortion only, not its legal status. In view of the great physical, financial and sometimes psychological costs of abortion, perhaps the legal arrangement most compatible with the proposed moral solution would be the absence of restrictions, that is, so-called abortion "on demand."

So I conclude, first, that application of our concept of a person will not suffice to settle the abortion issue. After all, the biological development of a human being is gradual. Second, whether a fetus is a person or not, abortion is justifiable early in pregnancy to avoid modest harms and seldom justifiable late in pregnancy except to avoid significant injury or death.

Study Questions

1. What would English say if a conservative right-to-lifer asked her: "Aren't you glad that your mother didn't abort you?" Presumably, she would say that yes, she was glad. The question would then be: "Why aren't you a right-to-lifer or conservative on abortion?"

2. Does the similarity of appearance of the fetus to that of a person have relevance to the question

of abortion? What if we encounter extraterrestrials one day who do not look anything like we do but who are rational, conscious, and can feel pain and pleasure? Would they have rights as we do?

■ Louise is twenty-eight years old and three months pregnant. Her father is diagnosed as having Parkinson's disease, a brain disease causing uncontrollable shaking of the hands. An experimental medical procedure has been introduced whereby fetal brain tissue is transplanted from aborted fetuses into the brains of Parkinson's patients. The procedure has been remarkably successful in alleviating the symptoms. Louise's father asks her to abort the fetus so that the brain tissue can be transplanted into his brain and perhaps cure him of his disease. She hates the idea of abortion, but her father tells her that she could have another child. He also offers to give her five thousand dollars if she agrees to have the abortion.

What should Louise do?
Is Louise's father making a fair request?

■ Margaret, a woman in her first year of college, meets a young man, Ron, in a bar and starts a relationship with him. One day she finds out that she is pregnant. She tells Ron about it, and he encourages her to do anything she wants, whether have an abortion, give the baby up for adoption, or get married and keep the baby. Her parents are strict Catholics who warn her that they will disown her if she has an abortion. Her friends tell her that she should have the abortion, finish college, and then have another baby for which she can provide a good life.

What should Margaret do?
Does it make a difference that Ron does not love her?
What if Ron changes his mind and says that he wants her to have the child, that his mother will take care of the infant, and that he now refuses to marry her?

■ Jane, aged sixteen, was born blind and deaf. She discovers that her mother had taken LSD and other drugs while she was pregnant with Jane. Jane sues her mother for monetary damages for causing her to be born disabled. The lawyer for the mother claims that the only alternative her mother had was to abort Jane. Because Jane's life with disabilities is better than no life at all, her mother believes that she made the right decision in carrying the fetus to term. Jane argues that if she had been aborted she would never have known about it and therefore it wouldn't matter to her.

If you were on the jury, how would you vote?

■ Barbara, a devout Catholic, is pregnant with her third child. After amniocentesis, she learns that the fetus has an incurable genetic defect that will cause the baby great pain after birth and that it will live for only about three months. Her husband recommends an abortion. Barbara, as a Catholic, does not believe in abortion, but she does not want the baby to suffer needlessly.

If you were Barbara, what would you do?

Suggested
Readings

Bayles, Michael D. *Reproductive Ethics.* Englewood Cliffs, N.J.: Prentice-Hall, 1984.

Beauchamp, Tom, and Walters, Leroy, eds. *Contemporary Issues in Bioethics.* Belmont, Calif.:

Wadsworth, 1982.

Regan, Tom, ed. *Matters of Life and Death.* New York: Random House, 1980.

Thomson, Judith Jarvis. "A Defense of Abortion." *Philosophy and Public Affairs* 1, no. 1 (Fall 1971).

Euthanasia

I f you found yourself dying from a painful and terminal disease, would you wish to hang on as long as possible, or would you prefer to die? *Euthanasia* originally meant a good death, and now it means mercy killing or ending a terminally ill patient's or severely deformed newborn's life. Euthanasia as helping another person to die must be distinguished from murder, which means the killing of a (healthy) person against his or her will, and from suicide, the killing of oneself.

Background

The practice of euthanasia is not new. According to scientific evidence, many primitive humans saw death as a rite of passage to another place of existence. Therefore, they probably did not see it as an absolute evil. The practice of infanticide, the killing of defective or unwanted newborns (especially females), existed in many ancient cultures, including Greece, and was acceptable to Aristotle. Several other philosophers of Greece and Rome viewed suicide and euthanasia as morally acceptable ways to escape unbearable pain. In other cultures, especially in nomadic groups, the old, sick, or otherwise incapacitated were abandoned to die or were killed directly. For example, in India, it was once customary to dispose of the old by throwing them into the Ganges River, and in ancient Sardinia in the Mediterranean, old men were clubbed to death by their own sons. With the increased influence of Judaism, Islam, and Christianity, which all regard the family and life itself to be sacred, suicide and euthanasia were prohibited. In recent times, euthanasia was widely practiced by Nazis under Adolf Hitler in Germany. Involuntary euthanasia of senile, terminally ill, genetically defective, and other "undesirable" people was widespread and legal in Nazi Germany.

Euthanasia presents a moral problem to the medical profession because euthanasia is apparently inconsistent with professional medical ethics. History does show, however, that ethical codes for professional conduct are the result of the prevailing understanding of what is moral. For example, the Code of Hammurabi (c. 1700 B.C.) required that the hands of a surgeon be cut off if the surgeon caused the death of a nobleman during the course of an operation. The Hippocratic oath, which all doctors are required to take today in some form, requires physicians to relieve suffering and prolong the life of the patient. What should a doctor do when these two duties conflict or when the patient requests to die? In its original form, the Hippocratic oath required that the teaching of medicine be free of charge, and it did not allow abortions, two precepts generally ignored today. In the United States presently, to actually kill a dying patient is illegal, although doctors are allowed to discontinue treatment of some patients. Those who do not wish to be kept alive by artificial means have developed a "living will." This document specifies an individual's wish that doctors not take measures to keep the individual alive when the person is irrevocably unconscious and dying. Many states accept these wills as legal.

Euthanasia can take place in different ways. *Active euthanasia* occurs when another person, such as a doctor or nurse, directly causes death in the patient by injection of a poison or by some other means. *Passive euthanasia* occurs when medical treatment is withheld from the patient, and then the disease kills the patient. Each of these types of euthanasia can be further subdivided. *Voluntary euthanasia* (active or passive) is euthanasia that is requested by the patient. *Nonvoluntary euthanasia* (active or passive) occurs when a patient is incapable of giving or withholding consent such as in the case of a comatose, extremely senile, or mentally ill person. *Involuntary euthanasia* means to let someone die or to kill someone against his or her will.

The question of mercy killing is related to the question of what death is and when it occurs. A religious definition used by many Christians, Jews, and Moslems states that death occurs when the soul, the life-giving principle, leaves the body and continues to exist in another dimension. The problem here, of course, is how to determine when in fact the soul has left the body. The traditional scientific definition states that death occurs when the heart stops beating. Today, however, medical technology has provided us with machines such as respirators that can keep the heart and lungs working indefinitely, even though the patient is in an irreversible coma (unconscious state). This has led some to adopt a third theory of death based on the death of the brain, the irreversible loss of consciousness, or irreversible coma. This view holds that a person is dead if the brain is dead, even if the heart is still beating.

According to E. Kübler-Ross, the physical dimension of death among persons is preceded by various psychological stages and attitudes toward death. The first stage upon hearing of one's impending death is usually shock, denial, and disbelief. These reactions are natural, given our virtually universal fear of death. The fear or dread of death involves several components. First, it consists of the dread of nonexistence and total annihilation of the self. Second, it involves fear of the suffering often associated with the dying process. Third, the fear focuses on the potential loss of dignity that may be experienced when one loses control over one's body. Finally, it involves fear of the unknown. These are all part of the first stage of dying, which continues to some extent until death.

The first stage of denial is usually replaced by a second stage of anger. The patient asks, "Why me?" and is bitter. The third stage is that of bargaining. The patient may seek ways to prolong his or her life. He or she may appeal for supernatural aid in exchange for various acts of devotion to the deity if the aid is given. When the bargaining fails, the patient usually goes into a depression, knowing that death is inevitable. At this stage, the patient must come to grips with the fact that he or she will lose everything and everyone. This usually results in withdrawal from the world and often, in the final stage, the acceptance of one's end.

A central part of the euthanasia debate concerns the proper degree of medical care and treatment of dying patients. Originally, the AMA (American Medical Association), the major professional organization of physicians, held that there is an obligation to give irreversibly unconscious terminal patients such "ordinary" treatment as food and water until they die; it was not necessary to provide "extraordinary" treatment (i.e., treatment that was expensive and not likely to provide long-term benefit). Extraordinary treatment, such as heart resuscitation or surgery, need not be provided to these patients. However, now the AMA believes that doctors may morally discontinue even ordinary treatment for brain dead patients. Part of the problem in this distinction is the exact definition of extraordinary and ordinary treatment.

Conservative Position: J. Gay-Williams

J. Gay-Williams argues against active euthanasia. He believes that euthanasia is against nature and human dignity. All living things desire to live, and to choose death is therefore unnatural. Gay-Williams further observes that medicine is not an exact science, and mistakes are possible in diagnosis and prognosis of a patient's disease. A patient could be erroneously misdiagnosed as terminal. If euthanasia were to be inflicted on this patient, the error would never be discovered, and the patient would have needlessly died.

Finally, we must consider the long-term consequences of practicing euthanasia. According to Gay-Williams, euthanasia could lead to the corruption of the medical profession, which has thus far been dedicated to the preservation of life, not its destruction. Once euthanasia becomes institutionalized,

perhaps nurses and doctors will not be as zealous in helping patients recover and live better and longer lives. This final point that Gay-Williams makes is sometimes called an example of the "slippery-slope" argument (i.e., if we allow something today, we might slip down the slope to even morally worse things tomorrow).

These arguments suggest important points for us to consider. It is certainly true that living things generally wish to live, yet do all living things wish to live under all conditions? Isn't it also natural to avoid pain and suffering? Isn't it conceivable that a terminal patient may choose to die rather than to live in pain? Again, it is true that medicine is not an exact science and that mistakes do occur, especially at the early stages of diagnosis, but is this true when a patient's disease has obviously progressed and the patient is clearly dying? Even if mistakes are possible at this point in prognosis, for cases of "miraculous" remissions and cures have occurred, still a patient fully aware of these possibilities might still choose to have control over his or her life and body and choose to die. Finally, what of the possible corruption of the medical profession's use of involuntary euthanasia in order to get rid of patients who are "too expensive" to keep alive or whose organs are needed by others? Some have suggested that euthanasia need not be actually performed by doctors or nurses. Medically trained persons who are experts on mercy killing could be responsible for the decision. Second, it is not clear which way the slippery slope will actually incline. If the absence of voluntary euthanasia leads to the overwhelming accumulation of terminally ill, senile, and comatose patients in hospitals who lead essentially vegetative existences, would this promote respect for life and human dignity? Many do not think so. Various legal restrictions and guidelines have been suggested to ensure that no one is killed or allowed to die against his or her will.

Liberal Position: James Rachels

Philosophers such as Gay-Williams believe that passive euthanasia is morally acceptable but reject active euthanasia as immoral. James Rachels questions the consistency of this view. Rachels points out that passive euthanasia, or allowing someone to die, can be cruel and nonhumanitarian, for it may needlessly prolong the suffering of a terminal patient. Killing someone is not necessarily morally worse than letting someone die. Rachels's example of Smith and Jones is intended to show this. In a realistic euthanasia case, the doctor does not choose to kill his or her patient for personal gain. According to Rachels, if it is humane and moral to let someone die, then it is at least as moral to kill them. Rachels believes that being moral means reducing suffering and that voluntary euthanasia, i.e., killing a terminal patient who requests it, is reducing suffering and therefore moral.

Moderate Position: Thomas D. Sullivan

Thomas D. Sullivan responds to the arguments of Rachels by making several points. According to Sullivan, the AMA prohibits a doctor from intentionally terminating the life of a patient, but it does allow the doctor to cease extraordinary treatment of the dying patient even if ceasing such treatment will allow death to occur. *Extraordinary treatment* is treatment that is expensive, inconvenient, and offers no reasonable hope of benefiting the patient. *Ordinary treatment,* however, is inexpensive and does benefit the patient; it includes feeding, massaging, and keeping the patient comfortable. For Sullivan, it is immoral to discontinue ordinary treatment under any circumstances.

Sullivan believes that doctors may discontinue extraordinary care in some cases. Here Sullivan asks us to distinguish between the intention of an action and the foreseeable consequence of an action. Not all foreseeable consequences of an action are intended. A doctor may therefore discontinue extraordinary care and not thereby intend to kill the patient, even if the patient does die.

James Rachels Responds

Rachels responds to Sullivan by challenging all of his major points. As far as the distinction between intention and consequence is concerned, Rachels believes that intention is useful in evaluating character and that consequences are useful in evaluating action. An action is not necessarily evil because of a bad intention but because of the utility it creates or takes away. Consequently, whether the doctor intends to kill the patient or not, the morality of the action must be evaluated based on the knowledge that this will result.

Rachels also rejects Sullivan's distinction between ordinary and extraordinary means. Rachels believes that in some cases it is moral to withhold even ordinary means (which the AMA now accepts for brain dead patients) and further points out that what is extraordinary depends on the patient in question. Spending ten thousand dollars on an elderly, terminally ill cancer patient with diabetes may be extraordinary and excessive, but not on a young cancer patient with diabetes. Finally, Rachels believes that the case for active euthanasia can be made on the basis of the utilitarian argument of reducing suffering and the Golden Rule. Rachels is careful to point out that we must never practice involuntary euthanasia (i.e., on those who do not wish to die).

Euthanasia As a Right

The issue of euthanasia, as in the question of abortion, concerns the rights that persons have. Liberals such as Rachels believe that a person has the right to control one's body and to end one's life. Conservatives believe that it is contrary to nature and God to wish to die and warn of the slippery slope leading to forced killing of the old, the retarded, and the unwanted. A related question concerns distributive justice; money and resources spent on the dying cannot be used by the young who are seriously ill. Death may be the taboo topic of conversation in our society today, but it is one that deserves serious discussion.

The Wrongfulness of Euthanasia

J. Gay-Williams is a philosopher living in the Midwest.

J. Gay-Williams

My impression is that euthanasia—the idea, if not the practice—is slowly gaining acceptance within our society. Cynics might attribute this to an increasing tendency to devalue human life, but I do not believe this is the major factor. The acceptance is much more likely to be the result of unthinking sympathy and benevolence. Well-publicized, tragic stories like that of Karen Quinlan elicit from us deep feelings of compassion. We think to ourselves, "She and her family would be better off if she were dead." It is an easy step from this very human response to the view that if someone (and others) would be better off dead, then it must be all right to kill that person.[1] Although I respect the compassion that leads to this conclusion, I believe the conclusion is wrong. I want to show that euthanasia is wrong. It is inherently wrong, but it is also wrong judged from the standpoints of self-interest and of practical effects.

Before presenting my arguments to support this claim, it would be well to define "euthanasia." An essential aspect of euthanasia is that it involves taking a human life, either one's own or that of another. Also, the person whose life is taken must be someone who is believed to be suffering from some disease or injury from which recovery cannot reasonably be expected. Finally, the action must be deliberate and intentional. Thus, euthanasia is intentionally taking the life of a presumably hopeless person. Whether the life is one's own or that of another, the taking of it is still euthanasia.

It is important to be clear about the deliberate and intentional aspect of the killing. If a hopeless person is given an injection of the wrong drug by mistake and this causes his death, this is wrongful killing but not euthanasia. The killing cannot be the result of accident. Furthermore, if the person is given an injection of a drug that is believed to be necessary to treat his disease or better his condition and the person dies as a result, then this is neither wrongful killing nor euthanasia. The intention was to make the patient well, not kill him. Similarly, when a patient's condition is such that it is not reasonable to hope that any medical procedures or treatments will save his life, a failure to implement the procedures or treatments is not euthanasia. If the person dies, this will be as a result of his injuries or disease and not because of his failure to receive treatment.

The failure to continue treatment after it has been realized that the patient has little chance of benefitting from it has been characterized by some as "passive euthanasia." This phrase is misleading and mistaken.[2] In such cases, the person involved is

1. For a sophisticated defense of this position see Philippa Foot, "Euthanasia," *Philosophy and Public Affairs,* vol. 6 (1977), pp. 85–112. Foot does not endorse the radical conclusion that euthanasia, voluntary and involuntary, is always right.

2. James Rachels rejects the distinction between active and passive euthanasia as morally irrelevant in his "Active and Passive Euthanasia," *New England Journal of Medicine,* vol. 292, pp 78–80. But see the criticism by Foot, pp. 100–103.

not killed (the first essential aspect of euthanasia), nor is the death of the person intended by the withholding of additional treatment (the third essential aspect of euthanasia). The aim may be to spare the person additional and unjustifiable pain, to save him from the indignities of hopeless manipulations, and to avoid increasing the financial and emotional burden on his family. When I buy a pencil it is so that I can use it to write, not to contribute to an increase in the gross national product. This may be the unintended consequence of my action, but it is not the aim of my action. So it is with failing to continue the treatment of a dying person. I intend his death no more than I intend to reduce the GNP by not using medical supplies. His is an unintended dying, and so-called "passive euthanasia" is not euthanasia at all.

1 The Argument from Nature

Every human being has a natural inclination to continue living. Our reflexes and responses fit us to fight attackers, flee wild animals, and dodge out of the way of trucks. In our daily lives we exercise the caution and care necessary to protect ourselves. Our bodies are similarly structured for survival right down to the molecular level. When we are cut, our capillaries seal shut, our blood clots, and fibrogen is produced to start the process of healing the wound. When we are invaded by bacteria, antibodies are produced to fight against the alien organisms, and their remains are swept out of the body by special cells designed for clean-up work.

Euthanasia does violence to this natural goal of survival. It is literally acting against nature because all the processes of nature are bent towards the end of bodily survival. Euthanasia defeats these subtle mechanisms in a way that, in a particular case, disease and injury might not.

It is possible, but not necessary, to make an appeal to revealed religion in this connection.[3] Man as trustee of his body acts against God, its rightful possessor, when he takes his own life. He also violates the commandment to hold life sacred and never to take it without just and compelling cause. But since this appeal will persuade only those who are prepared to accept that religion has access to revealed truths, I shall not employ this line of argument.

It is enough, I believe, to recognize that the organization of the human body and our patterns of behavioral responses make the continuation of life a natural goal. By reason alone, then, we can recognize that euthanasia sets us against our own nature.[4] Furthermore, in doing so, euthanasia does violence to our dignity. Our dignity comes from seeking our ends. When one of our goals is survival, and actions are taken that eliminate that goal, then our natural dignity suffers. Unlike animals, we are conscious through reason of our nature and our ends. Euthanasia involves acting as if this dual nature—inclination towards survival and awareness of this as an end—did not exist. Thus, euthanasia denies our basic human character and requires that we regard ourselves or others as something less than fully human.

2 The Argument from Self-Interest

The above arguments are, I believe, sufficient to show that euthanasia is inherently wrong. But there are reasons for considering it wrong when judged by standards other than reason. Because death is final and irreversible, euthanasia contains within it the possibility that we will work against our own interest if we practice it or allow it to be practiced on us.

Contemporary medicine has high standards of excellence and a proven record of accomplishment, but it does not possess perfect and complete knowledge. A mistaken diagnosis is possible, and so is a mistaken prognosis. Consequently, we may believe that we are dying of a disease when, as a matter of fact, we may not be. We may think that we have no hope of recovery when, as a matter of fact, our chances are quite good. In such circumstances, if euthanasia were permitted, we would die need-

---

3. For a defense of this view see J. V. Sullivan, "The Immorality of Euthanasia," in Marvin Kohl, ed., *Beneficent Euthanasia* (Buffalo, New York: Prometheus Books, 1975), pp. 34–44.

4. This point is made by Ray V. McIntyre in "Voluntary Euthanasia: The Ultimate Perversion," *Medical Counterpoint*, vol. 2, pp. 26–29.

lessly. Death is final and the chance of error too great to approve the practice of euthanasia.

Also, there is always the possibility that an experimental procedure or a hitherto untried technique will pull us through. We should at least keep this option open, but euthanasia closes it off. Furthermore, spontaneous remission does occur in many cases. For no apparent reason, a patient simply recovers when those all around him, including his physicians, expected him to die. Euthanasia would just guarantee their expectations and leave no room for the "miraculous" recoveries that frequently occur.

> *"Euthanasia is inherently wrong because it violates the nature and dignity of human beings."*

Finally, knowing that we can take our life at any time (or ask another to take it) might well incline us to give up too easily. The will to live is strong in all of us, but it can be weakened by pain and suffering and feelings of hopelessness. If during a bad time we allow ourselves to be killed, we never have a chance to reconsider. Recovery from a serious illness requires that we fight for it, and anything that weakens our determination by suggesting that there is an easy way out is ultimately against our own interest. Also, we may be inclined towards euthanasia because of our concern for others. If we see our sickness and suffering as an emotional and financial burden on our family, we may feel that to leave our life is to make their lives easier.[5] The very presence of the possibility of euthanasia may keep us from surviving when we might.

3 The Argument from Practical Effects

Doctors and nurses are, for the most part, totally committed to saving lives. A life lost is, for them, al-

most a personal failure, an insult to their skills and knowledge. Euthanasia as a practice might well alter this. It could have a corrupting influence so that in any case that is severe doctors and nurses might not try hard enough to save the patient. They might decide that the patient would simply be "better off dead" and take the steps necessary to make that come about. This attitude could then carry out to their dealings with patients less seriously ill. The result would be an overall decline in the quality of medical care.

Finally, euthanasia as a policy is a slippery slope. A person apparently hopelessly ill may be allowed to take his own life. Then he may be permitted to deputize others to do it for him should he no longer be able to act. The judgment of others then becomes the ruling factor. Already at this point euthanasia is not personal and voluntary, for others are acting "on behalf of" the patient as they see fit. This may well incline them to act on behalf of other patients who have not authorized them to exercise their judgment. It is only a short step, then, from voluntary euthanasia (self-inflicted or authorized), to directed euthanasia administered to a patient who has given no authorization, to involuntary euthanasia conducted as part of a social policy.[6] Recently many psychiatrists and sociologists have argued that we define as "mental illness" those forms of behavior that we disapprove of.[7] This gives us license then to lock up those who display the behavior. The category of the "hopelessly ill" provides the possibility of even worse abuse. Embedded in a social policy, it would give society or its representatives the authority to eliminate all those who might be considered too "ill" to function normally any longer. The dangers of euthanasia are too great to all to run the risk of approving it in any form. The first slippery step may well lead to a serious and harmful fall.

I hope that I have succeeded in showing why the benevolence that inclines us to give approval of euthanasia is misplaced. Euthanasia is inherently wrong because it violates the nature and dignity of

---

5. See McIntyre, p. 28.

6. See Sullivan, "Immorality of Euthanasia," pp. 34–44, for a fuller argument in support of this view.

7. See, for example, Thomas S. Szasz, *The Myth of Mental Illness,* rev. ed. (New York: Harper & Row, 1974).

human beings. But even those who are not convinced by this must be persuaded that the potential personal and social dangers inherent in euthanasia are sufficient to forbid our approving it either as a personal practice or as a public policy.

Suffering is surely a terrible thing, and we have a clear duty to comfort those in need and to ease their suffering when we can. But suffering is also a natural part of life with values for the individual

and for others that we should not overlook. We may legitimately seek for others and for ourselves an easeful death, as Arthur Dyck has pointed out.[8] Euthanasia, however, is not just an easeful death. It is a wrongful death. Euthanasia is not just dying. It is killing.

---

8. Arthur Dyck, "Beneficent Euthanasia and Benemortasia," Kohl, *op. cit.*, pp. 117–129.

Study Questions

1. Is it always immoral to want to die?

2. Will the legalization of euthanasia lead to forced killing of the old and the senile?

Active and Passive Euthanasia

James Rachels is a professor of philosophy at the University of Alabama, Birmingham. His most recent publication is The Elements of Moral Philosophy.

James Rachels

The distinction between active and passive euthanasia is thought to be crucial for medical ethics. The idea is that it is permissible at least in some cases, to withhold treatment and allow a patient to die, but it is never permissible to take any direct action designed to kill the patient. This doctrine seems to be accepted by most doctors, and it is endorsed in a statement adopted by the House of Delegates of the American Medical Association on December 4, 1973:

Reprinted by permission from *The New England Journal of Medicine*, vol. 292, no. 2 (Jan. 9, 1975), pp. 78–80.

The intentional termination of the life of one human being by another—mercy killing—is contrary to that for which the medical profession stands and is contrary to the policy of the American Medical Association.

The cessation of the employment of extraordinary means to prolong the life of the body when there is irrefutable evidence that biological death is imminent is the decision of the patient and/or his immediate family. The advice and judgment of the physician should be freely available to the patient and/or his immediate family.

However, a strong case can be made against this doctrine. In what follows, I will set out some of the relevant arguments, and urge doctors to reconsider their views on this matter.

To begin with a familiar type of situation, a patient who is dying of incurable cancer of the throat is in terrible pain, which can no longer be satisfactorily alleviated. He is certain to die within a few days, even if present treatment is continued, but he does not want to go on living for those days since the pain is unbearable. So he asks the doctor for an end to it, and his family joins in the request.

Suppose the doctor agrees to withhold treatment, as the conventional doctrine says he may. The justification for his doing so is that the patient is in terrible agony, and since he is going to die anyway, it would be wrong to prolong his suffering needlessly. But now notice this. If one simply withholds treatment, it may take the patient longer to die, and so he may suffer more than he would if more direct action were taken and a lethal injection given. This fact provides strong reason for thinking that, once the initial decision not to prolong his agony has been made, active euthanasia is actually preferable to passive euthanasia, rather than the reverse. To say otherwise is to endorse the option that leads to more suffering rather than less, and is contrary to the humanitarian impulse that prompts the decision not to prolong his life in the first place.

Part of my point is that the process of being "allowed to die" can be relatively slow and painful, whereas being given a lethal injection is relatively quick and painless. Let me give a different sort of example. In the United States about one in 600 babies is born with Down's syndrome. Most of these babies are otherwise healthy—that is, with only the usual pediatric care, they will proceed to an otherwise normal infancy. Some, however, are born with congenital defects such as intestinal obstructions that require operations if they are to live. Sometimes, the parents and the doctor will decide not to operate, and let the infant die. Anthony Shaw describes what happens then:

> … When surgery is denied [the doctor] must try to keep the infant from suffering while natural forces sap the baby's life away. As a surgeon whose natural inclination is to use the scalpel to fight off death, standing by and watching a salvageable baby die is the most emotionally exhausting experience I know. It is easy at a conference, in a theoretical discussion, to decide that such infants should be allowed to die. It is altogether different to stand by in the nursery and watch as dehydration and infection wither a tiny being over hours and days. This is a terrible ordeal for me and the hospital staff—much more so than for the parents who never set foot in the nursery.[1]

I can understand why some people are opposed to all euthanasia, and insist that such infants must be allowed to live. I think I can also understand why other people favor destroying these babies quickly and painlessly. But why should anyone favor letting "dehydration and infection wither a tiny being over hours and days?" The doctrine that says that a baby may be allowed to dehydrate and wither, but may not be given an injection that would end its life without suffering, seems so patently cruel as to require no further refutation. The strong language is not intended to offend, but only to put the point in the clearest possible way.

My second argument is that the conventional doctrine leads to decisions concerning life and death made on irrelevant grounds.

Consider again the case of the infants with Down's syndrome who need operations for congenital defects unrelated to the syndrome to live. Sometimes, there is no operation, and the baby dies, but when there is no such defect, the baby lives on. Now, an operation such as that to remove an intestinal obstruction is not prohibitively difficult. The reason why such operations are not performed in these cases is, clearly, that the child has Down's syndrome and the parents and doctor judge that because of that fact it is better for the child to die.

But notice that this situation is absurd, no matter what view one takes of the lives and potentials of such babies. If the life of such an infant is worth preserving, what does it matter if it needs a simple operation? Or, if one thinks it better that such a baby should not live on, what difference does it

---

1. A. Shaw: "Doctor, Do We Have a Choice?" *The New York Times Magazine,* Jan. 30, 1972, p. 54.

make that it happens to have an unobstructed intestinal tract? In either case, the matter of life and death is being decided on irrelevant grounds. It is the Down's syndrome, and not the intestines, that is the issue. The matter should be decided, if at all, on that basis, and not be allowed to depend on the essentially irrelevant question of whether the intestinal tract is blocked.

What makes this situation possible, of course, is the idea that when there is an intestinal blockage, one can "let the baby die," but when there is no such defect there is nothing that can be done, for one must not "kill" it. The fact that this idea leads to such results as deciding life or death on irrelevant grounds is another good reason why the doctrine should be rejected.

One reason why so many people think that there is an important moral difference between active and passive euthanasia is that they think killing someone is morally worse than letting someone die. But is it? Is killing, in itself, worse than letting die? To investigate this issue, two cases may be considered that are exactly alike except that one involves killing whereas the other involves letting someone die. Then, it can be asked whether this difference makes any difference to the moral assessments. It is important that the cases be exactly alike, except for this one difference, since otherwise one cannot be confident that it is this difference and not some other that accounts for any variation in the assessments of the two cases. So, let us consider this pair of cases:

In the first, Smith stands to gain a large inheritance if anything should happen to his six-year-old cousin. One evening while the child is taking his bath, Smith sneaks into the bathroom and drowns the child, and then arranges things so that it will look like an accident.

In the second, Jones also stands to gain if anything should happen to his six-year-old cousin. Like Smith, Jones sneaks in planning to drown the child in his bath. However, just as he enters the bathroom Jones sees the child slip and hit his head, and fall face down in the water. Jones is delighted; he stands by, ready to push the child's head back under if it is necessary, but it is not necessary. With only a little thrashing about the child drowns all by himself, "accidentally," as Jones watches and does nothing.

Now Smith killed the child, whereas Jones "merely" let the child die. That is the only difference between them. Did either man behave better, from a moral point of view? If the difference between killing and letting die were in itself a morally important matter, one should say that Jones's behavior was less reprehensible than Smith's. But does one really want to say that? I think not. In the first place, both men acted from the same motive, personal gain, and both had exactly the same end in view when they acted. It may be inferred from Smith's conduct that he is a bad man, although that judgment may be withdrawn or modified if certain further facts are learned about him—for example, that he is mentally deranged. But would not the very same thing be inferred about Jones from his conduct? And would not the same further consider-

> "... [K]illing is not in itself any worse than letting die; ... it follows that active euthanasia is not any worse than passive euthanasia."

ations also be relevant to any modification of this judgment? Moreover, suppose Jones pleaded, in his own defense, "After all, I didn't do anything except just stand there and watch the child drown. I didn't kill him; I only let him die." Again, if letting die were in itself less bad than killing, this defense should have at least some weight. But it does not. Such a "defense" can only be regarded as a grotesque perversion of moral reasoning. Morally speaking, it is no defense at all.

Now, it may be pointed out, quite properly, that the cases of euthanasia with which doctors are concerned are not like this at all. They do not involve personal gain or the destruction of normally healthy children. Doctors are concerned only with cases in which the patient's life is of no further use to him, or in which the patient's life has become or will soon become a terrible burden. However, the point is the same in these cases: the bare difference between killing and letting die does not, in itself, make a moral difference. If a doctor lets a patient die, for humane reasons, he is in the same moral position as if he had given the patient a lethal injection for humane reasons. If his decision was wrong—if, for example, the patient's illness was in fact curable—the decision would be equally regrettable no matter which method was used to carry it out. And if the doctor's decision was the right one, the method used is not in itself important.

The AMA policy statement isolates the crucial issue very well; the crucial issue is "the intentional termination of the life of one human being by another." But after identifying this issue, and forbidding "mercy killing," the statement goes on to deny that the cessation of treatment is the intentional termination of a life. This is where the mistake comes in, for what is the cessation of treatment, in these circumstances, if it is not "the intentional termination of the life of one human being by another?" Of course, it is exactly that, and if it were not, there would be no point to it.

Many people will find this judgment hard to accept. One reason, I think, is that it is very easy to conflate the question of whether killing is, in itself, worse than letting die, with the very different question of whether most actual cases of killing are more reprehensible than most actual cases of letting die. Most actual cases of killing are clearly terrible (think, for example, of all the murders reported in the newspapers), and one hears of such cases every day. On the other hand, one hardly ever hears of a case of letting die, except for the actions of doctors who are motivated by humanitarian reasons. So one learns to think of killing in a much worse light than of letting die. But this does not mean that there is something about killing that makes it in itself worse than letting die, for it is not the bare difference between killing and letting die that makes the difference in these cases. Rather, the other factors—the murderer's motive of personal gain, for example, contrasted with the doctor's humanitarian motivation—account for different reactions to the different cases.

I have argued that killing is not in itself any worse than letting die; if my contention is right, it follows that active euthanasia is not any worse than passive euthanasia. What arguments can be given on the other side? The most common, I believe, is the following:

"The important difference between active and passive euthanasia is that, in passive euthanasia, the doctor does not do anything to bring about the patient's death. The doctor does nothing, and the patient dies of whatever ills already afflict him. In active euthanasia, however, the doctor does something to bring about the patient's death: he kills him. The doctor who gives the patient with cancer a lethal injection has himself caused his patient's death; whereas if he merely ceases treatment, the cancer is the cause of the death."

A number of points need to be made here. The first is that it is not exactly correct to say that in passive euthanasia the doctor does nothing, for he does do one thing that is very important: he lets the patient die. "Letting someone die" is certainly different, in some respects, from other types of action—mainly in that it is a kind of action that one may perform by way of not performing certain other actions. For example, one may let a patient die by way of not giving medication, just as one may insult someone by way of not shaking his hand. But for any purpose of moral assessment, it is a type of action nonetheless. The decision to let a patient die is subject to moral appraisal in the same way that a decision to kill him would be subject to moral appraisal: it may be assessed as wise or unwise, compassionate or sadistic, right or wrong. If a doctor deliberately let a patient die who was suffering from a routinely curable illness, the doctor would certainly be to blame for what he had done, just as he would be to blame if he had needlessly killed the patient. Charges against him would then be appropriate. If so, it would be no defense at all for him to insist that he didn't "do anything." He would have done something very serious indeed, for he let his patient die.

Fixing the cause of death may be very important from a legal point of view, for it may determine whether criminal charges are brought against the doctor. But I do not think that this notion can be used to show a moral difference between active and passive euthanasia. The reason why it is considered bad to be the cause of someone's death is that death is regarded as a great evil—and so it is. However, if it has been decided that euthanasia—even passive euthanasia—is desirable in a given case, it has also been decided that in this instance death is no greater an evil than the patient's continued existence. And if this is true, the usual reason for not wanting to be the cause of someone's death simply does not apply.

Finally, doctors may think that all of this is only of academic interest—the sort of thing that philosophers may worry about but that has no practical bearing on their own work. After all, doctors must be concerned about the legal consequences of what they do, and active euthanasia is clearly forbidden by the law. But even so, doctors should also be concerned with the fact that the law is forcing upon them a moral doctrine that may well be indefensible, and has a considerable effect on their practices. Of course, most doctors are not now in the position of being coerced in this matter, for they do not re-

gard themselves as merely going along with what the law requires. Rather, in statements such as the AMA policy statement that I have quoted, they are endorsing this doctrine as a central point of medical ethics. In that statement, active euthanasia is condemned not merely as illegal but as "contrary to that for which the medical profession stands," whereas passive euthanasia is approved. However, the preceding considerations suggest that there is really no moral difference between the two, considered in themselves (there may be important moral differences in some cases in their *consequences*, but, as I pointed out, these differences may make active euthanasia, and not passive euthanasia, the morally preferable option). So, whereas doctors may have to discriminate between active and passive euthanasia to satisfy the law, they should not do any more than that. In particular, they should not give the distinction any added authority and weight by writing it into official statements of medical ethics.

Study Questions

1. Will legalizing active euthanasia corrupt the medical profession?
2. Will allowing active euthanasia lead to killing patients for their organs against their will?

2. Is it moral to keep brain dead patients "living" on respirators so that all of their useful organs can be transplanted into those who need them (farming the dead)?

Active and Passive Euthanasia: An Impertinent Distinction?

Thomas D. Sullivan

Because of recent advances in medical technology, it is today possible to save or prolong the lives of

Thomas D. Sullivan is a professor of philosophy at the College of St. Thomas in St. Paul, Minnesota.

Reprinted with permission from *The Human Life Review,* vol. III, no. 3 (Summer 1977), pp. 40–46. Copyright © 1977 by The Human Life Foundation, Inc.

many persons who in an earlier era would have quickly perished. Unhappily, however, it often is impossible to do so without committing the patient and his or her family to a future filled with sorrows. Modern methods of neurosurgery can successfully close the opening at the base of the spine of a baby born with severe myelomeningocoele, but do nothing to relieve the paralysis that afflicts it from the waist down or to remedy the patient's incontinence of stool and urine. Antibiotics and skin grafts can spare the life of a victim of severe and massive burns, but fail to eliminate the immobilizing contractions of arms and legs, the extreme pain, and the hideous disfigurement of the face. It is not surprising, therefore, that physicians and moralists in increasing number recommend that assistance should not be given to such patients, and that some have even begun to advocate the deliberate hastening of death by medical means, provided informed consent has been given by the appropriate parties.

The latter recommendation consciously and directly conflicts with what might be called the "traditional" view of the physician's role. The traditional view, as articulated, for example, by the House of Delegates of the American Medical Association in 1973, declared:

> The intentional termination of the life of one human being by another—mercy killing—is contrary to that for which the medical profession stands and is contrary to the policy of the American Medical Association.
>
> The cessation of the employment of extra-ordinary means to prolong the life of the body when there is irrefutable evidence that biological death is imminent is the decision of the patient and/or his immediate family. The advice and judgment of the physician should be freely available to the patient and/or his immediate family.

Basically this view involves two points: (1) that it is impermissible for the doctor or anyone else to terminate intentionally the life of a patient, but (2) that it is permissible in some cases to cease the employment of "extraordinary means" of preserving life, even though the death of the patient is a foreseeable consequence.

Does this position really make sense? Recent criticism charges that it does not. The heart of the complaint is that the traditional view arbitrarily rules out all cases of intentionally acting to terminate life, but permits what is in fact the moral equivalent, letting patients die. This accusation has been clearly articulated by James Rachels in a widely-read article that appeared in a recent issue of the *New England Journal of Medicine,* entitled "Active and Passive Euthanasia."[1] By "active euthanasia" Rachels seems to mean *doing something* to bring about a patient's death, and by "passive euthanasia," not doing anything, i.e., just letting the patient die. Referring to the A.M.A. statement, Rachels sees the traditional position as always forbidding active euthanasia, but permitting passive euthanasia. Yet, he argues, passive euthanasia may be in some cases morally indistinguishable from active euthanasia, and in other cases even worse. To make his point he asks his readers to consider the case of a Down's syndrome baby with an intestinal obstruction that easily could be remedied through routine surgery. Rachels comments:

> I can understand why some people are opposed to all euthanasia, and insist that such infants must be allowed to live. I think I can also understand why other people favor destroying these babies quickly and painlessly. But why should anyone favor letting 'dehydration and infection wither a tiny being over hours and days?' The doctrine that says that a baby may be allowed to dehydrate and wither, but may not be given an injection that would end its life without suffering, seems so patently cruel as to require no further refutation.[2]

Rachels' point is that decisions such as the one he describes as "patently cruel" arise out of a misconceived moral distinction between active and passive euthanasia, which in turn rests upon a distinction between killing and letting die that itself has no moral importance.

One reason why so many people think that there is an important moral difference between active and passive euthanasia is that they think killing someone is morally worse than letting someone

---

1. *The New England Journal of Medicine,* vol. 292 (Jan. 9, 1975), pp. 78–80.
2. *Ibid.,* pp. 78–79.

die. But is it? . . . To investigate this issue, two cases may be considered that are exactly alike except that one involves killing whereas the other involves letting someone die. Then, it can be asked whether this difference makes any difference to the moral assessments. . . .

In the first, Smith stands to gain a large inheritance if anything should happen to his six-year-old cousin. One evening while the child is taking his bath, Smith sneaks into the bathroom and drowns the child, and then arranges things so that it will look like an accident.

In the second, Jones also stands to gain if anything should happen to his six-year-old cousin. Like Smith, Jones sneaks in planning to drown the child in his bath. However, just as he enters the bathroom Jones sees the child slip and hit his head, and fall face down in the water. Jones is delighted; he stands by, ready to push the child's head back under if it is necessary. but it is not necessary. With only a little thrashing about the child drowns all by himself, "accidentally," as Jones watches and does nothing.[3]

Rachels observes that Smith killed the child, whereas Jones "merely" let the child die. If there's an important moral distinction between killing and letting die, then, we should say that Jones' behavior from a moral point of view is less reprehensible than Smith's. But while the law might draw some distinctions here, it seems clear that the acts of Jones and Smith are not different in any important way, or, if there is a difference, Jones' action is even worse.

In essence, then, the objection to the position adopted by the A.M.A. of Rachels and those who argue like him is that it endorses a highly questionable moral distinction between killing and letting die, which, if accepted, leads to indefensible medical decisions. Nowhere does Rachels quite come out and say that he favors active euthanasia in some cases, but the implication is clear. Nearly everyone holds that it is sometimes pointless to prolong the process of dying and that in those cases it is morally permissible to let a patient die even though a few hours or days could be salvaged by procedures that would also increase the agonies of the dying. But if it is impossible to defend a general distinction between letting people die and acting to terminate their lives directly, then it would seem that active euthanasia also may be morally permissible.

> *"The traditional view is that the intentional termination of human life is impermissible, irrespective of whether this goal is brought about by action or inaction."*

Now what shall we make of all this? It *is* cruel to stand by and watch a Down's baby die an agonizing death when a simple operation would remove the intestinal obstruction, but to offer the excuse that in failing to operate we didn't *do* anything to bring about death is an example of moral evasiveness comparable to the excuse Jones would offer for his action of "merely" letting his cousin die. Furthermore, it is true that if someone is trying to bring about the death of another human being, then it makes little difference from the moral point of view if his purpose is achieved by action or by malevolent omission, as in the cases of Jones and Smith.

But if we acknowledge this, are we obliged to give up the traditional view expressed by the A.M.A. statement? Of course not. To begin with, we are hardly obliged to assume the Jones-like role Rachels assigns the defender of the traditional view. We have the option of operating on the Down's baby and saving its life. Rachels mentions that possibility only to hurry past it as if that is not what his opposition would do. But, of course, that is precisely the course of action most defenders of the traditional position would choose.

Secondly, while it may be that the reason some rather confused people give for upholding the traditional view is that they think killing someone is

---

3. *Ibid.,* p. 79.

always worse than letting them die, nobody who gives the matter much thought puts it that way. Rather they say that killing someone is clearly morally worse than not killing them, and killing them can be done by acting to bring about their death or by refusing ordinary means to keep them alive in order to bring about the same goal.

What I am suggesting is that Rachels' objections leave the position he sets out to criticize untouched. It is worth noting that the jargon of active and passive euthanasia—and it is jargon—does not appear in the resolution. Nor does the resolution state or imply the distinction Rachels attacks, a distinction that puts a moral premium on overt behavior—moving or not moving one's parts—while totally ignoring the intentions of the agent. That no such distinction is being drawn seems clear from the fact that the A.M.A. resolution speaks approvingly of ceasing to use extra-ordinary means in certain cases, and such withdrawals might easily involve bodily movement, for example unplugging an oxygen machine.

In addition to saddling his opposition with an indefensible distinction it doesn't make, Rachels proceeds to ignore one that it does make—one that is crucial to a just interpretation of the view. Recall the A.M.A. allows the withdrawal of what it calls extra-ordinary means of preserving life; clearly the contrast here is with ordinary means. Though in its short statement those expressions are not defined, the definition Paul Ramsey refers to as standard in his book, *The Patient as Person,* seems to fit.

Ordinary means of preserving life are all medicines, treatments, and operations, which offer a reasonable hope of benefit for the patient and which can be obtained and used without excessive expense, pain, and other inconveniences.

Extra-ordinary means of preserving life are all those medicines, treatments, and operations which cannot be obtained without excessive expense, pain, or other inconvenience, or which, if used, would not offer a reasonable hope of benefit.[4]

Now with this distinction in mind, we can see how the traditional view differs from the position Rachels mistakes for it. The traditional view is that the intentional termination of human life is impermissible, irrespective of whether this goal is brought about by action or inaction. Is the action or refraining *aimed* at producing a death? Is the termination of life *sought, chosen or planned?* Is the intention deadly? If so, the act or omission is wrong.

But we all know it is entirely possible that the unwillingness of a physician to use extra-ordinary means for preserving life may be prompted not by a determination to bring about death, but by other motives. For example, he may realize that further treatment may offer little hope of reversing the dying process and/or be excruciating, as in the case when a massively necrotic bowel condition in a neonate is out of control. The doctor who does what he can to comfort the infant but does not submit it to further treatment or surgery may foresee that the decision will hasten death, but it certainly doesn't follow from that fact that he intends to bring about its death. It is, after all, entirely possible to foresee that something will come about as a result of one's conduct without intending the consequence or side effect. If I drive downtown, I can foresee that I'll wear out my tires a little, but I don't drive downtown with the intention of wearing out my tires. And if I choose to forego my exercises for a few days, I may think that as a result my physical condition will deteriorate a little, but I don't omit my exercise with a view to running myself down. And if you have to fill a position and select Green, who is better qualified for the post than her rival Brown, you needn't appoint Mrs. Green with the intention of hurting Mr. Brown, though you may foresee that Mr. Brown will feel hurt. And if a country extends its general education programs to its illiterate masses, it is predictable the suicide rate will go up, but even if the public officials are aware of this fact, it doesn't follow that they initiate the program with a view to making the suicide rate go up. In general, then, it is not the case that all the foreseeable consequences and side effects of our conduct are necessarily intended. And it is because the phy-

4. Paul Ramsey, *The Patient As Person* (New Haven and London: Yale University Press, 1970), p. 122. Ramsey abbreviates the definition first given by

Gerald Kelly, S. J., *Medico-Moral Problems* (St. Louis, Mo.: The Catholic Hospital Association, 1958), p. 129.

sician's withdrawal of extra-ordinary means can be otherwise motivated than by a desire to bring about the predictable death of the patient that such action cannot categorically be ruled out as wrong.

But the refusal to use ordinary means is an altogether different matter. After all, what is the point of refusing assistance which offers reasonable hope of benefit to the patient without involving excessive pain or other inconvenience? How could it be plausibly maintained that the refusal is not motivated by a desire to bring about the death of the patient? The traditional position, therefore, rules out not only direct actions to bring about death, such as giving a patient a lethal injection, but malevolent omissions as well, such as not providing minimum care for the newborn.

The reason the A.M.A. position sounds so silly when one listens to arguments such as Rachels' is that he slights the distinction between ordinary and extra-ordinary means and then drums on cases where *ordinary* means are refused. The impression is thereby conveyed that the traditional doctrine sanctions omissions that are morally indistinguishable in a substantive way from direct killings, but then incomprehensibly refuses to permit quick and painless termination of life. If the traditional doctrine would approve of Jones' standing by with a grin on his face while his young cousin drowned in a tub, or letting a Down's baby wither and die when ordinary means are available to preserve its life, it would indeed be difficult to see how anyone could defend it. But so to conceive the traditional doctrine is simply to misunderstand it. It is not a doctrine that rests on some supposed distinction between "active" and "passive euthanasia," whatever those words are supposed to mean, nor on a distinction between moving and not moving our bodies. It is simply a prohibition against intentional killing, which includes both direct actions and malevolent omissions.

To summarize—the traditional position represented by the A.M.A. statement is not incoherent. It acknowledges, or more accurately, insists upon the fact that withholding ordinary means to sustain life may be tantamount to killing. The traditional position can be made to appear incoherent only by imposing upon it a crude idea of killing held by none of its more articulate advocates.

Thus the criticism of Rachels and other reformers, misapprehending its target, leaves the traditional position untouched. That position is simply a prohibition of murder. And it is good to remember, as C. S. Lewis once pointed out:

> No man, perhaps, ever at first described to himself the act he was about to do as Murder, or Adultery, or Fraud, or Treachery.... And when he hears it so described by other men he is (in a way) sincerely shocked and surprised. Those others "don't understand." If they knew what it had really been like for him, they would not use those crude "stock" names. With a wink or a titter, or a cloud of muddy emotion, the thing has slipped into his will as something not very extraordinary, something of which, rightly understood in all of his peculiar circumstances, he may even feel proud.[5]

I fully realize that there are times when those who have the noble duty to tend the sick and the dying are deeply moved by the sufferings of their patients, especially of the very young and the very old, and desperately wish they could do more than comfort and companion them. Then, perhaps, it seems that universal moral principles are mere abstractions having little to do with the agony of the dying. But of course we do not see best when our eyes are filled with tears.

---

5. C. S. Lewis, *A Preface to Paradise Lost,* London: Oxford University Press, 1970, p. 126.

Study Questions

1. Is it immoral to intentionally kill someone who is dying and wants to die?

2. Can it ever be moral to discontinue ordinary treatment for the terminal patient? If so, when?

More Impertinent Distinctions and a Defense of Active Euthanasia

James Rachels is a professor of philosophy at the University of Alabama, Birmingham. His most recent publication is The Elements of Moral Philosophy.

James Rachels

Many thinkers, including almost all orthodox Catholics, believe that euthanasia is immoral. They oppose killing patients in any circumstances whatever. However, they think it is all right, in some special circumstances, to allow patients to die by withholding treatment. The American Medical Association's policy statement on mercy killing supports this traditional view. In my paper "Active and Passive Euthanasia"[1] I argued, against the traditional view, that there is in fact no moral difference between killing and letting die—if one is permissible, then so is the other.

Professor Sullivan[2] does not dispute my argument; instead he dismisses it as irrelevant. The traditional doctrine, he says, does not appeal to or depend on the distinction between killing and letting die. Therefore, arguments against that distinction "leave the traditional position untouched."

Is my argument really irrelevant? I don't see how it can be. As Sullivan himself points out,

> Nearly everyone holds that it is sometimes pointless to prolong the process of dying and that in those cases it is morally permissible to let a patient die even though a few hours or days could be salvaged by procedures that would also increase the agonies of the dying. But if it is impossible to defend a general distinction between letting people die and acting to terminate their

lives directly, then it would seem that active euthanasia also may be morally permissible.

But traditionalists like Professor Sullivan hold that active euthanasia—the direct killing of patients—is *not* morally permissible; so, if my argument is sound, their view must be mistaken. I cannot agree, then, that my argument "leaves the traditional position untouched."

However, I shall not press this point. Instead I shall present some further arguments against the traditional position, concentrating on those elements of the position which Professor Sullivan himself thinks most important. According to him, what is important is, first, that we should never *intentionally* terminate the life of a patient, either by action or omission, and second, that we may cease or omit treatment of a patient, knowing that this will result in death, only if the means of treatment involved are *extraordinary*.

Intentional and Nonintentional Termination of Life

We can, of course, distinguish between what a person does and the intention with which he does it. But what is the significance of this distinction for ethics?

---

1. "Active and Passive Euthanasia," *The New England Journal of Medicine,* vol. 292 (Jan. 9, 1975), pp. 78–80.
2. "Active and Passive Euthanasia: An Impertinent Distinction?" *The Human Life Review,* vol. III (1977), pp. 40–46.

The traditional view [says Sullivan] is that the intentional termination of human life is impermissible, irrespective of whether this goal is brought about by action or inaction. Is the action or refraining *aimed at* producing a death? Is the termination of life *sought, chosen or planned?* Is the intention deadly? If so, the act or omission is wrong.

Thus on the traditional view there is a very definite sort of moral relation between act and intention. An act which is otherwise permissible may become impermissible if it is accompanied by a bad intention. The intention makes the act wrong.

There is reason to think that this view of the relation between act and intention is mistaken. Consider the following example. Jack visits his sick and lonely grandmother, and entertains her for the afternoon. He loves her and his only intention is to cheer her up. Jill also visits the grandmother, and provides an afternoon's cheer. But Jill's concern is that the old lady will soon be making her will; Jill wants to be included among the heirs. Jack also knows that his visit might influence the making of the will, in his favor, but that is no part of his plan. Thus Jack and Jill do the very same thing—they both spend an afternoon cheering up their sick grandmother—and what they do may lead to the same consequences, namely influencing the will. But their intentions are quite different.

Jack's intention was honorable and Jill's was not. Could we say on that account that what Jack did was right, but what Jill did was wrong? No; for Jack and Jill did the very same thing, and if they did the same thing, we cannot say that one acted rightly and the other wrongly.[3] Consistency requires that we assess similar actions similarly. Thus if we are trying

to evaluate their *actions,* we must say about one what we say about the other.

However, if we are trying to assess Jack's *character,* or Jill's, things are very different. Even though their actions were similar, Jack seems admirable for what he did, while Jill does not. What Jill did—comforting an elderly sick relative—was a morally good thing, but we would not think well of her for it since she was only scheming after the old lady's money. Jack, on the other hand, did a good thing *and* he did it with an admirable intention. Thus we think well, not only of what Jack did, but of Jack.

The traditional view, as presented by Professor Sullivan, says that the intention with which an act is done is relevant to determining whether the act is right. The example of Jack and Jill suggests that, on the contrary, the intention is not relevant to deciding whether the *act* is right or wrong, but instead it is relevant to assessing the character of the person who does the act, which is very different.

Now let us turn to an example that concerns more important matters of life and death. This example is adapted from one used by Sullivan himself. A massively necrotic bowel condition in a neonate is out of control. Dr. White realizes that further treatment offers little hope of reversing the dying process and will only increase the suffering; so, he does not submit the infant to further treatment—even though he knows that this decision will hasten death. However, Dr. White does not seek, choose, or plan that death, so it is not part of his intention that the baby dies.

Dr. Black is faced with a similar case. A massively necrotic bowel condition in a neonate is out of control. He realizes that further treatment offers little hope of saving the baby and will only increase its suffering. He decides that it is better for the baby to die a bit sooner than to go on suffering pointlessly; so, with the intention of letting the baby die, he ceases treatment.

According to the traditional position, Dr. White's action was acceptable, but Dr. Black acted wrongly. However, this assessment faces the same problem we encountered before. Dr. White and Dr. Black did *the very same thing:* their handling of the cases was identical. Both doctors ceased treatment, knowing that the baby would die sooner, and both did

---

3. It might be objected that they did not "do the same thing," for Jill manipulated and deceived her grandmother, while Jack did not. If their actions are described in this way, then it may seem that "what Jill did" was wrong, while "what Jack did" was not. However, this description of what Jill did incorporates her intention into the description of the act. In the present context we must keep the act and the intention separate, in order to discuss the relation between them. If they *cannot* be held separate, then the traditional view makes no sense.

so because they regarded continued treatment as pointless, given the infants' prospects. So how could one's action be acceptable and the other's not? There was, of course, a subtle difference in their *attitudes* toward what they did. Dr. Black said to himself, "I want this baby to die now, rather than later, so that it won't suffer more; so I won't continue the treatment." A defender of the traditional view might choose to condemn Dr. Black for this, and say that his character is defective (although I would not say that); but the traditionalist should not say that Dr. Black's *action* was wrong on that account, at least not if he wants to go on saying that Dr. White's action was right. A pure heart cannot make a wrong act right; neither can an impure heart make a right act wrong. As in the case of Jack and Jill, the intention is relevant, not to determining the rightness of actions, but to assessing the character of the people who act.

There is a general lesson to be learned here. The rightness or wrongness of an act is determined by the reasons for or against it. Suppose you are trying to decide, in this example, whether treatment should be continued. What are the reasons for and against this course of action? On the one hand, if treatment is ceased the baby will die very soon. On the other hand, the baby will die eventually anyway, even if treatment is continued. It has no chance of growing up. Moreover, if its life is prolonged, its suffering will be prolonged as well, and the medical resources used will be unavailable to others who would have a better chance of a satisfactory cure. In light of all this, you may well decide against continued treatment. But notice that there is no mention here of anybody's intentions. The intention you would have, if you decided to cease treatment, is not one of the things you need to consider. It is not among the reasons either for or against the action. That is why it is irrelevant to determining whether the action is right.

In short, a person's intention is relevant to an assessment of his character. The fact that a person intended so-and-so by his action may be a reason for thinking him a good or a bad person. But the intention is not relevant to determining whether the act itself is morally right. The rightness of the act must be decided on the basis of the objective reasons for

or against it. It is permissible to let the baby die, in Sullivan's example, because of the facts about the baby's condition and its prospects—not because of anything having to do with anyone's intentions. Thus the traditional view is mistaken on this point.

Ordinary and Extraordinary Means of Treatment

The American Medical Association policy statement says that life-sustaining treatment may sometimes be stopped if the means of treatment are "extraordinary"; the implication is that "ordinary" means of treatment may not be withheld. The distinction between ordinary and extraordinary treatments is crucial to orthodox Catholic thought in this area, and Professor Sullivan reemphasizes its importance: he says that, while a physician may sometimes rightly refuse to use extraordinary means to prolong life, "the refusal to use ordinary means is an altogether different matter."

However, upon reflection it is clear that it is sometimes permissible to omit even very ordinary sorts of treatments.

> Suppose that a diabetic patient long accustomed to self-administration of insulin falls victim to terminal cancer, or suppose that a terminal cancer patient suddenly develops diabetes. Is he in the first case obliged to continue, and in the second case obliged to begin, insulin treatment and die painfully of cancer, or in either or both cases may the patient choose rather to pass into diabetic coma and an earlier death? . . . What of the conscious patient suffering from painful incurable disease who suddenly gets pneumonia? Or an old man slowly deteriorating who from simply being inactive and recumbent gets pneumonia: Are we to use antibiotics in a likely successful attack upon this disease which from time immemorial has been called "the old man's friend"?[4]

These examples are provided by Paul Ramsey, a leading theological ethicist. Even so conservative a thinker as Ramsey is sympathetic with the idea that,

---

4. *The Patient as Person* (New Haven: Yale University Press, 1970), pp. 115–116.

in such cases, life-prolonging treatment is not mandatory: the insulin and the antibiotics need not be used. Yet surely insulin and antibiotics are "ordinary" treatments by today's medical standards. They are common, easily administered, and cheap. There is nothing exotic about them. So it appears that the distinction between ordinary and extraordinary means does not have the significance traditionally attributed to it.

But what of the *definitions* of "ordinary" and "extraordinary" means which Sullivan provides? Quoting Ramsey, he says that

> Ordinary means of preserving life are all medicines, treatments, and operations, which offer a reasonable hope of benefit for the patient and which can be obtained and used without excessive expense, pain, and other inconveniences.
>
> Extra-ordinary means of preserving life are all those medicines, treatments, and operations which cannot be obtained without excessive expense, pain, or other inconvenience, or which, if used, would not offer a reasonable hope of benefit.

Do these definitions provide us with a useful distinction—one that can be used in determining when a treatment is mandatory and when it is not?

The first thing to notice is the way the word "excessive" functions in these definitions. It is said that a treatment is extraordinary if it cannot be obtained without *excessive* expense or pain. But when is an expense "excessive"? Is a cost of $10,000 excessive? If it would save the life of a young woman and restore her to perfect health, $10,000 does not seem excessive. But if it would only prolong the life of Ramsey's cancer-stricken diabetic a short while, perhaps $10,000 is excessive. The point is not merely that what is excessive changes from case to case. The point is that what is excessive *depends on* whether it would be a good thing for the life in question to be prolonged.

Second, we should notice the use of the word "benefit" in the definitions. It is said that ordinary treatments offer a reasonable hope of *benefit* for the patient; and that treatments are extraordinary if they will not benefit the patient. But how do we tell if a treatment will benefit the patient? Remember that we are talking about life-prolonging treatments; the "benefit," if any, is the continuation of life. Whether continued life is a benefit depends on the details of the particular case. For a person with a painful terminal illness, a temporarily continued life may not be a benefit. For a person in irreversible coma, such as Karen Quinlan, continued biological existence is almost certainly not a benefit. On the other hand, for a person who can be cured and resume a normal life, life-sustaining treatment definitely is a benefit. Again, the point is that in order to decide whether life-sustaining treatment is a benefit we must *first* decide whether it would be a good thing for the life in question to be prolonged.

> *"Terminal patients sometimes suffer pain so horrible that it is beyond the comprehension of those who have not actually experienced it.... Euthanasia is justified because it provides an end to that."*

Therefore, these definitions do not mark out a distinction that can be used to help us decide when treatment may be omitted. We cannot, by using the definitions, invent distinction that can be used to help us decide when treatment may be omitted. We cannot by using the definitions identify which treatments are extraordinary, and then use that information to determine whether the treatment may be omitted. For the definitions require that we must *already* have decided the moral questions of life and death *before* we can answer the question of which treatments are extraordinary!

We are brought, then, to this conclusion about the distinction between ordinary and extraordinary means. If we apply the distinction in a straightforward, commonsense way, the traditional doctrine is false, for it is clear that it is sometimes permissible to omit ordinary treatments. On the other hand, if we define the terms as suggested by Ramsey and Sullivan, the distinction is useless in practical decision-making. In either case, the distinction provides no help in formulating an acceptable ethic of letting die.

To summarize what has been said so far, the distinction between killing and letting die has no moral importance; on that Professor Sullivan and I agree. He, however, contends that the distinctions between intentional and nonintentional termination of life, and ordinary and extraordinary means, must be at the heart of a correct moral view. I believe that the arguments given above refute this view. Those distinctions are no better than the first one. The traditional view is mistaken.

In my original paper I did not argue in favor of active euthanasia. I merely argued that active and passive euthanasia are equivalent: *if* one is acceptable, so is the other. However, Professor Sullivan correctly inferred that I do endorse active euthanasia. I believe that it is morally justified in some instances and that at least two strong arguments support this position. The first is the argument from mercy; the second is the argument from the golden rule.

The Argument from Mercy

Preliminary Statement of the Argument

The single most powerful argument in support of euthanasia is the argument from mercy. It is also an exceptionally simple argument, at least in its main idea, which makes one uncomplicated point. Terminal patients sometimes suffer pain so horrible that it is beyond the comprehension of those who have not actually experienced it. Their suffering can be so terrible that we do not like even to read about it or think about it; we recoil even from the descriptions of such agony. The argument from mercy says: Euthanasia is justified because it provides an end to *that*.

The great Irish satirist Jonathan Swift took eight years to die, while, in the words of Joseph Fletcher,

"His mind crumbled to pieces."[5] At times the pain in his blinded eyes was so intense he had to be restrained from tearing them out with his own hands. Knives and other potential instruments of suicide had to be kept from him. For the last three years of his life, he could do nothing but sit and drool; and when he finally died it was only after convulsions that lasted thirty-six hours.

Swift died in 1745. Since then, doctors have learned how to eliminate much of the pain that accompanies terminal illness, but the victory has been far from complete. So, here is a more modern example.

Stewart Alsop was a respected journalist who died in 1975 of a rare form of cancer. Before he died, he wrote movingly of his experiences as a terminal patient. Although he had not thought much about euthanasia before, he came to approve of it after rooming briefly with someone he called Jack:

> The third night that I roomed with Jack in our tiny double room in the solid-tumor ward of the cancer clinic of the National Institutes of Health in Bethesda, Md., a terrible thought occurred to me.
>
> Jack had a melanoma in his belly, a malignant solid tumor that the doctors guessed was about the size of a softball. The cancer had started a few months before with a small tumor in his left shoulder, and there had been several operations since. The doctors planned to remove the softball-sized tumor, but they knew Jack would soon die. The cancer had metastasized—it had spread beyond control.
>
> Jack was good-looking, about 28, and brave. He was in constant pain, and his doctor had prescribed an intravenous shot of a synthetic opiate—a pain-killer, or analgesic—every four hours. His wife spent many of the daylight hours with him, and she would sit or lie on his bed and pat him all over, as one pats a child, only more methodically, and this seemed to help control the pain. But at night, when his pretty wife had left (wives cannot stay overnight at the NIH clinic) and darkness fell, the pain would attack without pity.

---

5. *Morals and Medicine* (Boston: Beacon Press, 1960), p. 174.

At the prescribed hour, a nurse would give Jack a shot of the synthetic analgesic, and this would control the pain for perhaps two hours or a bit more. Then he would begin to moan, or whimper, very low, as though he didn't want to wake me. Then he would begin to howl, like a dog.

When this happened, either he or I would ring for a nurse, and ask for a pain-killer. She would give him some codeine or the like by mouth, but it never did any real good—it affected him no more than half an aspirin might affect a man who had just broken his arm. Always the nurse would explain as encouragingly as she could that there was not long to go before the next intravenous shot—"Only about 50 minutes now." And always poor Jack's whimpers and howls would become more loud and frequent until at last the blessed relief came.

The third night of this routine, the terrible thought occurred to me: "If Jack were a dog," I thought, "what would be done with him?" The answer was obvious: the pound, and chloroform. No human being with a spark of pity could let a living thing suffer so, to no good end.[6]

The NIH clinic is, of course, one of the most modern and best-equipped hospitals we have. Jack's suffering was not the result of poor treatment in some backward rural facility; it was the inevitable product of his disease, which medical science was powerless to prevent.

I have quoted Alsop at length not for the sake of indulging in gory details but to give a clear idea of the kind of suffering we are talking about. We should not gloss over these facts with euphemistic language, or squeamishly avert our eyes from them. For only by keeping them firmly and vividly in mind can we appreciate the full force of the argument from mercy: If a person prefers—and even begs for—death as the only alternative to lingering on *in this kind of torment,* only to die anyway after a while, then surely it is not immoral to help this person die sooner. As Alsop put it, "No human being with a spark of pity could let a living thing suffer so, to no good end."

---

6. "The Right to Die with Dignity," *Good Housekeeping,* August 1974, pp. 69, 130.

The Utilitarian Version of the Argument

In connection with this argument, the utilitarians should be mentioned. They argue that actions and social policies should be judged right or wrong *exclusively* according to whether they cause happiness or misery; and they argue that when judged by this standard, euthanasia turns out to be morally acceptable. The utilitarian argument may be elaborated as follows:

1. Any action or social policy is morally right if it serves to increase the amount of happiness in the world or to decrease the amount of misery. Conversely, an action or social policy is morally wrong if it serves to decrease happiness or to increase misery.
2. The policy of killing, at their own request, hopelessly ill patients who are suffering great pain, would decrease the amount of misery in the world. (An example would be Alsop's friend Jack.)
3. Therefore, such a policy would be morally right.

The first premise of this argument, (1), states the Principle of Utility, which is the basic utilitarian assumption. Today most philosophers think that this principle is wrong, because they think that the promotion of happiness and the avoidance of misery are not the *only* morally important things. Happiness, they say, is only one among many values that should be promoted: freedom, justice, and a respect for people's rights are also important. To take one example: People *might* be happier if there were no freedom of religion; for, if everyone adhered to the same religious beliefs, there would be greater harmony among people. There would be no unhappiness caused within families by Jewish girls marrying Catholic boys, and so forth. Moreover, if people were brainwashed well enough, no one would mind not having freedom of choice. Thus happiness would be increased. But, the argument continues, even if happiness *could* be increased this way, it would not be right to deny people freedom of religion, because people have a right to make their own choices. Therefore, the first premise of the utilitarian argument is unacceptable.

There is a related difficulty for utilitarianism, which connects more directly with the topic of euthanasia. Suppose a person is leading a miserable life—full of more unhappiness than happiness—but does *not* want to die. This person thinks that a miserable life is better than none at all. Now I assume that we would all agree that the person should not be killed; that would be plain, unjustifiable murder. Yet it *would* decrease the amount of misery in the world if we killed this person—it would lead to an increase in the balance of happiness over unhappiness—and so it is hard to see how, on strictly utilitarian grounds, it could be wrong. Again, the Principle of Utility seems to be an inadequate guide for determining right and wrong. So we are on shaky ground if we rely on *this* version of the argument from mercy for a defense of euthanasia.

Doing What Is in Everyone's Best Interests

Although the foregoing utilitarian argument is faulty, it is nevertheless based on a sound idea. For even if the promotion of happiness and avoidance of misery are not the *only* morally important things, they are still very important. So, when an action or a social policy would decrease misery, that is *a* very strong reason in its favor. In the cases of voluntary euthanasia we are now considering, great suffering is eliminated, and since the patient requests it, there is no question of violating individual rights. That is why, regardless of the difficulties of the Principle of Utility, the utilitarian version of the argument still retains considerable force.

I want now to present a somewhat different version of the argument from mercy, which is inspired by utilitarianism but which avoids the difficulties of the foregoing version by not making the Principle of Utility a premise of the argument. I believe that the following argument is sound and proves that active euthanasia *can* be justified:

1. If an action promotes the best interests of *everyone* concerned, and violates *no one's* rights, then that action is morally acceptable.
2. In at least some cases, active euthanasia promotes the best interests of everyone concerned and violates no one's rights.
3. Therefore, in at least some cases active euthanasia is morally acceptable.

It would have been in everyone's best interests if active euthanasia had been employed in the case of Stewart Alsop's friend, Jack. First, and most important, it would have been in Jack's own interests, since it would have provided him with an easier, better death, without pain. (Who among us would choose Jack's death, if we had a choice, rather than a quick painless death?) Second, it would have been in the best interests of Jack's wife. Her misery, helplessly watching him suffer, must have been almost equal to his. Third, the hospital staff's best interests would have been served, since if Jack's dying had not been prolonged, they could have turned their attention to other patients whom they could have helped. Fourth, other patients would have benefited since medical resources would no longer have been used in the sad, pointless maintenance of Jack's physical existence. Finally, if Jack himself requested to be killed, the act would not have violated his rights. Considering all this, how can active euthanasia in this case be wrong? How can it be wrong to do an action that is merciful, that benefits everyone concerned, and that violates no one's rights?

The Argument from The Golden Rule

"Do unto others as you would have them do unto you" is one of the oldest and most familiar moral maxims. Stated in just that way, it is not a very good maxim: Suppose a sexual pervert started treating others as he would like to be treated himself; we might not be happy with the results. Nevertheless, the basic idea behind the golden rule is a good one. The basic idea is that moral rules apply impartially to everyone alike; therefore, you cannot say that you are justified in treating someone else in a certain way unless you are willing to admit that that person would also be justified in treating *you* in that way if your positions were reversed.

Kant and the Golden Rule

The great German philosopher Immanuel Kant (1724–1804) incorporated the basic idea of the Golden Rule into his system of ethics. Kant argued that we should act only on rules that we are willing to have applied universally; that is, we should behave as we would be willing to have *everyone* behave. He held that there is one supreme principle of morality, which he called "the Categorical Imperative." The Categorical Imperative says:

> Act only according to that maxim by which you can at the same time will that it should become a universal law.[7]

Let us discuss what this means. When we are trying to decide whether we ought to do a certain action, we must first ask what general rule or principle we would be following if we did it. Then, we ask whether we would be willing for everyone to follow that rule, in similar circumstances. (This determines whether "the maxim of the act"—the rule we would be following—can be "willed" to be "a universal law.") If we would not be willing for the rule to be followed universally, then we should not follow it ourselves. Thus, if we are not willing for others to apply the rule to *us,* we ought not apply it to *them.*

In the eighteenth chapter of St. Matthew's gospel there is a story that perfectly illustrates this point. A man is owed money by another, who cannot pay, and so he has the debtor thrown into prison. But he himself owes money to the king and begs that *his* debt be forgiven. At first the king forgives the debt. However, when the king hears how this man has treated the one who owed him, he changes his mind and "delivers him unto the tormentors" until he can pay. The moral is clear: If you do not think that others should apply the rule "Don't forgive debts!" to *you,* then you should not apply it to others.

The application of all this to the question of euthanasia is fairly obvious. Each of us is going to die someday, although most of us do not know when or how. But suppose you were told that you would die in one of two ways, and you were asked to choose between them. First, you could die quietly, and without pain, from a fatal injection. Or second, you could choose to die of an affliction so painful that for several days before death you would be reduced to howling like a dog, with your family standing by helplessly, trying to comfort you, but

---

7. *Foundations of the Metaphysics of Morals,* p. 422.

going through its own psychological hell. It is hard to believe that any sane person, when confronted by these possibilities, would choose to have a rule applied that would force upon him or her the second option. And if we would not want such a rule, which excludes euthanasia, applied to us, then we should not apply such a rule to others.

Implications for Christians

There is a considerable irony here. Kant [himself] was personally opposed to active euthanasia, yet his own Categorical Imperative seems to sanction it. The larger irony, however, is for those in the Christian Church who have for centuries opposed active euthanasia. According to the New Testament accounts, Jesus himself promulgated the Golden Rule as the supreme moral principle—"This is the Law and the Prophets," he said. But if this is the supreme principle of morality, then how can active euthanasia be always wrong? If I would have it done to me, how can it be wrong for me to do likewise to others?

R. M. Hare has made this point with great force. A Christian as well as a leading contemporary moral philosopher, Hare has long argued that "universalizability" is one of the central characteristics of moral judgment. ('Universalizability' is the name he gives to the basic idea embodied in both the Golden Rule and the Categorical Imperative. It means that a moral judgment must conform to universal principles, which apply to everyone alike, if it is to be acceptable.) In an article called "Euthanasia: A Christian View," Hare argues that Christians, if they took Christ's teachings about the Golden Rule seriously, would not think that euthanasia is always wrong. He gives this (true) example:

> The driver of a petrol lorry [i.e., a gas truck] was in an accident in which his tanker overturned and immediately caught fire. He himself was trapped in the cab and could not be freed. He therefore besought the bystanders to kill him by hitting him on the head, so that he would not roast to death. I think that somebody did this, but I do not know what happened in court afterwards.
>
> Now will you please all ask yourselves, as I have many times asked myself, what you wish

that men should do to you if you were in the situation of that driver. I cannot believe that anybody who considered the matter seriously, as if he himself were going to be in that situation and had now to give instructions as to what rule the bystanders should follow, would say that the rule should be one ruling out euthanasia absolutely.[8]

---

8. Philosophic Exchange (Brockport, NY), II:I (Summer 1975) p. 45.

We might note that *active* euthanasia is the only option here; the concept of passive euthanasia, in these circumstances, has no application....

Professor Sullivan finds my position pernicious. In his penultimate paragraph he says that the traditional doctrine "is simply a prohibition of murder," and that those of us who think otherwise are confused, teary-eyed sentimentalists. But the traditional doctrine is not that. It is a muddle of indefensible claims, backed by tradition but not by reason.

Study Questions

1. Will voluntary active euthanasia lead to involuntary euthanasia?

2. Will doctors be less zealous in keeping terminal patients alive if active euthanasia becomes legal (especially if organs are needed to transplant into other, younger patients)?

Moral Dilemmas

- John and Ann, both in their late sixties, have been married for forty-five years. At the age of sixty-eight, Ann finds out that she has Alzheimer's disease, an incurable brain-degenerative illness that leads to progressive senility and death. Ann tells John that she does not want to see the day of her own degradation through senility and incontinence, and she asks John to promise to allow her to die before her condition gets too much worse. Eventually Ann begins to deteriorate to such a degree that she doesn't even recognize her own husband or children. John, recalling his promise, gives her an overdose of sleeping pills and kills her. He is found out and indicted for murder.

  Did John do the right thing?
  Is he guilty of murder?

- After a major car accident, three teenagers are brought to a hospital. After examination, Dr. Eileen Jackson determines that they each need an organ to survive: two need a kidney, and one needs a lung. At the same time, a middle-aged derelict is found asleep near the hospital. Dr. Jackson recognizes him as an alcoholic and petty thief who also happens to have cancer and who will die in less than six months. The doctor also knows that the derelict has no friends or relatives. She decides to have him brought to the hospital. While she is alone with him, she injects him with a deadly poison so that she can use his organs to save the teenagers.

  Did Dr. Jackson do the right thing?
  Isn't it better for one person to die rather than three?

■ Michael, a young private in the army, has been sent into the field of battle. His best friend Kevin, assigned to the same battalion, has just been shot in the chest and is critically wounded. They both know that medical assistance is impossible and that the enemy is known for its extremely cruel torture of captives. Kevin begs his buddy Michael to kill him, before the enemy gets to him.

What should Michael do?

Suggested Readings

Bayles, Michael D., and Dallas M. High, eds. *Medical Treatment of the Dying: Moral Issues.* Cambridge, Mass.: Schenkman Publishing Co., 1978.

Beauchamp, Tom L., and James F. Childress. *Principles of Biomedical Ethics.* New York: Oxford University Press, 1979.

Kamerman, Jack B. *Death in the Midst of Life.* Englewood Cliffs, N.J.: Prentice-Hall, 1988.

Rachels, James. *The End Of Life.* Oxford, England: Oxford University Press, 1986.

Veatch, Robert, M., ed. *Case Studies in Medical Ethics.* Cambridge, Mass.: Harvard University Press, 1977.

Punishment

E very society is ordered through laws of various kinds. The laws represent the society's understanding of general welfare and right and wrong. However, human beings are morally limited and sometimes violate the laws of their own community. If the community is to preserve itself, its values, and respect for its laws, it must take measures to minimize these illegal incidents. One way this is done is through punishment.

Background

Punishment can be defined as some unpleasant consequence or experience, such as a fine, imprisonment, torture, exile, or death, that the state imposes on an individual for violation of a legal rule. According to the earliest records available, an individual could be punished regardless of whether he or she intended to or knowingly violated the norm. Today, many legal systems recognize that most infractions of legal rules deserve punishment only if the individual in question performed the act voluntarily (i.e., was not coerced by external threats, or was not suffering from internal mental states such as insanity, excusable ignorance, or some other rationality-reducing condition). This mental component of voluntarily committing a crime is called *mens rea*. Usually, a person who commits a crime but lacks mens rea will not be punished or will be punished less severely.

Primitive societies often viewed crime as an insult to the dieties or ancestral spirits. They believed that these spirits would bring calamity on the community if the violator was not punished. Death was widely used as a form of punishment. The Code of Hammurabi, which is one of the oldest codes of laws in existence and which originated in ancient Mesopotamia along the Tigris and Euphrates rivers (now Iraq) about 1700 B.C., prescribed death for about thirty different offences, including incest, swearing, casting a spell, burglary, and (for women) drinking alcohol in public. Some sociologists argue that punishment is the ritual expression of outrage at the crime and is a reaffirmation of the societal values undermined by the criminal. Punishment, on this view, promotes social solidarity by reinforcing the foundational social values. More radical thinkers argue that punishment is usually imposed by the ruling economic and political class on the lower class in order to maintain the privileges of the upper class. The greater the gap between the classes, the more severe the punishment on the lower class tends to be. Still others reject punishment altogether, and consider crime to be a disease that must be treated like any other disease, not by inflicting pain.

Capital punishment, or the death penalty, has a long history among humanity. Death has been used as a penalty not only for murder but also for sexual and religious offences including incest, adultery, and heresy. Means of inflicting death have included hanging, burning, stoning, crucifixion, beheading, mutilation, drowning, shooting, keelhauling, poisoning, and electrocution. One of the most horrifying methods of execution was practiced in the ancient Middle East. This method, called "the boats," involved placing the condemned into one boat and placing another boat on top, allowing the victim's head to protrude through a hole. He or she was then force-fed and kept alive as long as possible while milk and honey was regularly poured on the person's face to attract insects and flies, which would breed there and eventually devour the victim alive. In the Middle Ages, the church and state joined forces to burn heretics at the stake. In the early part of colonial American history, witchcraft was punished by death. However, gradually a historical trend toward limiting capital punishment to fewer offences has emerged, and some countries have completely abolished the death penalty. Even in those countries that still have executions, they are no longer public spectacles for the entertainment of the masses, but are private and highly structured events.

Historically, the retributive theory, supported by Immanuel Kant, and others, has been the most prevalent. This theory holds that the criminal has taken something unfairly from society, and justice demands that the lawbreaker must suffer. This is the "eye-for-an-eye" view, which holds that the wrongdoer deserves to be punished in proportion to his or her crime. Criminals are like parasites on society; they want the benefits of social cooperation, such as wealth, but they are not willing to contribute their fair share or to abide by social rules. The retributive theory holds that the only justifications necessary for punishing a criminal are that the person in fact committed the crime and that the punishment fits the crime.

The utilitarian theory of punishment, held by Jeremy Bentham (1748–1832), Cesare Beccaria (1738–1794), J. S. Mill (1806–1873), R. M. Hare and others first fully appeared on the historical stage in the eighteenth century. The retributive view, which was heavily influenced by religious conceptions of moral guilt and the need for removal of this guilt through penance, waned as the social power of religion was increasingly challenged by more scientific conceptions of crime and rehabilitation. The utilitarian view holds that we must always act to reduce pain and to reduce suffering in all of our actions. Utilitarians believe that the retributive view is based on some irrational need for revenge that merely increases overall suffering. They hold that the only justification for punishment is to prevent or deter future criminal acts. Utilitarians see punishment as an evil necessary to prevent greater evils in the future. Deterrence involves a two-fold purpose: *Specific deterrence* seeks to prevent future antisocial acts on the part of the criminal, and *general deterrence* is directed as a warning to potential criminals in society. Utilitarians also usually believe that imprisonment should serve as an opportunity to reform and rehabilitate the inmate so that he or she can become a contributing member of society upon release.

Supreme Court

The death penalty has existed in the United States since colonial times. The Eighth Amendment to the U.S. Constitution states that there shall be no "cruel and unusual punishment," yet the framers of the Constitution did not mean by this the exclusion of capital punishment, for they practiced it extensively. However, in *Furman v. Georgia* (1972), the U.S. Supreme Court ruled that the death penalty as then administered in many states was unconstitutional. The majority argued that the death penalty was implemented in an arbitrary, capricious, and discriminatory manner that especially penalized blacks and the poor. The majority did not, however, claim that capital punishment was in itself unconstitutional or immoral. The minority, on the other hand, did hold that the death penalty was unconstitutional, barbaric, and unnecessary to the achievement of deterrence, which they believed life imprisonment could accomplish.

In response to the *Furman* decision, many states formulated new laws regarding capital punishment. The majority opinion in *Gregg v. Georgia* (1976), written by Justices Potter Stewart, John Paul Stevens and Lewis F. Powell, ruled that the death penalty was constitutional. They argued that the intent of the Eighth Amendment was intended to prevent torture, not death, as a form of punishment. For them, the death penalty is an acceptable form of punishment for some crimes because it is an expression of society's moral outrage at conduct that undermines the very fabric of society. As retribution, it is in harmony with human nature's desire for revenge, and as such it promotes social stability. The justices went on to argue that the death penalty may also be a deterrent in premeditated or cold-blooded murders. However, the majority cautioned the states that, since death is irrevocable, the courts must take every measure to ensure a just and fair trial for all.

Justice Thurgood Marshall vehemently disagreed with the majority in the *Gregg* decision. According to Marshall, the death penalty is cruel and therefore unconstitutional. He disputes the majority's claim that it has deterrent value any greater than life imprisonment. Marshall adds that if the American people were fully informed, they would reject the death penalty as immoral and as contrary to the dignity of all persons.

R. M. Hare

R. M. Hare defends the utilitarian theory of punishment. In itself, punishment seems to be evil because it increases the amount of evil or pain in the world, for punishing a murderer cannot bring back the victim. The utilitarian justification for punishment is based on the assumption that punishment is a necessary evil because it prevents or makes less likely greater evil (more crime) in the future. Hence, utilitarians favor the deterrence view: Punishment makes future criminal acts less likely to occur. Utilitarians look to the future, whereas retributivists look to the past (the crime) and believe punishment is justified simply because the criminal deserves it.

One major controversy concerning the utilitarian view of punishment is whether it would allow the punishment of innocent individuals. Critics allege that an innocent person could be knowingly falsely accused and convicted of a crime in order to bring about some social benefit or utility. These critics point out that if the public at large believed the person to be guilty, deterrence would still be achieved, as utilitarians require, but at the cost of injustice. Some utilitarians have attempted to respond to this criticism by arguing that the very meaning of "punishment" tells us that the person is guilty, for an innocent person cannot be punished, although he or she can, of course, be harmed unjustifiably. Hare rejects this approach, for a person can and sometimes is punished for something he or she didn't do. Hare, nevertheless, believes that his version of utilitarianism will not allow the punishing of the innocent because, among other reasons, one could never guarantee that such an obviously unjust act would never be discovered. If it were uncovered, it would cause a decrease in public confidence in the fairness of the courts, police, and government in general, which would lead to the spread of general anxiety and fear throughout the population, thus reducing utility or happiness.

James P. Sterba

James P. Sterba believes that our understanding of punishment must distinguish between just and unjust, or ideal and non-ideal, circumstances. Under *ideal circumstances,* punishment would have four functions: (1) reform or rehabilitation of the criminal, (2) deterrence, (3) fairness, or the restoration of the fair distribution of goods that existed prior to the crime by compensating the victim, and

(4) assurance to law-abiding members of society that others are required to obey the law. Sterba believes that utilitarianism can account for all of these purposes of punishment except the fairness condition. Sterba argues that, in some cases, imposing a burden on criminals to prevent them from benefiting from their crimes, as fairness demands, may not necessarily maximize utility overall, hence utility and fairness may conflict. Sterba favors the *social contract theory* as the better justification for punishment. This theory requires us to decide on moral principles without knowing our own particular interests or whether we will end up a criminal or a victim. Under these circumstances, we would agree on safeguards against punishing the innocent, and also we would favor the victims over the criminals because criminals can more easily avoid their fate (of being a criminal) than victims can. Under the *non-ideal circumstances* of an unjust society, however, criminals may be individuals who are denied equal rights and equal opportunity to lead a good life, and thus punishment may be reduced or not applied at all.

John Rawls

John Rawls's theory seeks to combine the utilitarian and retributive views. He does this by distinguishing between justifying a practice or institution and justifying a particular action under that practice. Retributivists argue that the criminal deserves the punishment simply because crime deserves punishment. Utilitarians argue that deterrence of future criminals is the only thing that matters. Rawls thinks that both of these views have difficulties. Utilitarianism can justify punishing the innocent, and retributivism may allow too much punishment. Rawls reconciles the best elements of both views by arguing that the practice or institution of punishment is justified on utilitarian grounds, whereas punishing an individual criminal is justified on retributive grounds. Rawls explains his position by reference to the legislator and the judge. The legislator frames laws concerning punishment that will benefit society, whereas the judge makes specific decisions about how much and what type of punishment to apply to a particular criminal.

The question of punishment gives rise to the philosophical problems of justice and free choice. Do criminals choose to act in the way they do, or is free choice simply the name we give for our ignorance of why people do the things they do? If our society is unjust in that not all members have the same starting conditions or the same opportunities for self-development and success, can crime be reduced without addressing this problem? Should most punishment be replaced by the education and training of criminals to lead productive lives on the outside?

Majority Opinion in *Gregg v. Georgia*

Justices Potter Stewart, Lewis F. Powell, Jr., and John Paul Stevens

The issue in this case is whether the imposition of the sentence of death for the crime of murder un-

Justice Potter Stewart (1915–1985) was an Associate Justice of the U.S. Supreme Court from 1958 to 1981. Justice Lewis F. Powell was an Associate Justice of the U.S. Supreme Court from 1971 to 1987. Justice John Paul Stevens is an Associate Justice of the U.S. Supreme Court. He received his appointment to the Court in 1975.

United States Supreme Court, 428 U.S. 153 (1976).

der the law of Georgia violates the Eighth and Fourteenth Amendments.

I

The petitioner, Troy Gregg, was charged with committing armed robbery and murder. In accordance with Georgia procedure in capital cases, the trial was in two stages, a guilt stage and a sentencing stage....

... The jury found the petitioner guilty of two counts of armed robbery and two counts of murder.

At the penalty stage, which took place before the same jury, ... the trial judge instructed the jury that it could recommend either a death sentence or a life prison sentence on each count.... The jury returned verdicts of death on each count.

The Supreme Court of Georgia affirmed the convictions and the imposition of the death sentences for murder.... The death sentences imposed for armed robbery, however, were vacated on the grounds that the death penalty had rarely been imposed in Georgia for that offense....

II

... The Georgia statute, as amended after our decision in *Furman v. Georgia* (1972), retains the death penalty for six categories of crime: murder, kidnaping for ransom or where the victim is harmed, armed robbery, rape, treason, and aircraft hijacking....

III

We address initially the basic contention that the punishment of death for the crime of murder is, under all circumstances, "cruel and unusual" in violation of the Eighth and Fourteenth Amendments of the Constitution. In Part IV of this opinion, we will consider the sentence of death imposed under the Georgia statutes at issue in this case.

The Court on a number of occasions has both assumed and asserted the constitutionality of capital punishment. In several cases that assumption provided a necessary foundation for the decision, as the Court was asked to decide whether a particular method of carrying out a capital sentence would be allowed to stand under the Eighth Amendment. But until *Furman v. Georgia* (1972), the Court never confronted squarely the fundamental claim that the punishment of death always, regardless of the enormity of the offense or the procedure followed in imposing the sentence, is cruel and unusual punishment in violation of the Constitution. Although this issue was presented and addressed in *Furman,* it was not resolved by the Court. Four Justices would have held that capital punishment is not unconstitutional *per se;* two justices would have reached the opposite conclusion; and three Justices, while agreeing that the statutes then before the Court were invalid as applied, left open the question whether such punishment may ever be imposed. We now hold that the punishment of death does not invariably violate the Constitution.

A

The history of the prohibition of "cruel and unusual" punishment already has been reviewed at length. The phrase first appeared in the English Bill of Rights of 1689, which was drafted by Parliament at the accession of William and Mary. The English version appears to have been directed against punishments unauthorized by statute and beyond the jurisdiction of the sentencing court, as well as those disproportionate to the offense involved. The American draftsmen, who adopted the English phrasing in drafting the Eighth Amendment, were primarily concerned, however, with proscribing "tortures" and other "barbarous" methods of punishment.

In the earliest cases raising Eighth Amendment claims, the Court focused on particular methods of execution to determine whether they were too cruel to pass constitutional muster. The constitutionality of the sentence of death itself was not at issue, and the criterion used to evaluate the mode of execution was its similarity to "torture" and other "barbarous" methods....

But the Court has not confined the prohibition embodied in the Eighth Amendment to "barbarous" methods that were generally outlawed in the 18th century. Instead, the Amendment has been interpreted in a flexible and dynamic manner. The Court early recognized that a "principle to be vital must be capable of wider application than the mischief which gave it birth." Thus the Clause forbidding "cruel and unusual" punishments "is not fastened to the obsolete but may acquire meaning as public opinion becomes enlightened by a humane justice." . . .

It is clear from the foregoing precedents that the Eighth Amendment has not been regarded as a static concept. As Mr. Chief Justice Warren said, in an oftquoted phrase, "[t]he Amendment must draw its meaning from the evolving standards of decency that mark the progress of a maturing society." Thus, an assessment of contemporary values concerning the infliction of a challenged sanction is relevant to the application of the Eighth Amendment. As we develop below more fully, this assessment does not call for a subjective judgment. It requires, rather, that we look to objective indicia that reflect the public attitude toward a given sanction.

But our cases also make clear that public perceptions of standards of decency with respect to criminal sanctions are not conclusive. A penalty also must accord with "the dignity of man," which is the "basic concept underlying the Eighth Amendment." This means, at least, that the punishment not be "excessive." When a form of punishment in the abstract (in this case, whether capital punishment may ever be imposed as a sanction for murder) rather than in the particular (the propriety of death as a penalty to be applied to a specific defendant for a specific crime) is under consideration, the inquiry into "excessiveness" has two aspects. First, the punishment must not involve the unnecessary and wanton infliction of pain. Second, the punishment must not be grossly out of proportion to the severity of the crime.

B

Of course, the requirement of the Eighth Amendment must be applied with an awareness of the limited role to be played by the courts. This does not mean that judges have no role to play, for the Eighth Amendment is a restraint upon the exercise of legislative power. . . .

But, while we have an obligation to insure that constitutional bounds are not overreached, we may not act as judges as we might as legislators. . . .

Therefore, in assessing a punishment selected by a democratically elected legislature against the constitutional measure, we presume its validity. We may

not require the legislature to select the least severe penalty possible so long as the penalty selected is not cruelly inhumane or disproportionate to the crime involved. And a heavy burden rests on those who would attack the judgment of the representatives of the people.

This is true in part because the constitutional test is intertwined with an assessment of contemporary standards and the legislative judgment weighs heavily in ascertaining such standards. "[I]n a democratic society legislatures, not courts, are constituted to respond to the will and consequently the moral values of the people."

The deference we owe to the decisions of the state legislatures under our federal system is enhanced where the specification of punishments is concerned, for "these are peculiarly questions of legislative policy." Caution is necessary lest this Court become, "under the aegis of the Cruel and Unusual Punishment Clause, the ultimate arbiter of the standards of criminal responsibility . . . throughout the country." A decision that a given punishment is impermissible under the Eighth Amendment cannot be reversed short of a constitutional amendment. The ability of the people to express their preference through the normal democratic processes, as well as through ballot referenda, is shut off. Revisions cannot be made in the light of further experience.

C

In the discussion to this point we have sought to identify the principles and considerations that guide a court in addressing an Eighth Amendment claim. We now consider specifically whether the sentence of death for the crime of murder is a *per se* violation of the Eighth and Fourteenth Amendments to the Constitution. We note first that history and precedent strongly support a negative answer to this question.

The imposition of the death penalty for the crime of murder has a long history of acceptance both in the United States and in England. . . .

It is apparent from the text of the Constitution itself that the existence of capital punishment was accepted by the Framers. At the time the Eighth Amendment was ratified, capital punishment was a common sanction in every State. Indeed, the First Congress of the United States enacted legislation providing death as the penalty for specified crimes. . . .

For nearly two centuries, this Court, repeatedly and often expressly, has recognized that capital punishment is not invalid *per se*. . . .

Four years ago, the petitioners in *Furman* and its companion cases predicated their argument primarily upon the asserted proposition that standards of decency had evolved to the point where capital punishment no longer could be tolerated. The petitioners in those cases said, in effect, that the evolutionary process had come to an end, and that standards of decency required that the Eighth Amendment be construed finally as prohibiting capital punishment for any crime regardless of its depravity and impact on society. This view was accepted by two Justices. Three other Justices were unwilling to go so far; focusing on the procedures by which convicted defendants were selected for the death penalty rather than on the actual punishment inflicted, they joined in the conclusion that the statutes before the Court were constitutionally invalid.

The petitioners in the capital cases before the Court today renew the "standards of decency" argument, but developments during the four years since *Furman* have undercut substantially the assumptions upon which their argument rested. Despite the continuing debate, dating back to the 19th century, over the morality and utility of capital punishment, it is now evident that a large proportion of American society continues to regard it as an appropriate and necessary criminal sanction.

The most marked indication of society's endorsement of the death penalty for murder is the legislative response to *Furman*. The legislatures of at least 35 States have enacted new statutes that provide for the death penalty for at least some crimes that result in the death of another person. And the Congress of the United States, in 1974, enacted a statute providing the death penalty for aircraft piracy that results in death. These recently adopted statutes have attempted to address the concerns expressed by the Court in *Furman* primarily (i) by specifying the factors to be weighed and the procedures to be followed in deciding when to impose a capital sentence, or (ii) by making the death penalty mandatory for specified crimes. But all of the post-*Furman* statutes make clear that capital punishment itself has not been rejected by the elected representatives of the people. . . .

The jury also is a significant and reliable objective index of contemporary values because it is so directly involved. The Court has said that "one of the most important functions any jury can perform in making . . . a selection [between life imprisonment and death for a defendant convicted in a capital case] is to maintain a link between contemporary community values and the penal system." It may be true that evolving standards have influenced juries in recent decades to be more discriminating in imposing the sentence of death. But the relative infrequency of jury verdicts imposing the death sentence does not indicate rejection of capital punishment *per se*. Rather, the reluctance of juries in many cases to impose the sentence may well reflect the humane feeling that this most irrevocable of sanctions should be reserved for a small number of extreme cases. Indeed, the actions of juries in many States since *Furman* are fully compatible with the legislative judgments, reflected in the new statutes, as to the continued utility and necessity of capital punishment in appropriate cases. At the close of 1974 at least 254 persons had been sentenced to death since *Furman,* and by the end of March 1976, more than 460 persons were subject to death sentences.

As we have seen, however, the Eighth Amendment demands more than that a challenged punishment be acceptable to contemporary society. The Court also must ask whether it comports with the basic concept of human dignity at the core of the Amendment. Although we cannot "invalidate a category of penalties because we deem less severe penalties adequate to serve the ends of penology," the sanction imposed cannot be so totally without penological justification that it results in the gratuitous infliction of suffering.

The death penalty is said to serve two principal social purposes: retribution and deterrence of capital crimes by prospective offenders.[1]

---

1. Another purpose that has been discussed is the incapacitation of dangerous criminals and the consequent prevention of crimes that they may otherwise commit in the future.

In part, capital punishment is an expression of society's moral outrage at particularly offensive conduct. This function may be unappealing to many, but it is essential in an ordered society that asks its citizens to rely on legal processes rather than self-help to vindicate their wrongs.

The instinct of retribution is part of the nature of man, and channeling that instinct in the administration of criminal justice serves as an important purpose in promoting the stability of a society governed by law. When people begin to believe that organized society is unwilling or unable to impose upon criminal offenders the punishment they "deserve," then there are sown the seeds of anarchy—of self-help, vigilante justice, and lynch law. *Furman v. Georgia* (Stewart, J., concurring).

> *". . . [T]he infliction of death as a punishment for murder is not without justification and thus is not unconstitutionally severe."*

"Retribution is no longer the dominant objective of the criminal law," but neither is it a forbidden objective nor one inconsistent with our respect of the dignity of men. Indeed, the decision that capital punishment may be the appropriate sanction in extreme cases is an expression of the community's belief that certain crimes are themselves so grievous an affront to humanity that the only adequate response may be the penalty of death.

Statistical attempts to evaluate the worth of the death penalty as a deterrent to crimes by potential offenders have occasioned a great deal of debate. The results simply have been inconclusive. . . .

Although some of the studies suggest that the death penalty may not function as a significantly greater deterrent than lesser penalties, there is no convincing empirical evidence either supporting or refuting this view. We may nevertheless assume safely that there are murderers, such as those who act in passion, for whom the threat of death has little or no deterrent effect. But for many others, the death penalty undoubtedly is a significant deterrent. There are carefully contemplated murders, such as murder for hire, where the possible penalty of death may well enter into the cold calculus that precedes the decision to act. And there are some categories of murder, such as murder by a life prisoner, where other sanctions may not be adequate.

The value of capital punishment as a deterrent of crime is a complex factual issue the resolution of which properly rests with the legislatures, which can evaluate the results of statistical studies in terms of their own local conditions and with a flexibility of approach that is not available to the courts. Indeed, many of the post-*Furman* statutes reflect just such a responsible effort to define those crimes and those criminals for which capital punishment is most probably an effective deterrent.

In sum, we cannot say that the judgment of the Georgia Legislature that capital punishment may be necessary in some cases is clearly wrong. Considerations of federalism, as well as respect for the ability of a legislature to evaluate, in terms of its particular State, the moral consensus concerning the death penalty and its social utility as a sanction, require us to conclude, in the absence of more convincing evidence, that the infliction of death as a punishment for murder is not without justification and thus is not unconstitutionally severe.

Finally, we must consider whether the punishment of death is disproportionate in relation to the crime for which it is imposed. There is no question that death as a punishment is unique in its severity and irrevocability. When a defendant's life is at stake, the Court has been particularly sensitive to insure that every safeguard is observed. But we are concerned here only with the imposition of capital punishment for the crime of murder, and when a life has been taken deliberately by the offender,[2] we

---

2. We do not address here the question whether the taking of the criminal's life is a proportionate sanction where no victim has been deprived of live—for example, when capital punishment is imposed for rape, kidnaping, or armed robbery that does not result in the death of any human being.

cannot say that the punishment is invariably disproportionate to the crime. It is an extreme sanction, suitable to the most extreme of crimes.

We hold that the death penalty is not a form of punishment that may never be imposed, regardless of the circumstances of the offense, regardless of the character of the offender, and regardless of the procedure followed in reaching the decision to impose it.

IV

We now consider whether Georgia may impose the death penalty on the petitioner in this case.

A

While *Furman* did not hold that the infliction of the death penalty *per se* violates the Constitution's ban on cruel and unusual punishments, it did recognize that the penalty of death is different in kind from any other punishment imposed under our system of criminal justice. Because of the uniqueness of the death penalty, *Furman* held that it could not be imposed under sentencing procedures that created a substantial risk that it would be inflicted in an arbitrary and capricious manner.... \

Furman mandates that where discretion is afforded a sentencing body on a matter so grave as the determination of whether a human life should be taken or spared, that discretion must be suitably directed and limited so as to minimize the risk of wholly arbitrary and capricious action.

It is certainly not a novel proposition that discretion in the area of sentencing be exercised in an informed manner. We have long recognized that "[f]or the determination of sentences, justice generally requires ... that there be taken into account the circumstances of the offense together with the character and propensities of the offender." ...

Jury sentencing has been considered desirable in capital cases in order "to maintain a link between contemporary community values and the penal system—a link without which the determination of punishment could hardly reflect 'the evolving standards of decency that mark the progress of a maturing society.'" But it creates special problems. Much of the information that is relevant to the sentencing decision may have no relevance to the question of guilt, or may even be extremely prejudicial to a fair

determination of that question. This problem, however, is scarcely insurmountable. Those who have studied the question suggest that a bifurcated procedure—one in which the question of sentence is not considered until the determination of guilt has been made—is the best answer.... When a human life is at stake and when the jury must have information prejudicial to the question of guilt but relevant to the question of penalty in order to impose a rational sentence, a bifurcated system is more likely to ensure elimination of the constitutional deficiencies identified in *Furman*.

But the provision of relevant information under fair procedural rules is not alone sufficient to guarantee that the information will be properly used in the imposition of punishment, especially if sentencing is performed by a jury. Since the members of a jury will have had little, if any, previous experience in sentencing, they are unlikely to be skilled in dealing with the information they are given. To the extent that this problem is inherent in jury sentencing, it may not be totally correctible. It seems clear, however, that the problem will be alleviated if the jury is given guidance regarding the factors about the crime and the defendant that the State, representing organized society, deems particularly relevant to the sentencing decision....

While some have suggested that standards to guide a capital jury's sentencing deliberations are impossible to formulate, the fact is that such standards have been developed. When the drafters of the Model Penal Code faced this problem, they concluded "that it is within the realm of possibility to point to the main circumstances of aggravation and of mitigation that should be weighed *and weighed against each other* when they are presented in a concrete case."[3] While such standards are by necessity somewhat general, they do provide guidance to

---

3. The Model Penal Code proposes the following standards: "(3) Aggravating Circumstances.

"(a) The murder was committed by a convict under sentence of imprisonment.

"(b) The defendant was previously convicted of another murder or of a felony involving the use or threat of violence to the person.

"(c) At the time the murder was committed the defendant also committed another murder.

"(d) The defendant knowingly created a great risk of death to many persons.

the sentencing authority and thereby reduce the likelihood that it will impose a sentence that fairly can be called capricious or arbitrary. Where the sentencing authority is required to specify the factors it relied upon in reaching its decision, the further safeguard of meaningful appellate review is available to ensure that death sentences are not imposed capriciously or in a freakish manner.

In summary, the concerns expressed in *Furman* that the penalty of death not be imposed in an arbitrary or capricious manner can be met by a care-

---

"(e) The murder was committed while the defendant was engaged or was an accomplice in the commission of, or an attempt to commit, or flight after committing or attempting to commit robbery, rape or deviate sexual intercourse by force or threat of force, arson, burglary or kidnapping.

"(f) The murder was committed for the purpose of avoiding or preventing a lawful arrest or effecting an escape from lawful custody.

"(g) The murder was committed for pecuniary gain.

"(h) The murder was especially heinous, atrocious or cruel, manifesting exceptional depravity.

"(4) Mitigating Circumstances.

"(a) The defendant has no significant history of prior criminal activity.

"(b) The murder was committed while the defendant was under the influence of extreme mental or emotional disturbance.

"(c) The victim was a participant in the defendant's homicidal conduct or consented to the homicidal act.

"(d) The murder was committed under circumstances which the defendant believed to provide a moral justification or extenuation for his conduct.

"(e) The defendant was an accomplice in a murder committed by another person and his participation in the homicidal act was relatively minor.

"(f) The defendant acted under duress or under the domination of another person.

"(g) At the time of the murder, the capacity of the defendant to appreciate the criminality [wrongfulness] of his conduct or to conform his conduct to the requirements of law was impaired as a result of mental disease or defect or intoxication.

"(h) The youth of the defendant at the time of the crime." ALI Model Penal Code § 210.6 (Proposed Official Draft 1962).

---

fully drafted statute that ensures that the sentencing authority is given adequate information and guidance. As a general proposition these concerns are best met by a system that provides for a bifurcated proceeding at which the sentencing authority is apprised of the information relevant to the imposition of sentence and provided with standards to guide its use of the information.

We do not intend to suggest that only the above-described procedures would be permissible under *Furman* or that any sentencing system constructed along these general lines would inevitably satisfy the concerns of *Furman,* for each distinct system must be examined on an individual basis. Rather, we have embarked upon this general exposition to make clear that it is possible to construct capital-sentencing systems capable of meeting *Furman's* constitutional concerns.

B

We now turn to consideration of the constitutionality of Georgia's capital-sentencing procedures. In the wake of *Furman,* Georgia amended its capital punishment statute, but chose not to narrow the scope of its murder provisions. Thus, now as before *Furman,* in Georgia "[a] person commits murder when he unlawfully and with malice aforethought, either express or implied, causes the death of another human being." All persons convicted of murder "shall be punished by death or by imprisonment for life."

Georgia did act, however, to narrow the class of murderers subject to capital punishment by specifying 10 statutory aggravating circumstances, one of which must be found by the jury to exist beyond a reasonable doubt before a death sentence can ever be imposed. In addition, the jury is authorized to consider any other appropriate aggravating or mitigating circumstances. The jury is not required to find any mitigating circumstance in order to make a recommendation of mercy that is binding on the trial court, but it must find a *statutory* aggravating circumstance before recommending a sentence of death.

These procedures require the jury to consider the circumstances of the crime and the criminal before it recommends sentence. No longer can a Georgia jury do as Furman's jury did: reach a finding of the defendant's guilt and then, without guidance or direction, decide whether he should live or die. Instead, the jury's attention is directed to the specific circumstances of the crime: Was it committed in the course of another capital felony? Was it committed for money? Was it committed upon a peace officer or judicial officer? Was it committed in a particularly heinous way or in a manner that endangered the lives of many persons? In addition, the jury's attention is focused on the characteristics of the person who committed the crime: Does he have a record of prior convictions for capital offenses? Are there any special facts about this defendant that mitigate against imposing capital punishment (*e.g.,* his youth, the extent of his cooperation with the police, his emotional state at the time of the crime). As a result, while some jury discretion still exists, "the discretion to be exercised is controlled by clear and objective standards so as to produce non-discriminatory application."

As an important additional safeguard against arbitrariness and caprice, the Georgia statutory scheme provides for automatic appeal of all death sentences to the State's Supreme Court. That court is required by statute to review each sentence of death and determine whether it was imposed under the influence of passion or prejudice, whether the evidence supports the jury's finding of a statutory aggravating circumstance, and whether the sentence is disproportionate compared to those sentences imposed in similar cases.

In short, Georgia's new sentencing procedures require as a prerequisite to the imposition of the death penalty, specific jury findings as to the circumstances of the crime or the character of the defendant. Moreover, to guard further against a situation comparable to that presented in *Furman,* the Supreme Court of Georgia compares each death sentence with the sentences imposed on similarly situated defendants to ensure that the sentence of death in a particular case is not disproportionate. On their face these procedures seem to satisfy the concerns of *Furman.* No longer should there be "no meaningful basis for distinguishing the few cases in which [the death penalty] is imposed from the many cases in which it is not." ...

V

The basic concern of *Furman* centered on those defendants who were being condemned to death capriciously and arbitrarily. Under the procedures before the Court in that case, sentencing authorities were not directed to give attention to the nature or circumstances of the crime committed or to the character or record of the defendant. Left unguided, juries imposed the death sentence in a way that could only be called freakish. The new Georgia sentencing procedures, by contrast, focus the jury's attention on the particularized nature of the crime and the particularized characteristics of the individual defendant. While the jury is permitted to consider any aggravating or mitigating circumstances, it must find and identify at least one statutory aggravating factor before it may impose a penalty of death. In this way the jury's discretion is channeled. No longer can a jury wantonly and freakishly impose the death sentence; it is always circumscribed by the legislative guidelines. In addition, the review function of the Supreme Court of Georgia affords additional assurance that the concerns that prompted our decision in *Furman* are not present to any significant degree in the Georgia procedure applied here.

For the reasons expressed in this opinion, we hold that the statutory system under which Gregg was sentenced to death does not violate the Constitution. Accordingly, the judgment of the Georgia Supreme Court is affirmed.

Study Questions

1. Is capital punishment cruel and inhumane?

2. Does the death penalty deter crime?

3. Does the possibility of executing innocent individuals make capital punishment immoral?

Dissenting Opinion in *Gregg v. Georgia*

Justice Thurgood Marshall is Associate Justice of the U.S. Supreme Court—the first and only black member to sit on the Court. He received his appointment in 1967.

Justice Thurgood Marshall

In *Furman v. Georgia* (1972) (concurring opinion), I set forth at some length my views on the basic issue presented to the Court in [this case]. The death penalty, I concluded, is a cruel and unusual punishment prohibited by the Eighth and Fourteenth Amendments. That continues to be my view.

I have no intention of retracing the "long and tedious journey" that led to my conclusion in *Furman*. My sole purposes here are to consider the suggestion that my conclusion in *Furman* has been undercut by developments since then, and briefly to evaluate the basis for my Brethren's holding that the extinction of life is a permissible form of punishment under the Cruel and Unusual Punishment Clause.

In *Furman* I concluded that the death penalty is constitutionally invalid for two reasons. First, the death penalty is excessive. And second, the American people, fully informed as to the purposes of the death penalty and its liabilities, would in my view reject it as morally unacceptable.

Since the decision in *Furman*, the legislatures of 35 States have enacted new statutes authorizing the imposition of the death sentence for certain crimes, and Congress has enacted a law providing the death penalty for air piracy resulting in death. I would be less than candid if I did not acknowledge that these developments have a significant bearing on a realistic assessment of the moral acceptability of the death penalty to the American people. But if the constitutionality of the death penalty turns, as I have urged, on the opinion of an *informed* citizenry,

---

United States Supreme Court, 428 U.S. 153 (1976).

then even the enactment of new death statutes cannot be viewed as conclusive. In *Furman*, I observed that the American people are largely unaware of the information critical to a judgment on the morality of the death penalty, and concluded that if they were better informed they would consider it shocking, unjust, and unacceptable. A recent study, conducted after the enactment of the post-*Furman* statutes, has confirmed that the American people know little about the death penalty, and that the opinions of an informed public would differ significantly from those of a public unaware of the consequences and effects of the death penalty.

Even assuming, however, that the post-*Furman* enactment of statutes authorizing the death penalty renders the prediction of the views of an informed citizenry an uncertain basis for a constitutional decision, the enactment of those statutes has no bearing whatsoever on the conclusion that the death penalty is unconstitutional because it is excessive. An excessive penalty is invalid under the Cruel and Unusual Punishment Clause "even though popular sentiment may favor" it. The inquiry here, then, is simply whether the death penalty is necessary to accomplish the legitimate legislative purposes in punishment, or whether a less severe penalty—life imprisonment—would do as well.

The two purposes that sustain the death penalty as nonexcessive in the Court's view are general deterrence and retribution. In *Furman*, I canvassed the relevant data on the deterrent effect of capital punishment. The state of knowledge at that point, after literally centuries of debate, was summarized as follows by a United Nations Committee:

"It is generally agreed between the retentionists and abolitionists, whatever their opinions about the validity of comparative studies of deterrence, that the data which now exist show no correlation between the existence of capital punishment and lower rates of capital crime."

The available evidence, I concluded in *Furman,* was convincing that "capital punishment is not necessary as a deterrent to crime in our society." . . .

. . . The evidence I reviewed in *Furman* remains convincing, in my view, that "capital punishment is not necessary as a deterrent to crime in our society." The justification for the death penalty must be found elsewhere.

The other principle purpose said to be served by the death penalty is retribution. The notion that retribution can serve as a moral justification for the sanction of death finds credence in the opinion of my Brothers STEWART, POWELL, and STEVENS. . . . It is this notion that I find to be the most disturbing aspect of today's unfortunate [decision].

The concept of retribution is a multifaceted one, and any discussion of its role in the criminal law must be undertaken with caution. On one level, it can be said that the notion of retribution or reprobation is the basis of our insistence that only those who have broken the law be punished, and in this sense the notion is quite obviously central to a just system of criminal sanctions. But our recognition that retribution plays a crucial role in determining who may be punished by no means requires approval of retribution as a general justification for punishment. It is the question whether retribution can provide a moral justification for punishment—in particular, capital punishment—that we must consider.

My Brothers STEWART, POWELL, and STEVENS offer the following explanation of the retributive justification for capital punishment:

> The instinct for retribution is part of the nature of man, and channeling that instinct in the administration of criminal justice serves an important purpose in promoting the stability of a society governed by law. When people begin to believe that organized society is unwilling or unable to impose upon criminal offenders the punishment they "deserve," then there are sown the

seeds of anarchy—of self-help, vigilante justice, and lynch law.

This statement is wholly inadequate to justify the death penalty. As my Brother BRENNAN stated in *Furman,* "[t]here is no evidence whatever that utilization of imprisonment rather than death encourages private blood feuds and other disorders." It simply defies belief to suggest that the death penalty is necessary to prevent the American people from taking the law into their own hands.

In a related vein, it may be suggested that the expression of moral outrage through the imposition of the death penalty serves to reinforce basic moral values—that it marks some crimes as particularly offensive and therefore to be avoided. The argument is akin to a deterrence argument, but differs in that it contemplates the individual's shrinking from antisocial conduct, not because he fears punishment, but because he has been told in the strongest possible way that the conduct is wrong. This contention, like the previous one, provides no support for the death penalty. It is inconceivable that any individual concerned about conforming his conduct to what society says is "right" would fail to realize that murder is "wrong" if the penalty were simply life imprisonment.

"The death penalty, . . . is an excessive penalty forbidden by the Eighth and Fourteenth Amendments."

The foregoing contentions—that society's expression of moral outrage through the imposition of the death penalty pre-empts the citizenry from taking the law into its own hands and reinforces moral values—are not retributive in the purest sense. They are essentially utilitarian in that they portray the death penalty as valuable because of its beneficial results. These justifications for the death penalty are inadequate because the penalty is, quite clearly I think, not necessary to the accomplishment of those results.

There remains for consideration, however, what might be termed the purely retributive justification for the death penalty—that the death penalty is appropriate, not because of its beneficial effect on society, but because the taking of the murderer's life is itself morally good. Some of the language of the opinion of my Brothers STEWART, POWELL, and STEVENS . . . appears positively to embrace this notion of retribution for its own sake as a justification for capital punishment. They state:

> [T]he decision that capital punishment may be the appropriate sanction in extreme cases is an expression of the community's belief that certain crimes are themselves so grievous an affront to humanity that the only adequate response may be the penalty of death.

They then quote with approval from Lord Justice Denning's remarks before the British Royal Commission on Capital Punishment:

> The truth is that some crimes are so outrageous that society insists on adequate punishment, because the wrong-doer deserves it, irrespective of whether it is a deterrent or not.

Of course, it may be that these statements are intended as no more than observations as to the popular demands that it is thought must be responded to in order to prevent anarchy. But the implication of the statements appears to me to be quite different—namely, that society's judgment that the murderer "deserves" death must be respected not simply because the preservation of order requires it, but because it is appropriate that society make the judgment and carry it out. It is this latter notion, in particular, that I consider to be fundamentally at odds with the Eighth Amendment. The mere fact that the community demands the murderer's life in return for the evil he has done cannot sustain the death penalty, for as JUSTICES STEWART, POWELL, and STEVENS remind us, "the Eighth Amendment demands more than that a challenged punishment be acceptable to contemporary society." To be sustained under the Eighth Amendment, the death penalty must "compor[t] with the basic concept of human dignity at the core of the Amendment;" the objective in imposing it must be "[consistent] with our respect for the dignity of [other] men." Under these standards, the taking of life "because the wrongdoer deserves it" surely must fail, for such a punishment has as its very basis the total denial of the wrongdoer's dignity and worth.

The death penalty, unnecessary to promote the goal of deterrence or to further any legitimate notion of retribution, is an excessive penalty forbidden by the Eighth and Fourteenth Amendments. I respectively dissent from the Court's judgment upholding the [sentence] of death imposed upon the [petitioner in this case].

Study Questions

1. What happens when a murderer is sentenced to life imprisonment and murders a guard or an inmate?

2. Is capital punishment unfairly reserved for and imposed on poor, uneducated, and black criminals?

3. Should murderers who kill for money be executed?

Punishment and Retributive Justice

A graduate research professor of philosophy at the University of Florida, R. M. Hare was formerly a professor of philosophy at Oxford. He has published several books on ethics, most recently Moral Thinking, *and numerous articles.*

R. M. Hare

Although the problem of the justification of punishment, and particular problems about the justification of particular punishments, remain as pressing as ever, and crucial political decisions depend on the solutions to them, the philosophical study of the subject has not advanced as much as could have been hoped in the last thirty years. This is my excuse for starting by discussing a famous early paper by Lord Quinton (as he now is)[1] which is still widely read, and, more surprisingly, even accepted as the prevailing orthodoxy, in spite of its containing a very obvious mistake, which has indeed been pointed out by others long ago.[2] This makes me think that, in spite of the mistake, there must be something important in the paper which deserves to be rescued; and this we can do by looking carefully at the mistake and seeing whether Quinton's main thesis can survive its correction.

His main thesis is that the moral justification of punishment as an institution is utilitarian, and that the truth in retributivism is a purely logical truth. A utilitarian myself, I should naturally like to defend such a thesis, although, as should be evident from my other writings, I do not accept the common dogma that utilitarianism has to be at odds with Kantianism or even with tenable forms of deontology.[3] When all these positions are carefully formulated, they cease to be in disagreement. However, I shall in this paper argue, like Quinton, as a utilitarian. Since punishment is thought to be a prime example of a question on which utilitarians disagree

with Kantians and deontologists, it will be useful to point out that they need not. Quinton himself has done a lot to help resolve this dispute.

Quinton claims that what is true and essential is the so-called retributive theory of punishment is analytically true in virtue of the meaning of the word 'punish.' He says

> For the necessity of not punishing the innocent is not moral but logical. It is not, as some retributivists think, that we *may* not punish the innocent and *ought* only to punish the guilty, but that we *cannot* punish the innocent and *must* only punish the guilty ... The infliction of suffering on a person is only properly described as punishment if that person is guilty. The retributivist thesis, therefore, is not a moral doctrine, but an account of the meaning of the word 'punishment' (p. 137).

It is because I agree with the general tendency of Quinton's argument, and with most of the utilitarian conclusions that he supports with this premiss about the *logical* character of the retributivist thesis, that I wish, by amending the premiss in one particular, to plug one hole in his argument. For as

From *Philosophical Topics* 14, no. 2 (Fall 1986) 211–223 and by permission of Prof. R. M. Hare.

1. A.M. Quinton, 'On Punishment,' *Analysis* 14 (1953/4), p. 133.
2. See K. Baier, 'Is Punishment Retributive?', *Analysis* 16 (1955/6), p. 25.
3. See my 'The Ethics of Clinical Experimentation on Human Children,' in *Logic, Methodology and Philosophy of Science VII,* Proc. of 7th Int. Congress of Logic, Ph. and M. of Sc., Salzburg, 1983, ed. R. B. Marcus, G. B. H. Dorn and P. Weingartner (N. Holland, Amsterdam).

it stands the claim that one logically cannot punish the innocent seems to me wholly unconvincing. Logical theses of this sort rest on linguistic intuitions,[4] and my linguistic intuitions do not at all tally with Quinton's.

Quinton does consider the objection that 'the innocent can be punished and scapegoats are not logical impossibilities.'[5] And Professor Flew, who maintains a similar thesis,[6] also tries to answer this objection, though in a different way. Flew appeals to the vagueness of the term 'punish,' and calls such cases as I shall mention later 'metaphorical, secondary or nonstandard.'[7] The question is, however, whether the word 'punish' is *ever* used in the restricted way that he and Quinton maintain. Quinton, on the other hand, puts his main reliance on a comparison between 'punish' and 'that now familiar class of verbs whose first-person-present use is significantly different from the rest' (p. 138). But he does not succeed in showing that the verb 'punish' belongs to this class; it is certainly not a performative verb, as are the examples he quotes (one cannot punish someone by *saying* 'I hereby punish you,' as one can make a promise to someone by saying 'I hereby promise you that …'). However, since this argument of his has been dealt with satisfactorily by Professor Baier,[8] I shall not amplify this criticism now.

Consider the statement 'I am punishing you for something that you have not done.' I can see nothing *logically* wrong with saying this, and the use does not seem to me in any way peripheral. We can well imagine a member of the Tsarist secret police saying it to an unfortunate prisoner; for it is said to have been a maxim of theirs that it is better to shoot the wrong man than not to shoot anybody. Indeed, it is not even a sign of wickedness to say this: as Baier points out, a conscientious hangman, convinced that there has been a miscarriage of justice, might say it to his victim.[9]

What may have misled Quinton and Flew is this. Punishment is always, in virtue of the meaning of the word, *for* something. In legal punishments, it is always *for* the offence for which it is appointed by law. It is easy, but wrong, to infer from this that the person who is punished for something must, logically, have done it. But we can know that a person has been punished for an offence without knowing whether he actually committed it or not. The argument went on in Britain for many years about whether Timothy Evans had actually committed a murder for which he had undoubtedly been punished by hanging. When in the end it was accepted that he had not, we did not stop saying that he had been punished; nor did we start using 'punish' in a different sense from that in which both parties had been using it all along—those who thought he had done the murder and those who did not.

It may help if we compare the use of the word 'pay.' A payment is always *for* something. If I hand somebody (say a beggar) some of my money to keep for himself, for nothing, it is not a payment but a gift. The *Oxford English Dictionary* defines 'payment' as '… the giving of money, etc., in return for something or in discharge of a debt.' But this does not mean that it is logically impossible to pay money that is not due, or even money that you know is not due. If I am presented often enough with a bill for goods which I never had, and am threatened with proceedings, I may, if the sum involved is not large, pay the bill (and not in scarce quotes either). The words in the definition 'in return for something' do not necessarily imply that something has to exist. Similarly, when the *O.E.D.* says that a punishment is 'the infliction of a penalty in retribution *for* an offence,' this does not imply that the offence must actually have been committed by the man who is punished, nor even at all, nor even that the people who do the punishing think so. Quinton has made an illegitimate step from 'Punishment must be for an offence' to 'Punishment must be of a person who committed the offence.' Admittedly, when I say 'He was punished for the murder,' I imply that there was a murder; but that is in virtue of the use of the definite description 'the murder,' and has nothing to do with the word 'punished.' I could have said, without changing the meaning 'punished,' 'He was punished for the al-

---

4. See my *Moral Thinkings* (*MT,* Oxford, Oxford U.P., 1981), p. 9.

5. Quinton, p. 138.

6. A. G. N. Flew, 'The Justification of Punishment," *Philosophy* 29 (1954), p. 291. Cf.

7. Flew, p. 294.

8. Baier, p. 30.

9. Baier, p. 30.

leged murder'; and then I should not have implied that there was a murder at all.

Part of the source of Quinton's confusion is to be traced to some typically hyperbolic and rhetorical remarks by Bradley, in a well-known essay to which Quinton refers. Notice that Bradley, a fine specimen of a retributivist, does not cleave consistently to the view which Quinton fathers on the retributivists. Bradley's central view is, rather, that punishment of the innocent must be wrong and unjust. But he confuses this with a quite different view, that no harm inflicted on an innocent man can be *called* punishment. The two views indeed seem incompatible; for what logically cannot exist (punishment of the innocent, on Quinton's view) can hardly be unjust. I have in the quotation from Bradley that follows put in italics the words that express what I shall call the standard retributivist view that punishment of the innocent is wrong; and I have put the words that express the Quintonian version of retributivism (that there logically cannot be punishment of the innocent) in capitals.

> If there is any opinion to which the man of uncultivated morals is attached, it is the belief in the necessary connexion of punishment and guilt. PUNISHMENT IS PUNISHMENT, ONLY WHERE IT IS DESERVED. We pay the penalty, because we owe it, and for no other reason; and *if punishment is inflicted for any other reason whatever than because it is merited by wrong, it is a gross immorality, a crying injustice, an abominable crime* and NOT WHAT IT PRETENDS TO BE ... Having once the right to punish, we may modify the punishment according to the useful and the pleasant; but these are external to the matter, they cannot give us a right to punish, and *nothing can do that but criminal desert ... I am not to be punished, on the ordinary view, unless I deserve it.*[10]

Note that Bradley does not say here 'I am not punished unless I deserve it' (which would support Quinton's interpretation), but 'I am not *to be* punished.' My own guess as to Bradley's meaning is that

the passages in capitals, which seem to support Quinton's view, are confused pieces of rhetoric, and that the other passages represent Bradley's real position.

Quinton's own text is not immune from this confusion. He can say things like 'Essentially, then, retributivism is the view that only the guilty *are to be* punished,' but slides from this, via 'guilt is the necessary condition of punishment' (which is equivocal), to the view, which is his central one, that 'we cannot punish the innocent.'[11]

However, leaving Bradley, something a bit like Quinton's thesis might be truly maintained, not about the word 'punishment,' but about the word 'penalty.' The difference in meaning between these two words was first pointed out to me by Baier, and is of great importance. A penalty is, according to the *O.E.D.*, 'a loss, disability or disadvantage of some kind ... *ordained by law* to be inflicted for an offence.' Punishment, on the other hand, is defined as 'the *action* of punishing or the fact of being punished, the *infliction* of a penalty in retribution for an offence.' Thus we might say that penalties are hypothetical, punishments actual. There is a penalty for a certain offence if it is the law that *if* the offence be committed a certain sort of punishment shall be inflicted. Thus there can be penalties even if there are no punishments. Somebody might say without self-contradiction, of a country with Draconian laws, 'In that country they never have any punishments, because all the penalties are so atrocious that nobody commits any crimes.' Note also the oddness of the question put to a schoolboy after an interview with the headmaster at an old-fashioned school, 'Did your penalty hurt very much?'.

Now it is true of penalties that they cannot be ordained for *not* committing offences against the law to which they are attached. That is indeed a logical impossibility, and the promulgation of the penalty would be self-contradictory; and this would be a good way of rephrasing the point which Quinton ought to have been making. One could not consistently put up in the park a notice saying 'Do not pick the flowers: penalty for not picking the flowers $50.' This logical impossibility is of some impor-

---

10. F. H. Bradley, *Ethical Studies* (Oxford, Oxford U.P., 1876, 2nd Edn. 1927), pp. 26f.

11. Quinton, p. 137.

tance in the controversy between the retributivists and the utilitarians; for it lends some support to the often-canvassed compromise between the two views which allows the retributivists to have their way with regard to individual acts of punishing (they ought, that is to say, to be inflicted only where the law has been broken) but allows the utilitarians to have *their* way with regard to the so-called 'legislator's question' of what penalties we ought to have, and for what. Thus it is possible to combine a utilitarian theory about penalties with a retributive theory about punishments. This would suit Quinton's book, and I shall shortly be elaborating a form of this compromise, in terms of my own two-level theory of moral thinking.[12] Reflection on the problem of punishment was one of the things which led me to develop the theory.

Another way of putting essentially the same point as I have just been making about punishments and penalties is in terms of what I have called functional words.[13] These are words such that, if we know their meaning, we know at least something about the function of an object or person of the kind in question. Thus to know what an auger is, or what the word 'auger' means, is to know that augers are carpenters' tools for boring holes in wood, and thus to know that, if an auger will not bore holes in wood, it cannot be a good one.[14] Similarly to know what a carpenter is, is to know that carpenters have as their function the making of things out of wood shaped and fastened together; so if a carpenter (otherwise than temporarily) cannot do this, he cannot be a good carpenter.

'Punishment' is at least rather like a functional word: punishment, in order to fulfill its function, has to be in retribution for an offence, and, if there has been no offence by the person punished, the punishment cannot be a just one. (I leave out of consideration vicarious punishments, which in any case are usually considered unjust.) The major change is that from 'good' to 'just'; and this is important. But it gives us what may be a correct way of putting the point incorrectly formulated by Quinton. Quinton's way of putting it is like saying of the word 'auger' that in virtue of its meaning augers logically cannot be used for digging up potatoes. But if I use an auger for digging up potatoes, it is still an auger, though I am not using it *as* an auger (not using it in the function for which augers are designed). There is nothing *logically* improper in saying 'I am going to use (or am using) this auger for digging up the potatoes.' But it is true in virtue of the meaning of 'auger' that this would be an improper use of an auger. It would be technically improper, not logically improper, though it is a logical truth that it *would* be technically improper.

> *"... [T]he best principles will be the ones whose general adoption will have the best consequences all told for all those affected, considered impartially."*

Similarly with 'payment.' If I pay money which is not due, I am not doing the logically impossible; but it is logically impossible to be properly required to pay money which is not due. In the same way, if I use a tool-for-boring-holes not for boring holes, I am not using it for what it is for; and if I inflict on someone suffering which should only be inflicted on him if he has committed an offence, I am inflicting on him suffering which I should not inflict. The 'should's here are technical or moral or legal, depending on the context; but the consequence is a logical one, arising out of the meaning of the word 'punish.'

Another parallel is this: if I am awarding the prize for the biggest pumpkin, it is perfectly possible for me to award it to someone who has not entered the biggest pumpkin; but it is not logically possible for me *properly* so to award it.

We might be tempted at this point to find here an easy way of deriving an 'ought' from an 'is'; but it will not work. The argument would go 'A prize is

12. See *MT,* ch. 2 and *passim.*
13. See my *The Language of Morals* (Oxford, Oxford U.P., 1952), p. 100.
14. See *The Language of Morals,* p. 101.

by definition *for* a certain achievement; but this person has not achieved the achievement; therefore it ought not to be awarded to him.' And similarly, substituting 'punishment' for 'prize' and 'offence' for 'achievement.' Here the first premiss is supposed to be about language; the second is an ordinary statement of fact; and the third is a moral or other evaluative judgment.

But this is too easy. The situation is rather like that out of which Professor Searle got so much mileage in his notorious paper 'How to derive "ought" from "is"', about promises, to which I replied in my almost equally notorious paper 'The Promising Game.'[15] The point there was that, if we are going to have the word 'promise' in our language (i.e. have the institution of promising), we have to have a prior commitment to a certain moral principle according to which there is a moral obligation to keep promises. And from the fact that having such a moral principle is a necessary condition for the adoption of the use of a certain word, it does not follow that the moral principle itself has the necessity that it would have if it were true by definition. It is not necessary, logically or otherwise, for us to adopt the use of the word 'promise' or the word 'punishment.' If we do adopt them, we shall be showing our adherence to the principle that there is an obligation to keep promises, or to punish only the guilty. But we could decide (at a cost) to do without those words.

It is a very common mistake in philosophy, committed among others by Wittgenstein in what he said about pain, or at least by some of his disciples in expounding him, to think that, if a certain word cannot be introduced unless a certain assumption is made, then the assumption logically has to be made. This is simply not so. We can perhaps do without the word. We have to assume a certain view about other people's experiences if we are to teach children the use of the word 'pain'; but it may be that we only *think* that we have been successful in teaching it: they do not have pains, but have only learnt to mouth the word on the occasions on which we think they have pains. But it would be too much of a digression to pursue this point.[16]

The upshot is that we have established certain logical features of the word 'punish'; but, as we have seen, these do not suffice (and this is indeed the useful part of Quinton's thesis) to prove any *moral* conclusions about when it is right to punish. We need a totally different approach in order to show this. That is to say, if we are to have the word 'punish' in our language in the sense that it currently has, we have to agree that only offenders can justly be punished; but why should we have it in language in that sense? More generally: there are certain logical relations between the language and the institution, and between both and the obligation to obey the principle constitutive of the institution. But why have we a duty to adopt any of these? To have the institution of punishing entails having principles of a certain form. But why should we have that institution or that kind of principles? And, even given that they have to be of that form, why should they have one *content* rather than another? That is to say, even given that we have, by adopting the word, taken on the formal obligation to punish only for offences, how do we decide what, if anything, is to be an offence, and what is to be the punishment for it?

Nobody should be surprised if I now say that these questions can be answered satisfactorily by a theory like mine,[17] which divides moral thinking into two levels. The theory is able to achieve this because it is at one and the same time Kantian and utilitarian. The problem of retributive justice is generally thought to be a crucial area of disagreement between Kantians and utilitarians; but, as I have already hinted, a carefully formulated Kantian theory and a carefully formulated utilitarianism do not need to disagree.

To show this, let us first look at the scene as it is. We find ordinary people, including ordinary judges, legislators, policemen, etc., firmly wedded (at least we hope so) to a set of principles of retri-

---

15. J. R. Searle, *Ph. Rev.* 73 (1964). R. M. Hare, 'The Promising Game,' *Rev. Int. de Ph.* 70 (1964).

16. See my 'Pain and Evil,' *Proc. of Arist. Soc.* supp. vol. 38 (1964), p. 104, and 'Descriptivism,' *Proc. of Br. Acad.* 49. repr. in my *Essays on the Moral Concepts* (London, Macmillan, 1972), s.f.

17. See my *MT*.

butive justice. By 'firmly wedded' I mean not merely that they have moral opinions in the sense of being ready to express them when asked. I mean that they have what are called 'consciences': if they feel tempted to break these principles, they at once experience a string feeling of repugnance; if others break them, they experience feelings of what Sir Stuart Hampshire calls 'outrage or shock.'[18] We can if we wish dignify these experiences by the name of 'moral intuitions.' They are what Courts of Human Rights are apt to appeal to, with good results provided (and it is a big proviso) that their members have been brought up, or have schooled themselves, in the light of sound critical moral thinking.

In such a situation, everything will proceed just as intuitionists say it does, at the intuitive level. However, what are we to say to the citizens of a country where they believe in arbitrary sentencing and atrocious penalties? What are we to say even among ourselves when some particular principle in the administration of the law, or some particular piece of legislation, is questioned? For this, we shall need to do some critical thinking. I have tried to show elsewhere[19] that the critical thinking has to be utilitarian in method; but my way of showing this owes almost everything to Kant. I argued on a basis similar to what Kant called 'the groundwork of the metaphysic of morals,' but which I like to call the logic of the moral concepts.

Suppose that we start asking moral questions about punishment. We are not, as I have admitted, logically bound to do this, though there are strong non-logical reasons for doing it. But *if* we ask these moral questions, the rules of critical thinking imposed by the logic of the words we are using in our questions will compel us to try to assess the acceptance utility of various moral principles about punishment that we might adopt. These will include, first of all principles about the practice of courts in arriving at their verdicts and their sentences; then, proceeding in one direction, principles about the conduct of the police in trying to bring offenders before the courts; and in the other, principles to be followed by the legislature when deciding what criminal laws to make and what penalties to attach to them.

Are the attitudes which judges, legislators and ordinary people generally have in Western countries with regard to the administration of justice able to stand up to such a scrutiny? On the whole they are; but no doubt there is room for improvement; in some respects there might be better arrangements. But it is no use our thinking about this if we have no method for determining what *would* be better. I am suggesting that proposed new principles of conduct in these matters should be judged in the light of the utility of bringing them into use. This involves seeing how the bringing into use of various principles would affect the satisfaction of the preferences of all those affected. In other words the best principles will be the ones whose general adoption will have the best consequences all told for all those affected, considered impartially.

As I hope I made clear in *Moral Thinking,* such a suggestion is at once Kantian and utilitarian. Kant himself did not distinguish clearly enough between the two levels, and this is one of the sources of the widespread misunderstanding of his intentions. But in the suggestion just made, Kantian elements appear at both levels. At the critical level, when selecting the principles which we are to use at the intuitive level, we are treating everybody equally as an end (that is, willing as our own ends what they (rationally) will as their ends, and giving equal weight impartially to everybody's ends). Thus we are, as legislating members of the kingdom of ends, selecting those maxims for general use which we can will to be universal laws, no matter who is at the receiving end. In so doing, we are trying to maximize the realization of the ends of those affected, i.e., what recent utilitarians have called the satisfaction of their (rational) preferences.

The maxims themselves cannot be of unlimited specificity, for good practical reasons—above all the reason that they have to be built into our characters, and for this purpose a certain degree of generality is requisite. But the thought that goes to their selection could, if we had the time and the knowledge, be as specific as was needed to establish their

18. S. Hampshire, 'Morality and Pessimism,' Leslie Stephen Lecture, Cambridge, 1972, repr. in his *Public and Private Morality* (Cambridge, Cambridge U.P., 1978), p. 6.
19. See *MT,* chh. 5, 6.

acceptance utility. Kant wanted his maxims to be highly general and simple (perhaps, because of this rigorist upbringing, more simple than his method will really justify). But we can agree that they have to be *fairly* general, just because to be useful they have to apply to many situations which resemble one another in important respects, and have to be a suitable guide for moral education, which cannot cope with principles of infinite specificity.

It would be out of place here to examine the text of Kant in any more detail. My point is merely that, by applying Kantian universalizing impartiality at the critical level, we are able to select, for use at the intuitive level in our ordinary moral thinking, general, fairly simple principles or maxims such as Kant desired. And, without labouring the point, the resemblance of this scheme to the kind of act-cum-rule-utilitarianism advocated in my *Moral Thinking* will be obvious.

Such a utilitarian proposal is not open to the vulgar objections that are commonly brought against it by intuitionists, and in particular not to those which relate to punishment and retributive justice. These consist in alleging that a utilitarian judge would have, in consistency with his theory, to sentence entirely on the strength of the consequences in the particular case, rather narrowly delimited. For example, if it would have the best consequences in a particular case to send an innocent man to prison, this is what, it is alleged, the utilitarian judge would do. And, the objection goes on, this runs counter to our deepest moral convictions (which is what these objectors call their intuitions when they are pulling the rhetorical stops out, as was Bradley in the passage I quoted earlier). The objection is usually based on highly artificial examples, for the good reason that no real ones are forthcoming which support the objectors' case.[20]

But now we can see that the objection misses the point. A thoroughgoing and well informed act-utilitarian (the archangel as I have called him[21]) would know that more harm than good would come in the long run from breakdown of public confidence in the fairness of our judicial procedures, or of the police, than could ever be compen-

sated for by the good achieved by sentencing an innocent man. The same applies in general to any kind of (as we should call it, having been brought up the way we have) judicial malpractice. In the real world, as opposed to the examples provided by philosophers with axes to grind, it is rather obvious that the principles of retributive justice in which we all believe have a very high acceptance utility.

I am far less confident in the general principles about legislation that are currently accepted—if indeed we can say that any are. Act-utilitarianism of the two-level kind that I am advocating can give good guidance to legislators too, and they need it. What they should consider, when contemplating setting up a new offence, or altering the penalties for an existing one (rape for example), is again the acceptance utility of the principle on which they act, and indeed, since the law itself is a kind of principle, of the actual law which is being proposed. In considering, for example, the abolition of the restoration of capital or corporal punishment, what we should be considering are the consequences for the preference-satisfactions of all, treated impartially, of various possible laws about these matters, and of various possible public attitudes.

I hope it will not be said that I have *abandoned* justice in favour of utility.[22] The foundation of moral thinking (in essentials a Kantian foundation) is the impartiality required by the demand that we will universally in making our moral judgments. This impartiality requires us to treat the equal (rational) preferences (or, as Kant put it, wills) of all affected parties as of equal weight, i.e., to be fair to them all. This is the formal principle of justice on which everything else depends. In judging proposed pieces of legislation by their acceptance utility, we are following this requirement of equal concern, or formal justice in one of the senses of that expression. Those who live in a society have varying and often conflicting interests, which are a function of what they rationally will. Between these we have to be fair. We shall be fair if we do not give anybody's interest extra weight for any other reason than that it is greater.

This approach leads us to treat retributive justice as, basically, a form of distributive justice.[23] We are

---

20. See *MT*, chh. 8, 9.
21. See *MT*, ch. 3.

22. See *MT*, ch. 9.
23. See my *Freedom and Reason* (Oxford, Oxford U.P., 1963), p. 125 and *MT*, p. 162.

distributing fairly between the members of society the benefits and harms which come from living in that society subject to those laws. This is to be fair and just to all, viewing their interests with equal concern. If this impartial view leads us to assign certain rights to certain classes of people, as having the highest acceptance utility, those are the rights they should have, for that is the most just allocation of benefits and harms.

It is fairly obvious that, in society as we know it, the right to a fair trial will be one of these. So will the right to equality before the law, and to a democratic voice in legislation. There is no room here to justify the according of these rights, or to spell out in detail what will be their precise content; but I have shown how we should decide this. We should do it by treating everybody as one and nobody as more than one (Bentham[24]) and treating humanity, whether our own or other people's, always as an end and never merely as a means (Kant[25]), and so seeking to do the best impartially for all—whether we are choosing principles for courts or police to follow, or attitudes for them and the public to adopt, or laws for the legislators to enact.

The purpose of a system of retributive justice is to further impartially the interests of those affected. What *will* most further them (deterrence, or all the other many consequences of a system of punishments, or attempts to rehabilitate criminals and fit them back into society, or no penalties at all) is a factual question, depending on what people will or would rationally prefer, and on what would conduce to this. It can be clearly addressed only by those who have understood the point of punishment, which is, like the point of all moral action, the impartial furthering of interests.[26]

24. See J. S. Mill, *Utilitarianism* (1863), ch. 5, s.f.
25. I. Kant, *Groundwork of the Metaphysic of Morals,* ch. 2, s.f.

26. I have to thank Professor Michael Bayles for reading this paper and making many helpful suggestions. If I have not incorporated every one of them, it is for reasons of space, not disagreement.

Study Questions

1. Could utilitarianism ever knowingly allow the imprisonment of an innocent person for the greater social utility?
2. Is deterrence the only just basis for punishment?

Is There a Rationale for Punishment?

James P. Sterba

James P. Sterba is a professor of philosophy at the University of Notre Dame. He authored The Demands of Justice, *the forthcoming* How to Make People Just, *and edited several books and numerous articles on ethics and political philosophy.*

It is a commonplace in moral philosophy that circumstances can change the morality of an act. Thus,

From *The American Journal of Jurisprudence* 29 (1984): 29–43.

a rationale for paying one's taxes under certain circumstances (e.g., when taxes are being used for the public good) may not be a rationale for paying one's taxes under other circumstances (e.g., when taxes are being used for grossly immoral purposes). Unfortunately, philosophers have not taken this commonplace sufficiently to heart when reflecting upon a rationale for punishment. For in evaluating various rationales for punishment, philosophers have rarely noted that a rationale for punishing for a broad range of criminal activity under ideal circumstances in which justice prevails may not be a rationale for punishing for the same range of criminal activity under non-ideal circumstances in which basic injustices obtain. Indeed, failure to note the importance of ideal and non-ideal circumstances to the task of providing a rationale for punishment has led many philosophers to overstate what rationale there is for punishment in the relatively non-ideal societies in which we live and work. In what follows, I hope to go some way toward rectifying this deficiency in previous philosophical accounts of punishment by first presenting what I take to be a morally defensible rationale for punishment under ideal circumstances and then presenting what I take to be a morally defensible rationale for punishment under the relatively non-ideal circumstances in which we live and work.

Punishment Under Ideal Circumstances

A rationale for punishment under ideal circumstances is a rationale for punishment under circumstances in which social institutions and practices conform to the requirements of morally defensible principles of distributive justice.[1] Under such circumstances, the basic moral rights of every person would be generally respected, with the consequence that criminals would rarely be in a position to complain that they engaged in criminal activity because their society deprived them of a reasonable opportunity to lead a good life. To be sure, those who engaged in criminal activity under such circumstances would generally be seeking to unfairly

favor their own interests over the interests of others. Assuming, then, that ideal circumstances of this sort obtained in a society, what would be the rationale for punishment?[2]

Obviously one possible rationale for punishing persons for engaging in criminal activity under such circumstances would be to deter others from engaging in similar activity. For if the hardship of punishment inflicted on persons who are generally considered to be guilty of criminal activity appeared to make them substantially worse off than other persons with similar talents and opportunities who are generally considered to be law-abiding, then surely it would succeed in deterring would-be criminals at least to some degree. And if, in fact, it appeared that most offenders were so punished, the deterrent effect on others would be significant indeed. For would-be criminals would soon come to believe that engaging in criminal activity is an extremely risky affair.

A second possible rationale for punishment under ideal circumstances would be to reform the criminal. Presumably, in a society in which social institutions and practices accord with the requirements of distributive justice, even criminals would have been socialized in such a manner that they still could be influenced by moral considerations. Consequently, an enforced rehabilitation program that focused on inculcating in criminals a greater respect for the rights of others would presumably be able to significantly reduce recidivism among criminals. And if this were the case, reform would definitely serve as a possible rationale for inflicting the hardship of punishment on criminals.

Nevertheless, some may object to a reform rationale, claiming that the reform programs that have been tried have been dismal failures. Robert Martinson, for example, takes such a stance on the basis of a study of reported efforts at reform undertaken between 1945 and 1967.[3] What this study showed, ac-

---

1. Later in the paper I attempt to characterize such principles.

2. By "punishment" I simply mean "enforced deprivation or treatment for an offense." For a discussion of the definition of punishment, see John Kleinig, *Punishment and Desert* (The Hague, 1973), Chapter II.

3. Robert Martinson, "What Works?—Questions and Answers about Prison Reform," *Public Interest* (1974), pp. 22–54.

cording to Martinson, is that these efforts at reform have had "no appreciable effect on recidivism." Others, however, dispute Martinson's conclusion, claiming that although no reform program has proven generally effective, many reform programs have worked quite well with specific types of offenders.[4] But whatever the failure rate of reform programs in existing societies, that rate need not undermine the justification for such programs under ideal circumstances. Indeed, it would probably be a good thing that reform programs failed in existing societies if such programs simply taught criminals not to challenge basic injustices in their societies.

Yet a third possible rationale for punishment under ideal circumstances would be to restore a fair distribution of benefits and burdens among all those affected by criminal activity. Now criminals, by disrupting the fair distribution of benefits and burdens which obtains under ideal circumstances, would seem to benefit in two ways. Firstly, when others have assumed the burden of self-restraint required by the criminal law, criminals benefit by renouncing that burden.[5] Secondly, criminals also benefit in a more crime-specific manner, either by illegally depriving others of goods they possess, as in cases of burglary or fraud, or by illegally using force against others to satisfy their desires, as in cases of murder, rape, or assault. More importantly still, criminals sometimes benefit from their crimes more than their victims are harmed by them, e.g., when a wealthy person is robbed of a small sum of money. At other times criminals harm their victims more than they benefit themselves, e.g., when someone is killed for her meager possessions. Taking into account these various ways in which criminals can disrupt a fair distribution of benefits and burdens, this rationale for punishment would impose on criminals burdens which either prevent them from gaining any benefit from their crimes or

which approximate the burdens the criminals inflicted on their victims in the first place, whichever is greater.[6] This would be accomplished by depriving criminals of the goods they possess (which are needed to meet compensation, enforcement, and other social welfare costs), and/or by forcing criminals to benefit others (e.g., by providing deterrence, reform, or products of their labor). Thus, according to this rationale for punishment, the burdens to be imposed on criminals would serve to benefit the victims of crime, the legal enforcement system, and the general public.

Of course this fair distribution rationale for punishment assumes a certain commensurability between benefits and burdens, and some philosophers would surely reject the possibility of such commensurability.[7] Yet the commensurability that is presupposed is actually less demanding than might initially appear. For the fair distribution rationale for punishment does not assume we can make any *cardinal* interpersonal comparisons of benefits and burden—as, for example, would be required by the claim that the benefit to the criminal from her crime was twice as great as the harm to her victim. Rather the fair distribution rationale only assumes we can make *ordinal* interpersonal comparisons— which simply allow us to claim that the benefit a criminal derives from her crime is either greater than, equal to, or less than the harm to her victim, without claiming anything more precise. And in

---

4. Ted Palmer, *Correctional Intervention and Research* Toronto, 1978).

5. Herbert Morris and Andrew von Hirsh appear to restrict the role of the fair distribution rationale to correcting for just this type of benefit to the criminal. (See Herbert Morris, "Persons and Punishment," The Monist (1968), pp. 475–501; and Andrew von Hirsh, *Doing Justice* (New York, 1976), pp. 160-I note #4).

6. In the case of criminal attempts, the harm caused by the criminal would be a disruption of social stability. On this point, see, Lawrence Becker, "Criminal attempt and the Law of Crimes," *Philosophy and Public Affairs,* (1974), pp. 262–94; and James B. Bardy, "Punishing Attempts," *The Monist* (1980), pp. 240–251.

7. See George Sher, "An Unsolved Problem about Punishment," *Social Theory and Practice* (1977), pp. 156–157; Hugo Bedau, "Retributivism and the Concept of Punishment," *The Journal of Philosophy* (1978), pp. 612–613; Richard Wasserstrom, *Philosophy and Social Issue* (Notre Dame, 1980), pp. 143–146. For a more general challenge to the possibility of such commensurability, see Kenneth Arrow, *Social Choice and Individual Values,* Second Edition (New Haven, 1963) and my response, "A Rawlsian Solution to Arrow's Paradox," *Pacific Philosophical Quarterly* (1981), pp. 288–292.

other contexts, we do seem to be able to make such comparisons. For instance, in deciding how to allocate family resources, we might judge that Johnny is better off having a new pair of shoes than Suzy is hurt by not having a new catcher's mitt. Or in assessing university policies on leaves and sabbaticals we might judge that students would benefit more from a policy of limiting leaves and sabbaticals than professors would be harmed by such a policy. Consequently, there seems to be no reason to think that we cannot make the same sort of ordinal interpersonal comparisons to implement the fair distribution rationale for punishment. Moreover, it would surely suffice for fixing the amount of punishment required by this rationale if we could simply compare the benefit that criminals *standardly* derive from particular crimes with the harm their victims *standardly* suffer from such crimes. In fact, it may be the case that all we are able to do on the basis of these factors is to group crimes into four or five different categories.[8] Of course, more precise information about the particular criminal and the particular victim(s) would certainly be relevant when available, but it would not be necessary to implement this rationale for punishment.

Doubtless other philosophers will still object to this fair distribution rationale for punishment on the grounds that if all that is morally required is a fair distribution of benefits and burdens then it would presumably be acceptable to avoid punishment altogether by simply paying for one's crime before committing it.[9] Thus, for example, a wealthy individual could avoid punishment for assault by compensating her victim(s) ahead of time with a huge sum of money. Now if it were the case that this rationale did generally sanction such "pre-paid crime," then it would conflict with what we take to be a strict prohibition of criminal activity, and that would be a strong objection to its moral defensibility. But, in fact, this rationale would only rarely sanction a "pre-paid crime." For a "pre-paid crime" not only requires compensation in advance to all primary victims who would be directly harmed by the crime, it also requires compensation in advance to all secondary victims who would suffer fear and anxiety from knowing that they might be a primary victim.[10] Since it would be extremely difficult to locate and compensate in advance all primary and secondary victims, a "pre-paid crime" would have to be a rare occurrence indeed. For all practical purposes, therefore, the fair distribution rationale for punishment requires a strict prohibition of criminal activity.

Needless to say, this fair distribution rationale for punishment would apply straightforwardly only in cases in which a person has been *fairly* determined to be fully culpable for committing a crime. In cases in which there is less than full culpability—that is, in cases in which various mitigating conditions obtain—the rationale would require the imposition of a proportionally lesser punishment on the person. And, in cases in which there happens to be no culpability at all, this rationale would only require that there be compensation for any harm done to those whose rights have been nonculpably violated (e.g., as in cases of strict liability). There would be no requirement to prevent the nonculpable violator from deriving any benefit from her action.

A fourth possible rationale for punishment under ideal circumstances would be to assure the law-abiding members of a society that having assumed the burden of obeying the criminal law, they will secure for themselves the benefits of the law-abiding behavior of others. Clearly, such assurance would result from effectively implementing the three previous rationales for punishment. Thus, if the deterrence rationale were effectively implemented, the law-abiding members of a society would derive assurance from knowing that would-be criminals had been sufficiently deterred by punishment to accept the burdens of self-restraint required by the criminal law. Similarly, if the reform rationale were effectively implemented, the law-abiding members of a society would derive assurance from knowing that recidivism had been significantly reduced among criminals. Likewise, if the fair distribution rationale were effectively implemented,

8. For a similar view, see von Hirsch, pp. 82–83.

9. See, for example, Herbert Fingarette, "Punishment and Suffering," *Proceedings and Addresses of the American Philosophical Association* (Lancaster, 1977), pp. 501–502.

10. On this point, See Robert Nozick, *State, Anarchy and Utopia* (New York, 1974), p. 68.

the law-abiding members of a society would derive assurance at least to the extent that restoring a fair distribution of benefits and burdens also resulted in either deterrence or reform. However, since sometimes what reforms criminals does not suffice to deter would-be criminals, and since sometimes what restores a fair distribution of benefits and burdens does not suffice either to deter would-be criminals or to reform actual criminals, a deterrence rationale would appear to provide more assurance to the law-abiding members of a society than either a reform rationale or a fair distribution rationale. And if this is the case, then the assurance and deterrence rationales for punishment would be mutually supporting as well as, to some degree, mutually in conflict with both the reform and fair distribution rationales, which, it appears, are also mutually in conflict with each other.

The Problem of Conflict

Then how are we to provide a morally defensible resolution of the conflicts among the various rationales for punishment? Such a resolution would presuppose a higher-order moral theory that is capable of accounting for much of what is valuable in each of the rationales as a specification of its own more general requirements. To achieve this result, the requirements of the higher-order moral theory would have to be common to defenders of the opposing rationales, even though these defenders would disagree concerning the practical implications of the requirements. Indeed, to resolve conflicts among opposing moral rationales a higher-order moral theory would have to demonstrate to everyone's satisfaction the correct practical implications of the common ground shared by those rationales.

Now a higher-order moral theory that is frequently appealed to for the purpose of resolving conflicts among opposing moral rationales is utilitarianism. Utilitarianism, as is well known, would require us to maximize total net utility or well being in society, and would interpret all other moral requirements as simply means to that goal. Accordingly, utilitarianism would never favor the well being of a minority at the expense of the greater well being of the majority in a society. And

thus, utilitarianism, if we were to employ it to resolve the conflicts among our four rationales for punishment, would tend to favor the deterrence and assurance rationales over the reform and fair distribution rationales. For both the deterrence and assurance rationales aim at the well being of the law-abiding members of a society, and under ideal circumstances, the law-abiding members of a society would clearly constitute the overwhelming majority of a society. Hence, securing the well being of this overwhelming majority would clearly be the most promising way of maximizing total utility in a society.

Utilitarianism is also capable of accounting for many of the requirements of the reform rationale as well. Obviously, there would be no problem in cases in which the punishment that is required to produce reform also suffices to produce deterrences. The main problem concerns cases in which what suffices for reform does not suffice for deterrences and cases in which what suffices for deterrence does not suffice for reform. However, provided that increasing punishment to the extent that is necessary to produce deterrence or reform does not preclude attaining the other goal as well, it is hard to see why those who favored one of these two rationales for punishment should not accept the other as well. Utilitarians, at least, would tend to justify such a blending of the rationales of reform and deterrence.[11]

The most serious issue, however, concerns the degree to which utilitarianism can accommodate the fair distribution rationale for punishment. Of course, there would be little problem in cases in which restoring a fair distribution of benefits and burdens also secures reform, deterrence, or assurance, since utilitarianism, by and large, can account for such requirements. The difficulty would lie in cases in which restoring a fair distribution of benefits and burdens conflicts with the requirements of these other rationales. In such cases it may be possible for utilitarians to sanction some of the re-

---

11. See, for example, Karl Menninger, *The Crime of Punishment* (New York, 1975); and T. L. S. Sprigge, "Punishment and Moral Responsibility," in *Punishment and Human rights* edited by Milton Goldinger (Cambridge, 1974), pp. 73–98.

quirements of the fair distribution rationale on the grounds that pursuing fairness in such cases produces utilities that are greater than those that result from these other rationales. For example, it may be the case that the utilities that would come from having certain procedural safeguards against punishing the innocent would be greater than those that would result from an unrestricted pursuit of either reform or deterrence. But clearly this would not hold true with respect to all the requirements of the fair distribution rationale. For some of the requirements of this rationale do conflict with the maximization of utility. For example, there will certainly be cases in which the requirement of imposing a burden on the criminal in order to prevent her from deriving any benefit from her crimes will not be justifiable in terms of the maximization of utility since society would not benefit from those impositions as much as the criminal would by her freedom. And something similar would hold true with respect to the requirement of imposing a burden on the criminal which approximates the burden of the criminal inflicted on her victim in the first place. For there certainly will be cases in which the harm to the criminal would be greater than any benefit society would reap from reform, deterrence, assurance, or other good consequences.

Faced with such conflicts between the requirements of the fair distribution rationale and the maximization of utility, utilitarians might respond by claiming either

1. that such conflicts are simply instances in which the requirements of a morally acceptable fair distribution rationale are overridden by considerations of utility or
2. that such conflicts indicate the moral preferability of some other standard of fairness whose requirements are more compatible with considerations of utility.

The first response, however, overlooks the frequency of the conflicts between the fair distribution rationale and considerations of utility. The frequency of such conflicts makes it reasonable to believe that at least sometimes the fair distribution rationale will override the demands of utility. Moreover, since fairness is generally regarded as an

ultimate moral value, the acceptability of utilitarianism as a moral theory has always depended on the ability of the theory to show that fairness and utility rarely conflict, and that when they do it is plausible to think that the requirements of utility are morally overriding. Consequently, to grant the moral acceptability of a standard of fairness that frequently conflicts with the maximization of utility is tantamount to admitting the inadequacy of utilitarianism as a moral theory. Nor is the second response any more promising. For while it does seek to recognize fairness as an ultimate moral value, it does so at the expense of being unconvincing to anyone who initially favored the fair distribution rationale for punishment. After all, why should one reject the fair distribution rationale because it conflicts with the goal of maximizing utility? Why not reject the goal of maximizing utility because it conflicts with the fair distribution rationale?

> "... [T]here will certainly be cases in which the requirement of imposing a burden on the criminal ... will not be justifiable in terms of the maximization of utility...."

To resolve this impasse what is needed is a higher-order moral theory that would be acceptable to both utilitarians and defenders of the fair distribution rationale alike and that can be used to reasonably resolve the differences between them. Utilitarianism, as we have seen, is capable of functioning as a higher-order moral theory with respect to the deterrence, reform, and assurance rationales. But it cannot similarly function with respect to the difference between these rationales and the fair distribution rationale since many of the practical recommendations of the fair distribution rationale appear to be directly opposed to the maximization of utility. To resolve these latter differences, then, another higher-order moral theory is required. Happily the desired sort of higher-order moral theory can be found in recent formulations of social contract theory, for social contract theory, especially when formulated hypothetically so as not to presuppose an actual contract, has been widely accepted by both utilitarians and defenders of the fair distribution rationale alike, and, as I shall show, it can be used to reasonably resolve the differences between them[12]

Now according to the formulation of social contract theory I would suggest, moral principles are those principles we would agree to if we were to discount the knowledge of which particular interests happen to be our own.[13] Since we obviously know what our own particular interests are, in employing this version of social contract theory, we would just not be taking that knowledge into account when formulating moral principles. Rather we would be reasoning from our knowledge of all the particular interests that would be affected by our decision, but not from our knowledge of which particular interests happen to be our own. In employing such a decision procedure, therefore, we, like members of a jury who heed the judge's instruction to discount certain information in order to reach a fair verdict, would be able to give a fair hearing to everyone's particular interests. If we assume, further, that we were well informed of all the particular interests that could be affected by our decision and that we were fully capable of rationally deliberating with respect to that information, then our deliberations would culminate in a unanimous decision. This is because each of us would be deliberating in a rationally correct manner with respect to the same information and would be using a decision procedure that leads to a uniform evaluation of the alternatives. As a result, each of us would favor the same moral principles.

But what principles would we select using this procedure? Would we select principles that favored utilitarianism or would we select principles that favored the fair distribution rationale for punishment? Since we would be discounting our knowledge of which particular interests happen to be our own we would be attempting to decide what principles we would find acceptable assuming that we might in fact turn out to occupy the position of any of those having an interest in the legal enforcement system. Accordingly, we would want our legal enforcement system to have certain safeguards against punishing behavior that was excusable for reasons of accident, mistake, provocation, duress, or insanity. This means that we would generally favor the view that punishment is morally justified only when it is inflicted on a person who has committed an offense with the cognitive and volitional conditions of *mens rea*. On the same account, we would want to have procedural safeguards against punishing the innocent, safeguards such as the requirement of conduct, the presumption of innocence, and the evidentiary restrictions of due process. After all, when using this decision procedure we would have no way of assessing with confidence the probability of our being accused of a crime of which we were innocent or for which excusing conditions would be relevant. Unless we chose a legal enforcement system with excusing conditions and procedural safeguards against punishing the innocent, then, there would be very little we could do to protect ourselves against such possibilities. While under normal conditions, we could avoid killing someone deliberately, there is very little we could do to avoid killing someone accidentally or to avoid being accused of a crime of which we are innocent. Moreover, when using this decision procedure we would not be impressed by the gains in deterrence that could be attained by restricting the use of excusing

---

12. Utilitarians who also accept the contractual approach include R. M. Hare [see his "Justice and Equality" in *Justice: Alternative Political Perspectives,* edited by James P. Sterba (Belmont, 1980), pp. 105–119] and John Harsanyi [see his *Rational Behavior and Bargaining Equilibrium in Games and Social Situations* (Cambridge, 1977)]. Immanuel Kant is the best known classical defender of the fair distribution rationale who also accepts the contractual approach. Contemporary defenders of this rationale who also accept the contractual approach include David Richards [see his *The Moral Criticism of the Law* (Encino, 1977), Chapter VI; and myself [see "Retributive Justice," *Political Theory* (1977), pp. 349–362].

13. See *The Demands of Justice* (Notre Dame, 1980), Chapter 2.

conditions or procedural safeguards since we would have no grounds for thinking that we ourselves might not have to be punished in order to secure such gains in deterrence. We would, in short, favor the following principle:

Principle of Criminal Procedure

Punishment is to be applied only when (1) there are excusing conditions based on a general requirement of *mens rea,* and (2) there are safeguards to protect the innocent, safeguards such as the requirement of conduct, the presumption of innocence, and the evidentiary restrictions of due process.

While certain restrictions of this sort might also be required for the maximization of utility, when using this decision procedure the risk aversion we would have to finding ourselves in circumstances in which excusing conditions or procedural safeguards would be relevant would lead us to interpret the principle as imposing stronger restrictions on the use of punishment than could be justified by the maximization of utility.

Furthermore, provided that the legal enforcement system accords with the above principle, we would have grounds when using this decision procedure to favor the interests of the victim of crime over those of the criminal. By comparing the opportunities available to criminals and victims of crime, we would realize that criminals, unlike victims of crime, would have had sufficient opportunities to avoid their fate. To be sure, criminals would not have been "compelled" to pursue their interests at the expense of others. They would have acted as they did simply to unfairly benefit themselves since under ideal conditions there would have been ample legal means of pursuing their own interests. Consequently, unlike victims of crime, criminals could have been reasonably expected to act otherwise. On this account, when using this decision procedure we would want to improve the situation of victims of crime by imposing appropriate burdens on criminals.

But what burdens would be appropriate? Would burdens that suffice to provide reform, deterrence, or assurance be acceptable if they did not restore a fair distribution of benefits and burdens in society? Clearly not, for that could involve preferring the interests of the criminal to those of the victim of crime, and, as we have seen, when using this decision procedure we would have grounds for preferring the interests of the victim of crime to those of the criminal. Nor would it do once a fair distribution of benefits and burdens had been restored, to impose a greater burden on criminals in order to secure more reform, deterrence or assurance, since when using this decision procedure we would generally want to avoid imposing an excessive burden on any position which we assume that we might in fact occupy. This means that we would generally limit the burden to be imposed on the criminal to whatever is necessary to restore a fair distribution of benefits and burdens. Accordingly, we would endorse the following principle for fixing the amount of punishment:

Principle for Restoring Fairness

Punishment is to be generally restricted to a burden which either prevents the criminal from gaining any benefit from her crime or approximates the burden the criminal inflicted on her victim in the first place, whichever is greater.[14]

Obviously, in endorsing this principle, we would be favoring the fair distribution rationale over the deterrence, reform, or assurance rationales in ways that seriously conflict with the maximization of utility.

Utilitarians who accept social contract theory as a higher-order moral theory are thus faced with a difficult choice: either give up their commitment to social contract theory or modify their commitment to utilitarian goals. Nor can utilitarians easily choose to give up their commitment to social contract theory. For social contract theory is simply an interpretation of a commonly accepted standard of fairness

---

14. Of course, if there were some noncoercive way of restoring a fair distribution of benefits and burdens, such an alternative would clearly be morally preferable to the use of punishment. However, it is hard to imagine how this would ever the the case. I owe this point to Hugo Bedau.

which now has been shown to frequently conflict with, and presumably at least sometimes morally override, the requirements of utility. Since the acceptability of utilitarianism as a moral theory has always depended on showing that such standards of fairness *rarely* conflict with the requirements of utility, and that when they do, it is plausible to think that the requirements of utility are morally overriding, it would seem that unless the derivation of the above principles from social contract theory can be challenged, utilitarians have little choice but to modify their commitment to utilitarian goals.

Finally, it is important to note that when using this decision procedure for ideal circumstances we would have no reason to limit the practical application of the above-stated principles. This is because under such circumstances the comparative opportunity judgment that the criminal, unlike the victim of crime, could have been reasonably expected to act otherwise would generally hold true for the broadest range of criminal activity. On this account, when using this contractual decision procedure we would have grounds to favor the strictest practical application of the above-stated principles.[15]

Punishment Under Non-Ideal Circumstances

Unfortunately, under non-ideal circumstances the situation would be radically different. For under non-ideal circumstances there would be widespread violations of persons' moral rights with the conse-

---

15. In an interesting article, George Schedler has argued that when we use such a contractual decision-procedure we would *not* favor any principles of punishment because we would realize that implementing such principles would sometimes result in unintentionally punishing the innocent. But while it is undeniable that implementing the above-stated principles would sometimes have this result, failure to implement these principles would clearly give rise to even greater injustices by encouraging more frequent and more serious crimes. On this account, when using this contractual decision-procedure we would choose, as the lesser evil, to implement the above-stated principles. See George Schedler, "Can Retributivists Support Legal Punishment?" *Monist* (1980), pp. 185–198.

quences that many persons would be deprived of a reasonable opportunity to lead a good life. Normally this deprivation of opportunity would also be reflected in an unjust distribution of property since the opportunities we have are frequently a function of the property we control or the property that is controlled by our family or friends. (For example, the lack of opportunity many persons experience in the United States is not unrelated to the fact that 5% of the population controls 83% of corporate stock and 63% of businesses and professions.) Of course, in order to know when people have been deprived of a reasonable opportunity to lead a good life we need to determine what are morally defensible principles of distributive justice. Fortunately, such principles can be determined by the same social contract decision procedure that we used to resolve the conflict among the rationales for punishment.

Obviously, when using this decision procedure to arrive at principles of distributive justice we would be quite concerned about the pattern according to which opportunities would be distributed in society. However, this does not mean that we would favor a pattern that secured the highest possible minimum for those who are least advantaged. For that would require sacrificing at least some of the non-basic needs of the productive persons in society in order to satisfy the non-basic needs of those who in fact choose to be unproductive. Nevertheless, we would still have grounds to ensure that each of us has the opportunities necessary for satisfying her basic needs in the society in which she lives. And as long as such a minimum is guaranteed, we would have reason to allow free agreement and private appropriation to determine the distribution of opportunities that remain.[16] Thus we would accept the following principle of distributive justice:

The Needs and Agreement Principle

The results of voluntary agreement and private appropriation are morally justified provided each person is guaranteed the opportunities that are necessary for meeting the normal costs of satisfy-

---

16. For further argument, see *The Demands of Justice,* Chapters 2 and 5.

ing her basic needs in the society in which she lives.[17]

Since under non-ideal circumstances this principle would not be strictly adhered to, under non-ideal circumstances, many persons would lack a reasonable opportunity to lead a good life, having been unfairly, albeit legally, deprived of the opportunity necessary for satisfying their basic needs in the society in which they live.

Now suppose that one of these persons who has been unfairly deprived commits a crime in order to secure for herself the opportunities necessary to meet her basic needs. Is there a morally defensible rationale for punishing such a person? As we have seen, the ultimate moral grounds for favoring the fair distribution rationale under ideal circumstances is a social contract assessment of the comparative opportunity judgment that the criminal, unlike the victim of crime, could have been reasonably expected to act otherwise. But while this comparative opportunity judgment generally holds true under ideal circumstances, it does not hold true in many cases under non-ideal circumstances. Consequently, when using this same contractual decision procedure, we would not choose to punish criminal activity in such cases.

But what specifically would characterize the cases in which we would not choose to punish criminal activity? Firstly, in these cases other options (e.g., legal protest, civil disobedience, or revolutionary action) would have to be either ineffective for achieving reasonable progress toward a just society or too costly for those persons they would be intended to benefit. Secondly, in these cases there would have to be only minimal violations of the moral rights of others as determined by the above principle of distributive justice. This means that in these cases the criminal activity would be directed at appropriating surplus goods from those in society who have more than a fair share of opportunities to lead a good life, and appropriating such goods with a minimum of physical force. Hence, criminal activity that harms the less advantaged in society would

not be justified. Nor would it be justified to kill or seriously injure the more advantaged, except in self-defense, when attempting to dispossess them of their unjust holdings. Accordingly, when using this contractual decision procedure we would favor the following principle:

Principle for Withholding Punishment

Punishment should be withheld from persons who engage in criminal activity that (1) is undertaken after other options for achieving reasonable progress toward a just society have proven ineffective or too costly for those whom they are intended to benefit and that (2) involves only minimal violations of the moral rights of others.

Moreover, we would choose to withhold punishment in accordance with the above-stated principle whether or not the criminal activity was effective in securing the opportunity as necessary to meet the criminal's basic needs in the society in which she lives.

We have seen, therefore, that the Principle of Criminal Procedure and the Principle for Restoring Fairness determine a morally defensible rationale for punishment under ideal circumstances and that these two principles combined with the Principle for Withholding Punishment determine a morally defensible rationale for punishment under non-ideal circumstances. Now although both sets of principles favor the fair distribution rationale over the deterrence, reform, and assurance rationales in cases of conflict, the first set of principles justifies the application of punishment to the broadest range of criminal activity while the second set of principles justifies the application of punishment to most crimes against persons but to only *some* crimes against property. Happily, for those who dislike the limited justification for punishment in the relatively non-ideal societies in which we live and work, there is an appropriate remedy: provide a fairer distribution of benefits and burdens in society and more punishment will then be justified.[18]

---

17. The reasons for formulating the principle in precisely this way are given in *The Demands of Justice,* Chapter 2.

18. To quote from the President's Crime Commission Report of over a decade ago, "the most significant action that can be taken against crime is action designed to eliminate slums and ghettos, to improve educations, to provide jobs...."

1. Would Sterba allow capital punishment?

2. Is utility consistent with fairness?

Two Concepts of Rules

John Rawls is a professor of philosophy at Harvard. He is the author of A Theory of Justice *and many articles.*

John Rawls

In this paper I want to show the importance of the distinction between justifying a practice[1] and justifying a particular action falling under it, and I want to explain the logical basis of this distinction and how it is possible to miss its significance. While the distinction has frequently been made,[2] and is now becoming commonplace, there remains the task of explaining the tendency either to overlook it altogether, or to fail to appreciate its importance.

To show the importance of the distinction I am going to defend utilitarianism against those objections which have traditionally been made against it

From "Two Concepts of Rules" by John Rawls, *The Philosophical Review,* Vol. 64 (1955), pp. 3–13. Reprinted by permission of the author and the publisher.

1. I use the word "practice" throughout as a sort of technical term meaning any form of activity specified by a system of rules which defines offices, roles, moves, penalties, defenses, and so on, and which gives the activity its structure. As examples one may think of games and rituals, trials and parliaments.
2. The distinction is central to Hume's discussion of justice in *A Treatise of Human Nature,* bk. III, pt. ii, esp. secs. 2–4. It is clearly stated by John Austin in the second lecture of *Lectures on*

Jurisprudence (4th ed.; London, 1873), I, 116ff. (1st ed., 1832). Also it may be argued that J. S. Mill took it for granted in *Utilitarianism;* on this point cf. J. O. Urmson, "The Interpretation of the Moral Philosophy of J. S. Mill," *Philosophical Quarterly,* vol. III (1953). In addition to the arguments given by Urmson there are several clear statements of the distinction in *A System of Logic* (8th ed.; London, 1872), bk. VI, ch. xii pars. 2, 3, 7. The distinction is fundamental to J. D. Mabbott's important paper, "Punishment," *Mind,* n.s., vol. XLVIII (April, 1939). More recently the distinction has been stated with particular emphasis by S. E. Toulmin in *The Place of Reason in Ethics* (Cambridge, 1950), see esp. ch. xi, where it plays a major part in his account of moral reasoning. Toulmin doesn't explain the basis of the distinction, nor how one might in connection with punishment and the obligation to keep promises. I hope to show that if one uses the distinction in question then one can state utilitarianism in a way which makes it a much better explication of our considered moral judgments than these traditional objections would seem to admit.[3] Thus the importance of the distinction is shown by the way it strengthens the utilitarian view regardless of whether that view is completely defensible or not.

To explain how the significance of the distinction may be overlooked, I am going to discuss two conceptions of rules. One of these conceptions conceals the importance of distinguishing between the justification of a rule or practice and the justification of a particular action falling under it. The other conception makes it clear why this distinction must be made and what is its logical basis.

The subject of punishment, in the sense of attaching legal penalties to the violation of legal rules, has always been a troubling moral question.[4] The trouble about it has not been that people disagree as to whether or not punishment is justifiable. Most people have held that, freed from certain abuses, it is an acceptable institution. Only a few have rejected punishment entirely, which is rather surprising when one considers all that can be said against it. The difficulty is with the justification of punishment: various arguments for it have been given by moral philosophers, but so far none of them has won any sort of general acceptance; no justification

is without those who detest it. I hope to show that the use of the aforementioned distinction enables one to state the utilitarian view in a way which allows for the sound points of its critics.

For our purposes we may say that there are two justifications of punishment. What we may call the retributive view is that punishment is justified on the grounds that wrongdoing merits punishment. It is morally fitting that a person who does wrong should suffer in proportion to his wrongdoing. That a criminal should be punished follows from his guilt, and the severity of the appropriate punishment depends on the depravity of his act. The state of affairs where a wrongdoer suffers punishment is morally better than the state of affairs where he does not; and it is better irrespective of any of the consequences of punishing him.

What we may call the utilitarian view holds that on the principle that bygones are bygones and that only future consequences are material to present decisions, punishment is justifiable only by reference to the probable consequences of maintaining it as one of the devices of the social order. Wrongs committed in the past are, as such, not relevant considerations for deciding what to do. If punishment can be shown to promote effectively the interest of society it is justifiable, otherwise it is not.

I have stated these two competing views very roughly to make one feel the conflict between them: one feels the force of *both* arguments and one wonders how they can be reconciled. From my introductory remarks it is obvious that the resolution which I am going to propose is that in this case one must distinguish between justifying a practice as a system of rules to be applied and enforced, and justifying a particular action which falls under these rules; utilitarian arguments are appropriate with regard to questions about practices, while retributive arguments fit the application of particular rules to particular cases.

We might try to get clear about this distinction by imagining how a father might answer the question of his son. Suppose the son asks, "Why was *J* put in jail yesterday?" The father answers, "Because he robbed the bank at *B*. He was duly tried and found guilty. That's why he was put in jail yesterday." But suppose the son had asked a different question, namely, "Why do people put other people

overlook its importance, as I try to in this paper, and in my review of this book (*Philosophical Review,* vol. LX [October, 1951]), as some of my criticisms show, I failed to understand the force of it. See also H. D. Aiken, "The Levels of Moral Discourse," *Ethics,* vol. LXII (1952), A. M. Quinton, "Punishment," *Analysis,* vol. XIV (June, 1954), and P. H. Nowell-Smith, *Ethics* (London, 1954), pp. 236–239, 271–273.

3. On the concept of explication see the author's paper *Philosophical Review,* vol. LX (April, 1951).

4. While this paper was being revised, Quinton's appeared; footnote 2 supra. There are several respects in which my remarks are similar to his. Yet as I consider some further questions and rely on somewhat different arguments, I have retained the discussion of punishment and promises together as two test cases for utilitarianism.

in jail?" Then the father might answer, "To protect good people from bad people" or "To stop people from doing things that would make it uneasy for all of us; for otherwise we wouldn't be able to go to bed at night and sleep in peace." There are two very different questions here. One question emphasizes the proper name: It asks why *J* was punished rather than someone else, or it asks what he was punished for. The other question asks why we have the institution of punishment: Why do people punish one another rather than, say, always forgiving one another?

Thus the father says in effect that a particular man is punished, rather than some other man, because he is guilty, and he is guilty because he broke the law (past tense). In his case the law looks back, the judge looks back, the jury looks back, and a penalty is visited upon him for something he did. That a man is to be punished, and what his punishment is to be, is settled by its being shown that he broke the law and that the law assigns that penalty for the violation of it.

On the other hand we have the institution of punishment itself, and recommend and accept various changes in it, because it is thought by the (ideal) legislator and by those to whom the law applies that, as a part of a system of law impartially applied from case to case arising under it, it will have the consequence, in the long run, of furthering the interests of society.

One can say, then, that the judge and the legislator stand in different positions and look in different directions: one to the past, the other to the future. The justification of what the judge does, *qua* judge, sounds like the retributive view; the justification of what the (ideal) legislator does, *qua* legislator, sounds like the utilitarian view. Thus both views have a point (this is as it should be since intelligent and sensitive persons have been on both sides of the argument); and one's initial confusion disappears once one sees that these views apply to persons holding different offices with different duties, and situated differently with respect to the system of rules that make up the criminal law.[5]

One might say, however, that the utilitarian view is more fundamental since it applies to a more fundamental office, for the judge carries out the legislator's will so far as he can determine it. Once the legislator decides to have laws and to assign penalties for their violation (as things are there must be both the law and the penalty) an institution is set up which involves a retributive conception of particular cases. It is part of the concept of the criminal law as a system of rules that the application and enforcement of these rules in particular cases should be justifiable by arguments of a retributive character. The decision whether or not to use law rather than some other mechanism of social control, and the decision as to what laws to have and what penalties to assign, may be settled by utilitarian arguments; but if one decides to have laws then one has decided on something whose working in particular cases is retributive in form.[6]

The answer, then, to the confusion engendered by the two views of punishment is quite simple: One distinguishes two offices, that of the judge and that of the legislator, and one distinguishes their different stations with respect to the system of rules which make up the law; and then one notes that the different sorts of considerations which would usually be offered as reasons for what is done under the cover of these offices can be paired off with the competing justifications of punishment. One reconciles the two views by the time-honored device of making them apply to different situations.

But can it really be this simple? Well, this answer allows for the apparent intent of each side. Does a person who advocates the retributive view necessarily advocate, as an *institution,* legal machinery whose essential purpose is to set up and preserve a correspondence between moral turpitude and suffering? Surely not.[7] What retributionists have rightly insisted upon is that no man can be punished unless he is guilty, that is, unless he has broken the law. Their fundamental criticism of the utilitarian ac-

---

5. Note the fact that different sorts of arguments are suited to different offices. One way of taking the differences between ethical theories is to regard them as accounts of the reasons expected in different offices.

6. In this connection see Mabbott, *op. cit.,* pp. 163–164.

7. On this point see Sir David Ross, *The Right and the Good* (Oxford, 1930), pp. 57–60.

count is that, as they interpret it, it sanctions an innocent person's being punished (if one may call it that) for the benefit of society.

On the other hand, utilitarians agree that punishment is to be inflicted only for the violation of law. They regard this much as understood from the concept of punishment itself.[8] The point of the utilitarian account concerns the institution as a system of rules: utilitarianism seeks to limit its use by declaring it justifiable only if it can be shown to foster effectively the good of society. Historically it is a protest against the indiscriminate and ineffective use of the criminal law.[9] It seeks to dissuade us from assigning to penal institutions the improper, if not sacrilegious, task of matching suffering with moral turpitude. Like others, utilitarians want penal institutions designed so that, as far as humanly possible, only those who break the law run afoul of it. They hold that no official should have discretionary power to inflict penalties whenever he thinks it for the benefit of society; for on utilitarian grounds an institution granting such power could not be justified.[10]

---

8. See Hobbes's definition of punishment in *Leviathan,* ch. xxviii; and Bentham's definition in *The Principle of Morals and Legislation,* ch. xii, par. 36, ch. xv, par. 28, and in *The Rationale of Punishment,* (London, 1830), bk. I, ch. i. They could agree with Bradley that: "Punishment is punishment only when it is deserved. We pay the penalty, because we owe it, and for no other reason; and if punishment is inflicted for any other reason whatever than because it is merited by wrong, it is a gross immorality, a crying injustice, an abominable crime, and not what it pretends to be." *Ethical Studies* (2nd ed.; Oxford, 1927), pp. 26–27. Certainly by definition it isn't what it pretends to be. The innocent can only be punished by mistake; deliberate "punishment" on the innocent necessarily involves fraud.

9. Cf. Leon Radzinowicz, *A History of English Criminal Law: The Movement for Reform 1750–1833* (London, 1948), esp. ch. xi on Bentham.

10. Bentham discusses how corresponding to a punitory provision of a criminal law there is another provision which stands to it as an antagonist and which needs a name as much as the punitory. He calls it, as one might expect, the *anaetiosostic,* and of it he says: "The punishment of guilt is the object of the former one: the preservation of innocence that of the latter." In

The suggested way of reconciling the retributive and the utilitarian justifications of punishment seems to account for what both sides have wanted to say. There are, however, two further questions which arise, and I shall devote the remainder of this section to them.

> "... [U]tilitarian arguments are appropriate with regard to questions about practices, while retributive arguments fit the application of particular rules to particular cases."

First, will not a difference of opinion as to the proper criterion of just law make the proposed reconciliation unacceptable to retributionists? Will they not question whether, if the utilitarian principle is used as the criterion, it follows that those who have broken the law are guilty in a way which satisfies their demand that those punished deserve to be punished? To answer this difficulty, suppose that the rules of the criminal law are justified on utilitarian grounds (it is only for laws that meet his criterion that the utilitarian can be held responsible). Then it follows that the actions which the criminal law specifies as offenses are such that, if they were tolerated, terror and alarm would spread in society. Consequently, retributionists can only deny that

---

the same connection he asserts that it is never thought fit to give the judge the option of deciding whether a thief (that is, a person whom he believes to be a thief, for the judge's belief is what the 300 tion must turn upon) should hang or not, and so the law writes the provision: "The judge shall not cause a thief to be hanged unless he have been duly convicted and sentenced in course of law" (*The Limits of Jurisprudence Defined,* ed. C. W. Everett [New York, 1945], pp. 238–239).

those who are punished deserve to be punished if they deny that such actions are wrong. This they will not want to do.

The second question is whether utilitarianism doesn't justify too much. One pictures it as an engine of justification which, if consistently adopted, could be used to justify cruel and arbitrary institutions. Retributionists may be supposed to concede that utilitarians *intend* to reform the law and to make it more humane; that utilitarians do not *wish* to justify any such thing as punishment of the innocent; and that utilitarians may appeal to the fact that punishment presupposes guilt in the sense that by punishment one understands an institution attaching penalties to the infraction of legal rules, and therefore that it is logically absurd to suppose that utilitarians in justifying *punishment* might also have justified punishment (if we may call it that) of the innocent. The real question, however, is whether the utilitarian, in justifying punishment, hasn't used arguments which commit him to accepting the infliction of suffering on innocent persons if it is for the good of society (whether or not one calls this punishment). More generally, isn't the utilitarian committed in principle to accepting many practices which he, as a morally sensitive person, wouldn't want to accept? Retributionists are inclined to hold that there is no way to stop the utilitarian principle from justifying too much except by adding to it a principle which distributes certain rights to individuals. Then the amended criterion is not the greatest benefit of society *simpliciter* [simply], but the greatest benefit of society subject to the constraint that no one's rights may be violated. Now while I think that the classical utilitarians proposed a criterion of this more complicated sort, I do not want to argue that point here.[11] What I want to show is that there is *another* way of preventing the utilitarian principle from justifying too much, or at least of making it much less likely to do so; namely, by stating utilitarianism in a way which accounts for the distinction between the justification of an institution and the justification of a particular action falling under it.

I begin by defining the institution of punishment

as follows: a person is said to suffer punishment whenever he is legally deprived of some of the normal rights of a citizen on the ground that he has violated a rule of law, the violation having been established by trial according to the due process of law, provided that the deprivation is carried out by the recognized legal authorities of the state, that the rule of law clearly specifies both the offense and the attached penalty, that the courts construe statutes strictly, and that the statute was on the books prior to the time of the offense.[12] This definition specifies what I shall understand by punishment. The question is whether utilitarian arguments may be found to justify institutions widely different from this and such as one would find cruel and arbitrary.

This question is best answered, I think, by taking up a particular accusation. Consider the following from Carritt:

> … the utilitarian must hold that we are justified in inflicting pain always and only to prevent worse pain or bring about greater happiness. This, then, is all we need to consider in so-called punishment, which must be purely preventive. but if some kind of very cruel crime becomes common, and none of the criminals can be caught, it might be highly expedient, as an example, to hang an innocent man, if a charge against him could be so framed that he were universally thought guilty; indeed this would only fail to be an ideal instance of utilitarian 'punishment' because the victim himself would not have been so likely as a real felon to commit such a crime in the future; in all other respect it would be perfectly deterrent and therefore felicific.[13]

Carritt is trying to show that there are occasions when a utilitarian argument would justify taking an action which would be generally condemned; and thus that utilitarianism justifies too much. But the failure of Carritt's argument lies in the fact that he makes no distinction between the justification of the general system of rules which constitutes penal institutions and the justification of particular applica-

---

11. By the classical utilitarians I understand Hobbes, Hume, Bentham, J. S. Mill, and Sidgwick.

12. All these features of punishment are mentioned by Hobbes; cf. *Leviathan*, ch. xxviii.
13. *Ethical and Political Thinking* (Oxford, 1947), p. 65.

tions of these rules to particular cases by the various officials whose job it is to administer them. This becomes perfectly clear when one asks who the "we" are of whom Carritt speaks. Who is this who has a sort of absolute authority on particular occasions to decide that an innocent man shall be "punished" if everyone can be convinced that he is guilty? Is this person the legislator, or the judge, or the body of private citizens, or what? It is utterly crucial to know who is to decide such matters, and by what authority, for all of this must be written into the rules of the institution. Until one knows these things one doesn't know what the institution is whose justification is being challenged; and as the utilitarian principle applies to the institution one doesn't know whether it is justifiable on utilitarian grounds or not.

Once this is understood it is clear what the countermove to Carritt's argument is. One must describe more carefully what the *institution* is which his example suggests, and then ask oneself whether or not it is likely that having this institution would be for the benefit of society in the long run. One must not content oneself with the vague thought that, when it's a question of *this* case, it would be a good thing if *somebody* did something even if an innocent person were to suffer.

Try to imagine, then, an institution (which we may call "telishment") which is such that the officials set up by it have authority to arrange a trial for the condemnation of an innocent man whenever they are of the opinion that doing so would be in the best interests of society. The discretion of officials is limited, however, by the rule that they may not condemn an innocent man to undergo such an ordeal unless there is, at the time, a wave of offenses similar to that with which they charge him and telish him for. We may imagine that the officials having the discretionary authority are the judges of the higher courts in consultation with the chief of police, the minister of justice, and a committee of the legislature.

Once one realizes that one is involved in setting up an *institution,* one sees that the hazards are very great. For example, what check is there on the officials? How is one to tell whether or not their ac-

tions are authorized? How is one to limit the risks involved in allowing such systematic deception? How is one to avoid giving anything short of complete discretion to the authorities to telish anyone they like? In addition to these considerations, it is obvious that people will come to have a very different attitude towards their penal system when telishment is adjoined to it. They will be uncertain as to whether a convicted man has been punished or telished. They will wonder whether or not they should feel sorry for him. They will wonder whether the same fate won't at any time fall on them. If one pictures how such an institution would actually work, and the enormous risks involved in it, it seems clear that it would serve no useful purpose. A utilitarian justification for this institution is most unlikely.

It happens in general that as one drops off the defining features of punishment one ends up with an institution whose utilitarian justification is highly doubtful. One reason for this is that punishment works like a kind of price system: By altering the prices one has to pay for the performance of actions, it supplies a motive for avoiding some actions and doing others. The defining features are essential if punishment is to work in this way; so that an institution which lacks these features, for example, an institution which is set up to "punish" the innocent, is likely to have about as much point as a price system (if one may call it that) where the prices of things change at random from day to day and one learns the price of something after one has agreed to buy it.[14]

_____

14. The analogy with the price system suggests an answer to the question how utilitarian considerations insure that punishment is proportional to the offense. It is interesting to note that Sir David Ross, after making the distinction between justifying a penal law and justifying a particular application of it, and after stating that utilitarian considerations have a large place in determining the former, still holds back from accepting the utilitarian justification of punishment on the grounds that justice requires that punishment be proportional to the offense, and that utilitarianism is unable to account for this. Cf. *The Right and the Good,* pp. 61–62. I do

If one is careful to apply the utilitarian principle to the institution which is to authorize particular actions, then there is *less* danger of its justifying too much. Carritt's example gains plausibility by its indefiniteness and by its concentration on the particular case. His argument will only hold if it can be shown that there are utilitarian arguments which

justify an institution whose publicly ascertainable offices and powers are such as to permit officials to exercise that kind of discretion in particular cases. But the requirement of having to build the arbitrary features of the particular decision into the institutional practice makes the justification much less likely to go through.

---

not claim that utilitarianism can account for this requirement as Sir David might wish, but it happens, nevertheless, that if utilitarian considerations are followed penalties will be proportional to offenses in this sense: the order of offenses according to seriousness can be paired off with the order of penalties according to severity. Also the absolute level of penalties will be as low as possible. This follows from the

---

assumption that people are rational (i.e., that they are able to take into account the "prices" the state puts on actions), the utilitarian rule that a penal system should provide a motive for preferring the less serious offense, and the principle that punishment as such is an evil. All this was carefully worked out by Bentham in *The Principles of Morals and Legislation*, chs. xiii–xv.

Study Questions

1. Has Rawls correctly presented the retributive view?

2. Has Rawls adequately addressed the problem of punishing the innocent in a utilitarian system?

Moral Dilemmas

- One night, you see your neighbor Bill brutally kill a motorcycle mechanic during a robbery. The man is never caught. Ten years later, you see Bill, and you find out that for more than eight years he has dedicated his life to helping the poor and sick.

  Should you call the police and turn him in?

- The police capture a terrorist known as "the Flame" for killing many innocent persons by placing bombs in busy intersections. He has an accomplice named Huey who has placed bombs

elsewhere, but the Flame refuses to say where the bombs are. In order to save innocent lives, Captain Owens takes the terrorist into his private office and tortures him by pulling his nails out one by one. Finally, unable to stand any more pain, the Flame tells where Huey hid the bombs.

Did the captain do the correct thing, even though torture is unconstitutional?

- Two neighbors, Ken and Joe, are constantly arguing. One night, after an argument in a bar, Ken breaks down Joe's door and shoots him in the stomach. Joe, realizing that he is about to die, tells Ken, "Shoot me again, I'm going to die anyway." Ken refuses and walks out. Joe crawls to his kitchen and cuts his own throat. He dies a few minutes later. Ken is arrested and accused of murder. His lawyer argues that Joe died from the cut throat and thus committed suicide; therefore, his client should be found innocent. The

prosecutor argues that Joe would have died anyway from the gun wound alone, and therefore Ken is guilty of murder. In fact, Ken is found guilty of manslaughter (the unlawful killing of a human being without express or implied malice).

If you were on the jury, how would you vote?

Suggested Readings

Bedau, Hugo Adam, ed. *The Death Penalty in America*. Oxford, England: Oxford University Press, 1982.

Cover, Robert M., and Owen M. Fiss, eds. *The Structure of Procedure*. Mineola, N.Y.: Mineola Foundation Press, 1979.

Murphy, Jeffrie, and Jules Coleman. *The Philosophy of Law*. Totowa, N.J.: Rowman & Allanheld, 1984.

Wilson, James Q. *Thinking About Crime*. New York: Random House, 1983.

Economic Justice

What is the morally proper way to distribute income and wealth? How can we know whether a person deserves his or her income and wealth? Should individual persons be allowed to own large corporations, or should corporations be owned by the state or the workers? Should the human needs for food, clothing, shelter, and health be the sole responsibility of each individual, or should society or government help to meet the needs of those who cannot help themselves?

Background

The nature of the problem of distributive justice changes with the kind of society involved and the way each society provides for its needs. In the early stages of human evolution, people found food through the hunting of animals and the gathering of fruits and berries. This hunting and gathering stage of human economic activity meant an essentially nomadic existence that did not allow for great accumulation of wealth, and private property probably consisted of hunting tools and clothes.

A dramatic change occurred in human life with the discovery of agriculture. The nomadic-hunter pattern of existence was transformed into forms of settled agrarian life that involved the domestication of animals and plants. The agricultural revolution, which occurred at different times in different parts of the world (but as early as fifteen thousand years ago), changed early human beings from food finders into food makers. This profound change in the manner of providing subsistence allowed greater security and stability within individual and group life.

It dramatically increased the supply of goods, which enabled a steep rise in population, resulting in far-reaching social and intellectual changes. This increase in population required the formulation of a political organization, or a group of decision makers, who would have authority to determine issues that affected the general welfare. Early religious beliefs and rituals were closely associated with food production. As populations grew, more complex political, social, and economic institutions continued to develop for the next ten thousand years. The discovery of agriculture allowed for greater accumulation of wealth and an expansion in the concept of private property. This led to greater inequality of wealth among persons, an inequality that was to be exacerbated by the industrial revolution.

The appearance of the industrial revolution in the eighteenth century further transformed human life. New technology and new energy sources greatly increased production. Like the agricultural revolution before it, the industrial revolution provided the conditions for increasingly larger cities and added a new component—the emergence of large centers of production (factories).

Throughout this economic and social evolution, a general trend toward the realization of the moral equality of all persons also became more evident. Although defended by the stoics and implied in some Christian writings, the belief in the equal rights of human beings (initially in the equal rights of men only) did not influence political institutions until about the seventeenth century. Belief in equality has meant the eventual global abolition of slavery, the growing acceptance of women's rights, as well as the declining power of racism.

This growth in moral equality has not necessarily implied a corresponding growth in economic equality. Though reliable data is incomplete and open to interpretation, capitalism and the industrial revolution have generally contributed to the concentration of wealth in fewer and fewer hands. Today in the United States, as few as one percent of the population owns about fifty percent of the corporate wealth. The concept of the corporation has existed since the Middle Ages, if not before then, but its modern manifestation, the public stock investment corporation, was essential for the expansion of industry and production. The public stock investment corporation developed to meet the demands of greater financial needs of a dynamic industrial system. The limited liability of stockholders (i.e., stockholders could lose only their investments, nothing more), the emergence of a professional managerial class, and the establishment of legal protection (the Fourteenth Amendment of the U.S. Constitution granted the corporation the status of "abstract person") all contributed to the birth of modern society. The social, political, and economic power of the corporation is second only to that of government itself. Eighty percent of all employment in the United States is in corporations with twenty or more employees. The multinationals, large firms that operate in many countries, have become a new force in international politics. The activities and influences of such large and powerful entities permeate our lives.

Although the ethical organization of economic life was a subject of philosophical reflection from the earliest days, in many ways the industrial revolution and its precursors stimulated philosophers in a major way to systematically address the moral and political questions of economic production. As society became more complex, interrelated, and interdependent, the question of just compensation became more difficult to resolve because the actual contribution of individuals became harder to determine. In an agricultural or hunting and gathering society, to see who plowed what field or caught what animal was relatively easy; however, in a factory or corporation where the end result is a function of many working together in many different ways, the issue of the just distribution of rewards, pay, and other benefits is more puzzling. Philosophers developed basically three different approaches to the problem of economic production and economic justice. Adam Smith formulated what we may call the traditional view of *free-market capitalism,* which stresses liberty and the right to accumulate as much private property as possible. The opposing view of Karl Marx, *socialism,* stresses human equality and the collective ownership of most property. The moderate position of John Rawls, *welfare liberalism,* argues for a combination of liberty and equality with a large role for government in regulating the economy and providing for basic human needs.

Adam Smith

Adam Smith (1723–1790) is often referred to as the father of laissez-faire, or of free-market capitalism—a form of capitalism that rejects government interference in the free market. Smith argued that "wealth" consists in the sum total of goods that all people can purchase and consume to meet their needs. He further claimed that individuals are motivated by self-interest, and if they are allowed to freely express their tendency to "truck, barter, and exchange" in the open, competitive market, society in general will benefit. The "invisible hand" of the market will translate individual self-interest into general welfare. The pursuit of gain or profit acts as an incentive for individuals to produce a large quantity of goods thus creating a high standard of living.

According to Smith, the greatest cause of increased and improved production is *division of labor*. Smith suggests through his now famous example of pin-making that when a complex process, such as pin-manufacture, is broken down or divided into small, simple tasks done by individual persons, production is greatly increased. The productivity of workers increases because the focusing on a single task over time (1) increases dexterity or skill, (2) saves time in that one need not move from one task to the next, and (3) helps to promote the invention of machinery that even further reduces labor.

Smith's contribution to our understanding of economic life cannot be underestimated. He clearly saw that the interference of the British government by granting monopolies to various producers was limiting competition in a way that was detrimental to the overall efficiency of the economy. However, some critics believe that changing social and economic conditions have brought new challenges to capitalism. Contemporary production, if unregulated by government, is often characterized by large corporations forming monopolies by buying out their competitors, thus reducing competition. In addition, many workers have organized into labor unions that limit competition for workers. The pollution of the environment, the depletion of natural resources, and the demand for improved quality of working conditions have necessitated increased governmental regulation of the economy. Finally, economic crises such as the Great Depression of the 1930s have suggested to many economists that near full-employment with stable economic growth requires that the government actively monitor and control the economy.

Karl Marx

Karl Marx (1818–1883) was familiar with Smith's work, but he was not as optimistic as Smith was about laissez-faire capitalism. We can summarize Marx's objections to capitalism under three distinct headings: (1) alienation, (2) exploitation, and (3) instability.

In his early writings, Marx spoke vehemently about the brutalized and dehumanized existence of workers in factories. The dull, repetitive assembly-line work that Smith praised as efficient division of labor Marx viewed as oppressive to workers. Such conditions deny workers the opportunity to develop their true human potential; thus, they are alienated. He believed that truly human labor must involve human beings physically, mentally, and emotionally; capitalism does not allow such total involvement.

In addition to alienating workers, capitalism also exploits them. Marx argued that profit, the goal of all capitalist activity, is possible only if the wage workers earn is less than the actual value of what they produce. Profit then, for Marx, is value created by workers but, in effect, stolen from them by capitalists. Thus, economic inequality becomes ever more extreme as two classes (the proletariat and the bourgeoisie) drift further apart.

Finally, Marx believed capitalism to be an inherently unstable system subject to periodic depression. As he saw it, the basic drive of capitalists is increased profit, which can be achieved by increasing production, eliminating competition (the tendency to monopolize), and cutting wages. To reduce wages, business would increasingly seek to replace workers with machines, which would cause higher unemployment. High unemployment would, in turn, decrease demand on goods, or buying power. This, in turn, would cause a decrease in production, which would again increase unemployment, which would decrease demand, and so on. In this way, a vicious cycle would ensue, and the economy would grind to a depressing halt. This economic crisis, Marx believed, would pave the way for the socialist revolution.

Marx's impact on world history has been immense and continues to hold a fascination for many. Many philosophers agree that Marx's contributions have increased our understanding of history and society. He brought dramatically to light the importance of economic factors in political and social conflicts. He correctly predicted the increasing concentration of wealth in fewer and fewer hands under capitalism and correctly foresaw economic depressions and the formation of unions. He called attention to the horrible conditions of factory workers and deplored child labor. He argued for free education for all and equal rights for women. Nevertheless, Marx overlooked certain other problems.

Marx's protest against the mistreatment of workers was more on the mark than his predictions about the fate of capitalism. Although the United States did experience a severe economic depression in the 1930s, private enterprise survived with the help of increased government control and regulation of the market. In this, many think that Marx underestimated the flexibility of capitalism to adapt to changing economic and social conditions. Marx claimed that the most fully developed capitalist countries would turn to socialism first, but in fact the Soviet Union, which had barely begun to industrialize, was first. Marx's belief that workers should run society and factories seems to overlook their need for education in order to do this. This is partly why Marx's idea of a "dictatorship of the proletariat" in practice became a dictatorship of the Communist party, the educated elite, in the Soviet Union.

Also unclear is whether a socialist economy can be as efficient as a capitalist economy. Capitalism, as Smith argued, provides for competition between private companies, which increases production, helps to develop new technology, and controls prices. Can competition exist when all of the corporations have one owner, the state? Recent reforms in China and the Soviet Union have tried to increase economic productivity by introducing more private ownership and economic incentives to promote competition. Other critics of Marxism point out the lack of freedom in most, if not all, socialist countries. Philosophers such as John Rawls believe that a free society must have a free press, a press

independent of government control, as well as certain human rights such as the right to free speech and the right to form and join more than one political party. The great concentration of economic and political power in the hands of the Communist party, according to the critics, makes a free society impossible.

John Rawls

John Rawls's theory of justice is based on the idea of an imaginary social contract or agreement. He believes that the correct principles of justice would arise from an agreement among free and rational persons in an imaginary situation that he calls the *original position* (OP). The OP would include all persons who will be part of the society that accepts the principles of justice. We must further imagine that no one in this OP knows his or her sex, age, wealth, talents, abilities, or personality traits. This "veil of ignorance" is imposed on members of the OP in order to exclude information that might bias the participants in an improper way. Because of this veil, all of the participants in the OP are, in a sense, equal. Furthermore, they are equal in that they desire the same "primary goods"; namely, rights, liberties, opportunities, income, wealth, and self-respect. What principles of justice would they choose to guarantee these goods for themselves?

Rawls believes that they would choose the principles of justice that he calls "justice as fairness." This theory consists of two principles: (1) Each person has the right to the greatest degree of liberty compatible with the like liberty for all; and (2) Inequalities of income and wealth are justified only if they are attached to positions open to all (fair equality of opportunity) and benefit everyone, especially the poorest members of society (difference principle). Members of the OP would choose these principles because no one would want to be a slave or have unequal rights and liberties. They would also agree that inequality of incomes and wealth can exist as long as everyone has an equal chance to achieve and as long as everyone benefits from these inequalities. By making sure that everyone benefits from inequality, inequality is kept at a minimum and greater social harmony results.

Rawls's theory has been criticized by those on the left (Marxists) and those on the right (followers of Smith). Those on the left argue that Rawls should have argued for socialism because capitalism allows for too much inequality (i.e., violates the difference principle) and does not provide for equal opportunity because the rich have better private schools, better health care, and other privileges. Marxists believe that the only way to have true equality of opportunity is to have a classless society. This is not possible in capitalism.

Critics on the right argue that Rawls is too egalitarian and unnecessarily restricts human liberty. They contend that the difference principle restricts economic productivity too much by requiring that all inequality of wealth benefit all, or raise all. Some critics believe that morality requires only that certain minimums of welfare be assured, and once these are provided, wealth can become as unequal as the free market allows. Others believe that even these minimums steal wealth from those who produce it and transfer it to the lazy and incompetent.

Joseph Grčić

Smith's emphasis on the free market is important, for if we value individual liberty, we must allow that individual wants and preferences must play at least some role in the production and sale of goods. Yet, Marx added to this idea the reality that the concrete market may mean economic depressions, monopolies, unemployment, pollution, and inefficiency. To deal with these problems, government must regulate and stabilize the market to provide greater security for all. Marx stressed that the growth of large corporations has decreased the impact of the market and the consumer and that these corporations exercise great influence over our political institutions. In response to this new development and in order to realize Marx's vision of greater autonomy for the workers, a restructuring of the large corporations may be in order, as I suggest. The largest corporate entities should be democratized so that workers, consumers, and stockholders share the power of running firms.

The argument for corporate democracy is based on the understanding of the nature of conscience. A person who has a conscience has internalized society's moral values and controls his or her behavior accordingly. Ideally, then, if a corporation had a conscience, it would be less likely to act contrary to social morality. Unfortunately, a corporation is not a real person but many persons who may not know or desire to act on what the social morality requires them to do. In order to preserve the social welfare of society (which is what morality is supposed to do), those in society who can protect society must act as a conscience for the corporation. Consumer, employee, and stockholder representation on the boards of directors and in the management of major corporations is the most effective way to promote corporate moral behavior. Democracy in the corporation combines elements of the ideas of Smith and Marx while promoting a more ethical business system.

Benefits of the Profit Motive

Adam Smith (1723–1790) Adam Smith was a Scottish economist and professor of philosophy. He is considered by some to be the father of capitalism.

Adam Smith

Book I

Of the causes of improvement in the productive powers of labor and of the order according to

From Adam Smith, *The Wealth of Nations,* Books I and IV (1776; rpt. Random House, Inc.)

which its produce is naturally distributed among the different ranks of the people

Chapter I
Of the Division of Labor

The greatest improvement in the productive powers of labor, and the greater part of the skill, dexterity, and judgment with which it is anywhere directed, or applied, seem to have been the effects of the division of labor....

To take an example, therefore, from a very trifling manufacture; but one in which the division of labor has been very often taken notice of, the trade of the pin-maker; a workman not educated to this business (which the division of labor has rendered a distinct trade), nor acquainted with the use of the machinery employed in it (to the invention of which the same division of labor has probably given occasion), could scarce, perhaps, with his utmost industry, make one pin in a day, and certainly could not make twenty. But in the way in which this business is now carried on, not only the whole work is a peculiar trade, but it is divided into a number of branches, of which the greater part are likewise peculiar trades. One man draws out the wire, another straights it, a third cuts it, a fourth points it, a fifth grinds it at the top for receiving the head; to make the head requires two or three distinct operations; to put it on is a peculiar business, to whiten the pins is another; it is even a trade by itself to put them into the paper; and the important business of making a pin is, in this manner, divided into about eighteen distinct operations, which in some manufactories, are all performed by distinct hands, though in others the same man will sometimes perform two or three of them. I have seen a small manufactory of this kind where ten men only were employed, and where some of them consequently performed two or three distinct operations. But though they were very poor, and therefore but differently accommodated with the necessary machinery, they could, when they exerted themselves, make among them about twelve pounds of pins in a day. There are in a pound upwards of four thousands pins of a middling size. Those ten persons,

therefore, could make among them upwards of forty-eight thousand pins in a day. Each person, therefore, making a tenth part of forty-eight thousand pins, might be considered as making four thousand eight hundred pins in a day. But if they had all wrought separately and independently, and without any of them having been educated to this peculiar business, they certainly could not each of them have made twenty, perhaps not one pin in a day; that is, certainly, not the two hundred and fortieth, perhaps not the four thousand eight hundredth part, of what they are at present capable of performing in consequence of a proper division and combination of their different operations.

In every other art and manufacture, the effects of the divisions of labor are similar to what they are in this very trifling one; though in many of them, the labor can neither be so much subdivided, nor reduced to so great a simplicity of operation. The division of labor, however, so far as it can be introduced, occasions, in every art, a proportionable increase of the productive powers of labor....

> *"This division of labor . . . is not originally the effect of any human wisdom. . . ."*

This great increase of the quantity of work, which in consequence of the division of labor, the same number of people are capable of performing, is owing to three different circumstances: first, to the increase of dexterity in every particular workman; secondly, to the saving of the time which is commonly lost in passing from one species of work to another; and lastly, to the invention of a great number of machines which facilitate and abridge labor, and enable one man to do the work of many.

First, the improvement of the dexterity of the

workman necessarily increases the quantity of the work he can perform; and the division of labor, by reducing every man's business to some one simple operation and by making this operation the sole employment of his life, necessarily increases very much the dexterity of the workman. A common smith, who, though accustomed to handle the hammer, has never been used to make nails, if upon some particular occasion he is obliged to attempt it, will scarce, I am assured, be able to make about two to three hundred nails in a day, and those too very bad ones. A smith who has been accustomed to make nails, but whose sole or principal business has not been that of a nailer, can seldom with his utmost diligence make more than eight hundred or a thousand nails in a day. I have seen several boys under twenty years of age who had never exercised any other trade but that of making nails, and who, when they exerted themselves, could make, each of them, upwards of two thousand three hundred nails in a day. The making of a nail, however, is by no means one of the simplest operations. The same person blows the bellows, stirs or mends the fire as there is occasion, heats the iron, and forges every part of the nail: In forging the head too he is obliged to change his tools. The different operations into which the making of a pin or of a metal button is subdivided, are all of them much more simple; and the dexterity of the person, of whose life it has been the sole business to perform them, is usually much greater. The rapidity with which some of the operations of those manufactures are performed exceeds what the human hand could, by those who had never seen them, be supposed capable of acquiring.

Secondly, the advantage which is gained by saving the time commonly lost in passing from one sort of work to another is much greater than we should at first view be apt to imagine it. It is impossible to pass very quickly from one kind of work to another, that is carried on in a different place, and with quite different tools. A country weaver who cultivates a small farm must lose a good deal of time in passing from his loom to the field, and from the field to his loom. When the two trades can be carried on in the same workhouse, the loss of time

is no doubt much less. It is even in this case, however, very considerable. . . .

Thirdly, and lastly, every body must be sensible how much labor is facilitated and abridged by the application of proper machinery. . . .

. . . A great part of the machines made use of in those manufactures in which labor is most subdivided were originally the inventions of common workmen, who, being each of them employed in some very simple operation, naturally turned their thoughts toward finding out easier and readier methods of performing it. Whoever has been much accustomed to visit such manufacturers must frequently have been shown very pretty machines which were the inventions of such workmen in order to facilitate and quicken their own particular part of the work. In the first fire-engines, a boy was constantly employed to open and shut alternately the communication between the boiler and the cylinder, according as the piston either ascended or descended. One of those boys, who loved to play with his companions, observed that, by tying a string from the handle of the valve which opened this communication to another part of the machine, the valve would open and shut without his assistance, and leave him at liberty to divert himself with his play-fellows. One of the greatest improvements that has been made upon this machine, since it was first invented, was in this manner the discovery of a boy who wanted to save his own labor. . . .

It is the great multiplication of the productions of all the different arts in consequence of the division of labor, which occasions, in a well-governed society, that universal opulence which extends itself to the lowest ranks of the people. Every workman has a great quantity of his own work to dispose of beyond what he himself has occasion for; and every other workman being exactly in the same situation, he is enabled to exchange a great quantity of his own goods for a great quantity, or, what comes to the same thing, for the price of a great quantity of theirs. He supplies them abundantly with what they have occasion for, and they accommodate him as amply with what he has occasion for, and a general plenty diffuses itself through all different ranks of the society. . . .

Chapter II
Of the Principle Which Gives Occasion to the Division of Labor

This division of labor, from which so many advantages are derived, is not originally the effect of any human wisdom which foresees and intends that general opulence to which it gives occasion. It is the necessary, through very slow and gradual, consequence of a certain propensity in human nature which has in view no such extensive utility: the propensity to truck, barter, and exchange one thing for another.

... In almost every other race of animals each individual, when it is grown up to maturity, is entirely independent, and in its natural state has occasion for the assistance of no other living creature. But man has almost constant occasion for the help of his brethren, and it is in vain for him to expect it from their benevolence only. He will be more likely to prevail if he can interest their self-love in his favor, and show them that it is for their own advantage to do for him what he requires of them. Whoever offers to another a bargain of any kind, proposes to do this. Give me that which I want, and you shall have this which you want, is the meaning of every such offer; and it is in the manner that we obtain from one another the far greater part of those good offices which we stand in need of. It is not from the benevolence of the butcher, the brewer, or the baker, that we expect our dinner, but from their regard to their own interest. We address ourselves, not to their humanity but to their self-love, and never talk to them of our own necessities but of their advantages. Nobody but a beggar chooses to depend chiefly upon the benevolence of his fellow-citizens. Even a beggar does not depend upon it entirely. The charity of well-disposed people, indeed, supplies him with the whole fund of his subsistence. But though this principle ultimately provides him with all the necessaries of life which he has occasion for, it neither does nor can provide him with them as he has occasion for them. The greater part of his occasional wants are supplied in the same manner as those of other people, by treaty, by barter, and by purchase. With the money which one man gives him he purchases food. The old clothes which another bestows upon him he exchanges for other old clothes which suit him better, or for lodging, or for food, or for money, with which he can buy either food, clothes, or lodging, as he has occasion.

As it is by treaty, by barter, and by purchase that we obtain from one another the greater part of those mutual good offices which we stand in need of, so it is this same trucking disposition which originally gives occasion to the division of labor. In a tribe of hunters or shepherds a particular person makes bows and arrows, for example, with more readiness and dexterity than any other. He frequently exchanges them for cattle or for venison with his companions; and he finds at last that he can in this manner get more cattle and venison than if he himself went to the field to catch them. From a regard to his own interest, therefore, the making of bows and arrows grows to be his chief business, and he becomes a sort of armorer. Another excels in making the frames and covers of their little huts or movable houses. He is accustomed to be of use in this way to his neighbors, who reward him in the same manner with cattle and with venison till at last he finds it his interest to dedicate himself entirely to this employment, and to become a sort of house carpenter. In the same manner a third becomes a smith or a brazier; a fourth a tanner or dresser of hides or skins, the principal part of the clothing of savages. And thus the certainty of being able to exchange all that surplus part of the produce of his own labor, which is over and above his own consumption, for such parts of the produce of other men's labor as he may have occasion for, encourages every man to apply himself to a particular occupation, and to cultivate and bring to perfection whatever talent or genius he may possess for that particular species of business.

The difference of natural talents in different men is, in reality, much less than we are aware of; and the very different genius which appears to distinguish men of different professions, when grown up to maturity, is not upon many occasions so much the cause as the effect of the division of labor. The difference between the most dissimilar characters, between a philosopher and a common street porter, for example, seems to arise not so much from nature as from habit, custom, and education. When they came into the world, and for the first six or eight years of their existence, they were perhaps, very much alike, and neither their parents nor play-fellows could perceive any remarkable difference. About that age, or soon after, they come to be employed in very different occupations. The difference of talent comes then to be taken notice of, and widens by degrees, till at last the vanity of the philosopher is willing to acknowledge scarce any resemblance. For without the disposition to truck, barter, and exchange, every man must have procured to himself every necessary and conveniency of life which he wanted. All must have had the same duties to perform, and the same work to do, and there could have been no such difference of employment as can alone give occasion to any great difference of talents. . . .

Book IV

Chapter II

Every individual is continually exerting himself to find out the most advantageous employment for whatever capital he can command. It is his own advantage, indeed, and not that of the society, which he has in view. But the study of his own advantage, naturally, or rather necessarily, leads him to prefer that employment which is most advantageous to the society. . . .

As every individual, therefore, endeavours as much as he can both to employ his capital in the support of domestic industry, and so to direct that industry that its produce may be of the greatest value, every individual necessarily labors to render the annual revenue of the society as great as he can. He generally, indeed, neither intends to promote the public interest nor knows how much he is promoting it. By preferring the support of domestic to that of foreign industry, he intends only his own security and by directing that industry in such a manner as its produce may be of the greatest value, he intends only his own gain, and he is in this, as in many other cases, led by an invisible hand to promote an end which was no part of his intention. Nor is it always the worse for the society that it was no part of it. By pursuing his own interest he frequently promotes that of the society more effectually than when he really intends to promote it. I have never known much good done by those who affected to trade for the public good. It is an affectation, indeed, not very common among merchants, and very few words need be employed in dissuading them from it.

Study Questions

1. What role should government have in the business world?

2. Would some of Smith's ideas be applicable in a socialistic society?

3. What would Smith say about American business today?

The Communist Manifesto

Karl Marx (1818–1883) Karl Marx was born in Germany. He wrote extensively on capitalism and socialism. After having moved to London in 1849, Marx was for a time a correspondent for the New York Tribune *and collaborated with Friedrich Engels (1820–1895) on many of his writings.*

Karl Marx and Friedrich Engels

I. Bourgeois and Proletarians

The history of all hitherto existing society is the history of class struggles.

Freeman and slave, patrician and plebeian, lord and serf, guildmaster and journeyman, in a word, oppressor and oppressed, stood in constant opposition to one another, carried on an uninterrupted, now hidden, now open fight, a fight that each time ended, either in a revolutionary reconstitution of society at large, or in the common ruin of the struggling classes.

In the earlier epochs of history, we find almost everywhere a complicated arrangement of society into various orders, a manifold gradation of social rank. In ancient Rome we have patricians, knights, plebeians, slaves; in the Middle Ages, feudal lords, vassals, guildmasters, journeymen, apprentices, serfs; and in almost all of these particular classes, again, other subordinate gradations.

The modern bourgeois society that has sprouted from the ruins of feudal society has not done away with class antagonisms. It has only established new classes, new conditions of oppression, new forms of struggle in place of the old ones.

Our epoch, the epoch of the bourgeoisie, shows, however, this distinctive feature: it has simplified the class antagonisms. Society as a whole is more and more splitting up into two great hostile camps, into two great classes directly facing each other: *bourgeoisie* and *proletariat.*

From the serfs of the Middle Ages sprang the chartered burghers of the earliest towns. From these burghers the first elements of the bourgeoisie were developed.

The discovery of America, the rounding of the Cape, opened the fresh ground for the rising bourgeoisie. The East-Indian and Chinese markets, the colonization of America, trade with the colonies, the increase in the means of exchange and in commodities generally, gave to commerce, to navigation, to industry, an impulse never before known, and thereby, to the revolutionary element in the tottering feudal society, a rapid development.

The feudal system of industry, under which industrial production was monopolized by closed guilds, now no longer sufficed for the growing wants of the new markets. The manufacturing system took its place. The guildmasters were pushed on one side by the manufacturing middle class; division of labor between the different corporate guilds vanished in the face of division of labor in each single workshop.

Meanwhile the markets kept on growing; demand went on rising. Manufacturing no longer was able to keep up with this growth. Then, steam and machinery revolutionized industrial production. The place of manufacture was taken by the giant, *modern industry;* the place of the industrial middle class, by industrial millionaires, the leaders of whole industrial armies, the modern bourgeois.

Modern industry has established the world market, for which the discovery of America paved the way. This market has given an immense development to commerce, to navigation, to communication by land. This development has, in its turn, reacted on the extension of industry; and in proportion as industry, commerce, navigation, railways extended, in the same proportion the bourgeoisie developed, increased its capital, and pushed into the background every class handed down from the Middle Ages.

We see, therefore, how the modern bourgeoisie is itself the product of a long course of development, of a series of revolutions in the modes of production and of exchange....

The need of a constantly expanding market for its products chases the bourgeoisie over the whole surface of the globe. It must nestle everywhere, settle everywhere, establish connections everywhere.

The bourgeoisie has through its exploitation of the world market given a cosmopolitan character to production and consumption in every country. To the great chagrin of reactionaries, it has drawn from under the feet of industry the national ground on which it stood. All old-established national industries have been destroyed or are daily being destroyed. They are dislodged by new industries, whose introduction becomes a life and death question for all civilized nations, by industries that no longer work up indigenous raw material, but raw material drawn from the remotest zones; industries whose products are consumed, not only at home, but in every quarter of the globe. In place of the old wants, satisfied by the productions of the country, we find new wants, requiring for their satisfaction the products of distant lands and climates. In place of the old local and national seclusion and self-sufficiency, we have intercourse in every direction, universal inter-dependence of nations. And as in material, so also in intellectual production. The intellectual creations of individual nations become common property. National one-sidedness and narrow-mindedness become more and more impossible, and from the numerous national and local literatures, there emerges a world literature.

The bourgeoisie, by the rapid improvement of all instruments of production, by the immensely facilitated means of communications, draws all, even the most backward, nations into civilization. The cheap prices of its commodities are the heavy artillery with which it batters down all Chinese walls, with which it forces the underdeveloped nations' intensely obstinate hatred of foreigners to capitulate. It compels all nations, on pain of extinction, to adopt the bourgeois mode of production; it compels them to introduce what it calls civilization into their midst, *i.e.,* to become bourgeois themselves. In one word, it creates a world in its own image.

The bourgeoisie has subjected rural areas to the rule of cities. It has created enormous cities, has greatly increased the urban population as compared with the rural, and has thus reduced a considerable part of the population from the idiocy of rural life. Just as it has made the country dependent on the cities, so has it made barbarian and semi-underdeveloped countries dependent on the civilized ones, nations of peasants on nations of bourgeois, the East on the West.

The bourgeoisie keeps more and more doing away with the scattered state of the population, of the means of production, and of property. It has agglomerated population, centralized means of production, and has concentrated property in a few hands. The necessary consequence of this was political centralization. Independent, or but loosely connected, provinces with separate interests, laws, governments, and systems of taxation became lumped together into one nation, with one government, one code of laws, one national class-interest, one frontier, and one customs-tariff.

The bourgeoisie, during its rule of scarcely one hundred years, has created more massive and more colossal productive forces than have all preceding generations together. Subjection of Nature's forces to man, machinery, application of chemistry to industry and agriculture, steam-navigation, railways, electric telegraphs, clearing of whole continents for cultivation, canalization of rivers, whole populations conjured out of the ground—what earlier century had even a presentiment that such productive forces slumbered in the lap of social labor?

We see then: the means of production and of exchange, on whose foundation the bourgeoisie built itself up, were generated in feudal society. At a certain stage in the development of these means of production and of exchange, the conditions under which feudal society produced and exchanged, the feudal organization of agriculture and manufacturing industry, in one word, the feudal relations of property became no longer compatible with the already developed productive forces; they became so many fetters. They had to be burst asunder; they were burst asunder.

Into their place stepped free competition, accompanied by a social and political constitution adapted to it, and by the economical and political sway of the bourgeois class.

A similar movement is going on before our own eyes. Modern bourgeois society with its relations of production, of exchange and of property, a society that has conjured up such gigantic means of production and of exchange, is like the sorcerer, who is no longer able to control the powers of the subterranean world which he has called up by his spells. For many decades now the history of industry and commerce has been but the history of the revolt of modern productive forces against modern conditions of production, against the property relations that are the conditions for the existence of the bourgeoisie and of its rule. It is enough to mention the commercial crises that by their periodical return put on trial, each time more threateningly, the existence of the entire bourgeois society. In these crises a great part not only of the existing products, but also of the previously created productive forces, are periodically destroyed. In these crises there breaks out an epidemic that, in all earlier epochs, would have seemed an absurdity—the epidemic of overproduction. Society suddenly finds itself put back into a state of momentary barbarism; it appears as if a famine, a universal war of devastation had cut off the supply of every means of subsistence; industry and commerce seem to be destroyed; and why? Because there is too much civilization, too much means of subsistence, too much industry, too much commerce. The productive forces at the disposal of society no longer tend to further the development of the conditions of bourgeois property; on the contrary, they have become too powerful for these conditions, by which they are fettered, and so soon as they overcome these fetters, they bring disorder into the whole of bourgeois society, endanger the existence of bourgeois property. The conditions of

bourgeois society are too narrow to comprise the wealth created by them. And how does the bourgeoisie get over these crises? On the one hand by enforced destruction of a mass of productive forces; on the other, by the conquest of new markets, and by the more thorough exploitation of the old ones. That is to say, by paving the way for more extensive and more destructive crises, and by diminishing the means whereby crises are prevented.

". . . [T]he theory of the Communists may be summed up in the single phrase: Abolition of private property."

The weapons with which the bourgeoisie felled feudalism to the ground are now turned against the bourgeoisie itself.

But not only has the bourgeoisie forged the weapons that bring death to itself; it has also called into existence the men who are to wield those weapons—the modern working class—the proletarians.

In proportion as the bourgeoisie, *i.e.,* capital, is developed, in the same proportion is the proletariat, the modern working class, developed—a class of laborers, who live only so long as they find work, and who find work only so long as their labor increases capital. These laborers, who must sell themselves piecemeal, are a commodity, like every other article of commerce, and are consequently exposed to all the vicissitudes of competition, to all the fluctuations of the market.

Owing to the extensive use of machinery and to division of labor, the work of the proletarians has lost all individual character, and, consequently, all charm for the workman. He becomes an appendage of the machine, and it is only the most simple, most monotonous, and most easily acquired knack that is required of him. Hence, the cost of production of a workman is restricted, almost entirely, to the means of subsistence that he requires for his maintenance, and for the propagation of his race. But the price of a commodity, and therefore also of labor, is equal to its cost of production. In proportion, therefore, as the repulsiveness of the work increases, the wage decreases. What is more, in proportion as the use of machinery and division of labor increases, in the same proportion the burden of toil also increases, whether by prolongation of the working hours, by increase of the work exacted in a given time or by increased speed of the machinery, etc.

Modern industry has converted the little workshop of the patriarchal master into the great factory of the industrial capitalist. Masses of laborers, crowded into the factory, are organized like soldiers. As privates of the industrial army they are placed under the command of a perfect hierarchy of officers and sergeants. Not only are they slaves of the bourgeois class, and of the bourgeois state; they are daily and hourly enslaved by the machine, by the foreman, and, above all, by the individual bourgeois manufacturer himself. The more openly this despotism proclaims gain to be its end and aim, the more petty, the more hateful, and the more embittering it is. . . .

But with the development of industry the proletariat not only increases in number; it becomes concentrated in greater masses, its strength grows, and it feels that strength more. The various interests and conditions of life within the ranks of the proletariat are more and more equalized, in proportion as machinery obliterates all distinctions of labor, and nearly everywhere reduces wages to the same low level. The growing competition among the bourgeoisie, and the resulting commercial crises, make the wages of the workers ever more fluctuating. The unceasing improvement of machinery, ever more rapidly developing, makes their livelihood more and more precarious; the collisions between individual workmen and individual bourgeoisie take more and more the character of collisions between two classes. Thereupon the workers begin to form combinations (trade unions) against the bourgeoisie; they club together in order to keep up the rate of wages; they found permanent associations in order to make provision beforehand for these occa-

sional revolts. Here and there the contest breaks out into riots.

From time to time the workers are victorious, but only for a time. The real fruit of their battles lies not in the immediate result, but in the ever-expanding union of the workers. This union is helped by the improved means of communication that are created by modern industry and that place the workers of different localities in contact with one another. It was just this contact that was needed to centralize the numerous local struggles, all of the same character, into one national struggle between classes. But every class struggle is a political struggle. And that union, to attain which the burghers of the Middle Ages, with their miserable highways, required centuries, the modern proletarians, thanks to railways, achieve in a few years. . . .

Hitherto, every form of society has been based, as we have already seen, on the antagonism of oppressing and oppressed classes. But in order to oppress a class, certain conditions must be assured to it under which it can, at least, continue its slavish existence. The serf, in the period of serfdom, raised himself to membership in the commune, just as the petty bourgeois, under the yoke of feudal absolutism, managed to develop into a bourgeois. The modern laborer, on the contrary, instead of rising with the progress of industry, sinks deeper and deeper below the conditions of existence of his own class. He becomes a pauper, and pauperism develops more rapidly than population and wealth. And here it becomes evident that the bourgeoisie is unfit any longer to be the ruling class in society, and to impose its conditions of existence upon society as an overriding law. It is unfit to rule because it is incompetent to assure an existence to its slave within his slavery, because it cannot help letting him sink into such a state, that it has to feed him, instead of being fed by him. Society can no longer live under this bourgeoisie, in other words, its existence is no longer compatible with society.

The essential condition for the existence, and for the sway of the bourgeois class, is the formation and augmentation of capital; the condition for capital is wage labor. Wage labor rests exclusively on competition between the laborers. The advance of industry, whose involuntary promoter is the bourgeoisie, replaces the isolation of the laborers, due to competition, by their revolutionary combination, due to association. The development of modern industry, therefore, cuts from under its feet the very foundation on which the bourgeoisie produces and appropriates products. What the bourgeoisie, therefore, produces, above all, is its own grave-diggers. Its fall and the victory of the proletariat are equally inevitable.

II. Proletarians and Communists

... All property relations in the past have continually been subject to historical change consequent upon the change in historical conditions.

The French Revolution, for example, abolished feudal property in favor of bourgeois property.

The distinguishing feature of communism is not the abolition of property generally, but the abolition of bourgeois property. But modern bourgeois private property is the final and most complete expression of the system of producing and appropriating products that is based on class antagonisms, on the exploitation of the many by the few.

In this sense, the theory of the Communists may be summed up in the single phrase: Abolition of private property.

We Communists have been reproached with the desire of abolishing the right of personally acquiring property as the fruit of a man's own labor, which property is alleged to be the groundwork of all personal freedom, activity and independence.

Hard-won, self-acquired, self-earned property! Do you mean the property of the petty artisan and of the small peasant, a form of property that preceded the bourgeois form? There is no need to abolish that; the development of industry has to a great extent already destroyed it, and is still destroying it daily.

Or do you mean modern bourgeois private property?

But does wage labor create any property for the laborer? Not a bit. It creates capital, *i.e.,* that kind of property that exploits wage labor, and that cannot increase except upon condition of begetting a new

supply of wage labor for fresh exploitation. Property, in its present form, is based on the antagonism of capital and wage labor. Let us examine both sides of this antagonism.

To be a capitalist, is to have not only a purely personal, but a social *status* in production. Capital is a collective product, and only by the united action of many members, nay, in the last resort, only by the united action of all members of society, can it be set in motion.

Capital is, therefore, not a personal, it is a social power.

When, therefore, capital is converted into common property, into the property of all members of society, personal property is not thereby transformed into social property. It is only the social character of the property that is changed. It loses its class character.

Let us now take wage labor.

The average price of wage labor is the minimum wage, *i.e.,* that quantum of the means of subsistence, which is absolutely requisite to keep the laborer in bare existence as a laborer. What, therefore, the wage laborer appropriates by means of his labor, merely suffices to prolong and reproduce a bare existence. We by no means intend to abolish this personal appropriation of the products of labor, an appropriation that is made for the maintenance and reproduction of human life, and that leaves no surplus wherewith to command the labor of others. All that we want to do away with is the miserable character of this appropriation, under which the laborer lives merely to increase capital, and is allowed to live only in so far as the interest of the ruling class requires it.

In bourgeois society, living labor is but a means to increase accumulated labor. In communist society, accumulated labor is but a means to widen, to enrich, to promote the existence of the laborer.

In bourgeois society, therefore, the past dominates the present; in communist society the present dominates the past. In bourgeois society capital is independent and has individuality, while the living person is dependent and has no individuality.

And the abolition of this state of things is called by the bourgeoisie, abolition of individuality and freedom! And rightly so. The abolition of bourgeois individuality, bourgeois independence, and bourgeois freedom is undoubtedly aimed at.

By freedom is meant, under the present bourgeois conditions of production, free trade, free selling and buying.

But if selling and buying disappears, free selling and buying disappears also. This talk about free selling and buying, and all the other "brave words" of our bourgeoisie about freedom in general, have a meaning, if any, only in contrast with restricted selling and buying, with the fettered traders of the Middle Ages, but have no meaning when opposed to the communistic abolition of buying and selling, of the bourgeois conditions of production, and of the bourgeoisie itself.

You are horrified at our intending to do away with private property. But in your existing society, private property is already done away with for nine-tenths of the population; its existence for the few is soley due to its non-existence in the hands of those nine-tenths. You reproach us, therefore, with intending to do away with a form of property, the necessary condition for whose existence is the non-existence of any property for the immense majority of society.

In one word, you reproach us with intending to do away with your property. Precisely so; that is just what we intend.

From the moment when labor can no longer be converted into capital money, or rent, into a social power capable of being monopolized, *i.e.,* from the moment when individual property can no longer be transformed into bourgeois property, into capital, from that moment, you say, individuality vanishes.

You must, therefore, confess that by "individual" you mean no other person than the bourgeois, than the middle-class owner of property. This person must, indeed, be swept out of the way, and made impossible.

Communism deprives no man of the power to appropriate the products of society; all that it does is to deprive him of the power to subjugate the labor of others by means of such appropriation.

It has been objected that upon the abolition of private property all work will cease, and universal laziness will overtake us.

According to this, bourgeois society ought long ago to have gone to the dogs through sheer idleness; for those of its members who work, acquire nothing, and those who acquire anything, do not work. The whole of this objection is but another expression of the tautology: that there can no longer be any wage labor when there is no longer any capital.

Study Questions

1. Is capitalism an immoral system?

2. Can capitalism be reformed to respond to most of Marx's criticisms and still be capitalistic?

3. Would Marx approve of the Soviet system?

4. Will America move closer to Smith's vision or to Marx's vision in the next one hundred years?

A Theory of Justice

John Rawls is a professor of philosophy at Harvard. He is the author of A Theory of Justice *and many articles.*

John Rawls

3. The Main Idea of the Theory of Justice

My aim is to present a conception of justice which generalizes and carries to a higher level of abstraction the familiar theory of the social contract as found, say, in Locke, Rousseau, and Kant.[1] In order to do this we are not to think of the original contract as one to enter a particular society or to set up a particular form of government. Rather, the guiding idea is that the principles of justice for the basic structure of society are the object of the original agreement. They are the principles that free and rational persons concerned to further their own interests would accept in an initial position of equality as defining the fundamental terms of their association. These principles are to regulate all further agreements; they specify the kinds of social cooperation that can be entered into and the forms of government that can be established. This way of regarding the principles of justice I shall call justice as fairness.

Thus we are to imagine that those who engage in social cooperation choose together, in one joint act, the principles which are to assign basic rights and duties and to determine the division of social benefits. Men are to decide in advance how they are to regulate their claims one against one another and what is to be the foundation charter of their society. Just as each person must decide by rational reflection what constitutes his good, that is, the system of ends which it is rational for him to pursue, so a group of persons must decide once and for all what is to count among them as just and unjust. The choice which rational men would make in this hypothetical situation of equal liberty, assuming for the present that this choice problem has a solution, determines the principles of justice.

In justice as fairness the original position of equality corresponds to the state of nature in the traditional theory of the social contract. This original position is not, of course, thought of as an actual historical state of affairs, much less as a primi-

---

---

1. As the text suggests, I shall regard Locke's *Second Treatise of Government,* Rousseau's *The Social Contract,* and Kant's ethical works beginning with *The Foundations of the Metaphysics of Morals* as definitive of the contract tradition. For all of its greatness, Hobbes's *Leviathan* raises special problems. A general historical survey is provided by J. W. Gough, *The Social Contract,* 2nd ed. (Oxford, The Clarendon Press, 1957), and Otto Gierke, *Natural Law and the Theory of Society,* trans. with an introduction by Ernest Barker (Cambridge, The University Press, 1934). A presentation of the contract view as primarily an ethical theory is to be found in G. R. Grice, *The Grounds of Moral Judgment* (Cambridge, The University Press, 1967).

tive condition of culture. It is understood as a purely hypothetical situation characterized so as to lead to a certain conception of justice.[2] Among the essential features of this situation is that no one knows his place in society, his class position or social status, nor does any one know his fortune in the distribution of natural assets and abilities, his intelligence, strength, and the like. I shall even assume that the parties do not know their conceptions of the good or their special psychological propensities. The principles of justice are chosen behind a veil of ignorance. This ensures that no one is advantaged or disadvantaged in the choice of principles by the outcome of natural chance or the contingency of social circumstances. Since all are similarly situated and no one is able to design principles to favor his particular condition, the principles of justice are the result of a fair agreement or bargain. For given the circumstances of the original position, the symmetry of everyone's relations to each other, this initial situation is fair between individuals as moral persons, that is, as rational beings with their own ends and capable, I shall assume, of a sense of justice. The original position is, one might say, the appropriate initial status quo, and thus the fundamental agreements reached in it are fair. This explains the propriety of the name "justice as fairness": it conveys the idea that the principles of justice are agreed to in an initial situation that is fair. The name does not mean that the concepts of justice and fairness are the same, any more than the phrase "poetry as metaphor" means that the concepts of poetry and metaphor are the same.

Justice as fairness begins, as I have said, with one of the most general of all choices which persons might make together, namely, with the choice of the first principles of a conception of justice which is to regulate all subsequent criticism and reform of institutions. Then, having chosen a conception of justice, we can suppose that they are to choose a constitution and a legislature to enact laws, and so on, all in accordance with the principles of justice initially agreed upon. Our social situation is just if it is such that by this sequence of hypothetical agreements we would have contracted into the general system of rules which defines it. Moreover, assuming that the original position does determine a set of principles (that is, that a particular concept of justice would be chosen), it will then be true that whenever social institutions satisfy these principles those engaged in them can say to one another that they are cooperating on terms to which they would agree if they were free and equal persons whose relations with respect to one another were fair. They could all view their arrangements as meeting the stipulations which they would acknowledge in an initial situation that embodies widely accepted and reasonable constraints on the choice of principles. The general recognition of this fact would provide the basis for a public acceptance of the corresponding principles of justice. No society can, of course, be a scheme of cooperation which men enter voluntarily in a literal sense; each person finds himself placed at birth in some particular position in some particular society, and the nature of this position materially affects his life prospects. Yet a society satisfying the principles of justice as fairness comes as close as a society can to being a voluntary scheme, for it meets the principles which free and equal persons would assent to under circumstances that are fair. In this sense its members are autonomous and the obligations they recognize self-imposed.

One feature of justice as fairness is to think of the parties in the initial situation as rational and mutually disinterested. This does not mean that the parties are egoists, that is, individuals with only certain kinds of interests, say in wealth, prestige, and domination. But they are conceived as not taking an interest in one another's interests. They are to presume that even their spiritual aims may be opposed, in the way that the aims of those of different religions may be opposed. Moreover, the concept of

---

2. Kant is clear that the original agreement is hypothetical. See *The Metaphysics of Morals,* pt. I (*Rechtslehre*), especially §§ 47, 52; and pt. II of the essay "Concerning the Common Saying: This May Be True in Theory but It Does Not Apply in Practice," in *Kant's Political Writings,* ed. Hans Reiss and trans. by H. B. Nisbet (Cambridge, The University Press, 1970), pp. 73–87. See Georges Vlachos, *La Pensée politique de Kant* (Paris, Presses Universitaires de France, 1962), pp. 326–335; and J. G. Murphy, *Kant: The Philosophy of Right* (London, Macmillan, 1970), pp. 109–112, 133–136, for a further discussion.

rationality must be interpreted as far as possible in the narrow sense, standard in economic theory, of taking the most effective means to given ends. I shall modify this concept to some extent, as explained later (§25), but one must try to avoid introducing into it any controversial ethical elements. The initial situation must be characterized by stipulations that are widely accepted.

In working out the conception of justice as fairness one main task clearly is to determine which principles of justice would be chosen in the original position. To do this we must describe this situation in some detail and formulate with care the problem of choice which it presents. These matters I shall take up in the immediately succeeding chapters. It may be observed, however, that once the principles of justice are thought of as arising from an original agreement in a situation of equality, it is an open question whether the principle of utility would be acknowledged. Offhand it hardly seems likely that persons who view themselves as equals, entitled to press their claims upon one another, would agree to a principle which may require lesser life prospects for some simply for the sake of a greater sum of advantages enjoyed by others. Since each desires to protect his interests, his capacity to advance his conception of the good, no one has a reason to acquiesce in an enduring loss for himself in order to bring about a greater net balance of satisfaction. In the absence of strong and lasting benevolent impulses, a rational man would not accept a basic structure merely because it maximized the algebraic sum of advantages irrespective of its permanent effects on his own basic rights and interests. Thus it seems that the principle of utility is incompatible with the conception of social cooperation among equals for mutual advantage. It appears to be inconsistent with the idea of reciprocity implicit in the notion of a well-ordered society. Or, at any rate, so I shall argue.

I shall maintain instead that the persons in the initial situation would choose two rather different principles: the first requires equality in the assignment of basic rights and duties, while the second holds that social and economic inequalities, for example inequalities of wealth and authority, are just only if they result in compensating benefits for everyone, and in particular for the least advantaged members of society. These principles rule out justifying institutions on the grounds that the hardships of some are offset by a greater good in the aggregate. It may be expedient but it is not just that some should have less in order that others may prosper. But there is no injustice in the greater benefits earned by a few provided that the situation of persons not so fortunate is thereby improved. The intuitive idea is that since everyone's well-being depends upon a scheme of cooperation without which no one could have a satisfactory life, the division of advantages should be such as to draw forth the willing cooperation of everyone taking part in it, including those less well situated. Yet this can be expected only if reasonable terms are proposed. The two principles mentioned seem to be a fair agreement on the basis of which those better endowed, or more fortunate in their social position, neither of which we can be said to deserve, could expect the willing cooperation of others when some workable scheme is a necessary condition of the welfare of all.[3] Once we decide to look for a conception of justice that nullifies the accidents of natural endowment and the contingencies of social circumstance as counters in quest for political and economic advantage, we are led to these principles. They express the result of leaving aside those aspects of the social world that seem arbitrary from a moral point of view.

The problem of the choice of principles, however, is extremely difficult. I do not expect the answer I shall suggest to be convincing to everyone. It is, therefore, worth noting from the outset that justice as fairness, like other contract views, consists of two parts: (1) an interpretation of the initial situation and of the problem of choice posed there, and (2) a set of principles which, it is argued, would be agreed to. One may accept the first part of the theory (or some variant thereof), but not the other, and conversely. The concept of the initial contractual situation may seem reasonable although the particular principles proposed are rejected. To be sure, I want to maintain that the most appropriate

---

3. For the formulation of this intuitive idea I am indebted to Allan Gibbard.

conception of this situation does lead to principles of justice contrary to utilitarianism and perfectionism, and therefore that the contract doctrine provides an alternative to these views. Still, one may dispute this contention even though one grants that the contractarian method is a useful way of studying ethical theories and of setting forth their underlying assumptions.

Justice as fairness is an example of what I have called a contract theory. Now there may be an objection to the term "contract" and related expressions, but I think it will serve reasonably well. Many words have misleading connotations which at first are likely to confuse. The terms "utility" and "utilitarianism" are surely no exception. They too have unfortunate suggestions which hostile critics have been willing to exploit; yet they are clear enough for those prepared to study utilitarian doctrine. The same should be true of the term "contract" applied to moral theories. As I have mentioned, to understand it one has to keep in mind that it implies a certain level of abstraction. In particular, the content of the relevant agreement is not to enter a given society or to adopt a given form of government, but to accept certain moral principles. Moreover, the undertakings referred to are purely hypothetical: a contract view holds that certain principles would be accepted in a well-defined initial situation.

The merit of the contract terminology is that it conveys the idea that principles of justice may be conceived as principles that would be chosen by rational persons, and that in this way conceptions of justice may be explained and justified. The theory of justice is a part, perhaps the most significant part, of the theory of rational choice. Furthermore, principles of justice deal with conflicting claims upon the advantages won by social cooperation; they apply to the relations among several persons or groups. The word "contract" suggests this plurality as well as the condition that the appropriate division of advantages must be in accordance with principles acceptable to all parties. The condition of publicity for principles of justice is also connoted by the contract phraseology. Thus, if these principles are the outcome of an agreement, citizens have a knowledge of the principles that others follow. It is characteristic of contract theories to stress the public nature of political principles. Finally there is the long tradition of the contract doctrine. Expressing the tie with this line of thought helps to define ideas and accords with natural piety. There are then several advantages in the use of the term "contract." With due precautions taken, it should not be misleading.

A final remark. Justice as fairness is not a complete contract theory. For it is clear that the contractarian idea can be extended to the choice of more or less an entire ethical system, that is, to a system including principles for all the virtues and not only for justice. Now for the most part I shall consider only principles of justice and others closely related to them; I make no attempt to discuss the virtues in a systematic way. Obviously if justice as fairness succeeds reasonably well, a next step would be to study the more general view suggested by the name "rightness as fairness." But even this wider theory fails to embrace all moral relationships, since it would seem to include only our relations with other persons and to leave out of account how we are to conduct ourselves toward animals and the rest of nature. I do not contend that the contract notion offers a way to approach these questions which are certainly of the first importance; and I shall have to put them aside. We must recognize the limited scope of justice as fairness and of the general type of view that it exemplifies. How far its conclusions must be revised once these other matters are understood cannot be decided in advance.

4. The Original Position and Justification

I have said that the original position is the appropriate initial status quo which insures that the fundamental agreements reached in it are fair. This fact yields the name "justice as fairness." It is clear, then, that I want to say that one conception of justice is more reasonable than another, or justifiable with respect to it, if rational persons in the initial situation would choose its principles over those of the other for the role of justice. Conceptions of justice are to be ranked by their acceptability to persons so circumstanced. Understood in this way the question of justification is settled by working out a problem of deliberation: we have to ascertain which principles it would be rational to adopt given the contractual situation. This connects the theory of justice with the theory of rational choice.

If this view of the problem of justification is to succeed, we must, of course, describe in some detail the nature of this choice problem. A problem of rational decision has a definite answer only if we know the beliefs and interests of the parties, their relations with respect to one another, the alternatives between which they are to choose, the procedure whereby they make up their minds, and so on. As the circumstances are presented in different ways, correspondingly different principles are accepted. The concept of the original position, as I shall refer to it, is that of the most philosophically favored interpretation of this initial choice situation for the purposes of a theory of justice.

But how are we to decide what is the most favored interpretation? I assume, for one thing, that there is a broad measure of agreement that principles of justice should be chosen under certain conditions. To justify a particular description of the initial situation one shows that it incorporates these commonly shared presumptions. One argues from widely accepted but weak premises to more specific conclusions. Each of the presumptions should by itself be natural and plausible; some of them may seem innocuous or even trivial. The aim of the contract approach is to establish that taken together they impose significant bounds on acceptable principles of justice. The ideal outcome would be that these conditions determine a unique set of principles; but I shall be satisfied if they suffice to rank the main traditional conceptions of social justice.

One should not be misled, then, by the somewhat unusual conditions which characterize the original position. The idea here is simply to make vivid to ourselves the restrictions that it seems reasonable to impose on arguments for principles of justice, and therefore on these principles themselves. Thus it seems reasonable and generally acceptable that no one should be advantaged or disadvantaged by natural fortune or social circumstances in the choice of principles. It also seems widely agreed that it should be impossible to tailor principles to the circumstances of one's own case. We should insure further that particular inclinations and aspirations, and persons' conceptions of their good do not affect the principles adopted. The aim is to rule out those principles that it would be rational to propose for acceptance, however little the chance of success, only if one knew certain things that are irrelevant from the standpoint of justice. For example, if a man knew that he was wealthy, he might find it rational to advance the principle that various taxes for welfare measures be counted unjust; if he knew that he was poor, he would most likely propose the contrary principle. To represent the desired restrictions one imagines a situation in which everyone is deprived of this sort of information. One excludes the knowledge of those contingencies which sets men at odds and allows them to be guided by their prejudices. In this manner the veil of ignorance is arrived at in a natural way. This concept should cause no difficulty if we keep in mind the constraints on arguments that it is meant to express. At any time we can enter the original position, so to speak, simply by following a certain procedure, namely, by arguing for principles of justice in accordance with these restrictions.

It seems reasonable to suppose that the parties in the original position are equal. That is, all have the same rights in the procedure for choosing principles; each can make proposals, submit reasons for their acceptance, and so on. Obviously the purpose of these conditions is to represent equality between human beings as moral persons, as creatures having a conception of their good and capable of a sense of justice. The basis of equality is taken to be similarity in these two respects. Systems of ends are not ranked in value; and each man is presumed to have the requisite ability to understand and to act upon whatever principles are adopted. Together with the veil of ignorance, these conditions define the principles of justice as those which rational persons concerned to advance their interests would consent to as equals when none are known to be advantaged or disadvantaged by social and natural contingencies.

There is, however, another side to justifying a particular description of the original position. This is to see if the principles which would be chosen match our considered convictions of justice or extend them in an acceptable way. We can note whether applying these principles would lead us to make the same judgments about the basic structure of society which we now make intuitively and in which we have the greatest confidence; or whether, in cases where our present judgments are in doubt and given with hesitation, these principles offer a resolution which we can affirm on reflection. There are questions which we feel sure must be answered in a certain way. For example, we are confident that religious intolerance and racial discrimination are unjust. We think that we have examined these things with care and have reached what we believe is an impartial judgment not likely to be distorted by an excessive attention to our own interests. These convictions are provisional fixed points which we presume any conception of justice must fit. But we have much less assurance as to what is the correct distribution of wealth and authority. Here we may be looking for a way to remove our doubts. We can check an interpretation of the initial situation, then, by the capacity of its principles to accommodate our firmest convictions and to provide guidance where guidance is needed.

In searching for the most favored description of this situation we work from both ends. We begin by describing it so that it represents generally shared and preferably weak conditions. We then see if these conditions are strong enough to yield a significant set of principles. If not, we look for further premises equally reasonable. But if so, and these principles match our considered convictions of justice, then so far well and good. But presumably there will be discrepancies. In this case we have a choice. We can either modify the account of the initial situation or we can revise our existing judgments, for even the judgments we take provisionally as fixed points are liable to revision. By going back and forth, sometimes altering the conditions of the contractual circumstances, at others withdrawing our judgments and conforming them to principle, I assume that eventually we shall find a description of the initial situation that both expresses reasonable conditions and yields principles which match our considered judgments duly pruned and adjusted.

This state of affairs I refer to as reflective equilibrium.[4] It is an equilibrium because at last our principles and judgments coincide; and it is reflective since we know to what principles our judgments conform and the premises of their derivation. At the moment everything is in order. But this equilibrium is not necessarily stable. It is liable to be upset by further examination of the conditions which should be imposed on the contractual situation and by particular cases which may lead us to revise our judgments. Yet for the time being we have done what we can to render coherent and to justify our convictions of social justice. We have reached a conception of the original position.

> *"The distribution of wealth and income, and the hierarchies of authority, must be consistent with both the liberties of equal citizenship and equality of opportunity."*

I shall not, of course, actually work through this process. Still, we may think of the interpretation of the original position that I shall present as the result of such a hypothetical course of reflection. It represents the attempt to accommodate within one scheme both reasonable philosophical conditions on principles as well as our considered judgments of justice. In arriving at the favored interpretation of the initial situation there is no point at which an appeal is made to self-evidence in the traditional sense either of general conceptions or particular convictions. I do not claim for the principles of jus-

---

4. The process of mutual adjustment of principles and considered judgments is not peculiar to moral philosophy. See Nelson Goodman, *Fact, Fiction, and Forecast* (Cambridge, Mass., Harvard University Press, 1955), pp. 65–68, for parallel remarks concerning the justification of the principles of deductive and inductive inference.

tice proposed that they are necessary truths or derivable from such truths. A conception of justice cannot be deduced from self-evident premises or conditions on principles; instead, its justification is a matter of the mutual support of many considerations, of everything fitting together into one coherent view.

A final comment. We shall want to say that certain principles of justice are justified because they would be agreed to in an initial situation of equality. I have emphasized that this original position is purely hypothetical. It is natural to ask why, if this agreement is never actually entered into, we should take any interest in these principles, moral or otherwise. The answer is that the conditions embodied in the description of the original position are ones that we do in fact accept. Or if we do not, then perhaps we can be persuaded to do so by philosophical reflection. Each aspect of the contractual situation can be given supporting grounds. Thus what we shall do is to collect together into one conception a number of conditions on principles that we are ready upon due consideration to recognize as reasonable. These constraints express what we are prepared to regard as limits on fair terms of social cooperation. One way to look at the idea of the original position, therefore, is to see it as an expository device which sums up the meaning of these conditions and helps us to extract their consequences. On the other hand, this conception is also an intuitive notion that suggests its own elaboration, so that led on by it we are drawn to define more clearly the standpoint from which we can best interpret moral relationships. We need a conception that enables us to envision our objective from afar: the intuitive notion of the original position is to do this for us. . . .

11. Two Principles of Justice

I shall now state in a provisional form the two principles of justice that I believe would be chosen in the original position. In this section I wish to make only the most general comments, and therefore the first formulation of these principles is tentative. As we go on I shall run through several formulations and approximate step by step the final statement to

be given much later. I believe that doing this allows the exposition to proceed in a natural way.

The first statement of the two principles reads as follows.

First: each person is to have an equal right to the most extensive basic liberty compatible with a similar liberty for others.

Second: social and economic inequalities are to be arranged so that they are both
(a) reasonably expected to be to everyone's advantage, and (b) attached to positions and offices open to all.

There are two ambiguous phrases in the second principle, namely "everyone's advantage" and "open to all." Determining their sense more exactly will lead to a second formulation of the principle in § 13. The final version of the two principles is given in § 46; § 39 considers the rendering of the first principle.

By way of general comment, these principles primarily apply, as I have said, to the basic structure of society. They are to govern the assignment of rights and duties and to regulate the distribution of social and economic advantages. As their formulation suggests, these principles presuppose that the social structure can be divided into two more or less distinct parts, the first principle applying to the one, the second to the other. They distinguish between those aspects of the social system that define and secure the equal liberties of citizenship and those that specify and establish social and economic inequalities. The basic liberties of citizens are roughly speaking, political liberty (the right to vote and to be eligible for public office) together with freedom of speech and assembly; liberty of conscience and freedom of thought; freedom of the person along with the right to hold (personal) property; and freedom from arbitrary arrest and seizure as defined by the concept of the rule of law. These liberties are all required to be equal by the first principle, since citizens of a just society are to have the same basic rights.

The second principle applies, in the first approximation, to the distribution of income and wealth and to the design of organizations that make use of differences in authority and responsibility, or chains of command. While the distribution of wealth and income need not be equal, it must be to everyone's advantage, and at the same time, positions of authority and offices of command must be accessible to all. One applies the second principle by holding positions open, and then, subject to this constraint, arranges social and economic inequalities so that everyone benefits.

These principles are to be arranged in a serial order with the first principle prior to the second. This ordering means that a departure from the institutions of equal liberty required by the first principle cannot be justified by, or compensated for, by greater social and economic advantages. The distribution of wealth and income, and the hierarchies of authority, must be consistent with both the liberties of equal citizenship and equality of opportunity.

It is clear that these principles are rather specific in their content, and their acceptance rests on certain assumptions that I must eventually try to explain and justify. A theory of justice depends upon a theory of society in ways that will become evident as we proceed. For the present, it should be observed that the two principles (and this holds for all formulations) are a special case of a more general conception of justice that can be expressed as follows.

> All social values—liberty and opportunity, income and wealth, and the bases of self-respect—are to be distributed equally unless an unequal distribution of any, or all, of these values is to everyone's advantage.

Injustice then, is simply inequalities that are not to the benefit of all. Of course, this conception is extremely vague and requires interpretation.

As a first step, suppose that the basic structure of society distributes certain primary goods, that is, things that every rational man is presumed to want. These goods normally have a use whatever a person's rational plan of life. For simplicity, assume that the chief primary goods at the disposition of society are rights and liberties, powers and opportunities, income and wealth. (Later on in Part Three the primary good of self-respect has a central place.) These are the social primary goods. Other primary goods such as health and vigor, intelligence and imagination, are natural goods; although their possession is influenced by the basic structure, they

are not so directly under its control. Imagine, then, a hypothetical initial arrangement in which all the social primary goods are equally distributed: everyone has similar rights and duties, and income and wealth are evenly shared. This state of affairs provides a benchmark for judging improvements. If certain inequalities of wealth and organizational powers would make everyone better off than in this hypothetical starting situation, then they accord with the general conception.

Now it is possible, at least theoretically, that by giving up some of their fundamental liberties men are sufficiently compensated by the resulting social and economic gains. The general conception of justice imposes no restrictions on what sort of inequalities are permissible; it only requires that everyone's position be improved. We need not suppose anything so drastic as consenting to a condition of slavery. Imagine instead that men forego certain political rights when the economic returns are significant and their capacity to influence the course of policy by the exercise of these rights would be marginal in any case. It is this kind of exchange which the two principles as stated rule out; being arranged in serial order they do not permit exchanges between basic liberties and economic and social gains. The serial ordering of principles expresses an underlying preference among primary social goods. When this preference is rational so likewise is the choice of these principles in this order.

In developing justice as fairness I shall, for the most part, leave aside the general conception of justice and examine instead the special case of the two principles in serial order. The advantage of this procedure is that from the first the matter of priorities is recognized and an effort made to find principles to deal with it. One is led to attend throughout to the conditions under which the acknowledgment of the absolute weight of liberty with respect to social and economic advantages, as defined by the lexical order of the two principles, would be reasonable. Offhand, this ranking appears extreme and too special a case to be of much interest; but there is more justification for it than would appear at first sight. Or at any rate, so I shall maintain (§82). Furthermore, the distinction between fundamental rights and liberties and economic and social benefits marks a difference among primary social goods that one should try to exploit. It suggests an important division in the social system. Of course, the distinctions drawn and the ordering proposed are bound to be at best only approximations. There are surely circumstances in which they fail. But it is essential to depict clearly the main lines of a reasonable concept of justice; and under many conditions anyway, the two principles in serial order may serve well enough. When necessary we can fall back on the more general conception.

The fact that the two principles apply to institutions has certain consequences. Several points illustrate this. First of all, the rights and liberties referred to by these principles are those which are defined by the public rules of the basic structure. Whether men are free is determined by the rights and duties established by the major institutions of society. Liberty is a certain pattern of social forms. The first principle simply requires that certain sorts of rules, those defining basic liberties, apply to everyone equally and that they allow the most extensive liberty compatible with a like liberty for all. The only reason for circumscribing the rights defining liberty and making men's freedom less extensive than it might otherwise be is that these equal rights as institutionally defined would interfere with one another.

Another thing to bear in mind is that when principles mention persons, or require that everyone gain from an inequality, the reference is to representative persons holding the various social positions, or offices, or whatever, established by the basic structure. Thus in applying the second principle I assume that it is possible to assign an expectation of well-being to representative individuals holding these positions. This expectation indicates their life prospects as viewed from their social station. In general, the expectations of representative persons depend upon the distribution of rights and duties throughout the basic structure. When this changes, expectations change. I assume, then, that expectations are connected: by raising the prospects of the representative man in one position we presumably increase or decrease the prospects of representative men in other positions. Since it applies to institutional forms, the second principle (or rather the first part of it) refers to the expectations of representative individuals. As I shall discuss below, neither principle applies to distributions of particular goods to particular individuals who may be identified by their proper names. The situation where someone is considering how to allocate certain commodities to needy persons who are known to him is not within the scope of the principles. They are meant to regulate basic institutional arrangements. We must not assume that there is much similarity from the standpoint of justice between an administrative allotment of goods to specific persons and the appropriate design of society. Our common sense intuitions for the former may be a poor guide to the latter.

Now the second principle insists that each person benefit from permissible inequalities in the basic structure. This means that it must be reasonable for each relevant representative man defined by this structure, when he views it as a going concern, to prefer his prospects with the inequality to his prospects without it. One is not allowed to justify differences in income or organizational powers on the ground that the disadvantages of those in one position are outweighed by the greater advantages of those in another. Much less can infringements of liberty be counterbalanced in this way. Applied to the basic structure, the principle of utility would have us maximize the sum of expectations of representative men (weighted by the number of persons they represent, on the classical view); and this would permit us to compensate for the losses of some by the gains of others. Instead, the two principles require that everyone benefit from economic and social inequalities. It is obvious, however, that there are indefinitely many ways in which all may be advantaged when the initial arrangement of equality is taken as a benchmark. How then are we to choose among these possibilities? The principles must be specified so that they yield a determinate conclusion. I now turn to this problem. . . .

5. For a similar view, see B. A. O. Williams, "The Idea of Equality," *Philosophy, Politics, and Society,* Second Series, ed. Peter Laslett and W. G. Runciman (Oxford, Basil Blackwell, 1962), p. 113.

26. The Reasoning Leading to the Two Principles of Justice

In this and the next two sections I take up the choice between the two principles of justice and the principle of average utility. Determining the rational preference between these two options is perhaps the central problem in developing the conception of justice as fairness as a viable alternative to the utilitarian tradition. I shall begin in this section by presenting some intuitive remarks favoring the two principles. I shall also discuss briefly the qualitative structure of the argument that needs to be made if the case for these principles is to be conclusive.

It will be recalled that the general conception of justice as fairness requires that all primary social goods be distributed equally unless an unequal distribution would be to everyone's advantage. No restrictions are placed on exchanges of these goods and therefore a lesser liberty can be compensated for by greater social and economic benefits. Now looking at the situation from the standpoint of one person selected arbitrarily, there is no way for him to win special advantages for himself. Nor, on the other hand, are there grounds for his acquiescing in special disadvantages. Since it is not reasonable for him to expect more than an equal share in the division of social goods, and since it is not rational for him to agree to less, the sensible thing for him to do is to acknowledge as the first principle of justice one requiring an equal distribution. Indeed, this principle is so obvious that we would expect it to occur to anyone immediately.

Thus, the parties start with a principle establishing equal liberty for all, including equality of opportunity, as well as an equal distribution of income and wealth. But there is no reason why this acknowledgment should be final. If there are inequalities in the basic structure that work to make everyone better off in comparison with the benchmark of initial equality, why not permit them? The immediate gain which a greater equality might allow can be regarded as intelligently invested in view of its future return. If, for example, these inequalities set up various incentives which succeed in eliciting more productive efforts, a person in the original position

may look upon them as necessary to cover the costs of training and to encourage effective performance. One might think that ideally individuals should want to serve one another. But since the parties are assumed not to take an interest in one another's interests, their acceptance of these inequalities is only the acceptance of the relations in which men stand in the circumstances of justice. They have no grounds for complaining of one another's motives. A person in the original position would, therefore, concede the justice of these inequalities. Indeed, it would be shortsighted of him not to do so. He would hesitate to agree to these regularities only if he would be dejected by the bare knowledge or perception that others were better situated; and I have assumed that the parties decide as if they are not moved by envy. In order to make the principle regulating inequalities determinate, one looks at the system from the standpoint of the least advantaged representative man. Inequalities are permissible when they maximize, or at least all contribute to, the long-term expectations of the least fortunate group in society.

Now this general conception imposes no constraints on what sorts of inequalities are allowed, whereas the special conception, by putting the two principles in serial order (with the necessary adjustments in meaning), forbids exchanges between basic liberties and economic and social benefits. I shall not try to justify this ordering here. From time to time in later chapters this problem will be considered (§§39, 82). But roughly, the idea underlying this ordering is that if the parties assume that their basic liberties can be effectively exercised, they will not exchange a lesser liberty for an improvement in economic well-being. It is only when social conditions do not allow the effective establishment of these rights that one can concede their limitation; and these restrictions can be granted only to the extent that they are necessary to prepare the way for a free society. The denial of equal liberty can be defended only if it is necessary to raise the level of civilization so that in due course these freedoms can be enjoyed. Thus in adopting a serial order we are in effect making a special assumption in the original position, namely, that the parties know that the conditions of their society, whatever they are, admit the effective realization of the equal liberties. The serial ordering of the two principles of justice eventually comes to be reasonable if the general conception is consistently followed. This lexical ranking is the long-run tendency of the general view. For the most part I shall assume that the requisite circumstances for the serial order obtain.

It seems clear from these remarks that the two principles are at least a plausible conception of justice. The question, though, is how one is to argue for them more systematically. Now there are several things to do. One can work out their consequences for institutions and note their implications for fundamental social policy. In this way they are tested by a comparison with our considered judgments of justice. Part II is devoted to this. But one can also try to find arguments in their favor that are decisive from the standpoint of the original position. In order to see how this might be done, it is useful as a heuristic device to think of the two principles as the maximin solution to the problem of social justice. There is an analogy between the two principles and the maximin rule for choice under uncertainty.[6] This is evident from the fact that the two principles are those a person would choose for the design of a society in which his enemy is to assign him his place. The maximin rule tells us to rank alternatives by their worst possible outcomes: we are to adopt the alternative the worst outcome of which is superior to the worst outcomes of the others. The persons in the original position do not, of course, assume that their initial place in society is decided by a malevolent opponent. As I note below, they should not reason from false premises. The veil of ignorance does not violate this idea, since an absence of information is not misinformation. But that the two principles of justice would be chosen if the

parties were forced to protect themselves against such a contingency explains the sense in which this conception is the maximin solution. And this analogy suggests that if the original position has been described so that it is rational for the parties to adopt the conservative attitude expressed by this rule, a conclusive argument can indeed be constructed for these principles. Clearly the maximin rule is not, in general, a suitable guide for choices under uncertainty. But it is attractive in situations marked by certain special features. My aim, then, is to show that a good case can be made for the two principles based on the fact that the original position manifests these features to the fullest possible degree, carrying them to the limit, so to speak.

Consider the gain-and-loss table below. It represents the gains and losses for a situation which is not a game of strategy. There is no one playing against the person making the decision; instead he is faced with several possible circumstances which may or may not obtain. Which circumstances happen to exist does not depend upon what the person choosing decides or whether he announces his moves in advance. The numbers in the table are monetary values (in hundreds of dollars) in comparison with some initial situation. The gain (g) depends upon the individual's decision (d) and the circumstances (c). Thus $g = f(d,c)$. Assuming that there are three possible decisions and three possible circumstances, we might have this gain-and-loss table.

Decisions	Circumstances		
	c_1	c_2	c_3
d_1	-7	8	12
d_2	-8	7	14
d_3	5	6	8

The maximin rule requires that we make the third decision. For in this case the worst that can happen is that one gains five hundred dollars, which is better than the worst for the other actions. If we adopt one of these we may lose either eight or seven hundred dollars. Thus, the choice of d_3 maximizes $f(d,c)$ for that value of c, which for a given d, minimizes f. The term "maximin" means the *maximum minimorum*; and the rule directs our attention to the worst that can happen under any proposed course of action, and to decide in the light of that.

6. An accessible discussion of this and other rules of choice under uncertainty can be found in W. J. Baumol, *Economic Theory and Operations Analysis,* 2nd ed. (Englewood Cliffs, N.J., Prentice-Hall Inc., 1965), ch. 24. Baumol gives a geometric interpretation of these rules, including the diagram used in §13 to illustrate the difference principle. See pp. 558–562. See also R. D. Luce and Howard Raiffa, *Games and Decisions* (New York, John Wiley and Sons, Inc., 1957), ch. XIII, for a fuller account.

Now there appear to be three chief features of situations that give plausibility to this unusual rule.[7] First, since the rule takes no account of the likelihoods of the possible circumstances, there must be some reason for sharply discounting estimates of these probabilities. Offhand, the most natural rule of choice would seem to be to compute the expectation of monetary gain for each decision and then to adopt the course of action with the highest prospect. (This expectation is defined as follows: let us suppose that g_{ij} represent the numbers in the gain-and-loss table, where it is the row index and j is the column index; and let p_j, j = 1, 2, 3, be the likelihoods of the circumstances, with $\Sigma p_j = 1$. Then the expectation for the ith decision is equal to $\Sigma \, p_j g_{ij}$.) Thus it must be, for example, that the situation is one in which a knowledge of likelihoods is impossible, or at best extremely insecure. In this case it is unreasonable not to be skeptical of probabilistic calculations unless there is no other way out, particularly if the decision is a fundamental one that needs to be justified to others.

The second feature that suggests the maximin rule is the following: the person choosing has a conception of the good such that he cares very little, if anything, for what he might gain above the minimum stipend that he can, in fact, be sure of by following the maximin rule. It is not worthwhile for him to take a chance for the sake of a further advantage, especially when it may turn out that he loses much that is important to him. This last provision brings in the third feature, namely, that the rejected alternatives have outcomes that one can hardly accept. The situation involves grave risks. Of course these features work most effectively in combination. The paradigm situation for following the maximin rule is when all three features are realized to the highest degree. This rule does not, then, generally apply, nor of course is it self-evident. Rather, it is a maxim, a rule of thumb, that comes into its own in special circumstances. Its application depends upon the qualitative structure of the possible

gains and losses in relation to one's conception of the good, all this against a background in which it is reasonable to discount conjectural estimates of likelihoods.

It should be noted, as the comments on the gain-and-loss table say, that the entries in the table represent monetary values and not utilities. This difference is significant since for one thing computing expectations on the basis of such objective values is not the same thing as computing expected utility and may lead to different results. The essential point though is that in justice as fairness the parties do not know their conception of the good and cannot estimate their utility in the ordinary sense. In any case, we want to go behind de facto preferences generated by given conditions. Therefore expectations are based upon an index of primary goods and the parties make their choice accordingly. The entries in the example are in terms of money and not utility to indicate this aspect of the contract doctrine.

Now, as I have suggested, the original position has been defined so that it is a situation in which the maximin rule applies. In order to see this, let us review briefly the nature of this situation with these three special features in mind. To begin with, the veil of ignorance excludes all but the vaguest knowledge of likelihoods. The parties have no basis for determining the probable nature of their society, or their place in it. Thus they have strong reasons for being wary of probability calculations if any other course is open to them. They must also take into account the fact that their choice of principles should seem reasonable to others, in particular their descendants, whose rights will be deeply affected by it. There are further grounds for discounting that I shall mention as we go along. For the present it suffices to note that these considerations are strengthened by the fact that the parties know very little about the gain-and-loss table. Not only are they unable to conjecture the likelihoods of the various possible circumstances, they cannot say much about what the possible circumstances are, much less enumerate them and foresee the outcome of each alternative available. Those deciding are much more in the dark than the illustration by a numerical table suggests. It is for this reason that I have spoken of an analogy with the maximin rule.

---

7. Here I borrow from William Fellner, *Probability and Profit* (Homewood, Ill., R. D. Irwin, Inc., 1965), pp. 140–142, where these features are noted.

Several kinds of arguments for the two principles of justice illustrate the second feature. Thus, if we can maintain that these principles provide a workable theory of social justice, and that they are compatible with reasonable demands of efficiency, then this conception guarantees a satisfactory minimum. There may be, on reflection, little reason for trying to do better. Thus much of the argument, especially in Part Two, is to show, by their application to the main questions of social justice, that the two principles are a satisfactory conception. These details have a philosophical purpose. Moreover, this line of thought is practically decisive if we can establish the priority of liberty, the lexical ordering of the two principles. For this priority implies that the persons in the original position have no desire to try for greater gains at the expense of the equal liberties. The minimum assured by the two principles in lexical order is not one that the parties wish to jeopardize for the sake of greater economic and social advantages. In parts of Chapters IV and IX the case for this ordering is discussed.

Finally, the third feature holds if we can assume that other conceptions of justice may lead to institutions that the parties would find intolerable. For example, it has sometimes been held that under some conditions the utility principle (in either form) justifies, if not slavery or serfdom, at any rate serious infractions of liberty for the sake of greater social benefits. We need not consider here the truth of this claim, or the likelihood that the requisite conditions obtain. For the moment, this contention is only to illustrate the way in which conceptions of justice may allow for outcomes which the parties may not be able to accept. And having the ready alternative of the two principles of justice which secure a satisfactory minimum, it seems unwise, if not irrational, for them to take a chance that these outcomes are not realized. . . .

Study Questions

1. Is the difference principle too egalitarian?
2. Can equality of opportunity exist in a capitalist system?

3. Is the original position a useful method for solving moral disputes?

Democratic Capitalism: Developing a Conscience for the Corporation

Joseph Grčić

Joseph Grčić was born in Olib, Yugoslavia, and currently teaches philosophy at the University of Florida.

Any discussion of ethical problems must consist of at least three components. First, a general account of the distinctive nature or role of moral rules as

From *The Journal of Business Ethics* 4 (1985) 145–150. © 1985 by Reidel Publishing Company. Reprinted by permission of Kluwer Academic Publishers.

contrasted with other rules, must be provided. Second, one must determine the scope of applicability or relevance of moral concepts. Third, once it has been established that moral categories are relevant, then the conditions or structures necessary for maximal compliance with the appropriate moral principles should be addressed. The first two dimensions are generally considered metaethical whereas the third would be in the realm of applied ethics and moral psychology.

The role of morality is to provide a set of fundamental principles which constitute the deep structure of the human community. This fabric of rules is intended to preserve order, harmony and promote the *general group welfare* as understood by that group.[1] This is one feature that distinguishes it from rules of etiquette or aesthetics, which, though important, are less crucial and basic. Because they are viewed as basic and essential for the existence of the group, moral rules are action guides that are *overriding* in character; they have priority over all other rules, such as courtesy or matters of taste. They must also be *universalizable* for they are rules that apply to every full-fledged member of the community. In addition, ascribing moral rules and moral responsibility determines for that group who the true members 'persons' of that community are; to attribute duties and responsibilities is to imply that the individual has a role in maintaining the basic structure of his community. The nature of moral rules as ultimate reasons for or against an action is understandable once we see that they are intended to articulate the necessary conditions for the survival and well-being of the community (as viewed by that community). Moral rules override all other considerations because the existence of the group overrides all other interests.

This is why there is often an underlying conflict or tension in the human community between individual self-interest and the general interest or welfare. Since the role of morality is to outline the deep-structure of guidelines for continued community existence, individuals or groups may be called

upon to sacrifice their welfare, as in a war, for the good of all. This tension then is a structural one for human society for it cannot always be the case that self-interest is consistent with the general interest. (Though, of course, they may and do often coincide.) It is the task of moral philosophers to analyze and assess this tension.

It seems reasonably clear that moral categories apply to only certain kinds of entities and only certain actions or non-actions of these entities. Attributing moral responsibility must presuppose the *identifiability* of an agent who has performed an action. That is, the event in question must be of the type not caused by some general force or condition but some entity locatable in space and time. In addition, the agent must have some *continuity* in time, i.e., if the agent is to be rewarded, punished or informed about the moral character of his or her behavior, the agent must continue to exist for a time into the future. Thirdly, the agent must have performed the action intentionally, i.e., the act must not be the result of ignorance or an uncontrollable spasm, but of a conscious and rational sort. Moral responsibility also requires that the agent was neither *externally* nor *internally coerced.* Examples of internal coercion in a person would be those mental states associated with mental illness such as forms of psychoses. External coercion would include threats of bodily harm and possibly severe harm to one's economic and social well-being. Finally, only those actions that substantially affect or impinge on the welfare of others are proper targets of moral evaluation.

Though questions can be raised about these criteria, it seems generally agreed that at least some actions of biological persons can be evaluated with these categories. The question, however, is can the corporation as a separate entity meet these conditions as well. The American legal system recognizes that the corporation is an agent that can be held accountable for its actions independently of the actions of any of its directors, executives or employee. For example, when Mr. Grinshaw filed for damages resulting from burns received when his Pinto exploded, he sued the Ford Motor Company, not any individual of Ford. The following analysis of the unique nature of corporate agency will suggest why this must be so at least in some cases.

---

1. I am referring only to the *role* of moral rules and not to the *correctness* of the *content* of these rules.

Each individual working for a corporation is hired to perform some clearly defined function. Thus, employees of a corporation can be said to work and act for the corporation as agents or instruments of that corporation. Let us define 'instrumental actions' as those actions executed by virtue of one's role in an institution; instrumental actions are role-actions. When a corporation acts, it acts by virtue of the results of the combined instrumental actions of its employees. Let us term this action which emerges from the set of instrumental actions a 'secondary action.'[2] A nation state, for example, may wage war based on the instrumental actions of certain politicians within the decision-making body and a corporation may make a product or contribute to a political campaign. For an instrumental action to be properly attributed as such, the agents constituting the institution must perform the act within the framework and rules determining proper procedure. That is, not every act of a person within a firm is an act of the firm, only those actions which are carried out as instances of one's defined function or rule. Let us call agents performing instrumental actions 'instrumental agents' and those performing secondary actions 'secondary agents.'

It is clear that instrumental agents contribute causally to the performance of secondary agents but the moral characteristics of these actions may be quite distinct. In other words, moral responsibility does not always transfer across from one kind of agency to the other. This occurs because the instrumental and secondary agents can be in quite distinct moral positions in terms of the information they may have to other individuals or groups.[3] For example, an employee may have moral qualms about some action he is to perform, yet he may decide his obligations to his family override the qualms. The bureaucratic nature of the firm explains how this is possible.

Bureaucratic decision-making is characterized by the use of committees at various levels in the hierarchy. Isolation may exist between these various levels which is exacerbated by the extensive use of professionals in decision-making. Additionally, decisions of one committee may be revised by others and the make-up of these committees may change. Individuals who drew up the charter and set goals for the firm may no longer be employees or in any way related to the firm.[4] No one individual or even group can act with the awareness of all the information necessary for a corporation to take action, consequently, the organization as a whole is responsible as a distinct agent. The structure of the corporation, including its founding charter, its hierarchy of authority, its definition of functions, its hiring policy, contributes a *formal* cause to the instrumental causes of the employees which produces the secondary action of the corporation. It is this formal component of instrumental actions that allows the distinguishing of moral culpability between instrumental actions and secondary actions. These considerations suggest some of the obstacles to the application of moral categories to corporate acts.

"We must, then, establish control of the corporation ... by installing in controlling positions individuals who directly and personally represent those social concerns."

As has been suggested above, moral responsibility presupposes the identifiability of the agent. Clearly, a corporation as a legal entity can be identified as an agent. The continuity condition can also be met in most cases, unless of course the corporation has ceased to function due to bankruptcy or

---

2. Cf. Copp, David, "Collective Actions & Secondary Actions," *American Philosophical Quarterly* 16, No. 3, July, 1979, pp. 177–186.

3. *Ibid,* p. 184.

4. Werhane, Patricia, *Persons, Rights, and Corporations,* Prentice-Hall, Englewood Cliffs, NJ: 1985.

the like. However, continuity is not met if it refers to any one individual in the firm, for there are large turnovers in an institution which is potentially immortal. On the other hand, some have argued that the intentionality condition cannot be met.[5] It may be true that the corporation acts for goals but the reasons individuals in the firm act for them may be quite diverse, e.g., profit, salary, promotion. Hence, the argument continues, corporate acts lack the unity of reasons necessary for intentionality. However, one must distinguish between what may be termed 'primary intentionality' which resides in conscious rational biological agents, which is the paradigm case of intentionality, and the 'secondary intentionality' of the corporation. Secondary intentionality is analogous to secondary action in that it is a decision made by an authorized corporate decision-making body to act for some corporate goal. Corporations can act for reasons or goals as set up by its charter, board of directors, etc., and thus intentionally even though the motivations of the constituting individual may differ.

The application of the non-coercion criterion is a complex one. Let us define 'coercion' as the limiting of a person's options for action such that any choice but one will result in physical, psychological or financial harm to a substantial degree. The corporation as a whole may experience coercion if its officers lose control of the corporation as may occur in a takeover by another corporation. In this case, the new corporate entity is the locus of action and responsibility.

The above analysis suggests moral categories are applicable to the corporation but not necessarily to the individuals within it when they act as its agents. The corporation can be considered an agent distinct from the individuals who constitute it at any one time. If this is the case, it follows that measures to ensure corporate moral behavior are separate from measures taken to ensure the moral behavior of its employees. Let us consider some of these measures.

American courts have given the corporation the status of a 'person.' In this way they sought to protect the constitutional right of persons to organize with full protection of the laws. But corporations are like persons also in that they behave to promote their interests, e.g., profit, which may or may not be consistent with the general group interest. Recent history has shown that pollution of the environment, monopolization, dangerous products, disregard of the health and safety of workers and consumers, and the depletion of natural resources may well be compatible with, indeed perhaps in some cases ensure, increased profit. To meet these problems, government sought to regulate businesses by passing laws limiting pollution, establishing minimal health and safety for the workers, etc. The problems attending morality by regulation are many and well known.[6]

Morality through positive law is limited in that law as a system of *general* rules cannot deal perfectly with all *specific* circumstances. Law is by nature a *reaction* to a problem that has already occurred, and thus will always allow certain immoral action to occur until the legislature acts. Thirdly law is usually *negative* in formulation, telling what not to do, but moral behavior does not just involve the avoidance of evil, but the promotion of good to some degree. Moreover, the law can never completely express the full content of morality, but only that enforceable component; being moral means more than just being law-abiding. Fourth, government officials may be too unfamiliar with concrete business practice to regulate it efficiently. Finally, the extensive lobbying and funding of political campaigns by corporations through political action committees may undermine the impartiality and independence of governmental agencies and individuals.

Christopher Stone's proposal for improving corporate behavior through outside public directors is also too limited.[7] The role of these public directors is to be an ethical watchdog on the affairs of the firm and be available for consultation with employees. The strength of Stone's idea lies in that the

---

5. Keeley, Michael, "Organizations as Non-Persons," *Journal of Value Inquiry* 15, 1981, pp. 149–155.

6. Cf. Copp, David, "Collective Actions and Secondary Actions," *American Philosophical Quarterly* 16, No. 3, July, 1979, pp. 177–186.

7. Stone, Christopher, *Where the Law Ends,* Harper & Row, New York, NY, 1975, pp. 122–174.

public director has no financial interest in the corporation, but it makes the determination of the public interest an *interpretation* of one individual, the public director. More importantly, there is the problem of selecting and maintaining the independence and moral integrity of the director.

Another approach that has been suggested is the formulation of a code of ethics for each corporation.[8] This too is helpful, but the question of detection and enforcement of violations is unresolved. Additionally, the pressures to immorality that attend a firm caught in a competitive market can be formidable. If any institution is struggling for its very existence, taking unilateral moral action can be detrimental to success of the firm in the market. Secondly, as we have seen the bureaucratic nature of corporate action may make immoral acts more anonymous and thus more tempting. Moreover, moral considerations often concern *long-term* consequences of actions, whereas the demands of profit maximalization are often *short-term*. The division of labor and function in the corporation has resulted in division, diffusion and obfuscation of responsibility. The answer is not in codes of ethics alone or regulation, but, as in the case of a biological person, the development of a conscience through internalization of moral norms.

As our discussion of the role of morality above suggested, human society is typified by occasional tension or conflicts between individual self-interest and group-interest. Communities that wish to survive and prosper *as* communities must ensure that this conflict be controlled and resolved without serious detriment to the group. Historically, this has been done by developing an elaborate theological sanction for the moral law, by systems of reward and punishment, by education and training through the family, schools, and churches. But, it seems clear, no community thus far has developed means to ensure moral behavior by overt reward and punishment alone for this would require omniscience of all individual actions on the part of the community leaders. Indeed, this is where the idea of divine

omniscience plays such a crucial role in theologically oriented communities. The only alternative is the development of a 'conscience,' or an internal monitor and control on the behavior of individuals.

'Conscience' consists of a cognitive element, in that it presupposes knowledge of concepts of right, wrong, duty, as well as an emotive element, the feelings of guilt or shame for falling short of one's sense of duty.[9] Conscience involves a responsibility for *past* actions and an awareness of obligations with respect to anticipated *future* actions. It consists in the capacity for self-observation, and criticism by comparing our actions with values, ideals and group-norms one accepts as correct. Conscience is the assimilation of the rules which provide for the common 'good.' The advantages of conscience to external monitoring and control are clear: the judgment of a properly formed conscience is ever present and certain, whereas external authority and punishment may be avoided, uncertain, and mistaken. But how can the corporation, a theoretical 'person,' which has no single unifying mind develop a conscience? The answer lies in structuring the control of the corporation in such a manner as to provide for the same results that a conscience provides. The role of a conscience is to provide for the general welfare by monitoring and controlling individual actions so that they do not override social needs. We must, then, establish control of the corporation (so that social welfare is not compromised) by installing in controlling positions individuals who directly and personally represent those social concerns. This would, of course, mean equal participation of consumers, workers and investors in the running of major corporations. This type of representation will be the institutional correlative to a person's conscience for it will protect those groups and interests the corporation is most likely to offend; it will be present to protect their interest and at the same time, the general interest. This is why worker representation alone is not sufficient, for the interest of workers is not always compatible with the social interest. Similarly, within the present

---

8. Brenner, S. N., Molander, E. A., "Is the Ethics of Business Changing," *Harvard Business Review,* Jan.–Feb., 1977.

9. Cf. Loevinger, Jane, *Ego Development: Conceptions and Theories,* Jossey-Bass Publishers, London, 1976, pp. 397–398.

system of capitalism, investors have a legitimate right to be represented to protect their investment. Managers must be represented to provide information for the democratized corporation as a whole.

The actual institutional arrangement can be only briefly suggested since many details will be determined by experience and discussion of the parties involved. Of utmost importance is that the democratization must take place fully at the level of the board of directors and to a more limited extent at the more immediate level of management. The board of directors should include equal, three part representation of the stockholders, consumers and employees. On the daily running of the firms, employee representation in a workers and managers council which meets regularly may be sufficient, though the meeting may include representatives of the general public as well.

Should these democratic structures apply to every firm? Clearly not. The moral nature of past corporate behavior must be considered. If the corporation has behaved in a morally acceptable way, it may not be necessary to alter its structure. The basic idea here is that control of the corporation reflect the scope of impact of corporate policy and actions. Full-scale democratic representation may not be economically feasible for small firms, where government regulation may be sufficient to ensure satisfactory moral performance. The experience of the West German model where, a similar program, though without consumer representation, has been instituted in some organizations may be useful.[10]

We have argued that the argument for democratic capitalism is based on the understanding of morality as a system of basic deep-structured rules that are necessary for community life and prosperity. As such, no individual or group has a right to jeopardize the general welfare in pursuit of its own welfare. Consequently, our suggestion cannot be attacked on the basis that it is a violation of the right to property or the freedom to contract. The right to property is a right which exists within the general

context of the basic structural fabric of a group's moral code. Consequently, the interpretation and application of that right must be compatible with other basic rights defining the general welfare. The laws against monopoly formation, for example, are restrictions on appropriation based on an understanding of the general value of a competitive market. In other words, the right to property is not absolute but contingent on its harmony with the other basic rights of life and liberty. Moreover, no right can be claimed *in such a manner* as to preclude the *moral exercise* of that right. Hence, if the argument here is correct, that the development of something like a conscience is a necessary presupposition for the moral exercise of property rights in the context of the corporation, then no one can legitimately object that a democratic corporate government is a violation of property rights.

Traditionally, the right to property has been interpreted as a two-termed relation. To say, 'Jones owns a car,' means Jones has certain special rights, with respect to that car that no one else does. However, this analysis is inadequate, for it omits the fact that property rights involve *obligations* to others and *limits* depending on overriding rights and the general communal welfare. For example, my right to my car may be overriden by a policeman who may need it to capture a mass murderer, or sabateur. This three-termed view, as has been suggested by others, is a more accurate reflection of property rights understood in the full context of morality.[11] The model of the corporation here defended is a reflection of this view of property. The strength of this model is that it *institutionalizes* this relationship and sets up a procedure where conflicting claims can be adjudicated in an ongoing manner.

The role of morality is not merely the negative one of preventing wrongdoing, but, also the positive one providing for a general welfare. The weakness of morality through regulation consists in the fact that it is merely negative and minimal in scope. This is why democratized capitalism is superior, for individuals who have no direct monetary interest in

10. Neuberger, Hugh, "Codetermination—The West German Experiment at a New State," *Columbia Journal of World Business,* Winter, 1978, pp. 104–111.

11. Chaudhuri, Joyotpaul, "Toward a Democratic Theory of Property and the Modern Corporation," *Ethics* 81, pp. 271–286.

the corporation, the consumers, have the opportunity to introduce *positive* moral concerns.

There is reason to believe that this democratic corporation will not only instrumentally enhance positive moral performance of the corporation, it will also intrinsically enhance the self-esteem and productivity of workers. A recent study by HEW shows that redesigning the workplace can result in higher productivity and greater job satisfaction. These features of the restructured workplace include worker participation in decision-making, greater control over the workplace, closer peer ties and job security.[12]

Conclusion

Most ethical theorists have focused their attention on individual moral behavior and its justification, not group action. Yet, the reality of contemporary life is one where major decisions and actions are made by governmental and corporate bureaucracies. This new mode of action requires a new mode of monitoring and controlling group behavior.

Though the role of morality is to provide for the basic structure in which individuals may more fully satisfy their needs, no moral system is complete or perfect at any one time. As man's knowledge and experience increases, so do possibilities, opportunities and needs expand. A rational society, therefore, must allow for the dynamic response to this evolving nature of human moral consciousness. This is the genuis of democracy, for it provides for a forum for discussion, debate and decision that allows for the expression of various interests and input from all sources and thus promotes stability and order.

---

12. *Work in America,* Report of a Special Task Force to the Secretary of HEW, MIT Press, Cambridge, MA, p. 87, 96–99.

Study Questions

1. Will corporate democracy make business more ethical?

2. What would Marx and Smith say about corporate democracy?

3. Will corporate democracy mean a more inefficient economy?

Moral Dilemmas

- Mike's wife, Gretchen, is dying from a curable but painful disease called opinionosis. The cure, a bottle of pills without which his wife will die, costs over twenty thousand dollars, money which Mike and Gretchen do not have, nor do they have insurance. No one is willing to lend them the money. Mike pleads with the pharmacist to give him the pills, promising to pay back the twenty thousand in installments over the next ten years. The pharmacist refuses. One night, while the drugstore is closed, Mike breaks in and steals the drug.

Did Mike do the moral thing?
How would you have handled the situation?

- Sharon, a young woman just out of college, works as an accountant for a large firm. She makes forty-five thousand dollars a year. Her friend Garet makes the same amount of money but lives a more affluent style. Sharon asks him about this, and Garet tells her that he cheats on his taxes every chance he gets. He justifies this by pointing out that the government is corrupt and that everybody is doing it. He ends by saying: "The tax law is like sausage; if you knew how it was made, you'd never eat it."

Do you agree with Garet?

- While jogging one day, Jim, a poor but brilliant student, finds a wallet containing five hundred dollars. The driver's license gives the name and address of the owner, and Jim decides to return the wallet and money. When he arrives at the address, he sees a large mansion with two Rolls Royces parked in the driveway. Jim needs the money to pay his rent and stay in school.

Should Jim keep the money?

- Mr. Lamme entrusts his old safe to Ms. Lucky and tells her to sell it. While examining the safe, Ms. Lucky finds a secret compartment containing ten thousand dollars. She sells the safe for fifty dollars, which she gives to Mr. Lamme. She keeps the ten thousand and says nothing about it. Mr. Lamme finds out about the money and claims that he should get the ten thousand dollars by virtue of prior ownership of the safe even though he didn't know the money was there and doesn't know who originally placed it there. Ms. Lucky claims that this is a case of "finders keepers, losers weepers," especially since the rightful owner of the money cannot be found.

Who should keep the ten thousand dollars?

Suggested Readings

Avineri, Shlomo. *The Social and Political Thought of Karl Marx.* Cambridge, Mass.: Harvard University Press, 1968.

DesJardins, Joseph, and John McCall, eds. *Contemporary Issues in Business Ethics.* Belmont, Calif.: Wadsworth, 1985.

Dworkin, Ronald. *Taking Rights Seriously.* Cambridge, Mass.: Harvard University Press, 1977.

Sterba, James. *The Demands of Justice.* Notre Dame, Ind.: Notre Dame Press, 1980.

Kolakowski, Leszek. *Main Currents of Marxism,* V. 1–3. Oxford, England: Clarendon Press, 1978.

Tucker, Robert C., ed. *Marx-Engels Reader.* New York: Norton, 1978.

Werhane, Patricia. *Persons, Rights and Corporations.* Englewood Cliffs, N.J.: Prentice-Hall, 1985.

Reverse Discrimination

T he world is full of all kinds of injustice. Some injustices involve one individual unjustifiably harming another individual; in this case, when the culprit is caught, he or she is punished and may be required to provide some form of compensation to the victim. What do we do when a society as a whole through its laws and institutions is systematically unjust to an entire group within its own borders? This type of social injustice has existed and still exists in racist and sexist societies. How does one rectify this kind of injustice without creating even more injustice?

Background

Almost universally throughout human history, women have not had the same rights as men. Before the early twentieth century, most women in most countries could not attend schools of higher education, did not have access to high-paying jobs, could not vote or run for political office, and could not sue for divorce. Although slavery in the United States was abolished over a hundred years ago, and women received the right to vote in 1920, blacks and women still do not have the social and economic status equal to that of white men. Even though school segregation was abolished by the Supreme Court in 1954, many blacks still do not receive an education equal to that of most whites. In general, black people also have a lower economic status than whites, a lower life-expectancy, and are more often victims of violent crimes than any other group in the United States.

Most women still earn less than men for doing the same work. Women account for only about eight percent of scientists, six percent of physicians, three percent of lawyers, and one percent of federal judges, although they make up over fifty percent of the population. The Civil Rights Act of 1964 sought to finally outlaw all forms of *racism* (the belief that race determines one's traits and capacities and that a particular race is inherently superior or inferior) and *sexism* (the belief that one's gender makes one by nature superior or inferior intellectually, physically, or morally). It gave women, blacks, and other minorities greater social and economic opportunities and equality.

To achieve the goal of equality, however, several approaches are possible. In the struggle against racism and sexism, some favor a strict policy of nondiscrimination. *Nondiscrimination* means that all decisions to admit individuals to colleges, professional schools, housing, and employment are made in a color-blind and sex-blind manner, taking into consideration only the qualifications of the applicants in terms of experience, ability, and education. This approach is based on the belief in *meritocracy;* that is, the view that only high achievement, not race or gender, is relevant in how individuals should be treated.

In 1972, the Civil Rights Act of 1964 was amended to include the Equal Employment Opportunity Act. This act ordered all corporations with over fifty employees that engaged in business with the federal government in amounts over fifty thousand dollars to take *affirmative action* to increase the number of women and minorities in their work force. This policy of affirmative action was consistent with the policy of nondiscrimination but required employers and colleges to actively seek out qualified members of discriminated groups in order to enlarge the pool of minority candidates, not necessarily to give them any preferential treatment in hiring. However, in many instances, affirmative action did involve preferential treatment of minorities and women over white males who may have been more qualified. The policy of preferential treatment uses race and gender as a "plus" in hiring and admissions. This is why some refer to it as reverse discrimination because this form of discrimination is the opposite of traditional racism and sexism. Preferential treatment can be in the form of quotas where a specified number of positions are set aside

for women and minority members, or it may simply set a nonspecific goal to increase the number of women and minorities.

University of California v. Bakke

Allen Bakke, a white male, applied to the Medical School of the University of California at Davis in 1978 and was rejected. The university had a policy of preferential treatment with a quota of sixteen places out of an entering class of one hundred to be set aside for minority students. Bakke sued the University of California, claiming that he was discriminated against on the basis of his race and that he should be admitted because he was more qualified than some of the sixteen minority members who were admitted. In a five-to-four decision, the Court ruled in favor of Bakke and against the use of quotas. However, Justice Lewis F. Powell and other justices argued that race could be used as a factor in admissions to universities but not in the form of quotas. Powell wrote that to prefer a person simply because of race is an unwise policy that seeks to rectify past injustices by placing burdens on a specific individual who is innocent. Additionally, he noted that preferential treatment may actually have the reverse effect than intended by perpetuating a stereotype that certain groups are inferior and unable to achieve social progress without special government aid. Powell did argue that race could be used as a factor in admitting students in order to provide a more diverse and therefore more intellectually stimulating student body.

The Court's decision was very controversial. Part of the debate over its decision concerns whether the diversity of the student body is really important in acquiring a good education. Will a loss of educational excellence result if some individuals are chosen on the basis of race, gender, or geographic location and not simply on academic qualifications? What is the difference in practice between a quota and simply using race as a factor? One must still ask in how many individuals race will be used as a factor and in how many it will not. Interestingly, in the case of *United Steelworkers v. Weber* (1979), the Court ruled that a quota giving preferences to blacks in a training program at Kaiser Aluminum Co. was constitutional. In that case, Justice William

Brennan argued that because the quota was a voluntary agreement between Kaiser and the union and its purposes was to eliminate racial segregation in the workplace, it was legal.

Liberal Position: Thomas Nagel

Thomas Nagel supports preferential treatment for blacks as a short-term policy necessary to bring about a more just and harmonious society. To follow the route of simple nondiscrimination would take too long to overcome the rigid racial caste system that still exists in the United States. Nagel believes that the arguments against preferential treatment, namely those of inefficiency, damage to self-esteem, and unfairness are weak. Inefficiency, he grants, may result from giving preferences to those who are not as qualified as other candidates who are white males, but he seems to think that this loss of efficiency is worth the gain in social justice. Some consider preferential treatment unfair to white males who are being rejected on the basis of race and sex. For Nagel, however, this is not racism or sexism because its purpose is quite different, namely to increase the social standing of a formerly victimized group, not to degrade any group. He agrees that his approach involves an element of unfairness, but it is of the type exemplified by the draft. In this process, men and women are not treated equally, yet most find this practice acceptable.

Nagel does not embrace the compensation argument to support his thesis. He believes the compensation claim, which holds that preferential treatment of blacks is just compensation for past discrimination, is not a compelling one because we have no way to identify those who have suffered most under racism or those who have benefited most from it. However, Nagel does take the self-esteem argument seriously. This position holds that the self-esteem of those preferred may suffer if they and others believe that they were chosen simply on the basis of race. Still, he contends that this is an acceptable risk, but that it argues for the end of preferential treatment as soon as possible.

Nagel's argument presents interesting points for us to consider. He is aware that preferential treatment is basically undesirable, but he thinks that it is necessary to achieve social justice. One must ask, nevertheless, whether he has adequately addressed the criticisms of his own position. Is the unfairness of a military draft, which applies only to males, the same unfairness found in preferential treatment? If so, perhaps the military should also draft women when and if the draft is reinstituted. Is preferential treatment similar to the government condemnation of private property in order to build a road as Nagel claims? Perhaps, but the government compensates the owners, whereas racial preference does not compensate the white male. One must further ask, When does racial preference end? Nagel says it should end in the beginning of the twenty-first century; why then? How will we know the appropriate time? Will racial quotas perpetuate racist stereotypes?

Conservative Position: Barry R. Gross

Barry R. Gross gives four objections to reverse discrimination: (1) there is no accurate way to identify the discriminated groups to be preferred, (2) it may have dangerous racist consequences, (3) it doesn't fit any model of compensation or reparation, and (4) it is unjust to those it favors and to those it discriminates against.

The problem of identification of discriminated groups is a serious one for Gross. Just because certain groups are underrepresented in certain professions doesn't mean that they have been discriminated against; perhaps they simply have no interest in those professions. What of other groups that have been discriminated against such as Jews, Asians, Native Americans, and others, shouldn't they too get preference? How seriously must a group be discriminated against to get preference? These questions have no clear answers, according to Gross.

Gross agrees that justice demands that individuals be compensated for past wrongs, but just reparation is difficult to achieve when groups are involved. Was every member of the group equally affected? What about their competence to do the job? Moreover, as Gross points out, the self-esteem of those preferred may be damaged when they realize that they were chosen because of their race, not because of their qualifications. Finally, Gross believes that preferential treatment perpetuates race consciousness and injures those who had no hand in past discrimination.

Even if we must grant the cogency of some of Gross's points, the question still remains: What do we do about past injustices and racism? Can we maintain social harmony and stability if the races have radically unequal economic and social status? Those like Gross who are against preferential treatment use as their explicit or implicit argument that society should be organized on the basis of a meritocracy. The arguments for meritocracy are twofold: First, meritocracy is based on the idea of fairness, such that persons who work hard will be rewarded with entrance into the best schools and will receive the best jobs. Second, it is based on the idea of efficiency, such that society will function more productively if the most qualified have positions of power. But the question now becomes: To what extent do we in fact have a meritocracy in the United States today? Why does the government give preferences to veterans in hiring? Is it proper that colleges give preferences to the children of alumnae and faculty in admissions, as many do? Aren't many individuals hired on the basis of who they know, not what they know? Gross would probably agree that we do not have a complete meritocracy yet, but he would probably say that we should strive for it as a goal. On the other hand, proponents of preferential treatment would probably argue that equality and justice are just as important as efficiency if not more so.

Most conservatives and liberals agree that justice demands that individuals be treated on an individual basis and not according to what group they belong. Clearly, as Nagel suggests, preferential treatment is at best a temporary, partial solution to the problem of racism and sexism. Perhaps a better approach would involve a theory such as that suggested by John Rawls in chapter 12, which requires directing governmental efforts to equalize the starting point and conditions of all persons in terms of education and welfare. If life is a race, then a fair race requires that all begin the race from the same starting line and that no one be held back by racism or sexism.

University of California v. Bakke

Justice Lewis F. Powell is a former Associate Justice of the U.S. Supreme Court who was appointed in 1971 and served until 1987.

Justice Lewis F. Powell

I

Over the past 30 years, this Court has embarked upon the crucial mission of interpreting the Equal Protection Clause with the view of assuring to all persons "the protection of equal laws," in a Nation confronting a legacy of slavery and racial discrimi-

United States Supreme Court. 438 U.S. 265 (1978).

nation. Because the landmark decisions in this area arose in response to the continued exclusion of Negroes from the mainstream of American society, they could be characterized as involving discrimination by the "majority" white race against the Negro minority. But they need not be read as depending upon that characterization for their results. It suffices to say that "[o]ver the years, this Court has consistently repudiated '[d]istinctions between citizens solely because of their ancestry' as being 'odious to a free people whose institutions are founded upon the doctrine of equality.'"

Petitioner urges us to adopt for the first time a more restrictive view of the Equal Protection Clause and hold that discrimination against members of the white "majority" cannot be suspect if its purpose can be characterized as "benign." The clock of our liberties, however, cannot be turned back to 1868. It is far too late to argue that the guarantee of equal protection to *all* persons permits the recognition of special wards entitled to a degree of protection greater than that accorded others. "The Fourteenth Amendment is not directed solely against discrimination due to a 'two-class theory'—that is, based upon differences between 'white,' and Negro." ...

II

We have held that in "order to justify the use of a suspect classification, a State must show that its purpose or interest is both constitutionally permissible and substantial, and that its use of the classification is 'necessary ... to the accomplishment' of its purpose or the safeguarding of its interest." The special admissions program purports to serve the purposes of: (i) "reducing the historical deficit of traditionally disfavored minorities in medical schools and in the medical profession"; (ii) countering the effects of societal discrimination; (iii) increasing the number of physicians who will practice in communities currently underserved; and (iv) obtaining the educational benefits that flow from an ethnically diverse student body. It is necessary to decide which, if any, of these purposes is substantial enough to support the use of a suspect classification.

A

If petitioner's purpose is to assure within its student body some specified percentage of a particular group merely because of its race or ethnic origin, such a preferential purpose must be rejected not as insubstantial but as facially invalid. Preferring members of any one group for no reason other than race or ethnic origin is discrimination for its own sake. This the Constitution forbids.

B

The State certainly has a legitimate and substantial interest in ameliorating, or eliminating where feasible, the disabling effects of identified discrimination. The line of school desegregation cases, commencing with *Brown v. Board of Education* (1954) attests to the importance of this state goal and the commitment of the judiciary to affirm all lawful means toward its attainment. In the school cases, the States were required by court order to redress the wrongs worked by specific instances of racial discrimination. That goal was far more focused than the remedying of the effects of "societal discrimination," an amorphous concept of injury that may be ageless in its reach into the past.

> *"... [I]t is evident that the Davis special admissions program involves the use of an explicit racial classification never before countenanced by this Court."*

We have never approved a classification that aids persons perceived as members of relatively victimized groups at the expense of other innocent individuals in the absence of judicial, legislative, or administrative findings of constitutional or statutory violations. After such findings have been made, the governmental interest in preferring members of the injured groups at the expense of others is substantial, since the legal rights of the victims must be vindicated. In such a case, the extent of the injury and the consequent remedy will have been judicially, legislatively, or administratively defined. Also, the remedial action usually remains subject to continuing oversight to assure that it will work the least harm possible to other innocent persons competing for the benefit. Without such findings of constitutional or statutory violations, it cannot be said that the government has any greater interest in helping one individual than in refraining from harming another. Thus, the government has no compelling justification for inflicting such harm.

Petitioner does not purport to have made, and is in no position to make, such findings. Its broad mission is education, not the formulation of any legislative policy or the adjudication of particular claims of illegality.... [I]solated segments of our vast governmental structures are not competent to make those decisions, at least in the absence of legislative mandates and legislatively determined criteria. Before relying upon these sorts of findings in establishing a racial classification, a governmental body must have the authority and capability to establish, in the record, that the classification is responsive to identified discrimination. Lacking this capability, petitioner has not carried its burden of justification on this issue.

Hence, the purpose of helping certain groups whom the faculty of the Davis Medical School perceived as victims of "societal discrimination" does not justify a classification that imposes disadvantages upon persons like respondent, who bear no responsibility for whatever harm the beneficiaries of the special admissions program are thought to have suffered. To hold otherwise would be to convert a remedy heretofore reserved for violations of legal rights into a privilege that all institutions throughout the Nation could grant at their pleasure to whatever groups are perceived as victims of societal discrimination. That is a step we have never approved.

C

Petitioner identifies, as another purpose of its program, improving the delivery of health-care services to communities currently underserved. It may be assumed that in some situations a State's interest in facilitating the health care of its citizens is sufficiently compelling to support the use of a suspect classification. But there is virtually no evidence in the record indicating that petitioner's special admissions program is either needed or geared to promote that goal. The court below addressed this failure of proof:

"The University concedes it cannot assure that minority doctors who entered under the program, all of whom expressed an 'interest' in practicing in a disadvantaged community, will actually do so. It may be correct to assume that

some of them will carry out this intention, and that it is more likely they will practice in minority communities than the average white doctor. Nevertheless, there are more precise and reliable ways to identify applicants who are genuinely interested in the medical problems of minorities than by race. An applicant of whatever race who has demonstrated his concern for disadvantaged minorities in the past and who declares that practice in such a community is his primary professional goal would be more likely to contribute to alleviation of the medical shortage than one who is chosen entirely on the basis of race and disadvantage. In short, there is no empirical data to demonstrate that any one race is more selflessly socially oriented or by contrast that another is more selfishly acquisitive."

Petitioner simply has not carried its burden of demonstrating that it must prefer members of particular ethnic groups over all other individuals in order to promote better health-care delivery to deprived citizens. Indeed, petitioner has not shown that its preferential classification is likely to have any significant effect on the problem.

D

The fourth goal asserted by petitioner is the attainment of a diverse student body. This clearly is a constitutionally permissible goal for an institution of higher education. Academic freedom, though not a specifically enumerated constitutional right, long has been viewed as a special concern of the First Amendment. The freedom of a university to make its own judgments as to education includes the selection of its student body.

Ethnic diversity, however, is only one element in a range of factors a university properly may consider in attaining the goal of a heterogeneous student body. Although a university must have wide discretion in making the sensitive judgments as to who should be admitted, constitutional limitations protecting individual rights may not be disregarded. Respondent urges—and the courts below have held—that petitioner's dual admissions program is a racial classification that impermissibly infringes his rights under the Fourteenth Amendment. As the interest of diversity is compelling in the context of a university's admissions program, the question remains whether the program's racial classification is necessary to promote this interest.

III

A

It may be assumed that the reservation of a specified number of seats in each class for individuals from the preferred ethnic groups would contribute to the attainment of considerable ethnic diversity in the student body. But petitioner's argument that this is the only effective means of serving the interest of diversity is seriously flawed. In a most fundamental sense the argument misconceives the nature of the state interest that would justify consideration of race or ethnic background. It is not an interest in simple ethnic diversity, in which a specified percentage of the student body is in effect guaranteed to be members of selected ethnic groups, with the remaining percentage an undifferentiated aggregation of students. The diversity that furthers a compelling state interest encompasses a far broader array of qualifications and characteristics of which racial or ethnic origin is but a single though important element. Petitioner's special admissions program, focused *solely* on ethnic diversity, would hinder rather than further attainment of genuine diversity.

Nor would the state interest in genuine diversity be served by expanding petitioner's two-track system into a multitrack program with a prescribed number of seats set aside for each identifiable category of applicants. Indeed, it is inconceivable that a university would thus pursue the logic of petitioner's two-track program to the illogical end of insulating each category of applicants with certain desired qualifications from competition with all other applicants.

The experience of other university admissions programs, which take race into account in achieving the educational diversity valued by the First Amendment, demonstrates that the assignment of a fixed number of places to a minority group is not a necessary means toward that end. An illuminating example is found in the Harvard College program:

"In recent years Harvard College has expanded the concept of diversity to include students from disadvantaged economic, racial and ethnic groups. Harvard College now recruits not only

Californians or Louisianans but also blacks and Chicanos and other minority students. . . .

"In practice, this new definition of diversity has meant that race has been a factor in some admission decisions. When the Committee on Admissions reviews the large middle group of applicants who are 'admissible' and deemed capable of doing good work in their courses, the race of an applicant may tip the balance in his favor just as geographic origin or a life spent on a farm may tip the balance in other candidates' cases. A farm boy from Idaho can bring something to Harvard College that a Bostonian cannot offer. Similarly, a black student can usually bring something that a white person cannot offer. . . .

"In Harvard college admissions the Committee has not set target-quotas for the number of blacks, or of musicians, football players, physicists or Californians to be admitted in a given year. . . . But that awareness [of the necessity of including more than a token number of black students] does not mean that the Committee sets a minimum number of blacks or of people from west of the Mississippi who are to be admitted. It means only that in choosing among thousands of applicants who are not only 'admissible' academically but have other strong qualities, the Committee, with a number of criteria in mind, pays some attention to distribution among many types and categories of students."

In such an admissions program, race or ethnic background may be deemed a "plus" in a particular applicant's file, yet it does not insulate the individual from comparison with all other candidates for the available seats. The file of a particular black applicant may be examined for his potential contribution to diversity without the factor of race being decisive when compared, for example, with that of an applicant identified as an Italian-American if the latter is thought to exhibit qualities more likely to promote beneficial educational pluralism. Such qualities could include exceptional personal talents, unique work or service experience, leadership potential, maturity, demonstrated compassion, a history of overcoming disadvantage, ability to communicate with the poor, or other qualifications deemed important. In short, an admissions program operated in this way is flexible enough to consider all pertinent elements of diversity in light of the particular qualifications of each applicant, and to place them on the same footing for consideration, although not necessarily according them the same weight. Indeed, the weight attributed to a particular quality may vary from year to year depending upon the "mix" both of the student body and the applicants for the incoming class.

This kind of program treats each applicant as an individual in the admissions process. The applicant who loses out on the last available seat to another candidate receiving a "plus" on the basis of ethnic background will not have been foreclosed from all consideration for that seat simply because he was not the right color or had the wrong surname. It would mean only that his combined qualifications, which may have included similar nonobjective factors, did not outweigh those of the other applicant. His qualifications would have been weighed fairly and competitively, and he would have no basis to complain of unequal treatment under the Fourteenth Amendment.

It has been suggested that an admissions program which considers race only as one factor is simply a subtle and more sophisticated—but no less effective—means of according racial preference than the Davis program. A facial intent to discriminate, however, is evident in petitioner's preference program and not denied in this case. No such facial infirmity exists in an admissions program where race or ethnic background is simply one element—to be weighed fairly against other elements—in the selection process. "A boundary line," as Mr. Justice Frankfurter remarked in another connection, "is none the worse for being narrow." And a court would not assume that a university, professing to employ a facially nondiscriminatory admissions policy, would operate it as a cover for the functional equivalent of a quota system. In short, good faith would be presumed in the absence of a showing to the contrary in the manner permitted by our cases.

B

In summary, it is evident that the Davis special admissions program involves the use of an explicit racial classification never before countenanced by this Court. It tells applicants who are not Negro, Asian, or Chicano that they are totally excluded from a specific percentage of the seats in an entering class. No matter how strong their qualifications, quantitative and extracurricular, including their own potential for contribution to educational diversity, they are never afforded the chance to compete with applicants from the preferred groups for the special admissions seats. At the same time, the preferred applicants have the opportunity to compete for every seat in the class.

The fatal flaw in petitioner's preferential program is its disregard of individual rights as guaranteed by the Fourteenth Amendment. Such rights are not absolute. But when a State's distribution of benefits or imposition of burdens hinges on ancestry or the color of a person's skin or ancestry, that individual is entitled to a demonstration that the challenged classification is necessary to promote a substantial state interest. Petitioner has failed to carry this burden. For this reason, that portion of the California court's judgment holding petitioner's special admissions program invalid under the Fourteenth Amendment must be affirmed.

C

In enjoining petitioner from ever considering the race of any applicant, however, the courts below failed to recognize that the State has a substantial interest that legitimately may be served by a properly devised admissions program involving the competitive consideration of race and ethnic origin. For this reason, so much of the California court's judgment as enjoins petitioner from any consideration of the race of any applicant must be reversed.

Study Questions

1. How important is student diversity in college?

2. Are quotas wrong? Why, or why not?

A Defense of Affirmative Action

Thomas Nagel is a professor of philosophy and law at New York University. He has published several books, most recently, What Does It All Mean?

Thomas Nagel

The term "affirmative action" has changed in meaning since it was first introduced. Originally it referred only to special efforts to ensure equal opportunity for members of groups that had been subject to discrimination. These efforts included public advertisement of positions to be filled, active recruitment of qualified applicants from the formerly excluded groups, and special training programs to help them meet the standards for admission or appointment. There was also close attention to procedures of appointment, and sometimes to the results, with a view to detecting continued discrimination, conscious or unconscious.

More recently the term has come to refer also to some degree of definite preference for members of these groups in determining access to positions from which they were formerly excluded. Such preference might be allowed to influence decisions only between candidates who are otherwise equally qualified, but usually it involves the selection of women or minority members over other candidates who are better qualified for the position.

Let me call the first sort of policy "weak affirmative action" and the second "strong affirmative action." It is important to distinguish them, because the distinction is sometimes blurred in practice. It is strong affirmative action—the policy of preference—that arouses controversy. Most people would agree that weak or precautionary affirmative action

Reprinted by permission of Professor Nagel and *QQ: Report from the Center for Philosophy and Public Policy.*

is a good thing, and worth its cost in time and energy. But this does not imply that strong affirmative action is also justified.

I shall claim that in the present state of things it is justified, most clearly with respect to blacks. But I also believe that a defender of the practice must acknowledge that there are serious arguments against it, and that it is defensible only because the arguments for it have great weight. Moral opinion in this country is sharply divided over the issue because significant values are involved on both sides. My own view is that while strong affirmative action is intrinsically undesirable, it is a legitimate and perhaps indispensable method of pursuing a goal so important to the national welfare that it can be justified as a temporary, though not short-term, policy for both public and private institutions. In this respect it is like other policies that impose burdens on some for the public good.

Three Objections

I shall begin with the argument against. There are three objections to strong affirmative action: that it is inefficient; that it is unfair; and that it damages self-esteem.

The degree of inefficiency depends on how strong a role racial or sexual preference plays in the process of selection. Among candidates meeting the basic qualifications for a position, those better qualified will on the average perform better, whether they are doctors, policemen, teachers, or electricians. There may be some cases, as in preferential college admissions, where the immediate usefulness of making educational resources available to an individual is thought to be greater because of the use to which the education will be put or because of the internal effects on the institution itself. But by and large, policies of strong affirmative action must reckon with the costs of some lowering in performance level: the stronger the preference, the larger the cost to be justified. Since both the costs and the value of the results will vary from case to case, this suggests that no one policy of affirmative action is likely to be correct in all cases, and that the cost in performance level should be taken into account in the design of a legitimate policy.

The charge of unfairness arouses the deepest disagreements. To be passed over because of membership in a group one was born into, where this has nothing to do with one's individual qualifications for a position, can arouse strong feelings of resentment. It is a departure from the ideal—one of the values finally recognized in our society—that people should be judged so far as possible on the basis of individual characteristics rather than involuntary group membership.

This does not mean that strong affirmative action is morally repugnant in the manner of racial or sexual discrimination. It is nothing like those practices, for though like them it employs race and sex as criteria of selection, it does so for entirely different reasons. Racial and sexual discrimination are based on contempt or even loathing for the excluded group, a feeling that certain contacts with them are degrading to members of the dominant group, that they are fit only for subordinate positions or menial work. Strong affirmative action involves none of this: it is simply a means of increasing the social and economic strength of formerly victimized groups, and does not stigmatize others.

There is an element of individual unfairness here, but it is more like the unfairness of conscription in wartime, or of property condemnation under the right of eminent domain. Those who benefit or lose out because of their race or sex cannot be said to deserve their good or bad fortune.

It might be said on the other side that the beneficiaries of affirmative action deserve it as compensation for past discrimination, and that compensation is rightly exacted from the group that has benefitted from discrimination in the past. But this is a bad argument, because as the practice usually works, no effort is made to give preference to those who have suffered most from discrimination, or to prefer them especially to those who have benefitted most from it, or been guilty of it. Only candidates who in other qualifications fall on one or other side of the margin of decision will directly benefit or lose from the policy, and these are not necessarily, or even probably, the ones who especially deserve it. Women or blacks who don't have the qualifications even to be considered are likely to have been handicapped more by the effects of discrimination than those who receive preference. And the marginal white male candidate who is turned down can evoke our sympathy if he asks, "Why me?" (A policy of explicitly *compensatory* preference, which took into account each individual's background of poverty and discrimination, would escape some of these objections, and it has its defenders, but it is not the policy I want to defend. Whatever its merits, it will not serve the same purpose as direct affirmative action.)

> *"While this condition is not met by all programs of affirmative action now in effect, it is met by those which address the most deep-seated, stubborn, and radically unhealthy divisions in the society..."*

The third objection concerns self-esteem, and is particularly serious. While strong affirmative action is in effect, and generally known to be so, no one in an affirmative action category who gets a desirable job or is admitted to a selective university can be sure that he or she has not benefitted from the policy. Even those who would have made it anyway fall under suspicion, from themselves and from others: it comes to be widely felt that success does not mean the same thing for women and minorities. This painful damage to esteem cannot be avoided. It should make any defender of strong affirmative action want the practice to end as soon as it has achieved its basic purpose.

Justifying Affirmative Action

I have examined these three objections and tried to assess their weight, in order to decide how strong a countervailing reason is needed to justify such a policy. In my view, taken together they imply that strong affirmative action involving significant preference should be undertaken only if it will substantially further a social goal of the first importance. While this condition is not met by all programs of affirmative action now in effect, it is met by those which address the most deep-seated, stubborn, and radically unhealthy divisions in the society, divisions whose removal is a condition of basic justice and social cohesion.

The situation of black people in our country is unique in this respect. For almost a century after the abolition of slavery we had a rigid racial caste system of the ugliest kind, and it only began to break up twenty-five years ago. In the South it was enforced by law, and in the North, in a somewhat less severe form, by social convention. Whites were thought to be defiled by social or residential proximity to blacks, intermarriage was taboo, blacks were denied the same level of public goods—education and legal protection—as whites, were restricted to the most menial occupations, and were barred from any positions of authority over whites. The visceral feelings of black inferiority and untouchability that this system expressed were deeply ingrained in the members of both races, and they continue, not surprisingly, to have their effect. Blacks still form, to a considerable extent, a hereditary social and economic community characterized by widespread poverty, unemployment, and social alienation.

When this society finally got around to moving against the caste system, it might have done no more than to enforce straight equality of opportunity, perhaps with the help of weak affirmative action, and then wait a few hundred years while things gradually got better. Fortunately it decided instead to accelerate the process by both public and private institutional action, because there was wide recognition of the intractable character of the problem posed by this insular minority and its place in the nation's history and collective consciousness. This has not been going on very long, but the results are already impressive, especially in speeding the advancement of blacks into the middle class. Affirmative action has not done much to improve the position of poor and unskilled blacks. That is the most serious part of the problem, and it requires a more direct economic attack. But increased access to higher education and upper-level jobs is an essential part of what must be achieved to break the structure of drastic separation that was left largely undisturbed by the legal abolition of the caste system.

Changes of this kind require a generation or two. My guess is that strong affirmative action for blacks will continue to be justified into the early decades of the next century, but that by then it will have accomplished what it can and will no longer be worth the costs. One point deserves special emphasis. The goal to be pursued is the reduction of a great social injustice, not proportional representation of the races in all institutions and professions. Proportional racial representation is of no value in itself. It is not a legitimate social goal, and it should certainly not be the aim of strong affirmative action, whose drawbacks make it worth adopting only against a serious and intractable social evil.

This implies that the justification for strong affirmative action is much weaker in the case of other racial and ethnic groups, and in the case of women. At least, the practice will be justified in a narrower range of circumstances and for a shorter span of time than it is for blacks. No other group has been treated quite like this, and no other group is in a comparable status. Hispanic-Americans occupy an intermediate position, but it seems to me frankly absurd to include persons of oriental descent as beneficiaries of affirmative action, strong or weak.

They are not a severely deprived and excluded minority, and their eligibility serves only to swell the numbers that can be included on affirmative action reports. It also suggests that there is a drift in the policy toward adopting the goal of racial proportional representation for its own sake. This is a foolish mistake, and should be resisted. The only legitimate goal of the policy is to reduce egregious racial stratification.

With respect to women, I believe that except over the short term, and in professions or institutions from which their absence is particularly marked, strong affirmative action is not warranted and weak affirmative action is enough. This is based simply on the expectation that the social and economic situation of women will improve quite rapidly under conditions of full equality of opportunity. Recent progress provides some evidence for this. Women do not form a separate hereditary community, characteristically poor and uneducated, and their position is not likely to be self-perpetuating in the same way as that of an outcast race. The process requires less artificial acceleration, and any need for strong affirmative action for women can be expected to end sooner than it ends for blacks.

I said at the outset that there was a tendency to blur the distinction between weak and strong affirmative action. This occurs especially in the use of numerical quotas, a topic on which I want to comment briefly.

A quota may be a method of either weak or strong affirmative action, depending on the circumstances. It amounts to weak affirmative action—a safeguard against discrimination—if, and only if, there is independent evidence that average qualifications for the positions being filled are no lower in the group to which a minimum quota is being assigned than in the applicant group as a whole. This can be presumed true of unskilled jobs that most people can do, but it becomes less likely, and harder to establish, the greater the skill and education required for the position. At these levels, a quota proportional to population, or even to representation of the group in the applicant pool, is almost certain to amount to strong affirmative action. Moreover it is strong affirmative action of a particularly crude and indiscriminate kind, because it permits no variation in the degree of preference on the basis of costs in efficiency, depending on the qualification gap. For this reason I should defend quotas only where they serve the purpose of weak affirmative action. On the whole, strong affirmative action is better implemented by including group preference as one factor in appointment or admission decisions, and letting the results depend on its interaction with other factors.

I have tried to show that the arguments against strong affirmative action are clearly outweighed at present by the need for exceptional measures to remove the stubborn residues of racial caste. But advocates of the policy should acknowledge the reasons against it, which will ensure its termination when it is no longer necessary. Affirmative action is not an end in itself, but a means of dealing with a social situation that should be intolerable to us all.

Study Questions

1. When should affirmative action end?

2. Is the unfairness of affirmative action to white males justifiable?

Is Turn About Fair Play?

Barry R. Gross is a professor of philosophy at York College, CUNY.

Barry R. Gross

... The balance of argument weighs against reverse discrimination for four interrelated sets of reasons. First, the procedures designed to isolate the discriminated are flawed. Second, the practice has undesirable and dangerous consequences. Third, it fails to fit any of the models of compensation or reparations. Fourth, it falls unjustly upon both those it favors and those it disfavors. I conclude that if to eliminate discrimination against the members of one group we find ourselves discriminating against another, we have gone too far.

Sociologically, groups are simply not represented in various jobs and at various levels in percentages closely approximating their percentage of the population. When universities in general and medical schools in particular discriminated heavily against them, Jews were represented in the medical profession in far greater percentages than their percentage of the population. At the same time, they were represented in far lower percentages in banking, finance, construction, and engineering than their percentage in the population, especially the population of New York City. A similar analysis by crudely drawn group traits—Jew, Roman Catholic, WASP, Irish, and so forth—of almost any trade, business or profession would yield similar results.

But the argument from population percentages may be meant not as an analysis of what is the case, but as an analysis of what ought to be the case. A

proponent might put it this way: It is true that groups are not usually represented in the work force by their percentage in the population at large, but minority C has been systematically excluded from the good places. Therefore, in order to make sure that they get some of them, we should systematically include them in the good places, and a clear way of doing it is by their percentage in the population. Or we might conclude instead: therefore, in order to make up for past exclusion, they should be included in the good places as reparation, and an easy way to do it is by their percentage in the population.

If the definition of a minority discriminated against is ipso facto their representation in certain jobs in percentages less than their percentage in the general population, then one has to remark that the reasoning is circular. For we are trying to prove: (1) that minority C is discriminated against.

We use a premise (3) that minority C is underrepresented in good jobs. Since (1) does not follow from (3) (mere underrepresentation not being even prima facie evidence of discrimination), it is necessary to insert (2) that their underrepresentation is due to discrimination. But this completes the circle.

A critic might reply that we know perfectly well what is meant. The groups discriminated against are blacks, Puerto Ricans, Mexican-Americans, American Indians, and women. He is correct, though his answer does not tell us *how to find out* who is discriminated against. This critic, for example, left out Jews and Orientals. If he should reply that Jews and Orientals do well enough, we point out that the question was not "Who fails to do well?" but rather,

"Who is discriminated against?" This argument shows that the mechanisms for identifying the victims of discrimination and for remedying it are seriously deficient.

Even if we allow that the percentage of the group in the work force versus its percentage in the population is the criterion of discrimination, who is discriminated against will vary depending upon how we divide the groups. We may discover that Republicans are discriminated against by our literary or intellectual journals—*New York Review, Dissent, Commentary.* We may also discover that wealthy Boston residents are discriminated against by the Los Angeles Dodgers, that women are discriminated against by the Army, and that idiots (we hope) are discriminated against by universities.

What employment or profession a person chooses depends upon a number of variables—background, wealth, parents' employment, schooling, intelligence, drive, ambition, skill, and not least, luck. Moreover, the analysis will differ depending upon what group identification or stratification you choose. None seems to have priority over the others. Every person can be typed according to many of these classifications. It seems, therefore, that the relevant analysis cannot even be made, much less justified.

In addition, some proponents of the population-percentage argument seem to hold: (4) From the contingent fact that members of the group C were discriminated against, it follows necessarily that they are underrepresented in the good positions. They then go on to assert (5) if members of group C were not discriminated against they would not be underrepresented, or (6) if they are underrepresented, then they are discriminated against.

But clearly (4) is itself a contingent, not a necessary truth. Clearly also neither (5) nor (6) follows from it, (5) being the fallacy of denying the antecedent and (6) the fallacy of affirming the consequent. Lastly, neither (5) nor (6) is necessarily true. The members of a group might simply lack interest in certain jobs (for example, Italians in the public-school system are in short supply). Could one argue that, even though neither (4), (5), nor (6) is *necessarily* true, the mere fact of underrepresentation in certain occupations does provide evidence of dis-

crimination? The answer is no—no more than the fact of "overrepresentation" in certain occupations is evidence of favoritism.

At most, underrepresentation can be used to support the contention of discrimination when there is *other* evidence as well.

Fair Play: Ought We to Discriminate in Reverse?

There are at least three difficulties with reverse discrimination: first, it is inconsistent; second, it licenses discrimination; third it is unfair.

> *"There are at least three difficulties with reverse discrimination: first, it is inconsistent; second, it licenses discrimination; third, it is unfair."*

If we believe the principle that equal opportunity is a right of everyone, then if members of group C are excluded from enjoying certain opportunities merely because they are members of group C, their right is being abrogated. They are entitled to this right, but so is everybody else, even those persons who presently deny it to them. If both are made to enjoy equal opportunity, then both are enjoying their right. To give either oppressors or oppressed more than equal opportunity is equally to deny the rights of one or the other in violation of the principle of equal opportunity.

Proponents of reverse discrimination seem to be caught on the horns of a dilemma: either discrimination is illegitimate or it is not. If it is illegitimate, then it ought not to be practiced against anyone. If it is not, then there exists no reason for *now* favoring blacks, Puerto Ricans, Chicanos, Indians, women, and so forth over whites.

Two strategies present themselves. Either we can analyze one disjunct with a view to showing that distinctions can be made which require compensation or reparations in the form of reverse discrimination to be made to wronged individuals or groups; or we can try to soften one of the disjuncts so as to make a case for exceptions in favor of the wronged. The first appeals both to our reason and our sense of justice. The second appeals to our emotions. I shall argue that neither strategy works.[1]

Now reverse discrimination can take several forms, but I think that what many of its proponents have in mind is a strong form of compensation—a form which requires us to discriminate against non-C members and favor C members even if less qualified. One may well wonder whether there is not a little retribution hidden in this form of compensation.

The "Softened" General Principle

The argument for construing reverse discrimination as compensation or reparation has a great appeal which can be brought out by contrasting it with another approach. One might agree that as a general rule reverse discrimination is illegitimate but that it need not be seen as universally illegitimate. In particular, in the case where people have been so heavily discriminated against as to make it impossible for them now to gain a good life, there is no possibility of their having a fair chance, no possibility of their starting out on anything like equal terms, then and only then is it legitimate to discriminate in their favor and hence against anyone else.

Against this "softened" general principle I shall urge two sorts of objections which I call respectively "practical" and "pragmatic." Against the reparations type of argument, I shall urge first that there is some reason to think that conditions for exacting and accepting them are lacking, and second that, owing to the peculiar nature of the reparations to be exacted (reverse discrimination), the very exaction of them is unreasonable and unfair to both parties—exactors and exactees.

I mention briefly two sorts of practical objections to the "softened" general principle. First, it is simply the case that when discrimination is made in favor of someone regardless of his qualifications, there is the greatest possible danger that the person getting the position will not be competent to fill it. Second, when a person is placed in a position because of discrimination in his favor, he may come to feel himself inferior.[2] This may easily lead to the permanent conferral of inferior status on the group, an inferiority which is all the stronger because self-induced. Its psychological effects should not be underestimated.

The pragmatic objection to the "softened" general principle is much stronger. Discrimination in any form is invidious. Once licensed, its licenses rebound upon its perpetrators as well as others. Principles tend to be generalized without consideration of restrictions or the circumstances to which they were intended to apply. Students of the Nazi movement will have noticed that in licensing the discrimination, isolation, persecution, and "final solution" of the Jews, the Nazis (foreign and German) licensed their own. (Hitler's plans for extermination included political groups, for example, the Rohm faction of the SA, as well as other racial groups, for example, Slavs and Balts who fought on the German side.) It is necessary to be quite careful what principles one adopts. In view of the long and bloody history of discrimination, one ought to be very chary of sanctioning it.

Compensations, Reparations, and Restitution

Because it escapes most of these objections, the reparations argument becomes very attractive. What is more obvious than the principle that people ought to be compensated for monetary loss, pain and suffering inflicted by others acting either as agents of government or as individuals? From the negligence suit to reparations for war damage, the principle is comfortable, familiar, and best of all, legal. For victims of broken sidewalks, open wells, ignored stop

---

1. For examples of these strategies, see the article by J. W. Nickel, "Classification by Race in Compensatory Programs," *Ethics,* vol. 84, 1974.

2. *Contra* this objection see Irving Thalberg, "Justifications of Institutional Racism," *The Philosophical Forum,* Winter 1972.

signs, the conditions under which damages are awarded are quite clear. (1) There is specific injury, specific victim, specific time and place. (2) A specific individual or set of individuals must be found responsible either (a) by actually having done the injury, or (b) by failing to act in such a way (for example, repairing the sidewalk, sealing the well) so as to remove a particular potential source of injury on their property. (3) A reasonable assessment of the monetary value of the claim can be made. In such cases no moral blame is attached to the person forced to pay compensation.

But reparations are somewhat less clear. How much does Germany owe France for causing (losing?) World War I? Can we say that *Germany* caused the war? Germany did pay, at least in part, based upon rough calculations of the cost of the Allied armies, including pensions, the loss of allied GNP, indemnities for death and for the destruction of property....

Inapplicability of These Paradigms

Can reverse discrimination be construed to fit any of these paradigms? Can favoring blacks, Chicanos, Indians, women, and so forth over whites or males be seen as compensation, reparations or restitution? The answer is no for two general reasons and for several which are specific to the various paradigms. The general reasons are, first, that responsibility for discrimination past and present and for its deleterious consequences is neither clearly assigned nor accepted. Some seem to think that the mere fact of its existence makes all whites (or males in the case of antifeminism) responsible.[3] But I do not know an analysis of responsibility which bears out this claim. Second, there is a great difficulty, if not an impossibility, in assigning a monetary value to the damage

done and compensation allegedly owed—that is to say, reverse discrimination.

If we turn to the negligence paradigm, all the conditions seem to fail. *Specific* injury is lacking, *specific* individual responsibility is lacking, and there is no way to assess the monetary value of the "loss." Indeed, in the case of reverse discrimination it is not monetary value which is claimed but preferential treatment. Under the large-scale reparations paradigm two conditions beyond responsibility are lacking. There are no governments or government-like agencies between which the transfer could take place, and there is no *modus agendi* for the transfer to take place.

Where the transfer is to be of preferential treatment, it is unclear how it is even to be begun. So we come to the third paradigm: individual restitution. This is much closer, for it deals with compensating individual victims of persecution. Again, however, it fails to provide a model, first, because reverse discrimination cannot be looked at in monetary terms, and second, even if it could, the restitution is designed to bring a person back to where he was before deprivation. In the case of the minorities in question, there can be no question of restoring them to former positions or property. Precisely, the point of the reparation is to pay them for what they, because of immoral social practices, never had in the first place....

Justice

Finally, if we ignore all that has been said and simply go ahead and discriminate in reverse, calling it reparation, it remains to ask whether it would be either reasonable or just? I think the answer is no. It is possible to hold that in some set of cases, other things being equal, compensation is required and yet to argue either that since other things are not equal compensation is not required, or that even if some compensation is required it ought not to take the form of reverse discrimination. Certainly, from the fact that some form of compensation or reparation must be made it does not follow that any *specific* form of compensation is in order. If X is discriminated against in awarding professorships because he is a member of C group, it scarcely follows that if compensation is in order it *must* take

---

3. See Thalberg. For an interesting catalogue of "irresponsible use of 'responsibility'" see Robert Stover, "Responsibility for the Cold War—A Case Study in Historical Responsibility," *History and Theory,* 1972. For a clear-cut analysis that more than mere presence on the scene is required to show responsibility, see S. Levinson, "Responsibility for Crimes of War," *Philosophy and Public Affairs,* Spring 1973.

the form of his being discriminated in favor of for another professorship, at least not without adopting the principle of "an eye for an eye" (and only an *eye* for an eye?). Consider X being turned down for an apartment because he is a C member. Must compensation consist just in his being offered another ahead of anybody else? Even if he has one already? To go from the relatively innocuous principle that where *possible* we ought to compensate for damages, to sanction reverse discrimination as the proper or preferred form of redress, requires us to go beyond mere compensation to some principle very much like "let the punishment mirror the crime." But here the person "punished," the person from which the compensation is exacted, is often not the "criminal." Nor will it help to say that the person deprived of a job or advancement by reverse discrimination is not really being punished or deprived, since the job did not belong to him in the first place. Of course it didn't; nor did it belong to the successful candidate. What belonged to both is equal consideration, and that is what one of them is being deprived of.[4]

There is an element of injustice or unfairness in all reparations. The money derived from taxes paid by all citizens is used for reparations regardless of whether they were responsible for, did nothing about, opposed, or actually fought the policies or government in question. Yet we say that this is the only way it can be done, that the element of unfairness is not great, and that on the whole it is better that this relatively painless way of appropriating

money from Jones, who is innocent, be used than that the victims of persecution or crime go uncompensated. But the consequences of reverse discrimination are quite different, especially when it is based upon group membership rather than individual desert. It is possible and is sometimes the case that though most C members are discriminated against, Y is a C member who has met with no discrimination at all. Under the principle that all C members should be discriminated in favor of, we would offer "compensation" to Y. But what are we compensating him *for*? By hypothesis he was no victim of discrimination. Do we compensate him for what happened to others? Do we pay Jones for what we buy from Smith? We seem to be compensating him for being a C member, but why? Do we secretly hold C members inferior? Some claim that society as a whole must bear the burden of reparation. But then reverse discrimination will hardly do the trick. It does not exact redress from the government, or even from all white (responsible?) citizens equally, but falls solely against those who apply for admissions, or jobs *for which blacks or other minorities are applying at the same time.* By the same token, it does not compensate or "reparate" all minority persons equally but merely those applying for admission, jobs, promotions, and so forth. Those whose positions are secure would not be paid. A white person who fought for civil rights for blacks may be passed over for promotion or displaced, a victim of reverse discrimination, while a Ku Klux Klan man at the top of the job ladder pays nothing. This would be a laughably flawed system if it were not seriously advocated by responsible people, and partly implemented by the government. Surely, it violates the principles of both compensatory and distributive justice.

---

4. See Gertrude Ezorsky, "It's Mine," *Philosophy and Public Affairs,* Spring 1974.

Study Questions

1. How is it possible to rectify an injustice to a large group?

2. Would it make sense to simply give blacks a large amount of money as compensation for past discrimination?

Moral Dilemmas

- You are the head of personnel for a large high-tech company. Your company has advertised for a researcher, and you have narrowed down the search to two people, a white male and a black female. The company vice-president has instructed you to hire more women and minorities. You believe that the white male is more qualified and you know that he has three children while the black female is single and not as qualified.

  As personnel director, what should you do?

- Jill is a black female working as the personnel director for a large firm. She was hired over a year ago, but no one really seems friendly toward her. While in the ladies' room, she overhears two other female employees talking. One says to the other: "The only reason Jill got that job is because she's black." Jill is shocked. She is thinking about quitting.

  If you were Jill, would you quit?

- A large accounting firm, Dowee, Cheetem and How, sees the need to terminate some staff due to a drop in business. One executive believes people should be fired on the basis of 'Last hired, first fired.' Another executive is concerned that if they take this approach, most of the minority affirmative action employees will be fired. A third executive argues that those that need the job most (employees with families, elderly employees, etc.) should be fired last.

  Should the firm terminate employees simply on the basis of seniority or should other considerations be relevant?

Suggested Readings

Blackstone, William T., and Robert Heslep, eds. *Social Justice and Preferential Treatment*. Athens: University of Georgia Press, 1977.

Cohen, Marshall, Thomas Nagel, and Thomas Scanlon, eds. *Equality and Preferential Treatment*. Princeton: Princeton University Press, 1977.

Katzner, Louis. "Is the Favoring of Women and Blacks in Employment and Educational Opportunities Justified?" in *Philosophy of Law*, ed. Joel Feinberg and Hyman Gross. Encino: Dickenson, 1975.

Wasserstrom, Richard. "A Defense of Programs of Preferential Treatment," *National Forum (The Phi Kappa Phi Journal)* 58, no. 1 (Winter 1978).

Business and the Environment

I s pollution the inevitable price of economic and technological progress? If pollution is to be reduced, what is the acceptable level, and who should bear the cost? Can economic growth continue if our natural resources such as coal and oil are finite? Do we need different kinds of technologies and sources of energy such as nuclear reactors? Are the traditional ethical theories such as those of Kant and Mill adequate to deal with the problems of environmental degradation? These are some of the questions confronting environmental ethics.

Background

Human beings must interact with nature in order to provide for their needs. In the most primitive societies, humans provided for their needs as hunters and gatherers in a world of plentiful natural resources. The human population was small, and pollution was virtually nonexistent. As humanity developed its intellectual powers, its control of and relation to nature became more complex. The first signs of this were the use of primitive stone and wood tools several million years ago and the discovery of fire about a million years ago.

The discovery of agriculture fundamentally transformed our way of life. Although agriculture developed at different times in different places, it first appeared about fifteen thousand years ago and changed human beings from food finders to food producers. This was a revolution in the full sense of the term because it allowed people to live in one area indefinitely, thus enabling the development of cities and culture. The increase in population was made possible by the dramatic increase and stability of the food supply. This more intensive relationship to nature contributed to greater environmental disruption such as the depletion of various essential minerals in the soil by overfarming.

Although the impact of the agricultural revolution on civilization and the environment was of great magnitude, this impact was dwarfed by that of the industrial revolution. The industrial revolution essentially began in the eighteenth century and involved social change on a vast and unprecedented scale. It involved the use of new machinery, technology, and energy sources. The use of steam power and electricity and the greater demand for coal and oil created the well-known image of factory smokestacks spewing smoke into the air as a sign of industry and commerce. The increasing centralization of production in the factories increased the size and population of cities, which brought with it health and environmental problems associated with overcrowding and waste disposal vividly described by the British writer Charles Dickens and Marx's collaborator, Friedrich Engels.

Our interaction with and control of nature has continued to grow in complexity and scope. The continuing development of new technology and growth in the population continues to place increased stress on the environment and natural resources. The rise of modern medicine has contributed to the population growth, which in turn has exerted greater demand for increased food production. To meet this rising demand for food, farmers, with the help of scientists, brought forth new chemicals to control insects (insecticides), to control weeds (herbicides), and to increase the productivity of the soil (fertilizers). Unfortunately, many of these chemicals have been found to cause long-term health problems in people and in other species. The continued pollution of the air caused by factories and automobiles contributes to respiratory illnesses. When pollution mixes with rain to produce acid rain, the fish in lakes and streams thousands of miles away can be destroyed. This poisoning of the air may be raising the temperature of the atmosphere (greenhouse effect), which may alter climates across the world and raise the sea level by

melting the polar ice caps. Air pollution has also been associated with the depletion of the gas ozone in our upper atmosphere. This has allowed more of the sun's ultraviolet radiation to reach the earth's surface, thus possibly causing a rise in the incidence of skin cancer. Indeed, some environmentalists estimate that as many as seventy to ninety percent of all human cancers are caused by pollution. In 1984 in Bhopal, India, an accident occurred at a chemical plant, killing two thousand persons and injuring two hundred thousand. Our control over nature through technology and scientific farming seems to have been bought at unforeseen and sometimes tragic costs.

In 1945 the first nuclear bomb was exploded in New Mexico, thus inaugurating the atomic age. This unleashing of the power of the atom gave humankind an unprecedented source of power. On August 6, 1945, the United States dropped a nuclear bomb on Hiroshima, Japan, killing about sixty-five thousand persons instantly and many more later. In 1957 the first commercial nuclear power plant began to generate electricity. Today, approximately twenty nations use atomic energy, and probably more will in the future. In 1979 at the Three Mile Island nuclear plant in Pennsylvania, the worst commercial nuclear accident in U.S. history occurred. It involved the leakage of radioactive steam over many miles around the plant. Although no deaths were immediately reported, the possibility of long-term effects from cancer and birth defects in the as yet unborn were greatly increased. In the Soviet Union's Chernobyl plant on April 1986, an explosion killed two persons. More died later from radiation poisoning, and 135,000 persons were evacuated from the surrounding area. The increased cancer deaths from exposure to the Chernobyl radiation are projected to be at least 24,000 within the next seventy years. These and other events have led some to ask whether nuclear energy is worth the risk. If not, will there be enough coal and oil to provide all with a decent standard of living? What will we do with radioactive wastes that continue to be radioactive for thousands of years? What about the rights of future generations to a livable environment?

The British economist Thomas Malthus (1766–1834) argued that population growth will always outpace food production, thus making starvation inevitable. Although Malthus's views have been challenged by those who believe that scientific farming and birth control can control population and increase the food supply, in reality thus far, science, medicine, and technology have contributed to the rising world population now estimated to be about five billion. The United States, which has only six percent of the world's population, uses about sixty percent of the world's minerals and energy resources. The livestock population of the United States consumes enough food to feed as many as a billion people in a world where about three and one-half million people (mostly children) starve to death each year. Though many Americans love their steak, how many know that it takes eight pounds of grain to produce one pound of meat protein?

In 1961 Rachel Carson published *Silent Spring* in which she argued that unless pollution of the environment is drastically curtailed, entire species will be destroyed and our own future endangered. In response to her warnings and other developments, the U.S. government initiated several measures to deal with some of these problems. In 1970 Congress created the Environmental Protection Agency (EPA) to control pollution. The Clean Air Act of the same year provided for the reduction of air pollution, and the Federal Water Pollution Control Act of 1972 sought to protect lakes and rivers from excessive degradation. And again in 1976, Congress established the Toxic Substances Control Act to regulate the production and disposal of new and potentially hazardous chemicals. As welcome as these measures were, many environmentalists believed that they did not go far enough.

Some environmentalists argue that the only way to adequately address the environmental crisis is to change our values and lifestyles. Traditionally, before the full impact of technology and pollution was evident, the environment was viewed as a free resource to be exploited for individual and common benefit. People felt free to pollute, produce, and reproduce at will. Humans saw themselves as superior to all of nature, which existed to satisfy their every wish. This anthropocentric moral perspective placed humanity at the center of creation and denied any rights to lower forms of life. Some have labeled this attitude toward other forms of life *speciesism,* or the belief that the human species is superior to other animals. Those who reject speciesism usually adopt some form of vegetarianism, the abstaining from the eating of meat, as the only morally correct position. They believe that we must adopt a non-anthropocentric ethic, which holds that nature and all animals have an intrinsic value independent of any instrumental or practical value they may have to meet human needs.

Wilfred Beckerman

Wilfred Beckerman is very critical of "extreme" environmentalists such as the Club of Rome. They argue that in order to reduce pollution and to preserve scarce natural resources, economic growth must halt. Beckerman agrees that pollution must be controlled to a reasonable level through governmental action because individual polluters have no economic incentive to do so on their own. However, he believes pollution can be controlled without halting economic growth. According to Beckerman, environmentalists such as the Club of Rome are mistaken on several counts. He points out that even zero economic growth will deplete nonrenewable resources but it will only take longer than if the present rate of economic activity continues. Most importantly, he notes that what counts as a "resource" is relative to available technology; prior to the development of the internal combustion engine, petroleum was not considered to be much of a resource, but rather a nuisance. Beckerman contends that new technology will create new resources from materials not considered as such now. Additionally, he observes that our knowledge about the total available resources is incomplete and unreliable. Finally, he observes that our quest for new technology should not be hampered by the possibility of the destruction of species.

Beckerman's provocative argument has been challenged by environmentalists. Should we disregard the effects of technology and economic development on other species? Don't we have an obligation to future generations to allow them at least the right to come into existence? Will new technology allow for economic growth without greatly increasing pollution? A more technological society means a more complex society; will democracy be able to survive in such a world?

William Ophuls

The concerns behind criticisms of positions like that of Beckerman are the focus of Ophuls's argument. The "tragedy of the commons" Ophuls speaks about refers to selfish use of the environment without regard for the long-term degradation or impact on others. He attacks thinkers like Beckerman because he believes that they overlook the political and social problems that an increasingly technological society will present. A highly technological society will be more prone to more severe accidents. A complex technological world will be dominated by experts, which puts into question the viability of democracy. If economic growth is to continue, government will have to take a greater role in planning the economy in order to preserve resources and to control pollution; this again means a loss of freedom.

Ophuls's only solution is to recommend a radical transformation of our traditional values. We must give up greed, pride, and materialism and adopt humility, frugality, and gentleness in their place. Without this moral revolution, Ophuls believes that our future looks bleak. Unfortunately, Ophuls does not say how this moral change will occur. Are such deeply ingrained moral and psychological attitudes subject to change? If so, how will they be changed, and how long will it take? These questions remain serious problems with which we must contend.

William Blackstone

William Blackstone is concerned that technology develop within the parameters of human rights. Traditional discussions of human rights include such rights as life, liberty, and property but do not mention the right to a livable environment. Blackstone argues that the right to a livable environment is a basic right because without a healthy environment, one cannot exercise any other right nor develop one's capacities as free and rational beings. This means that property rights must be restricted to control pollution and that technology must not conflict with human rights.

Blackstone's position is important because it reminds us that technology should serve humankind, not be our enemy. This can only exist if human rights are protected. However, as social and technological conditions change, it may be necessary to reexamine some traditional rights that come into conflict with human welfare. As suggested before, originally persons saw nature as infinite and to be freely used to increase one's wealth and property. As Blackstone points out, if property rights come into conflict with the right to a healthy and long life, the property rights must be modified; human rights supersede property rights.

No creature has transformed the face of the earth as humans have. The human mind has created science and technology, which has freed a large part of humanity from the tyranny of hunger, disease, and poverty. Technology has increased the quantity and quality of goods, unified the world through modern communication and transportation systems, and enriched the lives of many through the increased availability of humanity's highest artistic creations at the flick of a switch. Yet, these benefits have left in their wake an environment poisoned by chemicals and waste that threaten our very existence. Historically, the manner in which technology has developed has been a function of several conditions: needs, resources, knowledge, moral beliefs, and political realities. Clearly, if technology is to serve humanity, it must be controlled by a valid moral and political system that promotes human flourishing and individuality, not the enslavement of persons or the destruction of the beauty and integrity of the earth.

The Case for Economic Growth

Born in England, Wilfred Beckerman teaches at Oxford University and is the author of Pricing for Pollution *among other writings.*

Wilfred Beckerman

For some years now it has been very unfashionable to be in favor of continued long-run economic growth. Unless one joins in the chorus of scorn for the pursuit of continued economic growth, one is in danger of being treated either as a coarse Philistine, who is prepared to sacrifice all the things that make life really worth living for vulgar materialist goods, or as a short-sighted, complacent, Micawber who is unable to appreciate that the world is living on the edge of a precipice. For it is widely believed that if growth is not now brought to a halt in a deliberate orderly manner, either there will be a catastrophic collapse of output when we suddenly run out of key raw materials, or we shall all be asphyxiated by increased pollution. In other words, growth is either undesirable or impossible, or both. Of course, I suppose this is better than being undesirable and inevitable, but the antigrowth cohorts do not seem to derive much comfort from the fact. . . .

Hence it is not entirely surprising that the antigrowth movement has gathered so much support over the past few years even though it is 99 per cent nonsense. Not 100 per cent nonsense. There does happen to be a one per cent grain of truth in it.

This is that, in the absence of special government policies (policies that governments are unlikely to adopt if not pushed hard by communal action from citizens), pollution will be excessive. This is because—as economists have known for many

Reprinted with permission from the September 26, 1974 *Public Utilities Fortnightly.*

decades—pollution constitutes that is known in the jargon as an "externality." That is to say, the costs of pollution are not always borne fully—if at all—by the polluter. The owner of a steel mill that belches smoke over the neighborhood, for example, does not usually have to bear the costs of the extra laundry, or of the ill-health that may result. Hence, although he is, in a sense, "using up" some of the environment (the clean air) to produce his steel he is getting this particular factor of production free of charge. Naturally, he has no incentive to economize in its use in the same way as he has for other factors of production that carry a cost, such as labor or capital. In all such cases of "externalities," or "spillover effects" as they are sometimes called, the normal price mechanism does not operate to achieve the socially desirable pattern of output or of exploitation of the environment. This defect of the price mechanism needs to be corrected by governmental action in order to eliminate excessive pollution.

But, it should be noted that the "externality" argument, summarized above, only implies that society should cut out "excessive" pollution; not *all* pollution. Pollution should only be cut to the point where the benefits from reducing it further no longer offset the costs to society (labor or capital costs) of doing so.

Mankind has always polluted his environment, in the same way that he has always used up some of the raw materials that he has found in it. When primitive man cooked his meals over open fires, or hunted animals, or fashioned weapons out of rocks and stones, he was exploiting the environment. But to listen to some of the extreme environmentalists, one would imagine that there was something immoral about this (even though God's first injunction to Adam was to subdue the earth and every living thing that exists in it). If all pollution has to be eliminated we would have to spend the whole of our national product in converting every river in the country into beautiful clear-blue swimming pools for fish. Since I live in a town with a 100,000 population but without even a decent swimming pool for the humans, I am not prepared to subscribe to this doctrine.

Anyway, most of the pollution that the environmentalists make such a fuss about, is not the pollution that affects the vast mass of the population. Most people in industrialized countries spend their lives in working conditions where the noise and stench cause them far more loss of welfare than the glamorous fashionable pollutants, such as PCB's or mercury, that the antigrowth lobby makes such a fuss about. Furthermore, such progress as has been made over the decades to improve the working conditions of the mass of the population in industrialized countries has been won largely by the action of working-class trade unions, without any help from the middle classes that now parade so ostentatiously their exquisite sensibilities and concern with the "quality of life."

The extreme environmentalists have also got their facts about pollution wrong. In the Western world, the most important forms of pollution are being reduced, or are being increasingly subjected to legislative action that will shortly reduce them. In my recently published book ("*In Defense of Economic Growth*")[1] I give the facts about the dramatic decline of air pollution in British cities over the past decade or more, as well as the improvement in the quality of the rivers. I also survey the widespread introduction of antipollution policies in most of the advanced countries of the world during the past few years, which will enable substantial

cuts to be made in pollution. By comparison with the reductions already achieved in some cases, or envisaged in the near future, the maximum pollution reductions built into the computerized calculations of the Club of Rome[2] can be seen to be absurdly pessimistic.

> "... [O]nly a totalitarian regime could persist on the basis of an antigrowth policy that denied people their normal and legitimate aspirations for a better standard of living."

The same applies to the Club of Rome's assumption that adequate pollution abatement would be so expensive that economic growth would have to come to a halt. For example, the dramatic cleaning

---

1. Jonathan Cape, London. The U.S.A. edition, under the title *"Two cheers for the Affluent Society,"* was published by the St. Martins Press in the fall of 1974.

2. The Club of Rome is an informal international organization of educators, scientists, economists, and others which investigates what it conceives to be the overriding problems of mankind. Its study, "The Limits to Growth," has become the bible of no-growth advocates (Potomac Associates, 1707 L Street, N.W., Washington, D.C., $2.75). The study assembled data on known reserves of resources and asked a computer what would happen if demand continued to grow exponentially. Of course, the computer replied everything would break down. The theory of "Beckermonium" lampoons this. Since the author's grandfather failed to discover "Beckermonium" by the mid-1800s, the world has had no supplies of it at all. Consequently, if the club's equations are followed, the world should have come to a halt many years ago. "Beckermonium's" foundation is that the things man has not yet discovered as far more numerous and of greater importance than what has been discovered. (Editor's of *Public Utilities Fortnightly* Note.)

up of the air in London cost a negligible amount per head of the population of that city. And, taking a much broader look at the estimates, I show in my book that reduction in pollution many times greater than those which the Club of Rome purports to be the upper limits over the next century can, and no doubt will, be achieved over the next decade in the advanced countries of the world at a cost of only about one per cent to two per cent of annual national product.

When confronted with the facts about the main pollutants, the antigrowth lobby tends to fall back on the "risk and uncertainty" argument. This takes the form, "Ah yes, but what about all these new pollutants, or what about undiscovered pollutants? Who knows, maybe we shall only learn in a 100 years' time, when it will be too late, that they are deadly." But life is full of risk and uncertainty. Every day I run the risk of being run over by an automobile or hit on the head by a golf ball. But rational conduct requires that I balance the probabilities of this happening against the costs of insuring against it. It would only be logical to avoid even the minutest chance of some catastrophe in the future if it were costless to do so. But the cost of stopping economic growth would be astronomic. This cost does not merely comprise the loss of any hope of improved standards of living for the vast mass of the world's population, it includes also the political and social costs that would need to be incurred. For only a totalitarian regime could persist on the basis of an antigrowth policy that denied people their normal and legitimate aspirations for a better standard of living.

But leaving aside this political issue, another technical issue which has been much in the public eye lately has been the argument that growth will be brought to a sudden, and hence catastrophic, halt soon on account of the impending exhaustion of raw material supplies. This is the "finite resources" argument; i.e., that since the resources of the world are finite, we could not go on using them up indefinitely.

Now resources are either finite or they are not. If they are, then even zero growth will not save us in the longer run. Perhaps keeping Gross National Product at the present level instead of allowing it to rise by, say 4 per cent per annum, would enable the world's resources to be spread out for 500 years instead of only 200 years. But the day would still come when we would run out of resources. (The Club of Rome's own computer almost gave the game away and it was obliged to cut off the printout at the point where it becomes clear that, even with zero growth, the world eventually begins to run out of resources!) So why aim only at zero growth? Why not cut output? If resources are, indeed, finite, then there must be some optimum rate at which they should be spread out over time which will be related to the relative importance society attaches to the consumption levels of different generations. The "eco-doomsters" fail to explain the criteria that determine the optimum rate and why they happen to churn out the answer that the optimum growth rate is zero.

And if resources are not, after all, finite, then the whole of the "finite resources" argument collapses anyway. And, in reality, resources are not finite in any meaningful sense. In the first place, what is now regarded as a resource may not have been so in the past decades or centuries before the appropriate techniques for its exploitation or utilization had been developed. This applies, for example, to numerous materials now in use but never heard of a century ago, or to the minerals on the sea bed (e.g., "manganese nodules"), or even the sea water itself from which unlimited quantities of certain basic minerals can eventually be extracted.

In the second place, existing known reserves of many raw materials will never appear enough to last more than, say, twenty or fifty years at current rates of consumption, for the simple reason that it is rarely economically worthwhile to prospect for more supplies than seem to be salable, at prospective prices, given the costs of exploitation and so on. This has always been the case in the past, yet despite dramatic increases in consumption, supplies have more or less kept pace with demand. The "finite resource" argument fails to allow for the numerous ways that the economy and society react to changes in relative prices of a product, resulting from changes in the balance between supply and demand.

For example, a major United States study in 1929 concluded that known tin resources were only adequate to last the world ten years. Forty years later, the Club of Rome is worried because there is only enough to last us another fifteen years. At this rate, we shall have to wait another century before we have enough to last us another thirty years. Meanwhile, I suppose we shall just have to go on using up that ten years' supply that we had back in 1929.

And it is no good replying that demand is growing faster now than ever before, or that the whole scale of consumption of raw materials is incomparably greater than before. First, this proposition has also been true at almost any time over the past few thousand years, and yet economic growth continued. Hence, the truth of such propositions tells us nothing about whether the balance between supply and demand is likely to change one way or the other. And it is this that matters. In other words, it may well be that demand is growing much faster than ever before, or that the whole scale of consumption is incomparably higher, but the same applies to supply. For example, copper consumption rose about fortyfold during the nineteenth century and demand for copper was accelerating, around the turn of the century, for an annual average growth rate of about 3.3 per cent per annum (over the whole century) to about 6.4 per cent per annum during the period 1890 to 1910. Annual copper consumption had been only about 16,000 tons at the beginning of the century, and was about 700,000 tons at the end of it; i.e., incomparably greater. But known reserves at the end of the century were greater than at the beginning.

And the same applies to the postwar period. In 1946 world copper reserves amounted to only about 100 million tons. Since then the annual rate of copper consumption has trebled and we have used up 93 million tons. So there should be hardly any left. In fact, we now have about 300 million tons!

Of course, it may well be that we shall run out of some individual materials; and petroleum looks like one of the most likely candidates for exhaustion of supplies around the end of this century—if the price did not rise (or stay up at its recent level). But there are two points to be noted about this. First, insofar as the price does stay put at its recent level (i.e., in the $10 per barrel region) substantial

economies in oil use will be made over the next few years, and there will also be a considerable development of substitutes for conventional sources, such as shale oil, oil from tar sands, and new ways of using coal reserves which are, of course, very many times greater than oil reserves (in terms of common energy units).

Secondly, even if the world did gradually run out of some resources it would not be a catastrophe. The point of my apparently well-known story about "Beckermonium" (the product named after my grandfather who failed to discover it in the nineteenth century) is that we manage perfectly well without it. In fact, if one thinks about it, we manage without infinitely more products than we manage with! In other words, it is absurd to imagine that if, say, nickel or petroleum had never been discovered, modern civilization would never have existed, and that the eventual disappearance of these or other products must, therefore, plunge us back into the Dark Ages.

The so-called "oil crisis," incidentally, also demonstrates the moral hypocrisy of the antigrowth lobby. For leaving aside their mistaken interpretation of the technical reasons for the recent sharp rise in the oil price (i.e., it was not because the world suddenly ran out of oil), it is striking that the antigrowth lobby has seized upon the rise in the price of oil as a fresh argument for abandoning economic growth and for rethinking our basis values and so on. After all, over the past two or three years the economies of many of the poorer countries of the world, such as India, have been hit badly by the sharp rise in the price of wheat. Of course, this only means a greater threat of starvation for a few more million people in backward countries a long way away. That does not, apparently, provoke the men of spiritual and moral sensibility to righteous indignation about the values of the growth-oriented society as much as does a rise in the price of gasoline for our automobiles!

The same muddled thinking is behind the view that mankind has some moral duty to preserve the world's environment or supplies of materials. For this view contrasts strangely with the antigrowth lobby's attack on materialism. After all, copper, oil, and so on are just material objects, and it is difficult to see what moral duty we have to preserve indefinitely the copper species from extinction.

Nor do I believe that we have any overriding moral duty to preserve any particular animal species from extinction. After all, thousands of animal species have become extinct over the ages, without any intervention by mankind. Nobody really loses any sleep over the fact that one cannot now see a live dinosaur. How many of the people who make a fuss about the danger that the tiger species may disappear even bother to go to a zoo to look at one? And what about the web-footed Beckermanipus, which has been extinct for about a million years. . . .

In fact, I am not even sure that the extinction of the human race would matter. The bulk of humanity lead lives full of suffering, sorrow, cruelty, poverty, frustration, and loneliness. One should not assume that because nearly everybody has a natural animal instinct to cling to life they can be said, in any meaningful sense, to be better off alive than if they had never been born. Religious motivations apart, it is arguable that since, by and large (and present company excepted, of course), the human race stinks, the sooner it is extinct the better. . . .

Whilst economic growth alone may never provide a simple means of solving any of these problems, and it may well be that, by its very nature, human society will always create insoluble problems of one kind or another, the absence of economic growth will only make our present problems a lot worse.

Study Questions

1. Is the human race a mistake?

2. Is it immoral to destroy entire species?

3. What are our obligations to future generations?

4. Is the extreme environmentalist position compatible with democracy?

The Scarcity Society

Formerly a professor of political science at Yale University, William Ophuls is the author of Ecology and the Politics of Scarcity.

William Ophuls

. . . For the past three centuries, we have been living in an age of abnormal abundance. The bonanza of the New World and other founts of virgin resources, the dazzling achievements of science and technology, the availability of "free" ecological resources such as air and water absorb the waste products of industrial activities, and other lesser factors allowed our ancestors to dream of endless material growth. Infinite abundance, men reasoned, would result in the elevation of the common man to economic nobility. And with poverty abolished, inequality, injustice, and fear—all those flowers of evil alleged to have their roots in scarcity—would wither away. Apart from William Blake and a few other disgruntled romantics, or the occasional pessimist like Thomas Malthus, the Enlightenment ideology of progress was shared by all the West. The works of John Locke and Adam Smith, the two men who gave bourgeois political economy its fundamental direction, are shot through with the assumption that there is always going to be more—more land in the colonies, more wealth to be dug from the ground, and so on. Virtually all the philosophies, values, and institutions typical of modern capitalist society—the legitimacy of self-interest, the primacy of the individual and his inalienable rights, economic laissez-faire, and democracy as we know it—are the luxuriant fruit of an era of apparently endless abundance. They cannot continue to exist in their current form once we return to the more normal condition of scarcity.

Worse, the historic responses to scarcity have been conflict—wars fought to control resources, and oppression—great inequality of wealth and the political measures needed to maintain it. The link between scarcity and oppression is well understood by spokesmen for underprivileged groups and nations, who react violently to any suggested restraint in growth of output.

Our awakening from the pleasant dream of infinite progress and the abolition of scarcity will be extremely painful. Institutionally, scarcity demands that we sooner or later achieve a full-fledged "steady-state" or "spaceman" economy. Thereafter, we shall have to live off the annual income the earth receives from the sun, and this means a forced end to our kind of abnormal affluence and an abrupt return to frugality. This will require the strictest sort of economic and technological husbandry, as well as the strictest sort of political control.

The necessity for political control should be obvious from the use of the spaceship metaphor: po-

litical ships embarked on dangerous voyages need philosopher-king captains. However, another metaphor—the tragedy of the commons—comes even closer to depicting the essence of the ecopolitical dilemma. The tragedy of the commons has to do with the uncontrolled self-seeking in a limited environment that eventually results in competitive over-exploitation of a common resource, whether it is a commonly owned field on which any villager may graze his sheep, or the earth's atmosphere into which producers dump their effluents.

Francis Carney's powerful analysis of the Los Angeles smog problem indicates how deeply all our daily acts enmesh us in the tragic logic of the commons:

> Every person who lives in this basin knows that for twenty-five years he has been living through a disaster. We have all watched it happen, have participated in it with full knowledge.... The smog is the result of ten million individual pursuits of private gratification. But there is absolutely nothing that any individual can do to stop its spread.... An individual act of renunciation is now nearly impossible, and, in any case, would be meaningless unless everyone else did the same thing. But he has no way of getting everyone else to do it.

If this inexorable process is not controlled by prudent and, above all, timely political restraints on the behavior that causes it, then we must resign ourselves to ecological self-destruction. And the new political structures that seem required to cope with the tragedy of the commons (as well as the imperatives of technology) are going to violate our most cherished ideals, for they will be neither democratic nor libertarian. At worst, the new era could be an anti-Utopia in which we are conditioned to behave according to the exigencies of ecological scarcity.

Ecological scarcity is a new concept, embracing more than the shortage of any particular resource. It has to do primarily with pollution limits, complex trade-offs between present and future needs, and a variety of other physical constraints, rather than with a simple Malthusian over-population. The case for the coming of ecological scarcity was most forcefully argued in the Club of Rome study *The*

Limits to Growth. That study says, in essence, that man lives on a finite planet containing limited resources and that we appear to be approaching some of these major limits with great speed. To use ecological jargon, we are about to overtax the "carrying capacity" of the planet.

Critical reaction to this Jeremiad was predictably reassuring. Those wise in the ways of computers were largely content to assert that the Club of Rome people had fed the machines false or slanted information. "Garbage in, garbage out," they soothed. Other critics sought solace in less empirical directions, but everyone who recoiled from the book's apocalyptic vision took his stand on grounds of social or technological optimism. Justified or not, the optimism is worth examining to see where it leads us politically.

The social optimists, to put their case briefly, believe that various "negative feedback mechanisms" allegedly built into society will (if left alone) automatically check the trends toward ever more population, consumption, and pollution, and that this feedback will function smoothly and gradually so as to bring us up against the limits to growth, if any, with scarcely a bump. The market-price system is the feedback mechanism usually relied upon. Shortages of one resource—oil, for example—simply make it economical to substitute another abundant supply (coal or shale oil). A few of these critics of the limits-to-growth thesis believe that this process can go on indefinitely.

Technological optimism is founded on the belief that it makes little difference whether exponential growth is pushing us up against limits, for technology is simultaneously expanding the limits. To use the metaphor popularized during the debate, ecologists see us as fish in a pond where all life is rapidly being suffocated by a water lily that doubles in size every day (covering the whole pond in thirty days). The technological optimists do not deny that the lily grows very quickly, but they believe that the pond itself can be made to grow even faster. Technology made a liar out of Malthus, say the optimists, and the same fate awaits the neo-Malthusians. In sum, the optimists assert that we can never run out of resources, for economics and technology, like

modern genii, will always keep finding new ones for us to exploit or will enable us to use the present supply with ever-greater efficiency.

The point most overlooked in this debate, however, is that politically it matters little who is right: the neo-Malthusians *or* either type of optimist. If the "doomsdayers" are right, then of course we crash into the ceiling of physical limits and relapse into a Hobbesian universe of the war of all against all, followed, as anarchy always has been, by dictatorship of one form or another. If, on the other hand, the optimists are right in supposing that we can adjust to ecological scarcity with economics and technology, this effort will have, as we say, "side effects." For the collision with physical limits can be forestalled only by moving toward some kind of steady-state economy—characterized by the most scrupulous husbanding of resources, by extreme vigilance against the ever-present possibility of disaster should breakdown occur, and, therefore, by right controls on human behavior. However we get there, "Spaceship Earth" will be an all-powerful Leviathan—perhaps benign, perhaps not.

> *"The real shortage with which we are afflicted is that of moral resources."*

The scarcity problem thus poses a classic dilemma. It may be possible to avoid crashing into the physical limits, but only by adopting radical and unpalatable measures that, paradoxically, are little different in their ultimate political and social implications from the future predicted by the doomsdayers.

Why this is so becomes clear enough when one realizes that the optimistic critics of the doomsdayers, whom I have artificially grouped into "social" and "technological" tendencies, finally have to rest their different cases on a theory of politics, that is, on assumptions about the adaptability of leaders, their constituencies, and the institutions that hold them together. Looked at closely, these assumptions also appear unrealistic.

Even on a technical level, for example, the market-price mechanism does not coexist easily with environmental imperatives. In a market system a bird in the hand is always worth two in the bush.[1] This means that resources critically needed in the future will be discounted—that is, assessed at a fraction of their future value—by today's economic decision-makers. Thus decisions that are economically "rational," like mine-the-soil farming and forestry, may be ecologically catastrophic. Moreover, charging industries—and, therefore, consumers—for pollution and other environmental harms that are caused by mining and manufacturing (the technical solution favored by most economists to bring market prices into line with ecological realities) is not politically palatable. It clearly requires political decisions that do not accord with current values or the present distribution of political power; and the same goes for other obvious and necessary measures, like energy conservation. No consumer wants to pay more for the same product simply because it is produced in a cleaner way; no developer wants to be confronted with an environmental impact statement that lets the world know his gain is the community's loss; no trucker is likely to agree with any energy-conservation program that cuts his income.

We all have a vested interest in continuing to abuse the environment as we have in the past. And even if we should find the political will to take these kinds of steps before we collide with the physical limits, then we will have adopted the essential features of a spaceman economy on a piecemeal basis—and will have simply exchanged one horn of the dilemma for the other.

Technological solutions are more roundabout, but the outcome—greater social control in a planned society—is equally certain. Even assuming that necessity always proves to be the mother of invention, the management burden thrown on our leaders and institutions by continued technological expansion of that famous fishpond will be enormous. Prevailing rates of growth require us to double our capital stock, our capacity to control pollution, our agricultural productivity, and so forth every fifteen to thirty years. Since we already start from a very high absolute level, the increment of required new construction and new invention will be staggering. For example, to accommodate world population growth, we must, in roughly the next thirty years, build houses, hospitals, ports, factories, bridges, and every other kind of facility in numbers that almost equal all the construction work done by the human race up to now.

The task in every area of our lives is essentially similar, so that the management problem extends across the board, item by item. Moreover, the complexity of the overall problem grows faster than any of the sectors that comprise it, requiring the work of innovation, construction, and environmental management to be orchestrated into a reasonably integrated, harmonious whole. Since delays, planning failures, and general incapacity to deal effectively with even our current level of problems are all too obvious today, the technological response further assumes that our ability to cope with large-scale complexity will improve substantially in the next few decades. Technology, in short, cannot be implemented in a political and social vacuum. The factor in least supply governs, and technological solutions cannot run ahead of our ability to plan, construct, fund, and man them.

Planning will be especially difficult. For one thing, time may be our scarcest resource. Problems now develop so rapidly that they must be foreseen well in advance. Otherwise, our "solutions" will be too little and too late. The automobile is a critical example. By the time we recognized the dangers, it was too late for anything but a mishmash of stopgap measures that may have provoked worse symptoms than they alleviated and that will not even enable us to meet health standards without painful additional measures like rationing. But at this point we are al-

---

1. Of course, noneconomic factors may temporarily override market forces, as the current Arab oil boycott illustrates.

most helpless to do better, for we have ignored the problem until it is too big to handle by any means that are politically, economically, and technically feasible. The energy crisis offers another example of the time factor. Even with an immediate laboratory demonstration of feasibility, nuclear fusion cannot possibly provide any substantial amount of power until well into the next century.

Another planning difficulty: the growing vulnerability of a highly technological society to accident and error. The main cause for concern is, of course, some of the especially dangerous technologies we have begun to employ. One accident involving a eder reactor would be one too many: the most minuscule dose of plutonium is deadly, and any we release now will be around to poison us for a quarter of a million years. Thus, while we know that counting on perfection in any human enterprise is folly, we seem headed for a society in which nothing less than perfect planning and control will do.

At the very least, it should be clear that ecological scarcity makes "muddling through" in a basically laissez-faire socioeconomic system no longer tolerable or even possible. In a crowded world where only the most exquisite care will prevent the collapse of the technological society on which we all depend, the grip of planning and social control will of necessity become more and more complete. Accidents, much less the random behavior of individuals, cannot be permitted; the expert pilots will run the ship in accordance with technological imperatives. Industrial man's Faustian bargain with technology therefore appears to lead inexorably to total domination by technique in a setting of clockwork institutions. C. S. Lewis once said that "what we call Man's power over Nature turns out to be a power exercised by some men over other men with Nature as its instrument," and it appears that the greater our technological power over nature, the more absolute the political power that must be yielded up to some men by others.

These developments will be especially painful for Americans because, from the beginning, we adopted the doctrines of Locke and Smith in their most libertarian form. Given the cornucopia of the frontier, an unpolluted environment, and a rapidly developing technology, American politics could afford to be a more or less amicable squabble over the division of the spoils, with the government stepping in only when the free-for-all pursuit of wealth got out of hand. In the new era of scarcity, laissez-faire and the inalienable right of the individual to get as much as he can are prescriptions for disaster. It follows that the political system inherited from our forefathers is moribund. We have come to the final act of the tragedy of the commons.

The answer to the tragedy is political. Historically, the use of the commons was closely regulated to prevent overgrazing, and we need similar controls—"mutual coercion, mutually agreed upon by the majority of the people affected," in the words of the biologist Garrett Hardin—to prevent the individual acts that are destroying the commons today. Ecological scarcity imposes certain political measures on us if we wish to survive. Whatever these measures may turn out to be—if we act soon, we may have a significant range of responses—it is evident that our political future will inevitably be much less libertarian and much more authoritarian, much less individualistic and much more communalistic than our present. The likely result of the reemergence of scarcity appears to be the resurrection in modern form of the preindustrial polity, in which the few govern the many and in which government is no longer of or by the people. Such forms of government may or may not be benevolent. At worst, they will be totalitarian; in every evil sense of that word we know now, and some ways undreamed of. At best, government seems likely to rest on engineered consent, as we are manipulated by Platonic guardians in one or another version of Brave New World. The alternative will be the destruction, perhaps consciously, of "Spaceship Earth."

There is, however, a way out of this depressing scenario. To use the language of ancient philosophers, it is the restoration of the civic virtue of a corrupt people. By their standards, by the standards of many of the men who founded our nation (and whose moral capital we have just about squandered), we are indeed a corrupt people. We understand liberty as a license for self-indulgence, so that we exploit our rights to the full while scanting our duties. We understand democracy as a political means of gratifying our desires rather than as a system of government that gives us the precious freedom to impose laws on ourselves—instead of having some remote sovereign impose them on us without our participation or consent. Moreover, the desires we express through our political system are primarily for material gain; the pursuit of happiness has been degraded into a mass quest for what wise men have always said would injure our souls. We have yet to learn the truth of Burke's political syllogism, which expresses the essential wisdom of political philosophy: man is a passionate being, and there must therefore be checks on will and appetite; if these checks are not self-imposed, they must be applied externally as fetters by a sovereign power. The way out of our difficulties, then, is through the abandonment of our political corruption.

The crisis of ecological scarcity poses basic value questions about man's place in nature and the meaning of human life. It is possible that we may learn from this challenge what Lao-tzu taught two-and-a-half millennia ago:

> Nature sustains itself through three precious principles, which one does well to embrace and follow.

> These are gentleness, frugality, and humility.

A very good life—in fact, an affluent life by historic standards—can be lived without the profligate use of resources that characterizes our civilization. A sophisticated and ecologically sound technology,

using solar power and other renewable resources, could bring us a life of simple sufficiency that would yet allow the full expression of the human potential. Having chosen such a life, rather than having had it forced on us, we might find it had its own richness.

Such a choice may be impossible, however. The root of our problem lies deep. The real shortage with which we are afflicted is that of moral resources. Assuming that we wish to survive in dignity and not as ciphers in some ant-heap society, we are obliged to reassume our full moral responsibility. The earth is not just a banquet at which we are free to gorge. The ideal in Buddhism of compassion for all sentient beings, the concern for the harmony of man and nature so evident among American Indians, and the almost forgotten ideal of stewardship in Christianity point us in the direction of a true ethics of human survival—and it is toward such an ideal that the best among the young are groping. We must realize that there is no real scarcity in nature. It is our numbers and, above all, our wants that have outrun nature's bounty. We become rich precisely in proportion to the degree in which we eliminate violence, greed, and pride from our lives. As several thousands of years of history show, this is not something easily learned by humanity, and we seem no readier to choose the simple, virtuous life now than we have been in the past. Nevertheless, if we wish to avoid either a crash into the ecological ceiling or a tyrannical Leviathan, we must choose it. There is no other way to defeat the gathering forces of scarcity.

Study Questions

1. Is the pollution problem caused by our values and lifestyle?

2. How would a society go about changing its values?

Ethics and Ecology

William T. Blackstone (1931–1977) A former professor of philosophy at the University of Georgia, William Blackstone was the author of several books and articles.

William Blackstone

The Right to a Livable Environment as a Human Right

… Let us first ask whether the right to a livable environment can properly be considered to be a human right. For the purposes of this paper, however, I want to avoid raising the more general question of whether there are any human rights at all. Some philosophers do deny that any human rights exist.[1] In two recent papers I have argued that human rights do exist (even though such rights may properly be overridden on occasion by other morally relevant reasons) and that they are universal and inalienable (although the actual exercise of such rights on a given occasion is alienable).[2] My argument for the existence of universal human rights rests, in the final analysis, on a theory of what it means to be human, which specifies the capacities for rationality and freedom as essential, and on the fact that there are no relevant grounds for excluding any human from the opportunity to develop and fulfill his capacities (rationality and freedom) as a human. This is not to deny that there are criteria which justify according human rights in quite different ways or with quite different modes of treatment for different persons, depending upon the nature and degree of such capacities and the existing historical and environmental circumstances.

If the right to a livable environment were seen as a basic and inalienable human right, this could be a valuable tool (both inside and outside of legalistic frameworks) for solving some of our environmental problems, both on a national and on an international basis. Are there any philosophical and conceptual difficulties in treating this right as an inalienable human right? Traditionally we have not looked upon the right to a decent environment as a human right or as an inalienable right. Rather, inalienable human or natural rights have been conceived in somewhat different terms; equality, liberty, happiness, life and property. However, might it not be possible to view the right to a livable environment as being entailed by, or as constitutive of, these basic human or natural rights recognized in our political tradition? If human rights, in other words, are those rights which each human possesses in virtue of the fact that he is human and in virtue of the fact that those rights are essential in permitting him to live a human life (that is, in permitting him to live a human life (that is, in permitting him to fulfill his capacities as a rational and free being), then might not the right to a decent environment be properly categorized as such a human right? Might it not be conceived as a right which

---

Reprinted from *Philosophy and Environmental Crisis,* edited by William T. Blackstone, by permission of the University of Georgia Press. © 1972 by the University of Georgia Press.

---

1. See Kai Nielsen's "Scepticism and Human Rights," *Monist,* 52, no. 4 (1968); 571–94.
2. See my "Equality and Human Rights," *Monist,* 52, no. 4 (1968): 616–39 and my "Human Rights and Human Dignity," in Laszlo and Gotesky, eds., *Human Dignity.*

has emerged as a result of changing environmental conditions and the impact of those conditions on the very possibility of the realization of other rights such as liberty and equality?[3] Let us explore how this might be the case.

Given man's great and increasing ability to manipulate the environment, and the devastating effect this is having, it is plain that new social institutions and new regulative agencies and procedures must be initiated on both national and international levels to make sure that the manipulation is in the public interest. It will be necessary, in other words, to restrict or stop some practices and the freedom to engage in those practices. Some look upon such additional state planning, whether national or international, as unnecessary further intrusion on man's freedom. Freedom is, of course, one of our basic values, and few would deny that excessive state control of human action is to be avoided. But such restrictions on individual freedom now appear to be necessary in the interest of overall human welfare and the rights and freedoms of *all* men. Even John Locke with his stress on freedom as a inalienable right recognized that this right must be construed so that it is consistent with the equal right to freedom of others. The whole point of the state is to restrict unlicensed freedom and to provide the conditions for equality of rights for all. Thus it seems to be perfectly consistent with Locke's view and, in general, with the views of the founding fathers of this country to restrict certain rights or freedoms when it can be shown that such restriction is necessary to insure the equal rights of others. If this is so, it has very important implications for the rights to freedom and to property. These rights, perhaps

properly seen as inalienable (though this is a controversial philosophical question), are not properly seen as unlimited or unrestricted. When values which we hold dear conflict (for example, individual or group freedom and the freedom of all, individual or group rights and the rights of all, and individual or group welfare and the welfare of the general public) something has to give; some priority must be established. In the case of the abuse and waste of environmental resources, less individual freedom and fewer individual rights for the sake of greater public welfare and equality of rights seem justified. What in the past had been properly regarded as freedoms and rights (given what seemed to be unlimited natural resources and no serious pollution problems) can no longer be so construed, at least not without additional restrictions.

> *"What in the past had been properly regarded as freedoms and rights ... can no longer be so construed, at least not without additional restrictions."*

We must recognize both the need for such restrictions and the fact that none of our rights can be realized without a livable environment. Both public welfare and equality of rights now require that natural resources not be used simply according to the whim and caprice of individuals or simply for personal profit. This is not to say that all property rights must be denied and that the state must own all productive property, as the Marxist argues. It is to insist that those rights be qualified or restricted in the light of new ecological data and in the interest of the freedom, rights, and welfare of all.

The answer then to the question, Is the right to a livable environment a human right? is yes. Each person has this right qua being human and because a livable environment is essential for one to fulfill his human capacities. And given the danger to our

3. Almost forty years ago, Aldo Leopold stated that "there is as yet no ethic dealing with man's relationship to land and to the non-human animals and plants which grow upon it. Land, like Odysseus' slave girls, is still property. The land relation is still strictly economic entailing privileges but not obligations." (See Leopold's "The Conservation Ethic," *Journal of Forestry,* 32, no. 6 (October 1933): 634–43. Although some important changes have occurred since he wrote this, no systematic ethic or legal structure has been developed to socialize or institutionalize the obligations to use land properly.

environment today and hence the danger to the very possibility of human existence, access to a livable environment must be conceived as a right which imposes upon everyone a correlative moral obligation to respect.[4] . . .

Ecology and Economic Rights

We suggested above that it is necessary to qualify or restrict economic or property rights in the light of new ecological data and in the interest of the freedom, rights, and welfare of all. In part, this suggested restriction is predicated on the assumption that we cannot expect private business to provide solutions to the multiple pollution problems for which they themselves are responsible. Some companies have taken measures to limit the polluting effect of their operations, and this is an important move. But we are deluding ourselves if we think that private business can function as its own pollution police. This is so for several reasons: the primary objective of private business is economic profit. Stockholders do not ask of a company, "Have you polluted the environment and lowered the quality of the environment for the general public and for future generations?" Rather they ask, "How high is the annual dividend and how much higher is it than the year before?" One can hardly expect organizations whose basic norm is economic profit to be concerned in any great depth with the long-range effects of their operations upon society and future generations or concerned with the hidden cost of their operations in terms of environmental quality to society as a whole. Second, within a free enterprise system companies compete to produce what the public wants at the lowest possible cost. Such competition would preclude the spending of adequate funds to prevent environmental pollution, since this would add tremendously to the cost of

the product—unless all other companies would also conform to such antipollution policies. But in a free enterprise economy such policies are not likely to be self-imposed by businessmen. Third, the basic response of the free enterprise system to our economic problems is that we must have greater economic growth or an increase in gross national product. But such growth many ecologists look upon with great alarm, for it can have devastating long-range effects upon our environment. Many of the products of uncontrolled growth are based on artificial needs and actually detract from, rather than contribute to, the quality of our lives. A stationary economy, some economists and ecologists suggest, may well be best for the quality of man's environment and of his life in the long run. Higher GNP does not automatically result in an increase in social well-being, and it should not be used as a measuring rod for assessing economic welfare. This becomes clear when one realizes that the GNP

> aggregates the dollar value of all goods and services produced—the cigarettes as well as the medical treatment of lung cancer, the petroleum from offshore wells as well as the detergents required to clean up after oil spills, the electrical energy produced and the medical and cleaning bills resulting from the air-pollution fuel used for generating the electricity. The GNP allows no deduction for negative production, such as lives lost from unsafe cars or environmental destruction perpetrated by telephone, electric and gas utilities, lumber companies, and speculative builders.[5]

To many persons, of course, this kind of talk is not only blasphemy but subversive. This is especially true when it is extended in the direction of additional controls over corporate capitalism. (Some ecologists and economists go further and challenge whether corporate capitalism can accommodate a stationary state and still retain its major features.)[6] The fact of the matter is that the ecological attitude

---

4. The right to a livable environment might itself entail other rights, for example, the right to population control. Population control is obviously essential for quality human existence. This issue is complex and deserves a separate essay, but I believe that the moral framework explicated above provides the grounds for treating population control both as beneficial and as moral.

5. See Melville J. Ulmer, "More Than Marxist," *New Republic,* 26 December 1970, p. 14.

6. See Murdock and Connell, "All about Ecology," *Center Magazine,* 3, no. 1 (January–February 1970), p. 63.

forces one to reconsider a host of values which have been held dear in the past, and it forces one to reconsider the appropriateness of the social and economic systems which embodied and implemented those values. Given the crisis of our environment, there must be certain fundamental changes in attitudes toward nature, man's use of nature, and man himself. Such changes in attitudes undoubtedly will have far-reaching implications for the institutions of private property and private enterprise and the values embodied in these institutions. Given that crisis we can no longer look upon water and air as free commodities to be exploited at will. Nor can the private ownership of land be seen as a lease to use that land in any way which conforms merely to the personal desires of the owner. In other words, the environmental crisis is forcing us to challenge what had in the past been taken to be certain basic rights of man or at least to restrict those rights. And it is forcing us to challenge institutions which embodied those rights.

Much has been said ... about the conflict between these kinds of rights, and the possible conflict between them is itself a topic for an extensive paper. Depending upon how property rights are formulated, the substantive content of those rights, it seems plain to me, can directly conflict with what we characterize as human rights. In fact our moral and legal history demonstrate exactly that kind of conflict. There was a time in the recent past when property rights embodied the right to hold human beings in slavery. This has now been rejected, almost universally. Under nearly any interpretation of the substantive content of human rights, slavery is incompatible with those rights.

The analogous question about rights which is now being raised by the data uncovered by the ecologist and by the gradual advancement of the ecological attitude is whether the notion of property rights should be even further restricted to preclude the destruction and pollution of our environmental resources upon which the welfare and the very lives of all of us and of future generations depend. Should our social and legal system embrace property rights or other rights which permit the kind of environmental exploitation which operates to the detriment of the majority of mankind? I do not think so. The fact that a certain right exists in a social or legal system does not mean that it ought to exist. I would not go so far as to suggest that all rights are merely rule-utilitarian devices to be adopted or discarded whenever it can be shown that the best consequences thereby follow.[7] But if a right or set of rights systematically violates the public welfare, this is prima facie evidence that it ought not to exist. And this certainly seems to be the case with the exercise of certain property rights today.

In response to this problem, there is today at least talk of "a new economy of resources," one in which new considerations and values play an important role along with property rights and the interplay of market forces. Economist Nathaniel Wollman argues that "the economic past of 'optimizing' resource use consists of bringing into an appropriate relationship the ordering of preferences for various experiences and the costs of acquiring those experiences. Preferences reflect physiological-psychological responses to experience or anticipated experience, individually or collectively revealed, and are accepted as data by the economist. A broad range of noneconomic investigations is called for to supply the necessary information."[8]

Note that Wollman says that noneconomic investigations are called for. In other words the price system does not adequately account for a number of value factors which should be included in an assessment. "It does not account for benefits or costs that are enjoyed or suffered by people who were not parties to the transaction."[9] In a system which emphasizes simply the interplay of market forces as a criterion, these factors (such as sights, smells and other aesthetic factors, justice, and human rights—

---

7. Some rights, I would argue, are inalienable, and are not based merely on a contract (implicit or explicit) or merely upon the norm of maximizing good consequences. (See David Braybrooke's *Three Tests for Democracy: Personal Rights, Human Welfare, Collective Preference* (New York: Random House, 1968), which holds such a rule-utilitarian theory of rights, and my "Human Rights and Human Dignity," for a rebuttal.)
8. Nathaniel Wollman, "The New Economics of Resources," *Daedalus* 96, pt. 2, (Fall 1967): 1100.
9. Ibid.

factors which are important to the well-being of humans) are not even considered. Since they have no direct monetary value, the market places no value whatsoever on them. Can we assume, then, that purely economic or market evaluations provide us with data which will permit us to maximize welfare, if the very process of evaluation and the normative criteria employed exclude a host of values and considerations upon which human welfare depend? The answer to this question is plain. We cannot make this assumption. We cannot rely merely upon the interplay of market forces or upon the sovereignty of the consumer. The concept of human welfare and consequently the notion of maximizing that welfare requires a much broader perspective than the norms offered by the traditional economic perspective. A great many things have value and use which have no economic value and use. Consequently we must broaden our evaluation perspective to include the entire range of values which are essential not only to the welfare of man but also to the welfare of other living things and to the environment which sustains all of life. And this must include a reassessment of rights.

Ethics and Technology

I have been discussing the relationship of ecology to ethics and to a theory of rights. Up to this point I have not specifically discussed the relation of technology to ethics, although it is plain that technology and its development is responsible for most of our pollution problems. This topic deserves separate treatment, but I do want to briefly relate it to the thesis of this work.

It is well known that new technology sometimes complicates our ethical lives and our ethical decisions. Whether the invention is the wheel or a contraceptive pill, new technology always opens up new possibilities for human relationships and for society, for good and ill. The pill, for example, is revolutionizing sexual morality, for its use can preclude many of the bad consequences normally attendant upon premarital intercourse. *Some* of the strongest arguments against premarital sex have been shot down by this bit of technology (though certainly not all of them). The fact that the use of

the pill can prevent unwanted pregnancy does not make premarital sexual intercourse morally right, nor does it make it wrong. The pill is morally neutral, but its existence does change in part the moral base of the decision to engage in premarital sex. In the same way, technology at least in principle can be neutral—neither necessarily good nor bad in its impact on other aspects of the environment. Unfortunately, much of it is bad—very bad. But technology can be meshed with an ecological attitude to the benefit of man and his environment.

I am not suggesting that the answer to technology which has bad environmental effects is necessarily more technology. We tend too readily to assume that new technological developments will always solve man's problems. But this is simply not the case. One technological innovation often seems to breed a half-dozen additional ones which themselves create more environmental problems. We certainly do not solve pollution problems, for example, by changing from power plants fueled by coal to power plants fueled by nuclear energy, if radioactive waste from the latter is worse than pollution from the former. Perhaps part of the answer to pollution problems is less technology. There is surely no real hope of returning to nature (whatever that means) or of stopping *all* technological and scientific development, as some advocate. Even if it could be done, this would be too extreme a move. The answer is not to stop technology, but to guide it toward proper ends, and to set up standards of antipollution to which all technological devices must conform. Technology has been and can be used to destroy and pollute an environment, but it can also be used to save and beautify it. What is called for is purposeful environmental engineering, and this engineering calls for a mass of information about our environment, about the needs of persons, and about basic norms and values which are acceptable to civilized men. It also calls for priorities on goals and for compromise where there are competing and conflicting values and objectives. Human rights and their fulfillment should constitute at least some of those basic norms, and technology can be used to implement those rights and the public welfare.

Study Questions

1. Do human beings have a right to a livable environment?

2. Should our understanding of property rights be changed?

Moral Dilemmas

- While doing investigative reporting for a local newspaper, you discover that the local drug company is illegally polluting the river running through town. The pollution could cause birth defects in future generations. You threaten to go public with the information unless the company stops the pollution. The company president tells you that the local politicians know about it and have let it go on because the firm makes large campaign contributions to their election funds. Furthermore, the company would rather move to a location where there are less restrictive pollution laws than pay the extra costs to reduce pollution. If the company does move, five thousand people will lose their jobs.

  What should you do?

- Dennis is an engineer working for a large chemical company. He discovers one day that his company is secretly dumping carcinogenic wastes at night from a truck driving through the back roads of the community. He tells his immediate superior about this illegal activity, but his supervisor tells him that if he wants to keep his job, he better say no more about it. Dennis is fifty years old, married, and has two children to put through college; he can't really afford to lose his job.

  What should Dennis do?
  What recommendations would you make to prevent this kind of problem in the future?

- You are at an important meeting during which your boss takes credit for the ideas of a friend who is not at the meeting. You are due for a promotion.

  Do you defend your friend at the meeting?

Suggested Readings

Baum, Robert and Flores, Albert. *Ethical Problems in Engineering*. London: Routledge and Kegan Paul, 1965.

Grčić, Joseph, "The Ethics of Financing Elections," *The Southern Journal of Philosophy,* v. 25, N.3, 1987.

Passmore, John. *Man's Responsibility for Nature.*
New York: Scribner's, 1974.

Singer, Peter. *Animal Liberation*. New York: *New York Review,* 1975.

Shrader-Frechette, K. S. *Environmental Ethics.*
Pacific Grove, CA: Boxwood Press, 1981.

Walter, Edward. *The Immorality of Limiting Growth*. Albany: State University of New York Press, 1981.

Pornography

One of the most troublesome questions in political philosophy is the proper limit to freedom of expression. We are all familiar with the right to free speech and press as an essential component of a free and democratic society; yet, should one be free to publish and make films about explicit sexual behavior?

Background

Pornography, understood to be the depiction of sexual behavior in an erotic manner with intent to arouse sexual desire in the reader or viewer, has existed probably as long as humanity itself. Ancient Greek and Roman poetry and plays often used explicit sexual references for purposes of entertainment and arousal. The Greek festival in honor of the god Dionysus included many salacious events and poetry readings. Archeologists have found painted scenes and sculptures of sexual intercourse on the walls of the ancient city of Pompeii as well as on the walls of Hindu temples in India. Some of the writings of the Roman poet Ovid (43 B.C.–A.D. 18) are considered classic erotica. Although the growth of Christianity in Europe made erotica morally and legally unacceptable, it continued to exist through the Middle Ages. For example, Boccaccio's (1313–1375) *Decameron* is now generally accepted as a literary masterpiece with erotic content. The invention of printing by movable type in the fifteenth century made all types of literary works more available and affordable. Technological innovations such as the invention of photography in the nineteenth century, the motion picture in the twentieth, and even more recently, the videocassette recorder, combined with changes in social attitudes toward sexuality, have contributed immensely to the proliferation of erotica.

Laws concerning pornography have had a long history in the United States. Massachusetts had anti-pornography laws even in colonial times, but federal laws against it were not passed until the nineteenth century. Since then, public attitudes toward sexuality and sexually explicit materials have gradually changed toward greater tolerance, especially since the suppression of several literary works such as James Joyce's *Ulysses,* D. H. Lawrence's *Lady Chatterley's Lover,* and others that are generally regarded today as great literary works.

In 1968 President Richard Nixon appointed a panel of experts to study pornography. The Presidential Commission on Obscenity and Pornography reported its findings in 1970, but not all members of the commission agreed. A majority of twelve members recommended that all laws prohibiting the sale, distribution, and exhibition of erotic materials to consenting adults be repealed. They found no evidence that pornography causes antisocial behavior such as rape. On the positive side, they argued that erotica is a source of entertainment and a sexual aid for many married adults. Furthermore, they believed pornography to be undefinable and laws against it to be contrary to the constitutional right to free speech and press. They did however argue against child pornography and the public display of erotica to people who do not wish to see such materials.

The minority of eight on the Presidential Commission disagreed with many of the findings of the majority report. They claimed that the majority was biased and ignored the scientific evidence that showed a causal link between exposure to pornography and rape. Many sex offenders who were interviewed claimed that viewing pornography was a factor in their sex crimes.

In 1986 the U.S. government completed another study on pornography and came to quite different conclusions. The Attorney General's Commission on Pornography concluded that pornography can lead to sexual violence such as rape and that it degrades women. In addition, the Commission found a strong link between pornography and organized crime. The report also condemned the sexual promiscuity that is depicted in most pornographic films. The Commission recommended new laws to restrict pornography and to abolish child pornography.

As in the earlier report, not all members of the Commission agreed with the above conclusions, and many others criticized it. The critics argued that rape is probably caused more by widespread violence in our society than by violence found in pornographic films. The critics referred to countries in Europe where few or no restrictions on sexually explicit materials are in effect. The decreasing rape rate in these countries supports a more liberal attitude toward pornography.

Conservative Position: Supreme Court Majority

The Supreme Court struggled with the question of pornography for a long time. In *Roth v. the United States* (1957), the Court first attempted to define pornography as material that is offensive by community standards and that has no redeeming social value. This definition, of course, is rather vague. In the next case, *Miller v. the State of California* (1973), the Court tried again to define pornography. Justice Warren Burger wrote the majority opinion in which he defined pornography as a work that:
(1) the average person applying contemporary community standards would find arouses lust,
(2) depicts sexual conduct in an offensive way, and
(3) as a whole, lacks serious literary, artistic, political, or scientific value (LAPS test). Burger used this definition again in the case of *Paris Adult Theatre I v. Slaton* (1973). He argued that the state has a right to protect the community against influences that corrupt or debase family values and public safety. Here Burger was referring to the apparent tendency of pornography theatres to attract criminal types, including prostitutes and drug dealers. Burger went on to argue that the right to privacy did not protect pornography in this case because the case involved a public theatre. The majority further claimed that the First Amendment of the Constitution does not protect public expression that lacks literary, artistic,

political, or scientific (LAPS) value. Burger concluded from this that the individual states may, if they choose, restrict pornography in public places.

Supreme Court Minority

Justice William Brennan wrote the minority view in the same case, criticizing several of Burger's claims. One of the first problems he emphasized was the definition of pornography. The question he posed was, how do we decide whether something has literary or artistic value? Is there an objective test for art and literature? Furthermore, according to Brennan, the evidence did not prove that pornography leads to sex crimes such as rape. As for the right of privacy, Brennan maintained that no one forces others to go to a theatre to view pornography, and if consenting adults want to view sexually explicit films in a theatre, they should be allowed to do this. Finally, according to Brennan, the First Amendment was passed to protect all ideas, not just those that conform to the status quo or to traditional beliefs.

Moderate Position: Ann Garry

Burger and Brennan have suggested important points to consider about pornography. Issues of definition, privacy, free speech, and crime are all relevant for assessing the question of pornography. However, the issue of how pornography treats women remains. Ann Garry argues that pornography as it generally now exists degrades women. Pornography treats women as mere sex objects and recommends that women be treated as such. To treat anyone as a sex object degrades that person by depicting him or her as less than a full person. Garry goes on to point out that large segments of our culture still believe that sex is dirty and that a woman who enjoys sex is immoral. Thus, pornography promotes a stereotype that further harms women. However, Garry concedes that pornography does not have to degrade women if it presents men and women as having equal value and treats them with equal respect, not as objects of sexual pleasure for men.

Garry's paper brings out a possible aspect of pornography that the Court has not considered yet.

Does pornography degrade women? How can we be sure? Is pornography that influential in forming the attitudes and beliefs that people have about women and sex? What if someone freely chooses to be degraded and used as a sex object? But even granting Garry's point, how would a free-market society implement her proposal for nonsexist pornography? Would sexist pornography be outlawed? Who would decide what is sexist?

Liberal Position: G. L. Simons

G. L. Simons claims that we must look not just at the possible harm but also at the possible benefits of pornography. Simons believes that pornography can produce many positive consequences. The pleasure people get from viewing or reading pornography is a benefit, unless one believes in a form of puritanism or asceticism that holds that pleasure is immoral. Second, pornography can help people to develop their sexuality, and it can educate them to be more open to sexual experience. Inhibitions restrict one's ability to enjoy sex, and pornography can help to remove these inhibitions. Simons further suggests that there are lonely people who, for whatever reasons, do not have a sex partner and for whom pornography can provide a sexual outlet and release without which they may be more likely to commit rape or other violent acts out of frustration. Just as a person is innocent until proven guilty, so Simons concludes, pornography is a cultural phenomenon that must be allowed until it is proven guilty.

Simons presents some relevant ideas for our considerations, but questions still persist as to whether a connection exists between exposure to pornography and sex crimes. The majority of the members of the Commission on Obscenity and Pornography appointed by President Nixon in 1968 reported that no evidence shows that pornography causes antisocial or criminal behavior, whereas the Attorney General's report in 1986 claimed that such a link can be shown. Which report is right? How can we prove that a specific experience (viewing pornography) caused a crime (rape) and that the crime was not caused by some other experience or personality trait? Would the incidence of rape be reduced if pornography no longer existed?

The debate over pornography involves three central concerns: sex, freedom, and equality. Human beings are sexual creatures. Sexual expression is part of one's identity as a person and a fundamental way of relating to others. The right to freedom is the right to self-expression in politics, religion, art, and other areas, but it is usually limited. What the limit is depends on the overall political philosophy that informs the lawmakers of that society. Physical harm is recognized by most societies as a limit, but others add restrictions based on religious and moral beliefs. The controversy over pornography is partly factual (whether it causes rape and other crimes), partly moral (based on a religious moral system or a secular one), and partly political (whether it degrades women). The political aspect concerns the issue of the equality of men and women. Although pornography need not be sexist, most of it is, according to feminists. How one decides these questions for oneself will determine one's outlook on pornography.

Majority Opinion in *Paris Adult Theatre I v. Slaton*

Justice Warren Burger is a former Chief Justice of the U.S. Supreme Court who served from 1969 to 1986.

Chief Justice Warren Burger

We categorically disapprove the theory, apparently adopted by the trial judge, that obscene, pornographic films acquire constitutional immunity from state regulation simply because they are exhibited for consenting adults only. This holding was properly rejected by the Georgia Supreme Court. Although we have often pointedly recognized the high importance of the state interest in regulating the exposure of obscene materials to juveniles and unconsenting adults, this Court has never declared these to be the only legitimate state interests permitting regulation of obscene material. The States have a long-recognized legitimate interest in regulating the use of obscene material in local commerce and in all places of public accommodation, as long as these regulations do not run afoul of specific constitutional prohibitions. "In an unbroken series of cases extending over a long stretch of this Court's history, it has been accepted as a postulate that 'the primary requirements of decency may be enforced against obscene publications.'"

In particular, we hold that there are legitimate state interests at stake in stemming the tide of commercialized obscenity, even assuming it is feasible to enforce effective safeguards against exposure to juveniles and to the passerby. Rights and interests "other than those of the advocates are involved." These include the interest of the public in the quality of life and the total community environment, the tone of commerce in the great city centers, and, possibly, the public safety itself. The Hill-Link Minority Report of the Commission on Obscenity and Pornography indicates that there is at least an arguable correlation between obscene material and crime. Quite apart from sex crimes, however, there remains one problem of large proportions aptly described by Professor Bickel:

United States Supreme Court. 413 U.S. 49 (1973).

It concerns the tone of the society, the mode, or to use terms that have perhaps greater currency, the style and quality of life, now and in the future. A man may be entitled to read an obscene book in his room, or expose himself indecently there.... We should protect his privacy. But if he demands a right to obtain the books and pictures he wants in the market and to foregather in public places—discreet, if you will, but accessible to all—with others who share his tastes, *then to grant him his right is to affect the world about the rest of us, and to impinge on other privacies.* Even supposing that each of us can, if he wishes, effectively avert the eye and stop the ear (which, in truth, we cannot), what is commonly read and seen and heard and done intrudes upon us all, want it or not.

The Public Interest 25, 25–26 (Winter, 1971). (Emphasis supplied.)

As Chief Justice Warren stated there is a "right of the Nation and of the States to maintain a decent society...."

But, it is argued, there is no scientific data which conclusively demonstrates that exposure to obscene materials adversely affects men and women or their society. It is urged on behalf of the petitioner that, absent such a demonstration, any kind of state regulation is "impermissible." We reject this argument. It is not for us to resolve empirical uncertainties underlying state legislation, save in the exceptional case where that legislation plainly impinges upon rights protected by the Constitution itself. Mr. Justice Brennan, speaking for the Court in *Ginberg v. New York* (1968), said "We do not demand of legislatures 'scientifically certain criteria of legislation.'" Although there is no conclusive proof of a connection between antisocial behavior and obscene material, the legislature of Georgia could quite reasonably determine that such a connection does or might exist....

If we accept the unprovable assumption that a complete education requires the reading of certain books, and the well nigh universal belief that good books, plays, and art lift the spirit, improve the mind, enrich the human personality and develop character, can we then say that a state legislature may not act on the corollary assumption that commerce in obscene books, or public exhibitions focused on obscene conduct, have a tendency to exert a corrupting and debasing impact leading to antisocial behavior? "Many of these effects may be intangible and indistinct, but they are nonetheless real." Mr. Justice Cardozo said that all laws in Western civilization are "guided by a robust common sense...." The sum of experience, including that of the past two decades, affords an ample basis for legislatures to conclude that a sensitive, key relationship of human existence, central to family life, community welfare, and the development of human personality, can be debased and distorted by crass commercial exploitation of sex. Nothing in the Constitution prohibits a State from reaching such a conclusion and acting on it legislatively simply because there is no conclusive evidence or empirical data.

It is argued that individual "free will" must govern, even in activities beyond the protection of the First Amendment and other constitutional guarantees of privacy, and that Government cannot legitimately impede an individual's desire to see or acquire obscene plays, movies, and books. We do indeed base our society on certain assumptions that people have the capacity for free choice. Most exercises of individual free choice—those in politics, religion, and expression of ideas—are explicitly protected by the Constitution. Totally unlimited play for free will, however, is not allowed in ours or any other society. We have just noted, for example, that neither the First Amendment nor "free will" precludes States from having "blue sky" laws to regulate what sellers of securities may write or publish about their wares. Such laws are to protect the weak, the uninformed, the unsuspecting, and the gullible from the exercise of their own volition. Nor do modern societies leave disposal of garbage and sewage up to the individual "free will," but impose regulation to protect both public health and the appearance of public places. States are told by some that they must await a "laissez faire" market solution to the obscenity-pornography problem, paradoxically "by people who have never otherwise had a kind word to say for laissez-faire," particularly in solving urban, commercial, and environmental pollution problems.

The States, of course, may follow such a "laissez faire" policy and drop all controls on commercialized obscenity, if that is what they prefer, just as they can ignore consumer protection in the market place, but nothing in the Constitution *compels* the States to do so with regard to matters falling within state jurisdiction. . . .

It is asserted, however, that standards for evaluating state commercial regulations are inapposite in the present context, as state regulation of access by consenting adults to obscene material violates the constitutionally protected right to privacy enjoyed by petitioners' customers. Even assuming that petitioners have vicarious standing to assert potential customers' rights, it is unavailing to compare a theatre, open to the public for a fee, with the private home of *Stanley v. Georgia* (1969) and the marital bedroom of *Griswold v. Connecticut* (1965). This Court, has, on numerous occasions, refused to hold that commercial ventures such as a motion-picture house are "private" for the purpose of civil rights litigation and civil rights statutes. The Civil Rights Act of 1964 specifically defines motion-picture houses and theatres as places of "public accommodation" covered by the Act as operations affecting commerce.

Our prior decisions recognizing a right to privacy guaranteed by the Fourteenth Amendment included "only those personal rights that can be deemed 'fundamental' or 'implicit in the concept of ordered liberty.'" This privacy right encompasses and protects the personal intimacies of the home, the family, marriage, motherhood, procreation, and child rearing. Nothing, however, in this Court's decisions intimates that there is any "fundamental" privacy right "implicit in the concept of ordered liberty" to watch obscene movies in places of public accommodation.

If obscene material unprotected by the First Amendment in itself carried with it a "penumbra" of constitutionally protected privacy, this Court would not have found it necessary to decide *Stanley* on the narrow basis of the "privacy of the home," which was hardly more than a reaffirmation that "a man's home is his castle." Moreover, we have declined to equate the privacy of the home relied on in *Stanley* with a "zone" of "privacy" that follows a distributor or a consumer of obscene materials wherever he goes. The idea of a "privacy" right and a place of public accommodation are, in this context, mutually exclusive. Conduct or depictions of

conduct that the state police power can prohibit on a public street does not become automatically protected by the Constitution merely because the conduct is moved to a bar or a "live" theatre stage, any more than a "live" performance of a man and woman locked in a sexual embrace at high noon in Times Square is protected by the Constitution because they simultaneously engage in a valid political dialogue.

". . . [W]e have today reaffirmed the basic holding of Roth v. United States *(1957) that obscene material has no protection under the First Amendment."*

It is also argued that the State has no legitimate interest in "control [of] the moral content of a person's thoughts," and we need not quarrel with this. But we reject the claim that the State of Georgia is here attempting to control the minds or thoughts of those who patronize theatres. Preventing unlimited display or distribution of obscene material, which by definition lacks any serious literary, artistic, political, or scientific value as communication, is distinct from a control of reason and the intellect. Where communication of ideas, protected by the First Amendment, is not involved, nor the particular privacy of the home protected by *Stanley,* nor any of the other "areas or zones" of constitutionally protected privacy, the mere fact that, as a consequence, some human "utterances" or "thoughts" may be incidentally affected does not bar the State from acting to protect legitimate state interests. The fantasies of a drug addict are his own and beyond the reach of government, but government regulation of drug sales is not prohibited by the Constitution.

Finally, petitioners argue that conduct which directly involves "consenting adults" only has, for that sole reason, a special claim to constitutional protection. Our Constitution establishes a broad range of conditions on the exercise of power by the states, but for us to say that our Constitution incorporates the proposition that conduct involving consenting adults only is always beyond state regulation, that is a step we are unable to take. Commercial exploitation of depictions, descriptions, or exhibitions of obscene conduct on commercial premises open to the adult public falls within a State's broad power to regulate commerce and protect the public environment. The issue in this context goes beyond whether someone, or even the majority, considers the conduct depicted as "wrong" or "sinful." The States have the power to make a morally neutral judgment that public exhibition of obscene material, or commerce in such material, has a tendency to injure the community as a whole, to endanger the public safety, or to jeopardize in Chief Justice Warren's words, the States' "right . . . to maintain a decent society."

To summarize, we have today reaffirmed the basic holding of *Roth v. United States* (1957) that obscene material has no protection under the First Amendment. We have directed our holdings, not at thoughts or speech, but at depiction and description of specifically defined sexual conduct that States may regulate within limits designed to prevent infringement of First Amendment rights. We have also reaffirmed the holdings of *United States v. Reidel* (1971) and *United States v. Thirty-Seven Photographs* (1971) that commerce in obscene material is unprotected by any constitutional doctrine of privacy. In this case we hold that the States have a legitimate interest in regulating commerce in obscene material and in regulating exhibition of obscene material in places of public accommodation, including so-called "adult" theatres from which minors are excluded. In light of these holdings, nothing precludes the State of Georgia from the regulation of the allegedly obscene materials exhibited in Paris Adult Theatre I and II, provided that the applicable Georgia law, as written or authoritatively interpreted by the Georgia courts, meets the First Amendment standards set forth in *Miller v. California* (1973). . . .

Study Questions

1. Is pornography protected by the right to free speech?

2. Does pornography have a corrupting influence on society? How can one prove or disprove this?

3. Do people focus too much on sexually explicit materials and not enough on violence in our society?

Dissenting Opinion in *Paris Adult Theatre I v. Slaton*

A graduate of Harvard Law School, Justice William Brennan became an Associate Justice of the U.S. Supreme Court in 1956.

Justice William Brennan

Our experience since *Roth v. United States* (1957) requires us not only to abandon the effort to pick

United States Supreme Court. 413 U.S. 49 (1973).

out obscene materials on a case-by-case basis, but also to reconsider a fundamental postulate of *Roth:* that there exists a definable class of sexually oriented expression that may be totally suppressed by the Federal and State Governments. Assuming that such a class of expression does in fact exist, I am forced to conclude that the concept of "obscenity" cannot be defined with sufficient specificity and clarity to provide fair notice to persons who create and distribute sexually oriented materials, to prevent substantial erosion of protected speech as a byproduct of the attempt to suppress unprotected speech, and to avoid very costly institutional harms. Given these inevitable side-effects of state efforts to suppress what is assumed to be *unprotected* speech, we must scrutinize with care the state interest that is asserted to justify the suppression. For in the absence of some very substantial interest in suppressing such speech, we can hardly condone the ill-effects that seem to flow inevitably from the effort. . . .

Because we assumed—incorrectly, as experience has proven—that obscenity could be separated from other sexually oriented expression without significant costs either to the First Amendment or to the judicial machinery charged with the task of safeguarding First Amendment freedoms, we had no occasion in *Roth* to probe the asserted state interest in curtailing unprotected, sexually oriented speech. Yet as we have increasingly come to appreciate the vagueness of the concept of obscenity, we have begun to recognize and articulate the state interests at stake. Significantly, in *Redrup v. New York* (1967), where we set aside findings of obscenity with regard to three sets of material, we pointed out that

> [i]n none of the cases was there a claim that the statute in question reflected a specific and limited state concern for juveniles. In none was there any suggestion of an assault upon individual privacy by publication in a manner so obtrusive as to make it impossible for an unwilling individual to avoid exposure to it. And in none was there evidence of the sort of 'pandering' which the Court found significant in *Ginzburg v. United States* (1966).

The opinions in *Redrup* and *Stanley v. Georgia* (1969) reflected our emerging view that the state interests in protecting children and in protecting un-

consenting adults may stand on a different footing from the other asserted state interests. . . .

But whatever the strength of the state interests in protecting juveniles and unconsenting adults from exposure to sexually oriented materials, those interests cannot be asserted in defense of the holding of the Georgia Supreme Court in this case. The court assumed for the purposes of its decision that the films in issue were exhibited only to persons over the age of 21 who viewed them willingly and with prior knowledge of the nature of their contents. And on that assumption the state court held that the films could still be suppressed. The justification for the suppression must be found, therefore, in some independent interest in regulating the reading and viewing habits of consenting adults.

At the outset it should be noted that virtually all of the interests that might be asserted in defense of suppression, laying aside the special interests associated with distribution to juveniles and unconsenting adults, were also posited in *Stanley v. Georgia* where we held that the State could not make the "mere private possession of obscene material a crime." That decision presages the conclusions I reach here today.

> "... [T]he concept of 'obscenity' cannot be defined with sufficient specificity and clarity ..."

In *Stanley* we pointed out that "[t]here appears to be little empirical basis for" the assertion that "exposure to obscene materials may lead to deviant sexual behavior or crimes of sexual violence." In any event, we added that "if the State is only concerned about printed or filmed materials inducing antisocial conduct, we believe that in the context of private consumption of ideas and information we should adhere to the view that '[a]mong free men, the deterrents ordinarily to be applied to prevent crime are education and punishment for violations of the law. . . .'"

Moreover, in *Stanley* we rejected as "wholly inconsistent with the philosophy of the First Amendment," the notion that there is a legitimate state concern in the "control [of] the moral content of a person's thoughts," and we held that a State "cannot constitutionally premise legislation on the desirability of controlling a person's private thoughts." That is not to say, of course, that a State must remain utterly indifferent to—and take no action bearing on—the morality of the community. The traditional description of state police power does embrace the regulation of morals as well as the health, safety, and general welfare of the citizenry. And much legislation—compulsory public education laws, civil rights laws, even the abolition of capital punishment—are grounded at least in part of a concern with the morality of the community. But the State's interest in regulating morality by suppressing obscenity, while often asserted, remains essentially unfocused and ill-defined. And, since the attempt to curtail unprotected speech necessarily spills over into the area of protected speech, the effort to serve this speculative interest through the suppression of obscene material must tread heavily on rights protected by the First Amendment.

In *Roe v. Wade* (1973), we held constitutionally invalid a state abortion law, even though we were aware of

the sensitive and emotional nature of the abortion controversy, of the vigorous opposing views, even among physicians, and of the deep and seemingly absolute convictions that the subject inspires. One's philosophy, one's experiences, one's exposure to the raw edges of human existence, one's religious training, one's attitudes toward life and family and their values, and the moral standards one establishes and seeks to observe, are all likely to influence and to color one's thinking and conclusions about abortion.

Like the proscription of abortions, the effort to suppress obscenity is predicated on unprovable, although strongly held, assumptions about human behavior, morality, sex, and religion. The existence of these assumptions cannot validate a statute that substantially undermines the guarantees of the First Amendment, any more than the existence of similar assumptions on the issue of abortion can validate a

statute that infringes the constitutionally protected privacy interests of a pregnant woman.

If, as the Court today assumes, "a state legislature may ... act on the ... assumption that ... commerce in obscene books, or public exhibitions focused on obscene conduct, have a tendency to exert a corrupting and debasing impact leading to antisocial behavior," then it is hard to see how state-ordered regimentation of our minds can ever be forestalled. For if a State may, in an effort to maintain or create a particular moral tone, prescribe what its citizens cannot read or cannot see, then it would seem to follow that in pursuit of that same objective a State could decree that its citizens must read certain books or must view certain films. However laudable its goal—and that is obviously a question on which reasonable minds may differ—the State cannot proceed by means that violate the Constitution....

Recognizing these principles, we have held that so-called thematic obscenity—obscenity which might persuade the viewer or reader to engage in "obscene" conduct—is not outside the protection of the First Amendment:

It is contended that the State's action was justified because the motion picture attractively portrays a relationship which is contrary to the moral standards, the religious precepts, and the legal code of its citizenry. This argument misconceives what it is that the Constitution protects. Its guarantee is not confined to the expression of ideas that are conventional or shared by a majority. It protects advocacy of the opinion that adultery may sometimes be proper, no less than advocacy of socialism or the single tax. And in the realm of ideas it protects expression which is eloquent no less than that which is unconvincing. *Kingsley Int'l Pictures Corp. v. Regents* (1959).

Even a legitimate, sharply focused state concern for the morality of the community cannot, in other words, justify an assault on the protections of the First Amendment. Where the state interest in regulation of morality is vague and ill-defined, interference with the guarantees of the First Amendment is even more difficult to justify.

In short, while I cannot say that the interests of the State—apart from the question of juveniles and unconsenting adults—are trivial or nonexistent, I am compelled to conclude that these interests cannot justify the substantial damage to constitutional rights and to this Nation's judicial machinery that inevitably results from state efforts to bar the distribution even of unprotected material to consenting adults. I would hold, therefore, that at least in the absence of distribution to juveniles or obtrusive exposure to unconsenting adults, the First and Fourteenth Amendments prohibit the state and federal governments from attempting wholly to suppress sexually oriented materials on the basis of their allegedly "obscene" contents. Nothing in this approach precludes those governments from taking action to serve what may be strong and legitimate interests through regulation of the manner of distribution of sexually oriented material.

Study Questions

1. Can pornography be defined?

2. Does exposure to pornography cause some to commit rape?

3. Is the LAPS test constitutional?

Pornography and Respect for Women

Ann Garry is a professor of philosophy at California State University at Los Angeles.

Ann Garry

Pornography, like rape, is a male invention, designed to dehumanize women, to reduce the female to an object of sexual access, not to free sensuality from moralistic or parental inhibition.... Pornography is the undiluted essence of anti-female propaganda.

> Susan Brownmiller, *Against Our Will: Men, Women and Rape*[1]

It is often asserted that a distinguishing characteristic of sexually explicit material is the degrading and demeaning portrayal of the role and status of the human female. It has been argued that erotic materials describe the female as a mere sexual object to be exploited and manipulated sexually.... A recent survey shows that 41 percent of American males and 46 percent of the females believe that "sexual materials lead people to lose respect for women."... Recent experi-

---

This article first appeared in *Social Theory and Practice,* 4 (Summer 1978). It is reprinted here as it appears in Sharon Bishop and Marjorie Weinzweig, eds. *Philosophy and Women* (Wadsworth, 1979). Reprinted by permission of the author.

---

1. (New York: Simon and Schuster, 1975), p. 394.

ments suggest that such fears are probably unwarranted.

Presidential Commission on Obscenity and Pornography[2]

The kind of apparent conflict illustrated in these passages is easy to find in one's own thinking as well. For example, I have been inclined to think that pornography is innocuous and to dismiss "moral" arguments for censoring it because many such arguments rest on an assumption I do not share—that sex is an evil to be controlled. At the same time I believe that it is wrong to exploit or degrade human beings, particularly women and others who are especially susceptible. So if pornography degrades human beings, then even if I would oppose its censorship I surely cannot find it morally innocuous.

In an attempt to resolve this apparent conflict I discuss three questions: Does pornography degrade (or exploit or dehumanize) human beings? If so, does it degrade women in ways or to an extent that it does not degrade men? If so, must pornography degrade women, as Brownmiller thinks, or could genuinely innocuous, nonsexist pornography exist? Although much current pornography does degrade women, I will argue that it is possible to have nondegrading, nonsexist pornography. However, this possibility rests on our making certain fundamental changes in our conceptions of sex and sex roles.

I

First, some preliminary remarks: Many people now avoid using 'pornography' as a descriptive term and reserve 'obscenity' for use in legal contexts. Because 'pornography' is thought to be a judgmental word, it is replaced by 'explicit sexual material,' 'sexually oriented materials,' 'erotica,' and so on.[3] I use 'pornography' to label those explicit sexual materials intended to arouse the reader or viewer sexually. I seriously doubt whether there is a clearly defined class of cases that fits my characterization of pornography. This does not bother me, for I am interested here in obvious cases that would be uncontroversially pornographic—the worst, least artistic kind. The pornography I discuss is that which, taken as a whole, lacks "serious literary, artistic, political, or scientific merit."[4] I often use pornographic films as examples because they generate more concern today than do books or magazines.

What interests me is not whether pornography should be censored but whether one can object to it on moral grounds. The only moral ground I consider is whether pornography degrades people; obviously, other possible grounds exist, but I find this one to be the most plausible.[5] Of the many kinds of degradation and exploitation possible in the production of pornography, I focus only on the content of the pornographic work. I exclude from this discussion (i) the ways in which pornographic film makers might exploit people in making a film, distributing it, and charging too much to see it; (ii) the likelihood that actors, actresses, or technicians will be exploited, underpaid, or made to lose self-respect or self-esteem; and (iii) the exploitation and degradation surrounding the prostitution and crime that often accompany urban centers of pornography.[6] I want to determine whether pornography shows (expresses) and commends behavior or atti-

---

4. *Roth v. United States,* 354 U.S. 476, 489 (1957).

5. To degrade someone in this situation is to lower her/his rank or status in humanity. This is morally objectionable because it is incompatible with showing respect for a person. Some of the other moral grounds for objecting to pornography have been considered by the Supreme Court: Pornography invades our privacy and hurts the moral tone of the community. See *Paris Adult Theatre I v. Slaton,* 413 U.S. 49 (1973). Even less plausible than the Court's position is to say that pornography is immoral because it depicts sex, depicts an immoral kind of sex, or caters to voyeuristic tendencies. I believe that even if moral objections to pornography exist, one must preclude any simple inference from "pornography is immoral" to "pornography should be censored" because of other important values and principles such as freedom of expression and self-determination.

6. See Gail Sheehy, *Hustling* (New York: Dell, 1971) for a good discussion of prostitution, crime, and pornography.

---

2. *The Report of the Commission on Obscenity and Pornography* (Washington, D.C., 1970), p. 201. Hereinafter, *Report.*

3. *Report,* p. 3, n. 4; and p. 149.

tudes that exploit or degrade people. For example, if a pornographic film conveys that raping a woman is acceptable, then the content is degrading to women and might be called morally objectionable. Morally objectionable content is not peculiar to pornography; it can also be found in nonpornographic books, films, advertisements, and so on. The question is whether morally objectionable content is necessary to pornography.

II

At the beginning of this paper, I quoted part of a passage in which the Presidential Commission on Obscenity and Pornography tried to allay our fears that pornography will lead people to lose respect for women. Here is the full passage:

> It is often asserted that a distinguishing characteristic of sexually explicit material is the degrading and demeaning portrayal of the role and status of the human female. It has been argued that erotic materials describe the female as a mere sexual object to be exploited and manipulated sexually.
>
> One presumed consequence of such portrayals is that erotica transmits an inaccurate and uninformed conception of sexuality, and that the viewer or user will (a) develop a calloused and manipulative orientation toward women and (b) engage in behavior in which affection and sexuality are not well integrated. A recent survey shows that 41% of American males and 46% of the females believe that "sexual materials lead people to lose respect for women" (Abelson, *et al.* 1970). Recent experiments (Mosher 1970a, b; Mosher and Katz 1970) suggest that such fears are probably unwarranted.[7]

The argument to which the Commission addresses itself begins with the assumption that pornography presents a degrading portrayal of women as sex objects. If users of pornography adopt the view that women are sex objects (or already believe it and allow pornography to reinforce their beliefs), they will develop an attitude of callousness and lack

of respect for women and will be more likely to treat women as sex objects to be manipulated and exploited. In this argument the moral objection to be brought against pornography lies in the objectionable character of the acquired attitudes and the increased likelihood of objectionable behavior— treating women as mere sex objects to be exploited rather than as persons to be respected.

A second moral argument, which does not interest the Commission, is that pornography is morally objectionable because it exemplifies and recommends behavior that violates the moral principle to respect persons. This argument contains no reference to immoral consequences; there need be no increased likelihood of behavior degrading to women. Pornography itself treats women not as whole persons but as mere sex objects "to be exploited and manipulated sexually." Such treatment is a "degrading and demeaning portrayal of the role and status" (and humanity) of women.

I will explain and discuss the first argument here and the second argument in Part III of this paper. The first argument depends on an empirical premise—that viewing pornography leads to an increase in "sex calloused" attitudes and behavior.[8] My discussion of this premise consists of four parts: (1) examples of some who accept the premise (Susan Brownmiller and the Supreme Court); (2) evidence presented for its denial by Donald Mosher for the Presidential Commission; (3) a critical examination of Mosher's studies; and (4) a concluding argument that, regardless of who (Mosher or Brownmiller) is correct, moral grounds exist for objecting to pornography.

1

Although I know of no social scientist whose data support the position that pornography leads to an increase in sex calloused behavior and attitudes, this view has popular support. For example, the

---

7. *Report,* p. 201. References cited can be found in notes 12, 13, 14, and 22, below.

8. 'Sex callousness' is a term used by Donald Mosher in the studies to be discussed here. See notes 12 and 13 below. Although the concept of sex callousness will be explained later, the core of the meaning is obvious: To be a sex calloused male is to have attitudes toward women (e.g., lack of respect) conducive to exploiting them sexually.

Presidential Commission survey cited above finds it supported by 41 percent of American males and 46 percent of the females. In addition, passages from both Susan Brownmiller and the United States Supreme Court illustrate a similar but more inclusive view: that use of pornography leads to sex callousness or lack of respect for women (or something worse) and that we do not need social scientists to confirm or deny it.

The following passage from Brownmiller forms part of her support for the position that liberals should rethink their position on pornography because pornography is anti-female propaganda:

> The majority report of the President's Commission on Obscenity and Pornography tried to pooh-pooh the opinion of law enforcement agencies around the country that claimed their own concrete experience with offenders who were caught with the stuff led them to conclude that pornographic material is a causative factor in crimes of sexual violence. The commission maintained that it was not possible at this time to scientifically prove or disprove such a connection.
>
> But does one need scientific methodology in order to conclude that the anti-female propaganda that permeates our nation's cultural output promotes a climate in which acts of sexual hostility directed against women are not only tolerated but ideologically encouraged?[9]

In at least two 1973 opinions, the Supreme Court tried to speak to the relevance of empirical data. They considered antisocial acts in general, without any thought that "sex calloused" behavior would be particularly antisocial. In *Kaplan v. California,* the Court said:

> A state could reasonably regard the "hard-core" conduct described by *Suite 69* as capable of encouraging or causing anti-social behavior, especially in its impact on young people. States need not wait until behavioral experts or educators can provide empirical data before enacting controls of commerce in obscene materials unprotected by the First Amendment or by a constitutional right to privacy. We have noted the power

of a legislative body to enact such regulatory law on the basis of unprovable assumptions.[10]

From *Paris Theatre I v. Slaton:*

> But, it is argued, there is no scientific data which conclusively demonstrates that exposure to obscene materials adversely affects men and women or their society. It is urged on behalf of the petitioner that, absent such a demonstration, any kind of state regulation is "impermissible." We reject this argument.... Although there is no conclusive proof of a connection between antisocial behavior and obscene material, the legislature of Georgia could quite reasonably determine that such a connection does or might exist.[11]

The disturbing feature of these passages is not the truth of the view that pornography leads to sex callousness but that the Court and Brownmiller seem to have succumbed to the temptation to disregard empirical data when the data fail to meet the authors' expectations. My intention in citing these passages is not to examine them but to remind the reader of how influential this kind of viewpoint is. For convenience I call it "Brownmiller's view"—the position that pornography provides a model for male sex calloused behavior and has numbing effect on the rest of us so that we tolerate sex calloused behavior more readily.

2

Donald L. Mosher has put forward evidence to deny that use of pornography leads to sex callousness or lack of respect for women.[12] In a study for the Presidential Commission, Mosher found that "sexually arousing pornographic films did not trigger sexual behavior even in the [sex calloused] college males whose attitudes toward women were more conducive to sexual exploitation" (p. 306), and that sex

---

9. Brownmiller, *Against Our Will,* p. 395.

10. 413 U.S. 115, 120 (1973).
11. 413 U.S. 49, 60–61.
12. "Psychological Reactions to Pornographic Films," *Technical Report of the Commission on Obscenity and Pornography,* vol. 8 (Washington, D.C., 1970), pp. 255–312. Hereinafter, *Tech. Report,* often cited by page number only in body of text.

calloused attitudes toward women decreased after the viewers saw pornographic films.

Mosher developed the operative concept of "sex callousness" in one study for the Commission,[13] then used the concept as part of a more comprehensive study of the effects of pornography.[14] In the second study Mosher rated his 194 unmarried undergraduate male subjects for "sex callousness." Men who have sex calloused attitudes approve of and engage in "the use of physical aggression and exploitative tactics such as falsely professing love, getting their dates drunk, or showing pornography to their dates as a means of gaining coitus" (pp. 305–6). Men rated high in sex callousness believe that sex is for fun, believe that love and sex are separate (p. 306), and agree to statements such as "Promise a woman anything, but give her your ___," When a woman gets uppity, it's time to ___ her, and "___ teasers should be raped" (p. 314, expletives deleted in report). Mosher suggests that this attitude is part of the "*Macho* syndrome" (p. 323).

The highly sex calloused men rated the two pornographic films they saw as more enjoyable and arousing, and less offensive or disgusting than did other subjects; but, like all of the subjects, these men did not increase their sexual activity. Mosher

found no increase in "frequencies of masturbation, heterosexual petting, oral-genital sex, or coitus" in the twenty-four hours after the subjects saw the two films.[15] He did not indicate whether a change occurred in the proportion of exploitative sexual behavior to nonexploitative sexual behavior.

In addition, the data from all the male subjects indicated a *decrease* in their sex calloused attitudes. The sharpest decrease occurred in the twenty-four hours after they saw the films. Two weeks later, their level of sex callousness was still lower than before they viewed the films. Although Mosher used several "equivalent" tests to measure callousness and did not explain the differences among them, the test I saw (*Form B*) was presumably typical: It measured the extent to which the subjects agreed or disagreed with statements such as "___ teasers should be raped."

Mosher's explanation for the decrease in sex calloused attitudes is, in his own words, "speculative." Sex callousness is an expression of "exaggerated masculine style" that occurs during a period of male development ("ideally followed by an integration of love with exploitative sex" [pp. 322–23]). During this period, men, especially young men without occupational success, use the "macho" conquest mentality to reassure themselves of their masculinity. Mosher thinks that seeing a pornographic film in the company of only men satisfies the need for macho behavior—the same need that is satisfied by exploiting women, endorsing calloused attitudes, telling "dirty" jokes, or boasting about one's sexual prowess. Thus the immediate need to affirm the sex calloused statements about women decreases once the men have seen the pornographic films (pp. 322–23, 306–7).

3

For Mosher pornography is an outlet for the expression of calloused attitudes—not, as for Brownmiller, a model for calloused behavior. Some

---

13. "Sex Callousness toward Women," *Tech. Report,* vol. 8, pp. 313–25.

14. "Psychological Reactions to Pornographic Films." See note 12. Both of Mosher's experiments used the same questions to test "sex callousness"; I treat the experiments together, citing only page numbers in the body of the text. As far as I know, no other social scientists are working on the relationship between pornography and sex callousness toward women. Mosher made another study with Harvey Katz that is on even less secure ground. They asked undergraduate males to "aggress verbally" at female student assistants before and after seeing a pornographic film. No increase in verbal aggression occurred after they saw the film. The authors seem to be aware of many limitations of this study; particularly relevant here are the facts that only verbal aggression was tested and that the film did not show violent or aggressive behavior. "Pornographic Films, Male Verbal Aggression Against Women, and Guilt," *Tech. Report,* vol. 8, pp. 357–77.

15. *Tech. Report,* vol. 8, p. 255. In his "Conclusions" section, Mosher qualifies the claim that no increase occurred in sexual behavior for sex calloused males. He says that they "reported no increased heterosexual behavior" (p. 310).

of the limitations of Mosher's study are clear to him; others apparently are not. My comments on his study fall into three categories: the limitations of his design and method, difficulties with his conclusions about sexual behavior, and difficulties with his conclusions about calloused attitudes. I am not raising general methodological issues; for example, I do not ask what measures were used to prevent a subject's (or experimenter's) civil libertarian beliefs from influencing a subject's tendency to show less calloused attitudes after seeing the films.

Limitations of Design and Method   (i) Mosher's was a very short-term study: His last questions were asked of subjects two weeks after they saw the pornographic films. But since pornography is supposed to provide only a temporary outlet, this limitation may not be crucial. (ii) Mosher believes that, given the standard of commercial pornography, the films he showed displayed more than the usual amount of affection and less than the usual amount of exploitative, "kinky," or exclusively male-oriented appeal. (iii) His test was designed only to measure the most readily testable, gross ways of talking callously about, and acting callously toward, women. Women, especially recently, have become aware of many more and less subtle ways in which men can express hostility and contempt for them. An obvious example is a man who would deny that "most women are cunts at heart" but would gladly talk about women as "chicks" or "foxes" to be captured, conquered, and toyed with. In short, many more men than Mosher thinks might well fall into the "sex calloused" class; and the questions asked of all the men should have included tests for more subtle forms of callousness.

Conclusions About Sexual Behavior   One of the most problematic parts of Mosher's study is that he did not test whether exploitative sexual behavior increased after the films were viewed; he tested only whether *any* sexual behavior increased and whether the endorsement of statements expressing calloused attitudes increased. One learns only that no increase occurred in the sexual behavior of the subjects (both calloused and not so calloused). One wants to know how the sex calloused men treated their partners after they saw the films; the frequency

of sex, increased or not, implies nothing about the quality of their treatment of their female partners. It is not enough for Mosher to tell us that a decrease occurred in endorsing statements expressing calloused attitudes. Mosher himself points out the gap between verbal behavior in the laboratory and behavior in real-life situations with one's chosen partners.[16]

Conclusions About Calloused Attitudes   (i) The most serious difficulty is one that Mosher recognizes: There was no control for the possibility that the men's level of sex callousness was unusually high in the beginning as a result of their anticipation of seeing pornographic films. (ii) Nor was there a control for the declining "shock value" of the statements expressing calloused attitudes. (iii) No precise indication of the relative decreases in sex calloused attitudes for the high- and low-callousness groups was given. Mosher states the differences for high- and low-guilt groups and has told us that highly calloused men tend to feel less guilt than other men;[17] however, one wants to know more precisely what the different effects were, particularly on the high-callousness group. (iv) Mosher realizes that his explanation for the decrease in calloused attitudes is still speculative. If seeing pornography with a group of men provides an outlet for callousness, there should be a control group of subjects seeing pornography while isolated from others. There should also be a control group experience not involving pornography at all. For example, subjects in such a group could watch a film about a Nazi concentration camp or about the first American presidents.

4

Although I am obviously critical of Mosher's work, let us suspend for a moment our critical judgment about his data and their interpretation. Even if the

---

16. "Pornographic Films, Male Verbal Aggression Against Women, and Guilt," *Tech. Report,* vol. 8, pp. 372–73.

17. *Tech. Report,* vol. 8, p. 274. The low-guilt subjects showed a rebound in sex callousness two weeks after seeing the films; however, the level of callousness still did not reach the prefilm level.

experience of seeing pornographic movies with other undergraduate men provides an opportunity to let out a small amount of male contempt and hostility toward women, very little follows from this for social policy or moral judgments. No sensible person would maintain that a temporary outlet is an adequate substitute for getting to the root of a problem. Given the existence of a large reservoir of male contempt and hostility toward women, and given that our society is still filled with pressures to "affirm one's manhood" at the expense of women, there is little reason to suppose a "cathartic" effect to be very significant here. Much of the research on the effects of pornography indicates that *any* effect it has—positive or negative—is short lived. At best pornography might divert or delay a man from expressing his callousness in an even more blatantly objectionable manner.

One could make the point in moral terms as follows: Sex calloused attitudes and behavior are morally objectionable; if expressing one's sex calloused attitudes lessens them temporarily, they are still morally objectionable if they persevere at some level. The most that one could say for pornography is that expressing callousness by enjoying pornography in a male group is a lesser evil than, for example, rape or obnoxiously "putting down" a woman in person. This is saying very little on behalf of pornography; it is still morally objectionable.

If pornography is morally objectionable even if Mosher is correct, then given the two alternatives posed, it is surely morally objectionable. For Brownmiller's alternative, remember, was that pornography provides a model for sex calloused behavior and has a numbing effect on many of us so that we more readily tolerate this behavior. This view, much more obviously than Mosher's, implies that pornography is morally objectionable.[18]

Before leaving Mosher and Brownmiller, let me point out that their views are not wholly incompatible. They disagree about pornography's function as an outlet or a model, of course, but Mosher's data (as he interprets their significance) are compatible

with the numbing effect of pornography. Pornography may have numbed all of us (previously sex calloused or not) to the objectionable character of exploitative sex; the fact that the sex calloused men were numbed does not imply that they will feel the need to endorse calloused attitudes just after expressing their callousness in other ways. Further, Mosher's data have no bearing at all on the numbing influence on women; certainly Brownmiller means for her claim to apply to women too.

One final point remains to be considered. The Presidential Commission assumes a connection between sex callousness and the lack (or loss) of respect for women; for it appealed to Mosher's data about sex callousness to show that pornography probably will not lead people to lose respect for women.[19] But look at the results of replacing Mosher's talk about sex calloused attitudes with talk about respect for women: One could conclude that seeing pornography (with a group of men) leads to an increase in respect for women. The explanation would be that men who tend toward low respect for women can use pornography as a way of expressing their low respect. They then feel no need to endorse statements exemplifying their low respect because they have just expressed it. "Therefore" pornography provides the opportunity for their respect for women to increase. The last idea is bothersome: To think of viewing and enjoying pornography as a way of expressing lack of respect, and at the same time as a way of expressing or increasing respect, seems very strange. This is not to say that such a feat is impossible. Given our complex psychological make-up, we might be able to express both respect and lack of respect at the same time in different ways; it might also be possible to express disrespect that leads to respect (e.g., if shame at feeling disrespect leads to a temporary increase in respect). But one would need far more information about what actually happens before agreeing that any of these possibilities seems very plausible. It is necessary to spell out both the possible connections and suitable explanations for each. Without much more information, one would not

---

18. Of course, pornography might have no effect at all. If this were true, some other basis must be found before calling it morally objectionable.

19. *Report,* p. 201.

want to base either favorable moral judgments about pornography or social policy on the possibility that pornography can lead to more respect for women.

Although much more remains to be said about the connection between pornography and respect for women, I will defer discussion of it to Part III of this paper. For now, let us note that even if the Presidential Commission appropriately allayed our fears about being molested on street corners by users of pornography, it would not have been warranted in placating us with the view that pornography is morally acceptable. It is fortunate that it did not try.

III

The second argument I will consider is that pornography is morally objectionable, not because it leads people to show disrespect for women, but because pornography itself exemplifies and recommends behavior that violates the moral principle to respect persons. The content of pornography is what one objects to. It treats women as mere sex objects "to be exploited and manipulated" and degrades the role and status of women. In order to evaluate this argument, I will first clarify what it would mean for pornography itself to treat someone as a sex object in a degrading manner. I will then deal with three issues central to the discussion of pornography and respect for women: how "losing respect" for a woman is connected with treating her as a sex object; what is wrong with treating someone as a sex object; and why it is worse to treat women rather than men as sex objects. I will argue that the current content of pornography sometimes violates the moral principle to respect persons. Then, in Part IV of this paper, I will suggest that pornography need not violate this principle if certain fundamental changes were to occur in attitudes about sex.

To many people, including Brownmiller and some other feminists, it appears to be an obvious truth that pornography treats people, especially women, as sex objects in a degrading manner. And if we omit 'in a degrading manner,' the statement seems hard to dispute: How could pornography *not* treat people as sex objects?

First, is it permissible to say that either the content of pornography or pornography itself degrades

people or treats people as sex objects? It is not difficult to find examples of degrading content in which women are treated as sex objects. Some pornographic films convey the message that all women really want to be raped, that their resisting struggle is not to be believed. By portraying women in this manner, the content of the movie degrades women. Degrading women is morally objectionable. While seeing the movie need not cause anyone to imitate the behavior shown, we can call the content degrading to women because of the character of the behavior and attitudes it recommends. The same kind of point can be made about films (or books or TV commercials) with other kinds of degrading, thus morally objectionable, content—for example, racist messages.[20]

The next step in the argument is to infer that, because the content or message of pornography is morally objectionable, we can call pornography itself morally objectionable. Support for this step can be found in an anology. If a person takes every opportunity to recommend that men rape women, we would think not only that his recommendation is immoral but that he is immoral too. In the case of pornography, the objection to making an inference from recommended behavior to the person who recommends is that we ascribe predicates such as 'immoral' differently to people than to films or books. A film vehicle for an objectionable message is still an object independent of its message, its director, its producer, those who act in it, and those who respond to it. Hence one cannot make an unsupported inference from "the content of the film is morally objectionable" to "the film is morally objec-

---

20. Two further points need to be mentioned here. Sharon Bishop pointed out to me one reason why we might object to either a racist or rapist mentality in film: it might be difficult for a Black or a woman not to identify with the degraded person. A second point concerns different uses of the phrase 'treats women as sex objects.' A film treats a subject—the meaninglessness of contemporary life, women as sex objects, and so on—and this use of 'treats' is unproblematic. But one should not suppose that this is the same use of 'treats women as sex objects' that is found in the sentence 'David treats women as sex objects'; David is not treating the *subject* of women as sex objects.

tionable." Because the central points in this paper do not depend on whether pornography itself (in addition to its content) is morally objectionable, I will not try to support this inference. (The question about the relation of content to the work itself is, of course, extremely interesting; but in part because I cannot decide which side of the argument is more persuasive, I will pass.[21]) Certainly one appropriate way to evaluate pornography is in terms of the moral features of its content. If a pornographic film exemplifies and recommends morally objectionable attitudes or behavior, then its content is morally objectionable.

Let us now turn to the first of our three questions about respect and sex objects: What is the connection between losing respect for a woman and treating her as a sex object? Some people who have lived through the era in which women were taught to worry about men "losing respect" for them if they engaged in sex in inappropriate circumstances find it troublesome (or at least amusing) that feminists—supposedly "liberated" women—are outraged at being treated as sex objects, either by pornography or in any other way. The apparent alignment between feminists and traditionally "proper" women need not surprise us when we look at it more closely.

The "respect" that men have traditionally believed they have for women—hence a respect they can lose—is not a general respect for persons as autonomous beings; nor is it respect that is earned because of one's personal merits or achievements. It is respect that is an outgrowth of the "double standard." Women are to be respected because they are more pure, delicate, and fragile than men, have more refined sensibilities, and so on. Because some women clearly do not have these qualities, thus do not deserve respect, women must be divided into two groups—the good ones on the pedestal and the bad ones who have fallen from it. One's mother, grandmother, Sunday School teacher, and usually one's wife are "good" women. The appropriate behavior by which to express respect for good women would be, for example, not swearing or telling dirty jokes in front of them, giving them seats on buses, and other "chivalrous" acts. This kind of "respect" for good women is the same sort that adolescent boys in the back seats of cars used to "promise" not to lose. Note that men define, display, and lose this kind of respect. If women lose respect for women, it is not typically a loss of respect for (other) women as a class but a loss of self-respect.

> "Although much current pornography does degrade women, ... it is possible to have nondegrading, nonsexist pornography."

It has now become commonplace to acknowledge that, although a place on the pedestal might have advantages over a place in the "gutter" beneath it, a place on the pedestal is not at all equal to the place occupied by other people (i.e., men). "Respect" for those on the pedestal was not respect for whole, full-fledged people but for a special class of inferior beings.

If a person makes two traditional assumptions—that (at least some) sex is dirty and that women fall into two classes, good and bad—it is easy to see how that person might think that pornography could lead people to lose respect for women or that pornography is itself disrespectful to women.[22]

---

21. In order to help one determine which position one feels inclined to take, consider the following statement: It is morally objectionable to write, make, sell, act in, use, and enjoy pornography; in addition, the content of pornography is immoral; however, pornography itself is not morally objectionable. If this statement seems extremely problematic, then one might well be satisfied with the claim that pornography is degrading because its content is.

22. The traditional meaning of "lose respect for women" was evidently the one assumed in the Abelson survey cited by the Presidential Commission. No explanation of its meaning is given in the report of the study. See H. Abelson et al., "National Survey of Public Attitudes Toward and Experience with Erotic Materials," *Tech. Report,* vol. 6, pp. 1–137.

Pornography describes or shows women engaging in activities inappropriate for good women to engage in—or at least inappropriate for them to be seen by strangers engaging in. If one sees these women as symbolic representatives of all women, then all women fall from grace with these women. This fall is possible, I believe, because the traditional "respect" that men have had for women is not genuine, wholehearted respect for full-fledged human beings but half-hearted respect for lesser beings, some of whom they feel the need to glorify and purify.[23] It is easy to fall from a pedestal. Can we imagine 41 percent of men and 46 percent of women answering "yes" to the question, "Do movies showing men engaging in violent acts lead people to lose respect for men?"?

Two interesting asymmetries appear. The first is that losing respect for men as a class (men with power, typically Anglo men) is more difficult than losing respect for women or ethnic minorities as a class. Anglo men whose behavior warrants disrespect are more likely to be seen as exceptional cases than are women or minorities (whose "transgressions" may be far less serious). Think of the following: women are temptresses; Blacks cheat the welfare system; Italians are gangsters; but the men of the Nixon administration are exceptions—Anglo men as a class did not lose respect because of Watergate and related scandals.

The second asymmetry concerns the active and passive roles of the sexes. Men are seen in the active role. If men lose respect for women because of something "evil" done by women (such as appearing in pornography), the fear is that men will then do harm to women—not that women will do harm to men. Whereas if women lose respect for male politicians because of Watergate, the fear is still that male politicians will do harm, not that women will do harm to male politicians. This asymmetry might be a result of one way in which our society thinks of sex as bad—as harm that men do to women (or

to the person playing a female role, as in a homosexual rape). Robert Baker calls attention to this point in " 'Pricks' and 'Chicks': A Plea for 'Persons'."[24] Our slang words for sexual intercourse—'fuck,' 'screw,' or older words such as 'take' or 'have'—not only can mean harm but have traditionally taken a male subject and a female object. The active male screws (harms) the passive female. A "bad" woman only tempts men to hurt her further.

It is easy to understand why one's proper grandmother would not want men to see pornography or lose respect for women. But feminists reject these "proper" assumptions: good and bad classes of women do not exist; and sex is not dirty (though many people believe it is). Why then are feminists angry at the treatment of women as sex objects, and why are some feminists opposed to pornography?

The answer is that feminists as well as proper grandparents are concerned with respect. However, there are differences. A feminist's distinction between treating a woman as a full-fledged person and treating her as merely a sex object does not correspond to the good-bad woman distinction. In the latter distinction, "good" and "bad" are properties applicable to groups of women. In the feminist view, all women are full-fledged people—some, however, are treated as sex objects and perhaps think of themselves as sex objects. A further difference is that, although "bad" women correspond to those thought to deserve treatment as sex objects, good women have not corresponded to full-fledged people; only men have been full-fledged people. Given the feminist's distinction, she has no difficulty whatever in saying that pornography treats women as sex objects, not as full-fledged people. She can morally object to pornography or anything else that treats women as sex objects.

One might wonder whether any objection to treatment as a sex object implies that the person objecting still believes, deep down, that sex is dirty. I don't think so. Several other possibilities emerge.

23. Many feminists point this out. One of the most accessible references in Shulamith Firestone, *The Dialectic of Sex: The Case for the Feminist Revolution* (New York: Bantam, 1970), especially pp. 128–32.

24. In Richard Wasserstrom, ed., *Today's Moral Problems* (New York: Macmillan, 1975), pp. 152–71; see pp. 167–71. Also in Robert Baker and Frederick Elliston, eds., *Philosophy and Sex* (Buffalo, N.Y.: Prometheus Books, 1975).

First, even if I believe intellectually and emotionally that sex is healthy, I might object to being treated *only* as a sex object. In the same spirit, I would object to being treated *only* as a maker of chocolate chip cookies or *only* as a tennis partner, because only one of my talents is being valued. Second, perhaps I feel that sex is healthy, but it is apparent to me that you think sex is dirty; so I don't want you to treat me as a sex object. Third, being treated as any kind of object, not just as a sex object, is unappealing. I would rather be a partner (sexual or otherwise) than an object. Fourth, and more plausible than the first three possibilities, is Robert Baker's view mentioned above. Both (i) our traditional double standard of sexual behavior for men and women and (ii) the linguistic evidence that we connect the concept of sex with the concept of harm point to what is wrong with treating women as sex objects. As I said earlier, 'fuck' and 'screw,' in their traditional uses, have taken a male subject, a female object, and have had at least two meanings: harm and have sexual intercourse with. (In addition, a prick is a man who harms people ruthlessly; and a motherfucker is so low that he would do something very harmful to his own dear mother.)[25] Because in our culture we connect sex with harm that men do to women, and because we think of the female role in sex as that of harmed object, we can see that to treat a woman as a sex object is automatically to treat her as less than fully human. To say this does not imply that no healthy sexual relationships exist; nor does it say anything about individual men's conscious intentions to degrade women by desiring them sexually (though no doubt some men have these intentions). It is merely to make a point about the concepts embodied in our language.

Psychoanalytic support for the connection between sex and harm comes from Robert J. Stoller. Stoller thinks that sexual excitement is linked with a wish to harm someone (and with at least a whisper of hostility). The key process of sexual excitement can be seen as dehumanization (fetishization) in fantasy of the desired person. He speculates that this is true in some degree of everyone, both men and women, with "normal" or "perverted" activities and fantasies.[26]

Thinking of sex objects as harmed objects enables us to explain some of the first three reasons why one wouldn't want to be treated as a sex object: (1) I may object to being treated only as a tennis partner, but being a tennis partner is not connected in our culture with being a harmed object; and (2) I may not think that sex is dirty and that I would be a harmed object; I may not know what your view is; but what bothers me is that this is the view embodied in our language and culture.

Awareness of the connection between sex and harm helps explain other interesting points. Women are angry about being treated as sex objects in situations or roles in which they do not intend to be regarded in that manner—for example, while serving on a committee or attending a discussion. It is not merely that a sexual role is inappropriate for the circumstances; it is thought to be a less fully human role than the one in which they intended to function.

Finally, the sex-harm connection makes clear why it is worse to treat women as sex objects than to treat men as sex objects, and why some men have had difficulty understanding women's anger about the matter. It is more difficult for heterosexual men than for women to assume the role of "harmed object" in sex; for men have the self-concept of sexual agents, not of passive objects. This

---

25. Baker, in Wasserstrom, *Today's Moral Problems,* pp. 168–169.

26. "Sexual Excitement," *Archives of General Psychiatry* 33 (1976): 899–909, especially p. 903. The extent to which Stoller sees men and women in different positions with respect to harm and hostility is not clear. He often treats men and women alike, but in *Perversion: The Erotic Form of Hatred* (New York: Pantheon, 1975), pp. 89–91, he calls attention to differences between men and women especially regarding their responses to pornography and lack of understanding by men of women's sexuality. Given that Stoller finds hostility to be an essential element in male-oriented pornography, and given that women have not responded readily to such pornography, one can speculate about the possibilities for women's sexuality: their hostility might follow a different scenario; they might not be as hostile, and so on.

is also related to my earlier point concerning the difference in the solidity of respect for men and for women; respect for women is more fragile. Despite exceptions, it is generally harder for people to degrade men, either sexually or nonsexually, than to degrade women. Men and women have grown up with different patterns of self-respect and expectations regarding the extent to which they deserve and will receive respect or degradation. The man who doesn't understand why women do not want to be treated as sex objects (because he'd sure like to be) would not think of himself as being harmed by that treatment; a woman might.[27] Pornography, probably more than any other contemporary institution, succeeds in treating men as sex objects.

Having seen that the connection between sex and harm helps explain both what is wrong with treating someone as a sex object and why it is worse to treat a woman in this way, I want to use the sex-harm connection to try to resolve a dispute about pornography and women. Brownmiller's view, remember, was that pornography is "the undiluted essence of anti-female propaganda" whose purpose is to degrade women.[28] Some people object to Brownmiller's view by saying that, since pornography treats both men and women as sex objects for the purpose of arousing the viewer, it is neither sexist, antifemale, nor designed to degrade women; it just happens that degrading of women arouses some men. How can this dispute be resolved?

Suppose we were to rate the content of all pornography from most morally objectionable to least morally objectionable. Among the most objectionable would be the most degrading—for example,

"snuff" films and movies which recommend that men rape women, molest children and puppies, and treat nonmasochists very sadistically.

Next we would find a large amount of material (probably most pornography) not quite so blatantly offensive. With this material it is relevant to use the analysis of sex objects given above. As long as sex is connected with harm done to women, it will be very difficult not to see pornography as degrading to women. We can agree with Brownmiller's opponent that pornography treats men as sex objects, too, but we maintain that this is only pseudoequality: such treatment is still more degrading to women.[29]

In addition, pornography often exemplifies the active/passive, harmer/harmed object roles in a very obvious way. Because pornography today is male-oriented and is supposed to make a profit, the content is designed to appeal to male fantasies. Judging from the content of the most popular legally available pornography, male fantasies still run along the lines of stereotypical sex roles—and, if Stoller is right, include elements of hostility. In much pornography the women's purpose is to cater to male desires, to service the man or men. Her own pleasure is rarely emphasized for its own sake; she is merely allowed a little heavy breathing, perhaps in order to show her dependence on the great male "lover" who produces her pleasure. In addition, women are clearly made into passive objects in still photographs showing only close-ups of their genitals. Even in movies marketed to appeal to heterosexual couples, such as *Behind the Green Door,* the woman is passive and undemanding (and in this case kidnapped and hypnotized as well). Although

---

27. Men seem to be developing more sensitivity to being treated as sex objects. Many homosexual men have long understood the problem. As women become more sexually aggressive, some heterosexual men I know are beginning to feel treated as sex objects. A man can feel that he is not being taken seriously if a woman looks lustfully at him while he is holding forth about the French judicial system or the failure of liberal politics. Some of his most important talents are not being properly valued.

28. Brownmiller, *Against Our Will,* p. 394.

29. I don't agree with Brownmiller that the purpose of pornography is to dehumanize women; rather it is to arouse the audience. The differences between our views can be explained, in part, by the points from which we begin. She is writing about rape; her views about pornography grow out of her views about rape. I begin by thinking of pornography as merely depicted sexual activity, though I am well aware of the male hostility and contempt for women that it often expresses. That pornography degrades women and excites men is an illustration of this contempt.

many kinds of specialty magazines and films are gauged for different sexual tastes, very little contemporary pornography goes against traditional sex roles. There is certainly no significant attempt to replace the harmer/harmed distinction with anything more positive and healthy. In some stag movies, of course, men are treated sadistically by women; but this is an attempt to turn the tables on degradation, not a positive improvement.

What would cases toward the least objectionable end of the spectrum be like? They would be increasingly less degrading and sexist. The genuinely nonobjectionable cases would be nonsexist and nondegrading; but commercial examples do not readily spring to mind.[30] The question is: Does or could any pornography have nonsexist, nondegrading content?

IV

I want to start with the easier question: Is it possible for pornography to have nonsexist, morally acceptable content? Then I will consider whether any pornography of this sort currently exists.

Imagine the following situation, which exists only rarely today: Two fairly conventional people who love each other enjoy playing tennis and bridge together, cooking good food together, and having sex together. In all these activities they are free from hang-ups, guilt, and tendencies to dominate or objectify each other. These two people like to watch tennis matches and old romantic movies on TV, like to watch Julia Child cook, like to read the bridge column in the newspaper, and like to watch pornographic movies. Imagine further that this couple is not at all uncommon in society and that nonsexist pornography is as common as this kind of nonsexist sexual relationship. This situation sounds fine and healthy to me. I see no reason to think that an interest in pornography would disappear in these circumstances.[31] People seem to enjoy watching others experience or do (especially do well) what they enjoy experiencing, doing, or wish they could do themselves. We do not morally object to people watching tennis on TV; why would we object to these hypothetical people watching pornography?

Can we go from the situation today to the situation just imagined? In much current pornography, people are treated in morally objectionable ways. In the scene just imagined, however, pornography would be nonsexist, nondegrading, morally acceptable. The key to making the change is to break the connection between sex and harm. If Stoller is right, this task may be impossible without changing the scenarios for our sexual lives—scenarios that we have been writing since early childhood. (Stoller does not indicate whether he thinks it possible for adults to rewrite their scenarios or for social change to bring about the possibility of new scenarios in future generations.) But even if we believe that people can change their sexual scenarios, the sex-harm connection is deeply entrenched and has widespread implications. What is needed is a thorough change in people's deep-seated attitudes and feelings about sex roles in general, as well as about sex

---

30. Virginia Wright Wexman uses the film *Group Marriage* (Stephanie Rothman, 1973) as an example of "more enlightened erotica." Wexman also asks the following questions in an attempt to point out sexism in pornography films:
    Does it [the film] portray rape as pleasurable to women? Does it consistently show females nude but present men fully clothed? Does it present women as childlike creatures whose sexual interests must be guided by knowing experienced men? Does it show sexually aggressive women as castrating viragos? Does it pretend that sex is exclusively the prerogative of women under twenty-five? Does it focus on the physical aspects of lovemaking rather than the emotional ones? Does it portray women as purely sexual beings? ("Sexism of X-rated Films," Chicago Sun-Times, 28 March 1976.)

31. One might think, as does Stoller, that since pornography today depends on hostility, voyeurism, and sado-masochism (*Perversion*, p. 87) that sexually healthy people would not enjoy it. Two points should be noticed here, however: (1) Stoller need not think that pornography will disappear because hostility is an element of sexual excitement generally; and (2) voyeurism, when it invades no one's privacy, need not be seen as immoral; so although enjoyment of pornography might not be an expression of sexual health, it need not be immoral either.

and roles in sex (sexual roles). Although I cannot even sketch a general outline of such changes here, changes in pornography should be part of a comprehensive program. Television, children's educational material, and nonpornographic movies and novels may be far better avenues for attempting to change attitudes; but one does not want to take the chance that pornography is working against one.

What can be done about pornography in particular? If one wanted to work within the current institutions, one's attempt to use pornography as a tool for the education of male pornography audiences would have to be fairly subtle at first; nonsexist pornography must become familiar enough to sell and be watched. One should realize too that any positive educational value that nonsexist pornography might have may well be as short-lived as most of the effects of pornography. But given these limitations, what could one do?

Two kinds of films must be considered. First is the short film with no plot or character development, just depicted sexual activity in which nonsexist pornography would treat men and women as equal sex partners.[32] The man would not control the circumstances in which the partners had sex or the choice of positions or acts; the woman's preference would be counted equally. There would be no suggestion of a power play or conquest on the man's part, no suggestion that "she likes it when I hurt her." Sexual intercourse would not be portrayed as primarily for the purpose of male ejaculation—his orgasm is not "the best part" of the movie. In addition, both the man and woman would express their enjoyment; the man need not be cool and detached.

The film with a plot provides even more opportunity for nonsexist education. Today's pornography often portrays the female character as playthings even when not engaging in sexual activity. Nonsexist pornography could show women and men in roles equally valued by society, and sex equality would amount to more than possession of equally functional genitalia. Characters would customarily treat each other with respect and consideration, with no attempt to treat men or women brutally or thoughtlessly. The local Pussycat Theater showed a film written and directed by a woman (*The Passions of Carol*), which exhibited a few of the features just mentioned. The main female character in it was the editor of a magazine parody of *Viva*. The fact that some of the characters treated each other very nicely, warmly, and tenderly did not detract from the pornographic features of the movie. This should not surprise us, for even in traditional male-oriented films, lesbian scenes usually exhibit tenderness and kindness.

Plots for nonsexist films could include women in traditionally male jobs (e.g., long-distance truck driver) or in positions usually held in respect by pornography audiences. For example, a high-ranking female Army officer, treated with respect by men and women alike, could be shown not only in various sexual encounters with other people but also carrying out her job in a humane manner.[33] Or perhaps the main character could be a female urologist. She could interact with nurses and other medical personnel, diagnose illnesses brilliantly, and treat patients with great sympathy as well as have sex with them. When the Army officer or the urologist engage in sexual activities, they will treat their partners and be treated by them in some of the considerate ways described above.

In the circumstances we imagined at the beginning of Part IV of this paper, our nonsexist films could be appreciated in the proper spirit. Under these conditions the content of our new pornography would clearly be nonsexist and morally accept-

---

32. If it is a lesbian or male homosexual film, no one would play a caricatured male or female role. The reader has probably noticed that I have limited my discussion to heterosexual pornography, but there are many interesting analogies to be drawn with male homosexual pornography. Very little lesbian pornography exists, though lesbian scenes are commonly found in male-oriented pornography.

33. One should note that behavior of this kind is still considered unacceptable by the military. A female officer resigned from the U.S. Navy recently rather than be court-martialed for having sex with several enlisted men whom she met in a class on interpersonal relations.

able. But would the content of such a film be morally acceptable if shown to a typical pornography audience today? It might seem strange for us to change our moral evaluation of the content on the basis of a different audience, but an audience today is likely to see the "respected" urologist and Army officer as playthings or unusual prostitutes—even if our intention in showing the film is to counteract this view. The effect is that, although the content of the film seems morally acceptable and our intention in showing it is morally flawless, women are still degraded.[34] The fact that audience attitude is so important makes one wary of giving wholehearted approval to any pornography seen today.

The fact that good intentions and content are insufficient does not imply that one's efforts toward change would be entirely in vain. Of course, I could not deny that anyone who tries to change an institution from within faces serious difficulties. This is particularly evident when one is trying to change both pornography and a whole set of related attitudes, feelings, and institutions concerning sex and sex roles. But in conjunction with other attempts to change this set of attitudes, it seems preferable to try to change pornography instead of closing one's eyes in the hope that it will go away. For I suspect that pornography is here to stay.[35]

---

34. The content may seem morally acceptable only if one disregards such questions as, "Should a doctor have sex with her patients during office hours?" More important is the propriety of evaluating content wholly apart from the attitudes and reactions of the audience; one might not find it strange to say that one film has morally unacceptable content when shown tonight at the Pussycat Theater but acceptable content when shown tomorrow at a feminist conference.

35. Three "final" points must be made:
    1. I have not seriously considered censorship as an alternative course of action. Both Brownmiller and Sheehy are not averse to it. But as I suggested in note 5, other principles seem too valuable to sacrifice when other options are available. In addition, before justifying censorship on moral grounds one would want to compare pornography to other possibly offensive material: advertising using sex and racial stereotypes, violence on TV and films, and so on.
    2. If my nonsexist pornography succeeded in having much "educational value," it might no longer be pornography according to my definition. This possibility seems too remote to worry me, however.
    3. In discussing the audience for nonsexist pornography, I have focused on the male audience. But there is no reason why pornography could not educate and appeal to women as well.

    Earlier versions of this paper have been discussed at a meeting of the Society for Women in Philosophy at Stanford University, California State University, Los Angeles, Claremont Graduate School, Western Area Meeting of Women in Psychology, UCLA Political Philosophy Discussion Group, and California State University, Fullerton Annual Philosophy Symposium. Among the many people who made helpful comments were Alan Garfinkel, Jackie Thomason, and Fred Berger. This paper grew out of "Pornography, Sex Roles, and Morality," presented as a responding paper to Fred Berger's "Strictly Peeking: Some Views on Pornography, Sex, and Censorship" in a Philosophy and Public Affairs Symposium at the American Philosophical Association, Pacific Division Meeting, March 1975.

Study Questions

1. Does most pornography degrade women? How can one prove this?

2. How can nonsexist pornography be encouraged in a free-enterprise society?

Is Pornography Beneficial?

A British writer, G. L. Simons is the author of Sex and Superstition *and* A History of Sex *among other writings.*

G. L. Simons

It is not sufficient, for the objectors' case, that they demonstrate that some harm has flowed from pornography. It would be extremely difficult to show that pornography had *never* had unfortunate consequences, but we should not make too much of this. Harm has flowed from religion, patriotism, alcohol and cigarettes without this fact impelling people to demand abolition. The harm, if established, has to be weighed against a variety of considerations before a decision can be reached as to the propriety of certain laws. Of the British Obscenity Laws the Arts Council Report comments[1] that "the harm would need to be both indisputable and very dire indeed before it could be judged to outweigh the evils and anomalies inherent in the Acts we have been asked to examine."

The onus therefore is upon the anti-pornographers to demonstrate not only that harm is caused by certain types of sexual material but that the harm is considerable: if the first is difficult the second is necessarily more so, and the attempts to date have not been impressive. It is even possible to argue that easily available pornography has a number of benefits. Many people will be familiar with the *catharsis* argument whereby pornography is said to cut down on delinquency by providing would-be criminals with substitute satisfactions. This is considered later but we mention it here to indicate that access to pornography may be socially beneficial in certain instances, and that where this is possible the requirement for anti-pornographers to *justify* their objections must be stressed.

The general conclusion[2] of the U.S. Commission was that no adequate proof had been provided that pornography was harmful to individual or society— "if a case is to be made out against 'pornography' [in 1970] it will have to be made on grounds other than demonstrated effects of a damaging personal or social nature." ...

The heresy (to some ears) that pornography is harmless is compounded by the even greater impiety that it may be beneficial. Some of us are managing to adjust to the notion that pornography is unlikely to bring down the world in moral ruin, but the idea that it may actually do good is altogether another thing. When we read of Professor Emeritus E. T. Rasmussen, a pioneer of psychological studies in Denmark, and a government adviser, saying that there is a possibility "that pornography can be beneficial," many of us are likely to have *mixed* reactions, to say the least. In fact this thesis can be argued in a number of ways.

The simplest approach is to remark that people enjoy it. This can be seen to be true whether we rely on personal testimony or the most respectable index of all in capitalist society—"preparedness to pay." The appeal that pornography has for many

---

1. *The Obscenity Laws,* André Deutsch, 1969, p. 33.
2. *The Report of the Commission on Obscenity and Pornography.* Part Three, II, Bantam Books, 1970, p. 169.

people is hardly in dispute, and in a more sober social climate that would be justification enough. Today we are not quite puritan enough to deny that *pleasure* has a worthwhile place in human life: not many of us object to our food being tasty or our clothes being attractive. It was not always like this. In sterner times it was *de rigueur* to prepare food without spices and to wear the plainest clothes. The cult of puritanism reached its apotheosis in the most fanatical asceticism, where it was fashionable for holy men to wander off into a convenient desert and neglect the body to the point of cultivating its lice as "pearls of God." In such a bizarre philosophy pleasure was not only condemned in its sexual manifestations but in all areas where the body could conceivably take satisfaction. These days we are able to countenance pleasure in most fields but in many instances still the case for *sexual* pleasure has to be argued.

Pleasure is not of course its own justification. If it clearly leads to serious malaise, early death, or the *dis*pleasure of others, then there is something to be said against it. But the serious consequences have to be demonstrated: it is not enough to condemn certain forms of pleasurable experience on the grounds of *possible* ill effect. With such an approach *any* human activity could be censured and freedom would have no place. In short, if something is pleasurable and its bad effects are small or nonexistent then it is to be encouraged: opposition to such a creed should be recognized as an unwholesome antipathy to human potential. Pleasure is a good except where it is harmful (and where the harmfulness is *significant*). . . .

That pornography is enjoyable to many people is the first of the arguments in its favour. In any other field this would be argument enough. It is certainly sufficient to justify many activities that have—unlike a taste for pornography—demonstrably harmful consequences. Only in a sexually neurotic society could a tool for heightening sexual enjoyment be regarded as reprehensible and such as to warrant suppression by law. The position is well summarized[3] in the *first* of the Arts Council's twelve reasons for advocating the repeal of the Obscenity Publications Acts:

"It is not for the State to prohibit private citizens from choosing what they may or may not enjoy in literature or art unless there were incontrovertible evidence that the result would be injurious to society. There is no such evidence."

A further point is that availability of pornography may *aid,* rather than frustrate normal sexual development. Thus in 1966, for example, the New Jersey Committee for the Right to Read presented the findings of a survey conducted among nearly a thousand psychiatrists and psychologists of that state. Amongst the various personal statements included was the view that "sexually stimulating materials" might help particular people develop a normal sex drive.[4] In similar spirit, Dr. John Money writes[5] that pornography "may encourage normal sexual development and broadmindedness," a view that may not sound well to the anti-pornographers. And even in circumstances where possible dangers of pornography are pointed out conceivable good effects are sometimes acknowledged. In a paper issued[6] by the Danish Forensic Medicine Council it is pointed out that neurotic and sexually shy people may, by reading pornographic descriptions of normal sexual activity, be freed from some of their apprehension regarding sex and may thereby attain a freer and less frustrated attitude to the sexual side of life. . . .

One argument in favour of pornography is that it can serve as a substitute for actual sexual activity involving another person or other people. This argument has two parts, relating as it does to (1) people who fantasize over *socially acceptable* modes of

---

3. *The Obscenity Laws,* André Deutsch, 1969, p. 35.

4. Quoted by Isadore Rubin, "What Should Parents Do About Pornography?" *Sex in the Adolescent Years,* Fontana, 1969, p. 202.

5. John Money, contribution to "Is Pornography Harmful to Young Children?" *Sex in the Childhood Years,* Fontana, 1971, p. 181–5.

6. Paper from the Danish Forensic Medicine Council to The Danish Penal Code Council, published in The Penal Code Council Report on Penalty for Pornography, Report No. 435, Copenhagen, 1966, pp. 78–80, and as appendix to *The Obscenity Laws,* pp. 120–4.

sexual involvement, and (2) people who fantasize over types of sexual activity that would be regarded as illegal or at least immoral. The first type relates to lonely and deprived people who for one reason or another have been unable to form "normal" sexual contacts with other people; the second type are instances of the much quoted *catharsis* argument.

One writer notes[7] that pornography can serve as a substitute for both the knowledge of which some people have been deprived and the pleasure in sexual experience which they have not enjoyed. One can well imagine men or women too inhibited to secure sexual satisfaction with other adults and where explicit sexual material can alleviate some of their misery. It is facile to remark that such people should seek psychiatric assistance or even "make an effort": the factors that prevent the forming of effective sexual liaisons are just as likely to inhibit any efforts to seek medical or other assistance. Pornography provides *sex by proxy,* and in such usage it can have a clear justification.

It is also possible to imagine circumstances in which men or women—for reasons of illness, travel or bereavement—are unable to seek sexual satisfaction with spouse or other loved one. Pornography can help here too. Again it is easy to suggest that a person abstain from sexual experience, or, if having *permanently* lost a spouse, seek out another partner. Needless to say such advice is often quite impractical—and the alternative to pornography may be prostitution or adultery. Montagu notes that pornography can serve the same purpose as "dirty jokes," allowing a person to discharge harmlessly repressed and unsatisfied sexual desires.

In this spirit, Mercier (1970) is quoted by the U.S. Commission:

"... it is in periods of sexual deprivation—to which the young and the old are far more subject than those in their prime—that males, at any rate, are likely to reap psychological benefit from pornography."

And also Kenneth Tynan (1970):

"For men on long journeys, geographically cut off from wives and mistresses, pornography can act as a portable memory, a welcome shortcut to remembered bliss, relieving tension without involving disloyalty."

It is difficult to see how anyone could object to the use of pornography in such circumstances, other than on the grounds of a morbid anti-sexuality.

> *"The* catharsis argument *has long been put forward to suggest that availability of pornography will neutralize 'aberrant' sexual tendencies..."*

The *catharsis argument* has long been put forward to suggest that availability of pornography will neutralize "aberrant" sexual tendencies and so reduce the incidence of sex crime or clearly immoral behaviour in related fields. (Before evidence is put forward for this thesis it is worth remarking that it should not be necessary to demonstrate a *reduction* in sex crime to justify repeal of the Obscenity Laws. It should be quite sufficient to show that an *increase* in crime will not ensue following repeal. We may even argue that a small increase may be tolerable if other benefits from easy access to pornography could be shown: but it is no part of the present argument to put this latter contention.)

Many psychiatrists and psychologists have favoured the catharsis argument. Chesser, for instance, sees[8] pornography as a form of voyeurism in which—as with sado-masochistic material—the desire to hurt is satisfied passively. If this is so and the

---

7. Ashley Montagu, "Is Pornography Harmful to Young Children?" *Sex in the Childhood Years,* Fontana, 1971, p. 182.

8. Eustace Chesser, *The Human Aspects of Sexual Deviation,* Arrow Books, 1971, p. 39.

analogy can be extended we have only to look at the character of the voyeur—generally furtive and clandestine—to realize that we have little to fear from the pornography addict. Where consumers are preoccupied with fantasy there is little danger to the rest of us. Karpman (1959), quoted by the U.S. Commission, notes that people reading "salacious literature" are less likely to become sexual offenders than those who do not since the reading often neutralizes "aberrant sexual interests." Similarly the Kronhausens have argued that "these 'unholy' instruments" may be a safety-valve for the sexual deviate and potential sex offender. And Cairns, Paul and Wishner (1962) have remarked that *obscene materials* provide a way of releasing strong sexual urges without doing harm to others.

It is easy to see the plausibility of this argument. The popularity of all forms of sexual literature—from the superficial, *sexless,* sentimentality of the popular women's magazine to the clearest "hardcore" porn—has demonstrated over the ages the perennial appetite that people have for fantasy. To an extent, a great extent with many single people and frustrated married ones, the fantasy constitutes an important part of the sex-life. The experience may be vicarious and sterile but it self-evidently fills a need for many individuals. If literature, as a *symbol* of reality, can so involve human sensitivities it is highly likely that when the sensitivities are *distorted* for one reason or another the same sublimatory function can occur: the "perverted" or potentially criminal mentality can gain satisfaction, as does the lonely unfortunate, in *sex by proxy.* If we wanted to force the potential sex criminal onto the streets in search of a human victim perhaps we would do well to deny him sublimatory substitutes: deny him fantasy and he will be forced to go after the real thing. . . .

The importance of this possibility should be fully faced. If a causal connection *does* exist between availability of pornographic material and a *reduction* in the amount of sex crime—and the evidence is wholly consistent with this possibility rather than its converse—then people who deliberately restrict pornography by supporting repressive legislation are prime architects of sexual offences against the individual. The anti-pornographers would do well to note that their anxieties may be driving them into a position the exact opposite of the one they explicitly maintain—their commitment to reduce the amount of sexual delinquency in society.

The most that the anti-pornographers can argue is that at present the evidence is inconclusive. . . . But if the inconclusive character of the data is once admitted then the case for repressive legislation falls at once. For in a *free* society, or one supposedly aiming after freedom, social phenomena are, like individuals, innocent until proven guilty—and an activity will be permitted unless there is clear evidence of its harmful consequences. This point was well put—in the specific connection with pornography—by Bertrand Russell, talking[9] when he was well over 90 to Rupert Crawshay-Williams.

After noting how people beg the question of causation in instances such as the Moors murders (where the murders and the reading of de Sade *may* have a common cause), Russell ("Bertie") said that on the whole he disapproved of sadistic pornography being available. But when Crawshay-Williams put the catharsis view, that such material might provide a harmless release for individuals who otherwise may be dangerous, Russell said at once—"Oh, well, if that's true, then I don't see that there is anything against sadistic pornography. In fact it should be encouraged. . . ." When it was stressed that there was no preponderating evidence either way Russell argued that we should fall back on an overriding principle—"in this case the principle of free speech."

Thus in the absence of evidence of harm we should be permissive. Any other view is totalitarian. . . .

If human enjoyment *per se* is not to be condemned then it is not too rash to say that we *know* pornography does good. We can easily produce our witnesses to testify to experiencing pleasure. If in the face of this—and no other favourable argument—we are unable to demonstrate a countervailing harm, then the case for easy availability of por-

---

9. Rupert Crawshay-Williams, *Russell Remembered,* Oxford University Press, 1970, p. 144.

nography is unassailable. If, in such circumstances, we find some people unconvinced it is futile to seek out further empirical data. Once we commit ourselves to the notion that the evil nature of something is axiomatic we tacitly concede that evidence is largely irrelevant to our position. If pornography never fails to fill us with predictable loathing then statistics on crime, or measured statements by careful specialists, will not be useful: our reactions will stay the same. But in this event we would do well to reflect on what our emotions tell us of our own mentality. . . .

Study Questions

1. Is pornography socially and individually beneficial?

2. Can pornography retard sexual maturity?

3. Does pornography degrade women?

Moral Dilemmas

- Monica is an attractive college student who is studying art. Her parents are not supporting her, so she must find part-time work to help pay her school and living expenses. She reads an ad in the school newspaper for an art class model. She takes the job, which requires her to pose nude in front of students, and she is paid ten dollars an hour. A friend tells her one day that he is shooting a pornographic film and asks her whether she would like to star in it; she would get two hundred dollars an hour. She refuses because she believes that pornographic films degrade and use women as things.

Is Monica being consistent in accepting the modeling job and refusing the film offer?

- Don, a journalist in a small southern town, is investigating a fire in an adult theatre that killed several customers who were in the theatre at the time. He discovers that the local minister and the former mayor, outspoken opponents of pornography, were among the victims. His editor tells him to write that they died outside the theatre—that they were simply walking by. Don doesn't know what to do.

If you were Don, would you obey your editor?

Suggested Readings

Berger, Fred R. *Freedom of Expression*. Belmont, Calif.: Wadsworth, 1980.

Feinberg, Joel. *Offense to Others*. New York: Oxford University Press, 1985.

Grčić, Joseph, "Freedom of Speech and Access to Mass Media," *The International Journal of Applied Philosophy*, v. 4, N.1, 1988.

Leiser, Burton, ed. *Values in Conflict*. New York: Macmillan, 1981.

The Meaning of Life

Most ethical systems assume that life, and especially human life, has value. Kant's philosophy is explicitly based on the absolute value of persons, and other philosophers take this as their starting point. But, can human life have value if it is a chance product of blind natural forces? If there is no God and no purpose for human existence, can persons still have value? Some individuals become so depressed, in a lonely, heartless, and godless universe, that all things lose their value and meaning. In such a state of pessimism, morals and ethics seem to pale into triviality and insignificance.

Background

The question of the meaning of life probably did not exist for primitive people as it does for modern people. Meaning for primitive individuals was based on the traditions and customs of the tribe and clan. They saw themselves as part of nature and the cosmic order of things. Religious ritual, the rhythms of nature, and the concerns of survival and family life were sufficient to place primitive men and women into a scheme that they found meaningful and purposeful. Later, Christianity and other major religions provided a picture of reality that placed human existence at the center of the universe. Every human act and want was filled with transcendental significance. No problem about the meaning of life existed then.

The meaning of life became a problem when modern science began to question the traditional religious conception of humanity and the universe. Copernicus (1473–1543), Galileo (1564–1642), and others shattered the grandiose scheme of humankind's central place by arguing that the earth is not the center of the universe, that the sun does not move around the earth, but just the reverse. Galileo also claimed that the moon, the sun, and the heavenly bodies in general were not perfect spheres made of some heavenly substance but imperfect and made of the same kind of matter as the earth.

Darwin's (1809–1882) theory of evolution was an even greater shock to the traditional religious cosmic order. He argued that men and women evolved out of lower forms of life as a result of a series of chance events. This was a further attack on the position of humanity as somehow special, unique, and superior to other beings. The belief in a life after death was now more difficult to hold, given that human beings were a product of purely natural forces. Freud's (1856–1939) theory of the presence of sexuality from childhood to adulthood further undermined the belief that humanity was essentially rational, spiritual, and above all other creatures. Copernicus, Galileo, Darwin, and Freud collectively challenged the traditional religious view of humanity in the universe.

Modern science seems to present a vision of a universe without purpose or meaning. There is no loving God who created us for a reason; rather, the universe is cold and indifferent to us. Existentialism, a school of philosophy including such thinkers as Nietzsche (1844–1900), Sartre (1905–1980), Camus (1913–1960), and others stress the absurdity of human life and death. If human existence was not created for a purpose, if there is no life after death, and if our solar system will die when the sun dies, destroying our planet, our history, and every vestige of our existence forever, how can life be meaningful? If life is not meaningful, can it be valuable? If life is not valuable, of what use are ethics and morality?

Leo Tolstoy

Some philosophers still believe that only a religious answer can be given to the question of the meaning of human existence. Leo Tolstoy (1828–1910), al-

though not primarily a philosopher, argued in *My Confession* that only a religious perspective can give meaning to human existence. In the midst of financial and literary success, Tolstoy became obsessed with the idea of his own death as self-annihilation to such a degree that he felt he could not live; life lost its flavor, and emptiness took its place. After a long and agonizing search, he came to the conclusion that only faith in an infinite God can make the reality of death bearable and life livable.

Moving though Tolstoy's confession may be, it raises at least two philosophical problems. First, death as personal destruction does add a tragic dimension to life, but in itself it does not make life meaningless. This is clear from the consideration that if we were eternal, life would not by that fact alone be meaningful, it would simply be without death. Second, since Tolstoy does not take a rational or objective approach to the existence of God, the possibility of self-delusion through wish-fulfillment is a genuine concern.

Kurt Baier

Others, such as Kurt Baier, a contemporary philosopher, take an explicitly antireligious approach and contend that life can be meaningful by humanity's own actions and purposes in this world. Rejecting the religious worldview as not rationally based, and indeed demeaning, Baier argues that having purposes that transcend one's own private concerns gives meaning to live. He agrees that science has shown that human life has no purpose in the sense that we were not made for an end or goal by some super-intelligent creative mind or god, but he further contends that there can be meaning *in life* through adopting goals and concerns that go beyond one's limited existence.

Baier criticizes Tolstoy's argument by claiming that he places an irrational emphasis on death and suffering in this life. Tolstoy's pessimistic perspective on human earthly life is a value judgment based on an arbitrary standard. Tolstoy's standard, according to Baier, is that of Christianity, which denigrates our present, imperfect earthly existence by comparison with a supposedly perfect life after death. The correct standard, Baier contends, is *average of the kind,* or the placing and judging of one's own life according to where it falls in the spectrum of human experience and possibilities.

Baier does present a challenging alternative to Tolstoy's approach, but some issues may still need reflection. Specifically, has Baier presented the religious and Christian world-picture fairly, or has he simply attacked a strawman? Does Baier's standard of the 'average of the kind' mean that half of humanity has led a meaningless and fruitless existence?

Bertrand Russell

Bertrand Russell (1872–1970) agrees with Baier that science presents us with a world where humankind is the result of impersonal natural forces and death is the final and irreversible end of personal conscious existence. Yet, we are capable of knowledge and freedom, the basis of our dignity. Russell contends that life can be lived well if we worship, not the power of the dead gods, but the ideals of truth and beauty, which unite humanity and promote human freedom. Although much evil and suffering exist in the world, we must not submit to despair. Human imagination deals with evil through artistic expression, especially in the art of tragedy. Here, for Russell, is the evidence that we need to prove that humankind can endure great suffering and still continue to live.

Arthur Schopenhauer

The philosopher Arthur Schopenhauer (1788–1860), by contrast to Baier and Russell, sees the world and human existence in utterly pessimistic terms. Human finite existence is totally meaningless in the face of the infinity of time and space and the continual burdens of boredom and anxiety that confront us. Humanity is never satisfied with life, for our species is an instrument of a blind cosmic force or will that acts endlessly but for no purpose. The truth, if we have the courage to face it, is that human existence is a mistake and that existence itself has no value.

Some have argued that Schopenhauer's bleak portrayal of human existence has its roots more in his own unhappiness than in rational argumentation. It is not clear, for example, why our admittedly finite lives become meaningless in the face of the infinities of space and time, just as it is not obvious why infinity should be the proper time frame within which to judge human life. Is it true that our lives are nothing but a cycle of boredom and anxiety? Are there no experiences of happiness and joy, fleeting though they may be, in artistic participation and in human affection and friendship?

If we stand back a moment from the details of these apparently conflicting arguments, a basic consensus seems to emerge. Although Tolstoy on the one hand, and Baier and Russell on the other, disagree about such crucial matters as the existence of God, they agree that human existence acquires meaning by relating one's existence to a greater value, or being, outside of one's life. For Tolstoy, this being was God, for Baier and Russell, it consisted in the transcendent values of knowledge, artistic expression, the enhancement of individual freedom, and the collective welfare of humanity. Moral values, then, can make life meaningful in and of themselves by providing us with a purpose.

Psychological studies such as those done by Maslow (see chapter 4) indicate that a person whose life does not have a purpose beyond that of his or her own narrow self-interest experiences a life filled with boredom, emptiness, and a sense of meaninglessness. But why does the exclusive pursuit of one's selfish pleasure and profit result in boredom and meaninglessness? This is sometimes called the 'paradox of hedonism,' i.e., that a life solely devoted to egotistical pleasure-seeking usually does not bring happiness. The reason for this could be that we are creatures so constituted that happiness comes to us as a result or consequence of some other successful kind of activity or goal achieved. As Aristotle suggests, happiness is nature's reward for living properly. The totally selfish person seeks happiness, the reward, without the effort needed to acquire it. It could be that we are inextricably social creatures, not only in terms of our biology and our need for the care of adults to survive for the first few years of our lives but also in our mental need for the approval of others to have a sense of our own value as persons. Without this sense of self-value or self-esteem, our life becomes meaningless and so do the lives of others, which leads to the rejection of morality. For us to believe

that our own lives are valuable, we need to value the lives of others, which is to say, we must act morally toward them.

My Confession

Leo Tolstoy

Leo Tolstoy (1828–1910) A major Russian writer, Leo Tolstoy was the author of many novels and essays, including War and Peace.

Chapter I

I was christened and educated in the Orthodox Christian Faith; I was taught it in my childhood, and in my boyhood and youth. Nevertheless, when, at eighteen years of age, I left the university in the second year, I had discarded all belief in anything I had been taught.

To judge by what I can now remember, I never had a serious belief; I merely trusted in what my elders made their profession of faith, but even this trust was very precarious.

I remember once in my twelfth year, a boy, now long since dead, Volodinka M——, a pupil in the gymnasium, spent a Sunday with us, and brought us the news of the last discovery in the gymnasium. This discovery was that there was no God, and that all we were taught on the subject was a mere invention (this was in 1838). I remember well how interested my elder brothers were in this news; I was admitted to their deliberations, and we all eagerly accepted the theory as something particularly attractive and possibly quite true.

I remember, also, that when my elder brother, Dmitri, then at the university, with the impulsiveness natural to his character, gave himself up to a passionate faith, began to attend the church services regularly, to fast, and to lead a pure and moral life, we all of us, and some older than ourselves, never ceased to hold him up to ridicule, and for some incomprehensible reason gave him the nickname of Noah. I remember that Musin-Pushkin, then curator of the University of Kazan, having invited us to a ball, tried to persuade my brother, who had refused the invitation, by the jeering argument that even David danced before the Ark.

I sympathized then with these jokes of my elders, and drew from them this conclusion,—that I was bound to learn my catechism, and go to church, but that it was not necessary to take all this too seriously.

I also remember that I read Voltaire when I was very young, and that his tone of mockery amused without disgusting me.

This estrangement from all belief went on in me, as it does now, and always has done, in those of the same social position and culture. This falling off, as it seems to me, for the most part goes on thus: people live as others live, and their lives are guided, not by the principles of the faith that is taught them,

From *My Confession* by Leo Tolstoy, translated by Leo Wiener. Reprinted with permission from J. M. Dent and Sons.

but by their very opposite; belief has no influence on life, nor on the relations among men—it is relegated to some other sphere apart from life and independent of it; if the two ever come into contact at all, belief is only one of the outward phenomena, and not one of the constituent parts of life.

By a man's life, by his acts, it was then, as it is now, impossible to know whether he was a believer or not. If there be a difference between one who openly professes the doctrines of the Orthodox Church, and one who denies them, the difference is to the advantage of the former. Then, as now, the open profession of the Orthodox doctrines was found mostly among dull, stern, immoral men, and those who think much of their own importance. Intellect, honor, frankness, good nature, and morality are oftener met with among those who call themselves disbelievers.

The school-boy is taught his catechism and sent to church; chinovniks, or functionaries, are required to show a certificate of having taken the holy communion. But the man belonging to our class, who is done with school and does not enter the public service, may now live a dozen years—still more was this the case formerly—without being once reminded of the fact that he lives among Christians, and is reckoned as a member of the Orthodox Christian Church.

Thus it happens that now, as formerly, the influence of early religious teaching, accepted merely on trust and upheld by authority, gradually fades away under the knowledge and practical experience of life, which is opposed to all its principles, and that a man often believes for years that his early faith is still intact, while all the time not a trace of it remains in him.

A certain S‗‗‗‗, a clever and veracious man, once related to me how he came to give up his belief.

Twenty-six years ago, while he was off on a hunting expedition, he knelt down to pray before he lay down to rest, according to a habit of his from childhood. His elder brother, who was of the party, lay on some straw and watched him. When S‗‗‗‗ had finished, and was preparing to lie down, his brother said to him:—

"Ah, so you still keep that up?"

Nothing more passed between them, but that day S‗‗‗‗ ceased to pray and to go to church. For thirty years S‗‗‗‗ has not said a prayer, has not taken the communion, has not been in a church,—not because he shared the convictions of his brother, or even knew them,—not because he had come to any conclusions of his own,—but because his brother's words were like the push of a finger against a wall ready to tumble over with its own weight; they proved to him that what he had taken for belief was an empty form, and that consequently every word he uttered, every sign of the cross he made, every time he bowed his head during his prayers, his act was unmeaning. When he once admitted to himself that such acts had no meaning in them, he could not continue them.

Thus it has been, and is, I believe, with the large majority of men. I am speaking of men of our class, I am speaking of men who are true to themselves, and not of those who make of religion a means of obtaining some temporal advantage. (These men are truly absolute unbelievers; for if faith be to them a means of obtaining any worldly end, it is most certainly no faith at all.) Such men of our own class are in this position: the light of knowledge and life has melted the artificially constructed edifice of belief within, and they have either observed that and cleared away the superincumbent ruins, or they have remained unconscious of it.

The belief instilled from childhood in men, as in so many others, gradually disappeared, but with this difference; that as from fifteen years of age I had begun to read philosophical works, I became very early conscious of my own disbelief. From the age of sixteen I ceased to pray, and ceased, from conviction, to attend the services of the church and to fast. I no longer accepted the faith of my childhood, but I believed in something, though I could not exactly explain in what. I believed in a God,—or rather, I did not deny the existence of a God,—but what kind of God I could not have told; I denied neither Christ nor His teaching, but in what that teaching consisted I could not have said.

Now, when I think over that time, I see clearly that all the faith I had, the only belief which, apart from mere animal instinct, swayed my life, was a belief in the possibility of perfection, though what it was in itself, or what would be its results, I could not have said.

I tried to reach intellectual perfection; my studies were extended in every direction of which my life afforded me a chance; I strove to strengthen my will, forming for myself rules which I forced myself to follow; I did my best to develop my physical powers by every exercise calculated to give strength and agility, and by way of accustoming myself to patient endurance; I subjected myself to many voluntary hardships and trials of privation. All this I looked on as necessary to obtain the perfection at which I aimed.

At first, of course, moral perfection seemed to me the main end, but I soon found myself contemplating in its stead an ideal of general perfectibility; in other words, I wished to be better, not in my own eyes nor in God's, but in the sight of other men. And very soon this striving to be better in the sight of men feeling again changed into another,— the desire to have more power than others, to secure for myself a greater share of fame, of social distinction, and of wealth.

Chapter II

At some future time I may relate the story of my life, and dwell in detail on the pathetic and instructive incidents of my youth. I think that many and many have had the same experiences as I did. I desired with all my soul to be good; but I was young, I had passions, and I was alone, wholly alone, in my search after goodness. Every time I tried to express the longings of my heart to be morally good, I was met with contempt and ridicule, but as soon as I gave way to low passions, I was praised and encouraged.

Ambition, love of power, love of gain, lechery, pride, anger, vengeance, were held in high esteem.

As I gave way to these passions, I became like my elders and I felt that they were satisfied with me. A kind-hearted aunt of mine, a really good woman with whom I lived, used to say to me that there was one thing above all others which she wished for me—an intrigue with a married woman: *"Rien ne forme un jeune homme, comme une liaison avec une femme comme il faut."* Another of her

wishes for my happiness was that I should become an adjutant, and, if possible, to the Emperor; the greatest piece of good fortune of all she thought would be that I should find a very wealthy bride, who would bring me as her dowry as many slaves as could be.

I cannot now recall those years without a painful feeling of horror and loathing.

I put men to death in war. I fought duels to slay others, I lost at cards, wasted my substance wrung from the sweat of peasants, punished the latter cruelly, rioted with loose women, and deceived men. Lying, robbery, adultery of all kinds, drunkenness, violence, murder. There was not one crime which I did not commit, and yet I was not the less considered by my equals a comparatively moral man.

Such was my life during ten years.

During that time I began to write, out of vanity, love of gain, and pride. I followed as a writer the same path which I had chosen as a man. In order to obtain the fame and the money for which I wrote, I was obliged to hide what was good and to say what was evil. Thus I did. How often while writing have I cudgeled my brains to conceal under the mask of indifference or pleasantry those yearnings for something better which formed the real thought of my life. I succeeded in this also, and was praised.

At twenty-six years of age, on the close of the war, I came to Petersburg and made the acquaintance of the authors of the day. I met with a healthy reception and much flattery.

Before I had time to look around, the prejudices and views of life common to the writers of the class with which I associated became my own, and completely put an end to all my former struggles after a better life. These views, under the influence of the dissipation of my life, supplied a theory which justified it.

The view of life taken by these my fellow-writers was that life is a development, and the principal part in that development is played by ourselves, the thinkers, while among the thinkers the chief influence is again due to us, the artists, the poets. Our vocation is to teach men.

In order to avoid answering the very natural

question, "What do I know, and what can I teach?" the theory in question is made to contain the formula that it is not necessary to know this, but that the artist and the poet teach unconsciously.

I was myself considered a marvelous artist and poet, and I therefore very naturally adopted this theory. I, an artist and poet, wrote and taught I knew not what. For doing this I received money; I kept a splendid table, had excellent lodgings, women, society; I had fame. Naturally what I taught was very good.

The faith in poetry and the development of life was a true faith, and I was one of its priests. To be one of its priests was very advantageous and agreeable. I long remained in this belief, and never once doubted its truth.

But in the second, and especially in the third year of this way of life, I began to doubt the infallibility of the doctrine, and to examine it more closely. What first led me to doubt was the fact that I began to notice the priests of this belief did not agree among themselves. Some said:—

"We are the best and most useful teachers; we teach what is needful, and all others teach wrong."

They disputed, quarreled, abused, deceived, and cheated one another. Moreover, there were many among us who, quite indifferent to the question who was right or who was wrong, advanced only their own private interests by the aid of our activity. All this forced on me doubts as to the truth of our belief.

Again, having begun to doubt the truth of our literary faith, I began to study its priests more closely, and became convinced that almost all the priests of this faith were immoral men, most of them worthless and insignificant, and beneath the moral level of those with whom I associated during my former dissipated and military career; but conceited and self-satisfied as only those can be who are wholly saints, or those who know not what holiness is.

I grew disgusted with mankind and with myself, and I understood that this belief was a delusion. The strangest thing in all this was that, though I soon saw the falseness of this belief and renounced it, I did not renounce the rank given me by these men,—the rank of artist, poet, teacher. I was simple enough to imagine that I was a poet and artist, and could teach all men without knowing what I was teaching. But so I did.

By my companionship with these men I had gained a new vice,—a pride developed to a morbid extreme, and an insane self-confidence in teaching men what I myself did not know.

When I now think over that time, and remember my own state of mind and that of these men (a state of mind common enough among thousands still), it seems to me pitiful, terrible, and ridiculous; it excites the feelings which overcome us as we pass through a madhouse.

We were all then convinced that it behooved us to speak, to write, and to print as fast as we could, as much as we could, and that on this depended the welfare of the human race. And thousands of us wrote, printed, and taught, and all the while confuted and abused one another. Quite unconscious that we ourselves knew nothing, that to the simplest of all problems in life—what is right and what is wrong—we had no answer, we all went on talking together without one to listen, at times abetting and praising one another on condition that we were abetted and praised in turn, and again turning upon one another in wrath—in short, we reproduced the scenes in a madhouse.

Thousands of laborers worked day and night, to the limit of their strength, setting up the type and printing millions of words to be spread by the post all over Russia, and still we continued to teach, unable to teach enough, angrily complaining the while that we were not much listened to.

A strange state of things indeed, but now it is comprehensible to me. The real motive that inspired all our reasoning was the desire for money and praise, to obtain which we knew of no other means than writing books and newspapers, and so we did. But in order to hold fast to the conviction that while thus uselessly employed we were very important men, it was necessary to justify our occupation to ourselves by another theory, and the following was the one we adopted:—

Whatever is, is right: everything that is, is due to development; development comes from civilization; the measure of civilization is the diffusion of books and newspapers; we are paid and honored for the books and newspapers which we write, and we are therefore the most useful and best of men!

This reasoning might have been conclusive had we all been agreed; but, as for every opinion expressed by one of us there instantly appeared from another one diametrically opposite, we had to hesitate before accepting it. But we did not notice this; we received money, and were praised by those of our party, consequently we—each one of us—considered that we were in the right.

It is now clear to me that between ourselves and the inhabitants of a madhouse there was no difference: at the time I only vaguely suspected this, and, like all madmen, thought all were mad except myself.

Chapter III

I lived in this senseless manner another six years, up to the time of my marriage. During this time I went abroad. My life in Europe, and my acquaintance with many eminent and learned foreigners, confirmed my belief in the doctrine of general perfectibility, as I found the same theory prevailed among them. This belief took the form which is common among most of the cultivated men of our day. This belief was expressed in the word "progress." It then appeared to me this word had a real meaning. I did not as yet understand that, tormented like every other man by the question, "How was I to live better?" when I answered that I must live for progress, I was only repeating the answer of a man carried away in a boat by the waves and the wind, who to the one important question for him, "Where are we to steer?" should answer, "We are being carried somewhere."

I did not see this then; only at rare intervals my feelings, and not my reason, were roused against the common superstition of our age, which leads men to ignore their own ignorance of life.

Thus, during my stay in Paris, the sight of a public execution revealed to me the weakness of my superstitious belief in progress. When I saw the head divided from the body, and heard the sound with which they fell separately into the box, I understood, not with my reason, but with my whole

being, that no theory of the wisdom of all established things, nor of progress, could justify such an act; and that if all the men in the world from the day of creation, by whatever theory, had found this thing necessary, I knew it was not necessary, it was a bad thing, and that therefore I must judge of what was right and necessary, not by what men said and did, not by progress, but what I felt to be true in my heart.

Another instance for the insufficiency of this superstition of progress as a rule of life was the death of my brother. He fell ill while still young, suffered much during a whole year, and died in great pain. He was a man of good abilities, of a kind heart, and of a serious temper, but he died without understanding why he had lived, and still less what his death meant for him. No theories could give an answer to these questions, either to him or to me, during the whole period of his long and painful lingering.

But these occasions for doubt were few and far between; on the whole, I continued to live in the profession of the faith of progress. "Everything develops, and I myself am developing; and why this is so will one day be apparent," was the formula I was obliged to adopt.

On my return from abroad I settled in the country, and occupied myself with the organization of schools for the peasantry. This occupation was especially dear to my heart, because it was free from the spirit of falseness so evident to me in the career of a literary teacher.

Here again I acted in the name of progress, but this time I brought a spirit of critical inquiry to the system on which the progress rested. I said to myself that progress was often attempted in an irrational manner, and that it was necessary to leave a primitive people and the children of peasants perfectly free to choose the way of progress which they thought best. In reality I was still bent on the solution of the same impossible problem,—how to teach without knowing what I had to teach. In the highest spheres of literature I had understood that it was impossible to do this because I had seen that each taught differently, and that the teachers quarreled among themselves, and scarcely succeeded in concealing their ignorance from one another. Having now to deal with peasants' children, I thought that I would get over this difficulty by allowing the children to learn what they liked. It seems now absurd when I remember the expedients by which I carried out this whim of mine to teach, though I knew in my heart that I could teach nothing useful, because I myself did not know what was necessary.[1]

After a year spent in this employment with the school I again went abroad, for the purpose of finding out how I was to teach without knowing anything.

I believed that I had found a solution abroad, and, armed with all that essence of wisdom, I returned to Russia, the same year in which the peasants were freed from serfdom; and, accepting the office of arbitrator,[2] I began to teach the uneducated people in the schools, and the educated classes in the journal which I began to publish. Things seemed to be going on well, but I felt that my mind was not in a normal state and that a change was near. I might even then, perhaps, have come to that state of despair to which I was brought fifteen years later, if it had not been for a new experience in life which promised me safety—family life.

For a year I was occupied with arbitration, with the schools and with my newspaper, and got so involved that I was harassed to death; the struggle over the arbitration was so hard for me, my activity in the schools was so dubious to me, my shuffling in the newspaper became so repugnant to me, consisting as it did in forever the same thing,—in the desire to teach all people and to hide the fact that I did not know how or what to teach,—that I fell ill, more with a mental than physical sickness, gave up everything, and started for the steppes to the Bashkirs to breathe a fresher air, to drink kumiss, and live an animal life.

After I returned I married. The new circumstances of a happy family life completely led me away from the search after the meaning of life as a whole. My life was concentrated at this time in my family, my wife and children, and consequently in the care for increasing the means of life. The effort to effect my own individual perfection, already replaced by the striving after general progress, was again changed into an effort to secure the particular happiness of my family.

In this way fifteen years passed.

Notwithstanding that during these fifteen years I looked upon the craft of authorship as a very trifling thing, I continued all the time to write. I had experienced the seductions of authorship, the temptations of an enormous pecuniary reward and of great applause for valueless work, and gave myself up to it as a means of improving my material position, and of stifling in my soul all questions regarding my own life and life in general. In my writings I taught what for me was the only truth,—that the object of life should be our highest happiness and that of our family.

"The truth was, that life was meaningless."

Thus I lived; but, five years ago, a strange state of mind began to grow upon me: I had moments of perplexity, of a stoppage, as it were, of life, as if I did not know how I was to live, what I was to do, and I began to wander, and was a victim to low spirits. But this passed, and I continued to live as before. Later, these periods of perplexity began to return more and more frequently, and invariably took the same form. These stoppages of life always presented themselves to me with the same questions: "Why?" and "What after?"

At first it seemed to me that these were aimless, unmeaning questions; it seemed to me that all they asked about was well known, and that if at any time when I wished to find answers to them I could do so without much trouble—that just at that time I could not be bothered with this, but whenever I should stop to think them over I should find an answer. But these questions presented themselves to

---

1. See "School Scenes from Yasnaya Polyana," Vol. XV.
2. *Posrednik,* sometimes translated Justice of the Peace.

my mind with ever increasing frequency, demanding an answer with still greater and greater persistence, and like dots grouped themselves into one black spot.

It was with me as it happens in the case of every mortal internal ailment—at first appear the insignificant symptoms of indisposition, disregarded by the patient; then these symptoms are repeated more and more frequently, till they merge in uninterrupted suffering. The sufferings increase, and the patient, before he has time to look around, is confronted with the fact that what he took for a mere indisposition has become more important to him than anything else on earth, that it is death!

This is exactly what happened to me. I became aware that this was not a chance indisposition, but something very serious, and that if all these questions continued to recur, I should have to find an answer to them. And I tried to answer them. The questions seemed so foolish, so simple, so childish; but no sooner had I taken hold of them and attempted to decide them than I was convinced, first, that they were neither childish nor silly, but were concerned with the deepest problems of life; and, in the second place, that I could not decide them— could not decide them, however I put my mind upon them.

Before occupying myself with my Samara estate, with the education of my son, with the writings of books, I was bound to know why I did these things. As long as I do not know the reason "why" I cannot do anything. I cannot live. While thinking about the management of my household and estate, which in these days occupied much of my time, suddenly this question came into my head:—

"Well and good, I have now six thousand desyatins in the government of Samara, and three hundred horses—what then?"

I was perfectly disconcerted, and knew not what to think. Another time, dwelling on the thought of how I should educate my children, I asked myself, *"Why?"* Again, when considering by what means the well-being of the people might best be promoted, I suddenly exclaimed, "But what concern have I with it?" When I thought of the fame which my works were gaining me, I said to myself:—

"Well, what if I should be more famous than Gogol, Pushkin, Shakespear, Molière—than all the writers of the world—well, and what then?"

I could find no reply. Such questions will not wait; they demand an immediate answer; without one it is impossible to live; but answer there was none.

I felt that the ground on which I stood was crumbling, that there was nothing for me to stand on, that what I had been living for was nothing, that I had no reason for living.

Chapter IV

My life had come to a stop. I was able to breathe, to eat, to drink, to sleep, and I could not help breathing, eating, drinking, sleeping; but there was no real life in me because I had not a single desire, the fulfilment of which I could feel to be reasonable. If I wished for anything, I knew beforehand that, were I to satisfy the wish, or were I not to satisfy it, nothing would come of it. Had a fairy appeared and offered me all I desired, I should not have known what to say. If I had, in moments of excitement, I will not say wishes, but the habits of former wishes, at calmer moments I knew that it was a delusion, that I really wished for nothing. I could not even wish to know the truth, because I guessed in what it consisted.

The truth was, that life was meaningless. Every day of life, every step in it, brought me, as it were, nearer the precipice, and I saw clearly that before me there was nothing but ruin. And to stop was impossible; to go back was impossible; and it was impossible to shut my eyes so as not to see that there was nothing before me but suffering and actual death, absolute annihilation.

Thus I, a healthy and a happy man, was brought to feel that I could live no longer,—some irresistible force was dragging me onward to escape from life. I do not mean that I wanted to kill myself.

The force that drew me away from life was stronger, fuller, and more universal than any wish; it was a force like that of my previous attachment to life, only in a contrary direction. With all my force I struggled away from life. The idea of suicide came as naturally to me as formerly that of bettering my life. This thought was so attractive to me that I was compelled to practise upon myself as species of self-deception in order to avoid carrying it out too hastily. I was unwilling to act hastily, only because I wanted to employ all my powers in clearing away the confusion of my thoughts; if I should not clear them away, I could at any time kill myself. And here was I, a man fortunately situated, hiding away a cord, to avoid being tempted to hang myself by it to the transom between the closets of my room, where I undressed alone every evening; and I ceased to go hunting with a gun because it offered too easy a way of getting rid of life. I knew not what I wanted; I was afraid of life; I struggled to get away from it, and yet there *was* something I hoped for from it.

Such was the condition I had to come to, at a time when all the circumstances of my life were preeminently happy ones, and when I had not reached my fiftieth year. I had a good, loving, and beloved wife, good children, and a large estate, which, without much trouble on my part, was growing and increasing; I was more than ever respected by my friends and acquaintances; I was praised by strangers, and could lay claim to having made my name famous without much self-deception. Moreover, I was not mad or in an unhealthy mental state; on the contrary, I enjoyed a mental and physical strength which I have seldom found in men of my class and pursuits; I could keep up with a peasant in mowing, and could continue mental labor for eight or ten hours at a stretch, without any evil consequences. And in this state of things it came to this,—that I could not live, and as I feared death I was obliged to employ ruses against myself so as not to put an end to my life.

The mental state in which I then was seemed to me summed up in the following: My life was a foolish and wicked joke played on me by some one. Notwithstanding that fact that I did not recognize a "Some one," who may have created me, this conclusion that some one had wickedly and foolishly made a joke of me in bringing me into the world seemed to me the most natural of all conclusions.

I could not help reasoning that *there,* somewhere, is some one who is now diverting himself at my expense, as he watches me, as after from thirty to forty years of a life of study and development, of mental and bodily growth with all my powers matured and having reached that summit of life from which it is seen in its completeness, I stand like a fool on this height, understanding clearly that there is nothing in life, that there never was anything, and never will be. To him it must seem ridiculous.

But whether there is, or is not, such a being, in either case it did not help me. I could not attribute a reasonable motive to any single act in my whole life. I was only astonished that I could not have realized this at the very beginning. All this had so long been known to me! Illness and death would come (indeed, they had come), if not today, then tomorrow, to those whom I loved, to myself, and nothing remains but stench and worms. All my acts, whatever I did, would sooner or later be forgotten, and I myself be nowhere. Why, then, busy one's self with anything? How could men fail to see this, and live? How wonderful this is! It is possible to live only as long as life intoxicates us; as soon as we are sober again we see that it is all a delusion, and a stupid delusion! In this, indeed, there is nothing either ludicrous or amusing; it is only cruel and stupid!

There is an old Eastern fable about a traveler in the steppes who is attacked by a furious wild beast. To save himself the traveler gets into a waterless well; but at the bottom of it he sees a dragon with its jaws wide open to devour him. The unhappy man dares not get out for fear of the wild beast, and dares not descend for fear of the dragon, so he catches hold of the branch of a wild plant growing in a crevice of the well. His arms grow tired, and he feels that he must soon perish, death awaiting him on either side, but he still holds on; and he sees two mice, one black and one white, gradually making their way round the stem of the wild plant on which he is hanging, nibbling it through. The plant will soon give way and break off, and he will fall into the jaws of the dragon. The traveler sees this, and knows that he must inevitably perish; but, while still hanging, he looks around him, and, finding some drops of honey on the leaves of the wild plant, he stretches out his tongue and licks them.

Thus do I cling to the branch of life, knowing that the dragon of death inevitably awaits me, ready to tear me to pieces, and I cannot understand why such tortures have fallen to my lot. I also strive to suck the honey which once comforted me, but this honey no longer rejoices me, while the white mouse and the black, day and night, gnaw through the branch to which I cling. I see the dragon plainly, and the honey is no longer sweet. I see the dragon, from which there is no escape, and the mice, and I cannot turn my eyes away from them. It is no fable, but a living, undeniable truth, to be understood of all men.

The former delusion of happiness in life which hid from me the horror of the dragon no longer deceives me. However I may reason with myself that I cannot understand the meaning of life, that I must live without thinking, I cannot do this, because I have done so too long already. Now I cannot help seeing the days and nights hurrying by and bringing me nearer to death. I can see but this, because this alone is true—all the rest is a lie. The two drops of honey, which more than anything else drew my eyes away from the cruel truth, my love for my family and for my writings, to which later I gave the name of art, were no longer sweet to me.

"My family," I said to myself; "but a family—a wife and children—are also human beings, and subject to the same conditions as I myself; they must either be living in a lie, or they must see the terrible truth. Why should they live? Why should I love them, care for them, bring them up, and watch over them? To bring them to the despair which fills myself, or to make dolts of them? As I love them, I cannot conceal from them the truth—every step they take in knowledge leads them to it, and that truth is death."

"Art, poetry?" . . . .

Under the influence of success, and flattered by praise, I had long been persuading myself that this was a work which must be done notwithstanding the approach of death, which would destroy everything—my writings, and the memory of them; but I soon saw that this was only another delusion, I saw clearly that art is only the ornament and charm of life. Life having lost its charm for me, how could I make others see a charm in it? While I was not liv-

ing my own life, but one that was external to me was bearing me away on its billows, while I believed that life had a meaning, though I could not say what it was, the reflections of life of every kind in poetry and art gave me delight, it was pleasant to me to look at life in the mirror of art; but when I tried to discover the meaning of life, when I felt the necessity of living myself, the mirror became either unnecessary, superfluous, and ridiculous, or painful. I could no longer take comfort from what I saw in the mirror—that my position was stupid and desperate.

It was a genuine cause of rejoicing when in the depths of my soul I believed that my life had a meaning. Then this play of lights, the comic, the tragic, the pathetic, the beautiful, and the terrible in life, amused me. But when I knew that life was meaningless and terrible, the play in the mirror could no longer entertain me. No sweetness could be sweet to me when I saw the dragon, and the mice nibbling away my support.

Nor was that all. Had I simply come to know that life has no meaning, I might have quietly accepted it, might have known that was my allotted portion. But I could not rest calmly on this. Had I been like a man living in a forest, out of which he knows that there is no issue, I could have lived on; but I was like a man lost in a forest, and who, terrified by the thought that he is lost, rushes about trying to find a way out, and, though he knows each step leads him still farther astray, cannot help rushing about.

It was this that was terrible! And to get free from this horror, I was ready to kill myself. I felt a horror of what awaited me; I knew that this horror was more horrible than the position itself, but I could not patiently await the end. However persuasive the argument might be that all the same a blood-vessel in the heart would be ruptured or something would burst and all be over, still I could not patiently await the end. The horror of the darkness was too great to bear, and I longed to free myself from it as speedily as possible by a rope or a pistol ball. This was the feeling that, above all, drew me to think of suicide.

I lived for a long time in this madness, which, not in words, but in deeds, is particularly characteristic of us, the most liberal and learned of men. But, thanks either to my strange, physical love for the real working class, which made me understand it and see that it is not so stupid as we suppose, or to the sincerity of my conviction, which was that I could know nothing and that the best that I could do was to hang myself,—I felt that if I wanted to live and understand the meaning of life, I ought naturally to look for it, not among those who had lost the meaning of life and wanted to kill themselves, but among those billions departed and living men who had been carrying their own lives and ours upon their shoulders. And I looked around at the enormous masses of deceased and living men,—not learned and wealthy, but simple men,—and I saw something quite different. I saw that all these billions of men that lived or had lived, all, with rare exceptions, did not fit into my subdivisions, ... and that I could not recognize them as not understanding the question, because they themselves put it and answered it with surprising clearness. Nor could I recognize them as Epicureans, because their lives were composed rather of privations and suffering than of enjoyment. Still less could I recognize them as senselessly living out their meaningless lives, because every act of theirs and death itself was explained by them. They regarded it as the greatest evil to kill themselves. It appeared, then, that all humanity was in possession of a knowledge of the meaning of life, which I did not recognize and which I contemned. It turned out that rational knowledge did not give any meaning to life, excluded life, while the meaning which by billions of people, by all humanity, was ascribed to life was based on some despised, false knowledge.

The rational knowledge in the person of the learned and the wise denied the meaning of life, but the enormous masses of men, all humanity, recognized this meaning in an irrational knowledge. This irrational knowledge was faith, the same that I could not help but reject. That was God as one and three, the creation in six days, devils and angels, and all that which I could not accept so long as I had not lost my senses.

My situation was a terrible one. I knew that I should not find anything on the path of rational knowledge but the negation of life, and there, in faith, nothing but the negation of reason, which was still more impossible than the negation of life. From the rational knowledge it followed that life was an evil and men knew it,—it depended on men whether they should cease living, and yet they lived and continued to live, and I myself lived, though I had known long ago that life was meaningless and an evil. From faith it followed that, in order to understand life, I must renounce reason, for which alone a meaning was needed.

There resulted a contradiction, from which there were two ways out: either what I called rational was not so rational as I had thought; or that which to me appeared irrational was not so irrational as I had thought. And I began to verify the train of thoughts of my rational knowledge.

In verifying the train of thoughts of my rational knowledge, I found that it was quite correct. The deduction that life was nothing was inevitable; but I saw a mistake. The mistake was that I had not reasoned in conformity with the question put by me. The question was, "Why should I live?" that is, "What real, indestructible essence will come from my phantasmal, destructible life? What meaning has my finite existence in this infinite world?" And in order to answer this question, I studied life.

The solutions of all possible questions of life apparently could not satisfy me, because my question, no matter how simple it appeared in the beginning, included the necessity of explaining the finite through the infinite, and vice versa.

I asked, "What is the extra-temporal, extra-causal, extra-spatial meaning of life?" But I gave an answer to the question, "What is the temporal, causal, spatial meaning of my life?" The result was that after a long labour of mind I answered, "None."

In my reflections I constantly equated, nor could I do otherwise, the finite with the finite, the infinite with the infinite, and so from that resulted precisely what had to result: force was force, matter was matter, will was will, infinity was infinity, nothing was nothing,—and nothing else could come from it.

There happened something like what at times takes place in mathematics: you think you are solving an equation, when you have only an identity. The reasoning is correct, but you receive as a result the answer: $a = a$, or $x = x$, or $o = o$. The same happened with my reflection in respect to the question about the meaning of my life. The answers given by all science to that question are only identities.

Indeed, the strictly scientific knowledge, that knowledge which, as Descartes did, begins with a full doubt in everything, rejects all knowledge which has been taken on trust, and builds everything anew on the laws of reason and experience, cannot give any other answer to the question of life than what I received,—an indefinite answer. It only seemed to me at first that science gave me a positive answer,—Schopenhauer's answer: "Life has no meaning, it is an evil." But when I analyzed the matter, I saw that the answer was not a positive one, but that it was only my feeling which expressed it as such. The answer, strictly expressed, as it is expressed by the Brahmins, by Solomon, and by Schopenhauer, is only an indefinite answer, or an identity, $o = o$, life is nothing. Thus the philosophical knowledge does not negate anything, but only answers that the question cannot be solved by it, that for philosophy the solution remains insoluble.

When I saw that, I understood that it was not right for me to look for an answer to my question in rational knowledge, and that the answer given by rational knowledge was only an indication that the answer might be got if the question were differently put, but only when into the discussion of the question should be introduced the question of the relation of the finite to the infinite. I also understood that, no matter how irrational and monstrous the answers might be that faith gave, they had this advantage that they introduced into each answer the relation of the finite to the infinite, without which there could be no answer.

No matter how I may put the question, "How must I live?" the answer is, "According to God's law." "What real result will there be from my life?"—"Eternal torment or eternal bliss." "What is the meaning which is not destroyed by death?"—"The union with infinite God, paradise."

Thus, outside the rational knowledge, which had to me appeared as the only one, I was inevitably led to recognize that all living humanity had a certain other irrational knowledge, faith, which made it possible to live.

All the irrationality of faith remained the same for me, but I could not help recognizing that it alone gave to humanity answers to the questions of life, and, in consequence of them, the possibility of living.

The rational knowledge brought me to the recognition that life was meaningless,—my life stopped, and I wanted to destroy myself. When I looked around at people, at all humanity, I saw that people lived and asserted that they knew the meaning of life. I looked back at myself: I lived so long as I knew the meaning of life. As to other people, so even to me, did faith give the meaning of life and the possibility of living.

Looking again at the people of other countries, contemporaries of mine and those passed away, I saw again the same. Where life had been, there faith, ever since humanity had existed, had given the possibility of living, and the chief features of faith were everywhere one and the same.

No matter what answers faith may give, its every answer gives to the finite existence of man the sense of the infinite,—a sense which is not destroyed by suffering, privation, and death. Consequently in faith alone could we find the meaning and possibility of life. What, then, was faith? I understood that faith was not merely an evidence of things not seen, and so forth, not revelation (that is only the description of one of the symptoms of faith), not the relation of man to man (faith has to be defined, and then God, and not first God, and faith through him), not merely an agreement with what a man was told, as faith was generally understood,—that faith was the knowledge of the meaning of human life, in consequence of which man did not destroy himself, but lived. Faith is the power of life. If a man lives he believes in something. If he did not believe that he ought to live for some purpose, he would not live. If he does not see and understand the phantasm of the finite, he believes in that finite; if he understands the phantasm of the finite, he must believe in the infinite. Without faith one cannot live. . . .

In order that all humanity may be able to live, in order that they may continue living, giving a meaning to life, they, those billions, must have another, a real knowledge of faith, for not the fact that I, with Solomon and Schopenhauer, did not kill myself convinced me of the existence of faith, but that these billions had lived and had borne us, me and Solomon, on the waves of life.

Then I began to cultivate the acquaintance of the believers from among the poor, the simple and unlettered folk, of pilgrims, monks, dissenters, peasants. The doctrine of these people from among the masses was also the Christian doctrine that the quasi-believers of our circle professed. With the Christian truths were also mixed in very many superstitions, but there was this difference: the superstitions of our circle were quite unnecessary to them, had no connection with their lives, were only a kind of an Epicurean amusement, while the superstitions of the believers from among the labouring classes were to such an extent blended with their life that it would have been impossible to imagine it without these superstitions,—it was a necessary condition of that life. I began to examine closely the lives and beliefs of these people, and the more I examined them, the more did I become convinced that they had the real faith, that their faith was necessary for them, and that it alone gave them a meaning and possibility of life. In contradistinction to what I saw in our circle, where life without faith was possible, and where hardly one in a thousand professed to be a believer, among them there was hardly one in a thousand who was not a believer. In contradistinction to what I saw in our circle, where all life passed in idleness, amusements, and tedium of life, I saw that the whole life of these people was passed in hard work, and that they were satisfied with life. In contradistinction to the people of our circle, who struggled and murmured against fate because of their privations and their suffering, these people accepted diseases and sorrows without any perplexity or opposition, but with the calm and firm conviction that it was all for good. In contradistinction to the fact that the more intelligent we are, the less do we understand the meaning of life and the more do we see a kind of a bad joke in our suffering and death, these people live, suffer, and approach death, and suffer in peace and more often in joy. In contradistinction to the fact that a calm death, a death without terror or despair, is the greatest exception in our circle, a restless, insubmissive, joyless death is one of the greatest exceptions among the masses. And of such people, who are deprived of everything which for Solomon and for me constitutes the only good of life, and who withal experience the greatest happiness, there is an enormous number. I cast a broader glance about me. I examined the life of past and present vast masses of men, and I saw people who in like manner had understood the meaning of life, who had known how to live and die, not two, not three, not ten, but hundreds, thousands, millions. All of them, infinitely diversified as to habits, intellect, culture, situation, all equally and quite contrary to my ignorance knew the meaning of life and of death, worked calmly, bore privations and suffering, lived and died, seeing in that not vanity, but good.

I began to love those people. The more I penetrated into their life, the life of the men now living, and the life of men departed, of whom I had read and heard, the more did I love them, and the easier it became for me to live. Thus I lived for about two years, and within me took place a transformation, which had long been working within me, and the germ of which had always been in me. What happened with me was that the life of our circle,—of the rich and the learned,—not only disgusted me, but even lost all its meaning. All our acts, reflections, sciences, arts,—all that appeared to me in a new light. I saw that all that was mere pampering of the appetites, and that no meaning could be found in it; but the life of all the working masses, of all humanity, which created life, presented itself to me in its real significance. I saw that that was life itself and that the meaning given to this life was truth, and I accepted it.

Study Questions

1. Can life be meaningful without God?

2. Would immortality alone make life meaningful?

3. If God exists, what gives God meaning?

The Meaning of Life

Kurt Baier is a professor of philosophy at the University of Pittsburgh and author of The Moral Point of View *and other writings on moral philosophy.*

Kurt Baier

Tolstoy, in his autobiographical work, "A Confession," reports how, when he was fifty and at the height of his literary success, he came to be obsessed by the fear that life was meaningless.

> "At first I experienced moments of perplexity and arrest of life, as though I did not know what to do or how to live; and I felt lost and became dejected. But this passed, and I went on living as before. Then these moments of perplexity began to recur oftener and oftener, and always in the same form. They were always expressed by the questions: What is it for? What does it lead to? At first it seemed to me that these were aimless and irrelevant questions. I thought that it was all well known, and that if I should ever wish to deal with the solution it would not cost me much effort; just at present I had no time for it, but when I wanted to, I should be able to find the answer. The questions however began to repeat themselves frequently, and to demand replies more and more insistently and like drops of ink always falling on one place they ran together into one black blot." [1]

A Christian living in the Middle Ages would not have felt any serious doubts about Tolstoy's questions. To him it would have seemed quite certain that life had a meaning and quite clear what it was. The medieval Christian world picture assigned to man a highly significant, indeed the central part in the grand scheme of things. The universe was made for the express purpose of providing a stage on which to enact a drama starring Man in the title role.

To be exact, the world was created by God in the year 4004 B.C. Man was the last and the crown of this creation, made in the likeness of God, placed in the Garden of Eden on earth, the fixed centre of the universe, round which revolved the nine heavens of the sun, the moon, the planets and the fixed stars, producing as they revolved in their orbits the heavenly harmony of the spheres. And this gigantic universe was created for the enjoyment of man, who was originally put in control of it. Pain and death were unknown in paradise. But this state of bliss was not to last. Adam and Eve ate of the forbidden tree of knowledge, and life on this earth turned into a death-march through a vale of tears. Then, with the birth of Jesus, new hope came into the world. After He had died on the cross, it became at least possible to wash away with the purifying water of baptism some of the effects of Original Sin and to achieve salvation. That is to say, on condition of obedience to the law of God, man could now enter heaven and regain the state of everlasting, deathless bliss, from which he had been excluded because of the sin of Adam and Eve.

To the medieval Christian the meaning of human life was therefore perfectly clear. The stretch on earth is only a short interlude, a temporary incar-

---

Reprinted by permission from Professor Kurt Baier.

1. Count Leo Tolstoy, "A Confession," reprinted in *A Confession,. The Gospel in Brief, and What I Believe,* No. 229, The World's Classics (London: Geoffrey Cumberlege, 1940).

ceration of the soul in the prison of the body, a brief trial and test, fated to end in death, the release from pain and suffering. What really matters, is the life after the death of the body. One's existence acquires meaning not by gaining what this life can offer but by saving one's immortal soul from death and eternal torture, by gaining eternal life and everlasting bliss.

The scientific world picture which has found ever more general acceptance from the beginning of the modern era onwards is in profound conflict with all this. At first, the Christian conception of the world was discovered to be erroneous in various important details. The Copernican theory showed up the earth as merely one of several planets revolving round the sun, and the sun itself was later seen to be merely one of many fixed stars each of which is itself the nucleus of a solar system similar to our own. Man, instead of occupying centre of creation, proved to be merely the inhabitant of a celestial body no different from millions of others. Furthermore, geological investigations revealed that the universe was not created a few thousand years ago, but was probably millions of years old.

Disagreements over details of the world picture, however, are only superficial aspects of a much deeper conflict. The appropriateness of the whole Christian outlook is at issue. For Christianity, the world must be regarded as the "creation" of a kind of Superman, a person possessing all the human excellences to an infinite degree and none of the human weaknesses, Who has made man in His image, a feeble, mortal, foolish copy of Himself. In creating the universe, God acts as a sort of playwright-cum-legislator-cum-judge-cum-executioner. In the capacity of playwright, He creates the historical world process, including man. He erects the stage and writes, in outline, the plot. He creates the *dramatis personae* and watches over them with the eye partly of a father, partly of the law. While on stage, the actors are free to extemporise, but if they infringe the divine commandments, they are later dealt with by their creator in His capacity of judge and executioner.

Within such a framework, the Christian attitudes towards the world are natural and sound: it is natural and sound to think that all is arranged for the best even if appearances belie it; to resign oneself cheerfully to one's lot; to be filled with awe and veneration in regard to anything and everything that happens; to want to fall on one's knees and worship and praise the Lord. These are wholly fitting attitudes within the framework of the world view just outlined. And this world view must have seemed wholly sound and acceptable because it offered the best explanation which was then available of all the observed phenomena of nature.

As the natural sciences developed, however, more and more things in the universe came to be explained without the assumption of a supernatural creator. Science, moreover, could explain them better, that is, more accurately and more reliably. The Christian hypothesis of a supernatural maker, whatever other needs it was capable of satisfying, was at any rate no longer indispensable for the purpose of explaining the existence or occurrence of anything. In fact, scientific explanations do not seem to leave any room for this hypothesis. The scientific approach demands that we look for a natural explanation of anything and everything. The scientific way of looking at and explaining things has yielded an immensely greater measure of understanding of, and control over, the universe than any other way. And when one looks at the world in this scientific way, there seems to be no room for a personal relationship between human beings and a supernatural perfect being ruling and guiding men. Hence many scientists and educated men have come to feel that the Christian attitudes towards the world and human existence are inappropriate. They have become convinced that the universe and human existence in it are without a purpose and therefore devoid of meaning. . . .[2]

The Purpose of Man's Existence

Our conclusion in the previous section has been that science is in principle able to give complete and real explanations of every occurrence and thing

---

2. See e.g. Edwyn Bevan, *Christianity,* pp. 211–227. See also H. J. Paton, *The Modern Predicament* (London: George Allen and Unwin Ltd., 1955) pp. 103–116, 374.

in the universe. This has two important corollaries: (i) Acceptance of the scientific world picture cannot be *one's reason for* the belief that the universe is unintelligible and therefore meaningless, though coming to accept it, after having been taught the Christian world picture, may well have been, in the case of many individuals, *the only or the main cause* of their belief that the universe and human existence are meaningless. (ii) It is not in accordance with reason to reject this pessimistic belief on the grounds that scientific explanations are only provisional and incomplete and must be supplemented by religious ones.

In fact, it might be argued that the more clearly we understand the explanations given by science, the more we are driven to the conclusion that human life has no purpose and therefore no meaning. The science of astronomy teaches us that our earth was not specially created about 6,000 years ago, but evolved out of hot nebulae which previously had whirled aimlessly through space for countless ages. As they cooled, the sun and the planets formed. On one of these planets at a certain time the circumstances were propitious and life developed. But conditions will not remain favourable to life. When our solar system grows old, the sun will cool, our planet will be covered with ice, and all living creatures will eventually perish. Another theory has it that the sun will explode and that the heat generated will be so great that all organic life on earth will be destroyed. That is the comparatively short history and prospect of life on earth. Altogether it amounts to very little when compared with the endless history of the inanimate universe.

Biology teaches us that the species man was not specially created but is merely, in a long chain of evolutionary changes of forms of life, the last link, made in the likeness not of God but of nothing so much as an ape. The rest of the universe, whether animate or inanimate, instead of serving the ends of man, is at best indifferent, at worst savagely hostile. Evolution to whose operation the emergence of man is due is a ceaseless battle among members of different species, one species being gobbled up by another, only the fittest surviving. Far from being the gentlest and most highly moral, man is simply the creature best fitted to survive, the most efficient if not the most rapacious

and insatiable killer. And in this unplanned, fortuitous, monstrous, savage world man is madly trying to snatch a few brief moments of joy, in the short intervals during which he is free from pain, sickness, persecution, war or famine until, finally, his life is snuffed out in death. Science has helped us to know and understand this world, but what purpose or meaning can it find in it?

Complaints such as these do not mean quite the same to everybody, but one thing, I think, they mean to most people: science shows life to be meaningless, because life is without purpose. The medieval world picture provided life with a purpose, hence medieval Christians could believe that life had a meaning. The scientific account of the world takes away life's purpose and with it its meaning.

There are, however, two quite different senses of "purpose." Which one is meant? Has science deprived human life of purpose in both senses? And if not, is it a harmless sense, in which human existence has been robbed of purpose? Could human existence still have meaning if it did not have a purpose in that sense?

What are the two senses? In the first and basic sense, purpose is normally attributed only to persons or their behaviour as in "Did you have a purpose in leaving the ignition on?" In the second sense, purpose is normally attributed only to things, as in "What is the purpose of that gadget you installed in the workshop?" The two uses are intimately connected. We cannot attribute a purpose to a thing without implying that someone did something, in the doing of which he had some purpose, namely, to bring about the thing with the purpose. Of course, *his* purpose is not identical with *its* purpose. In hiring labourers and engineers and buying materials and a site for a factory and the like, the entrepreneur's purpose, let us say, is to manufacture cars, but the purpose of cars is to serve as a means of transportation.

There are many things that a man may do, such as buying and selling, hiring labourers, ploughing, felling trees, and the like, which it is foolish, pointless, silly, perhaps crazy, to do if one has no purpose in doing them. A man who does these things without a purpose is engaging in inane, futile pursuits. Lives crammed full with such activities devoid of purpose are pointless, futile, worthless. Such lives may indeed be dismissed as meaningless. But it should also be perfectly clear that acceptance of the scientific world picture does not force us to regard our lives as being without a purpose in this sense. Science has not only not robbed us of any purpose which we had before, but it has furnished us with enormously greater power to achieve these purposes. Instead of praying for rain or a good harvest or offspring, we now use ice pellets, artificial manure, or artificial insemination.

By contrast, having or not having a purpose, in the other sense, is value neutral. We do not think more or less highly of a thing for having or not having a purpose. "Having a purpose," in this sense, confers no kudos, "being purposeless" carries no stigma. A row of trees growing near a farm may or may not have a purpose: it may or may not be a windbreak, may or may not have been planted or deliberately left standing there in order to prevent the wind from sweeping across the fields. We do not in any way disparage the trees if we say they have no purpose, but have just grown that way. They are as beautiful, made of as good wood, as valuable, as if they had a purpose. And, of course, they break the wind just as well. The same is true of living creatures. We do not disparage a dog when we say that it has no purpose, is not a sheep dog or a watch dog or a rabbiting dog, but just a dog that hangs around the house and is fed by us.

Man is in a different category, however. To attribute to a human being a purpose in that sense is not neutral, let alone complimentary: it is offensive. It is degrading for a man to be regarded as merely serving a purpose. If, at a garden party, I ask a man in livery, "What is your purpose?" I am insulting him. I might as well have asked, "What are you *for*?" Such questions reduce him to the level of a gadget, a domestic animal, or perhaps a slave. I imply that *we* allot to *him* the tasks, the goals, the aims which he is to pursue; that *his* wishes and desires and aspirations and purposes are to count for little or nothing. We are treating him, in Kant's phrase, merely as a means to our ends, not as an end in himself.

The Christian and the scientific world pictures do indeed differ fundamentally on this point. The latter robs man of a purpose in this sense. It sees him as a being with no purpose allotted to him by anyone but himself. It robs him of any goal, purpose, or destiny appointed for him by any outside agency. The Christian world picture, on the other hand, sees man as a creature, a divine artefact, something halfway between a robot (manufactured) and an animal (alive), a homunculus, or perhaps Frankenstein, made in God's laboratory, with a purpose or task assigned him by his Maker.

> *"... [W]e call a person's life meaningful not only if it is worthwhile, but also if he has helped in the realization of some plan or purpose transcending his own concerns."*

However, lack of purpose in this sense does not in any way detract from the meaningfulness of life. I suspect that many who reject the scientific outlook because it involves the loss of purpose of life, and therefore meaning, are guilty of a confusion between the two senses of "purpose" just distinguished. They confusedly think that if the scientific world picture is true, then their lives must be futile because that picture implies that man has no purpose given him from without. But this is muddled thinking, for, as has already been shown, pointlessness is implied only by purposelessness in the other sense, which is not at all implied by the scientific picture of the world. These people mistakenly conclude that there can be no purpose *in* life because there is no purpose *of* life; that *men* cannot themselves adopt and achieve purposes because *man,* unlike a robot or a watchdog, is not a creature with a purpose.[3]

However, not all people taking this view are guilty of the above confusion. Some really hanker after a purpose of life in this sense. To some people the greatest attraction of the medieval world picture is the belief in an omnipotent, omniscient, and all-good Father, the view of themselves as His children who worship Him, of their proper attitude to what befalls them as submission, humility, resignation in His will, and what is often described as the "creaturely feeling."[4] All these are attitudes and feelings appropriate to a being that stands to another in the same sort of relation, though of course on a higher plane, in which a helpless child stands to his progenitor. Many regard the scientific picture of the world as cold, unsympathetic, unhomely, frightening, because it does not provide for any appropriate object of this creaturely attitude. There is nothing and no one in the world, as science depicts it, in which we can have faith or trust, on whose guidance we can rely, to whom we can turn for consolation, whom we can worship or submit to— except other human beings. This may be felt as a keen disappointment, because it shows that the meaning of life cannot lie in submission to His will, in acceptance of whatever may come, and in worship. But it does not imply that life can have *no* meaning. It merely implies that it must have a different meaning from that which it was thought to have. Just as it is a great shock for a child to find that he must stand on his own feet, that his father and mother no longer provide for him, so a person who has lost his faith in God must reconcile himself to the idea that he has to stand on his own feet, alone in the world except for whatever friends he may succeed in making.

But is not this to miss the point of the Christian teaching? Surely, Christianity can tell us the meaning of life because it tells us the grand and noble end for which God has created the universe and man. No human life, however pointless it may seem, is meaningless because in being part of God's plan, every life is assured of significance.

This point is well taken. It brings to light a distinction of some importance: we call a person's life meaningful not only if it is worthwhile, but also if he has helped in the realization of some plan or purpose transcending his own concerns. A person who knows he must soon die a painful death, can give significance to the remainder of his doomed life by, say, allowing certain experiments to be performed on him which will be useful in the fight against cancer. In a similar way, only on a much more elevated plane, every man, however humble or plagued by suffering, is guaranteed significance by the knowledge that he is participating in God's purpose.

What then, on the Christian view, is the grand and noble end for which God has created the world and man in it? We can immediately dismiss that still popular opinion that the smallness of our intellect prevents us from stating meaningfully God's design in all its imposing grandeur.[5] This view cannot possibly be a satisfactory answer to our

---

3. See e.g. "Is Life Worth Living?" B.B.C. Talk by the Rev. John Sutherland Bonnell in *Asking Them Questions,* Third Series, ed. by R. S. Wright (London: Geoffrey Cumberlege, 1950).

4. See e.g. Rudolf Otto, *The Idea of the Holy,* pp. 9–11. See also C. A. Campbell, *On Selfhood and Godhood* (London: George Allen & Unwin Ltd., 1957) p. 246, and H. J. Paton, *The Modern Predicament,* pp. 69–71.

5. For a discussion of this issue see the eighteenth century controversy between Deists and Theists, for instance, in Sir Leslie Stephen's *History of English Thought in the Eighteenth Century* (London: Smith, Elder & Co., 1902) pp. 112–119 and pp. 134–163. See also the attacks by Toland and Tindal on "the mysterious" in *Christianity not Mysterious* and *Christianity as Old as the Creation, or the Gospel a Republication of the Religion of Nature,* resp., parts of which are reprinted in Henry Bettenson's *Doctrines of the Christian Church,* pp. 426–431. For modern views maintaining that mysteriousness is an essential element in religion, see Rudolf Otto, *The Idea of the Holy,* esp. pp. 25–40, and most recently M. B. Foster, *Mystery and Philosophy* (London: S.C.M. Press, 1957) esp. Chs. IV. and VI. For the view that statements about God must be nonsensical or absurd, see e.g. H. J. Paton, op. cit. pp. 119–120, 367–369. See also "Theology and Falsification" in *New Essays in Philosophical Theology,* ed. by A. Flew and A. MacIntyre (London: S.C.M. Press, 1955) pp. 96–131; also N. McPherson, "Religion as the Inexpressible," ibid, esp. pp. 137–143.

question about the purpose of life. It is, rather, a confession of the impossibility of giving one. If anyone thinks that this "answer" can remove the sting from the impression of meaninglessness and insignificance in our lives, he cannot have been stung very hard.

If, then, we turn to those who are willing to state God's purpose in so many words, we encounter two insuperable difficulties. The first is to find a purpose grand and noble enough to explain and justify the great amount of undeserved suffering in this world. We are inevitably filled by a sense of bathos when we read statements such as this: "... history is the scene of a divine purpose, in which the whole of history is included, and Jesus of Nazareth is the centre of that purpose, both as revelation and as achievement, as the fulfillment of all that was past, and the promise of all that was to come ... If God is God, and if He made all these things, why did He do it? ... God created a universe, bounded by the categories of time, space, matter, and causality, because He desired to enjoy for ever the society of a fellowship of finite and redeemed spirits which have made to His love the response of free and voluntary love and service."[6] Surely this cannot be right? Could a God be called omniscient, omnipotent, *and* all-good who, for the sake of satisfying his desire to be loved and served, imposes (or has to impose) on his creatures the amount of undeserved suffering we find in the world?

There is, however, a much more serious difficulty still: God's purpose in making the universe must be stated in terms of a dramatic story many of whose key incidents symbolize religious conceptions and practices which we no longer find morally acceptable: the imposition of a taboo on the fruits of a certain tree, the sin and guilt incurred by Adam and Eve by violating the taboo, the wrath of God,[7]

the curse of Adam and Eve and all their progeny, the expulsion from paradise, the Atonement by Christ's bloody sacrifice on the cross which makes available by way of the sacraments God's Grace by which alone men can be saved (thereby, incidentally, establishing the valuable power of priests to forgive sins and thus alone make possible a man's entry to heaven[8]), Judgment Day on which the sheep are separated from the goats and the latter condemned to eternal torment in hell-fire.

Obviously it is much more difficult to formulate a purpose for creating the universe and man that will justify the enormous amount of undeserved suffering which we find around us, if that story has to be fitted in as well. For now we have to explain not only why an omnipotent, omniscient, and all-good God should create such a universe and such a man, but also why, foreseeing every move of the feeble, weak-willed, ignorant, and covetous creature to be created, He should nevertheless have created him and, having done so, should be incensed and outraged by man's sin, and why He should deem it necessary to sacrifice His own son on the cross to atone for this sin which was, after all, only a disobedience of one of his commands, and why this atonement and consequent redemption could not have been followed by man's return to Paradise—particularly of those innocent children who had not yet sinned—and why, on Judgment Day, this merciful God should condemn some to eternal torment.[9] It is not surprising that in the face of these and other difficulties, we find, again and again, a return to the first view: that God's purpose cannot meaningfully be stated.

It will perhaps be objected that no Christian to-day believes in the dramatic history of the world as

---

6. Stephen Neill, *Christian Faith To-day* (London: Penguin Books, 1955) pp. 240–241.

7. It is difficult to feel the magnitude of this first sin unless one takes seriously the words "Behold, the man has eaten of the fruit of the tree of knowledge of good and evil, and is become as one of us; and now, may he not put forth his hand, and take also of the tree of life, and eat, and live for ever?" Genesis iii, 22.

8. See in this connection the pastoral letter of 2nd February, 1905, by Johannes Katschtaler, Prince Bishop of Salzburg on the honour due to priests, contained in *Quellen zur Geschichte des Papsttums*, by Mirbt pp. 497–9, translated and reprinted in *The Protestant Tradition*, by J. S. Whale (Cambridge: University Press, 1955) pp. 259–262.

9. How impossible it is to make sense of this story has been demonstrated beyond any doubt by Tolstoy in his famous "Conclusion of A Criticism of Dogmatic Theology," reprinted in *A Confession, The Gospel in Brief, and What I Believe.*

I have presented it. But this is not so. It is the official doctrine of the Roman Catholic, the Greek Orthodox, and a large section of the Anglican Church.[10] Nor does Protestantism substantially alter this picture. In fact, by insisting on "Justification by Faith Alone" and by rejecting the ritualistic, magical character of the medieval Catholic interpretation of certain elements in the Christian religion, such as indulgences, the sacraments, and prayer, while at the same time insisting on the necessity of grace, Protestantism undermined the moral element in medieval Christianity expressed in the Catholics' emphasis on personal merit.[11] Protestantism, by harking back to St. Augustine, who clearly realized the incompatibility of grace and personal merit,[12] opened the way for Calvin's doctrine of Predestination (the intellectual parent of that form of rigid determinism which is usually blamed on science) and Salvation or Condemnation from all eternity.[13] Since Roman Catholics, Lutherans, Calvinists, Presbyterians and Baptists officially subscribe to the views just outlined, one can justifiably claim that the overwhelming majority of professing Christians hold or ought to hold them.

It might still be objected that the best and most modern views are wholly different. I have not the necessary knowledge to pronounce on the accuracy of this claim. It may well be true that the best and most modern views are such as Professor Braithwaite's who maintains that Christianity is, roughly speaking, "morality plus stories," where the stories are intended merely to make the strict moral teaching both more easily understandable and more palatable.[14] Or it may be that one or the other of the modern views on the nature and importance of the dramatic story told in the sacred Scriptures is the best. My reply is that, even if it is true, it does not prove what I wish to disprove, that one can extract a sensible answer to our question, "What is the meaning of life?" from the kind of story subscribed to by the overwhelming majority of Christians, who would, moreover, reject any such modernist interpretation at least as indignantly as the scientific account. Moreover, though such views can perhaps avoid some of the worst absurdities of the traditional story, they are hardly in a much better position to state the purpose for which God has created the universe and man in it, because they cannot overcome the difficulty of finding a purpose grand and noble enough to justify the enormous amount of undeserved suffering in the world.

Let us, however, for argument's sake, waive all these objections. There remains one fundamental hurdle which no form of Christianity can overcome: the fact that it demands of man a morally repugnant attitude towards the universe. It is now very widely held[15] that the basic element of the Christian religion is an attitude of worship towards a being supremely worthy of being worshipped and that it is religious feelings and experiences which apprise their owner of such a being and which inspire in him the knowledge or the feeling of complete dependence, awe, worship, mystery, and self-abasement. There is, in other words, a bi-polarity (the famous "I-Thou relationship") in which the object, "the wholly-other," is exalted whereas the subject is abased to the limit. Rudolf Otto has called this the "creature-feeling"[16] and he quotes as an expression of it, Abraham's words when venturing to plead for the men of Sodom: "Behold now, I have taken upon me to speak unto the Lord, which am but

10. See "The Nicene Creed," "The Tridentine Profession of Faith," "The Syllabus of Errors," reprinted in *Documents of the Christian Church*, pp. 34, 373 and 380 resp.
11. See e.g. J. S. Whale, *The Protestant Tradition*, Ch. IV., esp. pp. 48–56.
12. See ibid., pp. 61 ff.
13. See "The Confession of Augsburg" esp. Articles II., IV., XVIII., XIX., XX.; "Christianae Religion is Institutio," "The Westminster Confession of Faith," esp. Articles III., VI., IX., X., XI., XVI., XVII., "The Baptist Confession of Faith," esp. Articles III., XXI., XXIII., reprinted in *Documents of the Christian Church*, pp. 294 ff., 298 ff., 344 ff., 349 ff.

14. See e.g. his *An Empiricist's View of the Nature of Religious Belief* (Eddington Memorial Lecture).
15. See e.g. the two series of Gifford Lectures most recently published: *The Modern Predicament* by H. J. Paton (London: George Allen & Unwin Ltd., 1955) pp. 69 ff., and *On Selfhood and Godhood* by C. A. Campbell (London: George Allen & Unwin Ltd., 1957) pp. 231–250.
16. Rudolf Otto, *The Idea of the Holy*, p. 9.

dust and ashes." (Gen. XVIII.27). Christianity thus demands of men an attitude inconsistent with one of the presuppositions of morality: that man is not wholly dependent on something else, that man has free will, that man is in principle capable of responsibility. We have seen that the concept of grace is the Christian attempt to reconcile the claim of total dependence and the claim of individual responsibility (partial independence), and it is obvious that such attempts must fail. We may dismiss certain doctrines, such as the doctrine of original sin or the doctrine of eternal hellfire or the doctrine that there can be no salvation outside the Church as extravagant and peripheral, but we cannot reject the doctrine of total dependence without rejecting the characteristically Christian attitude as such.

The Meaning of Life

Perhaps some of you will have felt that I have been shirking the real problem. To many people the crux of the matter seems as follows. How can there be any meaning in our life if it ends in death? What meaning can there be in it that our inevitable death does not destroy? How can our existence be meaningful if there is no after-life in which perfect justice is meted out? How can life have any meaning if all it holds out to us are a few miserable earthly pleasures and even these to be enjoyed only rarely and for such a piteously short time?

I believe this is the point which exercises most people most deeply. Kirilov, in Dostoevsky's novel, *The Possessed,* claims, just before committing suicide, that as soon as we realize that there is no God, we cannot live any longer, we must put an end to our lives. One of the reasons which he gives is that when we discover that there is no paradise, we have nothing to live for.

"... there was a day on earth, and in the middle of the earth were three crosses. One on the cross had such faith that He said to another, 'To-day thou shalt be with me in paradise.' The day came to an end, both died, and they went, but they found neither paradise nor resurrection. The saying did not come true. Listen: that man on the highest of all on earth ... There has never been any one like Him before or since, and never will be ... And if that is

so, if the laws of Nature did not spare even *Him,* and made even Him live in the midst of lies and die for a lie, then the whole planet is a lie and is based on a lie and a stupid mockery. So the very laws of the planet are a lie and a farce of the devil. What, then, is there to live for?"[17] And Tolstoy, too, was nearly driven to suicide when he came to doubt the existence of God and an after-life.[18] And this is true of many.

What, then, is it that inclines us to think that if life is to have a meaning, there would have to be an after-life? It is this. The Christian world view contains the following three propositions. The first is that since the Fall, God's curse of Adam and Eve, and the expulsion from Paradise, life on earth for mankind has not been worth while, but a vale of tears, one long chain of misery, suffering, and unhappiness, and injustice. The second is that a perfect after-life is awaiting us after the death of the body. The third is that we can enter this perfect life only on certain conditions, among which is also the condition of enduring our earthly existence to its bitter end. In this way, our earthly existence which, in itself, would not (at least for many people if not all) be worth living, acquires meaning and significance: only if we endure it, can we gain admission to the realm of the blessed.

It might be doubted whether this view is still held to-day. However, there can be no doubt that even to-day we all imbibe a good deal of this view with our earliest education. In sermons, the contrast between the perfect life of the blessed and our life of sorrow and drudgery is frequently driven home and we hear it again and again that Christianity has a message of hope and consolation for all those "who are weary and heavy laden."[19]

It is not surprising, then, that when the implications of the scientific world picture begin to sink in, when we come to have doubts about the existence

---

17. Fyodor Dostoyevsky, *The Devils* (London: The Penguin Classics, 1953) pp. 613–614.
18. Leo Tolstoy, *A Confession, The Gospel in Brief, and What I Believe,* The World's Classics, p. 24.
19. See for instance J. S. Whale, *Christian Doctrine,* pp. 171, 176–178, &c. See also Stephen Neill, *Christian Faith To-day,* p. 241.

of God and another life, we are bitterly disappointed. For if there is no afterlife, then all we are left is our earthly life which we have come to regard as a necessary evil, the painful fee of admission to the land of eternal bliss. But if there is no eternal bliss to come and if this hell on earth is all, why hang on till the horrible end?

Our disappointment therefore arises out of these two propositions, that the earthly life is not worth living, and that there is another perfect life of eternal happiness and joy which we may enter upon if we satisfy certain conditions. We can regard our lives as meaningful, if we believe both. We cannot regard them as meaningful if we believe merely the first and not the second. It seems to me inevitable that people who are taught something of the history of science, will have serious doubts about the second. If they cannot overcome these, as many will be unable to do, then they must either accept the sad view that their life is meaningless or they must abandon the first proposition: that this earthly life is not worth living. They must find the meaning of their life in this earthly existence. But is this possible?

A moment's examination will show us that the Christian evaluation of our earthly life as worthless, which we accept in our moments of pessimism and dissatisfaction, is not one that we normally accept. Consider only the question of murder and suicide. On the Christian view, other things being equal, the most kindly thing to do would be for every one of us to kill as many of our friends and dear ones as still have the misfortune to be alive, and then to commit suicide without delay, for every moment spent in this life is wasted. On the Christian view, God has not made it that easy for us. He has forbidden us to hasten others or ourselves into the next life. Our bodies are his private property and must be allowed to wear themselves out in the way decided by Him, however painful and horrible that may be. We are, as it were, driving a burning car. There is only one way out, to jump clear and let it hurtle to destruction. But the owner of the car has forbidden it on pain of eternal tortures worse than burning. And so we do better to burn to death inside.

On this view, murder is a less serious wrong than suicide. For murder can always be confessed and repented and therefore forgiven, suicide cannot—unless we allow the ingenious way out chosen by the heroine of Graham Green's play, The Living Room, who swallows a slow but deadly poison and, while awaiting its taking effect, repents having taken it. Murder, on the other hand, is not so serious because, in the first place, it need not rob the victim of anything but the last lap of his march in the vale of tears, and, in the second place, it can always be forgiven. Hamlet, it will be remembered, refrains from killing his uncle during the latter's prayers because, as a true Christian, he believes that killing his uncle at that point, when the latter has purified his soul by repentance, would merely be doing him a good turn, for murder at such a time would simply despatch him to undeserved and everlasting happiness.

These views strike us as odd, to say the least. They are the logical consequence of the official medieval evaluation of this our earthly existence. If this life is not worth living, then taking it is not robbing the person concerned of much. The only thing wrong with it is the damage to God's property, which is the same both in the case of murder and suicide. We do not take this view at all. Our view, on the contrary, is that murder is the most serious wrong because it consists in taking away from some one else against his will his most precious possession, his life. For this reason, when a person suffering from an incurable disease asks to be killed, the mercy killing of such a person is regarded as a much less serious crime than murder because, in such a case, the killer is not robbing the other of a good against his will. Suicide is not regarded as a real crime at all, for we take the view that a person can do with his own possessions what he likes.

However, from the fact that these are our normal opinions, we can infer nothing about their truth. After all, we could easily be mistaken. Whether life is or is not worthwhile, is a value judgment. Perhaps all this is merely a matter of opinion or taste. Perhaps no objective answer can be given. Fortunately, we need not enter deeply into these difficult and controversial questions. It is quite easy to show that the medieval evaluation of earthly life is based on a misguided procedure.

Let us remind ourselves briefly of how we arrive at our value judgments. When we determine the merits of students, meals, tennis players, bulls, or bathing belles, we do so on the basis of some criteria and some standard or norm. Criteria and standards notoriously vary from field to field and even from case to case. But that does not mean that we have *no* idea about what are the appropriate criteria or standards to use. It would not be fitting to apply the criteria for judging bulls to the judgment of students or bathing belles. They score on quite different points. And even where the same criteria are appropriate as in the judgment of students enrolled in different schools and universities the standards will vary from one institution to another. Pupils who would only just pass in one, would perhaps obtain honours in another. The higher the standard applied, the lower the marks, that is, the merit conceded to the candidate.

The same procedure is applicable also in the evaluation of a life. We examine it on the basis of certain criteria and standards. The medieval Christian view uses the criteria of the ordinary man: a life is judged by what the person concerned can get out of it; the balance of happiness over unhappiness, pleasure over pain, bliss over suffering. Our earthly life is judged not worth while because it contains much unhappiness, pain, and suffering, little happiness, pleasure, and bliss. The next life is judged worth while because it provides eternal bliss and no suffering.

Armed with these criteria, we can compare the life of this man and that, and judge which is more worth while, which has a greater balance of bliss over suffering. But criteria alone enable us merely to make comparative judgments of value, not absolute ones. We can say which is more and which is less worth while, but we cannot say which is worthwhile and which is not. In order to determine the latter, we must introduce a standard. But what standard ought we to choose?

Ordinarily, the standard we employ is the average of the kind. We call a man and a tree tall if they are well above the average of their kind. We do not say that Jones is a short man because he is shorter than a tree. We do not judge a boy a bad student because his answer to a question in the Leaving Examination is much worse than that given in reply to the same question by a young man sitting for his finals for the Bachelor's degree.

The same principles must apply to judging lives. When we ask whether a given life was or was not worth while, then we must take into consideration the range of worthwhileness which ordinary lives normally cover. Our end poles of the scale must be the best possible and the worst possible life that one finds. A good and worthwhile lives is one that is well above average. A bad one is one well below.

The Christian evaluation of earthly lifes is misguided because it adopts a quite unjustifiably high standard. Christianity singles out the major shortcomings of our earthly existence: there is not enough happiness; there is too much suffering; the good and bad points are quite unequally and unfairly distributed; the underprivileged and underendowed do not get adequate compensation; it lasts only a short time. It then quite accurately depicts the perfect or ideal life as that which does not have any of these shortcomings. Its next step is to promise the believer that he will be able to enjoy this perfect life later on. And then it adopts as its standard of judgment the perfect life, dismissing as inadequate anything that falls short of it. Having dismissed earthly life as miserable, it further damns it by characterizing most of the pleasures of which earthly existence allows as bestial, gross, vile, and sinful, or alternatively as not really pleasurable.

This procedure is as illegitimate as if I were to refuse to call anything tall unless it is infinitely tall, or anything beautiful unless it is perfectly flawless, or any one strong unless he is omnipotent. Even if it were true that there is available to us an after-life which is flawless and perfect, it would still not be legitimate to judge earthly lives by this standard. We do not fail every candidate who is not an Einstein. And if we do not believe in an after-life, we must of course use ordinary earthly standards.

I have so far only spoken of the worthwhileness, only of what a person can get out of a life. There are other kinds of appraisal; clearly, we evaluate people's lives not merely from the point of view of what they yield to the persons that lead them, but also from that of other men on whom these lives have impinged. We judge a life more significant if the person has contributed to the happiness of others, whether directly by what he did for others, or by the plans, discoveries, inventions, and work he performed. Many lives that hold little in the way of pleasure or happiness for its owner are highly significant and valuable, deserve admiration and respect on account of the contributions made.

It is now quite clear that death is simply irrelevant. If life can be worthwhile at all, then it can be so even though it be short. And if it is not worthwhile at all, then an eternity of it is simply a nightmare. It may be sad that we have to leave this beautiful world, but it is so only if and because it is beautiful. And it is no less beautiful for coming to an end. I rather suspect that an eternity of it might make us less appreciative, and in the end it would be tedious.

It will perhaps be objected now that I have not really demonstrated that life has a meaning, but merely that it can be worthwhile or have value. It must be admitted that there is a perfectly natural interpretation of the question, "What is the meaning of life?" on which my view actually proves that life has no meaning. I mean the interpretation discussed in section 2 of this lecture, where I attempted to show that, if we accept the explanations of natural science, we cannot believe that living organisms have appeared on earth in accordance with the deliberate plan of some intelligent being. Hence, on this view, life cannot be said to have a purpose, in the sense in which man-made things have a purpose. Hence it cannot be said to have a meaning or significance in that sense.

However, this conclusion is innocuous. People are disconcerted by the thought that life as such has no meaning in that sense only because they very naturally think it entails that no individual life can have meaning either. They naturally assume that *this* life or *that* can have meaning only if *life as such* has meaning. But it should by now be clear that your life and mine may or may not have meaning (in one sense) even if life as such has none (in the other). Of course, it follows from this that your life may have meaning while mine has not. The Christian view guarantees a meaning (in one sense) to every life, the scientific view does not (in any sense). By relating the question of the meaningfulness of life to the particular circumstances of an individual's existence, the scientific view leaves it an open question whether an individual's life has meaning or not. It is, however, clear that the latter is the important sense of "having a meaning." Chris-

tians, too, must feel that their life is wasted and meaningless if they have not achieved salvation. To know that even such lost lives have a meaning in another sense is no consolation to them. What matters is not that life should have a guaranteed meaning, whatever happens here or here-after, but that, by luck (Grace) or the right temperament and attitude (Faith) or a judicious life (Works) a person should make the most of his life.

"But here lies the rub," it will be said. "Surely, it makes all the difference whether there is an afterlife. This is where morality comes in." It would be a mistake to believe that. Morality is not the meting out of punishment and reward. To be moral is to refrain from doing to others what, if they followed reason, they would not do to themselves, and to do for others what, if they followed reason, they would want to have done. It is, roughly speaking, to recognize that others, too, have a right to a worthwhile life. Being moral does not make one's own life worthwhile, it helps others to make theirs so.

Conclusion

I have tried to establish three points: (i) that scientific explanations render their explicanda as intelligible as pre-scientific explanations; they differ from the latter only in that, having testable implications and being more precisely formulated, their truth or falsity can be determined with a high degree of probability; (ii) that science does not rob human life of purpose, in the only sense that matters, but, on the contrary, renders many more of our purposes capable of realization; (iii) that common sense, the Christian world view, and the scientific approach agree on the criteria but differ on the standard to be employed in the evaluation of human lives; judging human lives by the standards of perfection, as Christians do, is unjustified; if we abandon this excessively high standard and replace it by an everyday one, we have no longer any reason for dismissing earthly existence as not worthwhile.

On the basis of these three points I have attempted to explain why so many people come to the conclusion that human existence is meaningless and to show that this conclusion is false. In my opinion, this pessimism rests on a combination of two beliefs, both partly true and partly false: the belief that the meaningfulness of life depends on the satisfaction of at least three conditions, and the belief that this universe satisfies none of them. The conditions are, first, that the universe is intelligible, second, that life has a purpose, and third, that all men's hopes and desires can ultimately be satisfied. It seemed to medieval Christians and it seems to many Christians to-day that Christianity offers a picture of the world which can meet these conditions. To many Christians and non-Christians alike it seems that the scientific world picture is incompatible with that of Christianity, therefore with the view that these three conditions are met, therefore with the view that life has a meaning. Hence they feel that they are confronted by the dilemma of accepting either a world picture incompatible with the discoveries of science or the view that life is meaningless.

I have attempted to show that the dilemma is unreal because life can be meaningful even if not all of these conditions are met. My main conclusion, therefore, is that acceptance of the scientific world picture provides no reason for saying that life is meaningless, but on the contrary every reason for saying that there are many lives which are meaningful and significant. My subsidiary conclusion is that one of the reasons frequently offered for retaining the Christian world picture, namely, that its acceptance gives us a guarantee of a meaning for human existence, is unsound. We can see that our lives can have a meaning even if we abandon it and adopt the scientific world picture instead. I have, moreover, mentioned several reasons for rejecting the Christian world picture: (i) the biblical explanations of the details of our universe are often simply false; (ii) the so-called explanations of the whole universe are incomprehensible or absurd; (iii) Christianity's low evaluation of earthly existence (which is the main cause of the belief in the meaninglessness of life) rests on the use of an unjustifiably high standard of judgment.

Study Questions

1. Are goals in life enough to make life meaningful?

2. Are the scientific and religious viewpoints contradictory?

A Free Man's Worship

Bertrand Russell (1872–1970) Born in England, Bertrand Russell taught philosophy at Cambridge University. In 1938 he moved to the United States and taught philosophy in several American universities. Russell received the Nobel Prize in Literature in 1950 for his numerous books on all aspects of philosophy.

Bertrand Russell

To Dr. Faustus in his study Mephistopheles told the history of the Creation, saying:

Bertrand Russell, "A Free Man's Worship," from *Mysticism and Logic;* Unwin Hyman Ltd., London.

The endless praises of the choirs of angels had begun to grow wearisome; for, after all, did he not deserve their praise? Had he not given them endless joy? Would it not be more amusing to obtain undeserved praise, to be worshiped by beings whom he tortured? He smiled inwardly, and resolved that the great drama should be performed.

For countless ages the hot nebula whirled aimlessly through space. At length it began to take shape, the central mass threw off planets, the planets cooled, boiling seas and burning mountains heaved and tossed, from black masses of cloud hot sheets of rain deluged the barely solid crust. And now the first germ of life grew in the depths of the ocean, and developed rapidly in the fructifying warmth into vast forest trees, huge ferns springing from the damp mold, sea monsters breeding, fighting, devouring, and passing away. And from the monsters, as the play unfolded itself, Man was born, with the power of thought, the knowledge of good and evil, and the cruel thirst for worship. And Man saw that all is passing in this mad, monstrous world, that all is struggling to snatch, at any cost, a few brief moments of life before Death's inexorable decree. And Man said: "There is a hidden purpose, could we but fathom it, and the purpose is good; for we must reverence something, and in the visible world there is nothing worthy of reverence." And Man stood aside from the struggle, resolving that God intended harmony to come out of chaos by human efforts. And when he followed the instincts which God had transmitted to him from his ancestry of beasts of prey, he called it Sin, and asked God to forgive him. But he doubted whether he could be justly forgiven, until he invented a divine Plan by which God's wrath was to have been appeased. And seeing the present was bad, he made it yet worse, that thereby the future might be better. And he gave God thanks for the strength that enabled him to forego even the joys that were possible. And God smiled; and when he saw that Man had become perfect in renunciation and worship, he sent another sun through the sky, which crashed into Man's sun; and all returned again to nebula.

"Yes," he murmured, "It was a good play; I will have it performed again."

Such, in outline, but even more purposeless, more void of meaning is the world which Science presents for our belief. Amid such a world, if anywhere, our ideals henceforth must find a home. That Man is the product of causes which had no prevision of the end they were achieving; that his origin, his growth, his hopes and fears, his lives and his beliefs, are but the outcome of accidental collocations of atoms; that no fire, no heroism, no intensity of thought and feeling, can preserve an individual life beyond the grave; that all the labors of the ages, all the devotion, all the inspiration, all the noonday brightness of human genius, are destined to extinction in the vast death of the solar system, and that the whole temple of Man's achievement must inevitably be buried beneath the debris of a universe in ruins—all these things, if not quite beyond dispute, are yet so nearly certain, that no philosophy which rejects them can hope to stand. Only within the scaffolding of these truths, only on the firm foundation of unyielding despair, can the soul's habitation henceforth be safely built.

How, in such an alien and inhuman world, can so powerless a creature as Man preserve his aspirations untarnished? A strange mystery it is that Nature, omnipotent but blind, in the revolutions of her secular hurryings through the abysses of space, has brought forth at last a child, subject still to her power, but gifted with sight, with knowledge of good and evil, with the capacity of judging all the works of his unthinking Mother. In spite of Death, the mark and seal of the parental control, Man is yet free, during his brief years, to examine, to criticize, to know, and in imagination to create. To him alone, in the world with which he is acquainted, this freedom belongs; and in this lies his superiority to the resistless forces that control his outward life.

The savage, like ourselves, feels the oppression of his impotence before the powers of Nature; but having in himself nothing that he respects more than Power, he is willing to prost[r]ate himself before his gods, without inquiring whether they are worthy of his worship. Pathetic and very terrible is the long history of cruelty and torture, of degradation and human sacrifice, endured in the hope of placating the jealous gods: surely, the trembling believer thinks, when what is most precious has been freely given, their lust for blood must be appeased, and more will not be required. The religion of Moloch—as such creeds may be generically called—is in essence the cringing submission of the slave, who dare not, even in his heart, allow the thought that his master deserves no adulation. Since the independence of ideas is not yet acknowledged, Power may be freely worshiped, and receive an unlimited respect, despite its wanton infliction of pain.

But gradually, as morality grows bolder, the claim of the ideal world begins to be felt; and worship, if it is not to cease, must be given to gods of another kind than those created by the savage. Some, though they feel the demands of the ideal, will still consciously reject them, still urging that naked Power is worthy of worship. Such is the attitude inculcated in God's answer to Job out of the whirlwind: the divine power and knowledge are paraded, but of the divine goodness there is no hint. Such also is the attitude of those who, in our own day, base their morality upon the struggle for survival, maintaining that the survivors are necessarily the fittest. But others, not content with an answer so repugnant to the moral sense, will adopt the position which we have become accustomed to regard as specially religious, maintaining that, in some hidden manner the world of fact is really harmonious with the world of ideals. Thus Man creates God, all-powerful and all-good, the mystic unity of what is and what should be.

But the world of fact, after all, is not good; and, in submitting our judgment to it, there is an element of slavishness from which our thoughts must be purged. For in all things it is well to exalt the dignity of Man, by freeing him as far as possible from the tyranny of non-human Power. When we have realized that Power is largely bad, that man, with his knowledge of good and evil, is but a helpless atom in a world which has no such knowledge, the choice is again presented to us: Shall we worship Force, or shall we worship Goodness? Shall our God exist and be evil or shall he be recognized as the creation of our own conscience?

The answer to this question is very momentous, and affects profoundly our whole morality. The worship of Force, to which Carlyle and Nietzsche and the creed of Militarism have accustomed us, is the result of failure to maintain our own ideals against a hostile universe: it is itself a prostrate submission to evil, a sacrifice of our best to Moloch. If strength indeed is to be respected, let us respect rather the strength of those who refuse that false "recognition of facts" which fails to recognize that facts are often bad. Let us admit that, in the world we know, there are many things that would be better otherwise, and that the ideals to which we do and must adhere are not realized in the realm of matter. Let us preserve our respect for truth, for beauty, for the ideal of perfection which life does not permit us to attain, though none of these things meet with the approval of the unconscious universe. If Power is bad, as it seems to be, let us reject it from our hearts. In this lies Man's true freedom: in determination to worship only the God created by our own love of the good, to respect only the heaven which inspires the insight of our best moments. In action, in desire, we must submit perpetually to the tyranny of outside forces; but in thought, in aspiration, we are free, free from our fellowmen, free from the petty planet on which our bodies impotently crawl, free even, while we live, from the tyranny of death. Let us learn, then, that energy of faith which enables us to live constantly in the vision of the good; and let us descend, in action, into the world of fact, with that vision always before us.

When first the opposition of fact and ideal grows fully visible, a spirit of fiery revolt, of fierce hatred of the gods, seems necessary to the assertion of freedom. To defy with Promethean constancy a hostile universe, to keep its evil always in view, always actively hated, to refuse no pain that the malice of Power can invent, appears to be the duty of all who will not bow before the inevitable. But indignation is still a bondage, for it compels our thoughts to be occupied with an evil world; and in the fierceness of desire from which rebellion springs there is a kind of self-assertion which it is necessary for the wise to overcome. Indignation is a submission of our thoughts, but not of our desires; the Stoic freedom in which wisdom consists is found in the submission of our desires, but not of our thoughts.

From the submission of our desires springs the virtue of resignation; from the freedom of our thoughts springs the whole world of art and philosophy, and the vision of beauty by which, at last, we half reconquer the reluctant world. But the vision of beauty is possible only to unfettered contemplation, to thoughts not weighted by the load of eager wishes; and thus Freedom comes only to those who no longer ask of life that it shall yield them any of those personal goods that are subject to the mutations of Time.

Although the necessity of renunciation is evidence of the existence of evil, yet Christianity, in preaching it, has shown a wisdom exceeding that of the Promethean philosophy of rebellion. It must be admitted that, of the things we desire, some, though they prove impossible, are yet real goods; others, however, as ardently longed for, do not form part of a fully purified ideal. The belief that what must be renounced is bad, though sometimes false, is far less often false than untamed passion supposes; and the creed of religion, by providing a reason for proving that it is never false, has been the means of purifying our hopes by the discovery of many austere truths.

But there is in resignation a further good element: even real goods, when they are unattainable, ought not to be fretfully desired. To every man comes, sooner or later, the great renunciation. For the young, there is nothing unattainable; a good thing desired with the whole force of a passionate will, and yet impossible, is to them not credible. Yet, by death, by illness, by poverty, or by the voice of duty, we must learn, each one of us, that the world was not made for us, and that, however beautiful may be the things we crave, Fate may nevertheless forbid them. It is the part of courage, when misfortune comes, to bear without repining the ruin of our hopes, to turn away our thoughts from vain regrets. This degree of submission to Power is not only just and right: it is the very gate of wisdom.

But passive renunciation is not the whole of wisdom; for not by renunciation alone can we build a temple for the worship of our own ideals. Haunting foreshadowings of the temple appear in the realm of imagination, in music, in architecture, in the untroubled kingdom of reason, and in the golden sunset magic of lyrics, where beauty shines and glows, remote from the touch of sorrow, remote from the fear of change, remote from the failures and disenchantments of the world of fact. In the contemplation of these things the vision of heaven will shape itself in our hearts, giving at once a touchstone to judge the world about us, and an inspiration by which to fashion to our needs whatever is not incapable of serving as a stone in the sacred temple.

Except for those rare spirits that are born without sin, there is a cavern of darkness to be traversed before that temple can be entered. The gate of the cavern is despair, and its floor is paved with the gravestones of abandoned hopes. There Self must die; there the eagerness, the greed of untamed desire must be slain, for only so can the soul be freed from the empire of Fate. But out of the cavern the Gate of Renunciation leads again to the daylight of wisdom, by whose radiance a new insight, a new joy, a new tenderness, shine forth to gladden the pilgrim's heart.

> "To abandon the struggle for private happiness, to expel all eagerness of temporary desire, to burn with passion for eternal things—this is emancipation, and this is the free man's worship."

When, without the bitterness of impotent rebellion, we have learnt both to resign ourselves to the outward rule of Fate and to recognize that the nonhuman world is unworthy of our worship, it becomes possible at last so to transform and refashion the unconscious universe, so to transmute it in the crucible of imagination, that a new image of shining gold replaces the old idol of clay. In all the multiform facts of the world—in the visual shapes of trees and mountains and clouds, in the events of the life of man, even in the very omnipotence of Death—the insight of creative idealism can find the reflection of a beauty which its own thoughts first made. In this way mind asserts its subtle mastery over the thoughtless forces of Nature. The more evil the material with which it deals, the more thwarting to untrained desire, the greater is its achievement in inducing the reluctant rock to yield up its hidden treasures, the prouder its victory in compelling the opposing forces to swell the pageant of its triumph. Of all the arts, Tragedy is the proudest, the most triumphant; for it builds its shining citadel in the very center of the enemy's country, on the very summit of his highest mountain; from its impregnable watchtowers, his camps and arsenals, his columns and forts, are all revealed; within its walls the free life continues, while the legions of Death and Pain and Despair, and all the servile captains of tyrant Fate, afford the burghers of that dauntless city new spectacles of beauty. Happy those sacred ramparts, thrice happy the dwellers on the all-seeing eminence. Honor to those brave warriors who, through countless ages of warfare, have preserved for us the priceless heritage of liberty, and have kept undefiled by sacrilegious invaders the home of the unsubdued.

But the beauty of Tragedy does but make visible a quality which, in more or less obvious shapes, is present always and everywhere in life. In the spectacle of Death, in the endurance of intolerable pain, and in the irrevocableness of a vanished past, there is a sacredness, an overpowering awe, a feeling of the vastness, the depth, the inexhaustible mystery of existence, in which, as by some strange marriage of pain, the sufferer is bound to the world by bonds of sorrow. In these moments of insight, we lose all eagerness of temporary desire, all struggling and striving for petty ends, all care for the little trivial things that, to a superficial view, make up the common life of day by day; we see, surrounding the narrow raft illumined by the flickering light of human comradeship, the dark ocean on whose rolling waves we toss for a brief hour; from the great night without, a chill blast breaks in upon our refuge; all the loneliness of humanity amid hostile forces is concentrated upon the individual soul, which must struggle alone, with what of courage it can command, against the whole weight of a universe that cares nothing for its hopes and fears. Victory, in this struggle with the powers of darkness, is the true

baptism into the glorious company of heroes, the true initiation into the overmastering beauty of human existence. From that awful encounter of the soul with the outer world, renunciation, wisdom, and charity are born; and with their birth a new life begins. To take into the inmost shrine of the soul the irresistible forces whose puppets we seem to be—Death and change, the irrevocableness of the past and the powerlessness of man before the blind hurry of the universe from vanity to vanity—to feel these things and know them is to conquer them.

This is the reason why the Past has such magical power. The beauty of its motionless and silent pictures is like the enchanted purity of late autumn, when the leaves, though one breath would make them fall, still glow against the sky in golden glory. The Past does not change or strive; like Duncan, after life's fitful fever it sleeps well; what was eager and grasping, what was petty and transitory, has faded away, the things that were beautiful and eternal shine out of it like stars in the night. Its beauty, to a soul not worthy of it, is unendurable; but to a soul which has conquered Fate it is the key of religion.

The life of Man, viewed outwardly, is but a small thing in comparison with the forces of Nature. The slave is doomed to worship Time and Fate and Death, because they are greater than anything he finds in himself, and because all his thoughts are of things which they devour. But, great as they are, to think of them greatly, to feel their passionless splendor, is greater still. And such thought makes us free men; we no longer bow before the inevitable in Oriental subjection, but we absorb it, and make it a part of ourselves. To abandon the struggle for private happiness, to expel all eagerness of temporary desire, to burn with passion for eternal things—this is emancipation, and this is the free man's worship. And this liberation is effected by a contemplation of Fate; for Fate itself is subdued by the mind which leaves nothing to be purged by the purifying fire of Time.

United with his fellow-men by the strongest of all ties, the tie of common doom, the free man finds that a new vision is with him always, shedding over every daily task the light of love. The life of Man is a long march through the night, surrounded by invisible foes, tortured by weariness and pain, towards a goal that few can hope to reach, and where none may tarry long. One by one, as they march, our comrades vanish from our sight, seized by the silent orders of omnipotent Death. Very brief is the time in which we can help them, in which their happiness or misery is decided. Be it ours to shed sunshine on their path, to lighten their sorrows by the balm of sympathy, to give them the pure joy of a never-tiring affection, to strengthen failing courage, to instill faith in hours of despair. Let us not weigh in grudging scales their merits and demerits, but let us think only of their need—of the sorrows, the difficulties, perhaps the blindnesses, that make the misery of their lives; let us remember that they are fellow sufferers in the same darkness, actors in the same tragedy with ourselves. And so, when their day is over, when their good and their evil have become eternal by the immortality of the past, be it ours to feel that, where they suffered, where they failed, no deed of ours was the cause; but wherever a spark of the divine fire kindled in their hearts, we were ready with encouragement, with sympathy, with brave words in which high courage glowed.

Brief and powerless is Man's life; on him and all his race the slow, sure doom falls pitiless and dark. Blind to good and evil, reckless of destruction, omnipotent matter rolls on its relentless way; for Man, condemned to-day to lose his dearest, to-morrow himself to pass through the gate of darkness, it remains only to cherish, ere yet the blow falls, the lofty thoughts that ennoble his little day; disdaining the coward terrors of the slave of Fate, to worship at the shrine that his own hands have built; undismayed by the empire of chance, to preserve a mind free from the wanton tyranny that rules his outward life; proudly defiant of the irresistible forces that tolerate, for a moment, his knowledge and his condemnation, to sustain alone, a weary but unyielding Atlas, the world that his own ideals have fashioned despite the trampling march of unconscious power.

Study Questions

1. Can the pursuit of knowledge, justice, and art make life meaningful?

2. If purpose is not enough to make life meaningful, what is lacking?

The Vanity of Existence

Arthur Schopenhauer

Arthur Schopenhauer (1788–1860) was a German philosopher who contributed to many areas of philosophy. His most famous work was The World as Will and Idea.

This vanity finds expression in the whole way in which things exist; in the infinite nature of Time and Space, as opposed to the finite nature of the in-

From "The Vanity of Existence," by Arthur Schopenhauer, in *The Essays of Arthur Schopenhauer*, translated by T. Bailey Saunders, 1951.

dividual in both; in the ever-passing present moment as the only mode of actual existence; in the interdependence and relativity of all things; in continual Becoming without ever Being; in constant wishing and never being satisfied; in the long battle which forms the history of life, where every effort is checked by difficulties, and stopped until they are overcome. Time is that in which all things pass away; it is merely the form under which the will to live—the thing-in-itself and therefore imperishable—has revealed to it that its efforts are in vain; it is that agent by which at every moment all things in our hands become as nothing, and lose any real value they possess.

That which *has been* exists no more; it exists as little as that which has *never* been. But of everything that exists you must say, in the next moment, that it has been. Hence something of great importance now past is inferior to something of little importance now present, in that the latter is a *reality,* and related to the former as something to nothing.

A man finds himself, to his great astonishment, suddenly existing, after thousands and thousands of years of non-existence: he lives for a little while; and then, again, comes an equally long period when he must exist no more. The heart rebels against this, and feels that it cannot be true. The crudest intellect cannot speculate on such a subject without having a presentiment that Time is something ideal in its nature. This ideality of Time and Space is the key to every true system of metaphysics; because it provides for quite another order of things than is to be met with in the domain of nature. This is why Kant is so great.

Of every event in our life we can say only for one moment that it *is;* for ever after, that it *was.* Every evening we are poorer by a day. It might, perhaps, make us mad to see how rapidly our short span of time ebbs away, if it were not that in the furthest depths of our being we are secretly conscious of our share in the exhaustible spring of eternity, so that we can always hope to find life in it again.

Consideration of the kind, touched on above, might, indeed, lead us to embrace the belief that the greatest *wisdom* is to make the enjoyment of the present the supreme object of life; because that is the only reality, all else being merely the play of

thought. On the other hand, such a course might just as well be called the greatest *folly:* for that which in the next moment exists no more, and vanishes utterly, like a dream, can never be worth a serious effort.

The whole foundation on which our existence rests is the present—the ever-fleeting present. It lies, then, in the very nature of our existence to take the form of constant motion, and to offer no possibility of our ever attaining the rest for which we are always striving. We are like a man running downhill, who cannot keep on his legs unless he runs on, and will inevitably fall if he stops; or, again, like a pole balanced on the tip of one's finger; or like a planet, which would fall into its sun the moment it ceased to hurry forward on its way. Unrest is the mark of existence.

"Human life must be some kind of mistake."

In a world where all is unstable, and nought can endure, but is swept onwards at once in the hurrying whirlpool of change; where a man, if he is to keep erect at all, must always be advancing and moving, like an acrobat on a rope—in such a world, happiness is inconceivable. How can it dwell where, as Plato says, *continual Becoming and never Being* is the sole form of existence? In the first place, a man never is happy, but spends his whole life in striving after something which he thinks will make him so; he seldom attains his goal, and when he does, it is only to be disappointed; he is mostly shipwrecked in the end, and comes into harbor with masts and rigging gone. And then, it is all one whether he has been happy or miserable; for his life was never anything more than a present moment always vanishing; and now it is over.

At the same time it is a wonderful thing that, in the world of human beings as in that of animals in general, this manifold restless motion is produced and kept up by the agency of two simple impulses—hunger and the sexual instinct; aided a little, perhaps, by the influence of boredom, but by nothing else; and that, in the theatre of life, these suffice to form the *primum mobile* of how complicated a machinery, setting in motion how strange and varied a scene!

On looking a little closer, we find that inorganic matter presents a constant conflict between chemical forces, which eventually works dissolution; and on the other hand, that organic life is impossible without continual change of matter, and cannot exist if it does not receive perpetual help from without. This is the realm of *finality*; and its opposite would be *an infinite existence,* exposed to no attack from without, and needing nothing to support it; the realm of eternal peace; some timeless, changeless state, one and undiversified; the negative knowledge of which forms the dominant note of the Platonic philosophy. It is to some such state as this that the denial of the will to live opens up the way.

The scenes of our life are like pictures done in rough mosaic. Looked at close, they produce no effect. There is nothing beautiful to be found in them, unless you stand some distance off. So, to gain anything we have longed for is only to discover how vain and empty it is; and even though we are always living in expectation of better things, at the same time we often repent and long to have the past back again. We look upon the present as something to be put up with while it lasts, and serving only as the way towards our goal. Hence most people, if they glance back when they come to the end of life, will find that all along they have been living *ad interim:* they will be surprised to find that the very thing they disregarded and let slip by unenjoyed, was just the life in the expectation of which they passed all their time. Of how many a man may it not be said that hope made a fool of him until he danced into the arms of death!

Then again, how insatiable a creature is man! Every satisfaction he attains lays the seeds of some new desire, so that there is no end to the wishes of each individual will. And why is this? The real reason is simply that, taken in itself, Will is the lord of all worlds: everything belongs to it, and therefore no one single thing can ever give it satisfaction, but only the whole, which is endless. For all that, it

must rouse our sympathy to think how very little the Will, this lord of the world, really gets when it takes the form of an individual; usually only just enough to keep the body together. This is why man is so very miserable.

Life presents itself chiefly as a task—the task, I mean, of subsisting at all, *gagner sa vie*. If this is accomplished, life is a burden, and then there comes the second task of doing something with that which has been won—of warding off boredom, which, like a bird of prey, hovers over us, ready to fall wherever it sees a life secure from need.. The first task is to win something; the second, to banish the feeling that it has been won; otherwise it is a burden.

Human life must be some kind of mistake. The truth of this will be sufficiently obvious if we only remember that man is a compound of needs and necessities hard to satisfy; and that even when they are satisfied, all he obtains is a state of painlessness, where nothing remains to him but abandonment to boredom. This is direct proof that existence has no real value in itself; for what is boredom but the feeling of the emptiness of life? If life—the craving for which is the very essence of our being—were possessed of any positive intrinsic value, there would be no such thing as boredom at all: mere existence would satisfy us in itself, and we should want for nothing. But as it is, we take no delight in existence except when we are struggling for something; and then distance and difficulties to be overcome make our goal look as though it would satisfy us—an illusion which vanishes when we reach it; or else when we are occupied with some purely intellectual interest—when in reality we have stepped forth from life to look upon it from the outside, much after the manner of spectators at a play. And even sensual pleasure itself means nothing but a struggle and aspiration, ceasing the moment its aim is attained. Whenever we are not occupied in one of these ways, but cast upon existence itself, its vain and worthless nature is brought home to us; and this is what we mean by boredom. The hankering after what is strange and uncommon–an innate and ineradicable tendency of human nature—shows how glad we are at any interruption of that natural course of affairs which is so very tedious.

That this most perfect manifestation of the will to

live, the human organism, with the cunning and complex working of its machinery, must fall to dust and yield up itself and all its strivings to extinction—this is the naive way in which Nature, who is always so true and sincere in what she says, proclaims the whole struggle of this will as in its very essence barren and unprofitable. Were it of any value in itself, anything unconditioned and absolute, it could not thus end in mere nothing.

If we turn from contemplating the world as a whole, and, in particular, the generations of men as they live their little hour of mock-existence and then are swept away in rapid succession; if we turn from this, and look at life in its small details, as presented, say, in a comedy, how ridiculous it all seems! It is like a drop of water seen through a microscope, a single drop teeming with *infusoria*; or a speck of cheese full of mites invisible to the naked eye. How we laugh as they bustle about so eagerly, and struggle with one another in so tiny a space! And whether here, or in the little span of human life, this terrible activity produces a comic effect.

It is only in the microscope that our life looks so big. It is an indivisible point, drawn out and magnified by the powerful lenses of Time and Space.

Study Questions

1. Is human existence a mistake?

2. Does human life have more happiness or more pain?

3. Does the destruction of the self at death make life meaningless?

4. What does boredom tell us about human existence?

Moral Dilemmas

- A friend of yours, Stewart, calls you in the middle of the night. He tells you that he has come to the realization that life is meaningless and absurd. He says nothing has any meaning or value for him since his girlfriend Jan left him. He doesn't believe in God or anything else and threatens suicide.

  What should you do, and what should you say to Stewart?

- Arthur and Alice have enjoyed a good marriage for several years. One day Alice suggests they have children. She feels having children is part of what it means to be human. Having children also helps satisfy the need to love and be loved in turn. She feels that creating new life is an experience everyone should have.

  Arthur is a man more pessimistic about human existence. He believes that life is meaningless and absurd; the world overpopulated with people suffering from hunger, disease, and poverty. He feels it is better to devote his time helping the needy people already in existence than bringing more people into existence.

  What should Arthur and Alice do?

Suggested Readings

Alvarez, Alfred. *The Savage God.* New York: Random House, 1972.

Bender, David L., ed., *Constructing a Life Philosophy.* St. Paul: Greenhaven Press, 1985.

Dahl, Norman. "Morality and the Meaning of Life: Some First Thoughts," *Canadian Journal of Philosophy* 17, no. 1 (1987).

Edwards, Paul. "Why?" *The Encyclopedia of Philosophy.* New York: Macmillan, 1967.

Klemke, E. D., ed., *The Meaning of Life.* New York: Oxford University Press, 1981.

Nagel, Thomas. *What Does It All Mean?* New York: Oxford University Press, 1987.

Porter, Burton F., ed. *Personal Philosophy.* New York: Harcourt Brace Jovanovich, 1976.

Sanders, Steven and David Cheney. eds., *The Meaning of Life.* Englewood Cliffs, N.J.: Prentice-Hall, 1980.

Schutte, Ofelia, *Beyond Nihilism: Nietzsche Without Masks,* Chicago: University of Chicago Press, 1984.

Index

F

Fetal development and the right to life, 291–93, 295–301
Folkways
    definition of, 55–56, 59–60
    due to false inference, 61
    ethnocentrism and, 63–64
    harmful, 61–62
    notions of true and right and, 62–63
    unconsciously made, 60–61
    See also Mores
Forms, Theory of, 54
Free–market capitalism, 370, 371, 373–77
Furman v. Georgia, 332, 334, 336–42

G

Ginzberg v. New York, 446, 449
Golden Rule, euthanasia and, 326–27
Good will, 57, 84–99
Gratification, delaying, 132
Greeks
    law and the, 142
    philosophy to the, 1–2
    virtues and the, 174–175, 176–79
Gregg v. Georgia, 332
    description of majority opinion on, 333–40
    dissenting opinion on, 341–43
Griswold v. Connecticut, 219, 447

H

Happiness, 58, 85
Harm principle, 142–43, 149
Herring v. State, 218
Homosexuality, 200–201, 209–14
    Bowers v. Hardwick, 202, 214–21
    Vatican and, 207

I

Immoral, definition of, 69
Immorality, treason and, 153–59
Incest, 224
Infanticide, 293–94, 304
Infants, euthanasia and, 312–13
Intimacy, sex and personal, 201–2, 226–38
Intuitionism, 7

J

Jealousy, 175–76, 180–84

K

Kaplan v. California, 454
Katz v. United States, 217
Kingsley Int'l Pictures Corp. v. Regents, 450
Koran, excerpt from the, 19–21

L

Laissez-faire, 370, 371, 373–77
Law
    divine will and, 141
    Greeks and, 142
    harm principle, 142–43, 149
    immorality and treason, 153–59
    of karma, 9
    liberty and, 144–51
    public morality and, 151–55
    role of government, 145–46
Legal moralism, 142, 143
Legal paternalism, 142, 143–44, 160–71
Life, meaning of
    historical background on, 471–72
    human existence as a mistake, 473, 502–5
    humanity's own actions and purposes and, 472–73, 486–97
    religious perspective on, 472, 474–85
    role of truth, beauty, and suffering, 473, 497–502
Living wills, 305
Logic, rules of, 1–2
Logical positivism, 7
Lying, 175, 184–90

M

Malice, 175–76, 180–84
Marriage
    communal, 241
    definition of, 240
    equality in, 241
    extended, 241
    inferiority of women, 241
    interpersonal relationships and, 254–57
    laws, 253–54
    monogamy, 240, 242, 243–61
    nuclear, 241

R

Racism, 405
Rape, 223
Reality, ways of understanding, 2
Reason
    divine law and, 24–32
    ethics and, 56–57
Redrup v. New York, 449
Relativism, 6–7, 55
Religion
    common characteristics of, 11–12, 15
    See also under type of
Rights, human, 7–8
Roe v. Wade, 218, 276, 278–84, 450
Roth v. the United States, 443, 448–49

S

Self-actualization, 125–30
Sermon at Benares, 16–18
Sermon on Abuse, 18
Sermon on the Mount, 22–24
Sex
    bestiality, 223–24
    Catholic Church on, 200, 203–8
    early cultures and, 199–200
    homosexuality, 200–201, 207, 209–14
    incest, 224
    masturbation, 207–8
    necrophilia, 224
    personal intimacy and, 201–2, 226–38
    premarital, 202–3, 206–7, 224–25
    promiscuity and adultery, 224–25
    rape, 223
    religious views on, 200
    voluntary consent and, 202, 221–26
Sexism, 405
Sexual instinct, 115–17
Social contract theory, 333, 357, 358–59
Socialism, 370, 371–72, 378–83
Specieism, 424
Stanley v. Georgia, 216–17, 447, 449–50
Stoicism, 54
Supererogatory behavior, 5

T

Technology, environmental ethics and, 440
Teleological theories, 4

Ten Commandments, the, 21–22
Theological voluntarism, 11
Theory of Forms or Ideas, 54
Theory of Justice, The, (Rawls), 384–96
Thornburgh v. American Coll. of Obst. & Gyn., 218, 219
Treason, immorality and, 153–59

U

Union Pacific R. Co. v. Botsford, 280
U.S. Supreme Court
    capital punishment and the, 331–32
    pornography and the, 443–44, 445–51
United States v. Reidel, 448
United States v. Thirty-Seven Photographs, 448
United States v. Vuitch, 280–81
United Steelworkers v. Weber, 405–6
University of California v. Bakke, 405–6, 407–11
Utilitarianism, 58
    background on, 100–102
    description of, 102–6
    proofs of happiness, 106–8
Utilitarian theory of punishment, 331, 332, 344–51

V

Vatican, sex and the, 200, 203–8
Vices
    jealousy, envy, and malice, 175–76, 180–84
    lying, 175, 184–90
Virtues, 56–57
    basic, 174–75
    Christianity and, 175
    community defined, 175, 176–79
    compassion, 176, 191–97
    courage, 177
    Greeks and, 174–175, 176–79
Voluntary euthanasia, definition of, 305

W

Welfare liberalism, 370, 372–73, 384–96
West Virginia Board of Education v. Barnette, 220
Wisconsin v. Yoder, 219
Wisdom, meaning of, 1
Women
    discrimination and, 404–5
    marriage and inferiority of, 241
    pornography and, 444, 451–65